The Society and Population
Health Reader

The Society and Population Health Reader

Volume I: Income Inequality and Health
Edited by Ichiro Kawachi, Bruce P. Kennedy, and Richard G. Wilkinson

Volume II: A State and Community Perspective
Edited by Alvin R. Tarlov and Robert F. St. Peter

The Society and Population Health Reader

Volume I
Income Inequality and Health

Edited by
ICHIRO KAWACHI,
BRUCE P. KENNEDY, AND
RICHARD G. WILKINSON

The New Press
New York

Published in the United States by The New Press, New York
Distributed by W. W. Norton & Company, Inc., New York

The New Press was established in 1990 as a not-for-profit alternative to the large, commercial publishing houses currently dominating the book publishing industry. The New Press operates in the public interest rather than for private gain, and is committed to publishing, in innovative ways, works of educational, cultural, and community value that are often deemed insufficiently profitable.

www.thenewpress.com

Printed in Canada

9 8 7 6 5 4 3 2 1

CONTENTS

PART FOUR: EFFECTS OF INCOME INEQUALITY ACROSS RACE AND GENDER

The Society and Population
Health Reader

INTRODUCTION

Ichiro Kawachi, Richard G. Wilkinson, and Bruce P. Kennedy

LIVING IN AN UNEQUAL WORLD

THIS volume brings together the key research articles, commentaries and debates that have contributed to the nascent field of income inequality and its effects on public health. Social scientists have long suspected that the widening income inequalities of the last two decades—both globally and within individual countries—exact a heavy social cost in terms of diminished labor productivity, social exclusion, rising incidence of crime, and the erosion of civil society. But it was not until comparatively recently that public health researchers entered the debate and began turning their attention to investigating the consequences of income inequality for population well-being.

The growing body of research suggests that economic inequality has real costs in the form of worse population health. In fact, what the evidence shows is that the distribution of income among members of society matters as much for their health and well-being as does their absolute standard of living. These research findings are increasingly important because the world's wealth is daily becoming concentrated in fewer hands. According to the 1996 Human Development Report (UNDP, 1996), the world's 358 richest individuals controlled assets equivalent to the combined annual incomes of countries in which 45 percent of the world's people live. Of the global gross domestic product (GDP) which amounted to $23 trillion in 1993, the industrialized nations accounted for $18 trillion, compared to only $5 trillion among the developing world, home to 80% of the globe's people. The poorest 20% of the world's population saw their share of global income drop from 2.3% to 1.4% in the past 30 years. Meanwhile the share of the richest 20% increased from 70% to 85%. That doubled the ratio of the shares of the richest to the poorest, from 30:1 to 61:1 (UNDP, 1996).

Polarization of assets has worsened within individual countries as well. The United States is one of the richest countries in the world, but it is also one of the most unequal in terms of how that wealth is shared (Atkinson et al., 1995). In 1968, a year after the U.S. Census Bureau began collecting data on the incomes of households, the top 20 percent of U.S. households earned on average $73,754, compared to $7,202 earned by households in the bottom 20 percent. Three decades later, in 1994, the average income of the top 20 percent had jumped 44 percent (after adjustment for inflation), to $105,945; whereas the incomes of the bottom 20 percent grew by just 7 percent, to $7,762 (Brown et al., 1997). During the years 1991–1995, the median annual pay of the Chief Executive Officers of America's 100 largest companies was $2.8 million (plus an additional $8.4 million in stock options), which amounted to 112 times the median earnings of full-time wage and salary workers in the rest of America ($24,908) (Hacker, 1997).

Inequalities in the distribution of wealth (as opposed to income) are even more skewed: the best-off 1 percent of the American population owns between 40 and 50 percent of the nation's wealth (Wolff, 1995; Hacker, 1997). According to *Forbes* magazine, which publishes an annual list of the world's top 200 working billionaires, the average worth of individuals in this list increased from $2.2 billion in 1994 to $4.7 billion in 1998. In contrast, at the bottom of the economic hierarchy, the poverty rate in America (13.7% in 1996) has remained virtually unchanged during the last 30 years, and currently some 36.5 million Americans are officially poor (US Census Bureau, 1997).

So what? Does it matter that the rich are getting richer, and the poor poorer? The answer depends on one's point of view. If one subscribes to the functionalist view of inequality, first articulated by Davis and Moore in 1945, social stratification is a good thing: it provides the motivation for innovation, hard work, and business growth. During the same period that income inequality surged in America, the stock market has been going through "history's greatest bull market" (Samuelson, 1998). The Dow Jones industrial average reached 1,000 for the first time in 1972, then hovered at that level for the next decade. It took another decade to reach 2,365 in October 1990, which is when most observers date the beginning of the current bull market. Between 1990 and 1998, the Dow rose more than 400%. Some 45 million American families, or 44% of American households, now own some share of the bull market (Leland, 1998).

On the other hand, if one chose to dissent from the idea of inequality as "healthy" espoused by Davis and Moore (1945) and conservative commentators such as George F. Will (1996), you might point to the considerable costs of inequality, such as latent social conflicts, declining support for public institutions and increasing racial tensions. One might also point to some direct costs of inequality that have a "zero-sum" quality to them, as eloquently described by Lester Thurow in his 1980 book of the same name. For instance, in the same issue of *News-week* that eulogized the bull market, an article described the decision of US Airways to squeeze the space in coach class in order to give more leg room for business travelers. The distance between rows in business class now stretches 55 inches, while at the back of the bus, it is 31.[1] The majority of passengers on US Air now travel in increased discomfort, so that business travelers can enjoy more leg room. Even if such zero-sum situations were to prove the exception in a booming economy, it is impossible to ignore the fact that the fruits of growth have not been equally shared.

Perhaps the most dramatic rebuttal to the Panglossian view of recent economic history is to point to alternative measures of national progress that reveal quite a sobering picture. For instance, Mark Miringoff and colleagues at the Fordham Institute have been tracking the nation's progress for several years through an Index of Social Health, which is a composite of indicators such as infant mortality, child abuse, teenage suicides, drug abuse, alcohol-related traffic fatalities, and homicide (Miringoff et al., 1996). Despite decades of sustained economic development, their Index of Social Health has steadily diverged from indicators of economic progress such as the per capita gross domestic product (GDP) and the Dow Jones average. As Figure 1 indicates, while the Dow Jones quadrupled between the mid-1970s and 1993, the Index of Social Health has remained stagnant, reaching its lowest recorded levels in recent years (Miringoff et al., 1996).

In fact, the theme of this book is that health is one of the most extraordinarily sensitive indicators of the social costs of inequality. Health is measured by many things: by how long we live (life expectancy), what illnesses we get (heart disease, cancer . . .), how we feel subjectively (quality of life), and so on. No matter how it is measured, though, health seems to mirror economic inequality. The burden of ill health, we shall argue, is a major reason why we should care

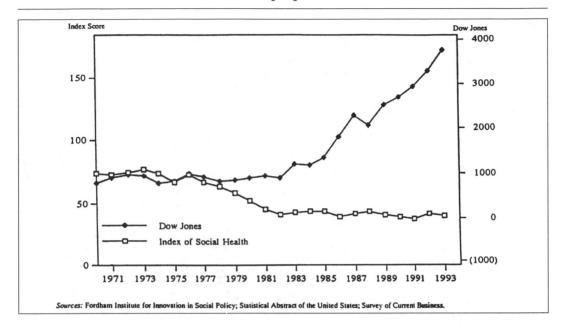

Figure 1.
Index of Social Health and Dow Jones Industrial Average, 1970–1993 (from Miringoff et al. 1996).

as a society about the growing economic distance between the top and bottom.

THE RELATIVE INCOME HYPOTHESIS

IN Figure 1, the growing disparity between economic growth and the nation's health seemingly violates the long-held faith in the ability of economic development to deliver improved quality of life. It is true that among less developed nations, a relationship can still be found between increasing GNP and an overall measure of health such as life expectancy (Figure 2). But beyond a relatively modest level of economic development (about $5,000 per capita), further advances in the standard of living seems to matter rather little; the linear relationship between income and life expectancy breaks down (Wilkinson, 1994). What, then, accounts for the health achievement of different societies? Stated differently, how is it that the United States,

which is the richest country in the world, ranks only 20th in the world, lagging behind poorer countries such as Costa Rica, Greece, and Spain?

One explanation is that the level of population wellbeing depends not just on the absolute size of the economic pie, but also on how the pie is sliced. For example, the more unequal the distribution of economic rewards, the lower the life expectancy (Wilkinson, 1992. 1994; 1997a). A series of cross-national studies have demonstrated this to be the case: the more egalitarian the distribution of income, the higher the life expectancy (Rodgers, 1979; Flegg, 1982; Wilkinson, 1986; LeGrand, 1987; Wilkinson, 1992; Waldman, 1992; Wennemo, 1993). The seminal studies demonstrating the income inequality/mortality relationship have been gathered in this volume. One of the earliest studies, by Rodgers (1979), examined data from 56 rich and poor countries to test the relationship between income distribution and three measures of health—life

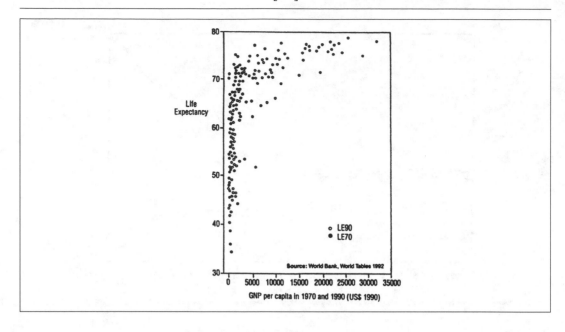

Figure 2.
Relationship between per capita GNP and life expectancy (from Wilkinson, 1996).

expectancy at birth, life expectancy at age 5, and infant mortality. Both per capita GNP and income distribution[2] were tightly linked with life expectancy at birth, together explaining about three-quarters of the variation between countries. The relationships were less strong for life expectancy at age 5 and infant mortality, though income distribution remained a significant predictor. Rodgers (1979) estimated that the difference between a relatively egalitarian and relatively inegalitarian country amounted to about 5 to 10 years in average life expectancy.

More generally, there is now substantial cross-national evidence on the health effects of income inequality. The "relative income hypothesis", as the idea has come to be called, has achieved prominence through the work of Richard Wilkinson (1986; 1990; 1992; 1994; 1996; 1997a). In a cross-sectional examination of eleven countries belonging to the Organization for Economic Cooperation and Development (OECD),

Wilkinson reported a striking correlation (r = −0.81, p < 0.0001) between the degree of income inequality and life expectancy (Wilkinson, 1986).[3] Similarly, a tight correlation (r = 0.86, p < 0.001) was found between the life expectancy of nine OECD countries and the proportion of income earned by the least well off 70% of the population (Wilkinson, 1992). The latter measure of income distribution, combined with GNP per capita, explained about three quarters of the variation in life expectancy between these countries. By itself, GNP per capita could explain less than 10 percent of the variation in life expectancy (Wilkinson, 1992). This quite surprising result revealed income inequality to be the crucial—and hitherto unrecognized—ingredient for the health achievement of societies.

The evidence linking income inequality to health has now been extended to studies within individual countries. Two studies published simultaneously in 1996 (Kaplan et al., (1996) and Kennedy, Kawachi, and Prothrow-Stith (1996)) examined the relationship of income inequality to health within the United States. Instead of life expectancy, these studies looked at the closely related measure of population death rates. The study by Kaplan et al. (1996) used as their measure of income distribution the share of total income earned by the less well off half of households in each state: if incomes were perfectly equally shared, the bottom half of households should account for exactly half of the aggregate income. In reality, the income shares going to the less well off half of households ranged from a low of 17.5 percent (Louisiana, the most unequal) to a high of 23.6 percent (New Hampshire, the most egalitarian). A strong correlation (r = − 0.62, p < 0.001) was found between this measure of inequality and death rates. Moreover, the effect was present in both men and women, and in whites as well as African-Americans. The other study by Kennedy, Kawachi and Prothrow-Stith (1996) looked at a measure of income distribution, appropriately termed "the Robin Hood Index". The Robin Hood Index is a measure of the proportion of total income that must be redistributed from rich to poor households in order to attain perfect equality of incomes. This measure was strongly correlated with death rates across the states. Inequality was associated not only with higher rates of death overall, but also with higher rates of dying from heart disease, cancers, homicide, and infant mortality. Income inequality and poverty could together account for about one quarter of the state variation in overall death rates, as well as just over half of the variation in murder rates. These findings held even after controlling for urban/rural residence, as well as health behaviors such as rates of cigarette smoking. After taking account of state differences in poverty rates and average incomes, a one percent increase in Robin Hood Index was associated with an excess of about 22 deaths per 100,000 population, suggest-

ing that if the relationship is real, then even a modest reduction in inequality could have an important impact on public health. For instance, it was calculated that if the level of inequality in the United States could be brought down to about the same level as Britain, overall death rates would have been about 7 percent lower, and heart disease rates about 25 percent lower.

In England, Ben Shlomo et al. (1996) examined the relationship between the extent of material deprivation in 369 local authorities, and their average death rates. As expected, death rates were strongly linked to levels of deprivation. Every 25% increase in the level of deprivation was associated with an increase of 26 deaths per 100,000 population (p < 0.001). However, death rates also varied as a function of the degree of variability in living standards across the areas that made up the local authorities. The more variable the extent of deprivation within an area, the higher was the death rate, with an average excess of 7 deaths per 100,000 population (P < 0.001) for every 25% increase in the degree of variability.

Most recently, Lynch, Kaplan, and Pamuk et al. (1998) examined the relationship between inequality and mortality at the level of metropolitan areas within the United States. Income inequality was measured in 282 US metropolitan areas, ranging in population size from Enid, Oklahoma (approximately 50,000), to New York City (over 18 million). Cities with high income inequality and low per capita income had the highest death rates compared to cities with low inequality and high per capita income. The difference in death rates, of 150 per 100,000 population, was estimated to be equivalent to eliminating all deaths from heart disease.

What all of these studies suggest is that income inequality causes a *shift* in the income/life expectancy curve (Figure 3), so that almost everyone pays the costs of inequality. If this is indeed the case, then almost every group in society (except perhaps the very rich) would reap the benefits of a more egalitarian distribution of income.

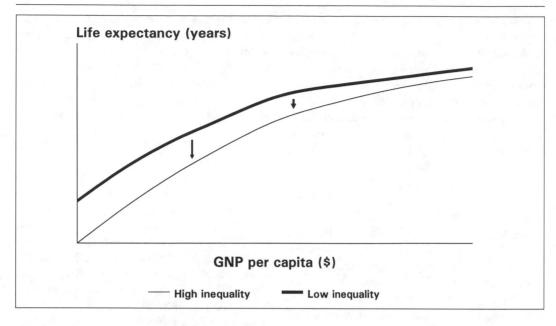

Figure 3.
Effect of a shift in the income/life expectancy curve.

This, in essence, is the thesis of this book. What the relative income hypothesis means is that an individual's health is affected not only by their own level of income, but by the scale of inequality in society as a whole. If true, the implications for social policy are far-reaching.

The higher health achievement of egalitarian societies makes a persuasive case for the redistribution of income. In the past, it has proved difficult to implement policies to improve the plight of the poor, if for no other reason than that the effect of income transfers were assumed to be a zero-sum game. Like changing the leg-room on an airplane, it was not thought possible to improve the health of the poor without worsening the status of the well off. The readings in this volume suggest a more compelling case for redistribution: that a more egalitarian distribution of income would improve the health of a large majority of the population without compensating losses among the rich.

CRITIQUES OF THE
RELATIVE INCOME HYPOTHESIS

THE relative income hypothesis is not without its critics. Three separate strands of criticism can be delineated: 1) that the relation between income distribution and health is an artefact produced by the so-called "ecologic fallacy" (Gravelle, 1998; Fiscella and Franks, 1997); 2) that the empirical evidence in support of the relative income hypothesis is methodologically flawed (Judge, 1995; Saunders, 1996); and 3) that the relative income hypothesis is inconsistent with what we know about the time trends in declining mortality rates throughout most of the industrialized world.

(a) *The Relative Income Hypothesis—*
Statistical Artefact or Real Association?

The first criticism centers on the charge that the relationship between income inequality and health is the result of a statistical aretfact. As shown on Figure 2, the shape of the curve linking absolute income (per capita GNP) and life expectancy is convex, i.e.g, as income rises, so does life expectancy, but there are diminishing returns so that the curve begins to flatten out around $5000 per capita. Given the shape of this curve (which has been replicated in countless cross-national as well as within-country studies), it is obvious that transferring income from the rich to the poor must result in a greater improvement in the life expectancy of the poor (where the curve is steeper), compared to the smaller drop in life expectancy expected among the rich (where the curve is flatter). On theoretical grounds alone, therefore, two societies with the same average standard of living will experience different levels of wellbeing, with the more egalitarian one exhibiting the higher average life expectancy (Kawachi et al., 1994; Gravelle, 1998).[4]

Gravelle (1998) and Fiscella and Franks (1997) have argued from this that aggregate-level studies of the type discussed in the previous section (referred to as "ecologic" studies) are incapable of ruling out the possibility that part or even all of the association between income inequality and health is simply due to the well-established relationship between individual income and individual health. In other words, an individual's risk of death may depend only on their own level of income (the absolute income hypothesis), and not on the income level of anyone else (the relative income hypothesis). The problem of drawing mistaken inferences about individual-level relationships from aggregate data is broadly referred to as the "ecologic fallacy."[5]

The only conclusive way to establish that income inequality has an effect on individual health independent of individual income is to do a study that collects information at both aggregate and individual levels (the so-called "multilevel" study). Fiscella and Franks (1997) reported the first of such studies, based on a followup study of 13,280 individuals in a nationally representative sample of Americans. The authors found that income inequality at the county level

was correlated with population death rates ($r = -0.34$, $p = 0.004$); however, when community income inequality was examined simultaneously with family income, the relationship of income inequality to individual risk of death disappeared ($p = 0.75$); meanwhile family income remained powerfully predictive of mortality risk ($p < 0.001$). These results therefore suggested that the relationship of income inequality to mortality could be explained entirely by one's own income alone.

However, following the publication of Fiscella and Franks' study, new studies have emerged that contradict their findings. Kennedy et al., (1998b) reported a multi-level study of over 200,000 individuals examining the effects of income inequality on the level of self-rated health. Self-rated health was assessed by asking individuals to rate their overall health along a continuum ranging from Excellent/Very Good to only Fair or Poor.[6] Controlling for individual income, educational attainment, cigarette smoking, overweight, and access to health care, individuals residing in the states with the highest levels of income inequality were still 25 percent more likely to report being in only fair to poor health, compared to those living in the most egalitarian states. Although low personal income was more strongly linked with poor self-rated health (for example, individuals from households earning less than $10,000 annually were more than three times as likely to report fair/poor health compared to those earning more than $35,000), the effect of income inequality was statistically significant, and independent of absolute income. The harmful effects of income inequality were most concentrated among individuals from households earning less than $20,000 per year. This study, as well as other forthcoming reports using different datasets (Soobader and LeClere, 1999; Lochner 1999) suggest that it is not simply a matter of individual income and health but that there is an environmental effect of income inequality on individual health status. It has been suggested that the divergent findings of the Fiscella and Franks (1997) study may reflect methodological differences (Kennedy et al., 1998b).

(b) *Methodological Issues*

A second strand of criticism of the relative income hypothesis focuses on a set of technical issues. Judge (1995) and Saunders (1996) have criticized the existing studies because of their lack of consistency in approaches to measuring income inequality. A variety of approaches exist for measuring income inequality (Sen, 1973; Cowell, 1977), and each study has chosen its own measure—for example, the share of the aggregate income earned by the bottom 50% of households (Kaplan et al., 1996), the Gini coefficient (Wilkinson, 1992), the Robin Hood Index (Kennedy et al., 1996), and so on. Such inconsistencies in the choice of measure has led critics to charge that the individual investigators picked the indicator that found the result that they were looking for. A somewhat related methodological criticism of the published studies is that they failed to adjust measures of income inequality for taxes, transfer payments, and household size. To the extent that taxes and transfer payments mitigate the extent of income inequality between households, failure to adjust for them might lead to misleading or biased tests of the relative income hypothesis. Moreover, two societies with the same median household income (say, $25,000) might have very different living standards depending on the average number of individuals living in each household among whom the incomes must be shared.

There is no consensus among economists about a "gold standard" measure of income inequality. On the other hand, most measures of income inequality turn out to be extremely tightly correlated with each other, and in turn, they each turn out to be associated with mortality (Kawachi and Kennedy, 1997a). Analyses of the relative income hypothesis have also been replicated using measures of income inequality adjusted for taxes, transfer payments, and household size (Kawachi and Kennedy, 1997a). The association of income inequality to mortality remained undiminished.

Finally, both Judge (1995) and Saunders (1996) have attempted to replicate Wilkinson's (1992) international studies, using the most recent data from the Luxembourg Income Study, and found that the relation between income inequality and life expectancy no longer holds. However, McIsaac and Wilkinson (1997) have countered that the results of analyses based on data from the Luxembourg Income Study appear to be sensitive to the response rates obtained from income surveys in participating countries. Specifically, data from some countries were based on response rates as low as 50 percent, which resulted in artificial truncation of the income distribution. Analyses that take account of this variable response bias suggest that there is an association between income inequality and life expectancy. More importantly, the validity of the relative income hypothesis no longer hinges on a single data set: there are now simply too many studies both internationally and within individual countries that find the same results (Wilkinson, 1995).

Faced with the large number of reports of an association between income inequality and mortality, these criticisms of the evidence have become entirely ad hoc.

(c) *Time Trends in Income Inequality and Life Expectancy*

A final criticism of the relative income hypothesis focuses on the apparent inconsistency between trends in rising income inequality over time and contemporaneous improvements in life expectancy. But this is a simple confusion. The evidence in this book does not suggest that income inequality is the only influence on health. There is a background rate of improvement in life expectancy which has continued for over a century, even when income distribution has remained unchanged. A narrowing or widening of income differences merely speeds up or slows down this rate of increase. Although the causes of this background rate of improvement have not been clearly identified, they do not appear to be closely related to the economic growth which has accompanied them (Preston, 1975; Wilkinson, 1996). They are likely to include elements as diverse as intergenerational factors, qualitative changes in the material and social environment, and advances in medical care.

TOWARD A THEORY OF INCOME DISTRIBUTION AND HEALTH

IN summary, the association between income inequality and health appears quite robust. What then are the mechanisms by which the societal distribution of income could affect an individual's health? When thinking about mechanisms, researchers often attempt to distinguish between the effects of absolute income on health, and the effects of relative income (or income distribution) on health. But this distinction may turn out to be largely artificial. Although within individual countries there is a strong health gradient related to personal income, if this reflected the impact of absolute income and living standards on health, one would expect the average levels of income for whole populations to be more strongly related to health than they actually appear to be in the developed world. Not only is the relation between GDP per capita and health among the developed countries remarkably flat (as shown in Figure 2), but among the 50 US states the weak correlation (r = 0.26) between median state income and mortality disappears altogether when it is controlled for income distribution in each state (Kaplan et al., 1996; Wilkinson, 1997a). The mismatch, between the strong associations of individual income and health within countries and the weak associations found when looking at differences between countries, may indicate that even at the individual level it is a person's income *relative* to others in society which impacts on health. The

main causal process may then have more to do with position in society than with absolute material living standards. Should this turn out to be the case, then the causal pathways involved in the links between individual income and health may not be so different from those involved in the link between societal income inequality and health. For instance, the quality of social relations is an important component of several of the suggested explanations of the income inequality effect which we discuss below in this section. The quality of social interaction may be partly a function of individual relative income and partly a societal generalization of more sociable norms of interaction in more egalitarian societies in which case individual and societal effects feed into the same processes. Emphasizing a distinction between the effects of individual income and of societal income inequality is of primary importance only to those who believe that they relate to very different processes—typically the effects of absolute material living standards on the one hand and more social processes on the other.

There are good reasons for thinking that both reflect processes centered on relative income. The relative income interpretation of the mismatch (above) of the way health is related to income differences within societies but not between them is confirmed by the way in which the relation between health and income inequality forms the opposite pattern. Income inequality is most closely related to mortality when measured over large areas—countries or US states—and tends to be more weakly related to health when measured across small areas—like counties or census tracts—within countries. Thus among the 50 states, mortality is strongly related to income inequality within them but not to the differences in median income between them. At the opposite extreme, mortality is strongly related to median income of census tracts, but weakly related—if at all—to income inequality within them (Soobader et al., 1999). Areas, like counties of intermediate size, show an intermediate position. Understanding this pattern is additionally important because it looks as if it also occurs in the relation between inequality and homicide and violent crime (Hsieh and Pugh, 1993).

These considerations suggest that what matters is relative income and social differences. Why the relationships reverse in the data for the smallest areas is that they loosen the social homogeneity which drives the income inequality effect. Thus death rates in Harlem are higher at most ages than the population of rural Bangladesh (McCord and Freeman, 1990) not because of the inequality within Harlem, but because most of the population are relatively poor compared to the wider society (Wilkinson, 1997b). Because of residential segregation, we are left at the most local level with something approaching socially homogenous single class neighborhoods. This in turn means that differences in median income between these small areas are related to mortality because they are serving as measures of the median income of the more homogenous local populations relative to the wider society: i.e. they serve to situate the median status of an area in relation to the society as a whole. If this interpretation is correct, it implies that the "reference groups" which could account for the income inequality effect are probably not neighbors, but that the defining social processes are those which give rise to class identity and position in relation to the wider society. If so, this would suggest that an important part of the income inequality effect works through the same processes as give rise to the social class gradient in mortality.

In theory, then, we can think of three plausible pathways by which income distribution could affect health: (a) by influencing individuals' access to life opportunities and material resources (such as access to health care, education, employment, decent housing); and (b) through social processes related to social cohesion, e.g., through mutual support and the benefits of better communication and cooperation; and (c) through directly psychosocial processes related for instance to latent social conflict and the quality of social relations. Importantly, these pathways are not mutually exclusive.

(a) *Access to Life Opportunities*

There is little doubt that truncated life opportunities explains an important part of the *absolute* income hypothesis: the less income we have, the less able we are to afford adequate housing and—particularly in the American context—health care and education. There are well-established and plausible reasons why access to each of these resources matters for the achievement of good health. But how could greater inequality lead to diminished access to these resources? Consider what happens to societies when they enter a spiral of increasing income inequality. As the social distance widens between the rich and poor, their interests begin to diverge, and groups find that they have less and less in common with each other. As economist Paul Krugman put it: "A family at the 95th percentile pays a lot more in taxes than a family at the 50th, but it does not receive a correspondingly higher benefit from public services, such as education. The greater the income gap, the greater the disparity in interests. This translates, because of the clout of the elite, into a constant pressure for lower taxes and reduced public services" (Krugman, 1996, p. 48). Reduced social spending, including educational spending, translates into diminished life opportunities, especially for those nearer the bottom of the economic hierarchy, making it difficult for them to improve their material circumstances.

Kaplan and colleagues (1996) have demonstrated striking correlations between the degree of income inequality at the state level and indicators of investment in human capital such as education. States with high income inequality (as measured by the proportion of total household income received by the less well off 50%) spent a smaller proportion of the state budget on education, and showed poorer educational outcomes, ranging from worse reading and math proficiency to higher high school dropout rates.

The economist Juliet Schor (1998) has described the process by which widening inequality in American society has given rise to a vicious cycle of upward social comparisons, and what she calls "competitive spending." As the rich get richer and acquire more consumer goods, the rest of society have to spend more and more to keep up with the rising standard of living.[7] Such patterns of competitive spending can have devastating consequences for family finances, especially during an era of stagnating middle-class incomes. Understandably, debts increased and savings declined and, as Schor points out:

"The intensification of competitive spending has affected more than family finances. There is also a boomerang effect on the public purse and collective consumption. As the pressures on private spending have escalated, support for public goods, and for paying taxes, has eroded. Education, social services, public safety, recreation, and culture are being squeezed. The deterioration of public goods then adds even more pressure to spend privately. People respond to inadequate public services by enrolling their children in private schools, buying security systems, and spending time at Discovery Zone rather than the local playground. These personal financial pressures have also reduced many Americans' willingness to support transfer programs to the poor and near-poor." (Schor, 1998; p. 21).

A further consequence of widening income inequality (not only in the United States) is that the more affluent households begin to move out of neighborhoods where social classes have traditionally mixed. Demographers have documented how affluent Americans have been relocating out of central cities into suburbs where they build their trophy houses and send their children to well-financed schools paid for out of higher property taxes. Economic residential segregation has increased dramatically during the period that income differences have widened. Between 1970 and 1990, the percentage of urban poor Americans living in nonpoor neighborhoods (defined as having poverty rates below 20%) declined from 45% to 31%, while the percentage living in poor neighborhoods (poverty rates between 20% and 40%) increased from 38% to 41% (Massey, 1996). These trends in the spatial concentration of the poor fail to capture what has happened at the opposite end of the income spectrum, among the affluent. According to Massey (1996), affluence in the US is even more highly concentrated spatially than poverty. In 1970, the typical affluent American family—defined as having an income level at last four times the poverty rate—lived in a neighborhood that was 39% affluent. By 1990, this had increased to 52%. In other words, the typical affluent person lived in a neighborhood where more than half the residents were also rich. Many metropolitan areas have become "hollowed out" as a consequence of these patterns of segregation. When affluent neighbors leave town, they take with them the money as well as the services, amenities, and employment opportunities. As one observer remarked: "When the social fabric thins, more affluent people can buy their way out with private schools, guarded or gated communities, private social clubs, and individual psychotherapy." (Kuttner, 1997)

These processes are exacerbated by a deterioration in the political process. Where income differences are wider, political participation (as measured by voting and other forms of engagement in politics) tends to be lower (Kawachi and Kennedy, 1997b), and ultimately, efficacy of government institutions is reduced (Putnam, 1993). Greater income inequality is closely correlated with lower levels of interpersonal trust (Kawachi et al., 1997a) which in turn is related to low levels of trust and confidence in public institutions (Brehm and Rahn, 1997). States with low levels of interpersonal trust are less likely to invest in human security, and to be less generous with their provisions for social safety nets. For example, the level of mistrust is highly inversely correlated (r = − 0.76) with the maximum welfare assistance as a percentage of per capita income in each state (Figure 4). Needless to say, less gener-

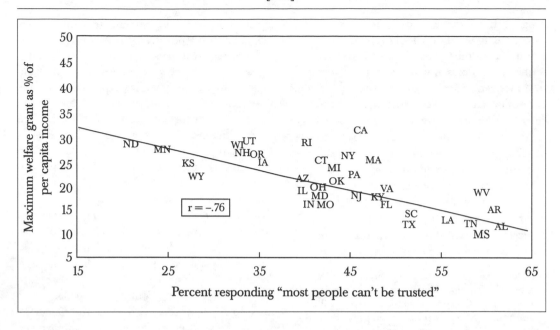

Figure 4.
Relationship between civic mistrust and maximum expenditure on welfare as a percentage of per capita income (from Kawachi and Kennedy, 1999).

ous states are likely to provide less hospitable environments for vulnerable segments of the population as lower political participation reduces support for policies which could ensure the security of all (Kawachi and Kennedy, 1997b; Kawachi et al., 1997b). As Putnam (1993) has argued, social capital is indispensable to the responsiveness and smooth functioning of civic institutions.

The difficulty with explanations such as these is that they do not seem powerful enough to explain more than a small part of the relation between income inequality and health. For instance, the likely effects of political divergence on social security safety nets will influence health through their impact on income distribution and so help to explain income distribution rather than the effects of any given income distribution on health. In addition, although lack of adequate funding for schools in poor areas is an important problem, it is likely that education affects health partly through the way in which it gives access to higher income occupations. This means that an important part of its influence on education would also be reflected in the income distribution figures themselves. Similarly, although the provision of public services, local amenities and recreational facilities is important and may suffer where wider income differences lead to residential segregation, it is not clear that any exert a major influence on population mortality rates.

(b) *Income Inequality and Social Cohesion*

A second set of processes by which income inequality affects health is via increases in intergroup conflict and the erosion of social cohesion (Wilkinson, 1996; Kawachi et al., 1997a). The wider the gap between the rich and poor, the greater the strain on the social fabric. In a 1953 essay on the dysfunctions of social stratification, Melvin Tumin speculated that "to the extent that inequalities in social rewards cannot be made fully acceptable to the less privileged in a society, social stratification systems function to encourage hostility, suspicion and distrust among the various segments of society and thus to limit the possibilities of extensive social integration." Wilkinson (1996) provides several case studies of societies which at certain points in history underwent either a rapid compression of the income distribution (Britain during the two World Wars), or a rapid widening of income differentials (the Italian-American community of Roseto in Pennsylvania during the 1960s). In the case of wartime Britain, narrowing of income differentials was accompanied by a greater sense of solidarity and social cohesion, as well as dramatic improvements in life expectancy. In contrast, the originally close-knit town of Roseto underwent a period of rapid economic change in the 1960s, which opened the gap between the rich and poor. The resulting breakdown of community cohesion was followed by a sharp increase in what had previously been its unusually low coronary disease mortality (Bruhn and Wolf, 1979).

Other evidence similarly suggests a close link between the extent of income inequality and the degree of social cohesion. Putnam (1993) noted a high correlation (r = 0.81) between the degree of income inequality in the regions of Italy and indicators of social cohesion (p. 224). And in the United States, Kawachi et al. (1997a) found high correlations between the degree of income inequality at the state level and the extent to which citizens said they trusted each other (r = 0.71). Talking of an egalitarian social ethos, Putnam went as far as saying "Equality is an essential feature of the civic community" (p. 105).

The concept of "social capital" has been introduced to refer to such features of social relations (Coleman, 1990; Putman, 1993; Woolcock, 1998). Using U.S. data aggregated at the state level, Kawachi et al. (1997a) reported strong correlations between indicators of social capital and mortality rates. In that study, social capital was measured by the degree of trust between citizens (the percent of survey respondents in each state answering that "most people can be trusted"); the existence of norms of reciprocity (percent respondents replying that "people are helpful"); and the per capita membership in voluntary associations of all kinds. The indicators of social capital were obtained from the General Social Surveys conducted by the National Opinions Research Center (NORC) between 1986 and 1990. Civic trust, perceptions of reciprocity, and associational membership were all strikingly correlated with lower mortality rates (r = -0.79, -0.71, and -0.49, respectively), even after adjustment for state median income and poverty rates.

But why and how does social cohesion, or the lack of it, affect individual health? One reason is that certain features of social relations—such as the level of trust between citizens, norms of reciprocity and mutual aid, and the ability to cooperate—represent resources for achieving collective ends (such as attaining health for all). In part this may be seen as the social background to the discussion of the provision of community resources above.

The link between social cohesion and community health status may simply reflect a higher concentration of socially-isolated individuals within communities that lack cohesiveness, because such places provide fewer opportunities for individuals to form local ties (Sampson, 1988). The well-established connection between social isolation and mortality risk will be discussed in the section on psychosocial explanations below. Apart from this rather obvious explanation, however, there are several other plausible mechanisms by which social cohesion might influence individual health through group-level effects (Kawachi et al., 1999b in press).

First, social cohesion may influence the *health behaviors* of neighborhood residents by promoting more rapid diffusion of health information, or increasing the likelihood of adoption of healthy norms of behavior such as exercise, or exerting social control over deviant health-related behavior, such as adolescent smoking, drinking, and drug abuse. For example, the theory of the diffusion of innovations (Rogers, 1983) suggests that innovative behaviors such as the use of preventive services spreads much more rapidly in communities that are cohesive and where members trust each other.[8] Alternatively, recent evidence from criminology suggests that the extent to which neighbors are willing to exert social control over deviant behavior may be critical for the prevention of delinquency and crime. In one study, "collective efficacy"—the degree to which residents of a neighborhood trusted each other and played an active role in helping each other—was strongly *inversely* associated with levels of neighborhood violence, violent victimization, as well as homicide rates (Sampson et al., 1997). In the light of such findings, it is noteworthy that social capital measured at the state level was most strongly correlated with homicide rates (r = 0.73), and that indicators of social capital such as levels of interpersonal trust could explain over half of the state-level variation in homicide rates (Kennedy et al., 1998a; Wilkinson et al., 1998).

A second way in which neighborhood social capital may affect health is through increasing access to local services and amenities. Evidence from criminology suggests that socially cohesive neighborhoods are more successful at uniting to ensure that budget cuts do not affect local services (Sampson et al., 1997). The same kind of organizational processes could conceivably ensure access to services such as transportation, community health clinics, or recreational facilities, that are directly relevant to health.

Although there seem to be a number of possible pathways which would tend to make more cohesive societies healthier, few of the *material* pathways seem likely to exert a major influence on population health. It is not clear whether collective efficacy, better access to amenities and services, and improved information flows where social networks are stronger will benefit health primarily through the direct effects of the material improvements they bring, or whether they reflect deeper psychosocial differences which in-

fluence health more directly. Similarly, if healthier behavior patterns diffuse more rapidly in more cohesive areas and less healthier behaviors diffuse more powerfully in less cohesive areas (Wallace and Wallace, 1997), then the explanatory problem perhaps has less to do with diffusion than with why such different behavior patterns (life preserving or life threatening) become common in areas with different amounts of cohesion.

(c) *Psychosocial Explanations of Income Inequality and Health*

Finally, there are more directly psychosocial pathways by which social cohesion might be expected to influence health. Research on the social gradient in health, and on the socioeconomic determinants of health more generally, has increasingly pointed to psychosocial pathways such as social support, hopelessness, sense of control, job insecurity to name but a few (Berkman, 1995; Everson et al., 1997; Bosma et al., 1997; Ferrie et al., 1995).

There is also a rapidly growing literature on the ways in which biological mechanisms such as those that are associated with chronic stress can give rise to a wide range of health problems (Lovallo, 1997; Chrousos et al., 1995; Sapolsky, 1994). Impacting on both the immune system and on cardiovascular health, the results may be analogous to more rapid aging and so provide the general vulnerability factor which the social gradient in health seems to imply (Kiecolt-Glaser and Glaser, 1995; Macintyre, 1986; Marmot et al., 1984).

Studies of the biological effects of social behavior in non-human primates have substantially strengthened this approach. Shively et al. (1994; 1997) manipulated social status among captive macaque monkeys (to ensure that physiological effects were not attributable to selection) and found that low social status gave rise to worse cholesterol profiles, increased atherosclerosis (clogging of the coronary arteries that predispose to heart attack), more obesity, and indications of behavioral depression. Because the diet and environment were controlled by the experimenter, it would be difficult to attribute the findings to anything other than the direct psychosocial effects of low social status. Studies of the physiological consequences of social status in human populations have found these same biological risk factors to be elevated among humans in lower status positions (Brunner, 1997): this strongly suggests common causes. Both Shively and Sapolsky (who studied the biological effects of social status among wild Baboons) attribute the physiological effects of low social status to chronic stress arising from low social status (Sapolsky et al., 1997; Sapolsky and Share , 1994; Sapolsky, 1993). In one of the first studies of these processes in human populations, Kristenson et al., (1998) reported that the same patterns of physiological alterations were an important part of the explanation of the social gradients in health in both Linkoping, Sweden and Vilnius, Lithuania, and that they also contributed to the health differences between the two cities.

The possible explanations for the association between income inequality and population health which we have already discussed deal primarily with the ways in which inequality and social cohesion may affect the provision of educational, medical and welfare services through their impact on the political process, and also the way in which social cohesion may affect other informal sources of interpersonal support, information flows and behavior. In this section, we flag up a more purely psychosocial hypothesis (pieced together by Wilkinson) which has so far received little research attention. Like the others, it also starts out from the evidence that there is a strong relationship between wider income differences and various measures of a poorer, less cohesive social environment. As we have seen, people seem less inclined to trust each other and regard others as less helpful where income differentials are greater (Kawachi et al., 1997a), homicide and

violent crime rates are higher (Hsieh and Pugh, 1993; Kennedy et al., 1998a; Wilkinson et al., 1998), and—at least among the regions of Italy—Putnam's index of "civic community" is strongly correlated with income inequality. In addition, the Minnesota hostility scores collected for ten US cities by Williams et al. (1995) are not only closely related to mortality but also to income inequality.

It is clear from this evidence that different measures of the strength or quality of social relations are close intercorrelated. A large body of evidence—including both observational and experimental work—has demonstrated that less socially integrated individuals are at increased risk of poor health outcomes (Berkman and Syme, 1979; Berkman, 1995; Kawachi et al., 1996; Cohen et al., 1997; House et al., 1988). Morbidity and mortality rates have been reported to be two, three, or even four times as high among those who are more isolated compared to those with good social networks. Just as a wide range of ecological measures of social relations are closely related to health, so also are a wide range of individual measures, including number of friends, people's involvement in community life, and whether or not they have a "confiding" relationship. Yet why social contact should have such a profound impact on health remains unclear. However, if different measures of the quality of social relations are closely intecorrelated, we should probably take none at face value on its own. Any single measure of the social environment probably serves as a proxy for the health impact of social relations or the social environment more generally, and it would be prudent to bear that in mind when interpreting correlations between any single measure and health. Just as Rose (1992) showed that measures of a range of health risk factors in populations—from heavy drinking to high blood pressure—are related to the population norms for drinking or blood pressure, so measures of violence or trust are perhaps different measures of where, on an axis ranging from highly sociable and supportive to highly conflictual and aggressive, the population's distribution of social interactions lies. What applies at the societal or ecological level perhaps also applies at the individual level in terms of the nature of the multiplicity of a person's social interactions—of the frequency with which they experience supportive or conflictual relations.

Interestingly, there are also suggestions that the biological effects of social subordination, common to human and non-human primates, are also involved in the effects of social isolation. Like subordinates, baboons with fewer social affiliations were reported to have elevated basal cortisol levels and attenuated cortisol responses (Sapolsky et al., 1997). The suggestion of similarities between the biological effects of subordinate status and social isolation is particularly intriguing alongside the association between greater income inequality and poorer social relations. Not only may they have similar biological effects, but there is an important sense in which social subordination and poor social affiliations are likely to be two sides of the same coin. Putnam (1993) referred to the egalitarian relations which are conducive to a stronger community life as "horizontal" relationships and contrasted them with what he called the "vertical" patron-client relations which dominated the regions of Italy in which he found community life to be much weaker. This contrast between horizontal and vertical relations is also apparent in studies of the social behavior of non-human primates: social affiliations are used by animals to protect or improve their position in the vertical dominance hierarchy. Among monkeys, social affiliations are created primarily through grooming which, as Jolly (1985) says, constitutes "the social cement of primates from lemur to chimpanzee" and creates obligations of reciprocity. In the highly egalitarian forms of social organization which dominated human existence as hunters and gathers (Erdal and Whiten, 1996), the social cement was instead provided by the ubiquitous practice of gift exchange and food sharing which, by making the clearest statement that people did not compete for resources, served to keep social relations sweet.

Friendship and dominance represent opposite principles of social organization: the social dominance hierarchy or pecking order is about access to resources based on power and coercion—regardless of the needs of others, whereas social affiliations are about mutuality, reciprocity and sharing of resources. (To suggest that these two powerful influences on health are two sides of the same coin does not of course mean that in social life—or epidemiological studies—they are the same variable: people can be low in the social hierarchy and have friends. What it does mean is that we should perhaps see that their common effects on the physiology of stress as rooted in the same underlying dynamic of social organization.) The relation between greater inequality and poor social relations could then hardly provide a more potent combination for population health. In terms of population attributable risk, if not in terms of relative risks alone, the two most powerful known risk factors for the health of populations in developed countries are perhaps social status and social relations. If wider income inequality marks the strengthening of the hierarchical principle in social life at the expense of more inclusive, sociable and egalitarian relations, then we would expect it to have a major health impact.

This brings us to the reasons why social relations tend to be weaker in a less egalitarian society. Plato remarked in *The Laws* "How correct the old saying is, that equality leads to friendship'! It's right enough and it rings true . . ." This is a principle of social life with which we are still only too familiar: only in fairy stories do princes often marry milkmaids. Indeed, the Cambridge Occupational Scale uses friendship patterns as the basis for classifying occupations hierarchically according to the social status distances between them (Prandy, 1990). (The method used was to ask a sample of people their own occupations and those of six friends. Occupations are then ranked on the assumption that occupations linked by many friendships are of similar social status, whereas those linked by few friendships are likely to be separated by a large hierarchical social distance.)

But although inequality and friendship tend to be inimical to each other, this is unlikely to be more than part of the explanation of why the social environment is less good among populations where income differences are larger. Even in highly unequal societies there is still no shortage of people at any given level in the hierarchy amongst whom to find friends, nor does the inequality associated with violence occur primarily between rich and poor. Overt violence—if not institutional violence—is greatest among the poor. There seems to be another social process at work linking relative deprivation, or low social status, to violence and less supportive social relations.

This process may reflect the tendency for people denied access to the usual economic sources of status and respect, to feel increasingly sensitive to signs of disrespect (Wilkinson et al., 1998; Gilligan, 1996). Where inferior social status makes people feel—in the words of Scheff et al., (1989)—"foolish, stupid, ridiculous, inadequate, defective, incompetent, awkward, exposed, vulnerable, insecure, helpless" (p.181) "rage and hostility increases proportionally to defend against loss of self-esteem." (p.188) ". . . hostility can be viewed as an attempt to ward off feelings of humiliation (shame) generated by inept, ineffectual moves, a sense of incompetence, insults, and a lack of power to defend against insults". (p.188) Using data for the US states, a paper exploring the links between income inequality, homicide and other causes of death (Wilkinson et al., 1998) concluded that the most plausible explanation of the close statistical links between homicide and other causes of death (which have also been reported using data for smaller areas)—was that the sense of inferiority, exclusion, and lack of respect, engendered both the violence and the chronic stress which leads to ill health.

Fundamentally, this view of health is based on a belief that human beings are highly attentive and sensitive to issues of social status and friendship. Adam Smith who in his *Theory of the Moral Sentiments* (1801) asked ". . . what are the advantages which we would propose to gain by that great purpose of human life which we call 'bettering our condition'?" He answered "To be observed, to be attended to, to be taken notice of with sympathy, complacency, and approbation, are all the advantages which we can propose to derive from it." (Adam Smith, Book i, ch. ii. 1, p.50). Several modern economists have also argued that pressure to consume is powerfully driven by competitive considerations of relative income and social position (Frank, 1985; Schor, 1998). Bourdieu (1984) has shown how aesthetic taste in different areas of life is used to express and maintain hierarchical social distinctions. Even experiments in which people are interviewed by either a higher or a lower status person, showed the effects of status differences on transient blood pressure (Long et al., 1982).

These sensitivities seem to reflect the dynamic which Scheff (1988; 1990) referred to as the "deference-emotion system". It works through ubiquitous processes of social comparison and monitoring, and gives rise to feelings of inferiority, inadequacy, incompetence and shame, which are likely to be heightened by greater inequalities and status differences. Individual differences in vulnerability will be strongly influenced by early attachment. According to this view then, we are dealing with highly social influences on health. But, despite the emphasis placed on the power of the social environment to influence health, this hypothesis treats the social environment as an expression of its economic foundations.

The Effects of Income Inequality Across Gender and Race

MUCH work remains to be carried out to elucidate the ways in which vertical hierarchy (along a dimension like income) expresses itself through inequalities along other dimensions like race and gender. It is a truism that the severity of income deprivation varies by race and gender. African-Americans are overrepresented among households in poverty. Poverty has also become feminized with the rise in single female-headed households (Danziger and Gottschalk, 1995). Preliminary work has begun to map out the effects of income maldistribution on the health of African-Americans and women. Kennedy and colleagues (1997) examined the relationship between income inequality and racial prejudice in the United States. States that tolerate high income inequalities also turn out to have high levels of racial prejudice, as revealed in public opinion polls. The General Social Survey, a nationally representative survey of American adults conducted by the National Opinions Research Center, asked citizens in 39 states to respond to the question: "On the average blacks have worse jobs, income, and housing than white people. Do you think the differences are: (a) Mainly due to discrimination? (yes/no); (b) Because most blacks have less in-born ability to learn? (yes/no); (c) Because most blacks don't have the chance for education that it takes to rise out of poverty? (yes/no); and (d) Because most blacks just don't have the motivation or will power to pull themselves up out of poverty? (yes/no)." The proportion of the population who believed that blacks have less in-born ability was correlated -0.44 with income inequality. In turn, the extent of racial prejudice was strongly correlated with black mortality rates (r = 0.56).

The status of women also tends to be the least advanced in areas with the widest income disparities. Kawachi et al. (1999) examined the relationships between income inequality and various composite indices of women's status, developed by the Institute for Women's Policy Research (1996). Indicators of women's status—including women's political participation, and women's economic autonomy—were negatively correlated with income inequality (r = -0.49 and -0.36, respectively; P < 0.05). Indicators of women's

status were, in turn, correlated with female mortality rates as well as mean days of activity limitations. These studies suggest ways in which the concepts of racism and sexism, which have been hitherto examined at the individual level (Krieger et al., 1993), can be fruitfully extended to the ecological level. It makes sense to attempt to measure racism and sexism as collective properties of society, and to begin to document their effects on population health.

WHAT CAN BE DONE?

MUCH concern has been expressed recently about the decline of social capital in American society over the past three decades. Between 1960 and 1993, the proportion of Americans saying that most people can be trusted fell by more than a third, from 58% to 37% (Putnam, 1995). Membership in all sorts of voluntary associations has also dropped. While the causes of the decline in civil society are still debated (Skocpol, 1996), the consequences of these trends are likely to be disproportionately borne by poor and working-class Americans.

What can be done about income inequality? We emphasize that the papers in this book are not dealing with the benefits of some unreachable egalitarian utopia. The statistical analyses they describe show the importance of the comparatively small differences in income distribution which currently exist between different US states or between different market democracies. What can be done to reduce income differentials depends on one's diagnosis of the problem. Economists have developed a lengthy laundry list of potential suspects, including "skill-based" technological change, globalization, deindustrialization, "winner take all" markets, and declining union membership, to name a few. Unfortunately, there is a tendency to view these suspected causes as necessary side effects of a free-market economy. But as James K. Galbraith (1998) has persuasively argued, it is a mistake to attribute the ongoing surge in inequality to inevitable market forces: "Relative wages are much more a matter of politics, and much less a matter of markets, than generally believed" (p. 10).

The Nobel laureate Amartya Sen has long taught that the quality of life in societies depends to a large extent on social policies and public action (Dreze and Sen, 1989; Sen, 1992; Sen, 1993). Taking famine as an example, few instances in history have been caused by crop failures or food shortages alone. Instead, government actions (or inaction) played a key role in most cases. For example, in the Indian state of Maharashtra, a series of severe droughts led to a drastic reduction in the amount of food produced. The response of the Indian government to this event was to institute public works programs—for example, the building of roads and wells. Such policies, Sen argued, actually *raise* the price of food by escalating total demand. But their net effect was to distribute the food shortage more equitably, since higher food prices lead to reduction in consumption by groups less affected by the shortage. Although the average amount of food available in Maharashtra was much lower than in the Sahel countries (Burkina Faso, Mauritania, Mali, Niger, Chad, and Senegal), there was little starvation in Maharashtra. By contrast, the Sahel suffered widespread famine due to their inability to dilute the effects of the food shortage by spreading the impact more equally.

Economic inequality, like famines, tends to be depicted as the inevitable consequence of natural forces. But the real cause of the current surge in inequality is, at least according to Galbraith (1998): "plainly visible to anyone with an open mind and a reasonable grasp of the evidence. Economic policy, and very specifically, monetary policy, changed. Beginning in 1970, the (U.S.) government abandoned the goal of full employment and instead turned its attention to a fight against inflation. For this purpose, only one instrument was deemed suitable: high interest rates brought into being by the Federal Reserve. There followed a repeated sequence of recessions, each justified at the time as the unfortunate conse-

quence of external shocks and events beyond national control. The high unemployment and recessions generated . . . the rise in inequality that destroyed the middle class." (p. 9).

The real story behind the surge in inequality during the 1980s and 1990s has been the destruction of middle class consensus and solidarity. Again, according to Galbraith (1998):

> "More equal societies will tend to have . . . less private capital, less debt, less conspicuous consumption and pecuniary emulation. People are willing to pay higher taxes for social insurance if they face a lower burden of private debts. Moreover, in a middle-class society, public services come to be seen as collective assets—something from which the population at large benefits directly. What might be a bad social bargain at 30 percent of the income, when benefits are thought to flow mainly to the unworthy, seems like a much better deal even at 40 percent of income, when benefits flow back to the population at large (for example, in the form of Canadian medical care, French trains and mass transit, and the German system of free universities)." (p. 16).

The blame for income inequality must rest, according to this view, squarely on the shoulders of government. Having dismantled welfare programs for the poor, the American government appears now to be rushing headlong into privatizing other social programs. Even as this book goes to press, debate rages on Capitol Hill over the future of Medicare and Social Security.

But if we accept that government policy is responsible for much of the recent surge in inequality, then it is also clear that government policy ought to be involved in the cure. A range of policy levers are available to address the problem of income inequality, spanning from the radical (a commitment to sustained full employment, collective wage bargaining, and progressive taxation) to the incremental (expansion of the earned income tax credit, increased child care credit, raising the minimum wage). As the papers in this book argue, society stands to reap a substantial health benefit from even a modest re- duction in income inequality. On current evi- dence, if the level of inequality in the United States were to be brought down to the level that existed at the height of Thatcherism in Britain, this would result in a reduction in overall mortal- ity rates of about 7 percent (Kennedy et al., 1996). We would expect a number of other benefits as well, including a more cohesive society, lower levels of violence and a reduction in a variety of other problems related to relative deprivation. As the eminent sociologist Sol Levine (1994) once argued, if our government really cared about the wellbeing of Americans, it would have to change its outlook significantly: "Health policy should not be separated from social and economic policy. Indeed, health leaders might find them- selves becoming involved in issues ordinarily viewed as distant from health concerns—such as tax policy, ways to fight inflation, and the kind of remedies we use for unemployment."

NOTES

1. Michael Meyer. "Tales from the Sardine Run". *News- week*, 1998, April 27, p. 60.

2. Income distribution was measured by the Gini coeffi- cient. For an explanation of how the Gini coefficient, as well as other measures of income distribution, are calculated, the reader is referred to the article by Kawachi and Kennedy (1997) included in section II of this volume.

3. We will use the correlation coefficient (r) and p-value throughout the text. The correlation coefficient measures the strength of linear relationship between two variables (in this instance, income inequality and life expectancy). The corre- lation coefficient can take values ranging from -1 (perfect negative relationship), through 0 (no relationship), to +1 (perfect positive relationship). P-values refer to tests of sta- tistical significance. P-values less than 0.05 are convention- ally regarded as "statistically significant". Income inequality in the study by Wilkinson (1986) was measured by Gini co- efficients of post-tax income standardized for differences in household size.

4. Although it should be borne in mind that in countries as rich as the USA, even those in relative poverty—on less than half the average income—lie on the relatively flat part of the curve.

5. It should be noted however that the issue of the level at which income distribution affects health is essentially an ar- gument about mechanisms: it does not reduce the policy sig- nificance of the relation itself.

6. Despite its apparently subjective nature, self-rated health has been found to predict subsequent risk of death in over two dozen studies (Idler and Benyamini, 1997).

7. In public opinion polls conducted back in 1978, people judged $19,600 (or $1,960 more than the median family in- come) as necessary for "reasonable comfort". In 1985, the in- come level for reasonable comfort had risen to $30,600 (compared to the median family income of $27,734). By 1994, the reasonable-comfort level had risen still further to $40,000 (Schor, 1998). A sizable proportion of American households in every stratum of society felt that their income was insuffi- cient "to afford to buy everything I really need," even those that earned well above the median income. Similarly, 46 per- cent of people in households earning $35,000 to $50,000, and 35 percent of those in households earning $50,000 to $70,000 responded that they spent "nearly all my money on the basic necessities of life" (Schor, 1998).

8. It is important to note in passing that there are also models of the diffusion of unhealthy behaviors (Wallace and Wallace, 1997).

REFERENCES

Atkinson AB, Rainwater L, Smeeding TM (1995). *Income distribution in OECD countries. Evidence from the Luxem- bourg Income Study*. Paris: Organization for Economic Cooperation and Development.

Ben-Shlomo Y, White IR, Marmot M (1996). Does the variation in the socioeconomic characteristics of an area affect mortality? *British Medical Journal* 312: 1013–14.

Berkman LF, Syme SL (1979). Social networks, host resis- tance and mortality: a nine-year follow-up study of Alameda County residents. *American Journal of Epidemi- ology* 109: 186–204.

Berkman LF. (1995). The role of social relations in health promotion. *Psychosomatic Research*; 57: 245–54.

Bosma H, Marmot MG, Hemingway H, Nicholson A, Brunner EJ, Stansfield S (1997). Low job control and risk of coronary heart disease in the Whitehall II study. *British Medical Journal*; 314: 558–65.

Bourdieu P (1984). *Distinction: a social critique of the judgement of taste*. Routledge, London.

Brehm J, Rahmn W (1997). Individual-level evidence for the causes and consequences of social capital. *American Journal of Political Science* 41: 999–1023.

Brown LR, Renner M, Flavin C, for the Worldwatch Institute (1997). *Vital Signs 1997*. New York: W.W. Norton & Company.

Bruhn JG, Wolf S (1979). *The Roseto Story*. Norman: University of Oklahoma Press.

Brunner E (1997). Stress and the biology of inequality. *British Medical Journal*, 314: 1472–6.

Chrousos GP, McCarty R, Pacak K, Cizza G, Sternbery E, Gold PW, Kvetnansky R (Editors) (1995). *Stress: basic mechanisms and clinical implications*. In: Annals of the New Your Academy of Sciences. New York Academy of Sciences.; Vol. 771.

Cohen S, Doyle WJ, Skoner DP, Rabin BS, Gwaltney JM (1997). Social ties and susceptibility to the common cold. *Journal of the American Medical Association*; 277: 1940–44.

Coleman JS (1990). *Foundations of Social Theory*. Cambridge, MA: Harvard University Press.

Cowell FA (1977). *Measuring Inequality*. Oxford: Philip Allan.

Danziger S and Gottschalk P (1995). *America Unequal*. Cambridge, MA: Harvard University Press.

Davis K, Moore WE (1945). Some principles of stratification. *American Sociologic Review*; 10: 242–49.

Dreze J and Sen A (1989). *Hunger and Public Action*. Oxford: Clarendon Press.

Erdal D, Whiten A (1996). Egalitarianism and Machiavellian intelligence in human evolution. In: *Modelling the early human mind*. Edited by Mellars P & Gibson K. McDonald Institute Monographs; 139–160.

Everson SA, Kaplan GA, Goldberg DE, Salonen R, Salonen JT (1997). Hopelessness and 4-year progression of carotid atherosclerosis. The Kuopio Ischemic Heart Disease Risk Factor Study. *Arteriosclerosis, Thrombosis & Vascular Biology*. 17: 1490–5.

Ferrie JE, Shipley MJ, Marmot MG, Stansfield S, Davey Smith G (1995). Health effects of anticipation of job change and non-employment: longitudinal data from the Whitehall II study. *British Medical Journal*; 311: 1264–9.

Fiscella K and Franks P (1997). Poverty or income inequality as predictor of mortality: longitudinal cohort study. *British Medical Journal* 314: 1724–1728.

Flegg AT (1982). Inequality of income, illiteracy and medical care as determinants of infant mortality in underdeveloped countries. *Population Studies* 36: 441–458.

Frank RH (1985). *Choosing the right pond: human behavior and the quest for status*. Oxford University Press.

Galbraith JK (1998). *Created Unequal. The Crisis in American Pay*. New York: The Free Press.

Gilligan J (1996). *Violence: Our Deadly Epidemic and Its Causes*. G.P. Putnam.

Gravelle H (1998). How much of the relation between population mortality and unequal distribution of income is a statistical artefact? *British Medical Journal*; 316: 382–5.

Hacker A (1997). *Money. Who has how much and why*. New York: Scribner.

House JS, Landis KR, Umberson D (1988). Social relationships and health. *Science* 214: 540–545.

Hsieh CC, Pugh MD (1993). Poverty, income inequality, and violent crime: a meta-analysis of recent aggregate data studies. *Criminal Justice Review;* 18: 182–202.

Idler EL, Benyamini Y (1997). Self-rated health and mortality: A review of twenty-seven community studies. *Journal of Health and Social Behavior* 38: 21–37.

Institute for Women's Policy Research (1996). *The Status of Women in the States*. Washington DC: Institute for Women's Policy Research (Library of Congress Card Catalogue Number 96–79874).

Jolly A (1985). *The evolution of primate behavior*. (2nd edition) Macmillian, NY.

Judge K (1995). Income distribution and life expectancy: a critical appraisal. *British Medical Journal*; 311: 1282–1285.

Kaplan GA, Pamuk ER, Lynch JW, Cohen RD, Balfour JL (1996). Inequality in income and mortality in the United States: analysis of mortality and potential pathways. *British Medical Journal* 312: 999–1003.

Kawachi I, Levine S, Miller SM, Lasch K, Amick BC III (1994). *Income inequality and life expectancy—theory, research, and policy*. Boston: The Health Institute, New England Medical Center.

Kawachi I, Colditz GA, Ascherio A, Rimm EB, Giovannucci E, Stampfer MJ, Willett WC (1996). A prospective study of social networks in relation to total mortality and cardiovascular disease incidence in men. *Journal of Epidemiology and Community Health* 50: 245–251.

Kawachi I, Kennedy BP (1997a). The relationship of income inequality to mortality—Does the choice of indicator matter? *Social Science & Medicine* 45: 1121–1127.

Kawachi I, Kennedy BP (1997b). Health and social cohesion: why care about income inequality? *British Medical Journal* 314: 1037–1040.

Kawachi I, Kennedy BP (1999). Income inequality and health: pathways and mechanisms. *Health Services Research* 34(1): 215–27.

Kawachi I, Kennedy BP, Lochner K, Prothrow-Stith D (1997a). Social capital, income inequality, and mortality. *American Journal of Public Health* 87: 1491–1498.

Kawachi I, Kennedy BP, Lochner K (1997b). Long live community. Social capital as public health. *The American Prospect* November/December, 56–59.

Kawachi I, Kennedy BP, Gupta V, Prothrow-Stith D. (1999). Women's status and the health of women and men: A view from the States. *Social Science & Medicine*.

Kawachi I, Kennedy BP, Glass R (1999). Social capital and self-rated health: A contextual analysis. *American Journal of Public Health*.

Kennedy BP, Kawachi I, Prothrow-Stith D (1996). Income distribution and mortality: cross-sectional ecological study of the Robin Hood Index in the United States. *British Medical Journal* 312: 1004–1007. And erratum: *British Medical Journal* 1996; 312: 1253.

Kennedy BP, Kawachi I, Lochner K, Jones CP, Prothrow-Stith D (1997). (Dis)respect and black mortality. *Ethnicity & Disease* 7: 207–214.

Kennedy BP, Kawachi I, Prothrow-Stith D, Lochner K, Gupta V (1998a). Social capital, income inequality, and firearm violent crime. *Soc Sci Med* 47: 7–17.

Kennedy BP, Kawachi I, Glass R, Prothrow-Stith D. (1998b). Income distribution, socioeconomic status, and self-rated health: A US multi-level analysis. *British Medical Journal* 317: 917–21.

Kiecolt-Glaser JK, Glaser R (1995). Psychoneuroimmunology and health consequences—data and shared mechanisms. *Psychosomatic Medicine* 57(3): 269–274.

Krieger N, Rowley DL, Herman AA, Avery B, Phillips MT (1993). Racism, sexism, and social class: implications for studies of health, disease, and well-being. *American Journal of Preventive Medicine* 9: 82–122.

Kristenson M, Orth-Gomér K, Kucinskienė Z, Bergdahl B, Calkauskas H, Balinkyniene I, Olsson AG (1998). Attenuated cortisol response to a standardised stress test in Lithuanian versus Swedish men: the LiVicordia Study. *International Journal of Behavioral Medicine* 5(1): 17–30.

Krugman P (1996). The spiral of inequality. *Mother Jones* November/December: 44–49.

Kuttner R (1997). *Everything for Sale. The virtues and limits of markets*. New York: Alfred Knopf.

LeGrand J (1987). Inequalities in health. Some international comparisons. *European Economic Review* 31: 182–191.

Leland J (1998). Blessed by the bull. *Newsweek*, April 27: 51–53.

Levine S (1994). If our government really cared about health. *Social Policy*, Spring: 6–12.

Lochner K, Kawachi I, Kennedy BP (1998 in press). Social capital: A guide to its measurement. *Health and Place*.

Lochner K (1999). State income inequality and individual mortality risk: A prospective multilevel study. Harvard University. PhD dissertation.

Long JM, Lynch JJ, Machiran NM, Thomas SA, Malinow K (1982). The effect of status on blood pressure during verbal communicaton. *Journal of Behavioral Medicine* 5: 165–71.

Lovallo WR (1997). *Stress and health: biological and psychological interactions*. Sage, London.

Lynch JW, Kaplan GA, Pamuk ER, Cohen RD, Heck KE, Balfour JL, Yen IH (1998). Income inequality and mortality in metropolitan areas of the United States. *American Journal of Public Health* 88: 1074–80.

Macintyre S (1986). The patterning of health by social position in contemporary Britain: directions for sociological research. *Social Science and Medicine*; 23: 393–415.

Marmot MG, Shipley MJ, Rose G (1984). Inequalities in death—specific explanations of a general pattern? *The Lancet*; May 5, 1003–1006.

Massey DS (1996). The age of extremes: concentrated affluence and poverty in the twenty-first century. *Demography* 33: 395–412.

McCord C, Freeman HP (1990). Excess mortality in Harlem. *New England Journal of Medicine*; 322: 173–7.

McIsaac SJ and Wilkinson RG (1997). Income distribution and cause-specific mortality. *European Journal of Public Health* 7: 45–53.

Miringoff M-L, Miringoff M, Opdycke S (1996). The growing gap between standard economic indicators and the nation's social health. *Challenge*; July–August 17–22.

Prandy K. (1990). The revised Cambridge scale of occupations *Sociology*, 24 (4): 629–655.

Preston SH (1975). The changing relation between mortality and level of economic development *Population Studies;* 29: 231–48.

Putnam RD (1993). *Making Democracy Work. Civic Traditions in Modern Italy*. Princeton, NJ. Princeton University Press.

Putnam RD (1995). Bowling alone. America's declining social capital. *Journal of Democracy* 6: 65–78.

Rodgers GB (1979). Income and inequality as determinants of mortality: an international cross-section analysis. *Population Studies;* 33: 343–351.

Rogers E (1983). *Diffusion of Innovations*. New York: Free Press.

Rose G (1992). *The strategy of preventive medicine*. Oxford: Oxford University Press.

Sampson RJ (1988). Local friendship ties and community attachment in mass society: a multilevel systemic model. *American Sociological Review* 53: 766–79.

Sampson RJ, Raudenbush SW, Earls F (1997). Neighborhoods and violent crime: a multilevel study of collective efficacy. *Science* 277: 918–924.

Samuelson RJ (1998). Why we're all married to the market. *Newsweek*, April 27: 47–50.

Sapolsky RM (1993). Endocrinology alfresco: psychoendocrine studies of wild baboons. *Recent Progresss in Hormone Research;* 48: 437–68.

Sapolsky RM (1994). *Why zebras don't get ulcers. A guide to stress, stress-related disease and coping*. WH Freeman, N.Y.

Sapolsky RM, Share LJ (1994). Rank-related differences in cardiovascular function among wild baboons: role of sensitivity to Glucocorticoids. *American Journal of Primateology,* 32: 261–75.

Sapolsky RM, Alberts SC, Altmann J (1997). Hypercortisolism associated wtih social subordinance or social isolation among wild baboons. *Archives of General Psychiatry,* 54, 12: 1137–1143.

Saunders P (1996). *Poverty, Income Distribution and Health: An Australian Study*. SPRC Reports and Proceedings No. 128. Sydney: Social Policy Research Center, University of New South Wales.

Scheff TJ (1988). Shame and conformity: the deference-emotion system. *American Sociological Review,* 53: 395–406.

Scheff TJ (1990). *Microsociology: discourse, emotion and social structure*. University of Chicago Press.

Scheff TJ, Retzinger SM, Ryan MT (1989). Crime, violence, and self-esteem: review and proposals. In: *The social importance of self-esteem*. Edited by Mecca AM, Smelser NJ, Vasconcellos J. University of California Press, Berkeley.

Schor JB (1998). *The Overspent American*. New York: Basic Books.

Sen A (1973). *On Economic Inequality*. Oxford: Oxford University Press.

Sen A (1992). *Inequality Re-examined*. Cambridge, MA: Harvard University Press.

Sen A (1993). The economics of life and death. *Scientific American*, May: 40–47.

Shively CA, Clarkson TB (1994). Social status and coronary artery atherosclerosis in female monkeys *Arteriosclerosis and Thrombosis;* 14: 721–6.

Shively CA, Laber-Laird K, Anton RF (1997). Behavior and physiology of social stress and depression in female cynomolgus monkeys. *Biological Psychiatry,* 41: 871–82.

Skocpol T (1996). Unraveling from above. *The American Prospect,* 25 (March–April): 20–25.

Smith, Adam (1801). The Theory of Moral Sentiments. 9th ed. London: A. Strahan.

Soobader M-J, LeClere FB (1999). Aggregation and the measurement of income inequality: effects on morbidity. *Social Science and Medicine* 48: 733–44.

Thurow LC (1980). *The Zero-Sum Society*. New York: Basic Books.

Tumin MM (1953). Some principles of stratification: a critical analysis. *American Sociological Review* 18: 387–94.

United Nations (1996). *Human Development Report 1996*. New York: Oxford University Press.

U.S. Bureau of the Census (1997). Income Inequality. March *Current Population Survey.*

Waldmann RJ (1992). Income distribution and infant mortality. *Quarterly Journal of Economics* 107: 1283–1302.

Wallace R, Wallace D (1997). Community marginalisation and the diffusion of disease and disorder in the United States. *British Medical Journal,* 314: 1341–5.

Wennemo I (1993). Infant mortality, public policy, and inequality—a comparison of 18 industrialised countries 1950–85. *Sociology of Health & Illness* 15: 429–446.

Wilkinson RG (1986). Income and inequality. In: *Class and health: Research and Longitudinal Data*, RG Wilkinson (ed). London: Tavistock.

Wilkinson RG (1990). Income distribution and mortality: a "natural" experiment. *Sociology of Health & Illness* 12: 391–412.

Wilkinson RG (1992). Income distribution and life expectancy. *British Medical Journal*; 304: 165–168.

Wilkinson RG (1994). The epidemiological transition: from material scarcity to social disadvantage? *Daedalus* 123: 61–77.

Wilkinson RG (1995). Commentary: A reply to Ken Judge: mistaken criticisms ignore overwhelming evidence. *British Medical Journal* 311: 1285–87.

Wilkinson RG (1996). *Unhealthy Societies. The Afflictions of Inequality*. London: Routledge.

Wilkinson RG (1997a). Health inequalities: relative or absolute material standards? *British Medical Journal* 314: 591–5.

Wilkinson RG (1997b). Income inequality and social cohesion. *American Journal of Public Health* 87: 104–6.

Wilkinson RG, Kawachi I, Kennedy BP (1998). Mortality, the social environment, crime and violence. *Sociology of Health & Illness*; 20(5): 578–97.

Will GF (1996). Healthy Inequality. Newsweek October 28, p. 92.

Williams RB, Feaganes J, Barefoot JC (1995). Hostility and death rates in 10 US cities. *Psychosomatic Medicine*; 57 (1): 94.

Wolff E (1995; 1996). *Top Heavy. The increasing inequality of wealth in America and What We Can Do About It*, revised and updated edition. New York: The New Press.

Woolcock M (1998). Social capital and economic development: Toward a theoretical synthesis and policy framework. *Theory and Society* 27: 151–208.

A NOTE ON USING THIS BOOK

SINCE Richard Wilkinson's seminal essay on the relative income hypothesis appeared in the January 18, 1992 issue of the *British Medical Journal*, a virtual cascade of papers has followed; in essence, a new field of scientific inquiry into the social determinants of health was born. The field is still comparatively young, as is evident from the chronology of articles gathered in this volume; most of them were published in the last six years. Nonetheless, there is now a sufficient corpus of work scattered throughout the public health and social sciences literature to justify pulling them together into one comprehensive volume.

The purpose of this anthology is two-fold: to serve as a resource for researchers embarking on the study of the relative income hypothesis; and secondly, to provide a curriculum guide for teachers and students in public health and allied social sciences who wish to familiarize themselves with this new field of research. The anthology is structured in four parts. The sections and their themes are:

(I) The relative income hypothesis—including a statement of the main hypothesis, followed by a review of the cross-national and within-country empirical evidence;

(II) Critiques of the relative income hypothesis, as well as responses to the critiques;

(III) The theory of income distribution and health—covering the major pathways by which income inequality is postulated to af-

fect health, including social cohesion and psycho-social processes; and

(IV) Effects of income inequality along ascriptive dimensions of gender and race/ethnicity.

Following the introductory chapter, each section of the book contains the key essays dealing with the topic area as they originally appeared. These articles were selected to ensure that introductory researchers and students will become acquainted with the most important concepts, findings and debates in the field. To guide the reader, at the beginning of each section, we have listed the types of questions and debates raised by the individual readings. In addition, we have included a list of important additional readings (some of book length) to supplement the articles reprinted in this volume.

One of the sections, on crime and the social environment (in section III), has no counterpart in the introductory chapter, though references to the findings in the criminological literature are made throughout the text of the Introduction. Given the crucial insights provided by the criminological literature on the relationship between the social environment and population well-being, we felt inserting a whole section of articles devoted to this topic to be important.

For readers who wish to glean an overview of the research on health inequalities up to 1996, an excellent source is the book *Unhealthy Societies: The Afflictions of Inequality* by Richard Wilkinson

(London: Routledge, 1996). In addition, for readers who wish to understand the measurement of income distribution, the sources of income inequality, and their trends over time, we refer them to the list of readings appended to the end of this volume.

Much work remains to be carried out in clarifying the link between income distribution and population health. We hope the readings in this anthology convey our sense of challenge and excitement, and inspire the reader to join in this research venture.

Part One

THE RELATIVE INCOME HYPOTHESIS

Part One

THE RELATIVE INCOME HYPOTHESIS

THE READINGS

Section A
Income Inequality and Health:
International Evidence

1. Rodgers GB (1979). Income and inequality as determinants of mortality: an international cross-section analysis. *Population Studies*, 33: 343–351.
2. Waldmann RJ (1992). Income distribution and infant mortality. *Quarterly Journal of Economics* 107: 1283–1302.
3. Wilkinson RG (1992). Income distribution and life expectancy. *British Medical Journal*, 304: 165–168.
4. Wilkinson RG (1994). The epidemiological transition: from material scarcity to social disadvantage? *Daedalus* 123: 61–77.

Section B
Income Inequality and Health:
Within-Country Evidence

5. Ben-Shlomo Y, White IR, Marmot M (1996). Does the variation in the socioeconomic characteristics of an area affect mortality? *British Medical Journal* 312: 1013–14.
6. Kaplan GA, Pamuk ER, Lynch JW, Cohen RD, Balfour JL (1996). Inequality in income and mortality in the United States: analysis of mortality and potential pathways. *British Medical Journal* 312: 999–1003.
7. Kennedy BP, Kawachi I, Prothrow-Stith D (1996). Income distribution and mortality: cross-sectional ecological study of the Robin Hood Index in the United States. *British Medical Journal* 312: 1004–1007, and erratum: *British Medical Journal* 1996; 312: 1253.
8. Lynch JW, Kaplan GA, Pamuk ER, Cohen RD, Balfour JL, Yen IH (1998). Income inequality and mortality in metropolitan areas of the United States. *American Journal of Public Health* 88: 1074–80.

COMMENT

THE articles reprinted in Part I provide the basic evidence for the relative income hypothesis, beginning with the original observation by Rodgers (1979) of an association between the extent of income inequality in society and its average life expectancy. Attempts to test the relative income hypothesis began in earnest following Wilkinson's (1992) statement of the problem. In 1996, three simultaneous publications in the same issue of the *British Medical Journal* (Kaplan et al. 1996; Kennedy et al. 1996; Ben Shlomo et al. 1996) extended the evidence in support of the relative income hypothesis to regional data within individual countries.

The types of questions and debate raised by these readings include:

• Is there an effect of income distribution on population health independent of individual income? Stated differently, does the size of the gap between the rich and poor matter for the health achievement of a society independently of the absolute standard of living enjoyed by all?
• Do the determinants of population health differ at various stages of a nation's economic development? What are the relative contributions of economic growth and the egalitarian distribution of economic gains on the health status of less developed countries compared to industrialized nations?
• Compared to income distribution, what are the relative contributions to population health status of: material scarcity (poverty), provision of health care, genetic factors and social selection, and lifestyle behaviors?
• Does the relationship of income inequality to health depend on the unit of analysis? At what level of geographic aggregation does income inequality matter for population health—at the level of nations, re-

gions within countries, cities, or communities/neighborhoods?
- What types of health outcomes (for example, life expectancy, all-cause and cause-specific mortality, disability, self-rated health, homicide and violence) are sensitive to the distribution of income?
- Do the effects of income inequality vary across the life course? For example, are the effects stronger and more consistent for infants and children, during mid-life, or at older ages?

SUGGESTIONS FOR FURTHER READING

Section A
Income Inequality and Health:
International Evidence

Flegg AT (1982). Inequality of income, illiteracy and medical care as determinants of infant mortality in underdeveloped countries. *Population Studies* 36: 441–458.

Wilkinson RG (1986). Income and mortality. In: *Class and health: Research and Longitudinal Data.* RG Wilkinson (ed). London: Tavistock.

LeGrand J (1987). Inequalities in health. Some international comparisons. *European Economic Review* 31: 182–191.

Wennemo I (1993). Infant mortality, public policy, and inequality—a comparison of 18 industrialised countries 1950–85. *Sociology of Health & Illness* 15: 429–446.

Duleep HO (1995). Mortality and income inequality among economically developed countries. *Social Security Bulletin* 58: 34–50.

Davey Smith G, Egger M (1996). Commentary: Understanding it all—health, meta-theories, and mortality trends. *British Medical Journal* 313: 1584–85.

van Doorslaer E, Wagstaff A, Bleichrodt H, Calonge S, Gerdtham U, Gerfin M, et al. (1997). Income-related inequalities in health: some international comparisons. *Journal of Health Economics* 16:93–122.

Walberg P, McKee M, Shkolnikov V, Chenet L, Leon DA (1998). Economic change, crime, and mortality crisis in Russia: regional analysis. *British Medical Journal* 317: 312–8.

Section B
Income Inequality and Health:
Within-Country Evidence

Wilkinson RG (1990). Income distribution and mortality: a "natural" experiment. *Sociology of Health & Illness* 12: 391–412.

Merva M, Fowles R (1993). *Effects of diminished economic opportunities and social stress: Heart attacks, stroke, and crime.* Washington DC: Economic Policy Institute.

Wilkinson RG (1994). Health, redistribution and growth. In: *Paying for Inequality: the Economic Cost of Social Injustice.* A. Glyn and D. Miliband (eds). Rivers Oram Press: London.

Steckel RH (1994). Heights and health in the United States. In: *Stature, Living Standards and Economic Development.* J. Komlos (ed). University of Chicago Press. [see also: Steckel RH (1983). Height and per capita income. *Historical Methods* 16: 1–7.]

Gorey KM (1994). The association of socioeconomic inequality with cancer incidence: an explanation for racial group cancer incidence. State University of New York at Buffalo: Ph.D. thesis.

Kahn HS, Tatham LM, Pamuk ER, Heath CW Jr (1998). Are geographic regions with high income inequality associated with risk of abdominal weight gain? *Social Science & Medicine* 47: 1–6.

Soobader M-J, LeClere FB (1999). Aggregation and the measurement of income inequality: effects on morbidity. *Social Science & Medicine* 48: 733–44.

One

INCOME AND INEQUALITY AS DETERMINANTS OF MORTALITY: AN INTERNATIONAL CROSS-SECTION ANALYSIS

G. B. Rodgers

INTRODUCTION

THE determinants of mortality change in less developed countries are not easy to unravel. Improvements in health technology and availability are evidently relevant; education certainly plays an important part; sanitation, clean water supply and a host of other environmental variables have undoubted effects. But empirically, the effects of these different factors are difficult to identify. The variables tend to be collinear with each other, and with many other aspects of development, making their isolation difficult. Moreover, there is a tendency for health programmes to be most intensive in the least healthy places, for obvious reasons, further confusing observed relationships.

Identifying the impact of factors such as these, which are directly associated with health, is well worth while for purposes of policy formulation; but it may not be critical for a description of mortality changes in the process of development. For behind these specific variables, the overall economic status of individuals is likely to dominate

health changes—through nutrition and other aspects of consumption, and also because economic status is a close correlate and determinant of many of the more specific variables noted above. Higher incomes may be a precondition for healthier environments and better health services, given competing demands on resources— this is self-evident at the community or national level but is also likely to hold at the individual level. Thus, for a general empirical analysis, it is quite reasonable to propose a sequence of causation which goes from income to mortality via a number of intermediate variables with which we need not necessarily concern ourselves.

THEORY

LET us suppose that at the individual level there is a relationship between income and life expectancy. Observations in developed countries suggest that this relationship is asymptotic; that is, there is a maximum life expectancy beyond which increases in income have no further effect. It is even possible that at very high in-

Originally published in *Population Studies*, 1979.

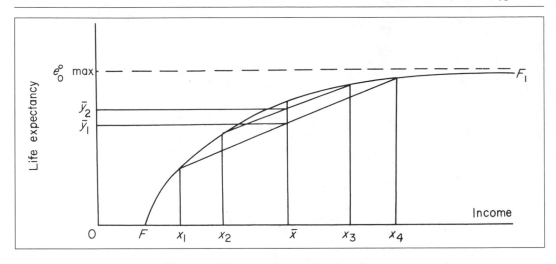

Diagram 1. *Life expectancy as a function of income.*

comes, diseconomies of excessive income might reduce life expectancy, but this we disregard for present purposes. The relation between income and life expectancy is thus non-linear, and we can reasonably suppose that it will take the form suggested by FF_1 in Diagram 1, with the slope of the curve declining (at a declining rate) with increasing income. This suggests the use of the reciprocal of income as a determinant of life expectancy. There is also some intuitive support for the proposition that a proportional change in income may be required for arithmetic changes in mortality, but the presumption here is weaker. If correct, this would suggest the use of the logarithm of income as the explanatory variable.

The relationship in Diagram 1 is defined for an individual. In practice, however, data for studying this type of relationship are available only at the aggregate level, if only because of the difficulty of generating appropriate, accurate micro-data. Thus, we need to formulate a relation between life expectancy at community or national level, and the incomes of the individuals composing the society concerned. With a linear relation between life expectancy and income, no problem arises; a corresponding linear relation-

ship between mean life expectancy and mean income can be defined. However, our function is non-linear, and mean life expectancy is a function not only of the mean income level, but also of the distribution of income. Without defining the distribution function for income, no complete relation can be established. But it is clear that there will be a tendency for greater dispersion of income to be associated with lower mean life expectancy. This can be seen by taking two income observations in Diagram 1, x_1 and x_4, with mean $\bar{x}$; their mean life expectancy is $\bar{y}_1$. If dispersion is reduced, by raising x_1 to x_2 and reducing x_4 to x_3, while holding $\bar{x}$ constant, mean life expectancy is raised to $\bar{y}_2$. This relationship is discussed in more detail in an appendix.[1] In theory, it holds only for the mean deviation measure of dispersion; in practice, however, different measures of disperson of income are highly correlated, so that under normal circumstances a similar negative relation may by expected between mean life expectancy and measures such as the variance or the Gini coefficient.

Our macro-model can therefore be specified as

$$Y = a + f(X) + bG + \epsilon$$

where Y is mortality or life expectancy
$f(X)$ is a function of mean income
G is a measure of income distribution
ϵ is an error term

The precise shape of this function depends on the joint relation between a number of other variables and income and mortality. General improvements in medical technology, for instance, will shift the asymptote upwards; this could be represented by introducing time explicitly into the function. More specific health improvements (e.g. eradication of malaria, exceptionally large health programmes, etc.) may also shift the func-

tion at lower income levels. It might, therefore, be possible to analyse the impact of such variables by looking at deviations from the trend relation with income. However, we do not treat these issues in the present paper.

DATA

THE function described above has been estimated using international cross-sectional data from 56 countries. The basic criterion for choice of the countries was that income distribution data were available. The distribution of in-

Table 1.

Dependent variable: life expectancy at birth; whole sample.*
Regression coefficients and t *values ($N = 56$). p: parameter multiplying income*

p	Independent variables			Asymptote	R^2
	$\dfrac{1}{\log(pY)}$	$\dfrac{1}{(\log Y)^2}$	Gini		
1.00	− 136.2 (11.85)	−	−	113.4	0.722
1.00	− 132.0 (12.27)		− 27.46 (3.10)	114.9	0.765
1.00	− 3.71 (0.56)	− 183.5 (3.79)	− 35.26 (3.55)	103.0	0.775
0.01	0.1889 (2.43)	−	− 44.30 (2.70)	63.5	0.188
0.02	− 3.323 (8.16)	−	− 56.01 (4.82)	71.7	0.600
0.03	− 11.74 (11.32)	−	− 47.52 (5.09)	78.9	0.736
0.06	− 28.15 (12.46)	−	− 38.85 (4.47)	87.2	0.770
0.08	− 35.98 (12.57)	−	− 36.58 (4.23)	90.3	0.773
0.10	− 42.49 (12.60)	−	− 35.12 (4.07)	92.6	0.7740
0.12	− 48.09 (12.60)	−	− 34.09 (3.95)	94.5	0.7741
0.15	− 53.30 (12.59)	−	− 32.98 (3.81)	96.7	0.7738

*Notes to tables are given after Table 6.

come data used are those of Paukert,[2] in some cases somewhat updated, with Thailand added and Lebanon deleted for lack of appropriate mortality information. Gini coefficients and quintile distributions were taken from this source.

Mortality data (life expectancy at ages 0 and 5, and infant mortality) were taken either from standard demographic sources[3] or from an ILO compilation.[4]

For the income variable, national income per head in United States dollars was taken for a year approximating as closely as possible to the year for which life expectancy data were available.[5] Some cases where the income and life expectancy referred to different dates have been dropped.

Results

A variety of different model specifications were tried, using three different dependent variables—expectation of life at birth, at fifth birthday, and infant mortality. The income variable was tried in a number of different specifications, including reciprocal, reciprocal quadratic and reciprocal logarithm. The income distribution variable used was the Gini coefficient, ex-

cept that in some runs the mean income of specified population groups was used rather than mean overall income, to combine income and its distribution into a single measure.[6]

(i) *Life Expectancy at Birth*

Results from three different specifications are given in Tables 1, 2 and 3. In general, it can be seen that both income and income distribution are highly significant, with R^2 mostly over 0.75.

In Table 1 a sequence of specifications based on logarithms of income is presented, parameterizing on a coefficient (p) multiplying income. Maximum explanation is achieved when this coefficient is 0.12. However, this gives an asymptotic life expectancy of about 95 years, which is unrealistic. On the other hand, if we select a value for the parameter p which gives us an asymptote of around 75 years, r^2 diminishes rapidly. Thus, there are some practical reasons for doubting the applicability of the formulation using the reciprocal logarithm and the Gini coefficient as independent variables. However, these are both highly significant.

Table 2 gives the results of an alternative formulation, using the reciprocal of income and its square, together with the Gini coefficient. All

Table 2.

Dependent variable: life expectancy at birth, whole sample.*
Regression coefficients and t values (N = 56).

Independent Variables			Asymptote	R^2
$\dfrac{1}{Y}$	$\dfrac{1}{Y^2}$	Gini		
− 4469 (6.40)	149900 (3.38)	–	72.9	0.712
− 2236 (12.11)	–	− 43.87 (4.94)	73.7	0.760
− 3389 (4.93)	76880 (1.74)	− 36.47 (3.76)	75.1	0.773

*Notes to tables are given after Table 6.

three variables are significant and the asymptote is more or less in line with *a priori* expectations. This is, therefore, a rather more satisfactory result.

In Table 3 we present the results of a different approach, using mean income of the lowest 20, 40, 60 and 80 per cent of the population respectively. Mean income for the population as a whole is also given for comparative purposes. The best results are achieved in the 60 per cent to 80 per cent levels in terms of the R^2s, and in the 20 per cent and 40 per cent levels in terms of the *t* values. When income in the population as a whole (the 100 per cent level) is used, the explanation is noticeably worse, thus further demonstrating the effect of income distribution on life expectancy. The asymptotes all fall within an acceptable range.

(ii) *Life Expectancy at Fifth Birthday*

Much of the international variation in life expectancy is due to infant mortality, and we may expect the factors affecting infant mortality to be somewhat different from those which influence adult and child mortality. Life expectancy at fifth birthday was, therefore, used as a dependent variable, partly as a proxy for adult mortality. The best results are given in Table 4. For reasons similar to those in the case of life expectancy at birth, the non-logarithmic formulation is preferable, and the most acceptable result is the simplest, using only the reciprocal of income and the Gini coefficient as explanatory variables. The squared reciprocal of income was nowhere significant. The level of explanation, as measured by R^2, is virtually as high as for life expectancy at birth.

(iii) *Infant Mortality*

The best results with infant mortality as dependent variable are given in Table 5. R^2 is generally lower than for life expectancy at birth or birthday five; but otherwise the pattern is similar. The negative asymptote in the logarithmic form is unsatisfactory, and the best results are found

Table 3.

*Dependent variable: life expectancy at birth; whole sample.**
Regression coefficients and t *values (N = 56). a: population percentiles*

a	Independent variables		Asymptote	R^2
	$\dfrac{1}{Y_a}$	$\dfrac{1}{(Y_a)^2}$		
20	− 1334 (8.26)	13751 (4.82)	75.0	0.724
40	− 1821 (8.83)	24987 (5.00)	75.0	0.770
60	− 2043 (7.41)	30799 (3.56)	73.9	0.781
80	− 2505 (7.17)	45466 (3.30)	73.4	0.782
100	− 4469 (6.40)	149900 (3.38)	72.9	0.712

*Notes to tables are given after Table 6.

Table 4.

*Dependent variable: life expectancy at fifth birthday; whole sample.**
Regression coefficients and t values (N = 43) (best results and results for comparative purposes)

a	p	Independent variables				Asymptote	R^2
		$\dfrac{1}{Y_a}$	$\dfrac{1}{(Y_a)^2}$	$\dfrac{1}{\log(p\,Y_a)}$	Gini		
100	–	− 1587 (11.10)	–	–	− 18.02 (2.49)	70.4	0.758
100	0.05	–	–	− 16.40 (11.05)	− 15.33 (2.12)	78.2	0.756
100	1	–	–	− 89.58 (9.57)	− 6.31 (0.79)	97.9	0.700
80	–	− 1299 (4.42)	11989 (1.05)	–	–	70.0	0.769
80	0.6	–	–	− 31.24 (10.71)	–	82.3	0.737
60	0.8	–	–	− 29.02 (10.81)	–	81.6	0.740

*Notes to tables are given after Table 6.

Table 5.

*Dependent variable: infant mortality; whole sample.**
Regression coefficients and t values (N = 51) (best results and result for comparative purposes)

a	p	Independent Variables				Asymptote	R^2
		$\dfrac{1}{Y_a}$	$\dfrac{1}{(Y_a)^2}$	$\dfrac{1}{\log(p\,Y_a)}$	Gini		
100	–	6275 (7.04)	–	–	112.5 (2.58)	21.1	0.543
100	0.05	–	–	66.61 (7.29)	103.9 (2.43)	− 11.5	0.559
100	1	–	–	385.6 (7.58)	64.1 (1.51)	− 90	0.577
60	–	7465 (5.45)	− 147433 (3.45)	–	–	14.0	0.581
80	1.6	–	–	229.1 (7.82)	–	− 55.4	0.555

*Notes to tables are given after Table 6.

when using income in the lowest 60 per cent of the population as the explanatory variable (with a squared term), and using overall income and the Gini coefficient.

(iv) *Less Developed Countries Only*

In order to test the possibility that the results merely reflect the difference between two groups of countries, one developed, the other less developed, a series of runs was undertaken using only data for countries with incomes per head of less than $1,000. Some results are given in Table 6, where it can be seen that significance is somewhat reduced by comparison with runs using the whole sample, particularly for infant mortality. However, the results on expectation of life at

Table 6.

Less developed countries only compared with all countries;
selected regressions for comparative purposes

Dependent	Independent variables				Asymptote	R^2
	$\dfrac{1}{Y}$	$\dfrac{1}{Y^2}$	$\dfrac{1}{\log Y}$	Gini		
Life expectancy at birth						
(i) less developed countries	–	–	– 150.1	– 37.96	124.6	0.646
			(8.47)	(3.25)		
(ii) all countries	–	–	– 132.0	– 27.46	114.9	0.765
			(12.27)	(3.10)		
(iii) less developed countries	– 3041	56682	–	– 41.30	74.6	0.646
	(2.95)	(0.94)		(3.34)		
(iv) all countries	– 3389	76880	–	– 36.47	75.1	0.773
	(4.93)	(1.74)		(3.76)		
Infant mortality						
(i) less developed countries	–	–	352.8	61.3	– 84	0.324
			(4.09)	(1.05)		
(ii) all countries	–	–	385.6	64.07	– 90	0.577
			(7.58)	(1.51)		
(i) less developed countries	4801	12751	–	78.67	38.1	0.333
	(0.91)	(0.04)		(1.26)		
(ii) all countries	10547	– 279611	–	83.30	72	0.558
	(2.99)	(1.25)		(1.69)		

Y = income per head in US dollars (not deflated for price differences and changes); 'Gini' is the Gini coefficient of income inequality.

Figures in the tables are estimated coefficients of the independent variables indicated, in a linear formulation, with t values in brackets. The asymptote is life expectancy (or mortality) as income tends to infinity, and equals the regression constant where only income variables are used. Where the Gini coefficient is included as an independent variable, it is assumed that it tends to 0.33 as income tends to infinity (see Paukert, *op. cit.* in footnote 2), and the overall asymptote reflects this.

The a coefficients refer to income in a certain proportion of the population. Thus for a = 60 we would have Y_{60} as the mean income per head in the 60 per cent of the population with the lowest incomes.

The p coefficients are merely designed to improve the logarithmic form by making it a three rather than a two-parameter model. The values reproduced are those giving the best or most interesting results.

birth (and also those at fifth birthday, not reported here), hold up quite well, with significance generally retained, and estimated coefficients not significantly different from those on all countries.

CONCLUSION

THE most striking result is the consistent significance of the income distribution variable. This is a very robust conclusion which holds across a variety of specifications and with each of the three dependent variables. Although a few specifications led to relatively low significance for income distribution, these were usually unacceptable for other reasons (e.g. poor asymptote), and the sign of the income distribution terms was always as expected—greater inequality being associated with higher mortality. The results for life expectancy at birth suggest that the difference in average life expectancy between a relatively egalitarian and a relatively inegalitarian country is likely to be as much as five to ten years. The distribution of income may not be the only factor operating, of course—inequality in income distribution is likely to be associated with inequality in access to health and social services, in education, and in a number of other aspects of society relevant to mortality.

The highly significant income terms are much more predictable, of course, but here, too, the form of the function is of interest. Asymptotes near the predicted level of 75 years for life expectancy at birth, 70 years at fifth birthday, and 15–20 per thousand for infant mortality are generated by functions using the reciprocal of income, or a quadratic expression in that variable, and these also tend to be among the best in terms of significance. These are functions which are sharply non-linear—in the last function in Table 2, for example, the rate of increase of life expectancy with income declines from 0.185 at $100 per head to 0.003 at $1,000 per head. The downward con-

cavity conforms to expectations,[7] and gives indirect support to the conclusions with respect to income distribution.

Finally, it is worth stressing again that the neglect of health, environmental and social variables does not imply that they are unimportant. Rather it is only after gaining an overall appreciation of the relations between mortality and economic status and inequality that their impact can be assessed.

APPENDIX

TAKE any function, $Y = f(x)$, concave downwards (of which our postulated relationship between life expectancy and income is a special case). Let X be a random variable with unknown distribution. Then we postulate that given $E(X)$, $E(Y)$ is a negative function of the dispersion of X.

The mean deviation of X is given by

$$\sum_{i=1}^{n} (\bar{x} - x_i) + \sum_{j=1}^{m} (x_j - \bar{x})$$

where there are n and m observations below and above the mean respectively.

$$E(Y) = \sum_{i=1}^{n} f(x_i) + \sum_{j=1}^{m} f(x_j)$$

Let there be a number of infinitesimal changes, such that $\Sigma(X)$ is unchanged, but the Σx_i is increased and Σx_j reduced (i.e. the mean deviation is reduced).

$$E^*(Y) = \sum_{i=1}^{n} f(x_i + \epsilon_i) + \sum_{j=1}^{m} f(x_j + \epsilon_j)$$

where $\Sigma\epsilon_i > 0$; $\Sigma\epsilon_j < 0$; $\Sigma(\epsilon_i + \epsilon_j) = 0$

Now

$$\Sigma f(x_i + \epsilon_i) \simeq \Sigma f(x_i) + \Sigma\epsilon_i f'(x_i)$$
$$\Sigma f(x_j + \epsilon_j) \simeq \Sigma f(x_j) + \Sigma\epsilon_j f'(x_j)$$
$$\Sigma^*(Y) \simeq E(Y) + \Sigma\epsilon_i f'(x_i) + \Sigma\epsilon_j f'(x_j)$$

So

By the definition of downward concavity,
$f'(x_i) > f'(x_j)$ for all i, j, since $x_i < x_j$.

therefore $\Sigma \epsilon_i f'(x_i) + \Sigma \epsilon_j f'(x_j) > 0$

since $\Sigma \epsilon_i = - \Sigma \epsilon_j$

Whence $E^*(Y) > E(Y)$

i.e. a reduction in the dispersion of X raises the expected value of Y.

Note that this result only applies to the mean deviation. For other measures of dispersion it is usually possible to find counter-examples. However, in general such counter-examples are rather extreme and, in practice, in sico-economic systems different measures of dispersion are usually monotonically related with each other.

This paper was written as part of a research project supported by UNFPA under the ILO's World Employment Programme. Thanks are due to Claude Castor for data processing and computational work. The ILO is not responsible for any statements or opinions expressed in this paper.

NOTES

1. Cf. also S. H. Preston. 'The Changing Relation between Mortality and Level of Economic Development'. *Population Studies*, 29, 2 (July, 1975), pp. 231–248.

2. F. Paukert, 'The Distribution of Income at Different Levels of Development', *International Labour Review*, 108, 2–3 (August–September 1973).

3. E.g., UN, *Demographic Yearbooks* (New York, various dates).

4. Due to Richard Anker. Sources for this compilation are given in R. Anker, 'An Analysis of Fertility Differentials in Developing Countries', *Review of Economics and Statistics*. 60, 4 (February 1978).

5. From UN, *Yearbooks of National Accounts Statistics* (New York, various dates).

6. Certain other specifications were tried out and dropped. In particular, (a) the year of the life expectancy data proved not to be significant in explaining asymptotic life expectancy; (b) a series of runs using income per adult equivalent rather than income per head gave virtually identical results, and was eliminated by applying Occam's razor; (c) experiments with non-asymptotic specifications of the income variable explained significantly less of the variance of life expectancy.

7. The quadratic forms have unpredictable shapes at incomes below the range of the observations, but are of the expected form from a certain income level—$68 per head in the case of the last function of Table 2.

Two

INCOME DISTRIBUTION
AND INFANT MORTALITY

Robert J. Waldmann

Comparing two countries in which the poor have equal real incomes, the one in which the rich are wealthier is likely to have a higher *infant mortality rate. This anomalous result does not appear to spring from measurement error in estimating the income of the poor, and the association between high infant mortality and income inequality is still present after controlling for other factors such as education, medical personnel, and fertility. The positive association of infant mortality and the income of the rich suggests that measured real incomes may be a poor measure of social welfare.*

COUNTRIES with unequal income distributions have higher rates of infant mortality than countries with similar levels of national product per capita but more equal income distributions [Flegg, 1982; Rogers, 1979]. This finding is not surprising. Infant mortality is concentrated among the poor. If the rich are richer and the average level of income is the same, the poor are poorer. What is surprising, however, is that infant mortality appears to be positively related to the income share of the rich (the upper 5 percent of the income distribution) when the incomes of the poor (the lowest 20 percent) are equalized among countries. In this pa-

per I first document this striking empirical regularity. To a first approximation, an increase in the wealth share of the rich while the incomes of the poor are held constant leaves the poor's command over resources unchanged. So why is such an increase associated with a decrease in the poor's ability to achieve the valued outcome—low infant mortality? The association presumably arises because an unequal income distribution is associated with another factor making for high infant mortality. This paper considers and tests several possible explanations, such as the provision of medical services, the degree of urbanization, the extent of female literacy, and differences in the composition of births among different income groups. None of these factors adequately accounts for the positive association between the incomes of the rich and infant mortality.

INFANT MORTALITY IS HIGHER WHEN THE INCOME OF THE RICH IS HIGHER

CONSIDER the following relationship to be estimated across nations:

(1)   log (Infant Mortality = β log (Nonrich Income)
+ γ Rich Share.

Originally published in *Quarterly Journal of Economics*, 1992.

In equation (1), β captures the association of infant mortality with the real incomes of the nonrich strata (conditional on the share of national income going to the rich). The coefficient γ captures the association of infant mortality with the share of national income received by the rich (conditional on the real incomes of the nonrich strata). Infant mortality is thus seen as a function of the real resources available to the nonrich, who face a significant hazard of infant mortality, and of the share of real national income accruing to the rich.[1]

In equation (1) the Rich Share coefficient γ would probably be expected to be negative since it captures the implications for infant mortality of the rich having more resources under their control, while other groups have the same resources. I shall demonstrate, however, that in an international cross section the coefficient γ is positive.

I define "the rich" as the top 5 percent of the household income distribution, and define "the poor" as the bottom 20 percent. The intermediate 75 percent are termed "the middle." Data on the income distribution, in the form of the income shares of the poorest 20 percent and the richest 5 percent of households, are taken from *World Tables 1976*, supplemented by Jain [1973].[2] Data on infant mortality rates are taken from *World Tables 1976*, in this case supplemented by the *U.N. Population and Vital Statistics Report* for 1974. The infant mortality rate is the number of deaths in the first year of life per thousand live births.

Real per capita GDP estimates are from Summers and Heston [1984] who calculate real per capita GDP for different countries in a consistent "international dollar" measure, which values different goods at prices intended to reflect the average structure of prices in the world. Estimates of the levels of real incomes of the poor were constructed by multiplying the income share of the poorest 20 percent from *World Tables* by the Summers and Heston estimates of real per capita GDP.

Data on the level and distribution of income, and on infant mortality, are available for 41 countries for each of the years 1960 and 1970. Data are available for both years for 25 countries. For sixteen countries data are available for 1960 only, and for sixteen countries data are available for 1970 only. In forming samples for regression analysis, data for 1970 are used if available; and if 1970 data are not available, then 1960 data are used. In all regressions a dummy indicator variable marks the year. Thirty of the countries for which 1970 data are available and twenty-three countries for which 1960 data are available are classified as "developing" by the World Bank. Table I presents summary statistics.[3]

Table II reports estimates of the equation,

$$(2) \quad \log(\text{Infant Mortality}) = \beta_o + \beta_1 \log(\text{Poor Income}) + \beta_2 \log(\text{Middle Income}) + \gamma \, \text{Rich Share} + \delta \, \text{Year 1970}.$$

In equation (2) Poor Income and Middle Income are the average income levels of the poorest 20 percent of the population, and of the middle strata of the income distribution lying between the twentieth and the ninety-fifth percentiles, respectively. Rich Share is the share of the country's total income received by the richest 5 percent of the population. Year 1970 is an indicator variable that flags data for 1970. Equation (2) thus contains two variables to control for the real resources commanded by the nonrich: the real income of the poorest 20 percent, who are the group most at risk of infant mortality; and the second is the real income of the middle strata, who in most developing nations face a lower but still sizable risk.

The first two columns of Table II report estimates of equation (2) for two samples: one sample composed of all nations for which data are available, and a second that includes only the developing nations. The larger sample in Table II includes data from 57 countries: 41 report data from 1970, and 16 report data from 1960. The smaller sample in Table II includes data from 41 developing countries.

Table I

Summary Statistics of Infant Mortality and Explanatory Variables

	Observations	Mean	Standard deviation	Minimum	Maximum
Full sample					
Infant mortality (per thousand)	57	73.98	56.90	13 (Japan)	229 (Gabon)
Share of richest 5%	57	24.38%	8.28	13 (Taiwan)	47 (Gabon)
Share of poorest 20%	57	4.99%	2.02	1 (Sierra Leone)	9 (Bangladesh)
RGDP* (Real GDP)	57	$2024.28	1651.21	258 (Burma)	6747 (USA)
ln(RGDP*)	57	$ 7.29	0.83		
ln(infant mortality)	57	3.99	0.84		
Doctors per 1000 (MD)	50	0.71	0.57	0.014 (Niger)	2.50 (Israel)
Medical workers per 1000 (nurse)	50	1.50	1.72	0.088 (Burma)	6.25 (Canada)
Percent urban	56	45.02%	23.31	4.0 (Barbados)	86.0 (Australia)
Primary school enrollment	56	89.59%	31.39	6.0 (Niger)	144.0 (France)
Gross reproductive rate (GRR)[a]	41[a]	2.43	0.84	1.0 (Japan)	3.7 (Pakistan)
Developing country sample					
Infant mortality (per thousand)	41	94.39	54.62	18 (Taiwan)	229 (Gabon)
Share of richest 5%	41	27.02%	8.03	13 (Taiwan)	47 (Gabon)
Share of poorest 20%	41	4.74%	1.93	1 (Sierra Leone)	9 (Bangladesh)
Real GDP	41	$1186.93	670.81	258 (Burma)	2743 (Argentina)
ln(RGDP)	41	$ 6.91	0.60		
ln(infant mortality)	41	4.37	0.64		
Doctors per 1000 (MD)	34	0.41	0.37	0.014 (Niger)	1.89 (Argentina)
Medical workers per 1000 (nurse)	34	0.60	0.53	0.088 (Burma)	2.32 (Barbados)
Percent urban	40	34.73%	21.52	4.0 (Barbados)	80.0 (Argentina)
Primary school enrollment	40	82.2%	33.1	6.0 (Niger)	130.0 (Brazil)
Female literacy rate	21	44.30%	33.19	0.3 (Niger)	91.0 (Uruguay)
Gross reproductive rate (GRR)[a]	31	2.77	0.65	1.4 (Barbados)	3.7 (Pakistan)

Source. See Data Appendix

a. Defined as live daughters born per mother. For 1970 observations only.

Table II

Estimates of the Effects of Income Levels and the Rich Share on Infant Mortalilty

	Dependent variables = Log(Infant Mortality Rate)			
	(1) All nations	(2) Developing only	(3) All nations	(4) Developing only
Constant	11.92	11.41	9.48	8.42
	(13.2)	(7.7)	(9.55)	(6.58)
1970 indicator variable	0.06	− 0.05	0.08	− 0.20
	(0.44)	(− 0.25)	(0.53)	(− 0.95)
Log poor income (β_1)	0.07	0.01	− 0.66	− 0.50
	(0.45)	(0.04)	(− 6.95)	(− 3.54)
Log middle income (β_2)	− 0.80	− 0.69		
	(− 5.57)	− (3.18)		
Rich Share (γ)	2.48	2.43	1.09	1.16
	(2.82)	(2.32)	(1.03)	(1.07)
Observations	57	41	57	41
R^2	0.79	0.56	0.66	0.44

Source. See text and Data Appendix.
t-statistics are in parentheses.
All regressions use data from 1970, supplemented by data from 1960 for countries with 1970 data absent.

For both samples the estimated value of the γ coefficient on the share of the richest 5 percent (Rich Share) is surprisingly positive. The estimates are 2.48 (with a *t*-statistic of 2.82) for the total sample, and 2.43 (with a *t*-statistic of 2.32) for the sample made up of developing countries only. Positive coefficients are also found for samples composed of data from 1960 only (1.15 with a *t*-statistic of 1.50), and of data from 1970 only (3.02 with a *t*-statistic of 2.06; these results are not shown). Note that the unexpected sign of the γ coefficient on the Rich Share variable does not appear to be an artifact of differences in structure between developed and developing nations. The coefficients in the first and second columns are similar.

The estimates from the first column of Table II imply, with 95 percent confidence,[4] that a rise in the real income of the rich by 1 percent of na-

tional income (holding the income of poorer strata constant) is associated with a rise in the infant mortality rate of between 0.72 and 4.24 percent of its original level. At the geometric mean of infant mortality in the larger sample (53.8 deaths per thousand), such an increase would raise infant mortality by between 0.39 and 2.28 infant deaths per thousand live births. The γ coefficient reported in the first column accounts for 3.2 percent of the sample variance in the log of Infant Mortality, and for 13.6 percent of the residual variance that remains once the year of the observation and the levels of income received by the nonrich strata are taken into account.[5]

These results do not by themselves immediately justify the claim that an increase in the wealth of the rich raises infant mortality—and thus may reduce social welfare. The results must be examined more closely.

The first potential problem is that the regressions are sensitive to outlying observations;[6] least square places a high priority on fitting regression lines that do not pass too far from extreme observations. Figure I plots the residuals from a regression of the log of Infant Mortality on all explanatory variables except the Rich Share against the residuals from a regression of the log of the Rich Share on the other explanatory variables. It thereby shows the partial scatter of infant mortality against the rich share. The slope of this plot corresponds to the estimated γ. From the figure Taiwan appears to be an influential data point, but the coefficient on the share of the rich remains positive in regressions that do not include Taiwan.[7] Other countries with surprising infant mortality rates—Fiji, Honduras, and the United States—have rich shares close to the value expected given the other variables and therefore have little influence on the estimate of γ. The other countries with a surprising rich share—Panama and Gabon—have opposite effects on the estimate of γ. The effects of these

data points on estimates of γ cancel almost exactly.

A second potential problem is the impact of errors in measuring the income of the poor. A high value for the Rich Share suggests that income is likely to be distributed unequally throughout the bottom 95 percent of the household income distribution as well. Equation (2) includes the income level of the middle 75 percent as well as the income of the poorest 20 percent to partially control for this effect. If estimates of the poor's income contain significant errors, the coefficient will be biased toward zero: it will be biased upward, since infant mortality is expected to be a decreasing function of the income of the poorest strata.

Since the shares of the rich, the middle, and the poor must sum to 100 percent, it is likely that measurement error in the share of income received by the poor is negatively correlated with measurement error in the share received by the rich. This will impart a negative bias to the coefficient on the Rich Share. When the income of

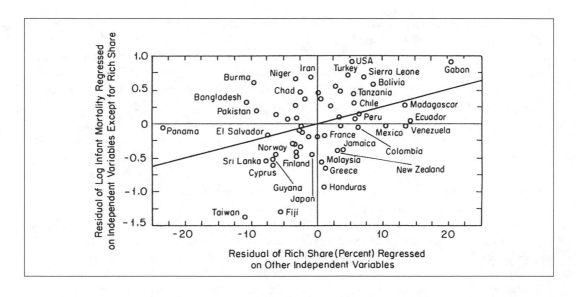

Figure 1
Partial Scatter of Infant Mortality Against Rich Share

the poor is underestimated, the share of the rich will be overestimated, and the infant mortality rate will be lower than would be expected given the (mismeasured) income of the poor. A high measured share for the rich will therefore be a signal that the real incomes of the poor are underestimated. A high measured Rich Share will thus be associated with a low infant mortality rate. This most likely form of measurement error biases the coefficient on the Rich Share downward and makes the estimated coefficient more negative in expectation than the true structural γ.

Measurement error in the income of the poor that does not induce negatively correlated measurement error in the share of the rich could bias the coefficient on the rich share upward, since a high Rich Share is likely to be associated with lower real incomes of the poor. It is worthwhile to attempt to place a bound on this upward bias. One way to do this is to estimate an equation that deliberately imparts a downward bias to the coefficient on the Rich Share.

Equation (3) omits the income of the middle 75 percent:

$$(3)\quad \log(\text{Infant Mortality}) = \beta_0 + \beta_1 \log(\text{Poor Income}) + \beta_2 \text{ Rich Share}.$$

Conditional on the income of the poor, a high Rich Share is associated with high real incomes and low infant mortality among the middle strata. This bias introduced by the complete omission of the middle income is of opposite sign and plausibly larger than any bias in γ induced by errors in measuring the income of the poor. The downward bias on γ in equation (3) comes from the correlation of the Rich Share with the (omitted) real income of the middle; the possible upward bias arises as a consequence of the bias in the poor income coefficient induced by errors in variables. Performing an auxiliary regression of the log income of the middle on the income of the poor, an indicator variable for 1970, and the share of the rich, the coefficient on the Rich Share is 1.75 (*t*-statistic of 2.16) for the entire

sample and 1.83 (*t*-statistic of 2.52) for the developing country sample. Conditional on poor income, a high value for Rich Share indicates that the middle strata are relatively rich as well and will suffer relatively low infant mortality. Equation (3) will thus generate deliberately downward-biased estimates of γ.

Two regressions with the income of the middle omitted, as in equation (3), are reported in columns (3) and (4) of Table II. The estimated γ coefficients are 1.16 (with a standard error of 1.00) using data on developing countries only, and 1.09 (with a standard error of 1.06) using data on all countries. As expected, the estimated coefficients are lower than those in the basic regressions. The deliberate attempt to bias them downward succeeds, but the coefficients remain positive although not statistically significant.

POSSIBLE EXPLANATIONS

WHY might increased income of the rich be correlated with increased infant mortality? In this section several explanations are proposed and tested, including changes in the relative accessibility of health care with increased income inequality, lower literacy rates with increased inequality, increased fertility of the poor with increased infant mortality, and compositional factors in aggregate infant mortality. Table III reports regressions with additional explanatory variables chosen to evaluate such explanations.

The relative prices of medical care, pure water, or food, for example, could be positively correlated with income inequality across countries. Since health care is plausibly a superior good, an increase in the income going of the rich could increase the relative cost of health care, leading to positive observed γ. Available data do not make it possible to test this explanation based on relative prices. The positive correlation between the Rich Share and infant mortality could also be given a related, but noncausal, explanation. A high Rich Share may indicate uneven regional develop-

Table III

Estimates of the Determinants of Infant Mortality Including Additional Explanatory Variables

	Dependent Variable = Log(Infant Mortality)					
	(1) All nations	(2) Developing only	(3) Developing only	(4) All nations	(5) All nations	(6) All nations
Constant	10.56 (6.29)	9.56 (3.79)	6.67 (1.82)	11.70 (11.64)	8.80 (5.01)	10.72 (5.23)
1970 indicator	0.01 (0.07)	− 0.23 (− 1.03)	− 0.09 (− 0.31)	0.10 (0.85)	− 0.04 (− 0.29)	
Log poor income (β_1)	0.06 (0.39)	− 0.06 (− 0.26)	− 0.15 (− 0.35)	0.06 (0.41)	0.02 (0.15)	0.09 (0.35)
Log middle income (β_2)	− 0.57 (− 2.69)	− 0.38 (− 1.07)	0.02 (0.03)	− 0.75 (− 4.93)	− 0.44 (− 2.14)	− 0.72 (− 2.70)
Doctors · (1-Rich Share)	− 0.09 (− 0.95)	− 0.09 (− 0.68)	0.09 (0.40)		0.01 (0.10)	
Nurses · (1-Rich Share)	− 0.16 (− 1.96)	− 0.14 (− 1.11)	− 0.62 (− 1.79)		− 0.16 (− 1.90)	
Percent urban	0.16 (0.40)	0.34 (0.51)	0.44 (0.33)		0.20 (0.53)	
Female literacy			− 1.29 (− 2.92)			
Primary school enrollment				− 0.18 (− 0.80)		
GRR (gross reproductive rate)						2.68 (0.17)
Continent dummies						
Africa					0.73 (2.38)	
S. Asia					0.54 (2.06)	
E. Asia					0.10 (0.29)	
Latin America					0.31 (1.45)	
Rich Share (γ)	1.76 (2.09)	1.43 (1.43)	3.84 (2.75)	2.39 (2.84)	1.41 (1.66)	2.95 (2.06)
Observations	50	34	19	56	50	41
R^2	0.85	0.64	0.80	0.81	0.88	0.73
Estimated coefficients of the rich share: basic specification, restricted sample[a]						
Rich Share (γ)	1.96 (2.30)	1.58 (1.59)	2.43 (1.54)	2.31 (2.78)	1.96 (2.30)	3.03 (2.26)
Estimated coefficients of the rich share: altered specification, full sample with imputed values[b]						
Rich Share (γ)	2.30 (2.97)	2.25 (2.59)	2.09 (2.52)	2.56 (2.88)	1.63 (2.29)	2.37 (3.02)

Source. See text and Data Appendix.

t-statistics are in parentheses.

All regressions use data from 1970, supplemented by data from 1960 for countries with 1970 data absent.

a. The restricted sample excludes countries for which the additional explanatory variables are lacking. The number of countries included is reported in the first row of the table. The basic specification is that used in the first two columns of Table II.

b. Imputed values of percent urban are fitted values from a regression of percent urban on the variables in the basic specification. Imputed values for other variables are fitted values of regressions of those variables on percent urban and on the variables in the basic specification. Heteroskedasticity-robust standard errors are reported for coefficient estimates using imputed values.

ment, with the poor concentrated in backward rural areas with limited access to health care. Under this interpretation one might expect that low urbanization would be associated with high infant mortality and with a high share of income going to the rich.

To access whether a high Rich Share is standing in for urbanization, a low level of health services, or a pattern of health provision influenced by the demand for first-class medical services (and thus biased away from public health measures), additional explanatory variables are included: the log of the number of doctors per thousand persons, the log of the number of nurses per thousand persons, and the percent of the population living in cities. The resulting estimates of γ remained positive (results not shown).

When the rich are richer, they demand more medical services, leaving fewer medical resources for the poor and middle classes. There are no direct estimates of the share of medical care consumed by the rich, but proxies can be constructed by assuming that the nonrich consume the same share of medical services as they do of other goods and services, thus that the income elasticity of demand for medical services is one. Under this assumption the proxy quantity of medical services consumed by the nonrich is proportional to the nonrich share of national income times the average national consumption of medical services per capita.

Table III reports regressions that include, as additional explanatory variables, the proxy consumption of medical services by the nonrich, namely the log of the number of doctors (or nurses) per thousand multiplied by the share of the nonrich: log(Doctors(1-Rich Share)) and log(Nurses(1-Rich Share)). The estimated coefficient on the Rich Share remains positive, although somewhat reduced in size, as shown in columns (1) and (2) of Table III. The coefficient ranges from 1.76 to 1.43, with reported *t*-statistics of 2.09 and 1.43.

Data on doctors and nurses, and on urbaniza-

tion, are missing for ten country/date pairs: seven in 1960 and three in 1970. To determine whether the shifts in the Rich Share coefficient were due to the additional variables or to the loss of data points, the original regression equation was reestimated on the diminished sample.[8] An alternative is to use the full sample for the regressions with the additional variables, imputing values where the additional explanatory variables are missing.[9] The final lines of Table III report coefficients on the Rich Share estimated for the basic specification using the restricted sample, and for the added-variable specification with missing data values imputed. The table shows that the changes in the estimated γ are principally due to the change in the sample.[10]

The association of a high Rich Share with increased infant mortality does not appear to arise because a high Rich Share is associated with relatively limited access to medical care for the poor. Medical care consumption proxy variables are important, and they are significant determinants of infant mortality rates, but their inclusion does not reverse the central finding.

An important indicator of a family's capacity to protect its children's health is the literacy of the mother (see Repetto [1979, p. 26]). Greater female literacy could reduce infant mortality because literate women are more likely to know how to protect their infants' lives. It is also possible that literacy confers status on women, and that women use this higher status in the family to advance the interests of infants. Alternatively, high female literacy rates may indicate an egalitarian government devoted to primary education for all, which also places a high priority on public health.

Female adult literacy rates for developing countries, taken from the United Nations' *Population and Vital Statistics Report* [1974], are included as additional explanatory variables alongside the income distribution variables. Female adult literacy rates are available for only 29 of the developing countries in the sample. Column (3) of Table III reports estimates for the developing country sample including the medical care variables and the female literacy rate (Lit).[11]

The estimated coefficient on the female literacy rate is negative, as expected, and suggests that if an additional 1 percent of women are literate, the expected infant mortality rate is 1.29 percent lower, corresponding to a reduction of 1.16 deaths per thousand live births at the sample mean of infant mortality (89.8 deaths per thousand). The coefficient on the Rich Share, however, remains positive, and increases to 3.84, with a t-statistic of 2.75.[12] Female literacy appears to be an important and statistically significant factor affecting infant mortality, but it is not related to a possible spurious link between a high share of income received by the rich and high infant mortality.

Since female literacy rates were not available for many countries, the primary school enrollment rate from *World Tables* [1976] is also used as an alternative indicator of health and sanitation knowledge.[13] The primary school enrollment rate has a negative effect on infant mortality, as expected. But the coefficient is never statistically significant, and the inclusion of the primary school enrollment rate has almost no effect on the coefficient of the rich share. Results for the full sample are reported in column (4) of Table III. The hypothesis that the correlation between inequality and infant mortality reflects a link between inequality and poor female education as a proxy for household "technology" receives no support.

A wide variety of possible omitted social and cultural variables can be accounted for by controlling for the continent of the different countries. The basic specifications reported in the first columns of Table II were reestimated including continent dummy variables, and separating "east Asia" out from "other Asia." The effect of the continent dummies on the estimate of rich share coefficient γ is small, as column (5) of Table III reports. The t-statistic falls only slightly, and the point estimate is almost exactly the same.

The small effect of continent dummies on the estimate of γ is striking given the large magnitudes and robust statistical significance of the continent dummy variables. The coefficient on the Africa dummy minus the east Asia dummy is approximately one, indicating that infant deaths are more than two and a half times as common in Africa as one would expect given the experience of east Asia.[14]

Another potential explanation for the association between a high Rich Share and infant mortality is reverse causality: high infant mortality could cause income inequality. High infant mortality could be correlated with or even be caused by faster population growth, and faster population growth, especially among the poor, could produce low wages for unskilled labor and generate more inequality. To test for this possibility, a measure of fertility—the gross reproductive rate—was included as an additional explanatory variable.[15]

Data on gross reproductive rates were taken from *World Tables* [1976] and are available for all countries in the sample in 1970. Data on gross reproductive rates in 1960 are not available for most countries. Accordingly, infant mortality regressions using data from 1970 only were performed adding the gross reproductive rate as an additional explanatory variable. Column (6) of Table III shows that γ is not sensitive to the inclusion of the gross reproductive rate, and thus that the hypothesis that high infant mortality causes inequality by causing a high gross reproductive rate does not receive support.

Increased income for the middle classes and the rich could be associated with a higher infant mortality rate without any association between infant deaths and the share of the rich holding poor income constant. If fertility declines with income, increased income of the rich reduces the denominator (births) of the infant mortality rate proportionally more than it reduces the numerator (deaths).

A method immune to this criticism is to use a measure of infant deaths that does not have births in the denominator, such as the number of

Table IV

Determinants of Infant Deaths per Woman

Sample	All nations		Developing only		All nations		Developing only	
	(1)	(2)	(3)	(4)	(5)	(6)	(7)	(8)
Dependent variable	Deaths /woman[a]	Infant mortality[b]	Deaths /woman	Infant mortality	Deaths /woman	Infant mortality	Deaths /woman	Infant mortality
Constant	12.47	9.09	10.89	8.11	11.33	7.73	7.64	4.97
	(8.23)	(7.21)	(6.20)	(5.17)	(4.18)	(3.58)	(2.47)	(1.88)
Poor income (β_1)	−0.91	−0.61	−0.72	−0.49	−0.71	−0.39	−0.27	−0.05
	(−6.70)	(−5.40)	(−4.09)	(−3.13)	(−2.29)	(−1.56)	(−0.74)	(−0.17)
Doctors · (Poor Share)					0.11	0.03	−0.12	−0.14
					(0.55)	(0.19)	(−0.54)	(−0.75)
Nurses · (Poor Share)					−0.31	−0.26	−0.31	−0.26
					(−2.38)	(−2.51)	(−2.10)	(−2.07)
Rich Share (γ)	1.55	1.07	1.77	1.21	0.47	−0.08	0.63	−0.02
	(0.98)	(0.81)	(1.12)	(0.86)	(0.27)	(−0.06)	(0.39)	(−0.01)
Observations	41	41	31	31	38	38	28	28
R^2	0.75	0.66	0.52	0.39	0.80	0.74	0.57	0.45

Source. See text and Data Appendix.
a. The dependent variable (deaths/woman) is the log of the product of the gross reproductive rate and the infant mortality rate.
b. The dependent variable (infant mortality) is the log of the infant mortality rate.
t-statistics are in parentheses.
All data are from 1970 only.

infant deaths per woman, as the dependent variable. A proxy for infant deaths per woman is the product of the gross reproductive rate and the infant mortality rate. A comparison of the results with this proxy for deaths per woman as the dependent variable with the results using the infant mortality rate would reveal the extent to which the positive association between infant mortality and rich share is driven by shifts in the denominator of the infant mortality rate.

Table IV reports regressions with infant deaths per woman as the dependent variable. In every case the γ coefficient on the Rich Share, and its t-statistic, are higher when infant deaths per woman is the dependent variable. Table IV reports four such regressions. The estimate of γ and its t-statistic are higher when infant deaths per woman is the dependent variable for all specifications reported in this article. There is no evidence that increased rich income causes an increased infant mortality rate because it reduces the fertility of the rich.

It is possible that relatively high fertility in rich families causes an equal income distribution because of, e.g., dilution of bequests. High fertility of rich families relative to the fertility of poor families should cause low infant mortality rates by affecting the composition of births. It is possible to compare this correlation between income and fertility in different countries to evaluate the compositional bias explanation of positive γ. Such a comparison reinforces the suggestion that the results of this paper not caused by compositional bias. Visaria [1980], for example, reports the average size of families by income or consumption decile in four countries: Malaysia, Sri Lanka, Nepal, and Taiwan; and two Indian provinces, Maharashtra and Gujarat. Although his sample is small, it is informative: Taiwan has both a very low share of the rich and a very low infant mortality rate. Taiwan is thus a prime candidate for a country in which the rich have a large share of births, which leads to a low aggregate infant mortality rate. Yet the rich have a small share of births in Taiwan compared with other countries in Visaria's sample whether families are stratified on the basis of income, per capita income, consumption, or per capita consumption.

Conclusion

CONTROLLING for the real incomes of the poor, for indicators of the amount of health care available to the relatively poor, and for other variables, a greater share of income going to the rich is correlated with higher infant mortality. This positive estimated coefficient on the rich share does not appear to be caused by the omission from the regression of doctors per capita, nurses per capita, urbanization indicators, female literacy, or gross reproductive rates. When these variables are included, the estimated coefficient on the share of income received by the rich remains positive and is little changed. Moreover, the positive sign of the Rich Share coefficient γ does not appear to be driven by errors in variables.

It is possible that the positive estimated γ arises from some unobserved factor which affects both inequality and infant mortality, but considerable exploration in this paper has failed to turn up such a factor. No single easily measured and identified factor appears to account for the positive estimated γ.

Limitations of the data set used make it impossible to decisively rule out two such explanations. Since I do not have data on relative prices, I cannot rule out the possibility that the results are caused by a positive correlation of the rich share and the relative price of, e.g., health care. Since I have very limited data on the correlation of household income and family size, I cannot rule out the possibility that a larger fraction of babies are born to poor families in countries with a high Rich Share. Neither explanation is supported by the limited or indirect evidence available, but they are not ruled out by the data.

Another remaining possibility is that higher incomes for the rich are associated with increased infant mortality because both are significantly affected by governmental policies. This explanation could be evaluated by assessing the government's relative concern with the rich and the poor by, for example, examining the share of health care spending devoted to hospitals (which treat the relatively rich almost exclusively). A final remaining possibility is that higher incomes for the rich distort the preferences and the judgment of the poor. One possible indicator of such distortions—and a leading explanation of the risk of infant mortality—is the prevalence of breast feeding [DaVanzo et al. 1982; Palloni and Milman, 1986].

Welfare comparisons often take a semi-Pareto condition as a building block: a country must be better off if every income percentile receives a higher *measured* real income than the same percentile in some reference country. Yet economists also believe that social indicators like the infant mortality rate are good measures of social welfare. The surprising positive sign of γ thus implies that measured incomes may be a poor measure of social welfare. When incomes are unequally distributed, the true welfare of the poor may be lower than measured real income suggests.

Data Appendix

DATA on income shares of the richest 5 percent of households and of the poorest 20 percent of households are taken from the International Bank for Reconstruction and Development's *World Tables 1976*. The shares are described by the International Bank for Reconstruction and Development as "typically" the percentage of private income both in cash and in kind accruing to the richest 5 percent and poorest 20 percent of households, respectively. The data from *World Tables 1976* are supplemented by Jain [1973] for Japan in 1970, Germany in 1970, Australia in 1970, and Taiwan in both 1960 and 1970. The share of the middle 75 percent of households was derived as a residual. All of the income distribution estimates are measured with consider-

able potential error, hence the attention paid in the text to the possible consequences of such measurement error.

Data on infant mortality rates are taken from *World Tables 1976*, supplemented by the United Nations' *Population and Vital Statistics Report* for the year 1974 to obtain an estimate for Honduras in 1970. The infant mortality rate is defined as the number of deaths before the age of one per 1000 live births. The most important potential sources of inconsistency across nations lie in the classification of live births and still births, and in the recording of infant deaths, especially among the very poor. It is more likely that such deaths are recorded if they occur in hospitals, causing possible bias. I thank an anonymous referee for pointing this out to me.

Real per capita GDP estimates are taken from Summers and Heston [1984], who calculate real per capita GDP for different countries in a consistent "international dollar" measure, which values different goods at prices intended to reflect the average structure of prices in the world. Estimates of the poor income and middle income variables are constructed by multiplying the poor and middle shares of income by the Heston and Summers real per capita national income measures.

Female adult literacy rates for developing countries are taken from the United Nations' *Population and Vital Statistics Report* [1974]. The rate is defined as the percentage of women over fifteen who can read and write.

Data on the number of doctors per thousand, on health workers per thousand, on the percent of the population living in cities, and on the gross reproductive rate are also taken from *World Tables 1976*. The doctors per thousand variable is defined as the number of practicing physicians (those who have qualified by attending a medical school at the university level) divided by the population. The health workers per thousand variable is defined as the sum of the number of (a) practicing graduate nurses, (b) "trained" or "certified" nurses, and (c) auxiliary personnel with either some professional training or practical experience, divided by the population. Data on doctors per thousand and health workers per thousand are missing for Taiwan, Benin, Chad, Ecuador, Guyana, Brazil, and Jamaica in 1960, and for Bangladesh, Taiwan, and Fiji in 1970. Data for Taiwan in 1960, Ecuador in 1960, and Brazil in 1960 were not used in the basic regressions because 1970 data were available for those countries. And so the sample restricted to those countries reporting data on doctors per thousand and health workers per thousand contains seven fewer countries than the full sample.

Data on the percent of the population living in urban areas are available from all countries except for Bangladesh in 1970. This does not further reduce the sample because data on health workers are also not reported by Bangladesh.

The gross reproductive rate is the average number of live daughters who would be born per woman if every woman were to survive to the end of her reproductive period and bear children at current rates. Data on the gross reproductive rate are available for all countries in 1970, and for a few countries from 1960. Only data from 1970 are used.

Primary school enrollment rates are taken from *World Tables 1976*. The primary school enrollment rate is available for all countries except for Fiji in 1970. The variable is total enrollment of all ages in primary schools as a percentage of the population of primary school age. Note that this statistic can easily be more than 100 percent.

World Tables is not a set of statistics compiled by an independent organization. It collects statistics reported by individual national governments. Statistics thus differ widely in reliability across countries.

References

DeVanzo, J., J. P. Habicht, K. Hill, and S. Preston, *Quantitative Studies of the Mortality Decline in Developing Countries*, World Bank Staff Working Paper #683 (Washington, DC: International Bank for Reconstruction and Development, 1982).

Flegg, A. "Inequality of Income, Illiteracy, and Medical Care as Determinants of Infant Mortality in Developing Countries," *Population Studies*, XXXVI (1982), 441–58.

International Bank for Reconstruction and Development, *World Tables 1976* (Baltimore, MD: Johns Hopkins University Press, 1976).

Jain, S., *The Size Distribution of Income: Compilation of Data*. Development Research Center Discussion Paper #4 (Washington, DC: International Bank for Reconstruction and Development, 1973).

Palloni, A., and S. Millman, "Effects of Inter-birth Intervals and Breast Feeding on Infant and Early Childhood Mortality," *Population Studies*, XXXX (1986), 215–36.

Repetto, R., *Economic Equality and Fertility in Developing Countries* (Baltimore, MD: Johns Hopkins University Press, 1979).

Rogers, G., "Income and Inequality as Determinants of Mortality: An International Cross Sectional Analysis," *Population Studies*, XXXIII (1979), 343–52.

Summers, R., and A. Heston, "Improved International Comparisons of Real Product and Its Composition, 1950–1980," *Review of Income and Wealth*, XXXIII (1984), 207–62.

United Nations, *Population and Vital Statistics Report 1974*, Department of Economic and Social Affairs Statistical Papers Series A, XXXVI (New York: United Nations, 1974).

Visaria, Pravan, *Poverty and Living Standards in Asia*, World Bank Working Paper (Washington, DC: International Bank for Reconstruction and Development, 1980).

NOTES

1. The log-log specification in infant mortality and real income is used. Preliminary inspection of scatter plots suggested an approximately log-linear relationship between real per capita GDP and infant mortality. The results reported below are not caused by the imposition of the log-linear functional form, since estimates of γ are little changed with more flexible functional forms.

2. Published income distribution data for Liberia are inconsistent. In 1970 Liberia reported that the richest 5 percent of families received 60 percent of national income. It also reported that the poorest 20 percent of families received 13 percent of national income. These statistics are grossly inconsistent. Given the claimed income share of the poor, the rich share could be no more than 39 percent of national income. Liberia was excluded from the sample throughout.

3. Additional details are in the Data Appendix.

4. The endpoints of 95 percent confidence interval are constructed by adding 2.01 and −2.01 to the *t*-statistic and multiplying by the standard error.

5. An alternative specification to equation (2) is

(f1) log(Infant Mortality) = β_0 + β_1 log(Poor Income) + β_2 log(Middle Income)

$$+ \gamma \log(\text{Rich Income}) + \delta \text{ Year 1970}.$$

In this specification, γ' captures the effect of raising the real income—not the share of national product—of the rich, while holding the real incomes of nonrich strata constant. Specification (2) was chosen over specification (f1) for a priori reasons. Variation in per capita income levels across nations is great. As a result, it seemed likely that across countries the incomes of households in different percentile ranges would be collinear. Specification (2) was chosen to eliminate this possible collinearity, which it was feared might prevent precise estimation of coefficients. When the regression is estimated with the share of the rich replaced by the log income of the rich as in equation (f1), the *t*-statistic in the regression corresponding to column 1 is 2.84 with a coefficient of 0.477, corresponding at the sample mean to a γ coefficient of 1.96 (compared with 2.48). With the developing country sample, the *t*-statistic is 2.50 with a coefficient corresponding at the sample mean to 1.88 (compare with 2.43). This suggests that the collinearity between the income of the rich and the income of the poor is not as high as feared.

6. When all data are used, only one striking outlier is found: Liberia. The residual from the regression of the Rich Share on the other explanatory variables is equal to 30.5 percent of national income. As noted earlier, all the results reported including summary statistics and the graph exclude Liberia.

7. Some regressions that do not include Taiwan in the sample are reported in Table III below. In Table III, columns (1), (2), and (3) omit Taiwan from the sample. Data for medical personnel in Taiwan are not reported by international organizations, and so all regressions that include medical personnel variables among the independent variables omit Taiwan.

8. For example, Taiwan is removed, and Taiwan has a low rich share and also a low rate of infant mortality.

9. Imputation uses the coefficients from a regression of the additional variable on the basic explanatory variables. Since the conventional standard errors of the regressions with imputed values are understated, heteroskedastic-robust standard errors are reported for these regressions.

10. Regressions with the added medical care and urbanization variables were also estimated with the income of the middle strata excluded, and with the number of doctors (or nurses) per capita multiplied not by the Nonrich Share but by the Poor Share. The coefficient on the Rich Share remained positive for all samples. For the developing country sample, the estimated coefficient was 0.82 (with a standard error of 0.97). Recall that this specification produces a downward-biased estimate of the coefficient on the Rich Share.

11. Additional regressions estimated included as well the urbanization variable and the proxies for health care consumed by the nonrich constructed above.

12. This is primarily due to the reduced sample.

13. Data were available for all countries except for Fiji in 1970.

14. In regressions including indicators of health care and urbanization, all of the continent dummies are positive, implying that even east Asia is doing poorly compared with the log-log infant mortality-income relationship extrapolated from the developed countries. As noted above, the effect of the added variables is probably due to the reduction of the sample and, in particular, to the elimination of Taiwan, which has surprisingly low infant mortality.

15. The gross reproductive rate is the average number of live daughters who would be born per woman if all women survived to the end of their potential reproductive periods. The appropriate variable would be the gross reproductive rate for the poor, but data on fertility by income class are not available for any substantial sample.

Three

INCOME DISTRIBUTION
AND LIFE EXPECTANCY

Richard G. Wilkinson

I N Britain, as in other developed countries, variations in morbidity and mortality have been associated with a wide variety of measures of socioeconomic status including car ownership, housing tenure, occupational class, overcrowding, education, and unemployment.[1-5] Associations with income have also been reported.[6-8] The cross sectional relation between income and health seems to be strictly non-linear. Figure 1 shows this relation in the 7000 people studied in the example, the health and lifestyles survey.[6] For three different measures of morbidity standards of health improved rapidly as income increased from the lowest towards the middle of the range. No further gains in health accompanied increases in income beyond that point. (Such a strongly non-linear relation may sometimes have been missed by researchers using linear methods.)

In a test of the causal significance of the relation between income and mortality during 1971–81 changes in occupational mortality were significantly related to changes in the proportion of people in each occupation earning less than about 60% of average earnings and also to changes in the proportion unemployed.[7] Changes in the proportions of people in higher earnings categories seemed to have less impact on mortality. If there are sharply diminishing health returns to increases in income, income redistribution might improve the health of the less well off while having little effect on the health of the better off. The end result would be to improve the average standard of health of the population.

Cross sectional evidence suggesting that there is a significant tendency for mortality to be lower in countries with a more egalitarian distribution of income does exist.[7-10] That this relation has been identified in different groups of countries, at different times, and with different measures of income distribution, suggests that it is robust. Correlation coefficients above 0–8 have been reported, [7-8] suggesting that the underlying relation may be important and should be pursued further. Nevertheless, if such an association exists it is surprising that mortality in developed countries has been found not to be closely related to measures of average income such as gross national product per head.[11]

Originally published in *British Medical Journal*, 1992.

ANALYSIS OF DATA

I collected data to investigate the cross sectional relation between income distribution and mortality and its possible interactions with gross national product per head and to access

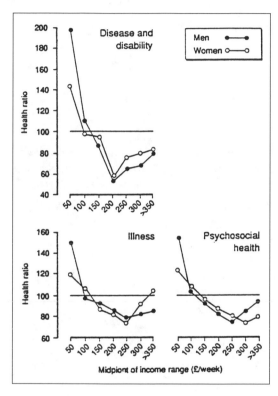

Figure 1

Age standardised health ratios for disease and disability, illness, and psychosocial health in relation to weekly income (£) in 1981 of men and women aged 40–59[6]

whether changes in income distribution over time are related to changes in mortality in developed countries. Throughout the following analyses mortality is measured by combined male and female life expectancy at birth. Data are from the *World Tables*,[11] supplemented by figures for Italy and Portugal from the *World Health Statistics Annuals*[13] and for the United Kingdom from the

Government Actuary's Department (personal communication).

Gross National Product Per Head

The relation between average income and life expectancy was assessed using figures of gross national product per head (based on purchasing power parities) for 23 countries in the Organisation for Economic Cooperation and Development.[14] The Pearson correlation coefficient for the cross sectional relation between life expectancy and gross national product per head in 1986–7 was 0·38 (p<0·05). The correlation between the increases in gross national product per head and in life expectancy over the 16 years 1970–1 to 1986–7 was almost non-existent at 0·07. These data seem to confirm that there is, at best, only a weak relation between gross national product per head and life expectancy in developed countries.[9-11]

Income Distribution

Unfortunately, internationally comparable data on the distribution of income within each country are scarce. The data used here were originally put together for reasons unrelated to health, and in each case all the countries given in the sources were included in the analyses. The measures of income distribution were also limited by the sources.

For a few countries the data bank of the Luxembourg Income Study provides income distribution data of "an unparalleled degree of comparability between countries."[15] The study gives data on the share of total income going to successive tenths in the income distribution in nine countries: Australia 1981, Canada 1981, the Netherlands 1983, Norway 1979, Sweden 1981, Switzerland 1982, West Germany 1981, United Kingdom 1979, and the United States 1979.[15] Income was family net cash income, defined as gross original income plus public and private transfers and minus direct (income and payroll) taxes. The table shows the Pearson correlation

coefficients for the relation between life expectancy in 1981 and the share of total income going
to successive tenths of the population, starting
with the poorest and ending with the richest, in
each of these nine countries. The coefficients in
the first column show the relation between life
expectancy and the proportion of total income
going to each tenth of the population taken separately. The second column is a cumulative version of the first column: it shows the correlation
between life expectancy and the proportion of income going to the combined population below
each successive decile of income distribution.
Here the strength of the correlation peaks at the
seventh decile—that is, with the proportion of
income going to the least well off 70% of the
population. Figure 2 shows the relation between
average life expectancy and the proportion of income received by the least well off 70% of the
population in different countries.

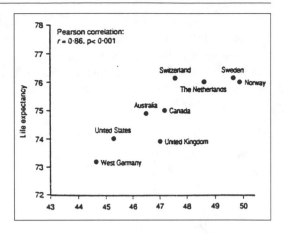

Figure 2
*Relation between life expectancy at birth (male and
female combined) and percentage of post tax and
benefit income received by least well off 70% of families, 1981*

*Pearson correlation coefficients for relation between life expectancy (male
and female at birth) and income distribution in nine countries in the Organisation for Economic Cooperation and Development[15]*

| | | Everyone below each decile | |
Income distribution	Each interdecile group separately	Controlling for gross national product/head	
Decile 1	0·13	0·13	0·28
Decile 2	0·63*	0·45	0·57
Decile 3	0·76**	0·57*	0·66*
Decile 4	0·92***	0·65**	0·73*
Decile 5	0·64*	0·75**	0·83**
Decile 6	0·28	0·84***	0·91***
Decile 7	0·18	0·86***	0·90***
Decile 8	0·17	0·80**	0·81**
Decile 9	0·11	0·68*	0·68*
Decile 10	− 0·68*		

*p<0·05, **p<0·01, ***p<0·001.

The third column of the table shows partial
correlation coefficients which repeat the cumulative analysis in the second column while controlling for gross national product per head (a
measure of the average income in each country).
Regressing life expectancy on gross national
product per head and the proportion of income

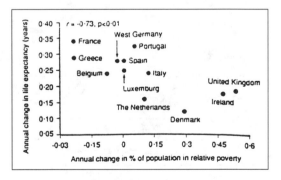

Figure 3
*Annual rate of change in life expectancy and in pro-
portion of population in relative poverty in 12 European Community countries, 1975–85*

going to everyone below the seventh decile in
each country produced an equation with a correlation coefficient of 0·90 and an adjusted R^2 suggesting that three quarters of the variation in life
expectancy is accounted for by these two variables alone. However, gross national product per
head does not make a significant independent
contribution to the equation. The change in R^2
produced by bringing gross national product per

head into the equation suggests that it contributes less than 10% to the proportion of the variance explained. This existence of a strong cross sectional relation between life expectancy and income distribution stands in marked contrast to the weak relation with gross national product per head.

Effect of Changes in Income Distribution

To provide a more demanding test of the relation with income distribution changes in income distribution between two dates were compared with changes in life expectancy in different countries. Only two small sets of data with internally consistent definitions of income and of the income receiving unit could be found from which figures of changes in income distribution could be derived. Results are also reported from a third source which falls short of these standards.

The first data set comes from a European Commission project to provide estimates of changes in the prevalence of relative poverty in 12 European Community countries between 1975 and 1985.[16] Relative poverty is defined as the proportion of the population living on less than 50% of the national average disposable income. As the initial estimates of poverty for some countries varied during 1973–7, resulting in estimates of change over different time spans, changes in both poverty and life expectancy were expressed as average annual rates of change. Figure 3 shows the relation between the annual rates of change in life expectancy and the proportion of the population in poverty. The correlation coefficient was -0.73 ($p<0.01$), showing that among these countries a fall in the prevalence of relative poverty was significantly related to a more rapid improvement in life expectancy.

The second data set contains the income distribution in some countries in the Organisation of Economic Cooperation and Development at varying dates.[17] Changes in the proportion of total disposable income received by the least well off 60% of households can be calculated over one

period for five countries, and over two periods for a sixth, to provide seven observations of change in all. As the length of the periods varied from five to 11 years, all changes were again expressed as annual rates (fig 4). To ensure the independence of the observations, the two periods shown for Japan were combined, and a correlation coefficient of 0.80 ($p<0.05$) across the six countries suggested once more that increases in the share of income going to the least well off were associated with faster increases in life expectancy.

The last set of data on changes in income distribution comes from the *World Development Reports*.[18] Changes in the proportion of income received by the least well off 60% can be calculated for 15 developed countries (Australia, Canada, Denmark, Finland, France, Italy, Japan, the Netherlands, Norway, West Germany, Spain, Sweden, Switzerland, United Kingdom, and the United States). This data set is larger than the last two partly because data are included that are often not strictly comparable. There are variations both in the definition of income and in the income receiving unit.[19] The correlation coefficient between the annual rate of change in life expectancy and in the proportion of income received by the least well off 60% of the population was 0.47 ($p<0.05$).

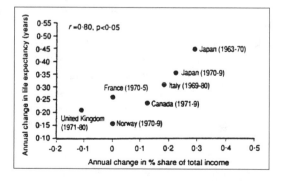

Figure 4
Annual change in life expectancy and percentage of income received by least well off 60% of population. (Two figures for Japan were combined when calculating correlation coefficient)

DISCUSSION

THE relation between income distribution and life expectancy is sufficiently strong to produce significant associations in analyses of cross sectional data and of data covering changes over time, despite the small number of countries for which compatible data are available. Because several countries appear in more than one data set, the four analyses reported here cannot be regarded as strictly independent. Nevertheless, data on income distribution from 19 developed countries has been included and the data on changes over time are independent of the cross sectional data given for nine countries. Other countries have been included in previous analyses.[8-10] Overall, there is clear evidence of a strong relation between a society's income distribution and the average life expectancy of its population.

How should this relation be interpreted? Four possibilities may be suggested. The first two concern potential intervening variables. The strength of the relation (correlation coefficients as high as 0·8 and 0·9) reduces the likelihood that it could be a byproduct of a closer underlying relation. Countries with a more egalitarian income distribution are likely to have better public services which benefit health, but medical services are unlikely to have a decisive influence on national mortality. Even the small proportion of deaths from conditions regarded as wholly amenable to medical treatment seem less influenced by differences in medical provision than they are by differences in socioeconomic factors.[20] Deaths from many other important causes are only marginally affected by medical care. In addition, it has been shown statistically that neither public nor private expenditure on medical care can account for the relation.[10] Although the effects of other areas of public expenditure still await examination, it is hard to imagine which could give rise to spurious correlations as strong as these.

The second possibility is that ethnic minority communities may have poor health and widen the income distribution as a result of discrimination in employment. The evidence suggests that ethnic minorities, at least in Britain, have very little effect on national standards of health.[21] In addition, such a hypothesis cannot explain the relation between changes in income distribution and life expectancy during years when international migration (especially of the unskilled) was tightly controlled. Lastly, the scale of the effect of income distributions on health is too large to be accounted for by minorities.

The third possibility is reverse causality. If sickness is sometimes a cause of poverty, a higher proportion of sick people would widen the income distribution. Processes of this kind have been found to make only a small contribution to the differences in mortality between social classes.[22-24] Class differentials in mortality are measured among economically active people of working age, among whom such effects might be expected to be at their strongest. As the current analyses have used life expectancy at birth for the total population, the impact of reverse causality will be reduced still further: children, pensioners, and those who are not economically active are unlikely to suffer any loss of income when ill.

If reverse causality were the main explanation of the association reported here, it would imply that changes in income distribution were mainly determined by autonomous changes in health. That would mean denying the contribution of economic factors like unemployment, taxes, benefits, profits, and wage bargaining to income distribution. Lastly, there is direct evidence from other sources that mortality is responsive to changes in income.[7-8]

The fourth possibility is that mortality is affected by income distribution. This interpretation is consistent with the curvilinear relation between income and mortality found in Britain (fig 1) and the suggestion that health is more responsive to changes in income among the least well off.[7-8] The contrasting experiences of Britain and Japan illustrate the possible effects of income distribution on health. In 1970 income distribution and life expectancy were similar in the two countries and fairly typical of other countries in the Organisation for Economic Cooperation and Development.[8] Since then they have diverged: Japan now has the highest life expectancy in the world. Marmot and Davey Smith found no obvious explanation (in changing diet, health services, or other aspects of life) for the rapid improvement in Japanese life expectancy.[25] They did, however, observe that Japan now has the most egalitarian income distribution of any country on record. In Britain, on the other hand, income distribution has widened since the mid-1980s and mortality among men and women aged 15–44 years has increased.[26] That these divergent trends in mortality are related to what has happened to socioeconomic differentials is confirmed by the tendency for mortality to fall most rapidly among the upper class in Britain and the lower classes in Japan.[25]

Size of the Effect

If Britain was to adopt an income distribution more like the most egalitarian European countries the slope of the regression equation suggests that about two years might be added to the population's life expectancy. As people in social class V account for less than 6% of the economically active population, reducing their death rates to the average would add only a few months to the life expectancy of the whole population. To account for the whole two year increase in life expectancy requires the assumption that the least well off half of the population overcome a mortality disadvantage almost as great as that of social class V. The fact that such a large group of the population at such high risk has not yet been identified[1] implies that the benefits may be more widespread.

It is not only the scale of the health benefits which suggest that income distribution may improve the health of the majority of the population. The pattern of correlations in the table and

the shape of the curve relating income to mortality in figure 1 carry the same implication. The table suggests that the health of the least well off 60–70% of the population may benefit from income redistribution. Although the correlations with the lowest tenth were not significant, the fact that changes in life expectancy and the proportion of the population in poverty were significantly related (fig 3) suggests that the income data used in the table are least accurate among the poor.

As income distribution is skewed, so that a little over 60% of the population live on less than the average, we may be seeing a demarcation between the potential beneficiaries of a more egalitarian income redistribution living on less than the average income and the 35% or so above the average income. In this context, the negative association between income and health among the most well off is interesting. That it has previously been found in women's mortality suggests that it should not be ignored.

Relative or Absolute Income?

Gross national product per head ceases to be an important determinant of national mortality only among developed countries.[27] In 1984 few countries achieved an average life expectancy at birth of 70 years or more until gross national product per head approached a threshold of almost $5000 a year. Beyond that level it seems that there is little systematic relation between gross national product per head and life expectancy. Thus despite the long term tendency for life expectancy and the standard of living to increase, among the developed countries the two are no longer closely connected.

This suggests that the association between health and income distribution is a result of factors to do with relative rather than absolute income. Increasingly social scientists have emphasised the importance of relative poverty and of the way it excludes people, socially and materially, from the normal life of society.[28]

Many national and international statistical agencies now measure poverty in relative terms.[17][29] But the sense of relative deprivation, of being at a disadvantage in relation to those better off, probably extends far beyond the conventional boundaries of poverty. A shift in emphasis from absolute to relative standards indicates a fall in the importance of the direct physical effects of material circumstances relative to psychosocial influences. The social consequences of people's differing circumstances in terms of stress, self esteem, and social relations may now be one of the most important influences on health. There is little evidence to guide further speculation on the mechanisms that may lie behind this relation, though the strength of the relation suggests that a wide variety of factors may be acting. Indeed, if confirmed, the importance of relative poverty to public health may lie in the possibility it provides of influencing unknown as well as known risk factors.

These results should caution against using the lack of a close relation between national mortality and gross national product per head to infer that health inequalities within societies cannot be a reflection of income differentials.[30] Indeed, if health differences within the developed countries are principally a function of income inequality itself, this would explain why social class differences in health have not narrowed despite growing affluence and the fall of absolute poverty.

I thank the Economic and Social Research Council (grant No. R000232685) for financial support.

NOTES

1. Goldblatt P. Mortality and alternative social classifications. In: Goldblatt P. ed. *Lunguainal study 1971–1981.* London: HMSO, 1990:163–92. (OPLS series LS: No. 6)

2. Townsend P. Phillimore P. Beattie A. *Health and deprivanon: inequality and the north.* London: Croom Helm, 1988.

3. Beale N. Nethercott S. The nature of unemployment morbidity 2. Description. *J R Cull Gen Prace* 1988:38:200–2.

4. Moser K, Goldblatt P, Fox J. Unemployment and mortality. In: Goldblatt P. ed. *Longitudinal study 1971–1981.* London: HMSO, 1990P81–97. (OPCS series LS No 6.)

5. Fox J, ed. *Health inequalities in European countries.* Aldershot: Gower, 1989.

6. Blaxter M. *Health and lifestyles.* London: Tavistock, 1990.

7. Wilkinson RG. Income distribution and mortality: a "natural" experiment *Sociology of Health and Illness* 1990:12:391–412.

8. Wilkinson RG. Income and mortality. In: Wilkinson RG, ed. *Class and health: research and longindinal data.* London: Tavistock, 1986:88–114.

9. Rodgers GB. Income and inequality as determines of mortality: an international cross-section analysis. *Population Studies* 1979:33:343–51.

10. LeGrand J. Inequalities in health: some international comparisons. *European Economic Review* 1987:31:182–91.

11. Preston S. *Mortality patterns in national populations.* London: Academic Press, 1976.

12. World Bank. *World Tables.* Baltimore: Johns Hopkins University Press, 1990.

13. World Health Organization. *World health stances annual.* Geneva: WHO, 1979–90.

14. Organisation for Economic Cooperation and Development. *National accounts: main aggregates.2 Vol. 1. 1960–89.* Paris: OECD, 1991.

15. Bishop JA, Formby JP, Smith WJ. *International comparisons of income inequality.* Luxembourg: Luxembourg Income Study, 1989. (Working paper 26.)

16. O'Higgins M. Jenkins SP. Poverty in the EC. IN: Teekens R. van Praag BMS. eds. *Analysing poverty in the European Community.* Luxembourg: EUROSTAT. 1990.

17. Organization for Economic Cooperation and Development. Living conditions in OECD countries: a compendium of social indicators. Paris: OECD, 1986.

18. World Bank, *World development report* 1979–90. Oxford: Oxford University Press, 1990.

19. World Bank, *World development report 1990.* Oxford: Oxford University Press, 1990.

20. Mackenbach JP, Bouvier-Colle MH, Jougla E. Avoidable mortality and health services: a review of aggregate studies. J *Epidemol Community Health* 1990:44:106–11.

21. Balarian R. Bulusu L. Mortality among immigrants in England and Wales 1979–93. In: Britton M, ed. *Mortality and geography*. London: HMSO. 1990:103–21. (OPCS series DS: No 9.)

22. Power C. Manor O, Fox AJ, Fogelman K. Health in childhood and social inequalities in health in young adults. *Journal of the Royal Statistical Society* 1990:153:17–28.

23. Fox J, Goldblatt P, Jones D. Social class mortality differentials: artifact, selection or life circumstances? In: *Longitudal study 1971–1981*. London: HMSO. 19990:99–108. (OPCS series LS: No 6.)

24. Wilkinson RG, Socio-economic differences in mortality: interpreting the data on the size and trends. In: Wilkinson RG, ed. *Class and health: research and longitudinal data*. London: Tavistock, 1986:1–20.

25. Marmot MG, Davey Smith G.Why are the Japanese living longer? BMJ 1989–299:1547–51.

26. Department of Health. *On the state of the public health for the year 1989*. London: HMSO, 1990.

27. Marsh C, *Exploring data*. Cambridge: Polity Press, 1988.

28. Townsend P. *Poverty in the United Kingdom*. Harmondsworth: Penguin, 1979.

29. Department of Social Security. *Households below average income: a statistical analyses 1981–87. London: Government Statistical Service, 1990*.

30. Baker D, Illsley R. Trends in inequality in health in Europe. *Int J Health Sciences* 1990:1–2:89–111.

Four

THE EPIDEMIOLOGICAL TRANSITION: FROM MATERIAL SCARCITY TO SOCIAL DISADVANTAGE?

Richard G. Wilkinson

INTRODUCTION

H EALTH and wealth have always appeared to be closely related. But within that relationship there is an important historical discontinuity which not only tells us about the changing determinants of health, but also marks a fundamental change in the limiting constraints on the quality of life in modern societies. Mortality rates in the developed world are no longer related to per capita economic growth, but are related instead to the scale of income inequality in each society. This represents a transition from the primacy of material constraints to social constraints as the limiting condition on the quality of human life.[1]

The implications of this change are not confined to health. Health can be viewed as a general indicator of welfare and the effects of social and economic change. If health is influenced more by income distribution than by economic growth, then the same is likely to be true of other aspects of human welfare. Furthermore, if increases in the quality of life now depend primarily on improving the social fabric of society rather than on

general rises in prosperity, then we must ask whether further *undifferentiated* economic growth is worth the environmental risks.

LIFE EXPECTANCY AND GROSS NATIONAL PRODUCT PER CAPITA

R ISING living standards were the basis of the historical decline of mortality in the developed world. While it is possible to argue the relative historical contributions of better nutrition, sewers, clean water supplies, improved housing, and, eventually, immunization to the long decline in mortality rates in the developed world, there can be no doubt that the enabling and sustaining power of economic growth was behind them all.

Evidence of the broad relationship between economic growth and increasing life expectancy can be found not only in the history of the developed countries, but also in the Third World today. *Figure 1* shows the relationship between Gross National Product per capita (GNPpc) and life expectancy at birth in rich and poor countries in 1970 and in 1990.

Originally published in *Daedalus*, 1994.

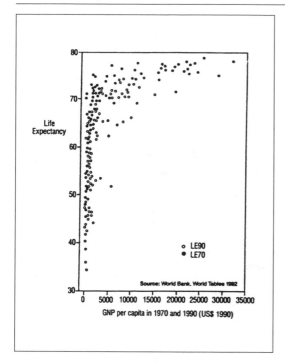

Figure 1
Life Expectancy at Birth (Male and Female) in Relation to GNP per capita, 1970 and 1990

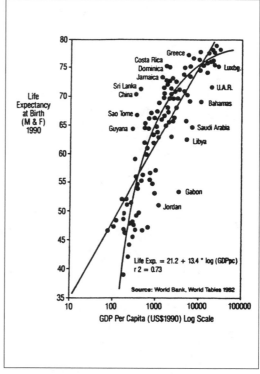

Figure 2
Life Expectancy and GDP per capita, 1990

Although it is clear that life expectancy rises steeply with increased GNPpc among the poorer countries, the data in *Figure 1* also suggests that the relationship between GNPpc and mortality peters out in the developed world. Apparently, there is some minimum level of income (around $5,000 per capita in 1990) above which the absolute standard of living ceases to have much impact on health.

Putting income on a log scale, as in *Figure 2*, it appears more accurate to think in terms of radically diminishing health returns to increasing income. However, as the curve in *Figure 2* indicates, as countries get richer even equally large *proportional* changes in incomes produce diminishing absolute returns in life expectancy.

Figure 3 shows that between 1970 and 1990 there was very little correspondence between changes in the Gross Domestic Product per capita (GDPpc) and life expectancy in the developed countries. In this example, GDPpc is converted at purchasing power parities to provide more accurate comparisons of the real material standard of living.

Figures 1, 2, and *3* show that regardless of whether one looks at Organization for Economic Cooperation and Development (OECD) countries at a single point in time or over several decades, there is no strong relationship between income and health among the developed countries.[2] People in one country can be twice as well-off on average as those in another without benefit to their mortality rates. As *Figure 3* shows, one country's economy can grow twice as fast as another's for twenty years without having an effect on life expectancy.

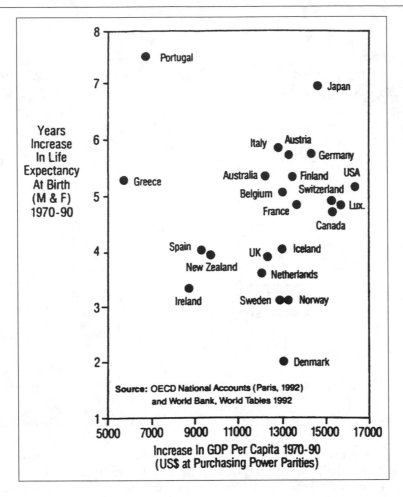

Figure 3
Increases in Life Expectancy Related to Increases
in GDP per capita in OECD Countries, 1970–1990

APPROACHING LIMITS OF
HUMAN LIFE EXPECTANCY?

ONE obvious explanation for the virtual disappearance of a relationship between GNPpc and life expectancy is that it reflects the approaching limits of human life expectancy. However, this fails to explain why the rate of improvement in life expectancy is not slowing down where longevity is already high. Life expectancy continues to increase at 2 to 2.5 years per decade among the rich countries, as it has during most of this century (wartime excluded). In addition, it appears that in several developed countries the fastest improvements are coming from those sections of the population where life expectancy is highest. For these reasons, we must assume that the leveling of the curve of rising life expectancy with GNPpc (shown in *Figure 1*) indicates the declining health benefits of further increases in the standard of living in the developed world.

THE EPIDEMIOLOGICAL TRANSITION

THE "epidemiological transition" is the shift in the main causes of death—from infectious diseases to degenerative cardiovascular diseases and cancers. It marks a fundamental change in the main determinants of health and seems to indicate the point in economic development at which the vast majority of the population gained reliable access to the basic material necessities of life.

The impact of medical science is not reflected in the epidemiological transition. In fact, the transition would have happened (and largely did happen) without it. The great infectious diseases of the nineteenth and early twentieth centuries dwindled to a fraction of what they had been long before immunization or effective medical treatment became available. Strongly associated with poverty, in the past as in the Third World today, the decline of the great infections reflected improved living standards and conditions.

The effect of economic development is also illustrated by the way in which the epidemiological transition saw the so-called "diseases of affluence" transformed into the diseases of the poor. No longer primarily "businessmen's diseases," coronary heart disease, stroke, and obesity have all become more common among the less well-off.[3] That this transition was associated with the attainment of a certain level of material wealth is shown by the associated reversal in the social gradient in smoking and in the consumption of refined foods such as white bread and sugar. In all but a few countries the evidence on cardiovascular diseases is fragmentary, but it seems likely that many developed countries went through the same transition and experienced the same change in the class distribution of these diseases, although at different times.

The change in the social class distribution of obesity is much more widely recognized. Throughout most of history obesity was a condition which affected only the privileged, and in many cultures was a status symbol—embodied proof of prosperity. The rich were fat and the poor were thin. This remained true in the developed world well into the present century when rising living standards began to enable the poor to be fat, and is still true in some parts of the Third World.

In Britain the change appears to have been accelerated by nutritional changes during World War II.[4] The Chief Medical Officer in the British Ministry of Education commented on the increasing incidence of obesity in schoolchildren in his annual reports of 1956–1957 and 1960–1961.[5] As if to confirm Pierre Bourdieu's thesis of the importance of the desire to express social distinction in aesthetic judgments, as soon as the poor became able to be fat, obesity ceased to be a status symbol.[6]

A further indication of the widespread attainment of adequate material standards for the populations of developed countries comes from trends in the proportion of babies with birth weights below 2,500 grams. Although perinatal and infant mortality rates have continued to decline rapidly, since the 1950s in England and Wales there has been no further marked decline in the proportion of low birth weight babies: between 6 and 7 percent of babies have weighed less than 2,500 grams ever since.[7] This proportion of low birth weight babies seems to represent a residual core which is unaffected by improvements in average prosperity.

Thus, it seems that in the later stages of industrial development countries go through a health climacteric after which the health of the vast majority of the population is no longer substantially affected by the absolute material standard of living.

INCOME DISTRIBUTION

AFTER the epidemiological transition, health remains closely associated with deprivation, but the relationship now is with relative rather than absolute deprivation. Health within developed countries continues to show a clear gradient with measures of socioeconomic status.[8] *Figure 4* shows how death rates vary according to income group in the United States. Evidence from Britain, covering most of the present century, suggests that the social class differences in death rates have increased or decreased as the proportion of the population living in *relative* poverty has increased or decreased.[9]

There is, however, a marked contrast between the well-ordered relationship between socioeconomic status and health within a country (as shown in *Figure 4*) and the lack of any clear relationship between socioeconomic status and health between countries (as shown in *Figures 1* and *3*). This contrast is extremely important. Given that the points in *Figures 1* and *3* are whole nations, the fact that they do not even begin to line up like those for income groups within the United States cannot be chalked up to sampling error or the like. Something quite different is going on. Health is affected by differences in *rela-*

tive income (differences between groups of people within the same society), not by the absolute level of average incomes for each society as a whole. This is confirmed by the surprisingly strong relationship between income distribution and mortality rates in developed countries.[10]

The countries with the longest life expectancy are not the wealthiest but those with the smallest spread of incomes and the smallest proportion of the population in relative poverty. Using a standard measure of income distribution, *Figure 5* shows that in 1970 the countries with the smallest income differences were also the countries where average life expectancy was longest. Since then the rate of growth of average life expectancy has been closely related to changes in income distribution. *Figure 6* shows that in the twelve member states of the European Community (EC), average life expectancy between 1975 and 1985 has grown fastest in those countries where relative poverty decreased fastest (or increased slowest).

The relationship implies that between one-half and three-quarters of the differences in average life expectancy from one developed country to another may be attributed solely to differences in income distribution. Controlling for GNPpc, public expenditure on medical care, or total public expenditure, does not suggest that the relationship with income distribution is a proxy for an effect of better public services. Nor are such factors thought to have a sufficiently powerful influence on national mortality rates to make them potential candidates.

Because this relationship is established on national data it may prove to be an ecological fallacy. However, there is substantial evidence not only that individual health and income are related (as shown in *Figure 4*), but also that health is responsive to changes in income.[11] The function of the international evidence shown here is primarily to distinguish between relative and absolute income levels. As relative income is inherently a social concept it cannot be dealt with at an individual level: societies, not individuals, have income distributions.

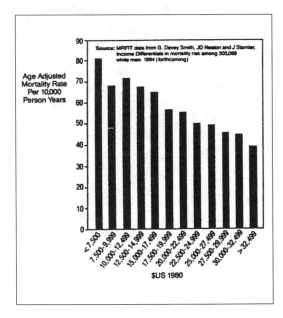

Figure 4
Income and Mortality among Three Hundred Thousand White US Men

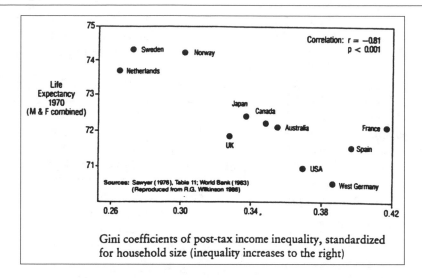

Figure 5
Life Expectancy and Income Distribution in OECD Countries

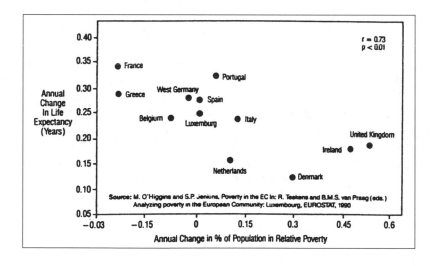

Figure 6
The Annual Rate of Change of Life Expectancy in Twelve EC Countries, 1975–1985
(with the rate of change in the percentage of the population in relative poverty)

A telling example of the influence of income distribution on health is the contrast between health trends in Britain and Japan. Since 1970 income distribution in Japan has narrowed significantly, making it the narrowest of any country reporting to the World Bank. At the same time, life expectancy in Japan has increased by 6.9 years and is now the highest in the world. In contrast, income distribution in Britain has widened, and Britain's position on the life expectancy table of OECD countries has fallen from tenth in 1970 to seventeenth in 1990, with a gain of only 3.9 years in life expectancy.

As income differences in Japan have narrowed, so have differences in death rates among social classes.[12] In Britain, on the other hand, both income and mortality differences have widened.[13] These divergent trends lie behind the contrasting gains in average life expectancy. The likelihood that there is a causal relationship between income distribution and national life expectancy is also confirmed by recent evidence of the relationship between inequalities in both health and income in different countries.[14]

Psychosocial Interpretation

THE fact that health seems to be influenced more by differences in income than by average level of income suggests that cognitive processes of social comparison are involved. The importance of relative income to health suggests that psychosocial factors related to deprivation and disadvantage are involved. That is to say, it is less a matter of the immediate physical effects of inferior material conditions than of the social meanings attached to those conditions and how people feel about their circumstances and about themselves.

The need to develop a psychosocial understanding of the impact of material differences on health is indicated by three other aspects of the relationship between health and socioeconomic status. *1*) The socioeconomic gradient in health does not distinguish merely between the poor

and the rest of society, but affects every rung of the social ladder. Thus, people who own houses and have two cars are healthier than those who rent houses and have one car;[15] administrative civil servants are healthier than executives;[16] and people in the highest income group are healthier than those only slightly less well-off (see *Figure 4*). *2*) Despite rising real incomes, which have undoubtedly reduced the incidence during the second half of this century of absolute material deprivation, the morality disadvantage of blue collar workers and their families appears to have increased in several countries. *3*) In Britain, now one of the poorer developed countries, absolute living standards among the *poorest* 20 percent of the population are remarkably high. In 1992, some 72 percent had central heating, almost all had televisions and refrigerators, 72 percent had telephones, and almost 60 percent had video-cassette recorders.[17]

The socioeconomic gradient in mortality (*Figure 4*) could only be attributed to the direct effects of material factors if it is assumed that increasing standards of comfort higher up the income scale have as great an effect as material improvements further down the scale. However, if this were so, there would be a closer association between changes in GDPpc and mortality than is shown in *Figure 3*.

There are a number of different ways in which psychosocial links might be involved in the association between socioeconomic status and health. For example, the stresses of economic insecurity or relative deprivation may impact directly on health, affecting both the endocrine and immune systems. Relatedly, psychosocial stress may cause people to start smoking or to engage in other behaviors which are detrimental to health.

Observational studies, actual experiments, and so-called "natural" experiments have repeatedly shown the power of psychosocial factors on physical health. For example, people in Bristol whose houses were flooded in 1969 were found to have a 50 percent higher mortality rate than members of a control group during the following year.[18] A study of the effects of job losses resulting from a factory closure found that health began to deteriorate when redundancies were first announced—before people actually became unemployed.[19] An Australian study of unemployment found health more closely related to the subjective experience of financial strain than to actual income.[20]

Workplace studies conducted in Sweden, the United States, Germany, and Britain found that the three most important health-related aspects of the work environment are the amount of control people have over their work, the pressure of work, and the social support they get from colleagues.[21] These three factors seem likely to apply as much to domestic circumstances as to working conditions. Indeed, numerous studies have confirmed the beneficial effects on health of more and better social contacts between people.[22] Friendships are often seen as protective against the effects of stress. One study showed that they are specifically protective against the stresses of economic hardship.[23] However, poorer people and people in lower status occupations are likely to have less social contact.[24]

Like social support, most of the psychosocial factors which are deleterious to health are more likely to occur in relatively deprived circumstances. Studies designed to show the links between relative deprivation and health have shown, not unexpectedly, that deprivation causes stress,[25] that socioeconomic status affects "fatalism" and attributional style,[26] that economic hardship reduces people's ability to fulfill their roles—whether as "breadwinner" or "homemaker"—and can therefore lead to depression.[27]

It may be that income affects health primarily as a determinant of social status. For example, Eastern Europe (prior to 1989) was an exception to the rule that narrower income differences are beneficial to health. The most likely explanation seems to be that income was often not a good guide to status: in several countries the average manual wage was higher than the average non-

manual wage. It seems that other factors, like party membership, were more important determinants of status.[28]

It may still seem surprising that income distribution affects us sufficiently to exert a major influence on health through psychosocial pathways. There is, however, no shortage of evidence of the centrality of the sense of social status, feelings of inferiority, and relative deprivation in human social life. Even in early childhood, standards are relative.[29] Rather than getting enough care, love, and attention in absolute terms, what is salient in children's minds is any sign that they are less favored than a sibling. If such feelings become part of a pattern they can have a deep emotional impact.

SOME WIDER IMPLICATIONS OF INCOME DISTRIBUTION

IF the psychological consequences of wider differences in income are powerful enough to exert a major influence on death rates, it is implausible that they do not also have other social implications. Although no one doubts that poorer areas suffer disproportionately from a wide range of social problems (including drugs, crime, violence, poor educational performance, and ill health), proving causality is not easy.

Given the controversy over the extent to which the ills of modern society should be blamed on changes in family structure rather than on relative poverty, there is perhaps one international comparison that is worth making. In terms of family structures, Japan and Sweden are at opposite ends of the spectrum. Japan remains closest to the two-parent family with very few births outside marriage and low divorce rates, while in Sweden over half of births occur outside marriage.[30] Yet, these two countries do almost equally well in terms of child welfare and health. What these countries have in common (or had until recently) is a narrow income distribution.

It is also interesting to note that Japan is almost the only developed country which appears not to have been affected by the general rise in crime. In Japan, homicide, robbery, rape, violence, and bodily injury have all shown a long-term decline.[31] Many Japanese attribute this decline to rapid economic growth, arguing that robbery has decreased because rising incomes mean that fewer people need to steal. This explanation sounds improbable to Westerners who are more likely to believe that improved living standards have somehow made us all more materialistic and selfish. A more plausible explanation is that a component of crime is related less to what has been happening to economic growth and *absolute* living standards than to what has been happening to income distribution and trends in *relative* poverty. While Japan has experienced a long-term decline in income differences, most other developed countries have seen either a worsening or little change in income distribution. Crime in Japan has declined faster in the larger cities, and its association with relative deprivation has weakened. If low *relative* income were a contributing factor, these are the trends which might be expected during a period of declining inequality.

If the relationship between health and income distribution is evidence of a powerful psychosocial effect of relative income, could it be said that each individual's desire for more income is more a desire to improve his relative standing in society than it is a desire for a higher level of material consumption? Such a desire would not be well served by general increases in prosperity, which leave relativities essentially unchanged. Indeed, it would mean that it is not legitimate to sum individual desires for more income into an aggregate societal demand for economic growth.

Beyond that, however, the psychosocial effect of relative income suggests that the quality of life is better served by reducing relative poverty and narrowing income distribution than it is by further haphazard economic growth. Because health is sensitive to the quantitative as well as qualitative aspects of both material and social change, it could be claimed that it is a better guide to the quality of life than is any mix of economic indicators. Economic indices can only reflect change by reducing qualitative change to quantitative increase, thereby ignoring the social dimension of life. In this context, the fact that in the developed world the predominant position of material factors as determinants of health has given way to social factors has profound implications.

At a time when the environmental impact of economic development is causing increasing concern, it is particularly important to know whether its advantages outweigh its disadvantages. In the developed world the answer to this question can no longer be taken for granted.[32] Clearly there are substantial reasons for thinking we need to be more selective about the direction and form which economic growth takes. We continue to think of it as desirable largely because of the short-term discomfort of recession and the need to keep unemployment down and profits up. This is not to suggest that it is time for the industrialized world to bring to a close its two hundred year involvement with economic development. But, rather than seeing innovation as serving the single goal of increasing per capita incomes, we should set it as a means of resolving growing environmental and social problems.

The environment cannot be safeguarded without major technical innovation, just as relative deprivation cannot be diminished except through income growth among the least well-off. Somehow growth has to be put into a new harness. Fortunately, there is increasing evidence that, in addition to the contribution it makes to welfare, income redistribution is also beneficial to productivity and growth. Among OECD countries, those with the fastest increases in productivity tend to be those with narrower income differences.[33] Among seventy rich and poor countries, investment was higher where income differences were narrower. In addition, eight of the rapidly growing East Asian economies narrowed their income differences between 1960 and 1980,[34] and Japan has the narrowest income differentials in the developed world.

This suggests that the pursuit of narrower income differentials may be complementary to growth. Social environments which are less divisive, less undermining of self-confidence, less productive of social antagonism, and which put greater resources into developing skills and abilities, may well turn out to be more innovative and better able to adapt to the environmental problems we face. The health data suggests that the quality of the social fabric, rather than increases in average wealth, may now be the primary determinant of the real subjective quality of human life. With this knowledge let us create high quality social environments where we will be less dependent on the destructive quick fix of indiscriminate economic growth.

NOTES

1. This change was also marked by the decline of mortality from infectious diseases which had been associated with absolute poverty and by the reversal of the social class distribution of heart disease when the so-called "diseases of affluence" became the diseases of the relatively poor in affluent societies.

2. Richard G. Wilkinson, "The Impact of Income Inequality on Life Expectancy," in Stephen Platt, H. Thomas, S. Scott, and G. Williams, eds., *Locating Health: Sociological and Historical Explorations* (Aldershot: Avebury, 1993).

3. Michael G. Marmot, Abe Adelstein, Nicola Robinson, and Geoffrey Rose, "Changing Social Class Distribution of Heart Disease," *British Medical Journal* II (1978): 1109–12. Steve Wing, "Social Inequalities in the Decline of Coronary Mortality," *American Journal of Public Health* 78 (1988): 1415–16. Aaron Antonovsky, "Social Class and the Major Cardiovascular Diseases," *Journal of Chronic Diseases* 21 (1968): 65–106.

4. British Medical Association, *Report of the Committee on Nutrition* (London: BMA, 1950).

5. Ministry of Education, *The Health of the School Child, 1956–7 and 1960–1,* Report of the Chief Medical Officer (London: HMSO, 1958 and 1962).

6. Pierre Bourdieu, *Distinction: A Social Critique of the Judgement of Taste* (London: Routledge, 1984).

7. Alison Macfarlane and Miranda Mugford, *Birth Counts: Statistics of Pregnancy and Childbirth* (London: HMSO, 1984). Chris Power, "National Trends in Birthweight and Future Adult Disease," *British Medical Journal* (forthcoming).

8. John Fox, ed., *Health Inequalities in European Countries* (London: Gower, 1989).

9. Richard G. Wilkinson, "Class Mortality Differentials, Income Distribution and Trends in Poverty 1921–1981," *Journal of Social Policy* 18 (3) (1989): 307–35.

10. Richard G. Wilkinson, "Income Distribution and Life Expectancy," *British Medical Journal* (1992): 165–68, 304. Irene Wennemo, "Infant Mortality, Public Policy and Inequality—A Comparison of 18 Industrialised Countries, 1950–85," *Sociology of Health and Illness* 15 (1993): 429–46.

11. Richard G. Wilkinson, "Income Distribution and Mortality: A 'Natural' Experiment," *Sociology of Health and Illness* 12 (1990): 391–411. Barbara H. Kehrer and Charles M. Wolin, "Impact of Income Maintenance on Low Birthweight," *Journal of Human Resources* XIV (1979): 434–62.

12. Michael G. Marmot and George Davey-Smith, "Why are the Japanese Living Longer?," *British Medical Journal* 299 (1989): 1547–51.

13. Michael G. Marmot and Michael E. McDowall, "Mortality Decline and Widening Social Inequalities," *Lancet* II (1986): 274–76.

14. "The rank order of countries in terms of income inequalities strongly corresponds to their rank order in terms of inequalities in mortality. Thus our material corroborates Wilkinson's inferences." Anton E. Kunst and Johan P. Mackenbach, "The Size of Mortality Differences Associated with Educational Level: A Comparison of Nine Industrialized Countries," *American Journal of Public Health* (forthcoming).

15. Peter Goldblatt, ed., *1971–81 Longitudinal Study: Mortality and Social Organisation,* OPCS Series LS 6 (London: HMSO, 1990).

16. George Davey-Smith, Martin J. Shipley, and Geoffrey Rose, "Magnitude and Causes of Socioeconomic Differentials in Mortality: Further Evidence from the Whitehall Study," *Journal of Epidemiology and Community Health* 44 (1990): 265–70.

17. Department of Social Security, *Households Below Average Income, 1979–1990/1* (London: HMSO, 1993).

18. Edward H. Conduit, "If A-B Does Not Predict Heart Disease, Why Bother With It? A Clinician's View," *British Journal of Medical Psychology* 65 (1992): 289–96.

19. Norman Beale and Susan Nethercott, "Job-Loss and Family Morbidity: A Study of Factory Closure," *Journal of the Royal College of General Practitioners* 35 (1988): 510–14.

20. Philip Ullah, "The Association between Income, Financial Strain and Psychological Well-Being among Unemployed Youths," *Journal of Occupational Psychology* 63 (1990): 317–30.

21. Jeffrey V. Johnson and Ellen M. Hall, "Job Strain, Work Place Social Support, and Cardiovascular Disease: A Cross-Sectional Study of a Random Sample of the Swedish Working Population," *American Journal of Public Health* 78 (1988): 1336–42. Robert A. Karasek et al., "Job Characteristics in Relation to the Prevalence of Myocardial Infarction in the U.S.," *American Journal of Public Health* 78 (1988):910–18. Johannes Siegrist, Richard Peter, Astrid Junge, Peter Cremer, and Dieter Seidel, "Low Status Control, High Effort at Work and Ischaemic Heart Disease: Prospective Evidence from Blue-Collar Men," *Social Science and Medicine* 31 (1990): 1127–34. Michael G. Marmot, George Davey-Smith, Stephen Stansfield et al., "Health Inequalities among British Civil Servants: The Whitehall II Study," *Lancet* (1991).

22. James S. House, Karl R. Landis, and Debra Umberson, "Social Relationships and Health," *Science* 241 (1988): 540–45.

23. Christopher T. Whelan, "The Role of Social Support in Mediating the Psychological Consequences of Economic Stress," *Sociology of Health and Illness* 15 (1993): 86–101.

24. Peter Townsend, *Poverty in the United Kingdom* (Harmondsworth: Penguin, 1979). Michael G. Marmot, "Social Inequalities in Mortality: The Social Environment," in Richard G. Wilkinson, ed., *Class and Health: Research and Longitudinal Data* (London: Tavistock, 1986).

25. Whelan, "The Role of Social Support in Mediating the Psychological Consequences of Economic Stress," 86–101.

26. Blair Wheaton, "The Sociogenesis of Psychological Disorder: An Attributional Theory," *Journal of Health and Social Behaviour* 21 (1980): 100–23.

27. Catherine E. Ross and Joan Huber, "Hardship and Depression," *Journal of Health and Social Behaviour* 26 (1985): 312–27.

28. Edmund Wnuk-Lipinski and Raymond Illsley, "Introduction," *Social Science and Medicine* 31 (1990): 833–36.

29. Judy Dunn and Robert Plomin, *Separate Lives: Why Siblings are so Different* (New York: Basic Books, 1990).

30. The statistics show that even single parents are well protected from relative poverty in Sweden and their children's health is good. Kathleen Kiernan and Valerie Estaugh, *Cohabitation, Extra-Marital Childbearing and Social Policy* (London: Family Policy Studies Centre, 1993).

31. Statistics Bureau, *Japan Statistical Yearbook 1990* (Japan: Management and Coordination Agency, 1990).

32. The various attempts to adjust GNPpc to produce better measures of economic welfare have also cast doubt on the benefits of undifferentiated economic growth. In Britain and the United States economic welfare has been declining despite increases in GNPpc. Herman E. Daley and John B. Cobb, *For the Common Good* (London: Green Print, 1990). Tim Jackson and Nic Marks, *U.K. Index of Sustainable Economic Welfare* (Sweden: Stockholm Environment Institute in cooperation with the New Economic Foundation, 1994).

33. Andrew Glyn and David Miliband, eds., *Paying for Inequality* (London: Rivers Oram, 1994).

34. The World Bank, *The East Asian Miracle* (Oxford: Oxford University Press, 1993).

Five

DOES THE VARIATION IN THE SOCIOECONOMIC CHARACTERISTICS OF AN AREA AFFECT MORTALITY?

Yoav Ben-Shlomo, Ian R. White, and Michael Marmot

O UR research in England has shown that the more deprived an area the greater its incidence of premature mortality.[1] Wilkinson has agreed that in the developed world income distribution is a more important predictor of life expectancy between countries than simply mean income.[2] We aimed to determine whether the risk of mortality in a geographical area was related to the degree of socioeconomic variation within that area as well as the average level of deprivation.

METHODS AND RESULTS

F OR each of the 8464 wards in England we obtained the Townsend deprivation index from the 1981 census[1] and directly standardised all cause mortality for 1981–5. Mortality under the age of 65 was used as an indicator of premature mortality. Male and female mortality rates were averaged for each ward. Twenty four wards were excluded because we could not compute the mortality rate, and two local authorities were excluded because each contained only one ward.

The remaining 369 local authorities contained an average of 23 wards (6–47).

For each local authority we computed the median of the ward Townsend scores as a measure of overall deprivation and their interquartile range as a measure of variation in deprivation (correlation between the two measures 0·33). We also computed the average of the ward mortality rates. The local authorities were divided according to their quartile of deprivation and variation and the mean mortality for each group computed. We then constructed models in which mortality was regressed on quartile of variation within each quartile of deprivation. Because deprivation still varied between wards within a quartile of deprivation "fully adjusted" analyses also controlled for deprivation as a continuous variable in each model.

Mortality was strongly positively associated with average deprivation (table). The trend for mortality was 26 per 100 000 per quartile of deprivation (95% confidence interval 23 to 28, P<0·001). Mortality was also positively associated with variation: the average fully adjusted

---

Originally published in *British Medical Journal*, 1996.

Mean mortality of local authorities by average deprivation and variation of deprivation. Values are mean mortality per 100 000 (and number of local authorities) for each quartile of variation and deprivation and trend in mortality

	Mortality				Trend in mortality per 100 000 per quartile of variation (95% confidence interval)	
	Least variable quartile (1·03–2·14)†	Second quartile (2·15–3·01)	Third quartile (3·03–4·13)	Most variable quartile (4·15–9·55)	Simple	Fully adjusted‡
Most affluent quartile (− 4·87 to −2·00)*	249 (30)	254 (36)	253 (19)	261 (7)	3 (− 3 to 9)	2 (− 3 to 8)
Second quartile (− 1·98 to − 0·71)	256 (34)	273 (26)	270 (23)	298 (10)	11 (6 to 16)	11 (6 to 15)
Third quartile (− 0·69 to 1·41)	272 (19)	278 (15)	292 (22)	302 (32)	10 (6 to 15)	8 (4 to 12)
Most deprived quartile (1·48 to 9·21)	358 (9)	330 (15)	334 (29)	342 (38)	− 1 (− 6 to 4)	4 (− 1 to 9)

*Median value of Townsend deprivation score.
†Interquartile range of Townsend deprivation score.
‡Adjusted for residual differences in deprivation scores.

trend was 7 per 100 000 per quartile of variation (4 to 9, P<0·001). Although this effect appeared to be stronger in the middle quartiles of deprivation, the trends did not differ significantly (P=0·09 for heterogeneity).

Results were similar using mean and standard deviation, all age mortality, and male and female mortality separately; after ward mortality had been transformed by taking either the square root or the square; and after we had adjusted for the number of wards both as a continuous and a quartile variable.

COMMENT

O UR results confirm a strong gradient in mortality related to deprivation, together with a positive association between degree of variation within an area and increased mortality (P<0·001). These results support the hypothesis that variations in income contribute an additional effect on mortality over the effect of deprivation alone.

This analysis cannot show which wards in an area of greater inequality suffer higher mortality: all might, or only the most deprived. Alternatively, increased mortality for poor wards might not be balanced by decreased mortality for rich wards in the same area—that is, the relation may not be linear, but analyses on transformed data did not alter the effect of variation on mortality.

The association between variation and mortality appears to be least in the most affluent and most deprived areas, although the result of a het-erogeneity test was not significant. These findings deserve further investigation as some evidence exists that community solidarity may have a beneficial effect on all residents.[3]

Studies have produced contradictory results on whether area characteristics have a truly independent effect on mortality.[4][5] Although our analysis is based on areas, not individuals, it suggests that the characteristics of individuals are insufficient to account fully for differences between areas, as individuals in more variable areas appear to have worse mortality than their counterparts in more homogeneous areas.

NOTES

1. Eames M, Ben-Shlomo Y, Marmot MG. Social deprivation and premature mortality: regional comparison across England. *BMJ* 1993;307:1097–1102.

2. Wilkinson RG. Income distribution and life expectancy. *BMJ* 1992;304:165–8.

3. Putnam RD, Leonardi R, Nanetti RY. *Making democracy work: civic traditions in modern Italy.* Princeton, NJ: Princeton University Press, 1993.

4. Haan M, Kaplan GA, Camacho T. Poverty and health. Prospective evidence from the Alameda County Study. *Am J Epidemiol* 1987; 125:989–98.

5. Sloggett A, Joshi H. Higher mortality in deprived areas: community or personal disadvantage? *BMJ* 1994; 309:1470–14.

Six

INEQUALITY IN INCOME AND MORTALITY IN THE UNITED STATES: ANALYSIS OF MORTALITY AND POTENTIAL PATHWAYS

George A. Kaplan, Elsie R. Pamuk, John W. Lynch,
Richard D. Cohen, and Jennifer L. Balfour

Abstract

Objective—To examine the relation between health outcomes and the equality with which income is distributed in the United States.

Design—The degree of income inequality, defined as the percentage of total household income received by the less well off 50% of households, and changes in income inequality were calculated for the 50 states in 1980 and 1990. These measures were then examined in relation to all cause mortality adjusted for age for each state, age specific deaths, changes in mortalities, and other health outcomes and potential pathways for 1980, 1990, and 1989–91.

Main outcome measure—Age adjusted mortality from all causes.

Results—There was a significant correlation ($r=0.62$, $P<0.001$) between the percentage of total household income received by the less well off 50% in each state and all cause mortality, unaffected by adjustment for state median incomes. Income inequality was also significantly associated with age specific mortalities and rates of low birth weight, homicide, violent crime, work disability, expenditures on medical care and police protection, smoking, and sedentary activity. Rates of unemployment, imprisonment, recipients of income assistance and food stamps, lack of medical insurance, and educational outcomes were also worse as income inequality increased. Income inequality was also associated with mortality trends, and there was a suggestion of an impact of inequality trends on mortality trends.

Conclusions—Variations between states in the inequality of the distribution of income are significantly associated with variations between states in a large number of health outcomes and social indicators and with mortality trends. These differences parallel relative investments in human and social capital. Economic policies that influence income and wealth inequality may have an important impact on the health of countries.

Originally published in *British Medical Journal*, 1996.

INTRODUCTION

THE inverse association between socioeconomic level and risk of disease is one of the most pervasive and enduring observations in public health.[1-4] This association is found for most diseases for most measures of socioeconomic level and is generally consistent across age, time, place, and organ systems. For the most part, socioeconomic level, whether it is measured by income, education, occupation, social class, or other measures, has been conceptualised as a property of the individual. This is not surprising as one's economic resources can determine, to a great extent, the availability and quality of food, housing, medical care, and other necessities. Recent findings, however, suggest that it may also be important to consider the overall distribution of wealth as a characteristic of a society or group. In a sample of industrialised countries Wilkinson demonstrated that life expectancy increased as the distribution of income in these countries became more egalitarian, whereas it was relatively unrelated to average income. There was a correlation of -0·81 (P<0·001) between the proportion of the total income and benefits after tax received by the least well off 70% of the population and life expectancy. The correlation with gross national product per capita was only -0·38 (P<0·05). In addition, countries that had shown increases over time in the equality of income distribution had proportionally greater increases in life expectancy compared with countries that had shown increased inequality in income distribution.

These are compelling observations for several reasons. They suggest, as Wilkinson argues,[5] that within populations one's relative socioeconomic position not just the absolute level may be importantly associated with health. Understanding the mechanisms by which relative socioeconomic position leads to variations in health outcomes may help to understand the relatively consistent observation of a steady gradient of risk associated with variations in socioeconomic level, with even those near the top having higher rates of disease than those at the top. Furthermore, as governments, through taxation policy, benefits, income transfers, investment incentives, and other mechanisms, often alter the level of income inequality such actions may also alter mortality, for better or worse. If this is the case then it is important to document such health effects so that they may be considered within the context of economic decisions. This is particularly compelling given the striking rise in the inequality in distributions of both wealth and income that have occurred over the past decade or so in the United States.[6-10]

Based as it is on a single set of observations concerning a small number of countries, the association between variations in income distribution and life expectancy needs to be examined in other contexts. We studied the relation between variations in income distribution between states of the United States and a variety of health outcomes, including variations in mortalities adjusted for age. In addition, we examined some of the potential pathways, possibly reflecting investments in human capital and social resources, by which income inequality may be related to health outcomes. Finally, we considered the impact of income inequality and changes in income inequality on mortality trends.

METHODS

Calculation of Income Inequality

Income inequality is defined as the proportion of aggregated household income held by households whose income is below a specified centile on the distribution of household income. Income inequality has been calculated for the 10th to the 90th centiles for all 50 states and the United States as a whole. These measures were calculated by using data from the 1980 and 1990 censuses. For each state the distribution of household income for the year before the census was available. Annual household income (in dollars) was divided into 17 intervals in 1979 and 25 intervals in 1989. The distribution is given as the number of households in each income interval. In 1990, but not in 1980, the aggregate household income for households with annual incomes of less than the top coded category and in the top coded category was also available.

The distribution of household income was used to calculate the income corresponding to the 10th to the 90th centiles in steps of 10. This was done by calculating the cumulative percentage distribution, identifying the interval containing the desired centile, and using linear interpolation within that interval to calculate the income corresponding to that centile.

The aggregate income held by households below an income centile was then calculated as follows. For the closed intervals, the interval midpoint was multiplied by the number of households to determine the aggregate income in each interval. For 1990 the sum slightly exceeded the census value so the interval totals were adjusted downwards by multiplying them by the ratio of the census sum to the calculated sum. The cumulative percentage distribution of aggregate income was determined from the adjusted aggregate values and the census value for the last interval. Finally, linear interpolation was used to find the percentage of aggregate income that fell below each centile of the distribution of household income.

State Mortalities and Other Health Outcomes

State mortalities for 1980, 1990, and 1989–91 were based on the National Center for Health Statistics (NCHS) Compressed Mortality File and were adjusted for age by using the age distribution, divided into 13 groups, of the entire United States for 1990 and 1989–91. Data on low birth weight, live births, homicides, violent crimes, disability, and medical care expenditures were taken from United States Government sources published by NCHS.[11]

Potential Pathways

Information on per capita expenditures by state and local governments for police protection and correction were based on data from the United States Bureau of the Census, Government Division,[12] and rates of incarceration in the population were from the United States Bureau of Justice Statistics.[13] Rates of receipt of income assistance (AFDC) are compiled by the Bureau of the Census from reports of the United States Social Security Administration and the United

---

Table 1

Correlation of 1990 mortality adjusted for age for all causes with proportion of total household income received by households below specified centile by sex, with and without adjustment for median income: United States, 1990

Centile	Adjusted for income			Not adjusted for income		
	Total	Male	Female	Total	Male	Female
10th	− 0·67	− 0·57	− 0·58	− 0·70	− 0·60	− 0·58
20th	− 0·61	− 0·59	− 0·58	− 0·65	− 0·62	− 0·56
30th	− 0·62	− 0·57	− 0·58	− 0·66	− 0·61	− 0·53
40th	− 0·61	− 0·54	− 0·56	− 0·64	− 0·57	− 0·50
50th	− 0·59	− 0·51	− 0·54	− 0·62	− 0·54	− 0·49
60th	− 0·56	− 0·47	− 0·51	− 0·60	− 0·51	− 0·47
70th	− 0·53	− 0·42	− 0·48	− 0·57	− 0·47	− 0·45
80th	− 0·48	− 0·37	− 0·45	− 0·53	− 0·42	− 0·43
90th	− 0·39	− 0·27	− 0·38	− 0·44	− 0·33	− 0·37

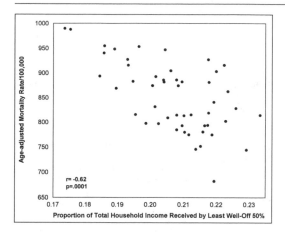

Figure 1
Inequality in income in the United States, 1990

States Administration for Children and Families.[14] Rates of receipt of food assistance (food stamps) come from the United States Department of Agriculture, Food and Nutrition Resources.[14] The Centers for Disease Control Behavioral Risk Factor Surveillance System was used for information on sedentary activity and smoking by state.[15] State rates on lack of health insurance were based on data from the Current Population Report,[16] and rates of high school graduation and drop out were from the 1990 Census of the Population.[17] Data from the National Assessment of Educational Progress were used for state 4th grade proficiency scores in reading and mathematics, which are published, together with the number of library books per capita and per capita spending on education, by the United States Department of Education, National Center for Education Statistics.[18] Unemployment rates are published by the United States Bureau of Labor Statistics.[19]

Statistical Methods

Pearson correlation coefficients were calculated to determine the association between measures of income inequality for the 50 states and age ad-

justed mortalities for males, females, and both sexes combined. Data for all other health outcomes and correlations between income inequality and potential pathways were based on fewer states as data were not available for all 50 in every case. To adjust for differences between states in absolute household income, partial correlation coefficients controlled for median income were also calculated. Because median income and expenditures per capita on medical care had highly skewed distributions a logarithmic transformation was applied before correlations were calculated. References to median income or total medical care expenditure refer to the natural log of the variable. For each state percentage changes between 1980 and 1990 in age adjusted mortalities, income inequality, and median income were also calculated.

RESULTS

Income Distribution and Mortality

Table 1 presents the association between 1990 state mortalities adjusted for age and income inequality for the total population and separately for males and females. The centile that designated the least well off proportion of each state varied from 10% to 90%. All correlations were significant (P<0·05) and were little influenced by adjustment for median income. Similar results were seen when the correlations were adjusted for mean income. Figure 1 shows the relation between the proportion of total household income received by the less well off 50% of the population in each state in 1990 and mortalities adjusted for age (*r*=0·62; P<0·001). When age specific death rates in broad categories were examined similar results were found, with the strongest correlation for deaths occurring at ages 25–64 years (*r*=0·76; P<0·0001) (table 2).

Income Distribution and Other Health Outcomes

Table 3 indicates that the proportion of total household income received by the less well off

50% was also related to various other health outcomes. The strongest correlations were with rate of homicide ($r=0.74$; $P<0.0001$) and violent crime ($r=0.70$; $P<0.0001$), expenditure per capita on medical care ($r=0.67$; $P<0.001$), and percentage of live born infants who weigh less than 2500 g ($r=0.65$; $P<0.001$). States that had greater inequality in the distribution of income also had significantly higher rates of smoking, sedentary behaviour, and disability as well as greater expenditure per capita on police protection.

Table 4

Correlation between social indicators and proportion of total household income received by less well off 50% of households, adjusted for median income: United States states, 1989–91

Indicator	r	P value
Unemployment (%)	−0·48	0·001
Prisoners (%)	−0·44	0·01
AFDC (%)*	−0·69	0·001
Food stamps (%)†	−0·72	0·001
No health insurance (%)	−0·45	0·002

*Income assistance to low income families with children.
†Food vouchers for people with low income.

Table 2

Correlation of 1989–91 mortality specific for age for all causes with proportion of total household income received by less well off 50% of households, with and without adjustment for median income: United States states, 1989–91

Age at death (years)	Adjusted for income	
	Yes	No
<1	−0·54	−0·49
1–24	−0·53	−0·36
25–64	−0·76	−0·74
≥65	−0·42	−0·37

Table 5

Correlation between education outcomes and indicators and proportion of total household income received by less well off 50% of households, adjusted for median income: United States states, 1989–91

Measure	r	P value
No high school (%)	−0·71	0·001
High school dropout (%)	−0·50	0·001
Reading proficiency (4th grade)	0·58	0·001
Maths proficiency (4th grade)	0·64	0·001
Education spending/total spending	0·32	0·02
Library books per capita	0·42	0·002

Table 3

Correlation between various health outcomes and risk factors and proportion of total household income received by less well off 50% of households, adjusted for median income: United States states, 1989–91

Outcome	r	P value
Proportion of live births <2500 g	−0·65	0·001
Homicides/100 000	−0·74	0·0001
Violent crimes/100 000	−0·70	0·0001
Proportion unable to work because of disability	−0·33	0·05
Per capita expenditures on protection	−0·38	0·007
Log per capita total medical care expenditures	−0·67	0·001
Proportion sedentary	−0·34	0·03
Proportion current smokers	−0·35	0·02

Income Distribution, Social Indicators, and Investments in Human and Social Capital

Tables 4 and 5 present correlations between the proportion of total household income received by the less well off 50% and several indicators of social resources and relative investments in human and social capital. States that had greater inequality in the distribution of income also had higher rates of unemployment, incarceration, people receiving income assistance and food stamps, and medically uninsured. They also spent a smaller proportion of total spending on education and had poorer educational outcomes, ranging from worse reading and proficiency in mathematics to lower rates of completion of high school education.

Trends in Mortality and Inequality

The association between income inequality and age adjusted mortality was slightly lower in 1980 than in 1990 (*r*=0·45; P<0·001 *v* *r*=0·62; P<0·001). Income inequality in 1980 was a strong predictor of trends in mortality, measured as percentage change in age adjusted mortality between 1980 and 1990 (*r*=0·62; P<0·0001). States that were more unequal in income distribution experienced smaller declines in mortality during the decade. When this was adjusted for changes in median income for each state, states with greater inequality in income continued to show smaller declines in mortality (*r*=0·51; P<0·002).

Inequality in income increased in all states except Alaska between 1980 and 1990. The share of total household income received by the less well off 50% of the population decreased by 6·1% (range – 11·5% to 2·9%). There was no important correlation between 1980–90 changes in state income inequality and 1980–90 trends in mortality (*r*=0·12; P>0·05), with or without adjustment for change in state median income or when various age specific mortalities were examined. When centile cuts for the income inequality measure were varied, however, there was a strong correlation between 1980–90 percentage change in the share of total income received by the least well off 10% of households and 1980-90 percentage change in age adjusted mortality (*r*=0·53; P<0·001), and this was not altered by adjustment for changes in state median incomes.

Discussion

THESE results indicate that variations in the relative equality of income distribution are significantly associated with various health outcomes, mortality over the life span, rates of behavioural risk factors, and markers for investment in human and social capital. As these analyses include all states, it cannot be argued that they are an artefact of the selection of a subset.[20] Strikingly, declines in mortality in the 1980s, experienced by all states, were smaller in states that had greater inequality in income at the beginning of the decade. When changes in income inequality were examined with respect to the worst off 10% of households in each state, increasing income inequality was associated with smaller declines in mortality over the decade.

Because these results are so striking it is important to consider various interpretive issues. It seems unlikely that these results are due only to differences in the average income between states. The correlation between median income and total mortality is weak (*r*=0·28; P<0·05) and is greatly reduced (*r*=0·06; P>0·05) with adjustment for the proportion of total household income received by the less well off 50%. On the contrary, the correlation between income inequality and total mortality is little influenced by adjustment for log median income (*r*=0·62 without adjustment and *r*=0·59 with adjustment).

Inspection of figure 1 indicates that many of the states in which the proportion of total household income received by the less well off 50% is low are those with a higher proportion of African Americans. Given the higher mortality for African Americans the correlation between income inequality and mortality may simply reflect higher proportions of a higher mortality group in high inequality states. If this were true then there would be no correlation between variations in income distribution and variations in mortality in white people. The correlation between the proportion of total household income received by the less well off 50%, however, is almost the same for mortality in white (*r*=0·51; P<0·0002) and African American people (*r*=0·52; P<0·0001).

If greater income inequality is associated with poorer health then areas with high income inequality could, over time, show increases in income inequality due to downward economic drift of those who are sick. Thus, income distribution would, to some extent, be a reflection of the distribution of disease. Such selection effects have not proved to be very important in other studies of the association between socioeconomic status and health,[21] but they must occur to some extent.

At any one time, however, relatively few people are sick, and the proportion of people in a state who are moving downward economically due to illness would be rather small; it is unlikely that this small proportion would have any major influence on income distribution, particularly in comparison with the impact of macroeconomic forces on distribution of income.

The Ecological Fallacy

These results also raise several interesting conceptual and methodological issues. Criticism is often directed at ecological analyses, of which these are an example, because it is not possible to control adequately for confounding and effect modification at the individual level—"the ecologic fallacy."[22] It should be recognised, however, that there are variables that can be measured only at this level.[23][24] The degree of income inequality is inherently such a variable because it is a property of the population not of the individual. Having said this, it is also important to ascertain the behavioural, psychosocial, and biological pathways by which income inequality affects the health experience of individual people. Such examinations will lead to an understanding of which segments of the population bear the burden on health of income inequality and the biological pathways that link income inequality to poor health. The results of these analyses suggest that the effects are quite strong and pervasive when the less well off 50% of the population are considered. Whether income distribution has similar effects on the health of poor, middle class, and rich people can be evaluated only through studies in which the health experience of individuals is examined in relation to income inequality.

In discussing his analyses of the relation between income distribution and differences in life expectancy between countries, Wilkinson argued that for developed nations it is not the absolute standard of living that is important but the levels of depression, isolation, insecurity, and anxiety that are associated with relative poverty.[5][25] Firstly, it should be recognised that these psychosocial characteristics are strongly patterned by socioeconomic level.[26] In addition, our results suggest that states with greater inequality in income have higher rates of violence, more disability, more people without health insurance, less investment in education and literacy, and poorer educational outcomes. It is reasonable to think that this translates, on average, into more difficult lives for those who live in such states. While there may be higher rates of adverse psychosocial outcomes in states with high inequality these may be only a reflection of the greater difficulties in life that are caused by the structural characteristics that distinguish between states with high and low inequality. From a prevention point of view it may be more important to deal with these structural features than their psychosocial consequences.

Geographical and Temporal Variations

The current analyses consider the association between state variations in income distribution and mortality. To understand the nature of the association between income distribution and health outcomes properly, however, it will be necessary to consider various different levels of geographical scale. Ideally, health outcomes could be associated with measures of income distribution calculated for geographical units ranging from the state, to counties, to neighbourhoods. Examination of the changes in the magnitude and nature of these associations at different geographic levels could add much to our understanding of the pathways by which income distribution influences health.

Observations of geographical and temporal variations in health outcomes are one of the foundations of epidemiological analysis, and there have been numerous presentations of such variations in mortality in many countries, including the United States.[27-30] Presumably such variations reflect the combined effects of historical, cultural, environmental, and socioeconomic forces on the distribution of risk factors. For the most part, however, the studies are descriptive, and there is considerable speculation but little understanding of the reasons for either geographical patterning or time trends in mortality.[31-32] The contribution of this study is to point out the possible role of income inequality in explaining some of the spatial and temporal variation in state mortality in the United States. This does not rule out the contribution of other factors, but there are few data available to assess the magnitude of their contribution or their association with income inequality. The macroeconomic forces that generate income inequality may also have a substantial impact on patterns of job creation and investment which, in turn, influence migration, distribution and concentration of community resources and demands, and maintenance and abandonment of practices specific to culture, thereby helping to shape the history of an area. Testing such a hypothesis, however, is beyond the scope of the current analyses.

Macroeconomic Effects

Because considerable increases in income and wealth inequality in the United States during the past 10 to 15 years have been reported (EN Wolff, 23rd general conference of the International Association for Research in Income and Wealth, St Andrews, New Brunswick, Canada, 1994) it was of interest to examine the association between secular trends in inequality and health outcomes. Such analyses are not necessarily informative as we do not know whether or not there are lags between changes in income inequality and mortality. Overall, however, there was no association between trends in income inequality and trends in mortality. This may reflect the small interstate variation in inequality increases: for 48 of 50 states the percentage change in inequality, defined at the 50th centile, varied only from −2% to −12%. Thus, the macroeconomic effects that re-

sulted in increases in income inequality may have influenced all states similarly. The largest variation was seen when we examined changes in the proportion of total household income received by the least well off 10% of the population. For this measure there was a mean decrease of 8·9% with a wide range (−32·4% to 23·8%), and there was a strong correlation with mortality changes ($r=0·53$). The macroeconomic effects on income inequality may be felt sooner at the bottom of the income distribution, and states may vary in the extent to which these effects are buffered by employment, taxation, and welfare policies. It is tempting to assume that the poorer mortality trends in those states in which income inequality increased are due to increased deaths rates among those who occupy the lower economic strata. Such a hypothesis cannot be tested, however, with the aggregate data used in the present analyses.

Conclusions

To our knowledge, this is the first report of an association between variations in income distribution within a single country and a variety of health outcomes. If these results are confirmed in other analyses there should be cause for concern. Given that inequalities in wealth are far greater than those for income in the United States[8] the health effects of inequality are likely to be even larger than those suggested by the current results. In addition, inequality in both wealth and income has increased dramatically in the United States, with wealth inequality reaching levels beyond those in other industrialised countries. While there is no complete consensus over the reasons for increases in inequality, factors identified generally include policies related to taxation, transfer payments, job creation and differential growth decay of various market sectors, and differential growth of assets—for example, housing v stocks. In the United States between 1981 and 1989 nearly half of the growth in wealth inequality was due to increases in income inequality and 21% due to increases in stock prices relative to housing (EN Wolff, 23rd general conference, New Brunswick, Canada, 1994). From 1983 to 1989, 66% of the total gain in net financial wealth was received by the top 1%, 37% by the next 19% of the population, and the bottom 80% lost 3%.[8] The current results suggest that either the mortality effects of these changes are focused on the very poor or that income inequality among the poor affects mortality trends among the entire population or that worsening income inequality among the poorest is a harbinger of trends in larger segments of the population. Whichever possibility is true there is cause for alarm given the increasing inequality of income and wealth in the United States.

While the present results do not prove that income inequality causes poor health, the results are dramatic and suggestive enough to make further research in this area a high priority. Because of the strength and consistency of the associations between income distribution and health outcomes, the impact of inequality on mortality trends, and the suggestive evidence concerning the impact of trends in inequality, it would be prudent to consider health effects, and the costs associated with them when the impact of economic policies is evaluated.

NOTES

1. Kaplan GA, Haan MN, Syme SL, Minkler M, Winkelby M. Socioeconomic status and health. In Amler RW, Dull HB, eds. *Closing the gap: the burden of unnecessary illness.* New York: Oxford University Press, 1987:125–9.

2. Haan MN, Kaplan GA, Syme SL. Socioeconomic status and health: old observations and new thoughts. In: Bunker JP, Gomby DS, Kehrer BH, eds. *Pathways to health: the role of social factors.* Menlo Park, CA: Henry J. Kaiser Family Foundation, 1989:76–135.

3. Syme SL, Berkman LF. Social class, susceptibility, and sickness. *Am J Epidermol* 1976;104:1–8.

4. Marmot MG, Kogenvas M, Elston MA. Social/economic status and disease. *Annu Rev Pubb: Health* 1987;8:111–35.

5. Wilkinson RG. Income distribution and life expectancy. *BMJ* 1992;304:165–8.

6. Kawachi I, Levine S, Miller M, Lasch K, Amuck B. *Income inequality and life expectancy: theory, research, and policy.* Boston: Society and Health Working Group, Health Institute, New England School of Medicine. 1994.

7. Thurow LC. *The zero-sum society.* New York: Basic Books, 1980.

8. Wolff EN. *Top heavy: a study of the increasing inequality of wealth in America.* New York: Twentieth Century Fund. 1995.

9. Fritzell J. Income inequality trends in the 1980s: a five-country comparison. *Acta Sociologica* 1993;36:47–62.

10. Dannger S, Gottschalk P, Smolensky E. How the rich have fared 1973–87. *American Economic Review* 1989; 79:310–4.

11. National Center for Health Statistics. *Health, United States, 1990.* Washington, DC: US Government Printing Office, 1991. (DHHS Pub No (PHS 91–1232.)

12. US Bureau of the Census. Government finances in 1990. Washington, DC: US Government Printing Office, 1992. (Series GF, No. 5.)

13. US Bureau of Justice Statistics.*Prisoners vs state and federal institutions: 1990. Correctional populations in the United States.* Washington, DC. US Government Printing Office, 1992.

14. US Bureau of the Census. *Statistical abstract of the United States, 1994.* Washington, DC. US Government Printing Office, 1994.

15. Centers for Disease Control, National Center for Chronic Disease Prevention and Health Promotion. Office of Surveillance and Analysis, Behavioral Survey Branch. *BRFSS summary prevalence report. Atlanta: Centers for Disease Control, 1990.*

16. US Bureau of the Census. *Money income of households, finances, and persons in the United States: 1990–1992. Consumer income.* Washington, DC: US Government Printing Office, 1992. (Current Population Reports. Series P-60, No. 184.)

17. US Bureau of the Census. *Social, economic, and housing characteristics. 1990 Census of population.* Washington, DC. US Government Printing Office, 1992. (CHP-L-96.)

18. National Center for Education Statistics. *Digest of education statistics, 1994.* Washington, DC: US Government Printing Office, 1994. (NCES 94–115.)

19. US Bureau of Labor Statistics. *Geographic profile of employment and unemployment, 1990.* Washington, DC. US Government Printing Office, 1993.

20. Judge K. Income distribution and life expectancy: a critical appraisal. *BMJ* 1995;311:1282–5.

21. Wilkinson, RG. *Class and health: research and longitudinal data.* London: Tavistock, 1986.

22. Morgenstern H. Uses of ecologic analysis in epidemiologic research. *Am J Public Health* 1982;139:1336–44.

23. Susser M. The logic in ecologic. I. The logic of analysis. *Am J Public Health* 1994;84:825–9.

24. Schwartz S. The fallacy of the ecological fallacy: the potential misuse of a concept and the consequences. *Am J Public Health* 1994;84:819–24.

25. Wilkinson RG. Income and health. In *Health, wealth and poverty.* London: Medical World/SHA. 1993.

26. Kaplan GA. Where do shared pathways lead? Some reflections on a research agenda. *Psychosom Med* 1995;57:208–12.

27. Cliff AD, Haggett P. *Atlas of disease distributions.* New York: Basil Blackwell, 1988.

28. Holland WW. *European community atlas of "avoidable death".* Oxford: Oxford University Press, 1992.

29. Mason, TJ, McKay FW. *US cancer mortality by county: 1950–69.* Washington, DC: US Government Printing Office, 1973. (DHEW Publication No. (NIH) 74–615.)

30. Stallones RA. The rise and fall of ischemic heart disease. *Sci Am* 1980;243:53–9.

31. Perry HM Jr, Gillespie KN, Romeis JC, Smith MM, Virgo KS, Carmody SE. Effects of stroke-belt residence, screening blood pressure and personal history risk factors on all-cause mortality among hypertensive veterans. *J Hypertens* 1994;12:315–21.

32. Kaplan GA, Cohn BA, Cohen RD, Guralnik J. The decline in ischemic heart disease mortality: prospective evidence from the Alameda county study. *Am J Epedemiol* 1986;127:1131–42.

Seven

INCOME DISTRIBUTION AND MORTALITY: CROSS-SECTIONAL ECOLOGICAL STUDY OF THE ROBIN HOOD INDEX IN THE UNITED STATES

Bruce P. Kennedy, Ichiro Kawachi, and Deborah Prothrow-Stith

ABSTRACT

Objective—To determine the effect of income inequality as measured by the Robin Hood index and the Gini coefficient on all cause and cause specific mortality in the United States.

Design—Cross sectional ecological study.

Setting—Households in the United States.

Main outcome measures—Disease specific mortality, income, household size, poverty, and smoking rates for each state.

Results—The Robin Hood index was positively correlated with total mortality adjusted for age ($r=0.54$; $P<0.05$). This association remained after adjustment for poverty ($P<0.007$), where each percentage increase in the index was associated with an increase in the total mortality of 21.68 deaths per 100 000. Effects of the index were also found for infant mortality ($P=0.013$); coronary heart disease ($P=0.004$); malignant neoplasms ($P=0.023$); and homicide ($P=0.001$). Strong associations were also found between the index and causes of death amenable to medical intervention. The Gini coefficient showed very little correlation with any of the causes of death.

Conclusion—Variations between states in the inequality of income were associated with increased mortality from several causes. The size of the gap between the wealthy and less well off—as distinct from the absolute standard of living enjoyed by the poor—seems to matter in its own right. The findings suggest that policies that deal with the growing inequities in income distribution may have an important impact on the health of the population.

INTRODUCTION

A small number of cross national studies have suggested a relation between income distribution and life expectancy: the greater the gap in income between the rich and poor in any given society the lower the average life expectancy.[1-5] In one study of 11 countries in the Organisation of Economic Cooperation and

Originally published in *British Medical Journal*, 1996.

Development a strong inverse correlation was found between income inequality—as measured by Gini coefficients of income after tax standardised for differences in household size—and average life expectancy.[2] This association seems to be independent of that between absolute income and life expectancy. In other words, it matters not only how well off a country is but also how economic gains are distributed among its members.

The mechanisms underlying the association between income distribution and mortality are poorly understood.[6 7] For instance, it is not clear whether income distribution is related to particular causes of death, such as infant mortality,[1 8] more than other causes. Published studies to date have focused almost exclusively on average life expectancy or overall mortality and have failed to report data on specific causes of death. Previous studies also have entailed comparisons across different countries, raising the question of comparability and completeness of income data. We examined the relation between income distribution and all cause and cause specific mortality within the United States.

METHODS

Sources of Data

Data on income, household size, and poverty were obtained from the 1990 United States census population and housing summary tape file 3A. This file provides annual data on household incomes for 25 income intervals. Counts of the number of households that fall into each income interval along with the total aggregate income and the median household income were obtained for each state. These data were used to calculate the Gini coefficient and the Robin Hood index. The Gini coefficient and the tenths of income distribution used in deriving the Robin Hood index were calculated by using the Gini and income distribution software developed by E Welniak (unpublished software, United States

Census Bureau, 1988). This program was developed specifically to be used with aggregate census data to generate Gini coefficients and income distributions.

The file also contains statistics on household size and poverty in which households are classified as being above or below the poverty level based on the revised federal poverty index originally developed by the Social Security Administration in 1964. The current poverty index is based purely on income from wages and does not reflect other sources of income such as non-cash benefits from food stamps, Medicaid, and public housing. Poverty thresholds are updated annually to reflect changes in the consumer price index. The poverty variable we used represents the percentage of households in a given state that were below the federal poverty level. In 1990, this represented an income of less than \$13 359 for households with four family members.[9]

All of the data on mortality adjusted for age for 1990 for each state were obtained from the compressed mortality files compiled by the National Center for Health Statistics, Centers for Disease Control and Prevention (CDC). The data were obtained from their database with the CDC WONDER/PC software.[10]

Data on prevalence of smoking in each state were obtained from the centre's smoking information page, available on the Internet. The data are from the current population survey (1989) and reflect the percentage of adults aged 18 years and older who are current smokers.

Measures of Income Distribution

We examined the relations of total and cause specific mortality with two alternative measures of income distribution: the Robin Hood index[11] and the Gini coefficient. The Robin Hood index was estimated from state specific data on the shares of total household income arranged by tenths of the distribution (see appendix, table A1 for the example of Massachusetts). The index is calculated by taking those groups whose share of the total income exceeds 10% then adding the excess of these shares over that level. In the example of Massachusetts, the value of the index is 30·26% (appendix, table A1). This value approximates the share of total income that has to be taken from those above the mean and transferred to those below the mean to achieve equality in the distribution of incomes.[11] The higher the value of the index the less egalitarian is the distribution of income. The Gini coefficient is another commonly used summary measure of income inequality where higher values indicate greater inequalities in income distribution (see appendix for its derivation).

All Cause and Cause Specific Mortality

All mortalities were directly standardised for age to the United States population and expressed as the number of deaths per 100 000 (except in the case of infant mortality, where death rates are expressed per 1000 live births). In addition to all cause mortality we examined the following major causes of death: coronary heart disease (defined by codes 410−414 of the *International Classification of Diseases*, 9th revision (ICD-9)); cerebrovascular disease (ICD-9 codes 430−438); malignant neoplasms (ICD-9 codes 140−239); and homicide (ICD-9 codes E960−969).

The association of income inequality with mortality may be partly mediated by lack of access to medical care. We tested this hypothesis indirectly by examining the relations of income inequality to cause of death amenable to medical intervention.[12-14] The specific causes of death examined were infectious and parasitic diseases (ICD-9 codes 001−139); tuberculosis (ICD-9 codes 010−018 and 137); pneumonia and bronchitis (ICD-9 codes 480−486 and 490); and hypertensive disease (ICD-9 codes 401−405).

Data Analysis

Ordinary least squares regression was used to examine separately the relations of the Robin Hood index and the Gini coefficient to measures of mortality. Two sets of models were examined for each outcome of interest. In the first set of models we adjusted for the proportion of households in each state with incomes below the federal poverty level (which was defined as an annual household income of less than $13 359 for a family of four in 1990). In the second set of models we adjusted for poverty as well as the state specific prevalence of smoking, median household income, and household size. Wherever appropriate, we examined mortality separately by race (white v black).

Table 1

Effects of Robin Hood index adjusted for poverty

Cause of death (ICD-9 code)	β (SE)	t (P value)	Adjusted r^2	$F_{2,47}$	P value
Total mortality	21·68 (7·68)	2·82 (0·007)	0·27	9·91	<0·008
Infant Mortality	0·45 (0·17)	2·59 (0·013)	0·20	7·31	<0·002
Heart disease (410−414)	9·96 (3·27)	3·06 (0·004)	0·18	6·20	<0·004
Malignant neoplasms (140−239)	5·09 (2·18)	2·34 (0·023)	0·07	2·73	<0·075
Cerebrovascular disease (430−438)	0·77 (0·01)	0·762 (0·449)	0·08	3·06	<0·056
Homicide (960−969)	2·22 (0·38)	5·78 (0·000)	0·52	27·09	<0·000

Table 2

Effects of Robin Hood index adjusted for poverty and smoking

Cause of death	β (SE)	t (P value)	Adjusted r^2	$F_{3,46}$	P value
Total mortality	11·83 (6·14)	1·93 (0·060)	0·567	22·36	<0·000
Infant mortality	0·31 (0·17)	1·87 (0·068)	0·32	8·52	<0·000
Heart disease	8·44 (3·33)	2·53 (0·015)	0·21	5·24	<0·003
Malignant neoplasms	2·36 (1·77)	1·33 (0·189)	0·43	13·22	<0·000
Cerebrovascular disease	0·38 (1·04)	0·366 (0·716)	0·09	2·68	<0·058
Homicide	2·11 (0·39)	5·26 (0·000)	0·52	18·60	<0·000

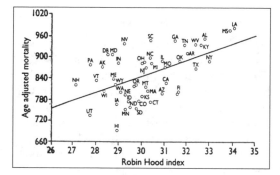

Figure 1

Mortality by inequality (Robin Hood index) in United States (abbreviations are for each state)

RESULTS

Robin Hood Index

The Robin Hood index for the United States overall in 1990 was 30·22% (range 27·13% for New Hampshire to 34·05% for Louisiana). The index had a significant correlation with total mortality adjusted for age (r=0·54; P<0·05) (fig 1). The association of the index to total mortality remained highly significant after adjustment for poverty in our regression model: each percentage increase in the index was associated with an increase in total mortality of 21·68 deaths per 100 000 (95% confidence interval 6·63 to 36·71) (table 1). The bivariate association of the index with total mortality was similar for both black people (r=0·39;

P<0·05) and white people (r=0·46; P<0·05). When the effects of poverty in each state were controlled for, the relation of the Robin Hood index to total mortality in black people (β=44·57; 95% confidence interval 12·57 to 76·57) was greater than to mortality in white people (β=15·04; 1·69 to 28·40). Adjustment for median household income and household size in each state did not materially alter these results (data not shown).

Strong associations with the index were also found for infant mortality (P=0·013); coronary heart disease (P=0·004); malignant neoplasms (P=0·023); and homicide (P<0·001) (table 1). In the case of homicide, the index variable alone explained 52·4% of the variance between states. The index was strongly associated with homicide rates among both black people (β=6·51; 2·82 to 10·18) and white people (β=1·81; 1·14 to 2·48).

Adjustment for smoking prevalence in addition to poverty generally attenuated the coefficients for total and cause specific mortality (table 2). As expected, smoking was an independent predictor of total mortality (β=12·37; P<0·0001) as well as deaths from cancer (β=3·42; P<0·0001). The association of the Robin Hood index with total mortality was of borderline significance (β=11·84; P=0·06). The index continued to be a powerful predictor of overall mortality from coronary heart disease (β=8·44; P=0·0148), although the association was confined to white people (β=9·36; P=0·009), the value being β=4·57

(P=0·471) for black people. Less egalitarian states continued to show higher rates of homicide, both among white people (β=1·82; P<0·0001) and black people (β=6·29; P=0·002).

Gini Coefficient

The Gini coefficient for the United States overall was 0·43 in 1990 (range 0·38 for Minnesota to 0·50 for Louisiana). Contrary to previous reports based on comparisons among European nations,[2] the Gini coefficient showed little correlation with any of the mortality outcomes in these data, with the exception of homicide (table 3).

The apparent discrepancy in findings with the Gini and the Robin Hood index was partly accounted for by differences in the meaning of the two measures. The Gini coefficient in these data was sensitive to the income accruing to the extremes of the distribution: a correlation of −0·92 with the proportion of income earned by households in the bottom 10% of the population and 0·93 with the proportion of income earned by the households above the 90th centile. On the other hand, the Gini coefficient correlated only modestly with the proportions of income earned by the bottom 50% and 60% of households (r=0·27 and −0·29, respectively).

The situation with the Robin Hood index was the reverse of that with the Gini coefficient: the index was highly correlated with the proportions of income earned by the bottom 50%, 60%, and 70% of households (r=0·99) but not with the proportion of income earned by the most poor (bottom 10%). The correlation between the Robin Hood index and the Gini coefficient was modest (r=0·29).

Treatable Causes of Mortality

Strong associations were found between the Robin Hood index and all of the indicators of treatable causes of mortality, which were independent of poverty and prevalence of smoking (table 4). No associations were found between the Gini coefficient and treatable causes of death (data not shown).

Discussion

THE relation between absolute living standards and mortality is well established.[15] The effects of relative deprivation on mortality, however, have been less well understood. Our study extends the findings of previous reports[2 4 5] in showing the association of income inequality (at least as measured by the Robin Hood index) to total and cause specific mortality within one country.

The mechanisms of the association between income inequality and mortality have not been completely elucidated.[7] Although the Robin Hood index correlated with poverty (r=0·73) and smoking (r=0·30), suggesting a potential problem due to multicolinearity, examination of the tolerance statistics and standard errors of the index regression coefficient when the poverty and

---

Table 3

Effects of Robin Hood index on treatable causes adjusted for poverty and smoking

Disease (ICD-9)	β (SE)	t (P value)	Adjusted r^2	$F_{3,46}$	P value
Infectious diseases (001–139)	4·57 (0·79)	5·80 (0·000)	0·39	11·49	<0·000
Hypertensive disease (401–405)	1·32 (0·53)	1·49 (0·016)	0·22	5·52	<0·003
Tuberculosis (010-018, 137)	0·15 (0·04)	4·04 (0·000)	0·44	13·55	<0·000
Pneumonia and bronchitis (480-486, 490)	1·38 (0·48)	2·87 (0·006)	0·10	2·81	<0·050

Table 4

Correlations between cause of death and Gini coefficient

Cause of death	r	P value
Total mortality	− 0·03	0·83
Infant mortality	0·06	0·67
Heart disease	0·09	0·52
Malignant neoplasms	− 0·19	0·18
Cerebrovascular disease	0·16	0·26
Homicide	0·28	0·04
Infectious diseases	0·08	0·60
Hypertensive disease	0·10	0·47
Tuberculosis	0·24	0·09
Pneumonia and bronchitis	− 0·05	0·70

smoking variables were entered into the model did not indicate that this was a serious problem. Several of the associations with cause specific mortality—in particular, coronary heart disease and homicide—remained significant after adjustment for these variables. We also estimated the regression models by adjusting for median household income and household size (data not shown) with essentially the same results. Although some researchers advocate the use of equivalency scales to take into account differences in household size, such scales ignore the effects of economies of scale. In our analyses there was no evidence that cross state variations in household size were related to mortality or measures of inequality.

Regions with a higher proportion of black residents tend to be overrepresented among the states with a high Robin Hood index (fig 1); none the less, when we stratified the analyses by race the association of the index with outcomes such as homicide remained just as strong for white people as for black people. In the case of coronary heart disease the association of the index with mortality was actually confined to white people.

Income distribution may be a proxy for other social indicators, such as the degree of investment in human capital. Communities that tolerate large degrees of inequality in income may be the same ones that tend to underinvest in social goods such as public education or accessible health care.[16] Our findings with regard to treatable causes of mortality suggest that lack of access to medical care may indeed be part of the mechanism by which income inequality produces higher mortality (although the contribution of treatable causes of death to overall mortality was rather small).

A limitation of the present study is its cross sectional design so that caution must be exercised in the interpretation of the observed associations. Some states may have a high proportion of sick people for reasons other than the hypothesis under investigation, and the less egalitarian distribution of income in such states merely reflects the reduced earning capacity of sick people, who are also at higher risk of dying. Further work should attempt to incorporate time series analyses of income inequality and mortality trends.

Another limitation of the present ecological study is its potential susceptibility to aggregation bias and unknown sources of confounding.[17] To some extent, aggregation of data is unavoidable in studies of this type since the main predictor of interest—namely, income dispersion—is itself an ecological variable. None the less, the ideal study design would incorporate collection of data at the individual level on other predictors of health, including health behaviours (such as smoking and drinking), access to health care, and social class.

Choice of Measure of Income Inequality
An unexpected finding of this study was that the choice of the measure of income inequality affected the relation with mortality. Thus strong associations were found between the Robin Hood index and cause specific mortality but not by using the Gini coefficient.

Previous studies have used different measures of income inequality (such as the Gini coefficient or the proportion of income earned by the bottom 60% of households) without detailed justification for the choice of measure.[18] In practice, it is recognised that there is a wide choice of indices to measure income inequality, but there is no consensus that a single measure, such as the Gini coefficient, ought to be standard.[19] Instead, the selection of the measure of income dispersion should be dictated by the underlying theory of cause of disease.

We found that the Gini coefficient was highly correlated with the proportion of income earned by the bottom 10% of households and hence acts as a proxy for extreme deprivation. By contrast, the Robin Hood index correlated much more with the share of income earned by most of the population. Although the wide choice of inequality indices creates the hazard that researchers will use the measure that proves the result they wish to find, our findings suggest that, at least in the United States, the use of the Gini coefficient may result in more of a test of the effects on health of extreme deprivation rather than relative deprivation. As a measure of income inequality the Robin Hood index has a plausible interpretation. For instance, the findings for mortality from coronary heart disease (adjusted for poverty and smoking) imply that a redistribution of incomes in the United States to achieve a reduction in the Robin Hood index (from 30% to 25%, which is roughly equivalent to the Robin Hood index in England) would be associated on average with about a 25% decline in age adjusted mortality for that disease (from 183 to 139 per 100 000). Furthermore, if there is a causal relation we might expect a reduction in total mortality of 7%.

Conclusion

Our findings provide some support for the notion that the size of the gap between the wealthy and less well off—as distinct from the absolute standard of living enjoyed by the poor—matters in its own right. This finding in no way diminishes the importance of measures to alleviate the burden of poverty. None the less, in an affluent society such as the United States, reliance on trickle down policies may not be enough—society must pay attention to the growing gap between the rich and the poor.

Funding: No special funding.
Conflict of interest: None.

APPENDIX:
DERIVATION OF THE GINI COEFFICIENT

THE Gini coefficient is derived from the Lorenz curve, which is a graphic device for representing the cumulative share of the total income accruing to successive income intervals (fig A1). The curve shows the share of income accruing to households in the bottom income interval, then the share going to households in the next income interval (which includes the previous income interval), and so on. If all incomes were equal the Lorenz curve would follow the 45° diagonal. As the degree of inequality increases so does the curvature of the Lorenz curve, and thus the area between the curve and the 45° line becomes larger. The Gini coefficient is calculated as the ratio of the area between the Lorenz curve and the 45° line divided by the whole area below the 45° line.

In figure A1 the Robin Hood index, also known as the Pietra ratio,[20] is equivalent to the

Table A1

Data on derivation of Robin Hood index for Massachusetts

Tenth	Percentage of total income
1	1·08
2	2·48
3	4·13
4	5·74
5	7·33
6	8·97
7	10·83
8	13·09
9	16·41
10	29·93

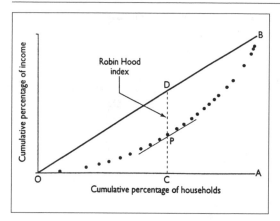

Figure A1
Derivation of the Robin Hood index from the
Lorenz curve and the Gini coefficient

maximum vertical distance between the Lorenz curve and the line of equal incomes (CD–CP). A more straightforward derivation of the index can be obtained from the tenths of an income distribution as shown in the example in table A1.

The Robin Hood index may also be calculated by summing the percentage of income for each tenth of an income distribution where the percentage exceeds 10% and subtracting from this the product of the number of tenths that meet this criterion times 10%. In this case four of the tenths (7–10) exceed 10%, so the Robin Hood index

=(10·84%+13·09%+16·41%+29·93%) – (4x10%)
=70·26% – 40%
=30·26.

NOTES

1. Rodgers GB. Income and inequality as determinants of mortality: an international cross-section analysis. *Population Studies* 1979;33:343–51.

2. Wilkinson RG. Income and mortality. In: Wilkinson RG, ed. *Class and heath: research and longitudinal data.* London: Tavistock, 1986.

3. Wilkinson RG. Income distribution and mortality: a "natural" experiment. *Sociology of Health and Illness* 1990; 12:391–412.

4. Wilkinson RG. Income distribution and life expectancy. *BMJ* 1992;304:165–8.

5. LeGrand J. Inequalities in health. Some international comparisons. *European Economic Review* 1987;31:182–91.

6. Kawachi I, Levine S, Miller SM, Lasch K, Amick B. *Income inequality and life expectancy—theory, research, and policy.* Boston: The Health Institute, New England Medical Center, 1994. (Working paper No 94–2).

7. Wilkinson RG. The epidemiological transition: from material scarcity to social disadvantage? *Daedalus* 1994;123: 61–77.

8. Flegg AT. Inequality of income, illiteracy and medical care as determinants of infant mortality in underdeveloped countries. *Population Studies* 1982;36:441–58.

9. US Bureau of the Census, *CD-ROM, income and poverty.* Washington, DC: US Bureau of the Census, 1993.

10. Friede A, Reid JA, Ory HW. CD WONDER: a comprehensive on-line public health information system of the Centers for Disease Control and Prevention. *Am J Public Health* 1993;83:1289–94.

11. Atkinson AB, Micklewright J. *Economic transformation in Eastern Europe and the distribution of income.* Cambridge: Cambridge University Press, 1992.

12. Charlton JRH, Velez R. Some international comparisons of mortality amenable to medical intervention. *BMJ* 1986;292:295–301.

13. Mackenbach JP, Bouvier-Colle MH, Jougla E. "Avoidable" mortality and health services: a review of aggregate data studies. *J Epidemiol Community Health* 1990;44: 106–11.

14. Marshall SW, Kawachi I, Pearce N, Borman B. Social class differences in mortality from diseases amenable to medical intervention in New Zealand. *In Int J Epidemiol* 1993; 22:255–61.

15. Townsend P, Davidson N. *Inequalities in health: the Black report.* Harmondsworth: Penguin, 1982.

16. Birdsall N, Ross D, Sabot R. *Inequality and growth reconsidered.* Boston: American Economic Association, 1994.

17. Morgenstern H. Uses of ecologic analysis in epidemiologic research. *Am J Public Health* 1982;139:1336–44.

18. Judge K. Income distribution and life expectancy: a critical appraisal. *BMJ* 1995;311:1282–5.

19. Buhmann B, Rainwater L, Schmaus G, Smeeding TM. Equivalence scales, well-being, inequality, and poverty: sensitivity estimates across ten countries using the Luxembourg income study (LIS) database. *Review of Income and Wealth* 1988;34:115–42.

20. Kondor Y. An old-new measure of income inequality. *Econometrica* 1971;39:1041–2.

Important correction

Income distribution and mortality: cross sectional ecological study of the Robin Hood index in the United States

A data transposition error occurred in table 4 of this paper, Bruce P. Kennedy *et al.* (20 April, pp 1004–7). The corrected data are presented below. This correction indicates that the Gini coefficient measure of income inequality is also strongly associated with mortality, contrary to the authors' initial conclusions.

Table 4

Correlations between cause of death and Gini coefficient

Cause of death	r	P value
Total mortality	0.51	<0.001
Infant mortality	0·47	<0.001
Heart disease	0·43	<0.002
Malignant neoplasms	0·21	<0.134
Cerebrovascular disease	0·28	<0.047
Homicide	0·72	<0.001
Infectious diseases	0·45	<0.001
Hypertensive disease	0·43	<0.002
Tuberculosis	0·67	<0.001
Pneumonia and bronchitis	0·30	<0.033

British Medical Journal 1996; 312: 1253

Eight

INCOME INEQUALITY AND MORTALITY IN METROPOLITAN AREAS OF THE UNITED STATES

*John W. Lynch, George A. Kaplan,
Elsie R. Pamuk, Richard D. Cohen,
Katherine E. Heck, Jennifer L. Balfour,
and Irene H. Yen*

ABSTRACT

Objectives. This study examined associations between income inequality and mortality in 282 US metropolitan areas.

Methods. Income inequality measures were calculated from the 1990 US Census. Mortality was calculated from National Center for Health Statistics data and modeled with weighted linear regressions of the log age-adjusted rate.

Results. Excess mortality between metropolitan areas with high and low income inequality ranged from 64.7 to 95.8 deaths per 100 000 depending on the inequality measure. In age-specific analyses, income inequality was most evident for infant mortality and for mortality between ages 15 and 64.

Conclusions. Higher income inequality is associated with increased mortality at all per capita income levels. Areas with high income inequality and low average income had excess mortality of 139.8 deaths per 100 000 compared with areas with low inequality and high income. The magnitude of this mortality difference is comparable to the combined loss of life from lung cancer, diabetes, motor vehicle crashes, human immunodeficiency virus (HIV) infection, suicide, and homicide in 1995. Given the mortality burden associated with income inequality, public and private sector initiatives to reduce economic inequalities should be a high priority.

INTRODUCTION

WHILE a large number of studies have demonstrated that absolute levels of income are related to morbidity and mortality.[1-5] two recent US reports have also shown strong associations between levels of income inequality

Originally published in *American Journal of Public Health*, 1998.

and mortality, after adjustment for absolute income differences, in the 50 US states.[6, 7] These findings suggest that it is not only the absolute amount of income that is important for health, but also the relative disparity with which income is distributed in a population.[8] The hypothesis that the size of the gap between the rich and the poor in a society is importantly related to health is intriguing and deserves further investigation. If relative position in the income distribution is an important determinant of health, then it is possible that more equitable societies may experience better overall levels of health than societies where there is a large gap between the rich and the poor. Examining the extent of income disparity may help us understand why people in countries with low income such as China, Bangladesh, and parts of India[9] have higher survival rates beyond ages 30 and 40 than African Americans living in Harlem, where real incomes are higher.[10]

To date, the small number of studies that have attempted to investigate associations between income inequality and health have largely focused on international comparisons.[11-13] There are many unanswered questions concerning this association,[14] and little is known about how disparities in income distribution affect health within the United States. We investigated the association of income inequality and mortality in metropolitan areas of the United States.[15] Our objectives were to examine whether associations varied according to the measure of income inequality and to gain estimates of the absolute magnitude of the effects of income inequality on mortality.

METHODS

ASSOCIATIONS between income inequality and mortality were studied in 283 metropolitan areas defined by the Federal Office of Management and Budget and used in the 1990 US Census. Metropolitan areas comprise a core area or city containing a large population nucleus and adjacent communities having a high degree of economic and social integration with the core. Metropolitan areas consist of entire counties, except in New England, where New England county metropolitan areas were used as the units of analysis. In total, 282 US metropolitan areas were included in these analyses (mortality data were not available for Anchorage, Alaska). In 1990, metropolitan area populations ranged from 56 735 for Enid, Okla, to 18 087 251 for New York, NY; the median population was 242 622.

Assessment of Income Inequality

To calculate income distributions, we used information on gross household income from all sources, including government transfers such as Aid to Families with Dependent Children, from the 1990 US Census Summary Tape File STF3C. Income distributions were based on the number of households in each of 25 income intervals, the midpoint of each interval, and the aggregate income in and below the top income interval (which is open-ended).

In general terms, measures of income inequality seek to represent the allocation of income in a population. There is no one best method for assessing income inequality,[16, 17] so a variety of measures were calculated on the basis of gross income distributions. We included measures commonly used in econometric analyses of income inequality, a measure used in our earlier analyses of US states[6] (income share at the 50th percentile), and income share ratios between the 90th, 50th, and 10th percentiles of the distribution. Preliminary analyses had shown somewhat larger variation in income shares at the bottom of the income distribution than at the top.

The 3 common measures of income inequality used in these analyses were the Gini coefficient, the Atkinson Deprivation Index, and the Theil Entropy Index. Detailed descriptions of their derivation and calculation are available elsewhere.[16] The Gini coefficient is discussed as an example of the logic behind the measurement of income inequality; it provides an overall estimate of income inequality derived from the relationship between cumulative proportions of the population, plotted against cumulative proportions of income. The Gini coefficient is calculated as a ratio of the area between the actual income distribution (the Lorenz curve) and the diagonal to the total area under the diagonal. Higher Gini coefficients mean greater income inequality and range from 0, meaning perfect equality, to 1, perfect inequality of income distribution. Perfectly equal income distribution would be achieved if 10% of the population received 10% of the total income, 20% of the population received 20% of the total income, and so on. If each percentile of the population received the equivalent share of total income, then the Gini coefficient would be 0. However, if only one household in the population received all the income, the Gini coefficient would be 1.

The Atkinson Deprivation Index is based on the ratio of the "equally distributed equivalent" income to the mean of the actual income distribution and incorporates a "social welfare function" that explicitly applies a normative weighting based on society's aversion to inequality.[18] The equation for the Atkinson index (A) is given below:

$$A = 1 - \frac{y_e}{\mu}.$$

In this equation, μ is the mean income in the metropolitan statistical area and y_e is given by the expression.

$$y_e = \left[\sum_{i=1}^{25} p_i y_i^{1-\epsilon} \right]^{\frac{1}{1-\epsilon}},$$

in which p_i is the proportion of households in the ith interval, y_i is the average income in the ith interval, ϵ is a parameter that reflects society's preference for equality, and the sum is taken over all 25 income intervals. Consistent with previous research, we used 2 values of this aversion weighting ($e = 0.5$ and 2.0 to indicate low and high aversion to inequality).[19, 20]

The Theil Entropy Index (T) is derived from information theory and likens the dispersion of income shares across the population to the concept of entropy.[21] In this equation, s_j is the share of total income in the jth income decile and the sum is taken over all deciles:

$$T = \sum_{j=1}^{10} [s_j \log(10) + s_j \log(s_j)].$$

In addition to these econometric indicators, we calculated income inequality measures on the basis of shares of total income. These measures related how much of the total income was received by a particular proportion of the population. From our previous study of US states, we used the income share held by the least well-off 50% of the population. A larger share indicates that the bottom half of the population receives more of the total income and suggests lower income inequality in the area.[6] We also calculated the ratio of income share held below the 50th percentile to the share held below the 10th, and the ratio of income share held below the 90th percentile to that below the 10th (higher ratios indicate greater income inequality).

Assessment of Mortality

Mortality information from the National Center for Health Statistics Compressed Mortality Files for 1989 through 1991 was used to calculate mortality rates in each metropolitan area. As mortality information is not routinely available for metropolitan areas, numbers of deaths and populations were aggregated for each county constituting the metropolitan area and were age-adjusted, with the 1990 US population divided into 13 age groups. Average mortality per 100 000 ranged from 642.5 to 1092.9; the average was 849.6. Excess mortality was calculated as the difference in mortality rates between high and low income inequality quartiles and indicates the absolute disease burden associated with differences in income inequality. We believe that absolute measures such as excess mortality are an appropriate yardstick for assessing the importance of income inequalities to population health.[22, 23]

Assessment of Covariates

For each metropolitan area, information on median household size, per capita income, and percentage of the population with incomes less than 200% of the federally designated poverty level ($12 674 for a four-person household) was obtained from the 1990 US Census Summary Tape File STF3C. The proportion of the population with incomes less than 200% of poverty is a widely used indicator of the prevalence of low-income households. Preliminary analyses using the proportion of the population in poverty produced almost identical results. Median household size was used to adjust for differences in the number of people supported by the income. Median household size, per capita income, and proportion of the population with incomes less than 200% of poverty were modeled continuously in all analyses except those that are reported in Figure 1, in which per capita income was divided into quartiles and modeled with indicator variables. Preliminary analyses stratified by, and then adjusted for, population and geographic size of the metropolitan area showed no evidence of interaction or confounding (data not shown).

Statistical Methods

Associations between income inequality and mortality were modeled with weighted linear regressions of the log age-adjusted or age-specific mortality rate. The distribution of each inequality measure was divided into quartiles, and indi-cator variables were used in all analyses, with the first (low) quartile as the reference. Observations were weighted by the reciprocal of the variance of the log mortality rate in each metropolitan area to account for differences in the variance of the rates.[24] Rates based on larger numbers of deaths and smaller variance received higher weighting than those based on smaller numbers. To check that results were robust with regard to the method of modeling, we also analyzed these associations with Poisson regression techniques and unweighted linear regression, and found almost identical results. Because the weighted linear regression technique offers more flexibility in adjustment for covariates, all analyses reported here are based on weighted linear regressions of the log mortality rate.

To calculate absolute mortality in the high and low quartiles of income inequality, we used median values of the covariates to evaluate the linear predictor from the model. These estimates of log mortality rate were then exponentiated to yield absolute mortality rates for each of the income inequality quartiles. The statistical significance of adding income inequality measures to models containing the covariates was tested with a general linear F test with 3 and 276 df.[24] Analyses were conducted with the PROC REG procedure in SAS version 6.12 on a Sun workstation.[25]

RESULTS

TABLE 1 shows medians, ranges, and Pearson correlations for age-adjusted mortality, income inequality measures, per capita income, proportion of the population with incomes less than 200% of poverty, and 1990 population size for the 282 metropolitan areas. Income inequality measures such as the ratio of the income share held below the 90th and 50th percentiles to that held below the 10th had the largest ranges (90th: 10th percentile ratio range = 39.48–95.21). The correlations displayed in Table 1 show that associations between the measures of income inequality ranged from $r = 0.55$ for the

Table 1

Pearson Correlation Coefficients for Age-Adjusted Total Mortality, Income Inequality Measures, Per Capita Income, Proportion of the Population with Incomes Less than 200% of Poverty, and Population Size: 282 US Metropolitan Areas, 1990

Variable (Median; Range)	Gini Coefficient	Theil Entropy Index	Atkinson Deprivation Index with ε = 0.5	Below 50th Percentile Share	50th:10th Percentile Share Ratio	Atkinson Deprivation Index with ε = 2.0	90th:10th Percentile Share Ratio	Per Capita Income	Proportion < 200% Poverty	Population Size
Age-adjusted total mortality (847.1; 642.5–1092.9)	0.25	0.21	0.27	−0.33	0.51	0.40	0.52	−0.28	0.26	0.05[a]
Gini coefficient (0.42; 0.36–0.50)		0.99	0.99	−0.98	0.58	0.89	0.70	−0.20	0.59	0.12[b]
Theil Entropy Index (0.29; 0.22–0.43)			0.99	−0.96	0.55	0.87	0.67	−0.15[c]	0.56	0.12[d]
Atkinson Deprivation Index with ε = 0.5 (0.16; 0.12–0.22)				−0.97	0.60	0.90	0.72	−0.20	0.58	0.12[b]
Below 50th percentile share (0.21; 0.15–0.25)					−0.61	−0.90	−0.76	0.30	−0.63	−0.08[e]
50th:10th percentile share ratio (16.79; 11.93–25.80)						0.81	0.97	−0.09[f]	0.27	0.12[b]
Atkinson Deprivation Index with ε = 2.0 (0.58; 0.47–0.68)							0.88	−0.05[g]	0.39	0.22
90th:10th percentile share ratio (55.4; 39.48–95.21)								−0.20	0.41	0.09[f]
Per capita income (12.93; 6.63–26.16)									−0.84	0.40
Proportion < 200% poverty (32.05; 14.35–69.27)										−0.22

Note. See Methods section of text for explanation of income inequality measures. All *P*'s <.001 unless otherwise noted.
[a]*P* = .35; [b]*P* = .05; [c]*P* = .009; [d]*P* = .18; [e]*P* = .04; [f]*P* = .12; [g]*P* = .36.

Table 2

Associations between Income Inequality and Age–Adjusted Total Mortality: 282 US Metropolitan Areas, 1989–1991

Income Inequality Measure[a]	Model 1 (Unadjusted)			Model 2 (Model 1 + Per Capita Income and Median Household Size)			Model 3 (Model 1 + Proportion < 200% Poverty and Median Household Size)		
	Excess Mortality per 100 000[b]	F[c]	Adjusted R^2	Excess Mortality per 100 000[b]	F[c]	Adjusted R^2	Excess Mortality per 100 000[b]	F[c]	Adjusted R^2
Gini coefficient	64.7	13.1	11.5	64.3	14.0	15.3	61.5	12.3	13.8
Theil Entropy Index	65.3	13.6	11.8	65.0	14.5	15.7	62.2	12.6	14.1
Atkinson Deprivation Index with e = 0.5	65.5	17.9	15.3	65.2	18.0	18.4	65.2	16.5	17.2
Below 50th percentile share	71.9	18.7	15.9	70.7	18.7	18.9	69.7	18.4	17.6
50th:10th percentile share ratio	89.4	31.3	24.4	112.2	41.3	32.6	92.8	30.2	26.4
Atkinson Deprivation Index with e = 2.0	89.4	28.0	22.4	108.7	38.8	31.4	87.6	26.2	23.9
90th:10th percentile share ratio	95.8	40.1	29.4	116.8	49.9	36.7	97.5	37.1	30.3

[a]See Methods section of text for explanation of income inequality measures.

[b]Excess mortality due to income inequality is calculated as the difference in age–adjusted mortality rates between the lowest and highest quartiles of income inequality.

[c]F statistic tests the overall significance of the income inequality measure in each model. All Ps <001.

Theil index and ratio of income share below 50th percentile to income share below 10th percentile to $r = 0.99$ for the Gini coefficient and both the Atkinson ($e = 0.5$) and Theil indices. The income inequality measures were all significantly related to mortality, although the strengths of association differed. The strongest correlations with mortality ($r = 0.52$ and $r = 0.51$) were observed for the ratios of income shares held below the 90th and 50th percentiles to that held below the 10th percentile of the income distribution. Both per capita income and proportion of the population with incomes less than 200% of poverty were modestly associated with mortality ($r = -0.28$ and $r = 0.26$, respectively), but the population size of the metropolitan area was unrelated.

Table 2 shows unadjusted associations between different measures of income inequality and age-adjusted total mortality (model 1), associations adjusted for per capita income and median household size (model 2), and associations adjusted for proportion of the population with incomes less than 200% of poverty and median household size (model 3). Per capita income and proportion with incomes less than 200% of poverty were not modeled together because they were highly correlated ($r = -0.84$). Preliminary analyses showed that models containing both were uninterpretable owing to problems of collinearity. No evidence of interaction was found between income inequality and absolute per capita income (data not shown). Each model presented in Table 2 shows the excess mortality in metropolitan areas in the high-inequality quartile compared with the low-inequality quartile. An F statistic tests the significance of the income inequality measure in each model, and the percentage of variance explained by the full model (adjusted R^2) indicates the overall model fit.

Excess mortality and the R^2 values indicated that the Atkinson Deprivation Index ($e = 2.0$, meaning high aversion to inequality) and income shares held below the 90th and 50th percentiles, compared with the share held below the 10th

percentile, had the strongest associations with mortality. However, income inequality was importantly related to mortality regardless of which measure was used and was a statistically significant addition to every model. The unadjusted excess mortality rate difference due to inequality varied form 64.7 per 100 000 when inequality was measured by the Gini coefficient to 95.8 per 100 000 when equality was measured by the ratio of income share held below the 90th percentile to the share held below the 10th percentile. Adjustment for per capita income and median household size in model 2 did not diminish the excess mortality associated with income inequality. Similar patterns were evident with adjustment for median household size and proportion with incomes less than 200% of poverty (model 3).

Table 3 shows associations between the inequality measure with the strongest mortality association—the ratio of income share held below the 90th percentile to the share held below the 10th percentile—and age-specific mortality. Mortality rates were also age-adjusted within each of the age-specific groups, except for infant mortality. Table 3 shows excess mortality due to income inequality, the attributable proportion (interpreted as the excess mortality between high- and low-inequality quartiles as a proportion of the mortality rate in the high-inequality quartile), an F statistic that tests the significance of the income inequality measure, and percentage of variance explained by the model (adjusted R^2). The effect of income inequality was most evident for infant mortality and mortality in age groups 15 to 34 years and 35 to 64 years. With regard to infant mortality, there were 210.5 excess deaths per 100 000 in the high- compared with the low-inequality metropolitan areas, after adjustment for differences in per capita income and household size. This suggests that in high-inequality metropolitan areas, 19.3% of the elevated infant mortality rate may be associated with the effects of income inequality. For mortality in the 35- to 64-year-old group, the measure of income inequality, per capita income, and

Table 3

Associations between Income Inequality (Ratio of Income Share Held below 90th Percentile to Share Held below 10th Percentile) and Age-Specific Mortality, Adjusted for Per Capita Income and Median Household Size: 282 US Metropolitan Areas, 1989–1991

Age Group, y	Excess Mortality per 100 000[a]	Attributable Proportion[b]	F[c]	Variance Explained by Whole Model, %
< 1	210.5	19.3	25.3	21.2
1–14	3.0	8.6	13.7	23.4
15–34	35.0	25.1	49.3	37.7
35–64	132.4	21.3	80.2	46.1
65+	459.9	8.8	18.0	23.3

[a]Excess mortality due to income inequality is calculated as the difference in mortality rates between the lowest and highest quartiles of income inequality, adjusted for per capita income and median household size.
[b]Attributable proportion is calculated as the excess mortality rate divided by the mortality rate in the highest quartile of income inequality.
[c] The F statistic tests the overall significance of the income inequality measure in each age-specific model. All P's <.001.

median household size explained 46.1% of the variance in total mortality across metropolitan areas.

Figure 1 shows the joint distribution of age-adjusted mortality for quartiles of income inequality (ratio of income share held below the 90th percentile to that held below the 10th percentile) and quartiles of per capita income. The figure is intended to demonstrate the joint effects of these factors on mortality differences between metropolitan areas. Significant mortality effects of income inequality were evident at every level of per capita income. When we compared the most extreme differences in the age-adjusted mortality rate between metropolitan areas with high income inequality and low per capita income (925.7 deaths per 100 000) and areas with low income inequality and high per capita income (785.9 deaths per 100 000), the excess mortality was 139.8 deaths per 100 000.

DISCUSSION

O UR findings show that metropolitan areas with high income inequality had significantly greater age-adjusted total mortality than those with low inequality, regardless of which measure of inequality was used. The mortality effects of income inequality differed by age, appearing to be concentrated in the age groups birth to 1 year and 15 to 64 years. The weakest effects were observed for deaths between the ages of 1 and 14, where average mortality was low (31.2 deaths per 100 000) and the major cause of death was accidents. The lack of effect of income inequality observed here was consistent with studies that have shown no overall association between individual socioeconomic status and risk of accidents in similar age groups.[26, 27] We should also note that we used data from metropolitan areas only, and so our findings do not address the relationship between income inequality and mortality in rural areas.

Associations between income inequality and mortality varied across inequality measures and were strongest for the ratios of income shares held below the 90th and 50th percentiles to that held below the 10th percentile. It is possible that overall inequality measures such as the Gini coefficient are less sensitive to associations with health status, because they have bounded ranges

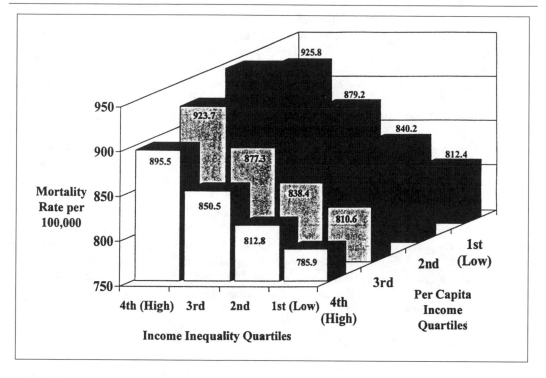

Figure 1

*Quartiles of income inequality and per capita income, adjusted for median household size,
and age-adjusted total mortality (per 100 000): 282 US metropolitan areas, 1989–1991.*

and do not explicitly incorporate variation at the bottom of the income distribution. The associations between different income inequality measures and mortality found in these data are consistent with a study of US states.[19] In addition, the present study was cross-sectional, so future research will have to clarify which measures are best suited to the complex task of examining changes in inequality[28] in regard to mortality.

The levels of inequality calculated here are consistent with those found in other data. Our results for metropolitan areas show a median Gini coefficient of 0.42, while US Census Bureau data show that the national Gini coefficient in 1990 was 0.43.[29] Gini coefficients of this size indicate a relatively high degree of inequality by international standards.[30] The differences among

metropolitan areas of the United States in terms of their levels of income inequality are as large as the differences observed among the countries of Europe. The Gini coefficient ranged from 0.36 to 0.50 among US metropolitan areas. While not strictly comparable with our data because they are based on different sources and definitions of income, data from the Luxembourg Income Study showed that Finland, a more equitable country, had a Gini coefficient for earnings inequality of 0.34, compared with Russia's Gini coefficient of 0.55.[31]

These data show that the mortality effects of income inequality were not diminished by adjustment for average per capita income, median household size, or proportion of the population with incomes less than 200% of poverty. This suggests that the elevated mortality observed in metropolitan areas with high income inequality was not due to the fact that these areas had lower average absolute income levels or that they had higher proportions of low-income households. However, we caution against a conclusion that absolute income levels are unimportant to health. As Figure 1 shows, higher per capita income was still significantly associated with lower mortality ($r = -0.21$), although this association was weaker than the effects of income inequality on mortality.

Furthermore, in a recent study of the association between "community income inequality," family income (measured at the individual level), and mortality, adjustment for family income reduced the effect of community income inequality on individual mortality to statistical insignificance.[32] We believe there are important issues in that study concerning the validity of using primary sampling units from a large national study to generate income distributions within local communities and the interpretation of the findings as an ecological fallacy.[32] Nevertheless, the cross-level confounding in those data by family-level income can be interpreted as indicating that areas with higher income inequality tended to have more families with lower incomes. We do not believe this represents an example of ecological fallacy—rather, it may demonstrate one of the mechanisms that link income inequality to individual mortality.

Inequality in the distribution of income should be understood as reflecting structural characteristics of the economy. Macroeconomics forces, such as differential monetary returns on education and skills, wage restraint pressures, and economic returns on capital compared with labor, influence the distribution of income.[33-35] These same forces are partly responsible for allocating low income to some families. Studies examining the cross-level relationships between ecological measures of income inequality, individual measures of income, and health are not tests of the validity of the ecological association between income inequality and health—they are elaborations of that ecological association.[36]

With regard to other potential confounders, metropolitan areas of the United States differ in many characteristics in addition to the extent of income inequality. Assessment of confounding of the association between income inequality and mortality should be based on conceptual models of disease causation that attempt to lay out the precursors and consequences of income inequality and their relationships to health. For example, it may not be appropriate to adjust for differences among metropolitan areas in workforce composition (e.g., numbers of professional, manufacturing, and service sector jobs). These jobs exist before income is allocated to the individuals who hold them, and so the distribution of particular types of jobs across metropolitan areas precedes and partly determines the income distribution of that area.

While these conceptual models remain largely undeveloped, this study showed that associations between income inequality and mortality were not due to differences in the size, population, average household size, per capita income, or proportion of low-income households among US metropolitan areas. Much remains to be understood about which factors act as confounders and which act as potential pathways linking income inequality to mortality. Our earliest research on US states has shown high correlations between income inequality and a variety of social indicators, including violent crime rates, per capita medical care expenditures, proportions of secondary behavior and smoking, percentage unemployed, educational spending, high school graduation rates, library books per capita, and fifth-grade reading and math scores.[6] It has also been shown that high income inequality may be associated with an undesirable psychosocial climate that directly influences health by affecting levels of social cohesion.[37]

At this stage there is little evidence about how income inequality might be linked to population health, but we propose a hypothesis that has 2 intertwining strands.[14] First, income inequality may be associated with a set of social processes and economic policies that systematically under-invest in physical and social infrastructure (such as education), and this underinvestment may have health consequences. Second, large dispari-ties in income distribution may have direct con-sequences on people's perceptions of their relative place in the social environment, leading to behavioral and cognitive states that influence health.[38]

By international standards, the United States has some of the highest levels of income inequal-ity in the world.[30] One obvious policy implica-tion of these findings is that serious steps should be taken to reduce income disparities within the United States. The standard political argument against income redistribution is framed in terms of a trade-off between overall economic growth and more equitable distribution of income. This approach is used whether the debate concerns economies of developed or developing countries, and it involves restraining wage increases, cut-ting social spending, delaying investment in pub-lic infrastructure, and abandoning redistribution of social goods to avoid stifling overall growth in the economy. According to this approach, the best way to improve the lot of those at the bottom of the income distribution is to enlarge the size of the economic pie. Evidence is mounting that this strategy of overall economic growth may be rela-tively ineffective in helping the disadvantaged members of the population and that a rising tide does not lift all boats evenly.[39, 40] Between 1979 and 1993, the bottom two-thirds of the popula-tion experienced stagnant or declining real in-comes, while income inequality reached a 60-year high.[29] Recent evidence suggests that there may be no intrinsic trade-off between long-run efficiency and equity. Policies that promote the accumulation of productive assets across the in-come spectrum are also important for achieving overall economic growth.[41]

CONCLUSIONS

UNDERSTANDING patterns of population health requires consideration of factors that lie well beyond specification in in-dividuals.[42] Inequitable distribution of income results from the complex interaction of particular economic, historical, and social factors. The size of the gap between rich and poor may be a useful summary indicator of the potential for these eco-nomic, historical, and social factors to influence levels of population health. Income inequality should be considered a structural characteristic of the economy, and although disparities in the dis-tribution of income are not measurable in indi-viduals, they may affect disease processes that occur in individuals.

The data shown in Figure 1 suggest that if metropolitan areas with the combination of high income inequality and low per capita income had the age-adjusted total mortality of areas with low inequality and high per capita income, mortality would be reduced by 139.8 deaths per 100 000. To place the magnitude of this difference in some perspective, an appropriate comparison would be that this mortality difference exceeds the com-bined loss of life from lung cancer, diabetes, mo-tor vehicle crashes, HIV infection, suicide, and homicide in 1995.[43] Given the mortality burden associated with income inequality, business, pri-vate, and public sector initiatives to reduce eco-nomic inequalities should be a high priority.

NOTES

1. Lynch JW, Kaplan GA, Shema SJ. Cumulative impact of sustained economic hardship on physical, cognitive, psy-chological, and social functioning. *N Engl J Med.* 1997;337:1889–1895.

2. Lynch JW, Kaplan GA, Cohen RD, Tuomilehto J, Sa-lonen JKT. Do cardiovascular risk factors explain the relation between socioeconomic status, risk of all-cause mortality, cardiovascular mortality and acute myocardial infarction? *Am J Epidemiol.* 1996;144:934–942.

3. Kaplan GA, Keil JE. Socioeconomic factors and car-diovascular disease: a review of the literature. *Circulation*, 1993;88:1973–1998.

4. Davey Smith G, Neaton JD, Wentworth D, Stamler R, Stamler J. Socioeconomic differentials in mortality risk among men screened for the Multiple Risk Factor Intervention Trial, 1: White men. *Am J Public Health.* 1996;86:486–496.

5. Sorlie PD, Backlund E, Keller JB. US mortality by economic demographic, and social characteristics: the National Longitudinal Mortality Study. *Am J Public Health.* 1995;85:949–956.

6. Kaplan GA, Pamuk ER, Lynch JW, Cohen RD, Balfour JL. Inequality in income and mortality in the United States: analysis of mortality and potential pathways. *BMJ.* 1996;312:999–1003.

7. Kennedy BP, Kawachi I, Prothrow-Stith D. Income distribution and mortality: cross-sectional ecologic study of the Robin Hood index in the United States. *BMJ.* 1996;312:1004–1007.

8. Wilkinson RG. *Unhealthy Societies: The Afflictions of Inequality.* London, England: Routledge; 1996.

9. Sen A. The economics of life and death. *Sci Am.* 1993; May:40–47.

10. McCord C, Freeman HP. Excess mortality in Harlem. *N Engl J Med.* 1990;322:173–177.

11. Rodgers GB. Income and inequality as determinants of mortality: an international cross-section analysis. *Popul Stud.* 1979;33:343–351.

12. Wilkinson RG. Income distribution and life expectancy. *BMJ.* 1992;304:165–168.

13. van Doorslaer E, Wagstaff A, Bleichrodt H, et al. Income-related inequalities in health: some international comparisons. *J Health Econ.* 1997;16:93–112.

14. Lynch JW, Kaplan GA. Understanding how inequality in the distribution of income affects health. *J Health Psychol.* 1997;2:297–314.

15. Rogot E, Sorlie PD, Johnson NJ, Schmitt C. *A Mortality Study of 1.3 Million Persons.* Bethesda, Md: National Institutes of Health; July 1992. NIH publication 92–3297.

16. Cowell FA. *Measuring Inequality.* London, England: Prentice Hall/Harvester Wheatsheaf; 1995.

17. Reed D, Haber MG, Mameesh L. *The Distribution of Income in California.* San Francisco: Public Policy Institute of California; 1996.

18. Atkinson AB. On the measurement of inequality. *J Econ Theory.* 1970;2:244–263.

19. Kawachi I, Kennedy BP. The relationship of income inequality to mortality—does the choice of indicator matter? *Soc Sci Med.* 1997;45:1121–1127.

20. Atkinson AB, Rainwater L, Smeeding T. *Income Distribution in OECD Countries. Evidence from the Luxembourg Income Study.* Paris, France: Organization for Economic Cooperation and Development, 1995.

21. Theil H. *Economic and Information Theory.* Amsterdam, the Netherlands: North Holland. 1967.

22. Mackenbach JP, Kunst AE, Cavelaars AE, et al. Socioeconomic inequalities in morbidity and mortality in western Europe. *Lancet.* 1997;349:1655–1659.

23. Vågerö D, Erikson R. Socioeconomic inequalities in morbidity and mortality in western Europe [letter]. *Lancet.* 1997;350:516.

24. Neter J, Wasseman W. *Applied Linear Statistical Models.* Homewood, Ill: RD Irwin Inc; 1974.

25. *SAS/Stat Users Guide, Version 6.* 4th ed. Vol 2. Cary, NC: SAS Institute Inc; 1989.

26. Williams JM, Currie CE, Wright P, Elton RA, Beattie TF. Socioeconomic status and adolescent injuries. *Soc Sci Med.* 1997;44:1881–1891.

27. Anderson R, Dearwater SR, Olsen T, Aaron DJ, Kriska AM, LaPorte RE. The role of socioeconomic status and injury morbidity risk in adolescents. *Arch Pediatr Adolesc Med.* 1994;148:245–249.

28. Wolfson MC. Divergent inequalities—theory and empirical results. *Rev Income Wealth.* December 1997;43:401–402.

29. Weinberg D. A brief look at postwar U.S. income inequality. Washington, DC: US Census Bureau; June 1996. *Current Population Reports.*

30. Gottschalk P, Smeeding TM. Cross-national comparisons of earnings and income inequality. *J Econ Lit.* 1997;35:633–686.

31. Smeeding TM, Gottschalk P. The international evidence on income distribution in modern economies: where do we stand? In: Bruno M, Mundlab Y, eds. *Contemporary Economic Development Reviewed.* London, England: Macmillan. In press.

32. Fiscella K, Franks P. Poverty or income inequality as predictor of mortality: longitudinal cohort study. *BMJ.* 1997;314:1724-1727.

33. Danziger SH, Gottschalk P. *America Unequal.* New York, NY: Russell Sage Foundation; 1995.

34. Dugger WM, ed. *Inequality*. Westport, Conn: Greenwood Press; 1996.

35. Iceland J. Urban labor markets and individual transitions out of poverty. *Demography*. 1997;34:429–441.

36. Daly M, Duncan G, Kaplan GA, Lynch JW. Macro-to-micro linkages in the inequality-mortality relationship. *Milbank Mem Fund Q*. In press.

37. Kawachi I, Kennedy BP, Lochner K, Prothrow-Stith D. Social capital, income inequality, and mortality. *Am J Public Health*. 1997;87:1491–1499.

38. Kaplan GA, Lynch JW. Whither studies on the socioeconomic foundations of population health [editorial]. *Am J Public Health*. 1997;87:1409–1411.

39. Cutler DM, Katz LF. Macroeconomic performance and the disadvantaged. *Brookings Papers on Economic Activity*. 1991;2:1–74.

40. Danziger SH, Gottschalk P, eds. *Uneven Tides: Rising Inequality in America*. New York, NY: Russell Sage Foundation; 1993.

41. Bruno M, Ravallion M, Squire L. Equity and growth in developing countries: old and new perspectives on the policy issues. Paper prepared for the International Monetary Fund Conference on Income Distribution and Sustainable Growth, Geneva, 1–2 June, 1995.

42. Evans RG, Barer ML, Marmor TR, eds. *Why Are Some People Healthy and Others Not?* New York, NY: Aldine de Gruyter; 1994.

43. National Center for Health Statistics. *Health United States 1996–97*. Hyattsville, Md: Public Health Service; 1997:168:Table 53.

Part Two

CRITIQUES OF THE
RELATIVE INCOME HYPOTHESIS

Part Two
CRITIQUES OF THE
RELATIVE INCOME HYPOTHESIS

COMMENT

THE articles reprinted in Part II summarize the main lines of criticism that have been directed so far at the relative income hypothesis. Early criticisms focused on the potential methodological flaws of the empirical studies in support of the relative income hypothesis (e.g., Judge, 1995). Responses to these criticisms (Wilkinson, 1995; Kawachi and Kennedy, 1997; McIsaac and Wilkinson, 1997) are also included in this section. Perhaps the most significant challenge to the relative income hypothesis is the charge that most or all of the association between income inequality and population health can be explained by the relationship of *individual* income to health (see Gravelle, 1998; Fiscella and Franks, 1997). If the relative income hypothesis is the result of a statistical artefact, as this view implies, then we need not be concerned about reducing income inequality; society should just focus on eliminating individual income poverty. The response to this criticism points out that there are likely to be a variety of pathways from income distribution to health, and that this fact should not detract from the need to reduce income differences to improve health. Moreover, a deleterious effect of income inequality on health has been demonstrated over and above the impact of individual income (Kennedy et al. 1998). Importantly, the relationship of individual income to health that we take for granted may itself reflect processes of *relative* deprivation. Thus, low income matters not just because it indicates absolute deprivation (e.g., lack of adequate food, clothing, shelter), but also because impoverished individuals feel deprived relative to what other people earn (a psychosocial effect) (Wilkinson, 1997). In other words, an individual's income summarizes the effects of both absolute and relative deprivation, and it may be the wrong question to ask whether relative income matters to health independently of absolute income.

The questions and debates raised by the paper in this section include:

- How robust is the relationship between income inequality and population health? Are there differences in the quality of income data across countries, and do these contribute to biases in the test of the relative income hypothesis cross-nationally?
- In the relation between income distribution and health, should the effects of individual income on health be regarded as statistical artefact? Is the association of income inequality to health independent of the well-established relationship between individual income and ill health?
- Does the relationship of income inequality to population health depend on the choice of the indicator used, e.g., the Gini coefficient versus the Robin Hood Index? Are the conclusions of studies sensitive to adjustments made to household incomes to take account of taxes, transfer payments, and household size? Do the different measures of income inequality capture different aspects of the relationship between income inequality and population health? Is there a "best way" to measure income inequality?
- What are the relevant and important confounding factors to consider in interpreting the relationship between income inequality and population health (e.g., poverty rates, average income, unemployment rates, race/ethnic composition, access to health care, lifestyle habits)?

- How do we account for the fact that income inequality has risen in many countries during periods that average life expectancy continued to improve?

SUGGESTIONS FOR FURTHER READING

Saunders P (1996). *Poverty, Income Distribution and Health: An Australian Study.* SPRC Reports and Proceedings No. 128. Sydney: Social Policy Research Center, University of New South Wales.

Davey Smith G (1996). Income inequality and mortality: Why are they related? *British Medical Journal* 312: 987–88.

Judge K, Benzeval M, Mulligan JA (1996). Income inequality and population health among rich industrial nations. *Journal of Epidemiology and Community Health* 50: 580.

Wilkinson RG (1997). Commentary: Income inequality summarises the health burden of individual relative deprivation. *British Medical Journal* 314: 1727–8.

Judge K, Mulligan JA, Benzeval M (1998). Income inequality and population health. *Social Science & Medicine* 46: 567–79.

Wilkinson RG (1998). Letter to the Editor (reply to Judge et al. Social Science & Medicine 1998; 46: 567–79). *Social Science & Medicine* 47: 411–12.

Judge K, Mulligan JA, Benzeval M (1998). Reply to Richard Wilkinson (letter). *Social Science & Medicine* 47: 983–85.

Nine

INCOME DISTRIBUTION AND LIFE EXPECTANCY: A CRITICAL APPRAISAL

Ken Judge

In a series of papers published during the past decade Richard Wilkinson has advanced the view that income inequality is the key determinant of variations in average life expectancy at birth among developed countries. Yet a careful examination of the two sources of data on income distribution most often used by Wilkinson suggests that if they are analysed more appropriately they do not lend support to his claims. More recent data on income distribution is now available for several countries in the Organisation for Economic Development and Cooperation in the mid-1980s and for Great Britain from 1961 to 1991. The use of these data also casts doubt on the hypothesis that inequalities in the distribution of income are closely associated with variations in average life expectancy at birth among the richest nations of the world.

A paradox inherent in the scientific method is that, attached though we are to the hypotheses we formulate, we must really subject them to assault and search for circumstances that really test their resilience.[1]

Life expectancy is one of the key indicators of population health and economic development.

Citizens of the poorest countries can expect to live for many decades less than those of the richest nations. Among the developed countries variations in the average expectation of life are not so great, but there are differences that cannot easily be explained by reference to economic prosperity. In 1988, for example, life expectancy at birth for men and women combined was almost five years greater in Japan than in Portugal.[2] Several reasons have been advanced to account for these differences—from dietary influences such as the consumption of olive oil or fish to cultural factors such as national perceptions of self esteem—but many of them are peculiar to one country or a small group of countries. In recent years, however, it has been suggested that the key determinant of variations in life expectancy at birth among developed societies is inequalities in the distribution of income within countries.

For almost a decade the evidence and arguments in support of this income inequality hypothesis have been most associated with a series of papers by Wilkinson.[3-10] A review of the primary sources of income distribution data used in these eight papers shows that two are used most

Originally published in *British Medical Journal*, 1995.

frequently: one in six of the papers[11]; and the other in five.[12]

The aim of this paper is critically to evaluate Wilkinson's use of the two key pieces of evidence on which his analyses are based and to suggest that the strength of the relation between income inequality and average life expectancy has been exaggerated. I also use more recently published data about income distribution that cast doubts on the income inequality hypothesis.

Cross Sectional Comparisons

THE two key sources of income distribution data used by Wilkinson to support his income inequality hypothesis examine cross sectional comparisons for one group of countries in about 1981[11] and changes over time for a slightly different selection of countries from the mid-1970s to 1984–5.[12]

The aim of the first source, produced by Bishop *et al*,[11] was to compare the degree of relative inequality in nine countries: Australia, Canada, the Netherlands, Norway, Sweden, Switzerland, West Germany, the UK, and the USA. Two main series of income distribution data were produced: one for family incomes and the other for income per head. In each case estimates were made of the proportion of income received by cumulative deciles of either families or individuals. A summary statistic of the overall shape of the income distribution in a particular country—the Gini coefficient, which rises as inequality increases—was also reported for each series.

Wilkinson shows that about three quarters of the observed variation in life expectancy among the nine countries is accounted for by differences in the proportion of family income going to the poorest 70% of families.[3 5-10] However, he gives no satisfactory explanation about why "the poorest 70%" should be chosen, and the suspicion must be that the choice is derived from the data. Moreover, Wilkinson makes no reference to the data about income per head.

The consequences of using family income rather than income per head as the indicator of economic inequality are illustrated in table 1. Correlation coefficients between average life expectancy at birth and the proportion of income going to cumulative deciles as well as the respective Gini coefficients are shown for the two series. Most of the coefficients associated with measures of family income are statistically significant and positive: they appear to lend support to the income inequality hypothesis. In contrast, the measures of income per head do not. This is important because the data about family incomes are unadjusted for differences in family size between countries. Bishop *et al* warn of the need for caution when using the measure of family income because: "international differences in variation in the size of families as the level of income changes has (sic) important implications for cross country comparisons of income inequality."[11]

Table 1

Income distribution and life expectancy:
Correlation coefficients 1979–1983[2 11]

Income decile†	Family income	Income per head
1	0·0879	– 0·1989
2	0·4435	0·0285
3	0·5703	0·1172
4	0·6529*	0·1673
5	0·7366**	0·2056
6	0·8089***	0·2527
7	0·8053***	0·3116
8	0·7310**	0·3849
9	0·6310*	0·4809
Gini coefficient	– 0·7737**	– 0·1886

†Cumulative share of income available to successive deciles.
*P < 0·1, **P < 0·05, ***P < 0·01.

Revised Data

In a later paper, not used by Wilkinson, Bishop *et al* deal with this problem by including data on family incomes adjusted for variations in household composition by using an appropriate equivalence scale.[13] They also report a number of revisions to the original data for various countries (Australia, Germany, the Netherlands, Switzerland, and the USA).

Analysis of the revised data is complicated by the fact that Wilkinson has expressed concern about the accuracy of the German data.[14] Nevertheless, whether the German data are used or not, the later data supplied by Bishop *et al*[13] do not support the income inequality hypothesis. Table II shows correlation coefficients between life expectancy and Gini coefficients—probably the best single summary statistic of income inequality—for the revised original data series and equivalent family incomes, both including and excluding Germany. No statistically significant relations can be identified. Even the previously significant association between the Gini coefficient for unadjusted family incomes and life expectancy reported in table I appears now to have been a product of errors in the underlying data.

CHANGES OVER TIME

The second of the two data sources most used by Wilkinson was produced by O'Higgins and Jenkins.[12] They were commissioned to provide estimates of the prevalence of poverty—the proportion of both persons and households—for the 12 countries of the European Commission in 1975, 1980, and 1985.

In several papers[6-10] Wilkinson uses some of these data to compare changes in income distribution with changes in life expectancy in the belief that this provides "a more demanding test"[6] of the income inequality hypothesis. The results suggest "that among these countries a fall in the prevalence of relative poverty was significantly related to a more rapid improvement in life expectancy."[6]

There is, however, a major problem in accepting the validity of this finding because O'Higgins and Jenkins explicitly stated that any: "examination of the patterns of change within countries is hampered by the limited number of calculations for each country, *since it is not appropriate to use the estimated observations for this purpose* [my emphasis]."[12]

The scale of the problem can be gauged by the fact that, for at least one of the two years used to calculate rates of change in income inequality, relatively crude estimates—"our best guess" according to O'Higgins and Jenkins—had to be produced for eight of the 12 countries for both series of poverty data.

Thus it seems inappropriate to use O'Higgins and Jenkins's data to calculate changes over time for individual countries. If one persists nevertheless it seems advisable to use data for matching years for both life expectancy and income distribution and to use and compare the results associated with both series of poverty estimates—for families and individuals. On this basis the correlation coefficients between changes in individual and family poverty rates and life expectancy between 1973−7 and 1984−5 are − 0·1287 (P=0·690)

Table 2

Income distribution and life expectancy 1979−83[2][13]

	Correlation coefficient	
Gini coefficient	Including Germany	Excluding Germany
Unadjusted family income	−0·1006 (P=0·797)	−03426 (P=0·406)
Equivalised family income	−0·0097 (P=0·980)	−0·1990 (P=0·637)
Income per head	0·0491 (P=0·900)	−0·1014 (P=0·811)

and +0·0719 (P=0·824) respectively. Neither is statistically significant. Wilkinson's result appears to be the consequence of using an incorrect poverty estimate for Portugal and not matching income and life expectancy data for the same years.

NEW EVIDENCE

IT is difficult to see how the two studies most cited by Wilkinson[??][??] can be regarded as lending support to the income inequality hypothesis. What do more recent data reveal? I have linked income distribution data taken from two recent studies to life expectancy data as new tests of the income inequality hypothesis.

Cross Sectional Comparisons

The first piece of evidence draws on a study by Förster of income distribution in 13 countries of the Organisation for Economic Cooperation and Development (OECD)—Australia, Austria, Belgium, Canada, France, Germany, Ireland, Italy, Luxembourg, the Netherlands, Sweden, the UK, and the USA—during the mid-1980s (1984–7).[15] The wide range of data obtained from the *Luxembourg Income Study* provides a good opportunity to test whether the income inequality hypothesis is particularly sensitive to one or more specific measures of income distribution.

For this analysis I correlated a selection of Förster's income distribution indicators with life expectancy data obtained from the World Bank.[2] The measures chosen include the Gini coefficient for the whole population and various measures of the poverty rate based on different proportions of the population receiving less than 40% or 50% or 60% of median equivalent income. In addition, four different equivalence scales are used with one particular poverty rate: the proportion of the population with less than 50% of the median equivalent income. The rationale for this procedure is that Buhmann *et al*[16] have shown that the choice of equivalence scale

can affect comparative assessments of income inequalities.

Equivalence scales are commonly used to compare the incomes of households that vary in terms of their composition on the assumption that there are economies of scale in consumption. The problem is that there is no consensus about the extent of economies of scale: numerous equivalence scales have been produced that vary "according to how great the adjustment for family size is in the range from no adjustment to per capita adjustment."[16] A common way of expressing the difference between scales is in terms of an equivalence elasticity that varies between 0 and 1. The larger the value the smaller are the economies of scale assumed by the equivalence scale.

Table III uses equivalence scales with elasticities ranging from 0·33 to 1·00 and shows the correlation coefficients between seven summary measures of income distribution and life expectancy in the 13 OECD countries for the appropriate year between 1984 and 1987. Support for the

Table 3

Life expectancy and income inequality in selected OECD countries 1984–7[2][15]

Income inequality	Correlation coefficient‡
Gini coefficient	− 0·1824
Low income rate*	
− 40%	0·1023
− 50%	− 0·0810
− 60%	− 0·1710
Equivalence elasticity†	
− 0·33	− 0·0815
− 0·72	− 0·1482
− 1·00	− 0·1830

*The proportion of the population with less than the stated percentage of median equivalent income assuming an equivalence elasticity of 0·55.

†The proportion of the population with less than 50% of median equivalent income for various equivalence elasticities.

‡None of the coefficients are statistically significant by conventional criteria.

income inequality hypothesis would be provided by any reasonably large and statistically significant negative relation with life expectancy, although ideally one would like to see support from more than a single statistic. In fact, none of the measures fulfil these requirements.

Many other indicators of income distribution could be computed for this group of 13 countries and so it is not possible to rule out the possibility that one or more of them might be found to be associated with life expectancy. However, seeking for such associations would be a fruitless exercise in the absence of any theoretical rationale for selecting one indicator rather than another. Simply identifying some statistical associations that contradict those reported here would not be sufficient on their own. If support for the income inequality hypothesis turns out to depend on the choice of income distribution indicator then a clear rationale for selecting one measure rather than another is essential.

Trends in the UK

The second piece of recent evidence comes from a report prepared for the Joseph Rowntree Foundation's *Inquiry into Income and Wealth* by Goodman and Webb.[17] This study offers perhaps the best opportunity to test the income inequality hypothesis because there are a reasonably large number of observations for a single country—which significantly reduces problems of data comparability—during a period when there were substantial changes in the distribution of income.

Goodman and Webb report a number of different indicators of income distribution, but whichever is selected the trends are almost identical. Between 1961 and the early 1980s there were relatively modest fluctuations in the values of the different measures, but since about 1984 every indicator of the distribution of disposable income shows a substantial increase in inequality. For the purposes of comparison with changes in average life expectancy over time, therefore, it does not

matter which indicator is chosen; the broad pattern of results is the same.

The example which has been computed here to test the income inequality hypothesis is the relation between annual percentage changes in the Gini coefficient (after adjusting for housing costs) and yearly improvements in life expectancy, using data supplied by the Government Actuary. The relation is not statistically significant ($R= -0.2022$, $P=0.284$).

A more plausible hypothesis might postulate a lagged relation between average life expectancy and income inequality. No clear evidence for this has yet been identified during the period of 1961–91, but it may take some time for the substantial increase in inequality in the late 1980s to manifest itself in terms of reduced life expectancy.

CONCLUSION

ONE of the main reasons for taking the income inequality hypothesis so seriously is that it has influenced a wide range of authoritative reports emanating from all corners of the glove. For example, Wilkinson's findings have been used by the National Health Strategy Unit in Australia,[18] the World Bank,[19] the Canadian Program in Population Health,[20] the European region of the World Health Organisation,[21] and the Commission on Social Justice in Britain.[22] In addition, the *Social Sciences Citation Index* shows that, since Wilkinson's seminal article on the subject was published in the *BMJ* in January 1992[6] it has been cited in at least 30 articles, reviews, and editorials in 16 major journals by authors other than himself.

Despite this popular acclaim, a careful review of the evidence does not support the hypothesis that inequalities in income distribution largely explain differences in average life expectancy among rich countries. In retrospect, it seems extraordinary that a predominantly monocausal explanation of international variations in life expectancy should ever have been regarded as plausible. It is much more likely that they are the product of many influences, which probably interact over long periods of time.

These critical observations, however, should not be interpreted as challenging the view that inequalities in living standards are associated with health differences within countries, as distinct from average levels between nations. For example, many international studies indicate that the poorest people have the worst health.[18 23 24] Similarly, Mackenbach and Looman have argued that regional differences in European living standards are associated with indicators of population health.[25] They make the point, however, that a statistically significant relation can be identified only "after taking into account potential confounders."

This point suggests that any future exploration of the relation between income distribution and life expectancy should use more sophisticated multivariate methods. It is certainly possible that a significant relation could be found after adjusting for other factors. Nevertheless, one recent attempt to do this "failed to support the hypothesis that an egalitarian distribution of income is related to higher levels of health."[26]

More generally, it is important that any future attempt to investigate the income inequality hypothesis should specify a priori what measures of income distribution might be expected to be associated with life expectancy and why. Considerable progress has been made recently in making available internationally comparable data about income distribution, but considerable traps remain for the unwary. Despite the very substantial efforts made by the *Luxembourg Income Study*, for example, unavoidable differences in population coverage and non-response rates across countries can influence judgments about the extent of economic inequality, especially for particular subgroups of the population.[27]

This paper does not claim to have taken account of all of these factors. What it has tried to do is to examine a reasonably representative range of indicators of income inequality and to show that these are not statistically significantly related to average life expectancy at birth among rich countries.

I thank Michaela Benzeval for her advice and encouragement and several other colleagues, including an anonymous referee, who made helpful suggestions.

NOTES

1. Paneth N, Susser M. Early origin of coronary heart disease (the "Barker hypothesis"). *BMJ* 1994;310:411–2.

2. World Bank, *Social indicators of development 1993*. Washington DC: World Bank, 1993.

3. Quick A, Wilkinson RG. *Income and health*. London: Socialist Health Association, 1991.

4. Wilkinson RG. Income and mortality. In: Wilkinson RG, ed. *Class and health: research and longitudinal data*. London: Tavistock, 1986:88–114.

5. Wilkinson RG. Income distribution and mortality: a "natural" experiment. *Sociology of Health and Illness* 1900; 12:391–412.

6. Wilkinson RG. Income distribution and life expectancy. *BMJ* 1992;304:165–8.

7. Wilkinson RG. Income and health. In: Ross R, Iliffe S, eds. *Health wealth and poverty*. London: Medical World/ Socialist Health Association, 1993:6–11.

8. Wilkinson RG. The impact of income inequality on life expectancy. In: Platt S, Thomas H, Scott S, Williams G, eds. *Locating health: sociological and historical explanations*. Aldershot: Avebury, 1993:7–28.

9. Wilkinson RG. Health, redistribution and growth. In: Glyn A, Miliband D, eds. *Paying for inequality: the economic cost of social injustice*. London: IPPR/Rivers Oram Press, 1994:24–43.

10. Wilkinson RG. *Unfair shares: the effects of widening income differences on the welfare of the young*. Ilford, Essex: Barnados, 1994.

11. Bishop JA, Formby JP, Smith WJ. *International comparisons of income inequality: tests for Lorenz dominance across nine countries*. Luxembourg: LIS Working Paper 26, 1989.

12. O'Higgins M, Jenkins SP. Poverty in the EC: 1975, 1980, 1985. In: Teekens R, van Praag BMS, eds. *Analysing poverty in the European Community*. Luxembourg: Eurostat, 1990:187–211.

13. Bishop JA, Formby JP, Smith WJ. International comparisons of income inequality: tests for Lorenz dominance across nine countries. *Economica* 1991;58:461–77.

14. Wilkinson RG. Research note: German income distribution and infant mortality. *Sociology of Health and Illness* 1994;16:2.

15. Förster MF. *Comparing poverty in 13 OECD countries: traditional and synthetic approaches.* Luxembourg: LIS, 1993 (Working paper 100).

16. Buhmann B, Rainwater L, Schmaus G, Smeeding TM. Equivalence scales, well-being, inequality, and poverty: sensitivity estimates across ten countries using the Luxembourg Income Study (LIS) database. *Review of Income and Wealth* 1988:34:115–42.

17. Goodman A, Webb S. *For richer for poorer: the changing distribution of income in the United Kingdom, 1961–91.* London: Institute for Fiscal Studies, 1994.

18. *Enough to make you sick: how income and environment affect health.* Canberra: Department of Health 1992 (Research paper 1).

19. World Bank. *World development report 1993: investing in health.* New York: Oxford University Press, 1993.

20. Evans RG, Barer MI, Marmor TR, eds. *Why are some people healthy and others not?* New York: Aldine de Gruyter, 1994.

21. Lundberg O, Fritzell J. Income distribution, income change and health. In: *Economic change, social welfare and health in Europe.* Copenhagen: WHO, 1994 (European series No 54).

22. Commission on Social Justice. *Social Justice: strategies for national renewal.* London: Vintage, 1994.

23. Pappas G, Queen S, Hadden W, Fisher G. The increasing disparity in mortality between socioeconomic groups in the United States, 1960 and 1986. *N Engl J Med* 1993:329:103–9.

24. O'Donnell O, Propper C. Equity and the distribution of UK National Health Service resources. *Journal of health Economics* 1991:10:1–19.

25. Mackenbach JP, Looman CWN. Living standards and mortality in the European Community. *J Epidemiol Community Health* 1994:48:140–5.

26. Matsaganis M. *An economic approach to international and inter-regional mortality variations with special reference to Greece.* Bristol: University of Bristol, 1992 (PhD thesis).

27. Smeeding TM, Schmaus G. The LIS database: technical and methodological aspects. In: Smeeding TM, ed. *Poverty, inequality and income distribution in comparative perspective.* Hemel Hempstead: Harvester Wheatsheaf, 1990:1–19.

Ten

A REPLY TO KEN JUDGE: MISTAKEN CRITICISMS IGNORE OVERWHELMING EVIDENCE

Richard G. Wilkinson

Despite Judge's highly personal focus, mine is far from being the only evidence of an association between national mortality rates and income distribution. The criticisms that Judge directs at two of my five demonstrations of the relation would therefore, even if they had been accurate, leave the bulk of the evidence unscathed. As well as summarising the evidence which Judge ignores, I shall also show why we should not be surprised at a relation between mortality and income distribution, and then deal with methodological problems that he inadvertently raises.

ADDITIONAL EVIDENCE

THE association between mortality and income distribution was first reported by Rodgers using data from around 1965 from 56 developed and less developed countries.[1] Since then it has been found by many others. Flegg found that income distribution was related to national infant mortality among a group of 59 developing countries,[2] and Le Grand reported that it was related to average age of death in a group of 17 developed countries.[3] Analysing data from 70 rich and poor countries, Waldmann found that, if the real incomes of the poorest 20% were statistically held constant, increases in the incomes of the richest 5% were associated with rising rates of infant mortality.[4] Among developed countries Wennemo has shown close relations between infant mortality and measures of income distribution and relative poverty.[5] I have shown relations in developed countries between income distribution and life expectancy on two sets of cross sectional data and three sets of data on changes over time.[6-8] Most recently, Kaplan *et al* at Berkeley and Kennedy *et al* at Harvard have independently found income distribution and life expectancy to be closely associated in 50 states of the United States.[9][10] Lastly, using mid-century data for 20 countries at different stages of development, Steckel reported that height (which is closely related to health) is related to income distribution.[11][12]

Leaving height aside, a total of at least eight different research workers or groups have reported statistically significant relations between income distribution and measures of mortality using 10 separate sets of data. Of these eight, one has used data exclusively on developing countries,[2] two on a mixture of developed and developing countries,[1 4] and five exclusively on developed countries.[3 5-10] The association has been found to be independent of fertility, maternal literacy, and education in developing countries and of average incomes, absolute levels of poverty, smoking, racial differences, and various measures of the provision of medical services in developed countries.[1-4 7 9 10]

PLAUSIBILITY

S UCH an association is to be expected. By raising death rates among deprived people, relative deprivation will raise national mortality rates unless the excess mortality is mysteriously offset by improvements in mortality elsewhere. But if health were to suffer as a result of an increase in unemployment where would the balancing improvement come from? Is the rest of New York really healthier because Harlem has death rates as high as Bangladesh?[13] The existence of deprived areas with high levels of crime; drug use, and violence is likely to harm health more widely. National mortality rates would then be raised by poorer health in deprived areas as well as by some wider knock on effects.

The larger part of this relation probably reflects an association between inequalities in income and in health within societies. Using linked data for individuals in nine European countries, van Doorslaer *et al* found a close association between the extent of differences in income and in self reported morbidity within these countries.[14] (Coupled with the effects of income distribution, this implies that health inequalities may be significant determinants of average health.)

If, as Judge suggests, income were a monocausal explanation it would not be so difficult to unpack what it means. It is, of course, a determinant and indicator of a wide range of material factors, covering all aspects of the standard of living, as well as having a crucial impact on psycho-

social factors such as sense of control, security, status, prestige, social distance, and cohesion.

PROBLEMS OF MEASUREMENT AND DATA

Time Series

Having shown that a relation between income distribution and national mortality rates is plausible and that it has been found repeatedly, I will now look at what is wrong with Judge's analyses. Why does he fail to find a relation between annual changes in life expectancy and in income distribution in the United Kingdom in 1961–91? As he says, "between 1961 and the early 1980s there were relatively modest fluctuations" in income distribution. To some extent he is probably correlating changes in sampling error from income distribution surveys with annual changes in mortality affected by cold winters and passing epidemics.[15]

There is also the possibility of time lags: I have usually only shown relations between changes in income distribution and mortality over periods of 5–10 years to allow for lags. An exception was when I showed that the slower decline in national mortality rates during the later 1980s at ages below 45 years (to which the chief medical officer drew attention[16]) was exactly coincident with the most dramatic postwar widening of income differentials.[17] However, because this widening was concentrated among those of working age while the elderly fared better, mortality at older ages was unaffected by rising relative deprivation. Others have shown that it was among younger age groups in the poorest areas that mortality rose—or failed to fall—during the decade.[18 19] Combining all age groups in life expectancy can mask the impact on younger ages. Life expectancy has no special status as a summary of the effects of relative deprivation. Not only is the basic relation probably between the socio-economic experience of an age group and age specific mortality, but also there can be different trends in income distribution in different age groups. In contrast to Judge's time series analysis, however, during the 1980s we have a consistent picture of rapidly widening income differentials, widening mortality differentials between rich and poor areas, and a slowing of the decline in the appropriate national age specific mortality rates. As I pointed out elsewhere, changes in income distribution had previously been too slow to make it easy to identify their effects.[17]

Income Distribution Measures

A number of factors weakened Judge's chances of finding the expected cross sectional association among 13 countries of the Organisation of Economic Cooperation and Development (OECD). Firstly, his poverty measure in table III covered, respectively, averages of just 4·5%, 8·9%, and 15·2% of the population among the 13 countries.[20] Although I have once shown a relation with changes in relative poverty, the indications are that total mortality is influenced by what is happening to a larger proportion of the population. Rather than giving "no satisfactory explanation about why the poorest 70% of households [containing about 50 per cent of the population] should be chosen" in one of my analyses, my paper contains a table showing exactly how the strength of the association increased with the proportion of households included.[7] Indeed, that table shows that statistical significance was lost precisely when taking the income share of the poorest 10% alone. In addition, if the problem were not so often disregarded, it would seem ludicrous to expect to get useful income figures for the bottom 10% of the population from surveys which often have 30–40% non-response rates concentrated disproportionately among the poor.[21][22]

Judge claims, a priori, that Gini coefficients are "probably the best single summary statistic of income inequality." But what for? Kennedy *et al* report that Gini coefficients are weakly related to mortality among American states because they

were heavily influenced by the tails of the income distribution.[10] They found that measures less dominated by these extremes were closely associated with mortality. Although Judge's table I shows how important the difference between measures can be, he does not explore why. The contrast between the columns invites one to think about equivalence scales. But when he does look at equivalence scales in table III he again confines attention to what was, on average, less than the poorest 10%.

The seriousness of the problems with the "revised" Luxembourg Income Study data which Judge uses (table II) was confirmed when my attempts to find out why Germany had suddenly become an outlier in the relation between income distribution and mortality led the Luxembourg Income Study to discover that the data had become so badly corrupted that they would have to be removed from the database (Smeeding, personal communications 28 May 1992). This error detection suggests that the relation in question was sufficiently powerful for mortality to serve almost as a touchstone for the veracity of income distribution data.[23] Nevertheless, in her paper on infant mortality, Wennemo has shown that even the revised data show a significant relation with infant mortality.[5]

Picking and Choosing

The impression of picking and choosing between measures while exploring these relations is not as worrying as it looks. You have to choose between not just two or three alternatives but more like 50 to have just half a chance of finding a relation significant at the 1% level purely by chance. The number of reports of highly significant relations, among independent data-sets, means that there is now no possibility that the relation can be attributed to chance. Furthermore, in this subject, as in others, positive and negative findings are not equally important. A failure to find something does not prove that it does not exist, particularly when others report sightings.

Measurement problems and noise in the system are more likely to produce false negatives—such as Judge's—than the many highly significant relations which have been discovered.

Mistakes?

Judge believes there are two problems in my treatment of changes in relative poverty in European countries 1975–85.[7] Firstly, the figures I used for Portugal are not a mistake. Instead of taking the whole period 1975–85 as for other countries, I took Portuguese figures for 1981–5 which were also given in the source. I did this because Portuguese life expectancy was reported to have risen by an implausible two years during the three years 1977–80. I excluded these earlier years only after my letters to Lisbon had failed to confirm these figures. I regret omitting an explanatory note.

Secondly, when Judge accuses me of "not matching income and life expectancy data for the same years" he reveals he is unaware of an important problem in these analyses. Life expectancy in the OECD countries increases by 2–2·5 years each decade—even if income distribution remains unchanged. As I have pointed out, changes in income distribution are associated only with increases of decreases in this unexplained background rate of improvement.[8 24] This means that, when combining data from slightly different dates for each country (as the discontinuous sources of income data necessitate), the effect on life expectancy of taking different dates has to be taken into account. This may be done (*a*) by comparing change at annual rates; (*b*) by controlling life expectancy statistically for differences in the observation year, or (*c*) by taking life expectancy from each country for the central year in a cross sectional comparison. The rationale for *c* is that—unlike life expectancy—income distribution shows no clear secular trend and is relatively stable from year to year. Hence small differences in the year matter for life expectancy (particularly when bearing in mind the effects of the international business cycle) more than for income distribution. I have always used one of these methods whereas Judge's failure to recognise this issue means not only that his criticism of me is badly mistaken but that the analyses in his tables II and III confound the secular improvement in life expectancy with the effects of income distribution.

Even without these oversights, however, I suspect that the international relation which others have identified would still have remained obscured. McIsaac and I have just broken down the relation with life expectancy into its component age specific, sex specific, and cause specific death rates. Using income distribution data from the Luxembourg Income Study for OECD countries, we found strong evidence that reported income distribution in some countries is heavily influenced by the low response rates in sample surveys of household income. Indeed, there is now a statistically significant correlation between response rates and reported income distribution, consistent with evidence that the poor and the rich are more likely to be non-responders. We found some ways round this problem and will soon be publishing our results.

CONCLUSION

AFTER having arbitrarily selected just two of the 10 demonstrations of this relation Judge's criticisms missed their targets. His failure to replicate other people's findings probably reflects faulty methods and poor quality data. The recent tests of the association among the 50 states of the United States,[9 10] on data entirely independent of all earlier international comparisons, provide the strongest confirmation that population mortality is associated with income distribution and so vindicate the results of the work Judge questions.

Future research in this subject is likely to rely heavily on the superior quality and quantity of the data for the American states. My impression is that we need measures of income distribution which emphasise the economies of scale in large households, that do not confine attention to the poorest 10%, and which take seriously the problems of low response rates in the income surveys in some countries. Criticism which is personally selective and fails to address the wider body of evidence can now make little impression. The importance of negative findings will depend on the quality of the data and methods used.

NOTES

1. Rodgers GB. Income and inequality as determinants of mortality: an international cross-section analysis. *Population Studies* 1979;33:343–51.

2. Flegg A. Inequality of income, illiteracy, and medical care as determinants of infant mortality in developing countries. *Population Studies* 1982;36:441–58.

3. LeGrand J. Inequalities in health: some international comparisons. *European Economic Review* 1987;31:182–91.

4. Waldmann RJ. Income distribution and infant mortality. *Quarterly Journal of Economics* 1992;107:1283–1302.

5. Wennemo I. Infant mortality, public policy and inequality—a comparison of 18 industrialised countries 1950–85. *Sociology of Health and Illness* 1993;15:429–46.

6. Wilkinson RG. Income and mortality. In: Wilkinson RG, ed. *Class and health: research and longitudinal data.* London: Tavistock, 1986.

7. Wilkinson RG. Income distribution and life expectancy. *BMJ* 1992;304:165–8.

8. Wilkinson RG. Health, redistribution and growth. In: Glyn A, Miliband D, eds. *Paying for inequality: the economic cost of social injustice.* London: Rivers Oram Press, 1994.

9. Kaplan GA, Pamuk E, Lynch JW, Cohen RD, Balfour JL. *Income inequality and mortality in the United States.* (To be published soon.)

10. Kennedy BP, Kawachi I, Prothrow-Stith D. Income distribution and mortality: test of the Robin Hood Index in the United States. (To be published.)

11. Steckel RH. Height and per capita income. *Historical Methods* 1983;16:1–7.

12. Steckel RH. Heights and health in the United States. In: Komlos J, ed. *Stature, living standards and economic development.* Chicago: University of Chicago Press, 1994.

13. McCord C, Freeman HP. Excess mortality in Harlem. *N Engl J Med* 1990;322:173–7.

14. Van Doorslaer E, Wagstaff A, Bleichrodt H, Calonge S, Gerdtham UG, Gerfin M, *et al.* Socioeconomic inequalities in health: some international comparisons. *Journal of Health Economics* (in press).

15. Curwen M. Excess winter mortality: a British phenomenon? *Health Trends* 1990–1;22:169–75.

16. Department of Health. *On the state of the public health. Annual report of the chief medical officer 1990.* London: HMSO, 1991.

17. Wilkinson RG. *Unfair shares: the effects of widening income differentials on the welfare of the young.* London: Barnardos, 1994.

18. McLoone P, Boddy FA. Deprivation and mortality in Scotland: 1981 and 1991. *BMJ* 1994;309:1465–70.

19. Phillimore P, Beattie A, Townsend P. The widening gap. Inequality of health in northern England, 1981–1991. *BMJ* 1994;308:1125–8.

20. Förster M. *Comparing poverty in 13 OECD countries.* Luxembourg: Luxembourg Income Study, 1993 (LIS working paper 100).

21. Redpath B. Family Expenditure Survey: a second study of differential response, comparing census characteristics of FES respondents and non-respondents. *Statistical News* 1986;72:13–6.

22. Wolf W. Verzerrungen durch Antwortausfalle in der Konsumerhebung 1984 *Statistische Nachrichten* 1988;43:861–7.

23. Wilkinson RG. Research note: German income distribution and infant mortality. *Sociology of Health and Illness* 1994;16:260–2.

24. Wilkinson RG. Income and health. In: Health, wealth and poverty. *Medical World* 1993;special edition (London).

Eleven

HOW MUCH OF THE RELATION BETWEEN POPULATION MORTALITY AND UNEQUAL DISTRIBUTION OF INCOME IS A STATISTICAL ARTEFACT?

Hugh Gravelle

The absolute income hypothesis—that holding other factors constant, the higher an individual's income the better is their health—is supported by a considerable body of evidence.[1-3] However, according to the more recent relative income hypothesis, an individual's health is also affected by the distribution of income within society. Someone with a given income would have worse health if he or she lived in a society with greater inequality than in a society in which income is more equally distributed.[4] Several recent papers examining the relation between population mortality and income inequality seem to support the relative income hypothesis.[5-11] They suggest that greater inequality is associated with higher population mortality and that this relation persists even when account is taken of the average income of the population.

However, some scepticism has been expressed about the relative income hypothesis.[12] To quote one of the papers cited above, the "mechanisms underlying the association between income distribution and mortality are poorly understood."[7]

A STATISTICAL ARTEFACT MAY EXPLAIN THE RELATION

THERE may be a very simple explanation for some, or all, of the reported associations between inequality of income and population health used to support the relative income hypothesis. They may be, at least partly, a statistical artefact caused by using population data rather than individual data. A positive correlation between population mortality and income inequality can arise at aggregate level even if inequality has no effect on the individual risk of mortality. Thus, we do not need the relative income hypothesis to explain the observed associations between population health and income inequality—the absolute income hypothesis will serve.

Originally published in *British Medical Journal*, 1998.

MORTALITY RISK
AND ABSOLUTE INCOME

THE absolute income explanation can be illustrated with the help of the figure (the mathematical argument is presented in the appendix). In this, the individual risk of mortality depends only on the income of the individual, as shown by the heavy line. As income increases, the risk of mortality falls, but it does so at a declining rate. Thus, an increase in income reduces the risk of mortality by a smaller amount at high incomes than at low incomes. Note that this model assumes that there is no relation between the distribution of income and the health of any member of the population. The risk of mortality depends on the absolute income, not the relative income, of the individual.

Mortality Risk and Inequality Income

Now compare two countries where the average income is the same $\bar{y}$ but the distribution of income is different. To avoid cluttering the figure, suppose that in country A half the population has a low income of y_{1A} and a high risk of mortality m_{1A}. The other half has a higher income of y_{2A} and therefore a lower mortality risk of m_{2A}. The population mortality in country A is m_A (the av-

erage of m_{1A} and m_{2A}). In country B income inequality is greater—half the population has an income of y_{1B} (and a mortality risk of m_{1B}) and the other half an income of y_{2B} (and a mortality risk of m_{2B}). Although the difference in incomes between rich and poor is greater in country B, it has the same average income as country A. However, population mortality in country B. m_B (the average of m_{1B} and m_{2B}), is greater than the population mortality of country A.

SUMMARY POINTS

The absolute income hypothesis, which states that the higher an individual's income, the lower his or her risk of mortality, is supported by a considerable body of evidence

However, the relative income hypothesis—that the distribution of income in a society affects the individual's risk of mortality—is being used increasingly in empirical work

Associations between unequal income distribution and population health may be a statistical artefact resulting from the use of aggregate rather than individual data—an example of the "ecological fallacy"

Because studies using population data cannot distinguish between the absolute and relative income hypotheses, the effects of income redistribution policies on population health can only be judged from individual data, interpreted by models of behaviors that affect health

The spurious or artefactual correlation at population level between population mortality and income dispersion will always occur if the effect of individual income on the individual risk of mortality is smaller at higher incomes than at lower incomes. This will be so even if there is no underlying relation between the distribution of income and the risk of mortality at the level of the individual.

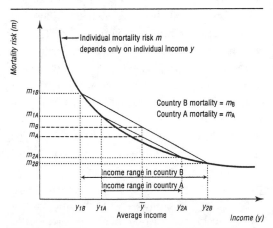

Effect of increased inequality of income on population mortality

Individual Mortality and Individual Risk

The greater population mortality in the country that has a less equal income distribution (country B), results entirely from the shape of the relation between individual income and the individual risk of mortality. The higher income of rich people in country B compared with rich people in country A reduces their risk of mortality by $m_{2A} - m_{2B}$ compared with rich people in country A. However, the lower income of poor people in country B compared with poor people in country A increases their risk of mortality by $m_{1B} - m_{1A}$ compared with poor people in country A. Because the impact of income on mortality is smaller at higher incomes, the reduced mortality of the rich is more than offset by the increased mortality of the poor and population mortality is therefore higher in country B.

If mortality declines with income, but at a decreasing rate, transferring income from the poor to the rich will increase the mortality risk of the poor more than it reduces the mortality risk of the rich. Overall population mortality increases when inequality increases, even though every individual's risk of mortality depends only on their own income level and not on the income level of anyone else.

Aggregate Estimates of Data May Distort Individual Risk

In a cross sectional study using population data for different countries or areas, the population mortality will be correlated positively with the degree of income inequality, even if income inequality does not affect the risk of mortality for individuals. The spurious or artefactual correlation at population level between population mortality and income dispersion will always occur if the effect of individual income on the individual risk of mortality is smaller at higher incomes than at lower incomes. This will be so even if there is no underlying relation between the distribution of income and the risk of mortality at the level of the individual.

The "artefactual argument" does not depend on the precise shape of the risk curve for individual mortality, provided only that the risk of mortality declines with income, but at a decreasing rate. Nor does it depend on the shapes of the income distributions or on using a particular measure of income inequality. The artefactual phenomenon can arise in very general circumstances.

INCOME AND HEALTH— A NON-LINEAR RELATION?

INCOME affects health because it influences individuals' consumption of commodities that affect health. Housing and tobacco are two obvious examples. The relation between income and health depends on the relation between income and the commodities that affect health, and on the relation between these commodities and health. What matters for the artefactual argument is that the resulting relation between health and income is not a straight line—it produces a curve like that in the figure. This could result from non-linear (or J shaped) relations between health and commodities or environmental factors that affect health,[15] or it could arise from non-linear associations between income commodities or environmental factors that affect health.[16] [17]

EVIDENCE FOR THE RELATIVE INCOME HYPOTHESIS

THE hypothesis that mortality is affected more by relative than absolute living standards has been supported by various types of evidence.[18] Several studies comparing different countries show that population mortality and income inequality are positively associated, even after differences in average income and other socioeconomic factors have been allowed for. But this is precisely what is predicted by the artefactual argument. The sheer volume of studies reporting population level correlations of health and inequality measures cannot in itself support either the relative income hypothesis or the artefactual argument.

Income and Mortality Are
More Closely Related Within Countries

The second type of evidence used to support the hypothesis that income distribution affects directly the individual risk of mortality is the regular gradient between income and mortality within countries, which contrasts sharply with the weak relation between countries. This, it is argued, is because income differences between groups within a society are associated with social stratification (and its detrimental effect on health) while per capita income differences between countries are not. However, if the artefactual argument is correct, we would expect to find that the income-mortality correlation within countries is stronger than the average income-mortality correlation between countries. The within country correlations would, in effect, be plotting the relation between individual mortality risk and individual income shown in the heavy line in the figure, provided the data for a single country were derived from the level of the individual or were aggregated across relatively homogeneous income groups. The correlation of population mortality against average income between countries would be confounded by the omission of measures of the variability of income in the different countries, resulting in a weaker correlation.

Marginal Effect of Income
Is Smaller in Richer Countries

The third argument is that in more developed (richer) societies the marginal effect of income on mortality is smaller, and the curve relating income to mortality is flatter. But this is what is required for the artefactual hypothesis to hold. If the artefactual hypothesis were an invalid explanation of the association between inequality and

population mortality, the income-mortality curve would have to be a straight line.[4]

MORE GENERAL
ARTEFACTUAL PROBLEMS
Hypotheses about Mechanisms

The artefactual problem can also arise in attempts to test hypotheses about the mechanism by which greater inequality affects individual health. For example, increased inequality might lead to greater stress in individuals, to greater alcohol consumption, and thus to worse health outcomes. One seemingly obvious way of testing this argument is to examine the relation between average alcohol consumption and income inequality. However, studies suggest that the relation between an individual's demand for alcohol and their income is non-linear—increases in income lead to greater than proportional increases in alcohol consumption.[15] If this is the case, an increase in income inequality will lead to an increase in average alcohol consumption because the increased consumption of the rich will more than outweigh the reduced consumption of the poor. Thus, any correlation between average alcohol consumption and income inequality would be at least partly artefactual, arising from the non-linearity of the relation at the level of the individual. Inequality could have no true effect on individual consumption.

Problems of Non-linear Relations
at Individual Level

Similar problems arise in examining the relation between inequality of income and health problems associated with alcohol. Studies suggest that the relation between alcohol consumption and health effects is non-linear—the deleterious effects increase more than proportionately with consumption, and consumption may even be protective at low levels.[16] This will be sufficient to generate a non-linear relation between income and alcohol related problems at the level of the individual, and therefore artefactual correlations between income inequality and alcohol related problems in the population.

The Ecological Fallacy

The artefactual argument is another example of the difficulties—known in epidemiology texts as the "ecological fallacy"—in inferring relations at the individual level from associations between variables at the population level.[18][19] The problem has been discussed in econometric reports on consumer behaviour, where it is known as the aggregation problem.[20] It was also noted in early work on income and health, and was emphasised in Rodgers's pioneering paper, to which reference is made in many recent reports on the link between mortality and income distribution.[21] I argue here that the problem is more general and therefore potentially more troubling for empirical work.

IMPLICATIONS OF THE ARTEFACTUAL ARGUMENT

SINCE the artefactual argument casts doubt on the methods and the interpretation of a large and growing body of empirical work, being clear about what is and what is not being suggested is important. I do not suggest that an individual's health is not affected by the overall distribution of income as well as by their own income. The point I am making is that correlations between population level measures of mortality and inequality provide biased estimates of the importance of any relative income effect, even after allowing for the levels of other potentially important determinants of mortality. If the relation between the individual risk of mortality and individual income is non-linear, at least part and possibly all of the correlation will be artefactual.

Both the absolute income and relative income hypotheses predict that a reduction in inequality of income can improve the health of a population. However, if policies that alter the distribution of income are to be judged at least partly by their effects on population health, knowing how large these effects are is important. Studies using population level data do not answer this question since they can not distinguish between the absolute income and relative income hypotheses. Individual data are necessary. Equally important are models of the behaviours that affect the health of individuals so that these data can be interpreted appropriately.[22-24]

I thank R Carr-Hill, G Davey Smith, T Sheldon, M Sutton, and R G Wilkinson for their comments and suggestions.

Funding: Support from the Department of Health to the National Primary Care Research and Development Centre is acknowledged. The views expressed are those of the author and not necessarily those of the Department of Health.

Conflict on interest: None.

Appendix: The Mathematical Argument

Suppose that the mortality risk of an individual with income y depends only on their income and is $m(y)$. Taking a second order approximation, we can express the mortality risk of an individual in terms of the individual's income y and the mean income $\bar{y}$ of the population where m' and m'' are the first and second derivatives of m.

$$m(y) \approx m(\bar{y}) + m'(\bar{y})(y - \bar{y}) + \tfrac{1}{2}m''(\bar{y})(y - \bar{y})^2$$

The mortality of the population as a whole is found by multiplying the risk of mortality for individuals with income y by their relative frequency in the population and summing over all income groups. If this operation is performed on both sides of the above expression, remembering that by definition the average deviation of incomes is zero, so that the second term disappears, the following equation is derived:

$$Em(y) \approx m(\bar{y}) + m'(\bar{y})E(y - \bar{y}) + \tfrac{1}{2}m''(\bar{y})E(y - \bar{y})^2 = m(\bar{y}) + \tfrac{1}{2}m''(\bar{y})\,Var(y)$$

where $Em(y)$ is the population mortality and $Var(y)$ is the variance of incomes across the population. Hence, provided only that $m'' > 0$. so that individual mortality risk declines with individual income at a decreasing rate (as in the figure), the population mortality will be positively correlated with mean income and the variance of incomes.

NOTES

1. Preston SH. The changing relation between mortality and level of economic development. *Popul Stud* 1975;29:231–48.

2. Pritchett L, Summers LH. Wealthier is healthier. *J Hum Resources* 1996;31:841–68.

3. Adler NE, Boyce W, Chesney MH, Folkman S, Fymes L. Socioeconomic inequalities in health: no easy solution. *JAMA* 1993;269:3140–5.

4. Wilkinson RG. *Unhealthy societies: the afflictions of inequality.* London: Routledge, 1996.

5. Ben-Shlomo Y, White IR, Marmot M. Does the variation in the socioeconomic characteristics of an area affect mortality? *BMJ* 1996;312:1013–4.

6. Kaplan GA, Parmuk ER, Lynch JW, Cophen RD, Baltour JG. Inequality in income and mortality in the United States: analysis of mortality and potential pathways. *BMJ* 1996;312:999–1003.

7. Kennedy BP, Kawachi I, Prothrow-Smith D. Income distribution and mortality: cross sectional ecological study of the Robin Hood index in the United States. *BMJ* 1996;312:1004–7.

8. Wilkinson RG. Income distribution and life expectancy. *BMJ* 1994;304:165–8.

9. Wilkinson RG. A reply to Ken Judge: mistaken criticisms ignore overwhelming evidence. *BMJ* 1995;311:1285–7.

10. Wilkinson RG. Health inequalities: relative or absolute material standards? *BMJ* 1997;314:591–5.

11. Waldman RJ. Income distribution and infant mortality. *Q J Econ* 1992;107:1283–302.

12. Davey Smith G. Income inequality and mortality: why are they related? *BMJ* 1996;312;987–8.

13. Atkinson AB. On the measurement of income inequality. *J Econ Theory* 1970;2:244–63.

14. Rothschild M, Stiglitz JE. Increasing risk I: a definition. *J Econ Theory* 1970;2:225–43.

15. Godfrey C. Factors influencing the consumption of alcohol and tobacco: the use end abuse of economic models. *Br J Addict* 1989;10:1123–38.

16. Edwards G, Babor TF, Anderson P. *Alcohol policy and the public good.* Oxford: Oxford University Press, 1994.

17. Atkinson AB, Gomulaka J, Stern NH. Spending on alcohol: evidence from the family expenditure survey. *Econ J* 1990;100:808–27.

18. Robinson WS. Ecological correlations and the behaviour of individuals. *Am Soc Rev* 1950;15:351–7.

19. Beaglehole R, Bonita R, Kjellstrom T. *Basic epidemiology.* Geneva: World Health Organisation, 1993.

20. Deaton A, Muellbauer J. *Economics of consumer behaviour.* Cambridge: Cambridge University Press, 1980.

21. Rodgers GB. Income and inequality as determinants of mortality: an international cross-section analysis. *Popul Stud* 1979;33:343–51.

22. Gravelle HSE. Time series analysis of mortality and unemployment. *J Health Econ* 1984;3:297–305.

23. Gravelle HSE, Backhouse M. International cross-section analyses of the determinants of mortality. *Soc Sci Med* 1987;25:427–41.

24. Ettner SL. New evidence on the relationship between income and health. *J Health Econ* 1996;15:67–86.

Twelve

POVERTY OR INCOME INEQUALITY AS A PREDICTOR OF MORTALITY: LONGITUDINAL COHORT STUDY

Kevin Fiscella and Peter Franks

ABSTRACT

Objective: To determine the effect of inequality in income between communities independent of household income on individual all cause mortality in the United States.

Design: Longitudinal cohort study.

Subjects: A nationally representative sample of 14 407 people aged 25–74 years in the United States from the first national health and nutrition examination survey.

Setting: Subjects were followed from initial interview in 1971–5 until 1987. Complete follow up information was available for 92.2% of the sample.

Main outcome measures: Relation between both household income and income inequality in community of residence and individual all cause mortality at follow up was examined with Cox proportional hazards survival analysis.

Results: Community income inequality showed a significant association with subsequent community mortality, and with individual mortality after adjustment for age, sex, and mean income in the community of residence. After adjustment for individual household income, however, the association with mortality was lost.

Conclusions: In this nationally representative American sample, family income, but not community income inequality, independently predicts mortality. Previously reported ecological associations between income inequality and mortality may reflect confounding between individual family income and mortality.

INTRODUCTION

STUDIES have documented the powerful association between a person's socioeconomic status and mortality.[1-4] Recently, ecological studies have suggested that income inequality is also correlated with overall mortality.[5] [6] Wilkinson reported a correlation of −0.81 between national income inequality among 11 industrialised countries and national life expectancy after controlling for gross national product per head.[7] Comparable findings were re-

Originally published in *British Medical Journal*, 1997.

cently reported using data at state level from the United States. Kaplan et al noted that state income inequality adjusted for state median income was significantly correlated (r=0.62) with all cause mortality, age specific mortality, low birth rate, homicide, violent crime, work disability, expenditures on medical care, and police protection.[8] Kennedy et al reported that state income inequality adjusted for levels of poverty was strongly correlated (r=0.54) with age adjusted total mortality, infant mortality, coronary heart disease, malignant neoplasms, and homicide.[9] Ben-Shlomo et al showed significant effects for income inequality measured at the British ward level on area mortality.[10]

These ecological or population level studies suggest that the relation between income and mortality in developed countries is a relative phenomenon. In other words, income inequality between countries, states, or communities, is more strongly associated with health than is poverty or mean per capita income. Income equality may be associated with mortality in several ways. Firstly, income inequality may affect health via cognitive processes such as perceived deprivation that promote hopelessness, hostility, or risk taking behaviour.[11-16] Secondly, income inequality may be a measure or cause, or both, of social forces such as reduced social cohesion that affect health.[17] Thirdly, income inequality may be a marker of a government's underinvestment in human resources.[18] Lastly, the association between income inequality and mortality may simply represent confounding by family income at the individual level.

Studies reporting an association between income inequality and mortality have provided limited insight into the nature of this relation. Conclusions from previous studies are limited by potential "ecological fallacy" because they cannot adequately control for confounding at the individual level.[19] In other words, the observed relation between income inequality and mortality observed at a population level may simply represent inadequately measured rates of income differences at the individual level. No published studies have specifically examined the effect of income inequality on mortality after adjustment for income at the individual level.

We examined whether inequality in income between communities predicts future individual mortality independent of family income. We used data from a nationally representative prospective cohort from the United States to assess whether residence in communities with greater income inequality was independently associated with mortality at follow up.

METHODS

Source of Data

The first national health and nutrition examination survey (NHANES I), conducted between 1971 and 1975 in the United States, collected sociodemographic data from multiple national probability samples of the civilian non-institutionalised population of adults aged 25 to 74 years.[20 21] The epidemiological follow up study (NHEFS) collected mortality data through follow up surveys conducted in 1982, 1984, 1986, and 1987.[22 23] Follow up data were derived from interview surveys, medical records from healthcare institutions, and all death certificates. The age, race, and sex specific mortality of the follow up cohort is comparable to that experienced by the American population.[23] In all, 14 407 people were in the original survey, 3.4% of whom had missing information on family income; mortality status at follow up was ascertained on 95.8% of the people for whom such information was available.

The first survey used multistage stratified probability samples of people from 105 areas or primary sampling units in the United States. The areas approximated to counties or combined county areas. People living in areas of poverty, women of childbearing age, and elderly people were oversampled (surveyed at disproportionately higher rates). A mean of 131 (range 48–323) people were surveyed in each primary sampling unit. The revised weights provided on the 1987 follow up study's "public use" tapes were used to adjust for survey oversampling and non-response to yield population estimates for each community surveyed.

Measure of Family Income

Household income was assessed through response to a single question in the first national health and nutrition examination survey. The question asked subjects to say which of 12 income groups represented their total family income for the previous 12 months, including all sources of income, such as wages, salaries, social security or retirement benefits, help from relatives, and rent from property. The income categories ranged from under $1000 and $25 000 and over. Subjects were assigned to the mean value within their income category. Subjects in the highest income category (4.6%) were assigned a mean value by extrapolation.

Measure of Income Inequality

Several indices of community income inequality have been described, though the relation of each index to mortality risk is similar.[9] We used an index that estimates the proportion of total income earned by the poorer half of the population in the area. The denominator for this index is the total aggregate income in the community (primary sampling unit), and the numerator is the aggregate income in the community earned by the poorer half of the population. The income inequality within the communities ranged from 0.18 to 0.37.

Statistical Analysis

Multilevel modelling is required to avoid the problems of clustering within a group.[24] We used the statistical package SUDAAN, which uses a Taylor series approximation method to compute variances that allow adjustment for multistage probability sampling.[25] A Cox proportional hazard survival analysis was performed that included the index of community income inequality, household income, family size, sex, and age as covariates in the predictive model for mortality. The assumptions of the model were tested and found valid.

RESULTS

OLDER age, residence at the time of the interview in a community with greater income inequality, and lower mean community income were all associated with the proportion of people in the community dying during follow up (table 1). Survival analysis showed that survival adjusted for age, sex, and family size was associated with income inequality (hazard ratio = 0.23, 95% confidence interval 0.06 to 0.86); additional

---

Table 1

Bivariate correlations between proportion of people in community dying during follow up and community level sociodemographic characteristics (n=105)

Variable (by community)	Mean (SD)	Correlation	P value
Age	46.61 (2.36)	0.64	0.001
Male (proportion)	0.47 (0.07)	0.13	0.184
Income ($000s)	12.03 (2.62)	− 0.48	0.001
Community income inequality*	0.28 (0.03)	− 0.34	0.004
Death (proportion)	0.15 (0.06)	NA	

NA=not applicable.
*Proportion of total area income earned by the poorer half of area residents.

Table 2

Survival analysis of factors affecting mortality hazard during follow up (n=13 280)

Risk factor	Hazard ratio (95% CI)	P value
Age	1.09 (1.08 to 1.09)	<0.001
Female sex	0.53 (0.49 to 0.57)	<0.001
Household income ($000s)	0.97 (0.96 to 0.98)	<0.001
Community income inequality*	0.81 (0.22 to 2.92)	0.752

Analysis is also adjusted for family size. Hazard ratios indicate the increase in risk of mortality during follow up based on a unit change in the risk factor.

*Proportion of total area income earned by the poorer half of community residents.

adjustment for mean community income did not greatly affect this relation (0.31, 0.10 to 0.90). However, after adjustment for household income, no significant relation between income inequality and mortality was evident (table 2). An analysis that excluded the income inequality measure showed no change in the effect size of income on mortality (0.97, 0.96 to 0.98).

Discussion

ANALYSES of data from a nationally representative prospective American cohort study show that individually measured family income strongly confounds the relation between community income inequality and mortality. Although aggregated data at the individual level simulated the findings of previous ecological studies,[7-10] community income inequality did not independently predict mortality after adjustment for family income. Conversely, exclusion of the variable of community income inequality did not affect the relation between family income and subsequent mortality. These findings suggest that the effect of income inequality reported in ecological studies may result from confounding by income at the individual level.

Our findings imply that income, as a measure of access to resources, and not relative inequality, better explains the relation between income and

mortality. Psychological or social factors related to income inequality may nevertheless have important health effects, as Wilkinson suggests.[17] We believe, however, that existing studies have not adequately tested his hypothesis. Future studies of the inequality hypothesis should control for income at the individual level and use direct measures of factors such as social cohesion and perceived socioeconomic deprivation to advance our understanding of the relative contribution of these factors to health.

These findings are subject to several important caveats. The appropriate unit of analysis for measuring income inequality is not known. Ecological studies have shown effects of inequality at the national level,[7] American state level,[8 9] and British ward level.[10] We used community (mostly American counties) income inequality as our unit of analysis and showed significant effects for income inequality in a simulated ecological analysis. The validity of our analysis is supported by the significant correlation between community income inequality and community mortality rates after adjustment for mean community income. Although the magnitude of this correlation was smaller than that reported in previous ecological studies, this may represent less nondifferential misclassification bias.[26] Because our ecological analysis used prospective data that had been carefully collected at the individual level, there may have been less misclassification than in ecological studies that have used national or state cross sectional data. Brenner et al showed that non-differential exposure misclassification in ecological studies as opposed to individual level studies can lead to significant overestimation of effects.[26] Further support for the validity of our findings is provided by preliminary data from the panel on income dynamics from the United States. In this study state income inequality showed no effect on mortality after individually measured income was controlled for (G Duncan, personal communication).

Limitations

Still larger units of analysis might yield different results. This hypothesis is particularly plausible if it is assumed that income inequality is simply a proxy for national policies that promote general social welfare and health.[8 27] However, if income inequality is assumed to influence health directly via cognitive processes then the appropriate unit remains speculative. For example, if people judge their socioeconomic status relative to that of their neighbours, then the community may be the appropriate level of analysis, but if they use national media sources as a frame of reference then analyses should focus on the national level. A stronger conceptual framework is needed to guide future studies in this area and also to provide direct testing of the hypothesis that individual perceptions of relative socioeconomic standing influence health.

These findings are limited by the area sampling methodology used by the first national health and nutrition examination survey. Although the survey was designed as a representative sample of the American population, sampling within communities was not random. The cluster sampling strategy underestimates the true variability in each community, thus underestimating community income inequality. Despite this bias, we found significant effects for income inequality in the ecological but not individual level analysis.

Our analysis does not account for an individual's relocation from one community to another during the study. Nor does our analysis account for increasing levels of income inequality in the United States during the study.[28] Such misclassification bias tends to overestimate the effects observed in an ecological study and to underestimate the effects observed in an individual level analysis. This bias operates similarly for family income. Both family size and income may change considerably over time, resulting in further misclassification bias. In addition, a selective bias resulting from greater loss to follow up among poorer people tends to understate the effect of poverty on mortality. Although each of these biases underestimates the effect of family income on mortality, we none the less found significant effects for family income.

Colinearity between family income and community income inequality may have masked the independent effect of community income inequality on mortality. The finding that the relation between family income and mortality was unaffected by adjustment for community income inequality suggests, at least, that family income is a far more powerful predictor of health status than community income inequality. Although our analysis does not exclude a modest effect of community income inequality on health, these findings militate against a large effect.

Conclusion

These findings suggest that community income inequality does not have large effects on mortality independent of the effects of family income. However, income inequality and family income are closely intertwined. Countries, states, or communities with large income inequalities are likely to have more poverty. Countries whose explicit goal has been eradication of poverty also have less income inequality. Thus, whether public policy focuses primarily on the elimination of poverty or on reduction in income disparity, neither goal is likely to be achieved in the absence of the other.

NOTES

1. Adler NE, Boyce T, Chesney MA, Cohen S, Folkman S, Kahn RL, et al. Socioeconomic status and health: the challenge of the gradient. *Am Psychol* 1994;49:15–24

2. Fein O. The influence of social class on health status: American and British research on health inequalities. *J Gen Int Med* 1995;10:577–86.

3. Kaplan GA, Keil JE. Socioeconomic factors and cardiovascular disease: a review of the literature. *Circulation* 1993;88:1973–98.

4. Sorlie PD, Backlund E, Keller JB. US mortality by economic, demographic, and social characteristics: the national longitudinal mortality study. *Am J Public Health* 1995;85:949–56.

5. LeGrand J. Inequalities in health. Some international comparisons. *Eur Economic Rev* 1987;31:182–91.

6. Rodgers GB. Income and inequality as determinants of mortality: an international cross-section analysis. *Population Studies* 1979;33:343–51.

7. Wilkinson RG. Income distribution and life expectancy. *BMJ* 1992;304:165–8.

8. Kaplan GA, Pamuk ER, Lynch JW, Cohen RD, Balfour JL. Inequality in income and mortality in the United States: analysis of mortality and potential pathways. *BMJ* 1996;312:999–1003.

9. Kennedy BP, Kawachi I, Prothrow-Stith D. Income distribution and mortality: cross sectional ecological study of the Robin Hood index in the United States. *BMJ* 1996;312:1004–7.

10. Ben-Shlomo Y, White IR, Marmot M. Does the variation in the socioeconomic characteristics of an area affect mortality? *BMJ* 1996;312:1013–4.

11. Barefoot J, Peterson B, Dahlstrom W, Siegler IC, Anderson NB, Williams RB. Hostility patterns and health implications: correlates of Cook-Medley hostility scale scores in a national survey. *Health Psychol* 1991;10:18–24.

12. Anderson NB, Armstead CA. Toward understanding the association of socioeconomic status and health: a new challenge for the biopsychosocial approach. *Psychosomatic Med* 1995;57:213–25.

13. Everson SA, Goldberg DE, Kaplan GA, Cohen RD, Pukkala E, Tuomilehto J, et al. Hopelessness and risk of mortality and incidence of myocardial infarction and cancer. *Psychosomatic Med* 1995;58:113–21.

14. Anda R, Williamson D, Jones D, Macera C, Eaker E, Glassman A, et al. Depressed affect, hopelessness, and the risk of ischemic heart disease in a cohort of US adults. *Epidemiology* 1993;4:285–94.

15. Miller TQ, Guijarro ML, Hallet AJ, Smith TW, Turner CW. A meta-analytic review of research on hostility and physical health. *Psychol Bull* 1996;119:322–48.

16. Miller TQ, Markides KS, Chiriboga DA, Ray LA. A test of the psychosocial vulnerability and health behaviour models of hostility: results from an 11-year follow-up study of Mexican Americans. *Psychosomatic Med* 1995;57:572–81.

17. Wilkinson RG. Mistaken criticisms ignore overwhelming evidence [commentary]. *BMJ* 1995;311:1285–7.

18. Smith GD. Income inequality and mortality: why are they related? *BMJ* 1996;312:987–8.

19. Selvin HC. Durkheim's "suicide" and problems of empirical research. *Am J Soc* 1958;63:607–19.

20. National Center for Health Statistics, Miller HW. *Plan and operation of the health and nutrition survey, United States, 1971–73.* Washington, DC: US Government Printing Office, 1977. (Vital and health statistics, series 1, No 10$_a$, 10$_b$. DHEW publication No (PHS) 73–1310.)

21. National Center for Health Statistics, Engel A, Murphy RS, Maurer K, Collins E. *Plan and operation of the NHANES I augmentation survey of adults 25–74 years, United States, 1974–75.* Washington, DC: US Government Printing Office, 1978. (Vital and health statistics, series 1, No 14, DHEW publication No (PHS) 78–1314.)

22. Cohen BB, Barbano HE, Cox CE, Feldman JJ, Finucane FF, Kleinman JC, et al. Plan and operation of the NHANES I epidemiologic followup study, 1982–84. Washington, DC: National Center for Health Statistics, US Government Printing Office, 1987. (Vital and health statistics, series 1, No 22. DHHS publication No (PHS) 87–1324.)

23. Madans JH, Cox CS, Kleinman JC, Makuc D, Feldman JJ, Finucane FF, et al. 10 Years after NHANES I: mortality experience at initial followup, 1982–84. *Public Health Reports—Hyattsville* 1986;101:474–81.

24. Morgenstern H. Ecologic studies in epidemiology: concepts, principles and methods. *Ann Rev Public Health* 1995;16:61–81.

25. *SUDAAN: professional software for survey data analysis.* Research Triangle Park, NC: Research Triangle Institute, 1991.

26. Brenner H, Savitz DA, Jockel K-H, Greenland S. Effects of nondifferential exposure misclassification in ecologic studies. *Am J Epidemiol* 1992;135:85–95.

27. Elola J, Daponte A, Navarro V. Health indicators and the organisation of health care systems in western Europe. *Am J Public Health* 1995;85:1397–401.

28. Plotnick RD. Changes in poverty, income inequality, and the standard of living in the United States during the Reagan years. *Int J Health Services* 1993;23:347–56.

Thirteen

THE RELATIONSHIP OF INCOME INEQUALITY TO MORTALITY: DOES THE CHOICE OF INDICATOR MATTER?

Ichiro Kawachi and Bruce P. Kennedy

ABSTRACT

Ecologic studies in the U.S. and elsewhere in the world have demonstrated that income inequality is strongly related to mortality and life expectancy: the greater the dispersion of income within a given society, the lower the life expectancy. However, the empirical studies have been criticized on the grounds that the choice of indicator may have influenced positive findings. Using a cross-sectional, ecologic design, we tested the relationships of six different income inequality indicators to total mortality rates in the 50 U.S. states. The following summary measures of income distribution were examined: the Gini coefficient; the decile ratio; the proportions of total income earned by the bottom 50%, 60%, and 70% of households; the Robin Hood Index; the Atkinson Index; and Theil's entropy measure. All were highly correlated with each other (Pearson r ≥ 0.94), and all were strongly associated with mortality (Pearson r ranging from 0.50 to 0.66), even after adjustment for median income and poverty. Thus, the choice of income distribution measure does not appear to alter the conclusion that income inequality is linked to higher mortality. Furthermore, adjustment for taxes and transfers, as well as household size (using equivalence scales), made no difference to the income inequality/ mortality association. From a policy perspective, the alternative income distribution measures perform differently under varying types of income transfers, so that theoretical considerations should guide the selection of an indicator to assess the impact of social and economic policies that address income inequality.

INTRODUCTION

THE relationship of poverty to poor health outcomes is by now well established, both internationally (World Bank, 1993) and within individual countries (Black *et al.*, 1988). Among poor countries in the world, there exists a strong relationship between the absolute level of income—as measured by per capita gross national product (GNP)—and life expectancy: the lower the GNP, the lower the average life expectancy (World Bank, 1993). However, once countries have attained some threshold level of income (around $5000 per capita in 1990), the relationship between the absolute standard of living and life expectancy disappears, so that further increases in GNP per capita are no longer associated with life expectancy gains (Wilkinson, 1996). On the other hand, what seems to strongly predict life expectancy in more affluent countries is the extent of *relative* deprivation, as measured by the size of the income gap between the rich and the poor (Wilkinson, 1992, 1996).

The relationship of income inequality to poor health status has been demonstrated in a growing number of studies, including cross-national

Originally published in *Social Science & Medicine*, 1997.

comparisons within the Organization for Economic Cooperation and Development (OECD) (Wilkinson, 1986, 1992, 1994), as well as within individual countries (Kennedy *et al.*, 1996; Kaplan *et al.*, 1996). The mechanisms by which income inequality is associated with worse health status are believed to include under-investment in human capital (Kaplan *et al.*, 1996); loss of social cohesion and disinvestment in social capital (Wilkinson, 1996); and the potentially harmful consequences of frustration brought about by relative deprivation (Kawachi *et al.*, 1994).

Notwithstanding the mounting evidence on the link between income inequality and mortality in a variety of settings, produced by different investigators, concern has been recently expressed about the apparently arbitrary way in which income inequality indicators have been selected in empirical studies (Judge, 1995). Different researchers have used different indicators of income distribution. Thus, Kennedy *et al.* (1996) reported that two indicators of income inequality—the Gini coefficient and the Robin Hood Index—were both strongly correlated with total and cause-specific mortality in the United States, even after adjusting for poverty, median income, and smoking rates. Using a different indicator of income inequality—the percentage of total income earned by the least well off 50% of households—Kaplan *et al.* (1996) independently demonstrated the existence of a link between income distribution and mortality. Repeated corroboration of the same hypothesis using different indicators of income inequality provides some reassurance about the robust nature of the association.

However, based on an analysis of life expectancy in 13 OECD countries between 1984 and 1987, Judge (1995) found no association with several summary measures of income distribution. The author concluded: "It is important that any future attempt to investigate the income inequality hypothesis should specify *a priori* what measures of income distribution might be expected to be associated with life expectancy and why".

The purpose of the present study was therefore to test a comprehensive range of income inequality indicators with respect to their relationships with total mortality in the United States.

METHODS

Data Sources

Data on income, household size, and poverty rates were obtained from the 1990 U.S. Census Population and Housing Summary Tape File 3A. This file provides annual data on household incomes for 25 income intervals. Counts of the number of households that fall into each income interval along with the total aggregate income and the median household income were obtained for each state. These data were used to calculate the six income inequality indices described below.

The file also contains data on household size and poverty rates, in which households are classified as being above or below the poverty level based on the federal poverty index originally developed by the Social Security Administration in 1964. The current poverty index is based purely on income from wages and does not reflect other resources of income such as non-cash benefits from food stamps, Medicaid, and public housing. Poverty thresholds are updated annually to reflect changes in the consumer price index. The poverty variable we used represents the percentage of households in a given state that were below the federal poverty threshold. In 1990, this represented an income of less than $13,359 for households with four family members (U.S. Bureau of the Census, 1993).

Age-standardized mortality rates (per 100,000 population) in 1990 were obtained for each state from the compressed mortality files compiled by the National Center for Health Statistics, Centers for Disease Control and Prevention (CDC). The data were obtained from their database with the CDC WONDER/PC® software (Friede *et al.*, 1993).

Measures of Income Distribution

We tested the associations of total mortality with a comprehensive range of income distribution measures (Theil, 1967; Atkinson, 1970; Sen, 1973; Cowell, 1977; Atkinson and Micklewright, 1993): the Gini coefficient; the decile ratio; the proportions of total income earned by the bottom 50%, 60%, and 70% of households; the Robin Hood Index; the Atkinson Index; and Theil's entropy measure.

GINI COEFFICIENT

The Gini coefficient is one of the most commonly used indicators of income inequality (Sen, 1973; Cowell, 1977; Atkinson and Micklewright, 1993). The Gini is derived from the Lorenz curve, which is a graphical device for displaying the cumulative share of total income accruing to successive income intervals. In Fig. 1 (example from Massachusetts data), the curve shows the shares of income earned by successive deciles of households, arrayed in order from the bottom 10% upwards. If incomes were equally distributed, the Lorenz curve would follow the 45° diagonal. As the degree of inequality increases, so does the curvature of the Lorenz curve, and thus the area between the curve and the 45° line becomes larger. The Gini is calculated as the ratio of the area between the Lorenz curve and the 45° line, to the whole area below the 45° line.

ROBIN HOOD INDEX

The Robin Hood Index is equivalent to the maximum vertical distance between the Lorenz curve and the line of equal incomes. We have previously described its algebraic derivation (Kennedy *et al.*, 1996). The value of the index approximates the share of total income that has to be taken from households above the mean and transferred to those below the mean to achieve equality in the distribution of incomes.

ATKINSON'S INDEX

The Atkinson Index is one of the few inequality measures that explicitly incorporates normative

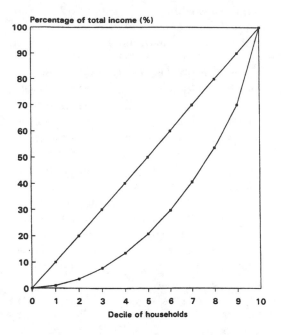

Figure 1
Lorenz curve for Massachusetts households, 1990.

judgments about social welfare (Atkinson, 1970). The index is derived by calculating the so-called equity-sensitive average income (y_e), which is defined as that level of per capita income which if enjoyed by everybody would make total welfare exactly equal to the total welfare generated by the actual income distribution. The equity-sensitive average income is given by:

$$y_e = (\sum_{i=1}^{n} f(y_i) . y_i^{1-\epsilon})^{1/(1-\epsilon)}$$

where y_i is the proportion of total income earned by the ith group, and ϵ is the so-called inequality aversion parameter. The parameter ϵ reflects the strength of society's preference for equality, and can take values ranging from zero to infinity. When $\epsilon > 0$, there is a social preference for equality (or an aversion to inequality). As ϵ rises, society attaches more weight to income transfers at the lower end of the distribution and less weight to transfers at the top. Following previous work (Atkinson, 1970; Sen, 1973; Cowell, 1977), we set $\epsilon = 0.5$, and 2.

The Atkinson Index (I) is then given by:

$$I = 1 - y_e/\mu$$

where μ is the actual mean income. The more equal the income distribution, the closer y_e will be to μ, and the lower the value of the Atkinson Index. For any income distribution, the value of I lies between 0 and 1.

THEIL'S ENTROPY MEASURE

A measure of inequality proposed by Theil (1967) derives from the notion of entropy in information theory. The entropy measure, T, is given by:

$$T = \sum_{i=1}^{n} s_i[\log s_i - \log(1 / n)]$$

where s_i is the share of the ith group in total income, and n is the total number of income groups. The index has a potential range from zero to infinity, with higher values (greater entropy) indicating more equal distribution of income.

OTHER MEASURES

The decile ratio was calculated by taking the income earned by the top 10% of households and dividing by the income earned by the bottom 10% of households. The proportions of income earned by the bottom 50%, 60%, and 70% of households were calculated from the cumulative percentage distributions of total aggregate income in each state.

Adjustment for Taxes,
Transfers, and Household Size

The income data in the present study were based upon *gross* income, and were not adjusted for fed-

eral and state taxes, or near-cash subsidies (such as food stamps, school lunches). Our focus on pre-tax incomes was justified on the grounds that the major part of income inequality in the United States is explained by the distribution of *pre-tax* incomes, and that taxes and transfers have a relatively modest impact on income distribution (Krugman, 1994). Moreover, since our unit of analysis was individual states within the U.S., the same federal income tax rates applied to households across states.

The income inequality measures in the present study were also unadjusted for household size. There was no relationship of average household size within a state to median income, poverty rates, mortality rates, or to measures of income inequality. Thus, household size was unlikely to be a confounding factor in the relationship of income inequality to mortality.

Nonetheless, in a sensitivity analysis, we did examine the effects of income distribution adjusted for both taxes and transfers, as well as household size. This was made possible by obtaining unpublished statistics courtesy of the Luxembourg Income Study (Timothy Smeeding, Project Director, personal communication). In this sensitivity analysis, we utilized the state-specific Gini coefficients calculated from disposable income, which adjusted for federal and state income and payroll taxes, and also accounted for cash or near-cash benefits including food stamps, the Earned Income Tax Credit (EITC), and school lunches. Adjustment for household size was accomplished using a household equivalence scale, which relates economic well-being (W) (or "adjusted income") to disposable income (D) and household size (S) in the following manner:

$$W = D/S^E$$

where E is the equivalence elasticity, which varies between 0 and 1. The value $E = 0$ corresponds to no adjustment for household size, while for $E > 0$, economies of scale are assumed, which reduce as E is increased, giving more generous "equivalents" for additional family members

(Buhmann *et al.*, 1988; Aronson *et al.*, 1994). For the purposes of the sensitivity analysis in the present study, E was set at 0.5, which is the established practice in the Luxembourg Income Study (Atkinson *et al.*, 1995), and provides a useful contrast between per capita income ($E = 1.0$), and no adjustment for household size ($E = 0$). Data for the adjusted Gini coefficients were calculated from the pooled 1991, 1992, and 1993 Current Population Surveys (Luxembourg Income Study, unpublished data).

Data Analysis

Ordinary least squares regress was used to examine the relationships of the various inequality measures to total mortality rates, adjusting for median income and poverty rates.

Results

THE means and standard deviations of the different income inequality measures for the U.S. are shown in Table 1. These data con-

firm reports that the degree of income inequality is high in the United States compared to other countries (Atkinson and Micklewright, 1993; Atkinson *et al.*, 1995). As expected, the choice of income aversion parameter (ε) in the Atkinson Index made a difference to the magnitude, though not the ranking, of the levels of inequality in each state. The higher the value of ε, the greater the implied social welfare loss due to inequality in the distribution of income, and hence the higher the value of the Atkinson Index.

All income inequality measures were very highly correlated with each other—in no instance did the correlation coefficient fall below 0.86 (Table 2). The Atkinson Index (ε = 2.0) was most strongly correlated with total mortality rates ($r = 0.66$), followed closely by the decile ratio ($r = 0.65$) (Table 3). The inequality indicators used in two recent published reports—the Robin Hood Index (Kennedy *et al.*, 1996), the Gini coefficient (Kennedy *et al.*, 1996), and the proportion of total income earned by the bottom

Table 1

Mean, standard deviation, and range of income inequality measures in 50 U.S. states, 1990

Income inequality measure	Mean	Standard deviation	Range
Gini	0.43	0.02	0.38–0.48
Decile ratio	28.47	6.81	18.65–49.07
Bottom 50%[a]	20.94	1.39	17.52–23.59
Bottom 60%[a]	29.79	1.61	15.94–32.87
Bottom 70%[a]	40.49	1.74	36.55–43.85
Robin Hood	30.22	1.61	27.13–34.05
Atkinson ε = 2	0.55	0.05	0.47–0.67
Atkinson ε = 0.5	0.15	0.02	0.12–0.19
Theil	0.13	0.01	0.10–0.16

[a]Percentage of total income accruing to bottom 50%, 60%, and 70% of households.

Table 2

Correlations among income inequality measures, 1990 U.S. data

	Gini	Decile ratio	Bottom 50%	Bottom 60%	Bottom 70%	Robin Hood	Atkinson ε = 2	Atkinson ε = 0.5	Theil
Gini	1.00	0.95	−0.98	−0.99	−1.0	0.99	0.95	0.99	1.00
Decile ratio		1.00	−0.96	−0.96	−0.94	0.96	0.99	0.97	0.86
Bottom 50%[a]			1.00	1.00	−0.98	−0.99	−0.98	−0.99	−0.97
Bottom 60%[a]				1.00	0.99	−1.00	−0.96	−1.00	−0.99
Bottom 70%[a]					1.00	−0.99	−0.94	−0.99	−1.00
Robin Hood						1.00	0.96	0.99	0.99
Atkinson ε = 2							1.00	0.97	0.94
Atkinson ε = 0.5								1.00	0.99
Theil									1.00

[a]Percentage of total income accruing to bottom 50%, 60%, and 70% of households.

50% of households (Kaplan *et al.*, 1996)—were among the measures less strongly correlated with total mortality (Pearson coefficients ranging from 0.51 to 0.58). Thus, there is no evidence to indicate that the authors somehow selected the inequality measures that provided strongest support for their hypothesis.

All the income inequality measures were correlated with poverty rates, as well as, to a lesser extent, median household income (Table 3). However, in multiple regression models adjusting for both poverty and median income, all inequality indicators were strongly associated with increased total mortality rates (Table 4). For example, a one unit increment in the Gini was associated with an increase in total mortality rates of 12.9 deaths per 100,000 (95% confidence interval: 2.0–23.8). The amount of variance in total mortality explained by the models ranged from 0.22 (proportion of total income earned by the bottom 70% of households) to 9.51 (decile ratio).

Adjustment for Taxes, Transfers, and Household Size

As expected, the Gini coefficients adjusted for taxes, transfers, and household size indicated a lower degree of income dispersion within states, compared to the unadjusted Gini coefficients. Nonetheless, there was a strong correlation between the adjusted and unadjusted Gini values (r = 0.73; P < 0.0001) (Fig. 2). Moreover, the correlation between the adjusted Gini coefficient and total mortality rates remained essentially unchanged compared to the unadjusted Gini coefficients (r = 0.54; P < 0.0001) (Table 5; Fig. 3). Similarly, the size of the regression coefficient for the adjusted Gini coefficient on mortality (β = 15.71; 95% confidence interval: 6.08–25.33; R^2 = 0.30) was very similar to the unadjusted Gini results (β = 12.91; 95% confidence interval: 2.01–23.81; R^2 = 0.23). Based on this sensitivity analysis, we therefore concluded that the income inequality/mortality link was unlikely to be ex-

plained by any biases resulting from not adjusting for taxes, transfers or household size.

Discussion

THE present study provides further empirical evidence for the relationship between income inequality and mortality. The fact that a broad range of standardly used income distribution indicators showed statistically significant associations with mortality provides some counterweight to recent concerns voiced about potential investigator bias in the choice of income inequality indicators (Judge, 1995). An analysis of data from 13 OECD countries failed to detect any relationship between life expectancy and several income distribution measures. The author commented that:

> Many other indicators of income distribution could be computed for this group of 13 countries and so it is not possible to rule out the possibility that one or more of them might be found to be associated with life expectancy. However, seeking for such associations would be a fruitless exercise in the absence of any theoretical rationale for selecting one indicator rather than another (Judge, 1995, p. 1284).

In practice, however, all income distribution measures were highly correlated with each other, so that the choice of indicator was unlikely to have influenced the conclusions reached in previous empirical tests of the income inequality hypothesis (Wilkinson, 1986, 1992, 1994; Kennedy *et al.*, 1996; Kaplan *et al.*, 1996). According to Wilkinson, the international evidence on income inequality and mortality appear to be sensitive to the response rates to income surveys in individual countries (Wilkinson, 1996). In the Luxembourg Income Study, countries with more equitable income distributions also tended to have poor response rates (<70%) to income surveys. Performing regression analyses without correcting for this non-response bias resulted in an attenuation of the income inequality/mortality link (Wilkinson, 1996). However, non-response bias was not

Table 3

Correlations of income inequality measures to median household income,
poverty rates, and total mortality rates

Income inequality measure	Median household income	Poverty rate (%)	Total mortality rate
Gini	− 0.42	0.67	0.51
Decile ratio	− 0.42	0.71	0.65
Bottom 50%[a]	0.49	− 0.75	− 0.58
Bottom 60%[a]	0.47	− 0.73	− 0.54
Bottom 70%[a]	0.42	− 0.69	− 0.50
Robin Hood	− 0.47	0.73	0.54
Atkinson $\epsilon = 2$	− 0.44	0.71	0.66
Atkinson $\epsilon = 0.5$	− 0.41	0.69	0.56
Theil	− 0.38	0.65	0.52

[a]Percentage of total income accruing to bottom 50%, 60%, and 70% of households.

Table 4

Relationships between income inequality measures and age-adjusted total mortality rates,
adjusted for median income and poverty rates

Income inequality measure	Regression coefficient[b]	95% confidence interval	*t*-statistic	*P*-value	R^2
Gini	12.91	2.01 to 23.81	2.32	0.02	0.23
Decile ratio	7.34	4.03 to 10.65	5.83	0.0001	0.39
Bottom 50%[a]	− 28.40	− 46.32 to − 10.49	− 3.11	0.003	0.29
Bottom 60%[a]	− 20.94	− 36.44 to − 5.43	− 2.65	0.01	0.26
Bottom 70%[a]	− 15.27	− 29.14 to − 1.41	− 2.16	0.04	0.22
Robin Hood	20.88	5.39 to 36.37	2.64	0.01	0.25
Atkinson $\epsilon = 2$	10.59	5.94 to 15.23	4.47	0.0001	0.40
Atkinson $\epsilon = 0.5$	23.07	7.69 to 38.44	2.94	0.005	0.28
Theil	20.80	3.62 to 37.97	2.37	0.02	0.24

[a]Percentage of total income accruing to bottom 50%, 60%, and 70% of households;
[b] regression coefficient for a one increment in inequality score, from multiple linear regression.

an issue in the U.S. data, where the response rate is about 95%.

Adjusting income for taxes and transfers is an important prerequisite to making valid international comparisons of income distribution. However, the U.S. evidence is neither influenced by taxes/transfers, nor differences in household size.

A more salient consideration in the choice of income distribution indicator is the differential

Table 5

Sensitivity analysis: relationships of adjusted and unadjusted Gini coefficient to median household income, poverty, and total mortality

	Median household income	Poverty rate (%)	Total mortality rate
Unadjusted Gini	− 0.42	0.67	0.51
Adjusted Gini[a]	− 0.15	0.42	0.54

[a]Adjusted for income and payroll taxes, cash and near-cash benefits, and household size (using equivalence elasticity $E = 0.05$).

sensitivity of alternative measures in detecting the effects of economic policies on income distribution. It is well documented that the various measures perform differently under alternative types of income transfers. For example, the Gini coefficient is much less sensitive to an income

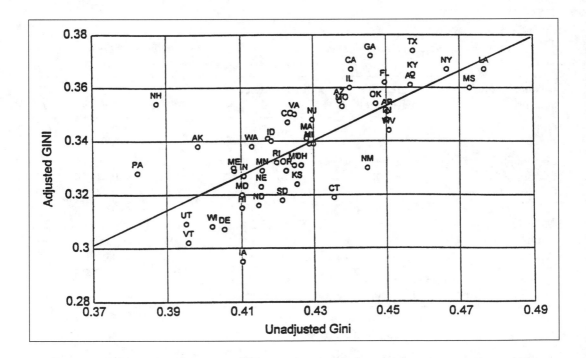

Figure 2

Scatterplot of unadjusted Gini coefficients to Gini coefficients adjusted for income and payroll taxes, cash and near-cash benefits, and household size (using equivalence elasticity, $E = 0.5$) ($r = 0.73$, $P < 0.0001$) (unpublished data courtesy of the Luxembourg Income Study).

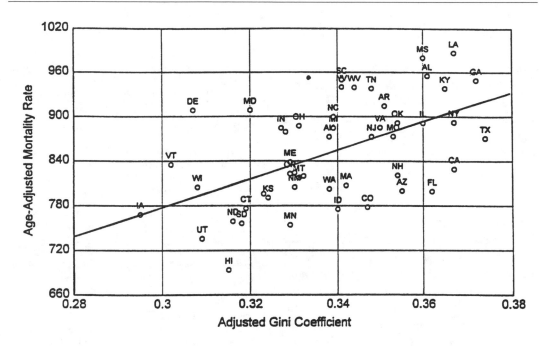

Figure 3
Scatterplot of adjusted Gini coefficients to total age-adjusted mortality rates within the U.S., 1990
($r = 0.54$, $P < 0.0001$).

transfer from a better off household to a less well off household if the two households lie near the middle of the income distribution than at either tail of the distribution (Cowell, 1977). Even more potentially problematic is the Robin Hood Index, which fails to register transfers from a well off household to a less well off household provided both lie on the same side of the mean income (Sen, 1973; Cowell, 1977). In other words, even if a policy achieves *some* redistribution in income from the more to the less well off, but the transfer occurs between household units below (or above) the mean income, then the overall value of the Robin Hood Index would remain unchanged. In this instance, the Robin Hood Index is clearly not the ideal indicator to evaluate

the impact of social policies, even though it may perform equally as well as the other indicators in demonstrating the existence of a basic relationship between income inequality and mortality.

The Atkinson Index is less susceptible to the above types of problems, and has the added advantage of incorporating explicit normative judgements about the social preference for income equality (Sen, 1973; Cowell, 1977). Higher values of the parameter, ϵ, denotes higher degrees of aversion to inequality, such that when ϵ equals infinity, society would give total priority to equality over any objective of raising incomes generally. Social welfare would then be determined solely by the position of the least advantaged in society. It is of interest to note that the

Atkinson Index using the higher value of the income aversion parameter (ϵ = 2.0) showed a stronger correlation with mortality rates (r = 0.66 vs 0.56 when ϵ = 0.5), as well as explained more of the variance in mortality in regression models (R^2 = 0.40 vs 0.28). In other words, the version of the index implying higher social welfare loss from inequality also correlated better with loss in welfare measured in health terms.

In summary, a theoretical justification for the choice of indicator is critical in assessing the impact of social and economic policies on income distribution and mortality. On the other hand, there is little evidence to suggest that the choice of indicator would have resulted in a different (i.e. negative) conclusion being reached about the cross-sectional relationship of income inequality to mortality. Given the fact that wealth in society is markedly more unequally distributed compared to income (for example, 1% of Americans own 40% of the aggregate wealth) (Wolff, 1995), further research should examine the association of mortality to the distribution of wealth.

This paper is dedicated to the memory of Sol Levine (1922–1996), Ph.D., whose encouragement and intellectual vision guided our research.

REFERENCES

Aronson, J. R., Johnson, P. and Lambert, P. J. (1994) Redistributive effect and unequal income tax treatment. *Economic Journal* **104**, 262–270.

Atkinson, A. B. (1970) On the measurement of inequality. *Journal of Economic Theory* **2**, 244–263.

Atkinson, A. B. and Micklewright, J. (1993) *Economic Transformation in Eastern Europe and the Distribution of Income*. Cambridge University Press, Cambridge.

Atkinson, A. B., Rainwater, L. and Smeeding, M. (1995) *Income Distribution in OECD Countries. Evidence from the Luxembourg Income Study*. Organization for Economic Cooperation and Development, Paris.

Black, D., Morris, J. N., Smith, C., Townsend, P. and Whitehead, M. (1988) *Inequalities in Health: The Black Report; The Health Divide*. Penguin, London.

Buhmann, B., Rainwater, L., Schmauss, G. and Smeeding, T. (1988) Equivalence scales, well-being, inequality and poverty: sensitivity estimates across 10 countries using the LIS database. *Review of Income and Wealth* **34**, 115–142.

Cowell, F. A. (1977) *Measuring Inequality*. Allan, Oxford.

Friede, A., Reid, J. A. and Ory, H .W. (1993) CDC WONDER: a comprehensive on-line public health information system of the Centers for Disease Control and Prevention. *American Journal of Public Health* **83**, 1289–1294.

Judge, K. (1995) Income distribution and life expectancy: a critical appraisal. *British Medical Journal* **311**, 1282–1285.

Kaplan, G. A., Pamuk, E. R., Lynch, J. W., Cohen, R. D., Balfour, J. L. (1996) Inequality in income and mortality in the United States: analysis of mortality and potential pathways. *British Medical Journal* **312**, 999–1003.

Kawachi, I., Levine, S., Miller, S. M., Lasch, K. and Amick, B., III (1994) *Income Inequality and Life Expectancy — Theory, Research and Policy*. Society and Health Working Paper Series No. 94–2, Harvard School of Public Health, Boston.

Kennedy, B. P., Kawachi, I. and Prothrow-Stith, D. (1996) Income distribution and mortality: cross-sectional ecological study of the Robin Hood Index in the United States. *British Medical Journal* **312**, 1004–1007 [also published *erratum*: (1996) *British Medical Journal* **312**, 1194].

Krugman, P. (1994) *Peddling Prosperity*. Norton, New York.

Sen, A. (1973) *On Economic Inequality*. Oxford University Press, Oxford.

Theil, H. (1967) *Economic and Information Theory*. North Holland, Amsterdam.

U.S. Bureau of the Census (1993) *Income and Poverty*, CD-ROM. U.S. Bureau of the Census, Washington, DC.

Wilkinson, R. G. (1986) Income distribution and infant mortality. In *Class and Health: Research and Longitudinal Data*, ed. R. G. Wilkinson. Tavistock, London.

Wilkinson, R. G. (1992) Income distribution and life expectancy. *British Medical Journal* **304**, 165–168.

Wilkinson, R. G. (1994) Health, redistribution and growth. In *Paying for Inequality: The Economic Cost of Social Injustice*, eds. A. Glyn and D. Miliband. Rivers Oram Press, London.

Wilkinson, R. G. (1996) *Unhealthy Societies. The Afflictions of Inequality*. Routledge, London.

Wolff, E. N. (1995) *Top Heavy. A Study of the Increasing Inequality of Wealth in America*. 20th Century Fund Press, New York.

World Bank (1993) *World Development Report 1993*. Oxford University Press, New York.

☙

Fourteen

INCOME DISTRIBUTION
AND CAUSE-SPECIFIC MORTALITY

Sandra J. McIsaac and Richard G. Wilkinson

ABSTRACT

The aim was to identify the age-, sex- and cause-specific premature mortality rates contributing to the association between life expectancy and income distribution in developed countries. Income distribution was calculated for the 13 OECD countries and years for which the Luxembourg Income Study held data. The potential years of life lost (1–65 years) by sex and cause, as well as the age- and sex-specific all-cause mortality rates and standardized mortality ratios for children 1–19 years were calculated from data supplied by the WHO. On finding evidence suggesting that reported income distribution is strongly affected by low response rates in some income surveys, we used 2 measures of income distribution: that among households where the 'head of household' was aged less than 65 years (weighted by response rates) and that among households with children (among whom response rates are thought to be higher). Partial correlations and regressions controlling for the year were used to analyse the relationship between mortality and income distribution. Both measures of income distribution showed broadly similar results. A more egalitarian distribution of income was related to lower all-cause mortality rates in both sexes in most age groups. All 6 major categories of cause of death contributed to this relationship. The causes of premature mortality contributing most were road accidents, chronic liver disease and cirrhosis, infections, ischaemic heart disease among women and other injuries among men. Income distribution was associated not only with larger absolute changes in mortality from these causes, but also with larger proportionate changes. Suicides and stomach cancer tended to be more common in more egalitarian countries.

THERE is evidence from a number of sources of a close association between the distribution of income within countries and the average life expectancy. This was first demonstrated by Rodgers[1] using data from around 1965 from 56 developed and less-developed countries. Le Grand[2] reported that the average age of death in a group of 17 developed countries was related to income distribution. Analysing data from 70 rich and poor countries Waldmann[3] found that if the real income of the poorest 20% of the population is statistically held constant, increases in the incomes of the richest 5% are associated with rising rates of infant mortality. Using mid-century data from some 20 countries at various stages of development Steckel[4] has shown that income distribution is an important determinant of height. He reported that the effect on height of a doubling of per capita income could be offset by 'a modest rise of 0.066 in the Gini coefficient' of income inequality.[5] Wennemo[6] has shown very close relationships between infant mortality

Originally published in *European Journal of Public Health*, 1997.

rates in developed countries and relative poverty. In a study of 59 countries Flegg[7] found that income distribution had an important effect on infant mortality which was independent of the effects not only of variations in GDP per capita, but also of the provision of doctors and nurses and of maternal education. These factors appeared to play much the same role in the determination of infant mortality rates in developed and in less-developed countries. Wilkinson[8, 9] has reported relationships between income distribution and life expectancy on 2 sets of cross-sectional data and 3 sets of data on changes over time—all among developed market economies. Working independently, both Kaplan et al.[10] and Kennedy et al.[11] have found income distribution and life expectancy to be closely associated within the 50 states of the United States, even after controlling for average incomes, absolute poverty and race.

In total, at least 8 different research workers or groups have reported statistically significant relationships between income distribution and measures of mortality and a ninth has reported a relationship with height. Of these 9, 1 has used data exclusively on developing countries,[7] 3 on a mixture of developed and developing countries[1, 3-5] and 5 exclusively on developed countries.[2, 6, 8-11] In all, the relationships with mortality have been shown using 10 separate sets of income distribution data. The association has been found to be independent of fertility, maternal literacy and education in developing countries and of average incomes, absolute poverty, racial differences, smoking and various measures of the provision of medical services in developed countries.[2-4, 10, 11]

To our knowledge no attempt to break down the association between income distribution and life expectancy or all-causes mortality into the component age-, sex- and cause-specific mortality rates has yet been published. This paper is intended to provide that analysis for a group of developed countries in the hope that it might shed light on the processes linking income distribution and mortality. We report here on premature mortality in the population aged under 65 years. This approximates the division between the population of working age, primarily dependent on earnings and the retired population dependent on pensions. Recent evidence suggests that in a number of developed countries widening income differences during the 1980s have been associated particularly with a widening of differences in earnings.[12]

Data and Methods

INCOME distribution data were taken from the Luxembourg Income Study (LIS) which holds electronic records of surveys of household incomes supplied by national governments. After some data preparation to improve international comparability, LIS makes SPSS data files available for analysis via electronic mail. While additional data sets are added from time to time, at the start of this project LIS provided access to data from some 16 developed countries for between 1 and 5 non-consecutive years between 1967–1991. We confined our analysis to 13 counties which are members of the Organization for Economic Cooperation and Development (OECD)—the rich marker economies. The 33 combinations of countries and years of data are shown in *table 1*. Because the aim was not to test the relationship but to identify the contributory age-specific and cause-specific mortality rates, we decided to use all the information available for these countries despite the recognition that several observations from the same country should not be regarded as truly independent. Observations which were always several years apart and sometimes spanned as much as 20 years were likely to contain valuable additional information which, given the paucity of data, should not be lost. Shares of personal disposable income (after taxes and benefits), were computed for each decile of the population, from the poorest to the richest, in each country at each date. To allow for the economies of scale accruing to households of 2 or more people, household income was adjusted for household size using the LIS 'subjective' equivalence scales (from surveys of incomes thought necessary 'to get along').[13] As a result of problems of the response rates in national surveys of household income (explained below) two sets of income distribution data were used: one confined to the distribution of income among households where the 'head of household' was under 65 years old (HHLT65) and another for all households with children aged 18 years and under (CHILDHSE). We calculated the proportion of income received by each decile within these populations.

The death rates for the countries and years shown in *table 1* were calculated from deaths and populations supplied by the WHO from the World Health Statistics Data Bank. Data for Germany prior to unification were missing. We calculated 14 age-specific 'all-causes' death rates for infants, 1–4 years and for the 12 remaining 5 year age groups to 64 years of age for males and females separately. In addition we used 2 summary measures of mortality across age groups: standardized mortality ratios for children 1–19 years and potential years of life lost (PYLL) from deaths occurring between the ages of 1 and 65 years for all causes combined and for each of the causes listed in *table 2*. Both were standardized on the total OECD population in 1985. The PYLL sum the differences between ages at death and 65 years according to formula 2.4 given by Romeder and McWhinnie[14] and are expressed per 100,000 of the standard population.

It is clear that there is an important long-term decline in mortality which continues even when income distribution is unchanged. We believe that changes in income distribution are among the factors which may affect the rate of this improvement. To remove the background difference in mortality associated simply with the different years for which data were available (*table 1*), all correlations reported below are first-order partial correlations controlling for the year and the year was entered in all regressions as the first independent variable.

Table 1

Countries, years and response rates for income distribution surveys: Luxembourg Income Study

Country	Year	Response rate (%)
Canada	1971	76
	1975	76
	1981	77
	1987	76
	1991	76
United States	1974	95
	1979	95
	1986	95
Belgium	1985	92
	1988	44
France	1979	82
	1981	82
	1984	82
Finland	1987	N/A
	1991	N/A
Ireland	1987	64
Italy	1986	61
The Netherlands	1983	56
	1987	60
Norway	1979	75
	1986	78
Sweden	1967	N/A
	1975	N/A
	1981	86
	1987	86
Switzerland	1982	98
United Kingdom	1969	70
	1974	68
	1979	67
	1986	69
Australia	1981	93
	1985	94
	1989	93

Response Rates

We encountered a serious problem related to the response rates in the sample surveys of household income in different countries. Although earlier reports using data for the smaller number of

Table 2

Causes of death for which potential years of life lost 1–65 years were calculated (ICD–9 basic list)

All causes	
Infectious and parasitic diseases	(01–07)
Malignant neoplasms	(08–14)
Malignant neoplasm of stomach	(091)
Malignant neoplasm of trachea, bronchus and lung	(101)
Malignant neoplasm of female breast	(113)
Disease of the circulatory system	(25–30)
Ischaemic heart disease	(27)
Cerebrovascular disease	(29)
Diseases of the respiratory system	(31–32)
Bronchitis, emphysema and asthma	(323)
Diseases of the digestive system	(33–34)
Chronic liver disease and cirrhosis	(347)
Injury and poisoning	(E47–E56)
Motor vehicle traffic accidents	(E471)
Suicide and self-inflicted injury	(E54)

countries previously available from the LIS had shown the expected strong relationship with life expectancy,[6, 8, 9] once the countries more recently added to the LIS were included we found only weak evidence of an association. The relationship we had intended to break down into its age-, sex- and cause-specific components seemed to have largely disappeared!

As shown in *table 1*, the response rates in surveys of household income sometimes fall as low as 50%. (The response rates shown in the table were taken from the LIS country files. Where response rates were given for a country in a particular year but not in others, we have assumed that the rate remained unchanged if subsequent income surveys were part of the same series using the same methods.) We found 4 pieces of evidence suggesting that the relationship with national mortality rates was hidden by a tendency for response rates to be disproportionately low among the poor and, to a lesser extent, the rich compared to the rest of the population.

First, despite the possibility that societies with genuinely narrow income distributions might be more cohesive and thus have higher response rates, producing an association between more equality and higher response rates, the LIS data shows an inverse relationship between response rates and equality. Regression analysis showed that lower response rates were associated with higher reported shares of income received by the lower deciles and lower shares by the higher deciles. The ratio of income received by the bottom 30% to the top 30% of households was significantly correlated (r-0.35, p=0.03) with non-response rates (*figure 1*). This suggests that low response rates may lose the poor and/or the rich and lead to an underestimation of the extent of income inequality. Although a genuinely narrow income distribution may be reported on the basis of low response rates, the conspicuous lack of data above the diagonal in *figure 1* shows that no country except Ireland has reported a wide income distribution using a survey with low response rates. It is also notable that Belgium is the only country to report a similar income distribution with very different response rates. Whereas other countries conduct new surveys at each date, the 1988 Belgium survey was a follow-up of people who had responded to the 1985 survey. The non-response here was, unlike that in other countries, a failure to contact people who had previously responded.

Second, when countries were weighted by the square of the proportion responding (the square was chosen not by inspection but in order to discount countries with low response rates more heavily) the expected relationship between mortality and income distribution appeared (see *table 3*).

Third, the Family Expenditure Survey, which is the source of the British data held by the LIS, has been found to underrepresent the poor and, to a lesser extent, the rich. Its response rates decrease with age, are lower among those born in Northern Ireland, the 'new commonwealth' and Pakistan and are lower among households with

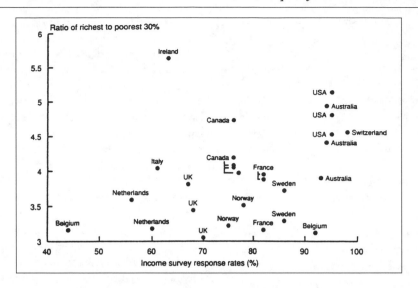

Figure 1
Relation between income survey response rate and ratio of incomes of richest and poorest 30%

more than two cars.[15] Response rates are also low among the self-employed who are known to be concentrated at both extremes of the income distribution.[16] Nor is the pattern of lower response rates among rich and poor unique to Britain.[17] Studies of response rates in social surveys more generally suggest that resentment of an invasion of privacy is among the most common reasons

Table 3

Partial correlation coefficients (controlling for year) between mortality measures and the proportion of income received by the poorest 30% in 2 population categories

Income distribution among		Households where head is <65 years old Unweighted	Weighted	Households with children Unweighted
Male	PYLL 1–65 years	−0.19 p=0.159	−0.68 p=0.000	−0.45 p=0.005
Female	PYLL 1–65 years	−0.39 p=0.014	−0.71 p=0.000	−0.62 p=0.000
Child	SMR 1–19 years	−0.44 p=0.007	−0.73 p=0.000	−0.67 p=0.000
Infant mortality		−0.32 p=0.039	−0.50 p=0.004	−0.53 p=0.001

PYLL: potential years of life lost
SMR: standardized mortality rates

for non-response and people are more likely to object to questions about money than almost any other subject.[18] Reluctance to cooperate on these grounds may be more common among people whose incomes lie outside the normal range.

The fourth pointer concerns households with children which is the largest group for whom response rates were consistently high in the Family Expenditure Survey.[13] Measures of the distribution of income exclusively among families with children were found to be strongly related to mortality rates whether or not the data was weighted. *Table 3* shows the weighted and unweighted correlations between various mortality rates and the share of income received by the poorest 30% in the HHLT65 and CHILDHSE income distributions.

In all analyses below we show how mortality is related to income distribution both among HHLT65 (weighted) and among CHILDHSE (unweighted) groups. This allows the results of 2 quite different ways of dealing with low response rates to be compared: the first discounts countries with low response rates and the second measures income distribution among families with children who are known to have higher response rates than the rest of the population. In terms of coverage, the former is more appropriate to mortality measured by PYLL before age 65 years, but a preference for unweighted data makes it desirable to include the CHILDHSE group though it covers 30–40% fewer people in most countries. Because of the large number of single mothers, the CHILDHSE group will cover a much smaller proportion of single men than women. This may be why the correlation between CHILDHSE and PYLL is not only weaker for men than women, but is weaker for men against CHILDHSE than against HHLT65 (*table 3*). As information was lacking on response rates in Finland and the first 2 of the 4 Swedish surveys (*table 1*), these cases are excluded from the weighted HHLT65 data.

RESULTS

Decile shares

Which part of the income distribution is most closely related to mortality? *Table 4* shows the strength of correlations between 3 all-causes mortality rates (infant mortality, SMRs 1–19 years and PYLL before age 65 years) and the share of income received by each decile separately. Correlations are negative among the poorer deciles showing that mortality rates tend to be lower where less well-off people receive a larger share of income. This pattern is reversed giving positive correlations among the richer deciles.

If the decile shares of income are *cumulated* to show the proportion of income received by everyone below the second, third, fourth decile, etc., the pattern of correlations with mortality reach their strongest with the proportion of income received by the poorest 30% (*table 5*). However, in contrast to the picture for separate deciles, when accumulating the proportion of income received across deciles, the correlation

Table 4

Partial correlations (controlling for year) between potential years of life lost from 'all causes' of death and shares of income received by each decile taken separately

Decile	HHLT65 Weighted		CHILDHSE Unweighted	
	Male	Female	Male	Female
1	−0.58**	−0.54**	−0.38*	−0.52**
2	−0.69**	−0.76**	−0.50**	−0.68**
3	−0.64**	−0.69**	−0.44**	−0.61**
4	−0.49**	−0.49**	−0.29	−0.43*
5	−0.28	−0.24	−0.12	−0.20
6	−0.02	+0.07	+0.15	+0.11
7	+0.24	+0.37*	+0.40*	+0.51**
8	+0.47**	+0.63**	+0.45*	+0.67**
9	+0.61**	+0.73**	+0.43*	+0.66**
10	+0.36*	+0.27	+0.21	+0.29

* p<0.05, ** p<0.01

Table 5

Partial correlations (controlling for year) between potential years of life lost from 'all causes' of death and the accumulated share of income received by population below successive deciles from the poorest upwards

Decile	HHLT65 Weighted		CHILDHSE Unweighted	
	Male	Female	Male	Female
1	−0.58**	−0.53**	−0.38*	−0.51**
2	−0.63**	−0.68**	−0.45*	−0.60**
3	−0.68**	−0.71**	−0.45*	−0.62**
4	−0.67**	−0.69**	−0.43*	−0.60**
5	−0.64**	−0.66**	−0.41*	−0.57**
6	−0.60**	−0.60**	−0.37*	−0.53**
7	−0.56**	−0.54**	−0.33	−0.48**
8	−0.49**	−0.44*	−0.29	−0.41*
9	−0.36*	−0.27	−0.21	−0.29

* p<0.05, ** p<0.01

weakens beyond the third but remains negative right up to the ninth.

Although the all-causes mortality rate is most closely related to the proportion of income received by the poorest 30%, each specific cause has its own pattern. *Table 6* shows the deciles over which the cumulated share of income is most clearly related to cause-specific mortality. Traffic accidents, for example, are most closely related to the share of income received by the poorest 20 or 30% (deciles 0−2 or 0−3) in each sex on both CHILDHSE and HHLT65. Here the correlations were close to 0.7 in all cases. Only statistically significant correlations (p<0.05) are shown in *table 6*.

Age and Sex

figures 2 and *3* show the correlations between the age-specific death rates at 0−65 years and the share of income received by the poorest 30% of the population. Correlations are strongest among children and younger adults but a more equitabale distribution of income is associated with lower mortality at most ages. The association weakens after age 25, particularly among men on the CHILDHSE income distribution.

This may partly reflect the exclusion of adults in households without children from these income figures. As in *tables 4* and *5*, the associations are slightly stronger with female than male mortality when using the CHILDHSE income distribution, but there is no clear sex difference when using income among HHLT65.

Causes of Death

The non-standardized regression coefficients showing the relation between changes in the share of income received by the bottom 30% of people among HHLT65 and CHILDHSE and PYLL from each cause are shown in the bar chart in *figure 4*. These provide estimates of the contributions of the different causes to the association between income distribution and the all-causes death rates. In both sexes and on both measures of income distribution, chronic liver diseases and cirrhosis, traffic accidents and infections come within the top 4 contributory causes. Eleven of the 12 regression coefficients for these 3 causes of death (for each sex on both measures of income distribution) were statistically significant: the exception was chronic liver disease and cirrhosis among women which just failed to

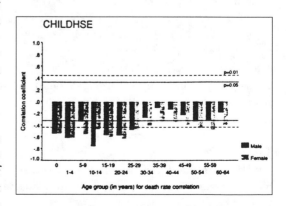

Figure 2

Partial correlations (controlling for year) between age-specific death rates and income share received by the poorest 30%

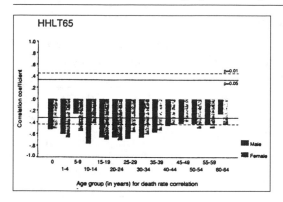

Figure 3
Partial correlations (controlling for year) between age-specific death rates and income share received by the poorest 30%

reach significance (p=0.06) in relation to the HHLT65 income share.

Among women but not among men, the contribution of ischaemic heart disease deaths and 'other' causes is statistically significant on both measures of income distribution. Among men the contribution of cancers is statistically significant against the CHILDHSE income share and deaths from 'other injuries' is significant on the HHLT65 income share.

Taking the PYLL from each cause per 100,000 of the OECD population as 100%, *figures 5* and *6* show the estimated percentage reduction in each cause associated with a 5% increase in the income share of the least well-off 30%. The percentage reductions in each cause associated with this decrease in relative deprivation tend to be larger in relation to HHLT65 than CHILDHSE. However, it is apparent on both bases that chronic liver diseases and cirrhosis, traffic accidents and infections are important contributors to the all-causes association partly because the conditions are disproportionately sensitive to changes in income distribution. Compared to CHILDHSE, income shares among HHLT65 are associated with bigger reductions in ischaemic heart disease, particularly

among women and in other injuries, particularly among men. The estimated impact on cancers, respiratory and 'other' causes is small on both bases.

DISCUSSION

THROUGHOUT this analysis levels of statistical significance must be treated with extreme caution. The requirement that observations are independent is compromised in the associations between mortality and HHLT65 income shares by weighting data and in all measures of association by the fact that wherever it was available (*table 1*) several years of income distribution data have been included for the same country. Although it is impossible to show weighted data in the form of a scattergram, *figure 7* shows the unweighted relation between CHILDHSE and childhood SMRs (1–19 years) recorded in *table 4*. Inspection shows that the relation is not dependent on outliers or on the points for any single country.

We believe that the importance of the underlying issues and the lack of better internationally comparable income distribution data justifies the flawed methods we have been obliged to use here. Indeed, we believe that it may not be possible to take analysis of these issues much further on the basis of international data currently available. The relationship between all-causes mortality and income distribution was well established: our purpose was merely to gain some insight into its age-, sex- and cause-specific components. The fact that the 2 measures of income distribution show broadly similar relationships to mortality (see *table 6* and *figures 4–6*), despite the major differences between them, suggests that the findings are fairly robust. Not only are the populations included in HHLT65 and CHILDHSE substantially different, but the weighting of HHLT65 discounts the data from countries with low response rates and shows again that the relationship is not wholly dependent on which groups of countries are examined.

Table 6

Maximum partial correlations (controlling for year) found between causes of death (PYLL) and the income shares received by various deciles. The range of deciles shows which part of the income distribution was most closely associated with mortality for each cause

PYLL by cause	Incomes among	Males Deciles	Males Correlation	Females Deciles	Females Correlation
All causes	CHILDHSE	0–3	−0.45	0–3	−0.62
	HHLT65	0–3	−0.68	0–3	−0.71
Infections	CHILDHSE	0–6	−0.35	0–3	−0.36
	HHLT65	0–6	−0.41	0–4	−0.47
Neoplasms	CHILDHSE	0–9	−0.62	0–4	−0.33
	HHLT65	0–9	−0.47	-	ns
Stomach neoplasms	CHILDHSE	0–1	+0.36	0–2	+0.67
	HHLT65	0–1	+0.56	0–2	+0.66
Lung neoplasms	CHILDHSE	0–7	−0.48	0–2	−0.49
	HHLT65	0–8	−0.39	0–2	−0.48
Breast neoplasms	CHILDHSE	-	-	0–6	−0.40
	HHLT65	-	-	-	ns
Circulatory diseases	CHILDHSE	-	ns	0–3	−0.39
	HHLT65	0–2	−0.43	0–3	−0.50
IHD	CHILDHSE	-	ns	0–2	−0.40
	HHLT65	0–2	−0.32	0–2	−0.53
CVD	CHILDHSE	-	ns	-	ns
	HHLT65	-	ns	-	ns
Respiratory diseases	CHILDHSE	-	ns	-	ns
	HHLT65	-	ns	-	ns
Digestive diseases	CHILDHSE	0–5	−0.32	0–5	−0.49
	HHLT65	0–5	−0.40	0–7	−0.44
Liver disease and cirrhosis	CHILDHSE	0–5	−0.36	0–5	−0.42
	HHLT65	0–5	−0.40	0–8	−0.36
Traffic accidents	CHILDHSE	0–2	−0.72	0–2	−0.68
	HHLT65	0–3	−0.68	0–2	−0.73
Suicide	CHILDHSE	0–6	+0.37	0–3	+0.55
	HHLT65	-	ns	0–3	+0.35
Other injury	CHILDHSE	-	ns	-	ns
	HHLT65	0–1	−0.63	0–1	−0.43

PYLL: potential years of life lost
IHD: ischaemic heart disease
CVD: cerebrovascular disease

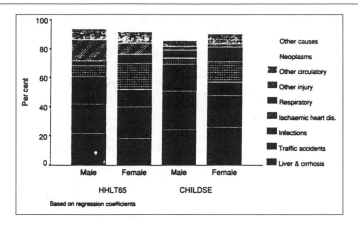

Figure 4
Cause-specific contributions to the association between potential years of life lost from all causes and the proportion of income received by the poorest 30%

The evidence suggests that the association between income distribution and mortality is spread over most of life. The variations in the strength of the association across the age range may be partly a reflection of differences in the age groups covered by HHLT65 and CHILDHSE and may also reflect the known tendency for response rates to decline with age.[13]

Although male mortality has sometimes appeared the more closely related of the 2 sexes to socioeconomic factors, our results provide no evidence that this is true in relation to income distribution. The stronger relation with female than with male mortality when using the CHILDHSE income shares (*tables 3* and *5*) may reflect the larger number of women included in

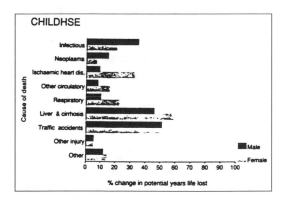

Figure 5
Per cent reduction in potential years of life lost from each cause associated with a 5% increase in income share received by the poorest 30%

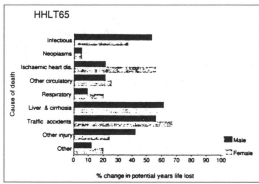

Figure 6
Per cent change in potential years of life lost associated with 5% change in share of income received by the poorest 30%

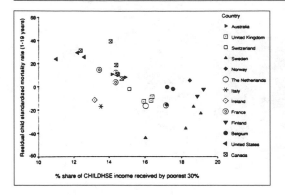

Figure 7
Relation between child standardized mortality rates
(1–19 years) and income share received by the poorest
30% (controlling for year)

households with children by virtue of their predominance as single parents. The analysis by cause of death suggests that the contribution of traffic accidents is central, both in terms of its size and statistical significance. It might be thought that this is largely due to the fact that PYLL (1–65 years) emphasizes the main causes of death at younger ages. However, *figures 5* and *6* show that a narrowing of income distribution is also associated with a bigger percentage reduction in deaths from traffic accidents than in deaths from most other causes. The association with chronic liver disease and cirrhosis appears substantial in each analysis and may indicate a relationship between alcohol consumption and income distribution which may also contribute to traffic accidents. However deaths from causes such as hepatitis are also included in this category. Deaths from 'other injuries' among men and women are significantly related only to income shares among HHLT65. This may be because HHLT65 will include many single people, particularly men, prone to high accident rates, while CHILDHSE covers only those adults with children who are likely to adopt safer lifestyles.

Suicides, which are included in 'other injuries'

and stomach cancer both show a tendency to be more common in more egalitarian countries (*table 6*). Some weight is lent to this finding by the fact that Japan, for which data was not available from the LIS, has narrow income differentials as well as high suicide and stomach cancer rates. However, in Britain, parasuicide has been linked to unemployment among men[19] and young men's, but not young women's, suicide rates have risen rapidly.[20] An association between male suicides and unemployment would run counter to any tendency for suicide to be more common in more egalitarian societies and may explain why that relationship is statistically stronger among women than men. Durkheim[21] suggested that there were different kinds of suicide related to the degree of social integration. If our results are to be believed, 'egotistic' suicide may be less important than Durkheim[21] other categories.

The likelihood that the association between income distribution and national mortality rates is accounted for largely by an effect of income distribution on health inequalities within countries is suggested by the very strong association (r=0.87) reported by Van Doorslaer et al.[22] between inequalities in self-reported morbidity and inequalities in income in 9 European countries. Their study was able to use income and mortality data for the same individuals.

Socioeconomic differences in mortality appear in different causes of death in different countries. Perhaps the underlying socioeconomic inequalities find expression through a variety of national cultural patterns. In France, alcohol and cirrhosis are major contributors to excess mortality, but heart disease is not.[23] In Britain differentials in respiratory and cardiovascular disease have been particularly large.[24] In Finland accidents and cardivoscular disease have been important. However, our results show that as well as these differences, there are also some causes of death which are more frequently raised where income differentials are large. These may represent the most direct expressions of the effects of greater socioeconomic inequality. If we were to take the causes of excess mortality in Harlem, New York, as exemplifying the extremes of relative deprivation in the Western world, it is interesting to note how much the pattern of cause-specific mortality has in common with the pattern found in our international data.[25] The 6 highest SMRs were for deaths caused by drug dependency, homicide, alcohol, cirrhosis, disorders of newborns and infections. Much as in our data, suicide was the only 1 of 17 separate causes which was actually slightly lower in Harlem than in the United States as a whole. Kaplan et al.[10] found that wider income differences were associated with higher homicide across the 50 states of the USA and there is evidence that the same relationship holds internationally.[26] Since Durkheim,[21] it has been widely recognized that suicide and homicide tend to vary inversely with each other.[27]

It is important to note that all the major categories of cause of death show at least some reduction associated with narrower income differences. Like health inequalities themselves, income distribution appears to involve a broad spectrum of conditions. It is likely that a number of social and psychosocial pathways relate mortality to income distribution. Deaths from traffic accidents, alcohol-related deaths and deaths from other injuries make a plausible group of 'social' causes which might be affected by socioeconomic stress. It is perhaps too early to say whether psychoneuroendocrinology and psychoneuroimmunology will lend weight to the possible involvement of heart disease among women and of infections in this picture.[28-30]

The prominent position of road accidents in a group of causes of death which may reflect socioeconomic stress is interesting. Road safety is clearly diminished by aggressive and competitive driving. Could it be that the amount of courtesy and cooperative behaviour road users show each other may be a sensitive indicator of people's attitudes to other members of society as unknown fellow citizens? Do they stop to let waiting pedestrians cross? Do they allow a car from a side road to enter a queue of slow moving traffic or do they more often cut each other up in an effort to gain individual advantage? Road accidents may be an example of a cause of death which would spread the increased risks associated with socioeconomic stress throughout society. The main findings of a recent review of studies of the psychological characteristics of people with injuries from accidents showed that people classified as having 'anti-social personality disorders' were at much greater risk.[31] Those suffering 'life event stresses' were also at greater risk. The involvement of alcohol and the possible link with homicide which others have reported, might lend plausibility to the hint in our data that deaths from 'other injuries' among single men are involved. 'Other injuries' includes homicide, all non-road accidents, poisonings and a proportion of deaths related to drug abuse. Perhaps we have here the beginnings of a picture of the effects of socioeconomic stress and lack of social cohesion.

This work was funded by the Economic and Social Research Council.

NOTES

1. Rodgers GB. Income and inequality as determinants of mortality: an international cross-section analysis. Populat Studies 1979;33:343–51.

2. Le Grand J. An international comparison of inequalities in health. Welfare State Programme Discussion Paper No. 16. London: London School of Economics, 1987.

3. Waldmann RJ. Income distribution and infant mortality. A J Econ 1992;107:1283–302.

4. Steckel RH. Height and per capita income. Historical Methods 1983;16:1–7.

5. Steckel RH. Heights and health in the United States. In: Komlos J, editor. Stature, living standards and economic development. Chicago: University of Chicago Press, 1994: 153–70.

6. Wennemo I. Infant mortality, public policy and inequality: a comparison of 18 industrialised countries 1950–85. Sociol Hlth Illness 1933;15:429–46.

7. Flegg, A. Inequality of income, illiteracy, and medical care as determinants of infant mortality in developing countries. Populat Studies 1982;36:441–58.

8. Wilkinson RG. Income distribution and life expectancy. BMJ 1992;304:165–8.

9. Wilkinson RG. Health, redistribution and growth. In: Glyn A, Miliband D, editors. Paying for inequality: the economic cost of social injustice. London: Rivers Oram Press, 1994:24–43.

10. Kaplan GA, Pamuk E, Lynch JW, Cohen RD, Balfour JL. Income inequality and mortality in the United States. BMJ 1996;312:999–1003.

11. Kennedy BP, Kawachi I, Prothrow-Stith D. Income distribution and mortality: test of the Robin Hood Index in the United States, BMJ 1996;312:1004–7.

12. Fritzell J. Income inequality trends in the 1980's: a five county comparison. Acta Sociol 1993;36:47–62.

13. Buhmann B, Rainwater L, Schmaus G, Smeeding TM. Poverty: sensitivity estimates across ten countries using the Luxembourg Income Study (LIS) database. Rev Income Wealth 1988;34:115–42.

14. Romeder JM, McWhinnie JR. Potential years of life lost between ages 1 and 70: an indicator of premature mortality for health planning. Int J Epidemiol 1977;6:143–51.

15. Redpath B. Family Expenditure Survey: a second study of differential response, comparing census characteristics of FES respondents and non-respondents. Stat News 1986;72:13–6.

16. Meager N, Court C, Moralee J. Self-employment and the income distribution. Brighton: Institute of Manpower Studies, University of Sussex, 1994.

17. Wolf W. Verzerrungen durch Antwortausfalle in der Konsumerhebung 1984. Statistische Nachrichten 1988;43(11):861–7.

18. Goyder J. The silent minority: non-respondents on sample surveys. Boulder, Co: Westview Press, 1987.

19. Platt S, Kreitman N. Trends in parasuicide and unemployment among men in Edinburgh, 1968–82. BMJ 1984;289:1029–32.

20. Charlton J, Kelly S, Dunnell K, Evans B, Jenkins R. Suicide deaths in England and Wales: trends in factors associated with suicide deaths. Populat Trends 1993;71:34–42.

21. Durkheim E. In: Simpson G, editor. Suicide. London: Routledge, 1952.

22. Van Doorslaer E, Wagstaff A, Bleichrodt H, et al. Socioeconomic inequalities in health: some international comparisons. J Hlth Econ 1997. In press.

23. Kunst A, Mackenbach J. International comparisons of socio-economic inequalities in mortality. Soc Sci Med 1997. In press.

24. Leclerc A, Lert F, Fabien C. Differential mortality: some comparisons between England and Wales, Finland and France, based on inequality measures. Int J Epidemiol 1990;19:1001–10.

25. McCord C, Freeman HP. Excess mortality in Harlem. New Engl J Med 1990;322:173–7.

26. Krahn H, Hartnagel TF, Gartrell JW. Income inequality and homicide rates: cross-national data and criminological theories. Criminology 1986:24:269–95.

27. James O. Juvenile violence in a winner-loser culture. London: Free Association Books, 1995.

28. Sapolsky RM. Endocrinology alfresco: psychoendocrine studies of wild baboons. Recent Prog Hormone Res 1993;48:437–68.

29. Siegrist J, Peter R, Junge A, Cremer P, Seidel D. Low status control, high effort at work and ischaemic heart disease: prospective evidence from blue-collar men. Soc Sci Med 1990;31:1127–34.

30. Kennedy S, Kiecolt-Glaser JK, Glaser R. Immunological consequences of acute and chronic stressors: mediating role of interpersonal relationships. Br J Med Psychol 1988;61:77–85.

31. McDonald AS, Davey GCL. Psychiatric disorders of accidental injury. Clin Psychiatric Rev 1996;16:105–27.

Fifteen

INCOME DISTRIBUTION, SOCIOECONOMIC STATUS, AND SELF-RATED HEALTH: A U.S. MULTI-LEVEL ANALYSIS

Bruce P. Kennedy, Ichiro Kawachi,
Roberta Glass, and Deborah Prothrow-Stith

Abstract

Objective—To determine the effect of state-level income inequality, as measured by the Gini coefficient, on self-rated health status controlling for individual socioeconomic status other individual characteristics.

Design—Cross-sectional multilevel study. Data were collected on income distribution in the 50 US states along with random probability samples of self-rated health, income, education, and other risk factors for each state.

Setting—The 1993 and 1994 Behavioral Risk Factor Surveillance System, a random digit dial survey of civilian, noninstitutionalized United States residents aged 18 years or older conducted in each of the 50 states.

Results—Controlling for household income and personal characteristics, persons living in the highest inequality states were 30% more likely to report their health as fair or poor than persons living in the states with the least income inequality.

Conclusions—Income inequality was associated with an adverse impact on health independent of the effects of household income.

Introduction

INEQUALITIES in health by socioeconomic status (SES) are large, pervasive, persistent, and widening. Whereas most theories that attempt to explain these inequalities have used *individual*-level indicators of SES—such as income, attainment, or occupation[1-4]—a major new hypothesis, first espoused by Richard Wilkinson, focuses on the societal *distribution* of income as a predictor of health. Numerous ecological studies have provided support for this hypothesis demonstrating that unequal income distribution is strongly associated with population mortality and life-expectancy both between and within nations.[5,6] Two recent US studies found that the degree of inequality in the distribution of income across the 50 states was strongly associated with all-cause and cause-specific mortality independent of poverty or median income.[7,8] Kennedy and Kawachi et al.[7] found that

Originally published in *British Medical Journal*, 1998.

two measures of income inequality, the Gini co-efficient and the Robin Hood Index, were both strongly associated with total mortality (r = .51 and r = .54 respectively). These associations held after controlling for poverty and median income. Income inequality was also a strong predictor of infant mortality and deaths from coronary heart disease, cancer and homicide. In independent study, Kaplan et al.[8] showed similar effects of income inequality using a different measure. Furthermore, state income inequality in 1980 predicted 1990 mortality rates where the states with higher income inequality in 1980 had lower reductions in mortality over the ten year period. A study conducted in Britain using ward-level data found a similar relationship.[9]

The mechanisms for these associations have not been completely elucidated. Income inequality may have a direct effect on individuals by increasing stress in response to their experience of relative deprivation depending on their position in the social hierarchy.[6,10] Income distribution may also indirectly impact the health status of populations through its effect on social structure and institutions. One potential pathway is that states or nations with higher income inequality under-invest in public goods such as education, public spaces (e.g., parks and libraries), and social welfare programs.[8,11] In fact, Kaplan et al.[8] has shown that in the US, wide income disparities at the state level are associated with high school drop-out rates, lower literacy rates, and reduced public spending on education. Other studies have shown that income inequality is associated with lower social capital or diminished social cohesion.[12] Kawachi and Kennedy et al.[12] found evidence that the effects of income inequality on health may be mediated through its effect on social capital. Income inequality was strongly associated with diminished social capital as measured by lack of social trust (r = .73) and membership in voluntary organizations (r = −.40). States with higher income inequality had much higher levels of social mistrust and lower per capita group memberships. These in turn were strongly associated with state variations in mortality (r = .77 and r = −.49 respectively) and were strongly associated with death rates due to infant mortality, heart disease, cancer, and unintentional injury as well.

These ecological studies indicate that income inequality may have extra-individual or contextual effects that structure the social environment in ways that impacts population health. However it is still not clear at what level of analysis (e.g., state, county, neighborhood) the effects of income inequality are best specified and whether it is more appropriate to test these effects using multi-level analyses (e.g., state and individual) that can adjust for individual level confounds.

Additionally, there have been several criticisms of the ecological studies linking income distribution to health outcomes. Some critics have argued that the relationship may simply be due to choice of inequality measure.[13] However, in a study that examined the most commonly used income inequality measures, Kawachi and Kennedy[14] showed that the relationship to mortality held across all measures and they concluded that the choice of indicator did not introduce a significant bias. Others have suggested that the relationship may simply be due to a statistical artefact produced from the curvilinear relationship of individual income to mortality.[15]

Other criticisms have argued that models using ecological data are more prone to mispecification due to a greater likelihood of unmeasured confounds at the individual level.[16] In a multi-level study that used both individual level and ecological level variables, Fiscella and Franks[16] found that the ecological effect of income inequality measured at the community level on mortality disappeared after controlling for family income. Based on this finding, they concluded that previous studies using purely ecological variables may have overstated the relationship of income inequality and mortality as they have not controlled for the confounding of income at the individual level.

The present study was conducted to further examine these issues by using state-level inequality measures to predict individual morbidity, as measured by self-rated health status, while adjusting for a number potential individual-level confounds including household income, education, age, gender, race, insurance status, smoking and obesity. Using a multi-level model that includes both ecological variables (in this case state income distribution) and individual-level variables mitigates against the possibility of model misspecification and the attribution of a contextual effect when none exists.[17,18]

DATA AND METHODS

Data Sources

Individual level data on self-rated health status, income, demographics, and health care access were drawn from the combined 1993 and 1994 Behavioral Risk Factor Surveillance System (BRFSS) surveys. The telephone survey is conducted by state health departments under the direction of the Behavioral Surveillance Branch (BSB), National Center for Chronic Disease Prevention and Health Promotion, Centers for Disease Control and Prevention. The states use probability samples in which all households with telephones have a non-zero chance of inclusion, designed to produce comparable state level estimates for the civilian, noninstitutinalized population aged 18 or older. The total sample size for the combined 1993 and 1994 data sets was 205,245, ranging from an *n* of 1259 in Wyoming to an *n* of 8,800 in Maryland.

In 1993 the BRFSS began asking questions about the health related quality of life. The perceived health question asks "Would you say that in general your health is: Excellent, Very good, Good, Fair, or Poor?"[19] From this item we created a dichotomous outcome measure equal to 1 if the respondent answered fair or poor. This measure of morbidity has demonstrated validity across numerous studies and is a strong predictor

of mortality.[20] For example, in the present study, the percentage of respondents within a state reporting fair to poor health was strongly correlated with state mortality rates (r = .58).

Demographic data included on the BRFSS survey include race, age, gender, education, and household income. The proportion of people reporting fair or poor health remains relatively constant until age 40, and then increases linearly. To model this relationship we created a variable that measures the number of years past age 40. Education is categorized as less than high school, high school, some college or trade school, and college graduate. Measures of health care access include whether the person currently has health insurance, and whether the person has had a check-up visit within the last two years. Household composition is categorized as one adult living alone, two or more adults with no children, one adult with any children, and two or more adults with children. We categorized race as white, black, and other races. Household income is categorized as less than $10,000, $10,000 to $14,999, $15,000 to $19,999, $20,000 to $24,999, $25,000 to $34,999, and $35,000 or more.

For our income inequality variable we used gini coefficient data generously provided by Professor Timothy Smeeding of the Luxembourg Income Study for the 50 US States.[21] The Gini is constructed using household income data from the Current Population Survey for the years 1990–92. The income data is adjusted for state differences in taxes and cash transfers as well as differences in household compositions using an equivalence scale (with the equivalence elasticity E = .5). The sample was then broken into four categories based on the Gini coefficient's distribution. Category 1 represents the states with low-income inequality and includes the states whose gini coefficients fall below one standard deviation below the mean gini for the United States. This includes nine states with gini less than 0.320: Connecticut, South Dakota, North Dakota, Hawaii, Utah, Wisconsin, Delaware, Vermont, and Iowa. Category 2 includes 13 states whose gini fall between one standard deviation below the mean and the mean (0.320 to 0.332) (RI, MT, OH, NM, WY, ME, MN, OR, PA, IN, KS, NE, and MD). Category 3 includes 18 states whose gini fall between the mean and one standard deviation above the mean (0.338–0.355) (AZ, NH, OK, MO, AR, VA, NJ, TN, CO, WV, MA, NV, SC, ID, MI, NC, AK, and WA). Category 4 contains the states with the highest levels of income inequality, those with gini above 0.360. Category 4 includes: TX, GA, CA, LA, NY, KY, FL, AL, IL, and MS.

DATA ANALYSIS

THE BRFSS employs a three stage sampling design, which requires special statistical techniques to account for clustering when calculating standard errors. The SUDAAN software package[22] Logistic regression procedure was used for all analyses. The Logistic procedure in SUDAAN accounts for the complex survey design when estimating the standard errors. SUDAAN can also be used for *hierarchical* or *multilevel models* using clustered data (individuals within states) such as was used in this study. The estimation procedure takes into account the violation of independence among individuals in the same cluster (state) and estimates the appropriate standard errors.

Logistic regression was employed to examine the relationship between state income inequality and self reported fair or poor health. A second logistic model examined the relationship adjusting for the demographic characteristics age, gender, and race. And a third model also adjusted for factors that may be pathways through which income inequality influences health status. These additional factors include health insurance status, recent use of health care services, family composition, smoking status, obesity, and education. Finally, we stratified by household income level (less than $20,000, $20,000 to $34,999, and $35,000 or more) and by race (white

and black) and employed adjusted models to determine whether the relationship between health status and income inequality differs by income stratum or race.

RESULTS

TABLE 1 summarizes the sample characteristics and bivariate relationships to fair/poor health. Women were slightly overrepresented in the sample (58.3% women vs. 41.7% men). In simple bivariate analyses, more women (15.4%) also reported fair/poor health than men (13.1%) as did blacks (20.3%) compared to whites (13.8%). In the bivariate associations, income was strongly associated with poor/fair health—for the whole sample, 32% of those in the lowest income category (<$10,000) reported fair/poor health compared with only 6.3% in the highest income category ($35,000+) representing a five-fold gradient effect for household income on morbidity. A similar gradient is seen for the education variable with 45% of those with no school or an elementary school education only reporting fair/poor health compared with 6% of college graduates. Obesity, smoking, marital status, health insurance coverage, and other demographic variables were also associated with fair/poor health (Table 1).

Table 2 presents the multivariate odds ratios for the effects of income inequality on individual morbidity. In model 1, the unadjusted odds ratio for income inequality (Gini) indicates about a 30% increased risk for morbidity for individuals living in states with higher income inequality. This effect is attenuated somewhat when the individual's household income is added to the model, yet the odds ratios remain statistically significant (Model 2, Table 2). The effect remains fairly stable even after adjusting for a number of individual demographics and risk factors such as age, race, smoking, obesity and health care utilization. The effect of income inequality on morbidity in the fully adjusted model (Model 4, Table 2) stratified by race was similar for blacks

Table 1

Sample Characteristics, Unweighted

Characteristic	N (percent)		% in Fair/Poor Health
Smoker	46,859	(22.8)	17.0
Non Smoker	157,901	(76.9)	13.4
Obese	53,283	(26.0)	20.5
Not Obese	151,962	(74.0)	12.3
Male	85,505	(41.7)	13.1
Female	119,740	(58.3)	15.4
Health Coverage	179,872	(87.6)	14.2
No Health Coverage	24,874	(12.1)	16.6
Check-up in Last 2 Years	166,903	(81.3)	15.5
No checkup in last 2 Years	38,342	(18.7)	10.0
Household Size 1	50,395	(24.6)	21.4
Household Size 2	66,120	(32.2)	15.8
Household Size 3	35,044	(17.1)	10.8
Household Size 4	31,818	(15.5)	8.0
Household Size 5	13,925	(6.8)	8.6
Household Size 6	4,930	(2.4)	10.5
Household Size 7+	2,755	(1.3)	12.7
One Adult, No Children	50,395	(24.6)	21.4
One Adult and Children	14,129	(6.9)	12.2
Two + Adults and Children	64,376	(31.4)	8.3
Two + Adults, No Children	76,345	(37.2)	15.5
Any Children	78,505	(38.3)	9.0
No Children	126,482	(61.6)	17.9
Excellent Health	50,452	(24.6)	
Very Good Health	68,538	(33.4)	
Good Health	56,118	(27.3)	
Fair Health	21,231	(10.3)	
Poor Health	8,448	(4.1)	

Table 1 (*continued*)

Sample Characteristics, Unweighted

Characteristic	N (percent)		% in Fair/Poor Health
Gini quartile 1 (lowest inequality states)	34,690	(16.9)	12.6
Gini quartile 2	52,536	(25.6)	13.2
Gini quartile 3	70,541	(34.4)	15.1
Gini quartile 4 (highest inequality states)	47,478	(23.1)	16.3
Income Missing or Refused	25,904	(12.6)	18.2
Income <$10,000	29,099	(14.2)	31.5
Income $10,000–$14,999	18,516	(9.0)	23.4
Income $15,000–$19,999	17,607	(8.6)	16.5
Income $20,000–$24,999	18,760	(9.1)	12.9
Income $25,000–$34,999	29,015	(14.1)	9.2
Income $35,000–$49,999	30,781	(15.0)	6.3
Income $50,000+	35,500	(17.3)	4.4
Education No School	1,504	(0.7)	21.7
Education Elementary or no school	10,919	(5.3)	45.0
Education Some High School	18,032	(8.8)	30.6
Education High School Grad/GED	67,995	(33.1)	15.2
Education Some College/Technical	55,038	(26.8)	10.1
Education College Graduate	51,295	(25.0)	5.8
Race White	176,037	(85.8)	13.8
Race Black	17,346	(8.5)	20.3
Race Other	11,614	(5.7)	15.7

(adjusted odds ratio for the highest inequality states, 1.37; 95% CI: 1.08–1.74) and for whites (adjusted odds ratio for the highest inequality states, 1.27; 95% CI: 1.19–1.36). Similarly, although women reported being in fair/poor health slightly more than men (15.4% vs. 13.1% for men, Table 1), this difference was not significant in the fully-adjusted model (OR for males, 1.05; 95% CI: 1.00–1.09; Model 4, Table 2)

We also examined the effects of income inequality stratified by income. These results are presented in Table 3. The effects of income in-

Table 2

Income inequality odds ratios for individual morbidity (fair/poor health) adjusted for individual characteristics

Independent Variables	Model 1[A] Odds Ratio	(95% CI)	Model 2[B] Odds Ratio	(95% CI)	Model 3[C] Odds Ratio	(95% CI)	Model 4[D] Odds Ratio	(95% CI)
Intercept	0.12	(0.12–0.13)	0.05	(0.04–0.05)	0.03	(0.03–0.03)	0.03	(0.03–0.03)
Gini (Highest Inequality)	1.32	(1.25–1.39)	1.23	(1.16–1.30)	1.27	1.19–1.34)	1.25	(1.17–1.33)
Gini (Higher Inequality)	1.29	(1.22–1.35)	1.23	(1.17–1.30	1.28	(1.21–1.36)	1.25	(1.18–1.32)
Gini (Lower Inequality)	1.19	(1.13–1.26)	1.14	(1.07–1.21)	1.15	(1.08–1.23)	1.11	(1.04–1.18)
Income < $10K			7.43	(6.99–7.89)	5.38	(5.05–5.74)	3.40	(3.16–3.65)
Income $10–$15K			5.38	(5.03–5.75)	3.93	(3.65–4.22)	2.65	(2.45–2.86)
Income $15–$20K			3.62	(3.37–3.89)	2.84	(2.63–3.06)	2.05	(1.89–2.21)
Income $20–$25K			2.71	(2.51–2.92)	2.26	(2.09–2.44)	1.76	(1.63–1.91)
Income $25–$35K			1.98	(1.84–2.12)	1.81	(1.69–1.95)	1.52	(1.41–1.63)
Income unknown			3.76	(3.52–4.01)	2.60	(2.43–2.79)	2.01	(1.87–2.16)
Age, yrs over 39					1.04	(1.04–1.04)	1.04	(1.04–1.04)
male					1.06	(1.02–1.10)	1.05	(1.00–1.09)
race—black					1.54	(1.45–1.63)	1.32	(1.25–1.41)
race—other					1.43	(1.32–1.55)	1.36	(1.26–1.48)
Smoker							1.52	(1.45–1.59)
Obese							1.75	(1.68–1.83)
health coverage							0.79	(0.74–0.84)
check-up							1.36	(1.28–1.43)
< HS education							1.72	(1.63–1.81)
some college							0.79	(0.75–0.83)
college graduate							0.54	(0.51–.058)
Lives alone							0.91	(0.87–0.95)
one parent family							0.91	(0.84–0.99)
two parent family							1.00	(0.95–1.06)

[A] Unadjusted odds ratio
[B] Odds ratios adjusted for individual income
[C] Odds ratios adjusted for individual income, gender and rac
[D] Odds ratios adjusted for individual income, gender, race and all other variables in the model

equality on morbidity were most pronounced in the lowest income category (income < $20,000) with an increased risk of about 30% in morbidity for individuals in the states with the highest income inequality. These effects remained stable after adjusting for a variety of individual characteristics (Table 3). Although not as pronounced as the lower income group, income inequality was also associated with an increased risk of morbidity of about 20% in middle income individuals

Table 3

Income inequality odds ratios for individual morbidity (fair/poor health)
adjusted for individual characteristics and stratified by income

Model	Category 4 (high Gini[1]) Odds Ratio (95% CI)	Category 3 Odds Ratio (95% CI)	Category 2 Odds Ratio (95% CI)	Category 1 (low Gini) Odds Ratio (95% CI)
Income < $20K				
Gini	1.29 (1.19–1.40)	1.26 (1.16–1.36)	1.16 (1.06–1.26)	1.00
Gini+ Demographic **(see model 3 in Table 2)**	1.39 (1.28–1.52)	1.32 (1.22–1.44)	1.18 (1.08–1.29)	1.00
Gini+ Demographic+ Other **(see model 4 in Table 2)**	1.33 (1.22–1.45)	1.25 1.15–1.36)	1.11 (1.01–1.22)	1.00
Income $20–$35K				
Gini	1.18 (1.04–1.34)	1.30 (1.16–1.46)	1.11 (0.97–1.26)	1.00
Gini+ Demographic	1.19 (1.05–1.36)	1.36 (1.20–1.53)	1.13 (0.99–1.30)	1.00
Gini+ Demographic+ Other	1.20 (1.05–1.37)	1.35 (1.19–1.52)	1.11 0.97–1.27)	1.00
Income $35K+				
Gini	1.13 (0.98–1.31)	1.08 (0.94–1.24)	1.13 (0.98–1.31)	1.00
Gini+ Demographic	1.08 (0.93–1.25)	1.07 (0.93–1.23)	1.14 (0.98–1.32)	1.00
Gini+ Demographic+ Other	1.09 (0.94–1.27)	1.07 (0.93–1.24)	1.13 (0.98–1.32)	1.00

[1] A higher Gini indicates greater income inequality

(20,000–35,000). Again, these effects remained stable after adjusting for numerous other risk factors (Table 3).

Discussion

THE relationship of income inequality to mortality has been repeatedly shown by ecological studies among nations[5,6] and within countries.[7-9] A recent study by Friscella and Franks has challenged the validity of the ecological approach with the finding that the ecological effect of income inequality at a community level disappears after including individual family income in the model.[16] Contrary to Fiscella and Franks, the present study found an independent effect for income inequality on self-rated health after adjusting for numerous potential individual confounds including household income. Furthermore, the effect of income distribution, although attenuated somewhat, did not change dramatically when household income was included in the model. When stratifying by income level, the effects of income inequality were strongest for those with lower incomes. The income inequality variable did not have a significant effect on the self-rated health of those in the highest income group, yet the effect was present for those with middle incomes.

Fiscella and Franks posited that the previous findings of ecological studies may have been confounded by individual income.[16] They suggested that income inequality was simply just capturing the compositional effect of individual income on mortality—areas with more poor individuals will have higher income inequality, and as being poor is associated with higher mortality there is a spurious association between income inequality and mortality. These findings do not support their conclusion, but instead suggest that there is an independent contextual effect of income distribution, when measured at the state level, on individual self-rated health status.

There are a number of potential explanations for the divergence between the two studies' findings. First, Fiscella and Franks used a different level of aggregation which may have been too small for income distribution to exert an effect independent from individual income. It is still not clear at what ecological level income inequality can be expected to be meaningful. For example, income inequality measured within very poor and very affluent communities would not have the same meaning as when measured across them. As Wilkinson points out, it is not the inequality within Harlem that matters, but how Harlem compares to the larger society.[23]

Secondly, this study used morbidity as measured by self-rated health as the outcome which may be more sensitive to income inequality. However numerous studies have shown that self-rated health is closely linked to mortality. For example, in a recent review of twenty-seven studies, Idler and Benyamini[20] concluded that the same self-rated health measure used in our study had high predictive validity for mortality. In our own data, morbidity aggregated to the state-level was strongly correlated with state total age-adjusted mortality rates (r=.58) and the correlation with Gini, although larger, was similar to that of mortality (.62 vs. .51 respectively).

Another reason for the divergence in findings may be due to measurement error in the calculation of income inequality. As Fiscella and Franks[16] note, their community samples were not meant to be representative of the communities to which the ecological variables were assigned. Furthermore, the inequality measures were derived from the income distributions of each area's sample and were truncated at $25,000 which may have resulted in the underestimation of the true degree of inequality, thus attenuating its effects in the multilevel model. A more appropriate index of inequality could be derived from independent income data by using county census data (as was done in the present study by using independent state income distributions from the census).

CONCLUSION

THE present study's findings indicate that state-level income inequality exerts an independent effect on individual risk for morbidity suggesting that the ecological relationship of income inequality to mortality is not simply an artefact due to the *compositional* effect of aggregated individual incomes as has been suggested by others.[15,16] Instead, there appears to be a clear *contextual* effect of income inequality on health. Recently, Gravelle[15] argued that the effect of income inequality on mortality risk was simply a statistical artefact resulting from: (a) the non-linear shape of the relationship between average income and mortality rates; and (b) the use of aggregate rather than individual data (in other words, the "ecologic fallacy"). These arguments are not new: some years ago, we suggested that the non-linear relation between average income and mortality is a *sufficient*, but not necessarily the *only* explanation for the association between income inequality and health.[24] The results of the present multi-level analysis suggests that the observed association is not simply a product of the ecologic fallacy, and that a contextual effect of income inequality is apparent even among individuals whose personal incomes are above the poverty line.

NOTES

1. Black D, Morris JN, Smith C, Townsend P, Whitehead M. *Inequalities in Health: The Black Report; The Health Divide*. London: Penguin Group, 1988.

2. Smith GD, Shipley MJ, Rose G. Magnitude and causes of socioeconomic differentials in mortality: further evidence from the Whitehall Study. *Journal of Epidemiology and Community Health* 1990;44:265–270.

3. Pappas G, Queen S, Hadden W, Fisher G. The increasing disparity in mortality between socioeconomic groups in the United States, 1960 and 1986. *NEJM* 1993;329:103–9.

4. Alder NE, Boyce T, Chesney MA, et al. Socioeconomic status and health: the challenge of the gradient. *American Psychologist* 1994;49:15–24.

5. Wilkinson RG. Income distribution and life expectancy. *BMJ* 1992;304: 165–8.

6. Wilkinson RG. *Unhealthy Societies: The Afflictions of Inequality*. London: Routledge, 1996.

7. Kennedy BP, Kawachi I, Prothrow-Stith D. Income distribution and mortality: cross-sectional ecological study of the Robin Hood Index in the United States. *BMJ* 1996;312: 1004–7. Also published erratum: *BMJ* 1996;312: 1194.

8. Kaplan GA, Pamuk ER, Lynch JW, Cohen RD, Balfour JL. Inequality in income and mortality in the United States: analysis of mortality and potential pathways. *BMJ* 1996; 312:999–1003.

9. Ben-Shlomo, White IR, Marmot M. Does the variation in the socioeconomic characteristics of an area affect mortality? BMJ 1996; 312: 1013–14.

10. Wilkinson RG. Health inequalities: relative or absolute material standards. *BMJ* 1996;987–8.

11. Smith, GD. Income inequality and mortality: why are they related? *BMJ* 1996;987–8.

12. Kawachi I, Kennedy BP, Lochner K, Prothrow-Stith D. Social capital, income inequality, and mortality. *Am J Public Health* 1997;87:1491–8.

13. Judge K. Income distribution and life expectancy: a critical appraisal. *BMJ* 1995; 311: 1282–5.

14. Kawachi I, Kennedy BP. The relationship of income inequality to mortality: does the choice of indicator matter? *Soc Sci Med* 1997;45:1121–1127.

15. Gravelle H. How much of the relation between population mortality and unequal distribution of income is a statistical artefact? *BMJ* 1998;316:382–5.

16. Fiscella K, Franks, P. Poverty or income inequality as predictor of mortality: longitudinal cohort study. *BMJ* 1997;314:1724–8.

17. Blalock H. Contextual effects models: Theoretical and methodological issues. *Am Rev Sociol* 1984;10:353–72.

18. Hauser R. Contextual effects model: A cautionary tale. *American Journal of Sociology* 1970;75:645–64.

19. Hagan HC, Moriarty DG, Zack MM, Scherr PA, Brackbill R. Measuring health-related quality of life for public health surveillance. *Public Health Reports* 1994;109:665–72.

20. Idler El, Benyamini Y. Self-rated health and mortality: A review of twenty-seven community studies. *J. Health and Soc Behav* 1997;38:21–37.

21. Unpublished data courtesy of Timothy Smeeding. *Luxembourg Income Study.* Atkinson AB, Rainwater L, Smeeding TM. *Income distribution in OECD countries: evidence from the Luxembourg Income Study.* Paris: OECD, 1995.

22. Shah BV. *Software for survey data analysis (SUDAAN) version 5.50.* Research Triangle Park, NC: Research Triangle Institute; 1991.

23. Wilkinson RG. Commentary: Income Inequality summarizes the health burden of individual deprivation. *BMJ* 1997;314;1728−9.

24. Kawachi I, Levine S, Miller SM, Lasch K, Amick B. Income inequality and life expectancy: theory, research and policy. Joint Program on Society and Health Working Paper series. Boston, MA: New England Medical Center, Working Paper No. 94−2, 1994.

Sixteen

HEALTH INEQUALITIES: RELATIVE
OR ABSOLUTE MATERIAL STANDARDS?

Richard G. Wilkinson

ABSTRACT

That mortality in developed countries is affected more by relative than absolute living standards is shown by three pieces of evidence. Firstly, mortality is related more closely to relative income within countries than to differences in absolute income between them. Secondly, national mortality rates tend to be lowest in countries that have smaller income differences and thus have lower levels of relative deprivation. Thirdly, most of the long term rise in life expectancy seems unrelated to long term economic growth rates. Although both material and social influences contribute to inequalities in health, the importance of relative standards implies that psychosocial pathways may be particularly influential. During the 1980s income differences widened more rapidly in Britain than in other countries; almost a quarter of the population now lives in relative poverty. The effects of higher levels of relative deprivation and lower social cohesion may already be visible in mortality trends among young adults.

The existence of wide—and widening—socioeconomic differences in health shows how extraordinarily sensitive health remains to socioeconomic circumstances. Twofold, threefold, or even fourfold differences in mortality have been reported within Britain, depending largely on the social classification used.[1-3] This series will illustrate some of the most important mechanisms involved in the generation of these differences.

Fundamental to understanding the causes of these differences in health is the distinction between the effects of relative and absolute living standards. Socioeconomic gradients in health are simultaneously an association with social position and with different material circumstances, both of which have implications for health—but which is more important in terms of causality? Is the health disadvantage of the least well off part of the population mainly a reflection of the direct physiological effects of lower absolute material standards (of bad housing, poor diets, inadequate heating, and air pollution), or is it more a matter of the direct and indirect effects of differences in psychosocial circumstances associated with social position—of where you stand in relation to others? The indirect effects of psychosocial circumstances here include increased exposure to behavioural risks resulting from psychosocial stress, including any stress related smoking, drinking, eating "for comfort," etc; most of the direct effects are likely to centre on the physiological effects of chronic mental and emotional stress.

Originally published in *British Medical Journal*, 1997.

Evidence from three sources suggests that the psychosocial effects of social position account for the larger part of health inequalities. If valid, this perspective would have fundamental implications for public policy and for our understanding of the pathways through which socioeconomic differences have an impact on human biology.

INCOME WITHIN
AND BETWEEN SOCIETIES

DESPITE the difficulty of disentangling material from social influences on health, it is possible to look at the relation between income and health in population groups where income differences are, and are not, associated with social status. Social stratification exists within rather than between societies. Therefore, while income differences among groups within the developed societies are associated with social status, the differences in average per capita incomes between developed societies are not. We may therefore compare the association of income and health within and between societies.

Within countries there is a close relation between most measures of health and socioeconomic circumstances. As an example, figure 1 uses data from 300 685 white American men in the multiple risk factor intervention trial to show the relation between mortality and the median family income in the postcode areas in which they lived.[4] Among black men in the trial, larger mortality differences are spread over a smaller income range.[5] In Britain, there are similar gradients in mortality and sickness absence among men and women.[6][7]

The regular gradients between income and mortality within countries contrast sharply with the much weaker relation found in the differences between rich developed societies. Figure 2 shows the cross sectional relation between life expectancy and gross domestic product per capita for 23 members of the Organisation of Economic Cooperation and Development (OECD) in 1993. Using data from the OECD countries reduces the influence of extraneous cultural differences by restricting the comparison to developed, democratic countries with market economies. Currencies have been converted at "purchasing power parities" to reflect real differences in spending in each country. The correlation coefficient of 0.08 shows that life expectancy and gross national product per capita are not related in this cross sectional data. Excluding government expenditure makes little difference: the correlation with private consumer's expenditure per capita is only 0.10.

Data on changes over time between countries show a weak but non-significant relation. During 1970−93 the correlation between increases in life expectancy and percentage increases in gross domestic product per capita among OECD countries was 0.30, suggesting that less than 10% of the increases in life expectancy were related to economic performance. Though the recent rise in national mortality in eastern Europe suggests

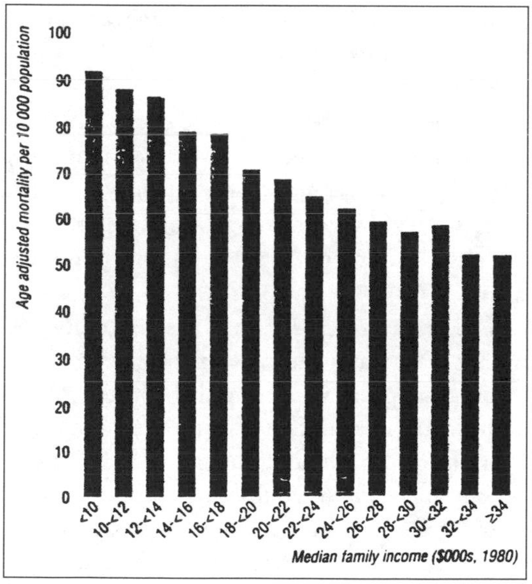

Figure 1
Age adjusted mortality of 300 685 white American men by median family income of zip code areas in the United States[4]

that time lags may be short, the period used here allows for the possibility of longer lags.[8]

As figure 2 uses data for whole countries, the contrast between it and the strong relation shown in figure 1 cannot arise from sampling error. A strong international relation is unlikely to be masked by cultural factors: not only are the international comparisons confined to OECD countries, but the picture is supported by comparisons among the 50 states of the United States, where cultural differences are smaller. The correlation reported between age adjusted mortality and median incomes in the states was −0.28.[9] As with the international comparisons, social stratification mainly occurs within rather than between American states.

Income and mortality are so strongly related within societies that this relation cannot be assumed to exist between developed societies but has somehow become hidden. Its robustness within societies shows not merely in mortality data but in measures as diverse as medically certified sickness absence among civil servants and prescription items issued per head of population in relation to local rates of unemployment.[7] [10] However, the contrast in the strength of the relation within and between societies would make sense if mortality in rich countries were influenced more by relative income than by absolute material standards.

INCOME DISTRIBUTION

A second source of evidence that relative income has a powerful influence on health comes from analyses of the relation between measures of income inequality and mortality both among developed countries[11] and among the 50 states of the United States.[12] Cross sectional data and data covering changes over time both show that mortality tends to be lower in societies where income differences are smaller, even after average incomes, absolute poverty, and a number of other socioeconomic factors have been controlled for. This relation has now been

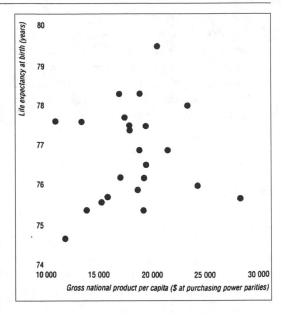

Figure 2
Relation of life expectancy and gross national product per capita in OECD countries, 1993 (based on data from OECD national accounts 1995 and World Bank's world tables 1996)

shown independently on over a dozen different datasets and has been reported absent only once.[11] The most plausible explanation is that mortality is lower in more egalitarian societies because the burden of relative deprivation is reduced.

The weak association between mortality and median (absolute) incomes of the 50 American states disappears when the distribution of income within each state is controlled for.[9] The correlation coefficient drops from −0.28 to −0.06, suggesting that absolute income is unrelated to mortality in the United States. Unfortunately, further exploration of the international relation between income distribution and mortality will depend on taking account of the differences in response to income surveys in different countries. Response rates vary by more than 30%, and as non-responders are concentrated particularly among the rich and poor, high non-response leads to smaller reported income differences.[13 14]

EPIDEMIOLOGICAL TRANSITION

THE third reason for thinking that health is influenced more by relative than absolute income centres on the epidemiological transition. Although absolute material standards remain important in less developed countries, there are indications that the epidemiological transition represents a stage in economic development after which further improvements in material standards have less influence on health. Not only do the infectious diseases of poor countries give way to degenerative diseases as the main causes of death, but the transition also coincides with a flattening of the curve relating life expectancy to gross domestic product per capita.[11 13] In addition, several of the so called "diseases of affluence" (including coronary heart disease, stroke, hypertension, obesity, and duodenal ulcers) reverse their social distribution to become more common among poor people in affluent societies, reflecting that the majority of the population has risen above a minimum threshold level of living.[11 16] When those who are less well off cease to be thin, obesity ceases to be associated with social status.

A THEORY OF HEALTH AND SOCIAL POSITION?

IF the association between health and socioeconomic status within societies — at least in the developed world — is not primarily the direct effect of material standards, then some might think it resulted simply from differential social mobility between healthy people and unhealthy people. However, many research reports show that this is not the major part of the picture,[17-20] and social selection is entirely unable to account for the relation between national mortality rates and income distribution.

This pushes us — inexorably though perhaps reluctantly — towards the view that socioeconomic differences in health within countries result primarily from differences in people's position in the socioeconomic hierarchy relative to others, leaving a less powerful role to the undoubted direct effects of absolute material standards. If health inequality had been a residual problem of absolute poverty it might have been expected to have diminished under the impact of postwar economic growth, and it would tend to distinguish primarily between the poor and the rest of the population — rather than running across society, making even the higher echelons less healthy than those above them (see figure 1).

Need for a Theory

A theory is needed which unifies the causes of the health inequalities related to social hierarchy with the effects of income inequality on national mortality rates. At its centre are likely to be factors affecting how hierarchical the hierarchy is, the depths of material insecurity and social exclusion which societies tolerate, and the direct and indirect psychosocial effects of social stratification.[21]

One reason why greater income equality is associated with better health seems to be that it tends to improve social cohesion and reduce the social divisions.[11] Qualitative and quantitative evidence suggests that more egalitarian societies are more cohesive. In their study of Italian regions, Putnam *et al* report a strong correlation (0.81) between income equality and their index of the strength of local community life.[22] They say, "Equality is an essential feature of the civic community." Kawachi *et al* have shown that measures of "social trust" provide a statistical link between income distribution and mortality in the United States.[23] Better integration into a network of social relations is known to benefit health.[24 25] This accords with the emphasis placed on relative poverty as a form of social exclusion, and with the evidence that racial discrimination has direct health effects.[26] However, social wellbeing is not simply a matter of stronger social networks. Low control, insecurity, and loss of self esteem are among the psychosocial risk factors known to mediate between health and socioeconomic circumstances. Indeed, integration in the economic life of society, reduced unemployment, material security, and narrower income differences provide the material base for a more cohesive society. Usually the effects of chronic stress will be closely related to the many direct effects of material deprivation, simply because material insecurity is always worrying. However, as Hogarth's *Gin Lane* shows, even absolute poverty has often killed through psychosocial and behavioural pathways.

Pathways

In terms of the pathways involved in the transition from social to biological processes, there is increasing interest in the physiological effects of chronic stress. Social status differences in physiological risk factors among several species of non-human primates have been identified. Animals lower in the social hierarchy hypersecreted cortisol, had higher blood pressure, had suppressed immune function, more commonly had central obesity, and had less good ratios of high density lipoproteins to low density lipoproteins—even when they were fed the same diet and social status was manipulated experimentally.[27] [28] Among humans, lower social status has also been associated with lower ratios of high to low density lipoproteins, central obesity, and higher fibrinogen concentrations.[29] In experiments in which social status was manipulated, subordinate monkeys "received more aggression, engaged in less affiliation, and spent more time alone than dominants . . . they spent more time fearfully scanning the social environment and displayed more behavioral depression than dominants."[30] Loss of social status resulting from being rehoused with more domi-

nant animals was associated with fivefold increases in coronary artery atherosclerosis.[31]

Although research has shown that psychosocial factors are related to both morbidity and mortality, differences in reporting make international comparisons of morbidity unreliable. Nevertheless, because patterns even of self reported morbidity are predictive of mortality rates, we can probably assume that mortality differences indicate differences in objectively defined morbidity.[32] [33] Although no obvious patterns have emerged from attempts to assess international differences in the extent of inequalities in self reported morbidity when people are classified by education or social class, across countries there is a close relation between the extent of inequalities in income and in self reported morbidity.[34] [35]

RELATIVE POVERTY AND MORTALITY

ALTHOUGH Britain had a greater increase in inequality during the 1980s than other developed market economies,[36] the proportion of the population living in relative poverty (below half the average income) may—for the first time in two decades—have decreased slightly during the early 1990s. It now stands at almost one in four of the whole population (incomes after deducting housing costs).[37] Among children the proportion is almost one in three. Particularly worrying is the likely increase in the proportion of children emotionally scarred by the tensions and conflicts of family life aggravated by living in relative poverty. During 1982–92 there were no improvements in national mortality rates among young men (aged 20–40) and smaller improvements among younger women (aged 15–24) than at most other ages.[38] Socioeconomic differences in mortality are at their maximum at these ages, and the national trends are likely to be partly a reflection of the increased burden of relative deprivation. Among young men, deaths from suicide, AIDS, violence, and cirrhosis increased. These causes suggest that the psychosocial effects of relative deprivation are unlikely to be confined to health. As in the international data, where death rates from accidents, violence, and alcohol related causes seem to be particularly closely related to wider income inequalities, the predominance of behavioural causes may reflect in social cohesion.[9] [13]

The papers in this series are intended to illustrate some of the processes which give rise to the relation between relative deprivation and health. What comes out of several of them may not have been so different had the subject been crime, drug misuse, or poor educational performance. Important aspects of the evidence suggest that the rest of society cannot long remain insulated from the effects of high levels of relative deprivation.

NOTES

1. Phillimore P, Beattie A, Townsend P. The widening gap. Inequality of health in northern England, 1981–91. *BMJ* 1994;308:1125–8.

2. Goldblatt P. Mortality and alternative social classifications. In: Goldblatt P, ed. *Longitudinal study 1971–1981: mortality and social organisation.* London: HMSO, 1990. (OPCS series LS, No 6.)

3. Davey Smith G, Shipley MJ, Rose G. Magnitude and causes of socioeconomic differentials in mortality: further evidence from the Whitehall Study. *J Epidemiol Community Health* 1990;44:265–70.

4. Davey Smith G, Neaton JD, Stamler J. Socioeconomic differentials in mortality risk among men screened for the multiple risk factor intervention trial. 1. White men. *Am J Public Health* 1996;86;486–96.

5. Davey Smith G, Wentworth D, Neaton JD, Stamler R, Stamler J. Socioeconomic differentials in mortality risk among men screened for the multiple risk factor intervention trial. 2. Black men. *Am J Public Health* 1996;86;497–504.

6. Office of Population Censuses and Surveys. *Registrar general's supplement on occupational mortality 1979–83.* London: HMSO, 1986.

7. North F, Syme SL, Feeney A, Head J, Shipley MJ, Marmot MG. Explaining socioeconomic differences in sickness absence: the Whitehall II study. *BMJ* 1993;306:361–6.

8. Hertzman C, Kelly S, Bobak M. *East-West life expectancy gap in Europe.* Dortrecht: Kluwer, 1996.

9. Kaplan GA, Pamuk E, Lynch JW, Cohen RO, Balfour JL. Income inequality and mortality in the United States: analysis of mortality and potential pathways. *BMJ* 1996;312:999–1003.

10. Office of Health Economics. *Compendium health statistics.* London: OHE, 1995.

11. Wilkinson RG. Unhealthy societies: the afflictions of inequality. London: Routledge, 1996.

12. Kennedy BP, Kawachi I, Prothrow-Stith D. Income distribution and mortality: cross sectional ecological study of the Robin Hood index in the United States. *BMJ* 1996;312:1004–7. (Important correction. *BMJ* 1996;312:1194.)

13. McIsaac SJ, Wilkinson RG. Income distribution and cause-specific mortality. *Eur J Public Health* (in press).

14. Wilkinson RG. Research note: German income distribution and infant mortality. *Sociology of Health and Illness* 1994;16:260–2.

15. World Bank. *World development report.* New York: Oxford University Press, 1993.

16. Wilkinson RG. The epidemiological transition: from material scarcity to social disadvantage? *Daedalus* 1994; 123(4):61–77.

17. Lundberg O. Childhood living conditions, health status, and social mobility: a contribution to the health selection debate. *European Sociological Review.* 1991;7:149–62.

18. Blane D, Davey Smith G, Bartley M. Social selection: what does it contribute to social class differences in health? *Sociology of Health and Illness* 1993;15:1–15.

19. Fox J, Goldblatt P, Jones D. Social class mortality differentials: artefact, selection or life circumstances? *J Epidemiol Community Health* 1985;39:1–8.

20. Power C, Manor O, Fox AJ, Fogelman K. Health in childhood and social inequalities in young adults. *J R Stat Soc (A)* 1990;153:17–28.

21. Sennett R, Cobb J. *The hidden injuries of class.* New York: Knopf, 1973.

22. Putnam RD, Leonardi R, Nanetti RY. Making democracy work: civic traditions in modern Italy. Princeton, NJ: Princeton University Press, 1993;102–5, 224.

23. Kawachi I, Kennedy BP, Lochner K, Prothrow-Stith D. Social capital, income inequality and mortality: *Am J Public Health* (in press).

24. House JS, Landis KR, Umberson D. Social relationships and health. *Science* 1988;241:540–5.

25. Berkman LF. The role of social relations in health promotion. *Psychosom Res* 1995;57:245–54.

26. Krieger N. Sidney S. Racial discrimination and blood pressure: the CARDIA study of young black and white adults. *Am J Public Health* 1996;86:1370–8.

27. Shively CA, Clarkson TB. Regional obesity and coronary artery atherosclerosis in females: a non-human primate model. *Acta Medica Scand* 1988:723(suppl):71–8.

28. Sapolsky RM. Endocrinology alfresco: psychoendocrine studies of wild baboons. *Recent Prog Hormone Res* 1993;48:437–68.

29. Brunner E. The social and biological basis of cardiovascular disease in office workers. In: Brunner E, Blane D, Wilkinson RG, eds. *Health and social organisation*. London: Routledge, 1996.

30. Shivley CA, Laird KI, Anton RF. The behavior and physiology of social stress and depression in female cynomolgus monkeys. *Biol Psychiatry* (in press).

31. Shively CA, Clarkson TB. Social status and coronary artery atherosclerosis in female monkeys. *Arteriosclerosis Thrombosis* 1994;14:721–6.

32. Ostlin P. Occupational history, self-reported chronic illness, and mortality: a follow up of 25,586 Swedish men and women. *J Epidemiol Community Health* 1990;44:12–6.

33. Arber S. Social class, non-employment, and chronic illness: continuing the inequalities in health debate. *BMJ* 1987;94:1069–73.

34. Kunst AK, Cavelaar AEJM, Groenhof F, Geurts JJM, Mackenbach JP. Socioeconomic inequalities in morbidity and mortality in Europe: a comparative study. Rotterdam: Erasmus University, 1997. (EU Working Group on Socio-Economic Inequalities in Health.)

35. Van Doorslaer E, Wagstaff A, Bleichrodt H, Calonge S, Gerdtham U, Gerfin M, *et al.* Socioeconomic inequalities in health: some international comparisons. *J Health Econ* (in press).

36. Hills J. *The future of welfare*. York: Joseph Rowntree Foundation, 1994.

37. Department of Social Security. *Households below average income 1979–1993/4.* London: Stationary Office, 1996.

38. Tickle L. Mortality trends in the United Kingdom, 1982–1992. *Population Trends* 1996;86:21–8.

Part Three

TOWARDS A THEORY
OF INCOME DISTRIBUTION AND HEALTH

Part Three

TOWARDS A THEORY
OF INCOME DISTRIBUTION AND HEALTH

standardized stress test in Lithuanian versus Swedish men: the LiVicordia Study. *International Journal of Behavioral Medicine* 5(1): 17–30.

COMMENT

IN Part III, the largest of the book, we have gathered together the papers that form the nucleus of the beginnings of a theory of how income inequality affects health. Two potential pathways are emphasized in particular: the link between income inequality and the disruption of social cohesion (a group-level phenomenon); and the growing evidence on how social status "gets under the skin" to produce deleterious health effects (an individual process, labeled by Tarlov (1996) as the "socio-biological translation").

The papers dealing with social cohesion and health are grouped under Section A. The role of supportive social relationships in promoting health is one of the most thoroughly corroborated findings in social epidemiology (House et al. 1988; Berkman, 1995; Kawachi et al. 1996). Indeed, based on a review of the available evidence in 1988, House and colleagues (1988) remarked that: "the theory and evidence on social relationships and health increasingly approximate that available at the time of the U.S. Surgeon General's 1964 report on smoking and health, with similar implications for future research and public policy" (p. 541).

Interestingly, social integration can be conceived of as both an individual characteristic and as a societal characteristic (Kawachi and Kennedy, 1997). A socially integrated individual is one who has many social connections, in the form of both intimate social contacts (spouse, friends, relatives) as well as more distal connections (membership of church groups and voluntary associations). At the group level, a socially integrated society is one that is endowed with stocks of "social capital", which consists partly of moral resources such as trust between citizens and norms of reciprocity. More socially inte-

grated societies seem to have lower rates of crime, suicide, and mortality from all causes (Wilkinson, 1996; Kawachi et al. 1997), as well as better overall quality of life (Kawachi et al. 1999 in press). Importantly, the degree of social integration (or cohesion) appears to vary according to the extent of social stratification: societies with more inegalitarian distributions of income suffer from higher levels of mistrust, social disorganization, and latent conflict. In the extreme case, such as in Russia following the transition to a market economy, the rapid decompression of the income distribution combined with the suppression of civil society during the Soviet regime appear to have created the conditions for an unprecedented collapse in life expectancy (Kennedy et al. 1998; Wilkinson, 1996).

In Section B we have selected studies that focus on the relationship between the social environment and crime. Crime, especially violent crime, is a sensitive mirror of the quality of social relations (Wilkinson et al. 1998). Criminologists have been long aware of the associations between income inequality, social disorganization, and rates of crime and violence (Hsieh and Pugh, 1993). Recent work has begun to chart the theoretical and empirical linkages between social cohesion and crime rates at the regional (Kennedy et al. 1998) and community (Sampson et al. 1997) levels.

Finally, how do differences in social status "get under the skin" to produce deleterious effects on health? Section C includes up to date reviews of the evidence from observational and experimental work depicting the sociobiological translation (Taylor et al. 1997; McEwen, 1998). Studies in both non-human primates (Shively and Clarkson, 1994; Shively et al. 1997; Sapolsky et al. 1997) and increasingly, human populations (Kristenson et al. 1998), demonstrate the deleterious health effects of stress associated with lower social status. The concept of "allostatic load" (McEwen and Stellar, 1993; McEwen, 1998) has been put forward to describe the "wear and tear" resulting from chronic stress on the endocrine, immune, and physiologic systems of organisms. This is a rapidly evolving area of research that holds the promise of linking macro-level structures (vertical social hierarchy) to micro-level processes (neuro-endocrine disturbances) at the individual level.

The questions and debates raised by the readings in this selection include:

- What are the pathways and mechanisms by which income inequality affects population and individual health? Do the mechanisms differ according to the unit of analysis—nations, states, cities, and neighborhoods?
- What are the mechanisms by which income inequality is related to social cohesion? Does income inequality inevitably lead to the disruption of social cohesion?
- What is social cohesion, and how does it influence health? Is social cohesion an unqualified social good (are there downsides to social cohesion)? Can we intervene to build social cohesion?
- How do differences in social status "get under the skin" to produce differences in health status? Does relative deprivation directly affect health, and if so, how?
- What factors explain the mortality crisis in post-Soviet societies following the transition to market economies? What are the relative contributions of the physical environment (e.g., pollution), material deprivation (e.g., lack of access to health services), lifestyle factors (e.g., excess alcohol consumption and poor diets), and the social environment (absence of civil society)?
- What social forces account for the variations in crime across space and time? Can we consider crime a "marker" for the quality of social relations? Do the determinants of violent crimes differ from property crimes?

SUGGESTIONS FOR FURTHER READING

General Readings

Wilkinson RG (1996). *Unhealthy Societies. The Afflictions of Inequality.* London: Routledge.

Kawachi I, Levin S, Miller SM, Lasch K, Amick BC III (1994). *Income inequality and life expectancy—theory, research, and policy.* Boston: The Health Institute, New England Medical Center.

Glyn A and Miliband D, eds (1994). *Paying for Inequality: The Economic Cost of Social Injustice.* Rivers Oram Press, London.

Section A
Social Cohesion and Health

Berkman LF, Syme SL (1979). Social networks, host resistance and mortality: a nine-year follow-up study of Alameda County residents. *American Journal of Epidemiology* 109: 186–204.

Bruhn JG, Wolf S (1979). *The Roseto Story.* Norman: University of Oklahoma Press.

Putnam RD (1993). *Making Democracy Work. Civic Traditions in Modern Italy.* Princeton, NJ. Princeton University Press.

Putnam RD (1995). Bowling alone. America's declining social capital. *Journal of Democracy* 6: 65–78.

Wilkinson RG (1996). *Unhealthy Societies. The Afflictions of Inequality.* London: Routledge.

Kawachi I, Kennedy BP, Lochner K (1997). Long live community. Social capital as public health. *The American Prospect* November/December, 56–59.

Wilkinson RG (1997). Comment: Income inequality and social cohesion. *American Journal of Public Health* 87: 104–6.

Kaplan G, Lynch JW (1997). Editorial: Whither studies on the socioeconomic foundations of population health? *American Journal of Public Health*

Section B
The Social Environment, Crime, and Violence

Braithwaite J, Braithwaite V (1980). The effect of income inequality and social democracy on homicide. *British Journal of Criminology* 20(1): 45–53.

Blau JR and Blau PM (1982). The cost of inequality. Metropolitan structure and violent crime. *American Sociological Review*, 47, 114–129.

Baily WC (1984). Poverty, inequality, and city homicide rates: some not so unexpected findings. *Criminology*, 22, 531–50.

Krahn H, Hartnagel TF, Gartrell JW (1986). Income inequality and homicide rates: cross-national data and criminological theories. *Criminology* 24: 269–95.

Messner SF (1989). Economic discrimination and societal homicide rates: further evidence on the cost of inequality. *American Sociological Review*, 54, 597–611.

Bailey WC, Peterson RD (1995). Gender inequality and violence against women. In: J. Hagan and RD Peterson (eds). *Crime and Inequality.* Stanford University Press: 174–205.

Kawachi I, Kennedy BP, Wilkinson RG (1999). Crime: social disorganization and relative deprivation. *Social Science & Medicine* 48: 719–31

Section C
The Socio-Biological Translation

Sapolsky RM (1993). Endocrinology alfresco: psychoendocrine studies of wild baboons. *Recent Progress in Hormone Research* 48: 437–68.
McEwen BS, Stellar E (1993). Stress and the individual: mechanisms leading to disease. *Archives of Internal Medicine* 153:2093–101.
Sapolsky RM (1994). *Why Zebras Don't Get Ulcers. A guide to stress, stress-related disease and coping.* New York: WH Freeman.
Adler NE, Boyce T, Chesney MA, Folkman S, Kahn RL, Syme SL (1994). Socioeconomic status and health: The challenge of the gradient. American Psychologist 49:15–24.

Brunner E (1997). Stress and the biology of inequality. *British Medical Journal* 314:1472–6.
Kelly S, Hertzman C, Daniels M (1997). Searching for the biological pathways between stress and health. *Annual Review of Public Health* 18: 437–62.
Tarlov AR (1996). Social determinants of health: the sociobiological translation. In: Blane D, Brunner EJ, Wilkinson RG (eds). *Health and Social Organization.* London: Routledge.

Seventeen

SOCIAL RELATIONSHIPS AND HEALTH

James S. House, Karl R. Landis, and Debra Umberson

Abstract

Recent scientific work has established both a theoretical basis and strong empirical evidence for a causal impact of social relationships on health. Prospective studies, which control for baseline health status, consistently show increased risk of death among persons with a low quantity, and sometimes low quality, of social relationships. Experimental and quasi-experimental studies of humans and animals also suggest that social isolation is a major risk factor for mortality from widely varying causes. The mechanisms through which social relationships affect health and the factors of social relationship remain to be explored.

Introduction

. . . my father told me of a careful observer, who certainly had heart-disease and died from it, and who positively stated that his pulse was habitually irregular to an extreme degree; yet to his great disappointment it invariably became regular as soon as my father entered the room.

—*Charles Darwin*[1]

Scientists have long noted an association between social relationships and health. More socially isolated or less socially integrated individuals are less healthy, psychologically and physically, and more likely to die. The first major work of empirical sociology found that less socially integrated people were more likely to commit suicide than the most integrated.[2] In subsequent epidemiologic research age-adjusted mortality rates from all causes of death are consistently higher among the unmarried than the married.[3-5] Unmarried and more socially isolated people have also manifested higher rates of tuberculosis,[6] accidents,[7] and psychiatric disorders such as schizophrenia.[8, 9] And as the above quote from Darwin suggests, clinicians have also observed potentially health-enhancing qualities of social relationships and contacts.

The causal interpretation and explanation of these associations has, however, been less clear. Does a lack of social relationships cause people to become ill or die? Or are unhealthy people less likely to establish and maintain social relationships? Or is there some other factor, such as a misanthropic personality, which predisposes people both to have a lower quantity or quality of social relationships and to become ill or die?

Such questions have been largely unanswerable before the last decade for two reasons. First, there was little theoretical basis for causal explanation. Durkheim[2] proposed a theory of how social relationships affected suicide, but this theory did not generalize to morbidity and mortality from other causes. Second, evidence of the association between social relationships and health, especially in general human populations, was al-

Originally published in *Science*, 1988.

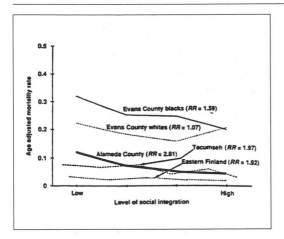

Figure 1
Level of social integration and age-adjusted mortality for males in five prospective studies. RR, the relative risk ratio of mortality at the lowest versus highest level of social integration.

most entirely retrospective or cross-sectional before the late 1970s. Retrospective studies from death certificates or hospital records ascertained the nature of a person's social relationships after they had become ill or died, and cross-sectional surveys of general populations determined whether people who reported ill health also reported a lower quality or quantity of relationships. Such studies used statistical control of potential confounding variables to rule out third factors that might produce the association between social relationships and health, but could do this only partially. They would not determine whether poor social relationships preceded or followed ill health.

In this article, we review recent developments that have altered this state of affairs dramatically: (i) emergence of theoretical models for a causal effect of social relationships on health in humans and animals; (ii) cumulation of empirical evidence that social relationships are a consequential predictor of mortality in human populations; and (iii) increasing evidence for the causal impact

of social relationships on psychological and physiological functioning in quasi-experimental and experimental studies of humans and animals. These developments suggest that social relationships, or the relative lack thereof, constitute a major risk factor for health—rivaling the effects of well-established health risk factors such as cigarette smoking, blood pressure, blood lipids, obesity, and physical activity. Indeed, the theory and evidence on social relationships and health increasingly approximate that available at the time of the U.S. Surgeon General's 1964 report on smoking and health,[10] with similar implications for future research and public policy.

THE EMERGENCE OF "SOCIAL SUPPORT" THEORY AND RESEARCH

THE study of social relationships and health was revitalized in the middle 1970s by the emergence of a seemingly new field of scientific research on "social support." This concept was first used in the mental health literature,[11, 12] and was linked to physical health in separate seminal articles by physician-epidemiologists Cassel[13] and Cobb.[14] These articles grew out of a rapidly developing literature on stress and psychosocial factors in the etiology of health and illness.[15] Chronic diseases have increasingly replaced acute infectious diseases as the major causes of disability and death, at least in industrialized countries. Consequently, theories of disease etiology have shifted from ones in which a single factor (usually a microbe) caused a single disease, to ones in which multiple behavioral and environmental as well as biologic and genetic factors combine, often over extended periods, to produce any single disease, with a given factor often playing an etiologic role in multiple diseases.

Cassel[13] and Cobb[14] reviewed more than 30 human and animal studies that found social relationships protective of health. Recognizing that any one study was open to alternative interpretations, they argued that the variety of study designs (ranging from retrospective to experimental), of life stages studied (from birth to death), and of health outcomes involved (including low birth weight, complications of pregnancy, self-reported symptoms, blood pressure, arthritis, tuberculosis, depression, alcoholism, and mortality) suggested a robust, putatively causal, association. Cassel and Cobb indicated that social relationships might promote health in several ways, but emphasized the role of social relationships in moderating or buffering potentially deleterious health effects of psychosocial stress or other health hazards. This idea of "social support," or something that maintains or sustains the organism by promoting adaptive behavior or neuroendocrine responses in the face of stress or other health hazards, provided a general, albeit simple, theory of how and why social relationships should causally affect health.[16]

Publications on "social support" increased almost geometrically from 1976 to 1981. By the late 1970s, however, serious questions emerged from the empirical evidence cited by Cassel and Cobb and the evidence generated in subsequent research. Concerns were expressed about causal priorities between social support and health (since the great majority of studies remained cross-sectional or retrospective and based on self-reported data), about whether social relationships and supports buffered the impact of stress on health or had more direct effects, and about how consequential the effects of social relationships on health really were.[17-19] These concerns have been addressed by a continuing cumulation of two types of empirical data: (i) a new series of prospective mortality studies in human populations and (ii) a broadening base of laboratory and field experimental studies of animals and humans.

PROSPECTIVE MORTALITY STUDIES OF HUMAN POPULATIONS

JUST as concerns began to surface about the nature and strength of the impact of social relationships on health, data from long-term, pro-spective studies of community populations provided compelling evidence that lack of social relationships constitutes a major risk factor for mortality. Berkman and Syme[20] analyzed a probability sample of 4775 adults in Alameda County, California, who were between 30 and 69 in 1965 when they completed a survey that assessed the presence or extent of four types of social ties—marriage, contacts with extended family and friends, church membership, and other formal and informal group affiliations. Each type of social relationship predicted mortality through the succeeding 9 years. A combined "social network" index remained a significant predictor of mortality (with a relative risk ratio for mortality of about 2.0, indicating that persons low on the index were twice as likely to die as persons high on the index) in multivariate analyses that controlled for self-reports in 1965 of physical health, socioeconomic status, smoking, alcohol consumption, physical activity, obesity, race, life satisfaction, and use of preventive health services. Such adjustment or control for baseline health and other risk factors provides a conservative estimate of the predictive power of social relationships, since some of their impact may be mediated through effects on these risk factors.

The major limitation of the Berkman and Syme study was the lack of other than self-reported data on health at baseline. Thus, House et al.[21] sought to replicate and extend the Alameda County results in a study of 2754 adults between 35 and 69 at their initial interview and physical examinations in 1967 through 1969 by the Tecumseh (Michigan) Community Health Study. Composite indices of social relationships and activities (as well as a number of the individual components) were inversely associated with mortality during the succeeding 10- to 12-year follow-up period, with relative risks of 2.0 to 3.0 for men and 1.5 to 2.0 for women, after adjustment for the effects of age and a wide range of biomedically assessed (blood pressure, cholesterol, respiratory function, and electrocardiograms) as well as self-reported risk factors of mortality. Analyzing data on 2059 adults in the Evans County (Georgia) Cardiovascular Epidemiologic Study, Schoenbach et al.[22] also found that a social network index similar to that of Berkman and Syme[20] predicted mortality for 11- to 13-year follow-up period, after adjustment for age and baseline measures of biomedical as well as self-reported risk factors of mortality. The Evans County associations were somewhat weaker than those in Tecumseh and Alameda County, and as in Tecumseh were stronger for males than females.

Studies in Sweden and Finland have described similar results. Tibblin, Welin, and associates[23,24] studied two cohorts of men born in 1913 and 1923, respectively, and living in 1973 in Gothenberg, Sweden's second largest city. After adjustments for age, baseline levels of systolic blood pressure, serum cholesterol, smoking habits, and perceived health status, mortality in both cohorts through 1982 was inversely related to the number of persons in the household and the men's level of social and outside home activities in 1973. Orth-Gomer et al.[25] analyzed the mortality experience through 1981 of a random sample of 17,433 Swedish adults aged 29 to 74 at the time of their 1976 or 1977 baseline interviews. Frequency of contact with family, friends, neighbors, and co-workers in 1976–77 was predictive of mortality through 1981, after adjustment for age, sex, education, employment status, immigrant status, physical exercise, and self-reports of chronic conditions. The effects were stronger among males than among females, and were somewhat nonlinear, with the greatest increase in mortality risk occurring in the most socially isolated third of the sample. In a prospective study of 13,301 adults in predominantly rural eastern Finland, Kaplan et al.[26] found a measure of "social connections" similar to those used in Alameda County, Tecumseh, and Evans County to be a significant predictor of male mortality from all causes during 5 years, again after adjustments for

other biomedical and self-reported risk factors. Female mortality showed similar, but weaker and statistically nonsignificant, effects.

These studies manifest a consistent pattern of results, as shown in Figs. 1 and 2, which show age-adjusted mortality rates plotted for the five prospective studies from which we could extract parallel data. The report of the sixth study[25] is consistent with these trends. The relative risks (*RR*) in Figs. 1 and 2 are higher than those reported above because they are only adjusted for age. The levels of mortality in Figs. 1 and 2 vary greatly across studies depending on the follow-up period and composition of the population by age, race, and ethnicity, and geographic locale, but the patterns of prospective association between social integration (that is, the number and frequency of social relationships and contacts) and mortality are remarkably similar, with some variations by race, sex, and geographic locale.

Only the Evans County study reported data for blacks. The predictive association of social integration with mortality among Evans County black males is weaker than among white males in Evans County or elsewhere (Fig. 1), and the relative risk ratio for black females in Evans County, although greater than for Evans County white females, is smaller than the risk ratios for white females in all other studies (Fig. 2). More research on blacks and other minority populations is necessary to determine whether these differences are more generally characteristic of blacks compared to whites.

Modest differences emerge by sex and rural as opposed to urban locale. Results for men and women are strong, linear, and similar in the urban populations of Alameda County (that is, Oakland and environs) and Gothenberg, Sweden (only men were studied in Gothenberg). In the predominantly small-town and rural populations of Tecumseh, Evans County, and eastern Finland, however, two notable deviations from the urban results appear: (i) female risk ratios are consistently weaker than those for men in the same rural populations (Figs. 1 and 2), and (ii) the results for men in more rural populations, although rivaling those in urban populations in terms of risk ratios, assume a distinctly nonlinear, or threshold, form. That is, in Tecumseh, Evans County, and eastern Finland, mortality is clearly among the most socially isolated, but declines only modestly, if at all, between moderate and high levels of social integration.

Explanation of these sex and urban-rural variations awaits research on broader regional or national populations in which the same measures are applied to males and females across the full rural-urban continuum. The current results may have both substantive and methodological explanations. Most of the studies reviewed here, as well as others,[27-29] suggest that being married is more beneficial to health, and becoming widowed more detrimental, for men than for women. Women, however, seem to benefit as much or more than men from relationships with friends and relatives, which tend to run along same-sex lines.[20, 30] On balance, men may benefit more from social relationships than women, especially in cross-gender relationships. Small communities may also provide a broader context of social integration and support that benefits most people, except for a relatively small group of socially isolated males.

These results may, however, have methodological rather than substantive explanations. Measures of social relationships or integration used in the existing prospective studies may be less valid or have less variance in rural and small town environments, and for women, thus muting their relationship with mortality. For example, the data for women in Fig. 2 are similar to the data on men if we assume that women have higher quality relationships and hence that their true level of social integration is moderate even at low levels of quantity. The social context of small communities may similarly provide a moderate level of social integration for everyone except

quite isolated males. Thus measures of frequency of social contact may be poorer indices of social integration for women and more rural populations than for men and urban dwellers.

Variations in the results in Figs. 1 and 2 should not, however, detract from the remarkable consistency of the overall finding that social relationships do predict mortality for men and women in a wide range of populations, even after adjustment for biomedical risk factors for mortality. Additional prospective studies have shown that social relationships are similarly predictive of all-cause and cardiovascular mortality in studies of people who are elderly[31-33] or have serious illness.[34, 35]

EXPERIMENTAL AND QUASI-EXPERIMENTAL RESEARCH

THE prospective mortality data are made more compelling by their congruence with growing evidence from experimental and clinical research on animals and humans that variations in exposure to social contacts produce psychological or physiological effects that could, if prolonged, produce serious morbidity and even mortality. Cassel[13] reviewed evidence that the presence of a familiar member of the same species could buffer the impact of experimentally induced stress on ulcers, hypertension, and neurosis in rats, mice, and goats, respectively, and the presence of familiar others has also been shown to reduce anxiety and physiological arousal (specifically secretion of free fatty acids) in humans in potentially stressful laboratory situations.[36, 37] Clinical and laboratory data indicate that the presence of or physical contact with another person can modulate human cardiovascular activity and reactivity in general, and in stressful concerns such as intensive care units.[38] Research also points to the operation of such processes across species. Affectionate petting by humans, or even their mere presence, can reduce the cardiovascular sequelae of stressful situations among dogs, cats, horses, and rabbits.[38] Nerem *et al.*[39] found that human handling also reduced the arteriosclerotic impact of a high fat diet in rabbits. Recent interest in the potential health benefits of pets for humans, especially the isolated aged, is based on similar notions, although the evidence for such efforts is only suggestive.[40]

Bovard[41] has proposed a psychophysiologic theory to explain how social relationships and contacts can promote health and protect against disease. He reviews a wide range of human and animal studies suggesting that social relationships and contacts, mediated through the amygdala, activate the anterior hypothalamic zone (stimulating release of human growth hormone) and inhibit the posterior hypothalamic zone (and hence secretion of adrenocorticotropic hormone, cortisol, catecholamines, and associated sympathetic autonomic activity). These mechanisms are consistent with the impact of social relationships on mortality from a wide range of causes and with studies of the adverse effects of lack of adequate social relationships on the development of human and animal infants.[42] This theory is also consistent with sociobiological processes which, due to the survival benefit of social relationships and collective activity, would promote genetic selection of organisms who find social contact and relatedness rewarding and the lack of such contact and relatedness aversive.[43]

The epidemiologic evidence linking social relationships and supports to morbidity in humans is limited and not fully consistent. For example, although laboratory studies show short-term effects of social relationships on cardiovascular functioning that would, over time, produce cardiovascular disease, and prospective studies show impacts of social relationships on mortality from cardiovascular disease, the link between social relationships and the incidence of cardiovascular morbidity has yet to be firmly demonstrated.[19, 44] Overall, however, the theory and evidence for the impact of social relationships on health are building steadily.[45, 46]

SOCIAL RELATIONSHIPS AS A RISK FACTOR FOR HEALTH: RESEARCH AND POLICY ISSUES

THE theory and data reviewed above meet reasonable criteria for considering social relationships a cause or risk factor of mortality, and probably morbidity, from a wide range of diseases.[10; 46; 47] These criteria include strength and consistency of statistical associations across a wide range of studies, temporal ordering or prediction from cause to effect, a gradient of response (which may in this case be nonlinear), experimental data on animals and humans consistent with nonexperimental human data, and a plausible theory[41] of biopsychosocial mechanisms explaining the observed associations.

The evidence on social relationships is probably stronger, especially in terms of prospective studies, than the evidence which led to the certification of the Type A behavior pattern as a risk factor for coronary heart disease.[48] The evidence regarding social relationships and health increasingly approximates the evidence in the 1964 Surgeon General's report[10] that established cigarette smoking as a cause or risk factor for mortality and morbidity from a range of diseases. The age-adjusted relative risk ratios shown in Figs. 1 and 2 are stronger than the relative risks for all cause mortality reported for cigarette smoking.[10] There is, however, less specificity in the associations of social relationships with mortality than has been observed for smoking, which is strongly linked to cancers of the lung and respiratory tract (with age-adjusted risk ratios between 3.0 and 11.0). Better theory and data are needed on the links between social relationships and major specific causes of morbidity and mortality.

Although a lack of social relationships has been established as a risk factor for mortality, and probably, morbidity, three areas need further investigation: (i) mechanisms and processes linking social relationships to health, (ii) determinants of levels of "exposure" to social relationships, and (iii) the means to lower the prevalence of relative social isolation in the population or to lessen its deleterious effects on health.

MECHANISMS AND PROCESSES LINKING SOCIAL RELATIONSHIPS TO HEALTH

ALTHOUGH grounded in the literature on social relationships and health, investigators on social support in the last decade leaped almost immediately to the interpretation that what was consequential for health abut social relationships was their supportive quality, especially their capacity to buffer or moderate the deleterious effects of stress or other health hazards.[13, 14] Many recent studies have reported either a general positive association between social support and health or a buffering effect in the presence of stress,[49] but these studies are problematic because the designs are largely cross-sectional or retrospective and the data usually self-reported. The most compelling evidence of the causal significance of social relationships on

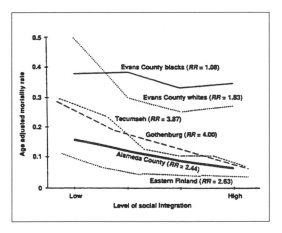

Figure 2

Level of social integration and age-adjusted mortality for females in five prospective studies. RR, *the relative risk ratio of mortality at the lowest versus highest level of social integration.*

health has come from the experimental studies of animals and humans and the prospective mortality studies reviewed above—studies in which the measures of social relationships are merely the presence or absence of familiar other organisms, or relative frequency of contact with them, and which often do not distinguish between buffering and main effects. Thus, social relationships appear to have generally beneficial effects on health, not solely or even primarily attributable to their buffering effects, and there may be aspects of social relationships other than their supportive quality that account for these effects.

We now need a broader theory of the biopsychosocial mechanisms and processes linking social relationships to health than can be provided by extant concepts or theories of social support. That broader theory must do several things. First, it must clearly distinguish between (i) the existence or quantity of social relationships, (ii) their formal structure (such as their density or reciprocity), and (iii) the actual content of these relationships such as social support. Only by testing the effects on health of these different aspects of social relationships in the same study can we understand what it is about social relationships that is consequential for health.

Second, we need better understanding of the social, psychological, and biological processes that link the existence, quantity, structure, or content of social relationships to health. Social support—whether in the form of practical help, emotional sustenance, or provision of information—is only one of the social processes involved here. Not only may social relationships affect health because they are or are not supportive, they may also regulate or control human thought, feeling and behavior in ways that promote health, as in Durkheim's[2] theory relating social integration to suicide. Current views based on this perspective suggest that social relationships affect health either by fostering a sense of meaning or coherence that promotes health[50] or by facilitating health-promoting behaviors such as proper sleep, diet, or exercise, appropriate use of alcohol, cigarettes, and drugs, adherence to medical regimens, or seeking appropriate medical care.[51] The negative or conflictive aspects of social relationships need also to be considered, since they may be detrimental to the maintenance of health of social relationships.[52]

We must further understand the psychological and biological processes or mechanisms linking social relationships to health, either as extensions of the social processes just discussed [for example, processes of cognitive appraisal and coping[53]] or as independent mechanisms. In the latter regard, psychological and sociobiological theories suggest that the mere presence of, or sense of relatedness with, another organism may have relatively direct motivational, emotional, or neuroendocrinal effects that promote health either directly or in the face of stress or other health hazards but that operate independently of cognitive appraisal or behavioral coping and adaptation.[38, 42, 43, 54].

DETERMINANTS OF SOCIAL RELATIONSHIPS: SCIENTIFIC AND POLICY ISSUES

ALTHOUGH social relationships have been extensively studied during the past decade as independent, intervening, and moderating variables affecting stress or health or the relations between them, almost no attention has been paid to social relationships as dependent variables. The determinants of social relationships, as well as their consequences, are crucial to the theoretical and causal status of social relationships in relation to health. If exogenous biological, psychological, or social variables determine both health and the nature of social relationships, then the observed association of social relationships to health may be totally or partially spurious. More practically, Cassel,[13] Cobb,[14] and others became interested in social support as a means of improving health. This, in

turn, requires understanding of the broader social, as well as psychological or biological, structures and processes that determine the quantity and quality of social relationships and support in society.

It is clear that biology and personality must and do affect both people's health and the quantity and quality of their social relationships. Research has established that such factors do not, however, explain away the experimental, cross-sectional, and prospective evidence linking social relationships to health.[55] In none of the prospective studies have controls for biological or health variables been able to explain away the predictive association between social relationships and mortality. Efforts to explain away the association of social relationships and supports with health by controls for personality variables have similarly failed.[56, 57] Social relationships have a predictive, arguably causal, association with health in their own right.

The extent and quality of social relationships experienced by individuals is also a function of broader social forces. Whether people are employed, married, attend church, belong to organizations, or have frequent contact with friends and relatives, and the nature and quality of those relationships, are all determined in part by their positions in a larger social structure that is stratified by age, race, sex, and socioeconomic status and is organized in terms of residential communities, work organizations, and larger political and economic structures. Older people, blacks, and the poor are generally less socially integrated,[58] and differences in social relationships by sex and place of residence have been discussed in relation to Figs. 1 and 2. Changing patterns of fertility, mortality, and migration in society affect opportunities for work, marriage, living and working in different settings, and having relationships with friends and relatives, and can even affect the nature and quality of these relations.[59] These demographic patterns are themselves subject to influence by both planned and unplanned economic and political change, which can also affect individuals' social relationships more directly—witness the massive increase in divorce during the last few decades in response to the women's movement, growth in women's labor force participation, and changing divorce law[60, 61].

In contrast with the 1950s, adults in the United States in the 1970s were less likely to be married, more likely to be living alone, less likely to belong to voluntary organizations, and less likely to visit informally with others.[62] Changes in marital and childbearing patterns and in the age structure of our society will produce in the 21st century a steady increase of the number of older people who lack spouses or children—the people to whom older people most often turn for relatedness and support. Thus, just as we discover the importance of social relationships for health, and see an increasing need for them, their prevalence and availability may be declining. Changes in other risk factors (for example, the decline of smoking) and improvements in medical technology are still producing overall improvements on health and longevity, but the improvements might be even greater if the quantity and quality of social relationships were also improving.

We are indebted to D. Buss, P. Converse, G. Duncan, R. Kahn, R. Kessler, H. Schuman, L. Syme, and R. Zajonc for comments on previous drafts, to many other colleagues who have contributed to this field, and to M. Klart for preparing the manuscript.

REFERENCES AND NOTES

1. C. Darwin, *Expression of the Emotions in Men and Animals* (Univ. of Chicago Press, Chicago, 1965 [1872]).

2. E. Durkheim, *Suicide* (Free Press, New York, 1951 [1897]).

3. A. S. Kraus and A. N. Lilienfeld, *J. Chcronic Dis.* 10, 207 (1959).

4. H. Carter and P. C. Glick, *Marriage and Divorce: A Social and Economic Study* (Harvard Univ. Press, Cambridge, MA, 1970).

5. E. M. Kitigawa and P. M. Hauser, *Differential Mortality in the United States: A Study in Socio-Economic Epidemiology* (Harvard Univ. Press, Cambridge, MA, 1973).

6. T. H. Holmes, in *Personality, Stress and Tuberculosis*, P. J. Sparer, Ed. (International Univ. Press, New York, 1956).

7. W. A. Tillman and G. E. Hobbs, *Am. J. Psychiatr.* 106, 321 (1949).

8. R. E. L. Faris, *Am. J. Sociol.* 39, 155 (1934).

9. M. L. Kohn and J. A. Clausen, *Am. Sociol. Rev.* 20, 268 (1955).

10. U.S. Surgeon General's Advisory Committee on Smoking and Health, *Smoking and Health* (U.S. Public Health Service, Wasignton, DC, 1964).

11. G. Caplan, *Support Systems and Community Mental Health* (Behavioral Publications, New York, 1974).

12. President's Commission on Mental Health, *Report to the President* (Government Printing Office, Washignton, DC, 1978), vols. 1 to 5.

13. J. Cassel, *Am. J. Epidemiol.* 104, 107 (1976).

14. S. Cobb, *Psychosomatic Med.* 38, 300 (1976).

15. J. Cassel, in *Social Stress*, S. Levine and N. A. Scotch, Eds. (Aldine, Chicago, 1970), pp. 189–209.

16. J. S. House, *Work Stress and Social Support* (Addison-Wesley, Reading, MA, 1981).

17. K. Heller, in *Maximizing Treatment Gains: Transfer Enhancement in Psychotherapy*, A. P. Goldstein and F. H. Kanter, Eds. (Academic Press, New York, 1979), pp. 353–382.

18. P. A. Thoits, *J. Health Soc. Behav.* 23, 145 (1982).

19. D. Reed *et al.*, *Am. J. Epidemiol.* 117, 384 (1983).

20. L. F. Berkman and S. L. Syne, *ibid.* 109, 186 (1979).

21. J. S. House, C. Robbins, H. M. Metzner, *ibid.* 116, 123 (1982).

22. V. J. Schoenbach *et al.*, *ibid.* 123, 577 (1986).

23. G. Tibblin *et al.*, in *Social Support: Health and Disease*, S. O. Isacsson and L. Janzon, Eds. (Almqvist & Wiksell, Stockholm, 1986), pp. 11–19.

24. L. Welin *et al.*, *Lancet* 1–?, 915 (1985).

25. K. Orth-Gomer and J. Johnson, *J. Chron. Dis.* 40, 949 (1987).

26. G. A. Kaplan *et al.*, *Am. J. Epidemiol.*, in press.

27. M. Stroebe and W. Stroebe, *Psychol. Bull.* 93, 279 (1983).

28. W. R. Gove, *Soc. Forces* 51, 34 (1972).

29. K. J. Helsing and M. Szklo, *Am. J. Epidemiol.* 114, 41 (1981).

30. L. Wheeler, H. Reis, J. Nezlek, *J. Pers. Soc. Psychol.* 45, 943 (1983).

31. D. Blazer, *Am. J. Epidemiol.* 115, 684 (1982).

32. D. M. Zuckerman, S. V. Kasl, A. M. Ostfeld, *ibid.* 119, 410 (1984).

33. T. E. Seeman *et al., ibid.* 126, 714 (1987).

34. W. E. Ruberman *et al., N. Engl. J. Med.* 311, 552 (1984).

35. K. Orth-Gomer *et al.,* in *Social Support: Health and Disease,* S. O. Isacsson and L. Janzon, Eds. (Almqvist & Wiksell, Stockholm, 1986), pp. 21–31.

36. L. S. Wrightsman, Jr., *J. Abnorm. Soc. Psychol.* 61, 216 (1960).

37. K. W. Back and M. D. Bogdonoff, *Behav. Sci.* 12, 384 (1967).

38. J. J. Lynch, *The Broken Heart* (Basic Books, New York, 1979).

39. R. M. Nerem, M. J. Levesque, J. F. Cornhill, *Science* 208, 1475 (1980).

40. J. Goldmeier, *Gerontologist* 26, 203 (1986).

41. E. W. Bovard, in *Perspectives on Behavioral Medicine,* R. B. Williams (Academic Press, New York, 1985), vol. 2.

42. J. Bowlby, in *Loneliness: The Experience of Emotional and Social Isolation,* R. S. Weiss, Ed. (MIT Press, Cambridge, MA, 1973).

43. S. P. Mendoza, in *Social Cohesion: Essays Toward a Sociophysiological Perspective,* P. R. Barchas and S. P. Mendoza, Eds. (Greenwood Press, Westport, CT, 1984).

44. S. Cohen, *Health Psychol.* 7, 269 (1988).

45. L. F. Berkman, in *Social Support and Health,* S. Cohen and S. L. Syme, Eds. (Academic Press, New York, 1985), pp. 241–262.

46. W. E. Broadhead *et al., Am. J. Epidemiol.* 117, 521 (1983).

47. A. M. Lilienfeld and D. E. Lilienfeld, *Foundations of Epidemiology* (Oxford Univ. Press, New York, 1980).

48. National Heart, Lung and Blood Institute, *Circulation* 63, 1199 (1982).

49. S. Cohen and S. L. Syme, *Social Support and Health* (Academic Press, New York, 1985).

50. A. Antonovsky, *Health, Stress and Coping* (Jossey-Bass, San Francisco, 1979).

51. D. Umberson, *J. Health Soc. Behav.* 28, 306 (1987).

52. K. Rock, *J. Pers. Soc. Psychol.* 46, 1097 (1984).

53. R. S. Lazarus and S. Folkman, *Stress, Appraisal, and Coping* (Springer, New York, 1984),

54. R. B. Zajonc, *Science* 149, 269 (1965).

55. J. S. House, D. Umberson, K. Landis, *Annu. Rev., Sociol., in press.*

56. S. Cohen, D. R. Sherrod, M. S. Clark, *J. Pers. Soc. Psychol.* 50, 963 (1986).

57. R. Schultz and S. Decker, *ibid.* 48, 1162 (1985).

58. J. S. House, *Socio, Forum* 2, 135 (1987).

59. S. C. Watkins, J. A. Menken, J. Bongaarts, *Am. Sociol. Rev.* 52, 346 (1987).

60. A. Cherlin, *Marriage, Divorce, Remarriage* (Harvard Univ. Press, Cambridge, MA, 1981).

61. L. J. Weitzman, *The Divorce Revolution* (Free Press, New York, 1985).

62. J. Veroff, E. Douvan, R. A. Kulka, *The Inner American: A Self-Portrait from 1957 to 1976* (Basic Books, New York, 1981.

Eighteen

THE ROLE OF SOCIAL RELATIONS
IN HEALTH PROMOTION

Lisa F. Berkman

ABSTRACT

In considering new paradigms for the prevention and treatment of disease and disability, we need to incorporate ways to promote social support and develop family and community strengths and abilities into our interventions. There is now a substantial body of evidence that indicates that the extent to which social relationships are strong and supportive is related to the health of individuals who live within such social contexts. A review of population-based research on mortality risk over the last 20 years indicates that people who are isolated are at increased mortality risk from a number of causes. More recent studies indicate that social support is particularly related to survival postmyocardial infarction. The pathways that lead from such socioenvironmental exposures to poor health outcomes are likely to be multiple and include behavioral mechanisms and more direct physiologic pathways related to neuroendocrine or immunologic function. For social support to be health promoting, it must provide both a sense of belonging and intimacy and must help people to be more competent and self-efficacious. Acknowledging that health promotion rests on the shoulders not only of individuals but also of their families and communities means that we must commit resources over the next decade to designing, testing, and implementing interventions in this area.

INTRODUCTION

AS our nation confronts a health care crisis and as disease, disability, and violence become centered more and more in the poorest, most isolated, and marginal segments of our populations, it is time to consider new paradigms for the prevention and treatment of disease and disability. In considering new preventive efforts, it is important to keep in mind that individuals do not live in a vacuum, rather they are enmeshed in a social environment and in a series of social relationships. There is now a substantial body of evidence that indicates that the extent to which these relationships are strong and supportive and individuals are integrated in their communities is related to the health of the individuals who live within such social contexts.

Almost 20 years ago, epidemiologists who

Originally published in *Psychosomatic Medicine*, 1995.

were interested in how social conditions might influence health status began to develop the idea that one of the most important factors that protected people from what seemed to be overwhelming insults, both natural and humanmade, was the extent to which people maintained close personal relationships with others, i.e., the degree to which they were socially integrated into their communities and had deep and abiding social and psychological resources.[1-4]

Unlike most epidemiologic research, the hallmark of much of this work from the start was its focus, i.e., not on any specific disease but rather on the degree to which these social conditions influence what was rather loosely termed "host resistance." In other words, in contrast to a host of other conditions and exposures, including psychological stressors, that result in classes of *specific* psychosomatic diseases, this class of experiences seemed to make people more vulnerable to a broad range of diseases and disabilities, which ranged from pregnancy complications and infant health in the early parts of life to disability in old age.[1] This idea was defended on the basis of principles articulated in the early part of this century by such scientists as Wade Hampton Frost,[5] who in speaking about declining rates of tuberculosis occurring in the first half of the century wrote

"One of the most important factors in the decline of tuberculosis has been progressively increasing human resistance due to environmental improvements such as better nutrition and relief from physical stress tending to raise what may be called *nonspecific resistance.*"[5]

To give you an idea of the novelty of the proposition that, first, social factors might be determinants of disease and, second, they might influence *a broad range of disease* outcomes, I would like to recount to you a small part of an exchange that took place during my doctoral comprehensive examinations in 1975. During these tests, candidates were asked to defend dissertation plans and underlying epidemiologic theory. The committee came quickly to a discussion of how social networks might influence health status. I offered the opinion that social support or networks influence many disease outcomes because these social conditions influence susceptibility to disease in general. I went on to add some hypothetical pathways involving neuroendocrine regulation and potential immune responses, which in turn might influence both diseases of an infectious nature and cancer and heart disease. At that point, the senior member of this committee, a man distinguished by his identification of viruses associated with major illnesses, proclaimed, "Over the last 150 years of medical research from Pasteur, Koch onward, research has proceeded *successfully* along the lines of identifying one cause of one disease with the theory of disease specificity being one of the major advances in our thinking over the last century." In fact, he correctly recounted, we often *name* diseases after specific etiologic agents once they are identified. He went on to question whether we should ignore this vast body of evidence and return to an era in which we invoke such vague concepts as "social forces" or perhaps "fevers," "miasma," and "consumption" and that furthermore we permit such forces to rule our current models of disease causation.

With more evidence than was available 20 years ago, I would like to respond to this issue today the way I responded to it then with a "yes."

Between 1979 with the Alameda County Study and 1994, there have been eight community-based prospective studies that reveal an association between what we have now come to call "social integration" and mortality rates, usually death from all causes.[6-13] Although there are substantial variations among these studies in measurement of social relationships, in types of communities under investigation, and in length of follow-up, they show remarkably consistent results. In almost all cases, those who are most socially isolated and "disconnected" are at increased risk.

In the first of these studies from Alameda County,[6] men and women who lacked ties to others (in this case, based on an index assessing contacts with friends and relatives, marital status, and church and group membership) were 1.9 to 3.1 times more likely to die in a 9-year follow-up period from 1965 to 1974 than those who had many more contacts.

The relative risks associated with social isolation were *not* centered in one cause of death; rather those who lacked social ties were at increased risk of dying from ischemic heart disease (IHD), cerebrovascular and circulatory disease, cancer, and a final category including respiratory, gastrointestinal, and all other causes of death. Clearly, this social condition is not associated exclusively with increased risks from, say, coronary heart disease (CHD).

Although this study opened the field to much work in this area, there were some methodologic problems with it. Perhaps the most important of which was that the Alameda County Study had no clinical assessment of health status and relied exclusively on subject's self-reports of conditions. Thus, it is open to the criticism that prevalent disease might influence the extent to which people could maintain active social relationships and this association might be the underlying reason why isolation is related to mortality risk. Although this is a viable hypothesis, a study of men and women in the North Karelia CHD Study supports the importance of this new social risk factor independently of prelavent CHD or other standard cardiovascular risk factors.[9] In this study, men and women were enrolled in a study of cardiovascular diseases. Prevalent cases of CHD were excluded; traditional CHD risk factors, blood pressure, cholesterol level, and other behavioral risk factors were assessed. The percentage of subjects who died from IHD and other causes was significantly associated with the level of social connectedness, a measure similar to the one used in Alameda County. Among men, those who were disconnected were at increased risk of dying of CHD and had an increased total mortality rate. There was no association between social ties and mortality rates among women, but it is important to note that women had very low mortality rates from any cause in this study of middle-aged men and women. The low prevalence of the outcome renders interpretation of risk difficult.

Data from these two studies of what I have called first-generation studies because they often used crude or post hoc measures of social networks are illustrative of the others in Table 1. Overall, they consistently show that people who are isolated are at increased mortality risk from a number of causes. Furthermore, they have several important methodologic strengths, which give us have confidence in the findings, as follows:

1. These studies are *prospective cohort* studies in which ascertainment of social ties is not biased by differential recall.
2. The studies are population based. They are not composed of cohorts of volunteers or small, nonrandom segments of the population.
3. The studies have remarkably few losses to follow-up. In Alameda County, less than 4% were lost to follow-up over a decade. In a more recent study of elderly men and women in the Established Population for the Epidemiologic Study of the Elderly (EPESE), less than 1% were lost to follow-up.[13]
4. This population-based sampling strategy coupled with small loss to follow-up leads to minimal selection bias.
5. Finally, when the studies are examined en masse, most relevant covariates have been included in most analyses, although certainly not all have been examined.

Thus, we can be confident that, based on these findings, risks are meaningful, consistent, and of sufficient magnitude that we are observing an important phenomenon.

In spite of this strong evidence, there is still much that is not known and will need to be known to improve health by modifying social conditions. For instance, we have little information on where along the spectrum of disease development these social factors have their greatest

Table 1

Social Network/Support Studies of All-Cause or CHD Mortality Rate

Study	Outcome	Sample Size	Age Range	Number of Outcome Events[a]	Average Follow-Up
Community-Based					
Alameda County, Berkman and Syme (6)	All-cause mortality	4725	30–69	371	9 years
Tecumseh, Michigan, House et al. (8)	All-cause mortality	2754	30–69	259	9–12 years
Duke, Blazer (7)	All-cause mortality	331	65	50	30 months
Swedish men, Welin et al. (7)	All-cause mortality	989	50, 60	151	9 years
Evans County, Georgia, Schoenbach et al. (11)	All-cause mortality	2059	15	530	12 years
Swedish population, Orth-Gomer and Johnson (10)	All-cause mortality	17,433	29–74	841	6 years
North Karelia, Finland, Kaplan et al. (9)	All-cause mortality	13,301	39–59	598	5 years
EPESE, Seeman et al. (13)	All-cause mortality		65+		5 years
East Boston		3807		892	
Iowa		3097		583	
New Haven		2788		803	
Survival Post-MI					
B-HAT, Ruberman et al. (14)	All-cause mortality	2320	30–69	184	3 years
Swedish men, Orth-Gomer et al. (15)	All-cause mortality	150	40–65	34	10 years
Diltiazem Post-Infarction Trial, Case et al. (17)	Recurrent nonfatal MI or cardiac death	1234	25–75	226	25 months
Angiography and coronary artery disease, Williams et al. (16)	Cardiovascular death	1368	46–58	237	4–11 years
EPESE, Berkman et al. (18)	All-cause mortality	194	65+	76	6 months

[a]Number of events = actual number of outcome events in the cohort described in outcome column (e.g., deaths from all causes, CHD, or recurrent nonfatal MIs).

impact. Do they influence the development of risk factors or health behaviors, subclinical disease, incidence of clinical events, or case fatality? Second, we need a much clearer understanding of the mechanisms or pathways that link socioenvironmental conditions to morbidity and mortality rates. Finally, of the utmost importance is the need to learn whether we can modify or intervene on these conditions to improve health status.

In the remainder of this discussion, I focus some attention on each of these issues.

Studies of Recovery from Myocardial Infarction (MI)

ALTHOUGH the previously mentioned community-based studies showed social isolation or lack of social ties to be related to mortality risk, these studies did not clarify where along the spectrum of disease social factors might have their greatest impact. For instance, do they influence the mortality rate by influencing the onset or progression of clinical disease or survival after an event?

Recently, researchers have began to address this question by examining the influence of social ties on survival in patients post-MI. In five studies, patients who lacked social support, lived alone, or had not been married had an elevated mortality risk post-MI (Table 1).[14-18] In the first of these, Ruberman et al.[14] explored 2320 male survivors of acute MI who were participants in the Beta-Blocker Heart Attack Trial. Patients who were socially isolated were more than twice as likely to die over a 3-year period than those who were less socially isolated. When this measure of social isolation was combined with a general measure of life stress, which included items related to occupational status, divorce, exposure to violent events, retirement, or financial difficulty, the risks associated with high-risk psychosocial status were even greater. Those in the high-risk psychosocial categories were four to five times as likely to die as those in the lowest

risk categories. This psychosocial characteristic was associated with death from all causes and sudden deaths. It made large contributions to mortality risk in both the high-arrhythmia and low-arrhythmia groups. In this study (and most of the studies in which subjects are recruited postevent), the investigators were not able to determine the temporal association between the assessment of psychosocial resources and the severity of disease. Nonetheless, it serves as a powerful model for future studies.

In a second Swedish study of 150 cardiac patients and patients with high-risk factor levels for CHD, the finding that lack of support predicts death was further confirmed.[15] Patients who were socially isolated had a three times higher 10-year mortality rate than did those who were socially active and integrated. Because these patients were examined extensively for cardiological prognostic factors at study entry, it was possible to disentangle effects of psychosocial and clinical characteristics.

In a third study, Williams et al.[16] enrolled 1368 patients who were undergoing cardiac catheterization from 1974 through 1980 and found to have significant coronary artery disease. They examined survival time until cardiovascular death through 1989. Men constituted 82% of the sample. In this study, men and women who were unmarried or without a confidant were over three times as likely to die within 5 years compared with those who had a close confidant or who were married (odds ratio (OR), 3.34; confidence interval (CI), 1.8–6.2). This association was independent of other clinical prognostic indicators and sociodemographic factors, including socioeconomic status.

In another study, Case et al.[17] examined the association between marital status and recurrent major cardiac events among patients post-MI who were enrolled in the placebo arm of a clinical trial, the Multicenter Diltiazem Post-Infarction Trial. These investigators reported that living alone was an independent risk factor with a hazard ratio of 1.54 (CI, 1.04–2.29) for recurrent major cardiac event, including both nonfatal infarctions or cardiac deaths.

In a fifth study, we explored the relationship between social networks and support and mortality rate among men and women hospitalized for a MI between 1982 and 1988 who are participants in the population-based New Haven EPESE.[18] Over the study period, 100 men and 94 women were hospitalized for an MI. Thirty-four per cent of women and 44% of men died in the 6-month period after MI (Figure 1).

Among both men and women, emotional support, measured prospectively, that is, before the MI was related to both early in-hospital death and later death over a 1-year period. Among those admitted to the hospital, almost 38% of those who reported no source of emotional support died in the hospital compared with 11.5% of those with two or more sources of support. The patterns remained steady throughout the follow-up period. At 6 months, the major end point of the study, 52.8% of those with no source of support had died compared with 36.0% of those with one source and 23.1% of those with two or more sources of support. These figures did not change substantially at 1 year. As Figure 1 shows, the patterns were remarkably consistent for both men and women, younger and older people, those with greater or lesser comorbidity, and those with more or less severe cardiovascular disease, as assessed by a Killip classification system. In multivariate models that control for sociodemographic factors, psychosocial factors, including living arrangements, depressive symptoms, and clinical prognostic indicators, men and women who reported no emotional support had almost three times the mortality risk compared with subjects who reported at least one source of support (OR, 2.9; 95% CI, 1.2–6.9).

The findings from these studies are strong and consistent, although the measures of support and the populations vary dramatically. Whereas they in no way preclude the possibility that these social factors influence the onset of CHD, they strongly suggest that they influence survival post-MI.

This large body of research focusing on mortality rates, and more recently case-fatality rates, specifically, is complemented by a more limited but growing body of literature on disease progression[19, 20] incidence and functional disability,[21-24] especially related to CHD and cerebrovascular disease. In considering ways in which we can maximize opportunities to make substantial progress in this area over the next years, we should investigate the influence of social relationships on the full spectrum of disease development to understand where interventions will be most effective.

PATHWAYS LEADING TO DISEASE: THE SEARCH FOR A BIOLOGIC LINK

S OCIAL networks and the degree to which individuals are embedded in supportive social relationships are related to many different outcomes, probably for many different reasons. For example, social networks are related to a broad array of health behaviors that range from the likelihood that women will engage in cancer screening,[25-27] dialysis,[28, 29] and smoking[30] and alcohol consumption.[31] They may influence health outcomes through these behavioral mechanisms or by more direct physiologic pathways. Although a thorough review of this physiologic literature is beyond the scope of this article, several recent studies are noteworthy and have provided important pieces to the puzzle of how such a fundamentally social experience could get "inside the body." These findings suggest that there are likely to be multiple biologic pathways involved in this linkage and, furthermore, that the pathways invoked are likely to cascade and influence a number of disease outcomes. By examining these mechanisms, we can begin to understand how several basic physiologic regulatory mechanisms, themselves intertwined, might be responsive to socioenvironmental stressors.[32-34] The notion of "generalized

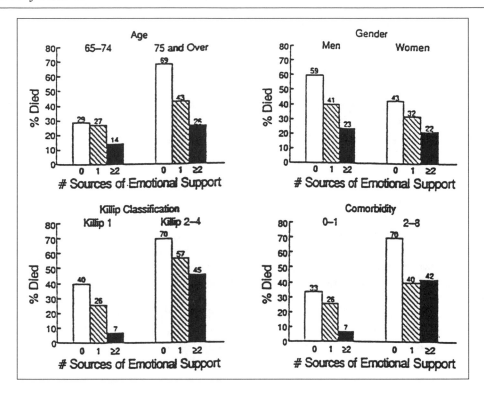

Figure 1
Percentage of patients with MIs who died within 6 months by level of social support. Adjustments were made for age (top left); gender (top right); severity of MI, as defined by Killip class (bottom left); and comorbidity (bottom right). (From Berkman et al.[18] with permission.)

resistance" or "susceptibility to disease" need not be interpreted literally as a single mechanism or pathway but, rather, as a more general route, referring to complex physiologic systems with feedback loops and potentials to cascade and influence an even broader array of end points.

The two physiologic systems that are the focus of most recent attention are the immunological and neuroendocrine systems, with the neuroendocrine systems being closely tied to cardiovascular reactivity. There are several excellent reviews in this field,[35-38] and the reader may refer to them for more extensive and detailed discussions. I take this opportunity to discuss several individual studies that, in themselves, are illustrative of the excellent work done in this area.

Early work on the link between immunological parameters and social relations was often focused on the effects of severe social losses and death of the spouse. These early landmark studies supported the idea that bereavement and loss were associated with suppressed immune function, particularly cellular immunity.[39, 40]

This work was followed by the study of caregivers living with chronically ill spouses.[41, 42] The findings of these more recent studies are generally consistent with those focused on bereaved men and women and support the general hypothesis that immune function, especially cellular immunity and natural killer cell activity, is influenced by aspects of social relationships.

However, because these losses or impending losses are so severe and involve so many other physical and economic stresses and psychological threats, it is hard to interpret these associations as specifically linking social support to changes in immune function. Only examination of specific findings within these studies gives stronger support for the direct importance of the influence of social relationships per se. For instance, in the study by Kiecolt-Glaser et al.[42] on family caregivers of patients with Alzheimer's disease (AD), it was reported that caregivers whose relatives were institutionalized did not differ significantly in most health behavioral or psychological parameters from those who lived with patients with AD. These data suggest that it was the emotional loss of the spouse or parent that was more critical to changes in immune function rather than the physical stresses associated with providing ongoing care to the patient with AD. Moritz et al.[43] reported similar findings with regard to depression among elderly couples in which one spouse is cognitively impaired.

Finally, other studies in which investigators examined a) the quality of marital relationships and loneliness[44-47] in less than tragic circumstances in humans and b) affiliation in nonhuman primates[48, 49] consistently point out the importance of the quality of social relationships in influencing cellular immune response.

The work in the area of neuroendocrine function and social relations is small, although there is a much larger body of work on social factors and cardiovascular reactivity and physiological arousal, which is closely linked to neuroendocrine function.[50] Animal studies consistently show that how animals are grouped and the degree to which they are isolated from mothers or any animal or touched influences neuroendocrine function, cardiovascular reactivity, lipid metabolism, and the development of atherogenesis.[51-56] In humans, much less is known specifically on the association between support and neuroendocrine function or reactivity, although several studies[57-59] have illustrated that touching

reduces cardiovascular reactivity. Seeman et al.[60] have just completed an analysis of neuroendocrine functioning and social relationships among older high-functioning men and women. In this study, social relationships, especially the quality of emotional support, was related to urinary levels of epinephrine, norepinephrine, and cortisol among older men and women independent of other behaviors or levels of comorbidity. Emotional support was more strongly and consistently associated with these neuroendocrine parameters than were measures of social ties (e.g., integration), instrumental support, or negative aspects of social relationships. This is one of the only studies to test the hypothesis that social support is directly associated with neuroendocrine function.

In regard to cardiovascular reactivity, Kamarck et al.[61] completed a recent well-designed experimental study that builds on much of the earlier work on the effects of touching or companionship on blood pressure and cardiovascular function.[62] In their study, subjects completed two laboratory tasks. One-half of the subjects worked alone. The other half had a friend accompany them. Subjects who had a supportive partner in the room during tasks showed significantly reduced heart rate activity and tended to have lower systolic and diastolic blood pressures. In addition, there was an interesting interaction between Type A behavior and social support, whereby support was associated with attenuated systolic blood pressure only for those individuals classified as being Type A. Among the potential mechanisms that might explain the association between having a supportive partner and decreased cardiovascular arousal, the authors suggest that the "friend's presence may have acted as a conditioned stimulus or a 'safety signal,' altering neural input to the heart during challenge" (p. 54).

The evidence linking social relationships and support to health outcomes by way of physiologic responses that involve neuroendocrine regulation and immunological function is plausible, yet progress in this area remains a major challenge, necessitating serious interdisciplinary collaboration and great sensitivity to measurement of both psychosocial and physiologic conditions.

A Call for the Development of Psychosocial Interventions

ALTHOUGH research based on observational studies will undoubtedly continue to yield productive insights into the role that social conditions play as etiologic factors and in the prognosis of disease, it now seems clear that we should take the next step forward to develop psychosocial interventions whereby we might attempt to alter or modify social networks and support to improve health outcomes. The development of such interventions is critical from both a scientific and a public health standpoint. From a scientific perspective, clinical trials and experimental work have important methodologic strengths that complement observational studies. Clinical trials allow us to test the principle that, by modifying exposure to risk, we change the disease outcome. Also, randomization provides us with confidence (although not assurance) that both measured and unmeasured covariates are equally distributed in the intervention and control groups. From a public health perspective, if we are unable to translate scientific discoveries into practices that will improve the health and well-being of the public, we have failed in our most fundamental mission.

There are several key theories that have guided our group at Yale in the development of interventions. A social network or support intervention is based on the premise that the individual who is ill or at risk and his or her network represent an interdependent and dynamic system. Thus, improvement or even maintenance of health in one individual is influenced not only by the individual's behavior but also by the behaviors of others in the network and their abilities to communicate optimally. These types of interventions build on social support group and family therapy theories in which the family or network is seen in its entirety as a functioning unit.[63-67]

Social learning theory also provides a useful model for understanding the acquisition of specific behaviors within social support interventions.[68] A central tenet in this theory is the role of self-efficacy or the belief that one can successfully perform behaviors to produce a desired outcome. Self-efficacy is believed to be shaped by past and present behavior and by the social environment through observation of behaviors in others and verbal support and persuasion. Thus, according to this theory, for social support to be health promoting, it must provide not only a sense of belonging and intimacy, but it must also help people to be more competent and self-efficacious. Support that encourages dependence may not be health promoting.[69, 70] Social learning and support group theories have been used successfully in the development of self-management programs aimed at minimizing the impact of chronic illness on functional capacity[71] and have been designed to help people manage a chronic condition.[72-76] Many programs aimed at altering specific behaviors have used support groups of patients to induce behavioral and psychological changes.[73, 77, 78] Finally, some programs have specifically been aimed at providing support and/or supportive counseling to improve health outcomes in patients with MIs,[79] cancer,[80, 81] and stroke.[82] These programs have an excellent potential to generalize to other areas with the use of intervention strategies that range in focus from patient support groups to individualized professional intervention with the patient and/or family. Our own bias in this regard is that interventions that aim at restructuring naturally occurring networks and resources for support will be more effective than those that rely on short-term constructed support groups. We recognize, however, that support groups often have the advantage of bringing people together with shared concerns or of providing opportunities for interaction among people who are socially isolated.

Because naturally occurring networks form the basis for long-term behaviors, we found an excellent intervention model that was developed at the Center for Family Research at George Washington University School of Medicine, which combines both natural and "constructed" supports.[83] This model brings both patients and families with different chronic illnesses together in small groups for a number of structured sessions. The multifamily discussion group as envisioned by the George Washington group has three components: a) educational, b) family issues, and c) affective. The model is designed to mix families with different chronic illnesses so that biomedical aspects of any single disease do not overwhelm the discussion of general psychosocial stressors. Such a multifamily intervention also has the advantages of not isolating the "sick" patient from other family members nor of focusing all intervention efforts on a single family or network so that they find it difficult to identify their situation as common or shared with others.

Over the next years, as more interventions are developed, we will undoubtedly see variations on this theme work with equal efficacy. Similarly, as other clinical trial methodologists have come to appreciate, individually tailored, stepped-care approaches will become better defined. It will also be important to remember that large-scale macrosocial, economic, and welfare policies influence the ability of families and communities to maintain high levels of social integration and support. In this vein, larger scale interventions aimed not at individuals but at communities or work sites may also make significant contributions to strengthening social ties.

In this era of health care reform, it is important to support efforts to promote financial access to medical care for all Americans; however, we cannot expect that such access will erase social inequalities in health. To improve health among vulnerable and high-risk populations, we will need to focus on preventive efforts that, at their core, promote social support and develop family and community strengths. Acknowledging that health promotion rests on the shoulders not only of individuals but also of their families and communities means that we must commit resources over the next decade to designing, testing, and implementing interventions in this area. This is a critical next step. For, as an African saying goes, "It takes an entire village to raise one child."

Supported in part by the National Institute of Aging grant R01 AG11042–01A1 and Claude Pepper Older Americans Independence Centers grant 1P60- AG10469–01A1.

I acknowledge the collaboration of Tom Glass, Teresa Seeman, Carlos Mendes de Leon, and Kelly Brownell in the development of psychosocial intervention models discussed in this article.

NOTES

1. Cassel J: The contribution of the social environment to host resistance. Am J Epidemiol 104:107–123, 1976

2. Cobb S: Social support as a moderator of life stress. Psychosom Med 38:300–314, 1976

3. Bruhn J, Wolf S: An Anatomy of Health: The Roseto Story. Oklahoma City, OK, University of Oklahoma Press, 1979

4. Matsumoto YS: Social stress and coronary heart disease in Japan: A hypothesis. Milbank Q 48:9–36, 1979

5. Frost WH: How much control of tuberculosis? Am J Public Health 27:759–766, 1937

6. Berkman LF, Syme SL: Social networks, host resistance and mortality: A nine year follow-up study of Alameda County residents. Am J Epidemiol 109:186–204, 1979

7. Blazer D: Social support and mortality in an elderly community population. Am J Epidemiol 115:684–694, 1982

8. House JS, Robbins C, Metzner HL: The association of social relationships and activities with mortality: Prospective evidence from the Tecumseh community health study. Am J Epidemiol 116:123–140, 1982

9. Kaplan JR, Salonen JT, Cohen RD, et al: Social connections and mortality from all causes and cardiovascular disease: Prospective evidence from Eastern Finland. Am J Epidemiol 128:370–380, 1988

10. Orth-Gomer K, Johnson J: Social network interaction and mortality: A six year follow-up of a random sample of the Swedish population. J Chronic Dis 40:949–957, 1987

11. Schoenbach VJ, Kaplan BG, Freedman L, et al: Social ties and mortality in Evans County, Georgia. Am J Epidemiol 123:577–591, 1986

12. Welin L, Tibblin G, Svardsudd K, et al: Prospective study of social influences on mortality: The study of men born in 1913 and 1923. Lancet 1:915–918, 1985

13. Seeman TE, Berkman LF, Kohout F, et al: Intercommunity variations in the association between social ties and mortality in the elderly: A comparative analysis of three communities. Ann Epidemiol 3:325–335, 1993

14. Ruberman W, Weinblatt E, Goldberg JD, et al: Psychosocial influences on mortality after myocardial infarction. N Engl J Med 311:552–559, 1984

15. Orth-Gomer K, Unden AL, Edwards ME: Social isolation and mortality in ischemic heart disease. Acta Med Scand 224:205–215, 1988

16. Williams RB, Barefoot JC, Califf RM, et al: Prognostic importance of social and economic resources among medically treated patients with angiographically documented coronary artery disease. JAMA 267:520–524, 1992

17. Case RB, Moss AJ, Case N, et al: Living alone after myocardial infarction. JAMA 267:515–519, 1992

18. Berkman LF, Leo-Summers L, Horwitz RI: Emotional support and survival following myocardial infarction: A prospective population-based study of the elderly. Ann Intern Med 117:1003–1009, 1992

19. Seeman TE, Syme SL: Social networks and coronary artery disease: A comparison of the stucture and function of social relationships as predictors of disease. Psychosom Med 49:340–353, 1987

20. Kaplan JR, Manuck SB, Clarkson TB, et al: Social status, environment, and atherosclerosis in cynomolgus monkeys. Arteriosclerosis 2:359–368, 1982

21. Orth-Gomer K, Rosengren A, Wilhelmsen L: Lack of social support and incidence of coronary heart disease in middle-aged Swedish men. Psykchosom Med 55:37–43, 1993

22. Glass TA, Matchar DB, Belyed M, et al: The impact of social support on outcome in first stroke. Stroke 24:67–70, 1993

23. Evans RL, Bishop DS, Matlock AL, et al: Prestroke family interaction as a predictor of stroke outcome. Arch Phys Rehab Med 68:508–512, 1987

24. Colantonio, A, Kasl S, Ostfield A, et al: Psychosocial predictors of stroke outcomes in an elderly population. J Gerontol 48:S261–S268, 1993

25. Suarez L, Lloyd L, Weiss N, et al: Effect of social networks on cancer-screening behavior of older Mexican American women. J Natl Cancer Inst 86:775–779, 1994

26. Calnan M: Patterns in preventive behavior: A study of women in middle age. Soc Sci Med 20:263–268, 1985

27. Kang SH, Bloom JR: Social support and cancer screening among older black Americans. J Natl Cancer Inst 85:737–742, 1993

28. Steidl JH, Finkelstein FO, Wexler JP, et al: Medical condition, adherence to treatment regimes and family functioning: Their interactions in patients receiving long-term dialysis treatment. Arch Gen Psychiatry 37:1025–1027, 1980

29. Kaplan De-Nour A: Dialysis within the context of the family. Int J Fam Psychiatry 1:61–75, 1980

30. Mermelstein R, Cohen S, Lichtenstein F, et al: Social support and smoking cessation maintenance. J Consult Clin Psychol 54:447–453, 1986

31. Berkman LF, Breslow L: Health and Ways of Living. New York, Oxford University Press, 1983

32. Rabin BS, Cohen S, Ganguli R, et al: Bidirectional interaction between the central nervous system and immune system. Crit Rev Immunol 9:279–312, 1989

33. Brindley DN, Rolland Y: Possible connections between stress, diabetes, obesity, hypertensioin and altered lipoprotein metabolism that may result in atherosclerosis. Clin Sci 77:453–461, 1989

34. Selye H, Tuchweber B: Stress in relation to aging and disease. In Everitt A, Burgess J (eds), Hypothalamus, Pituitary and Aging. Springfield, IL, Charles C. Thomas, 1975, 553–569

35. Seeman TE, Robbins RJ: Aging and hypothalamic-pituitary-adrenal response to challenge in humans. Endocr Rev 15:233–260, 1994

36. Cohen S: Psychosocial models of the role of support in the etiology of physical disease. Health Psychol 7:265–297, 1988

37. Kennedy S, Kiecolt-Glaser JK, Glaser R: Social support, stress, and the immune system. In Sarason BR, Sarason IG, Pierce GR (eds), Social Support: An Interactional View. New York, Wiley & Sons, 1990, 253–266

38. Ader R, Felten DL, Cohen N: Psychoneuroimmunology, 2nd Edition. New York, Academic Press, 1991

39. Schleifer SJ, Keller SE, Camerino M, et al: Suppression of lymphocyte stimulation following bereavement. JAMA 250:374–377, 1983

40. Bartrop RW, Luckhurst E, Lazarus L, et al: Depressed lymphocyte function after bereavement. Lancet 1:834–836, 1977

41. Baron RS, Cutrona CE, Hicklin D, et al: Social support and immune function among spouses of cancer patients. J Pers Soc Psychol 59:344–352, 1990

42. Kiecolt-Glaser JK, Glaser R, Suttleworth EC, et al: Chronic stress and immunity in family caregivers of Alzheimer's disease victims. Psychosom Med 49:523–535, 1987

43. Moritz DJ, Kasl SV, Berkman LF: The health impact of living with a cognitively impaired spouse: Depressive symptoms and social functioning. J. Gerontol 44:S17–S27, 1989

44. Kiecolt-Glaser JK, Fisher LD, Ogrocki P, et al: Marital quality, marital disruption and immune function. Psychosom Med 49:13–34, 1987

45. Thomas PD, Goodwin JM, Goodwin JS: Effect of social support on stress-related changes in cholesterol level, uric acid level, and immune function in an elderly sample. Am J Psychiatry 142:735–737, 1985

46. Glaser R, Kiecolt-Glaser JK, Speicher CE, et al: Stress, loneliness and changes in herpes virus latency. J Behav Med 8:249–260, 1985

47. Kiecolt-Glaser JK, Garner W, Speicher CE, et al: Psychosocial modifiers of immunocompetence in medical students. Psychosom Med 46:7–14, 1984

48. Cohen S, Kaplan JR, Cunnick J, et al: Chronic social stress, affiliation and cellular immune response in nonhuman primates. Psychol Sci 4:301–310, 1992

49. Kaplan JR, Manuck SB, Heise EB, et al: The relationship of agonistic and affiliative behavior patterns to cellular-mediated immune function among cynomolgus monkeys *Macaca fascicularis* living in unstable social groups. Am J Primatology 25:157–173, 1991

50. Krantz DS, Manuck SB: Acute psycho-physiologic reactivity and risk of cardiovascular disease. A review and methodologic critique. Psychol Bull 96:435–464, 1984

51. Clarkson TB, Kaplan JR, Adams MR, et al: Psychosocial influences in the pathogenesis of atherosclerosis among nonhuman primates. Circulation 76(Suppl 1):I29–40, 1987

52. Stanton ME, Patterson JM: Social influences on conditioned cortisol secretion in the squirrel monkey. Psychoneuroendocrinology 10:125–134, 1985

53. Meaney MJ, Aitken DH, Van Berkel C, et al: Effects of neonatal handling on age-related impairments associated with the hippocampus. Science 239:766–768, 1988

54. Shively CA, Clarkson TB, Kaplan JR: Social deprivation and coronary artery atherosclerosis in female cynomolgus monkeys. Atherosclerosis 77:69–76, 1989

55. Shively CA, Adams MR, Kaplan JR, et al: Social stress, ovarian function and coronary artery atherosclerosis in primates. In Zajkowski SM, Hill D, Clarkson TB (eds), Women, Behavior and Cardiovascular Disease (Publication No. NIH, 94–3309). Bethesda, MD, National Institutes of Health, 1994. 127–144

56. Sapolsky RM: Endocrine aspects of social instability in the olive baboon. Am J Primatology 5:365–379, 1983

57. Drescher VM, Whitehead WE, Morril-Corbin ED, et al: Physiological ankd subjective reactions to being touched. Psychophysiology 22:96–100, 1985

58. Lynch JJ, Thomas SA, Paskewitz DA, et al: Human contact and cardiac arrhythmia in a coronary care unit. Psychosom Med 39:188–192, 1977

59. Whitcher ST, Fisher JD: Multidimensional reaction to therapeutic touch in a hospital setting. J Pers Soc Psychol 37:87–96, 1979

60. Seeman TE, Berkman LF, Blazer D, et al: Social ties and support and neuroendocrine function: The MacArthur Studies of Successful Aging, Ann Behav Med 16:95–106, 1994

61. Kamarck T, Manuck SB, Jennings JR: Social support reduces cardiovascular reactivity to psychological challenge: A laboratory model. Psychosom Med 52:42–58, 1991

62. Lynch JL: The Broken Heart: The Medical Consequences of Loneliness. New York, Basic Books, 1979

63. Speck R, Attneave C: Family Networks. New York, Vintage, 1973

64. Vaux A: Social Support: Theory Research and Intervention. New York, Praeger, 1988

65. Spiegal D, Spira J: Supportive Expressive Group Therapy: A Treatment Manual of Psychosocial Intervention for Women with Recurrent Breast Cancer. Stanford, CA, Psychosocial Treatment Laboratory, 1991

66. Minuchin S: Families and Family Therapy. Cambridge, MA, Harvard University Press, 1974

67. Rolland JS: Families, Illness and Disability: An Integrative Treatment Model, New York, Basic Books, 1994

68. Bandura A: Social Foundations of Thought and Action. A Social Cognitive Theory. Englewood Cliffs, NJ, Prentice Hall, 1986

69. Wortman C, Lehman D: Reactions to victims of life crisis: Support that doesn't help. In Sarason IG, Sarason BR (eds), Social Support: Theory, Research and Application. Dordrecht, Martinus Nijhoff, 1985

70. McLeroy KR, DeVillis R, DeVellis B, et al: Social support and physical recovery in a stroke population. J Soc Pers Relations 1:395–413, 1984

71. Tobin DL, Reynolds RVC, Hoylroyd KA, et al: Self-management and social learning theory. In Hoylroyd KA, Creer DL (eds), Self-Management of Chronic Disease: Handbook of Clinical Intervention and Research. Orlando, FL, Academic Press, 1985, 29–55

72. Lorig K, Cauvin J, Holman H: Arthritis self-management: A study of the effectiveness of patient education for the elderly. Gerontologist 24:455–457, 1984

73. Lorig K, Mazonson PD, Holman HR: Evidence suggesting that health education for self-management in patients with chronic arthritis has sustained health benefits while reducing health care costs. Arthritis Rheum 36:439–446, 1993.

74. Wilson W, Pratt C: Impact of diabetes education and peer support upon weight and glycemic control of elderly persons witlh noninsulin dependent diabetes mellitus (NIDDM). Am J Public Health 77:634–635, 1987

75. Clark NM, Rakowski W, Ostrander L, et al: Development of self-management for elderly heart patients. Gerontologist 28:491–494, 1988

76. Clark NM, Becker MH, Janz NK, et al: Self-management of chronic disease by older adults. J Aging Health 3:3–27, 1991

77. Ornish D, Brown SE, Scherwitz LW, et al: Can life-style changes reverse coronary heart disease? Lancet 336:129–133, 1990

78. Friedman M, Thoresen CE, Gill JJ, et al: Alteration of type A behavior and its effect on cardiac recurrences in post-myocardial infarction patients: Summary results of the recurrent coronary prevention project. Am Heart J 112:653–665, 1986

79. Frasure-Smith N, Prince R: Long-term follow-up of the ischemic heart disease life stress monitoring program. Psychosom Med 51:485–513, 1989

80. Spiegal D, Bloom JR, Yalom ID: Group support for metastatic cancer patients: A randomized prospective outcome study. Arch Gen Psychiatry 38:527–533, 1981

81. Fawzy FI, Kemeny ME, Fawzy NW, et al: A structured psychiataric intervention for cancer patients. II. Changes over time in immunologic measures. Arch Gen Psychiatry 47:729–735, 1990

82. Evans RL, Matlock AL, Bishop DS, et al: Family intervention after stroke: Does counseling or education help? Stroke 19:1243–1249, 1988

83. Gonzalez S, Steinglass P, Reiss D: Putting the illness in its place: Discussion groups for families with chronic medical illnesses. Fam Process 28:69–87, 1987.

Nineteen

A PROSPECTIVE STUDY OF SOCIAL NETWORKS IN RELATION TO TOTAL MORTALITY AND CARDIOVASCULAR DISEASE INCIDENCE IN MEN IN THE UNITED STATES

Ichiro Kawachi, Graham A. Colditz, Alberto Ascherio, Eric B. Rimm, Edward Giovannucci, Meir J. Stampfer, and Walter C. Willett

ABSTRACT

Study objective—Previous studies have established a relationship between low levels of social networks and total mortality, but few have examined cause specific mortality or disease incidence. This study aimed to examine prospectively the relationships between social networks and total and cause specific mortality, as well as cardiovascular disease incidence.

Design—This was a four year follow up study in an ongoing cohort of men, for whom information on social networks was collected at baseline. The main outcome measures were total mortality, further categorised into deaths from cardiovascular disease (stroke and coronary heart disease), total cancer, accidents/suicides, and all other causes; as well as stroke and coronary heart disease *incidence*.

Participants—Altogether 32 624 US male health professionals aged 42 to 77 years in 1988, who were free of coronary heart disease, stroke, and cancer at baseline.

Results—A total of 511 deaths occurred during 122 911 person years of follow up. Compared with men with the highest level of social networks, socially isolated men (not married, fewer than six friends or relatives, no membership in church or community groups) were at increased risk for cardiovascular disease mortality (age adjusted relative risk, 1·90; 95% CI 1·07, 3·37) and deaths from accidents and suicides (age adjusted relative risk 2·22; 95% CI 0·76, 6·47). No excess risks were found for other causes of death. Socially isolated men were also at increased risk of stroke incidence (relative risk, 2·21; 95% CI, 1·12, 4·35), but not incidence of non-fatal myocardial infarction.

Conclusions—Social networks were associated with lower total mortality by reducing deaths from cardiovascular disease and accidents/suicides. Strong social networks

Originally published in *Journal of Epidemiology & Community Health*, 1996.

were associated with reduced incidence of stroke, though not of coronary heart disease. However, social networks may assist in prolonging the survival of men with established coronary heart disease.

INTRODUCTION

THE association between social relationships and health was originally described by Durkheim,[1] who reported an increased risk of suicide among socially isolated individuals. Subsequent epidemiological research has established that social networks predict not only the risk of suicide, but all-cause mortality.[2] To date, eight prospective epidemiological studies have reported an increased risk of total mortality in socially isolated individuals.[3-10] Despite the wealth of evidence on social networks and total mortality, some important questions remain unanswered.

Firstly, it is not clear whether the increased risk of total mortality reflects a generalised susceptibility to illnesses among socially isolated individuals,[11] or whether such persons are at especially high risk of mortality from specific types of illness. There is some evidence that social isolation is associated with an increased risk of cardiovascular disease mortality[6 12] and total cancer mortality.[13] However, virtually all of the prospective studies to date have reported data on total, but not cause specific, mortality. Secondly, it is not known where along the spectrum of disease social networks exert their impact. The major prospective studies of social networks have examined mortality, but not disease incidence. Thus it is not clear whether social networks influence disease incidence, recovery, or case fatality.[14]

To address some of these unanswered questions about social networks, we prospectively studied the associations between social networks and subsequent disease incidence and cause specific mortality.

METHODS

THE health professionals follow-up study is a longitudinal study of risk factors for cardiovascular disease and cancer among 51 529 US men aged 40 to 75 years in 1986. The study population consists of 29 683 dentists, 10 098 veterinarians, 4185 pharmacists, 3745 optometrists, 2218 osteopathic physicians, and 1600 podiatrists. The study began in 1986, when cohort members completed a mailed questionnaire on heart disease and cancer risk factors, medical history, and diet. Follow up questionnaires were sent in 1990 and 1992 to update this information.

Assessment of Social Networks and Other Exposures

All participants in the study were asked to complete the Berkman-Syme social networks index as part of the 1988 mailed questionnaire. The social networks index was originally developed in the Alameda County study,[3] and is a composite measure of four types of social connection: marital status (married versus not married); sociability (frequency and number of contacts with extended family and close friends, rated on a scale of 1 to 5, with high values associated with many contacts and low values with few); church group membership (yes versus no); and membership in other community organisations (yes versus none). Responses to the index are categorised into four levels of social connection: low networks (level I)—for example, characterised by individuals with low intimate contacts (not married, fewer than six friends or relatives), and no membership in either church or community groups; medium networks (level II); medium-high networks (level III); and high networks (level IV). Further details of the construction of the social networks index are described elsewhere.[15]

In addition to the assessment of social networks, we obtained information from the baseline and follow up questionnaires on the participants' medical history, current smoking habits, body mass index, levels of physical activity, alcohol intake, parental history of myocardial infarction (including the age of each parent at the first event), and participants' self reported history of diabetes mellitus, hypertension, and hypercholesterolaemia. The accuracy of a self reported diagnosis of hypertension was confirmed and reported in a validation study among 100 cohort members.[16]

Assessment of Total and Cause Specific Mortality

The primary end points in our study comprised deaths from all causes that occurred between the return of the 1988 questionnaire and January 31, 1992. Most deaths were reported by next of kin, work associates, or postal authorities. In addition, the mortality surveillance systematic searches of the vital records using the national death index to discover deaths among participants who were persistent non-responders to the questionnaire mailings. We estimate that more than 98% of the deaths are ascertained by these methods.[17]

Physicians reviewed death certificates and hospital or pathology reports to classify individual causes of death. As well as analysing total mortality, the deaths were grouped into four broad categories: cardiovascular diseases (coronary heart disease, ICD 9th revision codes 410 to 414, and 798; and stroke, ICD codes 430 to 438); total cancers (ICD 9th revision codes 140 to 209); external causes of injury (all ICD "E" codes, which included deaths from accident, poisoning, suicide, and other trauma); and all remaining causes of death.

Assessment of Cardiovascular Disease Incidence

We also examined all incident cases of coronary heart disease and stroke occurring between the return of the 1988 questionnaire and January 31, 1992. We wrote to all participants reporting an incident myocardial infarction or stroke on the 1990 or 1992 questionnaires to request permission to review their medical records. A definite myocardial infarction was classified according to the criteria of the World Health Organization,[18] and required symptoms plus either typical electrocardiographic changes or high levels of cardiac enzymes. A definite stroke was classified as confirmed if the criteria of the national survey of stroke were met.[19] Incident cases of non-fatal myocardial infarction and non-fatal stroke were classified as "probable" if the hospital records could not be obtained but the event required admission to hospital and the diagnosis was corroborated by supplementary correspondence or telephone interview.

Fatal coronary heart disease was made up of cases of fatal myocardial infarction confirmed by hospital records or autopsy reports; cases of sudden cardiac death (defined below); plus other deaths from coronary heart disease as determined from death certificates, if evidence of *previous* coronary heart disease was available (either from hospital records or interviews with the next of kin) and this was the underlying and most plausible cause of death. In no instance did we use death certificate classification alone to categorise a death as due to coronary heart disease. Sudden cardiac death was defined as death occurring within 1 hour of the onset of symptoms in a man with no previous serious illness, for which no other plausible cause of death—other than coronary disease—was reported.

Death due to stroke was ascertained by physician review of hospital records and autopsy reports. In this study, 92% of the non-fatal myocardial infarction and fatal coronary heart disease, and 87% of the non-fatal and fatal strokes were classified as definite events.

Study Population and Data Analysis

Because the onset of major illness could itself influence an individual's social networks, we excluded from analyses all members of the cohort who reported a diagnosis of myocardial infarction, stroke, or cancer (except non-melanoma

Table 1

Age standardised distribution of risk factors in relation to level of social network index

Risk factor	Berkman-Syme social network index			
	IV (high)	III	II	I (low)
No (%)	16 807 (51·5)	6 216 (19·1)	7 706 (23·6)	1 895 (5·8)
Smoking (%)	7·3	9·1	9·5	12·1
Hypertension (%)	19·1	20·4	20·5	20·1
Diabetes (%)	2·7	2·5	2·8	2·8
High cholesterol (%)	16·8	18·0	17·4	16·4
Body mass index (kg/m²)	25·1	25·0	24·9	24·9
Parental history of MI before age 60 (%)	11·7	12·5	13·1	12·0
Alcohol intake >15 g/d (%)	11·4	16·0	17·0	19·6
Physical activity (MET-h/week)	20·0	19·5	19·5	20·1
Blood pressure check in past 2 years (%)	86·2	83·2	82·7	79·3
Cholesterol check in past 2 years (%)	70·4	68·6	65·8	62·1
Screening physical exam in past 2 years (%)	66·8	64·0	60·3	57·1

skin cancer) before the return of the 1988 questionnaire (n = 6115 men). We cannot exclude the possibility that some men had undiagnosed illnesses at baseline. On the other hand, there is no reason to believe that an undiagnosed illness would have affected an individual's social network. We additionally excluded 12 790 men who after three mailings did not complete the main 1988 questionnaire but instead answered a shorter questionnaire that did not include the Berkman-Syme social networks index. This left a total of 32 624 men available for follow up. After repeated mailings to non-respondents, including the use of certified mail, we obtained 96% response rate to the 1990 questionnaire, and a 94% response rate to the 1992 questionnaire.

In the analyses, each participant accumulated person-months of follow up from the date of return of the 1988 questionnaire to January 31, 1992 (or, for those who died or developed cardiovascular disease, up to the date of the event). Proportional hazards models were used to adjust for age (in 5 year age categories), cigarette smoking (categorized as current smokers of 1 to 14, 15 to 24, or 25+ cigarettes per day, past, or never smokers), alcohol intake (o·o g/day, o·o1–4·9, 5·0–14·9, 15·0–24·9–49·9, and 50·0 or more g/day), body mass index (deciles), history of hypertension, diabetes mellitus, hypercholesterolaemia, angina pectoris, family history of myocardial infarction before age 60, and physical activity (tertiles). When appropriate, we performed the Mantel test for linear trend across levels of social networks, and reported the two tailed p values.[20]

RESULTS

Characteristics of the Study Population

Altogether 5·8% of the study population were socially isolated (level I of the social networks index), while 23·6% were in level II (medium networks), 19·1% were in level III (medium-high networks), and 51·5% were socially well integrated (level IV). We compared the age standardised distributions of health behaviors and risk factors across the levels of social networks (table 1). Socially isolated individuals were more likely to be current smokers and to drink more than 15 g/day alcohol (p for linear trend across categories of social networks <o·oo01, for both smoking and drinking). Socially isolated men were also

Table 2

Age adjusted and multivariate relative risks of total and cause specific mortality
according to level of social network index 1988–92

| | Berkman–Syme social network index | | | | |
	IV (high)	III	II	I (low)	Test for trend, p
Total mortality					
Cases	234	101	133	43	
Age adjusted RR	1·00	1·11	1·22	1·57	
		(0·88, 1·41)	(0·99, 1·51)	(1·14, 2·17)	0·004
Multivariate RR*	1·00	1·06	1·13	1·38	
		(0·84, 1·35)	(0·91, 1·40)	(0·99, 1·93)	0·06
Cardiovascular disease (stroke and coronary heart disease)					
Cases	63	31	45	14	
Age adjusted RR	1·00	1·28	1·53	1·90	
		(0·83, 1·96)	(1·05, 2·24)	(1·07, 3·37)	0·006
Multivariate RR	1·00	1·21	1·44	1·76	
		(0·79, 1·87)	(0·98, 2·13)	(0·97, 3·16)	0·02
Total cancer					
Cases	100	41	39	12	
Age adjusted RR	1·00	1·05	0·84	1·02	
		(0·73, 1·52)	(0·58, 1·21)	(0·56, 1·84)	0·55
Multivariate RR	1·00	1·03	0·78	0·87	
		(0·71, 1·48)	(0·54, 1·13)	(0·47, 1·60)	0·25
Accidents and suicides					
Cases	16	10	18	4	
Age adjusted RR	1·00	1·68	2·48	2·22	
		(0·77, 3·66)	(1·29, 4·75)	(0·76, 6·47)	0·008
Multivariate RR	1·00	1·62	2·35	1·99	
		(0·73, 3·59)	(1·19, 4·62)	(0·66, 5·99)	0·02
Other causes					
Cases	55	19	31	13	
Age adjusted RR	1·00	0·88	1·23	1·97	
		(0·52, 1·48)	(0·79, 1·89)	(1·09, 3·58)	0·06
Multivariate RR	1·00	0·78	1·09	1·48	
		(0·46, 1·33)	(0·70, 1·70)	(0·79, 2·76)	0·32

*Multivariate relative risks adjusted for age (5 year age categories), time period (1988–90; 1990–92), smoking status (never, former, and current in categories of 1 to 14, 15 to 24, and 25 or more cigarettes per day), history of hypertension, diabetes mellitus, and hypercholesterolemia, diagnosis of angina pectoris, deciles of body mass index, parental history of myocardial infarction before age 60 (yes/no), daily alcohol intake (0, 0·41–4·9, 5·0–14·9, 15·0–49·9 or more g/day), and tertiles of physical activity.

less likely to have undergone a blood pressure check, a serum cholesterol check, or a physical examination during the past two years for screening purposes. Other health related habits were distributed similarly across the groups.

Total Mortality

During the four years of follow up, 511 deaths occurred in 122 911 person-years. One hundred and fifty three individuals died of cardiovascular diseases (135 coronary heart disease deaths and 18

Table 3

Age adjusted and multivariate relative risks of total, non-fatal, and fatal stroke incidence according to level of social network index 1988–92

	Berkman-Syme social network index				
	IV high	III	II	I (low)	Test for trend, p
Total stroke					
Cases	40	21	33	10	
Age adjusted RR	1·00	1·39	1·82	2·21	
		(0·82, 2·37)	(1·15, 2·87)	(1·12, 4·35)	0·002
Multivariate RR*	1·00	1·31	1·72	2·02	
		(0·77, 2·23)	(1·08, 2·73)	(1·00, 4·08)	0·008
Fatal stroke†					
Cases	5	0	6	2	
Age adjusted RR	1·00	—	2·64	3·64	
			(0·84, 8·27)	(0·78, 16·9)	0·04
Non fatal storke					
Cases	35	21	27	8	
Age adjusted RR	1·00	1·55	1·65	1·96	
		(0·90, 2·66)	(1·00, 2·71)	(0·91, 4·17)	0·02
Multivariate RR	1·00	1·50	1·61	1·86	
		(0·87, 2·60)	(0·97, 2·67)	(0·84, 4·06)	0·03

*Multivariate relative risks for age (5 year age categories), time period (1988–92), smoking status (never, former, and current in categories of 1 to 14, 15 to 24, and 25 or more cigarettes per day), history of hypertensin, diabetes mellitus, and hypercholesterolemia, diagnosis of angina pectoris, deciles of body mass index, parental history of myocardial infarction before age 60 (yes/no), daily alcohol intake (0-, 0·01–4·9, 15·0–24·9, 25·0–49·9, or 50 or more g/day), and tertiles of physical activity.
†Too few cases to perform multivariate analysis.

stroke deaths); 192 of total cancer, 48 of accidents and suicide; and 118 of other causes.

Compared with the group with the most social connections (level IV), socially isolated individuals (level I) were at 1·5 times the age adjusted risk of total mortality (p for trend across categories of social networks index=0·004) (table 2). Adjustment for a broad range of risk factors in multivariate analysis somewhat attenuated the association. The following components of the social networks index predicted total mortality (data not shown in tables): not being married (relative risk, 1·41; 95% CI 1·07, 1·87); not belonging to a church group (relative risk, 1·42; 95% CI 1·19, 1·70); and the absence of close relatives (relative risk, 1·34; 95% CI 1·01, 1·78).

Cause Specific Mortality

Socially isolated individuals were at increased risk of cardiovascular diseases (p for trend = 0·006), and accidents and suicides (p for trend = 0·008) though not total cancer (p for trend = 0·55). Of the individual components of the social networks index, being unmarried was the strongest predictor of cardiovascular disease mortality (relative risk, 1·44; 95% CI 0·88, 2·38). We analysed stroke mortality separately from coronary heart disease mortality (data not shown in tables). Compared with the group with the highest level of social ties (level IV), the age adjusted relative risk of stroke mortality was 1·31 (95% CI 0·24, 7·23) among men in the medium-high group (level III), 4·90 (95% CI 1·70, 14·16) among men in the medium group (level II), and 6·59 (95% CI 1·78, 24·38) among men in the low group (level I) (p for trend, 0·0008, based on 18 deaths). By contrast, the association between social networks and coronary mortality was weaker: relative to the group with the highest level of social ties (level IV), the age adjusted relative risk of coronary heart disease mortality was 1·28 (95% CI 0·82, 1·99) among men in the medium-high group (level III), 1·31 (95% CI 0·86, 1·98) among men in the medium group (level II), and 1·59 (95% CI 0·84, 3·02) among men in the low group (level I) (p for trend, 0·09, based on 135 deaths).

Three components of the social networks index strongly predicted mortality from accidents and suicides: not being married (relative risk, 2·92; 95% CI 1·50, 5·67); not belonging to a church group (relative risk 1·99; 95% CI 1·14, 3·47); and the absence of close relatives (relative risk, 3·83; 95% CI 1·97, 7·47). Twenty cases of suicide occurred during the four year study period. The age adjusted relative risk of suicide among individuals in the most socially isolated group (level I) was 3·22 (95% CI 0·92, 11·22) compared with those in the most well connected group (p for trend = 0·12). Previous studies have reported an association between social isolation and smoking related cancers.[13] However, we found no significant association between social isolation and lung cancer mortality (relative risk in men with fewest social connections = 1·48; 95% CI 0·43, 5·07; p for trend = 0·52, based on 39 cases).

Coronary Heart Disease and Stroke Incidence

Altogether 104 incident cases of stroke (91 cases of non-fatal stroke, and 13 cases of fatal stroke) and 403 cases of incident coronary heart disease (275 cases of non-fatal myocardial infarction, and 128 cases of fatal coronary heart disease) occurred during the four year follow up. If a participant developed a new episode of stroke or heart attack and died within the two year interval between two successive follow up questionnaires, then

this person was classified as having had an incident fatal event.

A strong dose-response gradient was found between the level of social networks and stroke incidence (p for trend, 0·008) (table 3). Increased risks were observed for both fatal and non-fatal stroke, although there were too few cases of fatal stroke to carry out multivariate analysis. In contrast to stroke, social isolation was not associated with the incidence of either total coronary heart disease or non-fatal myocardial infarction (table 4). There was a modest increase in risk of fatal coronary heart disease among individuals with the least social connections (multivariate relative risk, 1·42; 95% CI 0·72, 2·81). We examined this association in detail by separately analysing sudden cardiac death (45 cases) and non-sudden cardiac death (83 cases) (table 5). The rationale for performing this analysis was based on the theory that social relationships enhance disease survival through the provision of various types of support, for example, advice to stop smoking.[21] If improved survival among individuals with already established disease is indeed the mechanism by which social relationships affect mortality, we would not expect to find a protective effect of social networks for sudden cardiac death, since by definition, death occurs within one hour of the onset of symptoms. Consistent with this hypothesis, we found no association between level of social ties and sudden cardiac death (p for trend, 0·94), but a dose-response gradient with risk of non-sudden cardiac death (p for linear trend = 0·05) (table 5).

Finally, we assessed potential effect modification by smoking status and diagnosis of hypertension. Within strata of smoking status (never, former, and current smokers), the strongest association of social networks with total mortality was found among current smokers. The relative risk of total mortality in the least socially connected group was 2·16 (95% CI 1·10, 4·23) among smokers, 1·73 (95% CI 1·09, 2·76) among former smokers, and 1·10 (95% CI 0·53, 2·28) among never smokers. The smoking χ social isolation

Table 4

Age adjusted multivariate relative risks of total coronary heart disease, non-fatal myocardial infarction, and fatal coronary heart disease incidence according to level of social network, 1988–92

	Berkman-Syme social network index				
	IV (high)	III	II	I (low)	Test for trend, p
Total coronary heart disease					
Cases	188	90	100	25	
Age adjusted RR	1·00	1·27	1·16	1·17	
		(0·99, 1·63)	(0·91, 1·47)	(0·77, 1·77)	0·17
Multivariate RR*	1·00	1·26	1·13	1·14	
		(0·98, 1·62)	(0·89, 1·45)	(0·74, 1·73)	0·25
Fatal coronary heart disease					
Cases	56	25	37	10	
Age adjusted RR	1·00	1·16	1·41	1·52	
		(0·73, 1·86)	(0·93, 2·14)	(0·78, 2·98)	0·06
Multivariate RR*	1·00	1·10	1·34	1·42	
		(0·68, 1·77)	(0·88, 2·04)	(0·72, 2·81)	0·13
Non fatal myocardial infarction					
Cases	132	65	63	15	
Age adjusted RR	1·00	1·32	1·05	1·01	
		(0·98, 1·77)	(0·78, 1·41)	(0·59, 1·72)	0·69
Multivariate RR*	1·00	1·32	1·04	1·00	
		(0·98, 1·79)	(0·76, 1·40)	(0·58, 1·71)	0·19

*Multivariate relative risks adjusted for age (5 year age categories), time period (1988–90; 1990–92), smoking status (never, former, and current in categories of 1 to 14, 15 to 24, and 25 or more cigarettes per day), histoiry of hypertension, diabetes mellitus, and hypercholesterolemia, diagnosis of angina pectoris, deciles of body mass index, parental history of myocardial infarction before age 60 (yes/no), daily alcohol intake (0, 0·01–4·9, 5·0–14·9, 15·0–24·9, or 50 or more g/day), and tertiles of physical activity.

Table 5

Age adjusted and multivariate relative risks of sudden cardiac death and non-sudden cardiac death, according to level of social network index 1988–92

	Berkman-Syme social network index				
	IV (high)	III	II	I (low)	Test for trend, p
Sudden cardiac death					
Cases	21	10	12	2	
Age adjusted RR	1·00	1·24	1·22	0·82	
		(0·58, 2·63)	(0·60, 2·49)	(0·19, 3·52)	0·78
Multivariate RR*	1·00	1·22	1·10	0·68	
		(0·57, 2·60)	(0·54, 2·26)	(0·16, 2·96)	0·94
Non-sudden cardiac death					
Cases	35	15	25	8	
Age adjusted RR	1·00	1·12	1·52	1·94	
		(0·61, 2·03)	(0·91, 2·54)	(0·91, 4·14)	0·04
Multivariate RR*	1·00	1·05	1·48	1·89	
		(0·57, 1·94)	(0·88, 2·49)	(0·87, 4·13)	0·05

interaction term was statistically significant (p<0·001). The impact of poor social networks on cardiovascular mortality was stronger in men with a diagnosis of hypertension (relative risk, 2·62; 95% CI 1·07, 6·45) than in men without hypertension (relative risk, 1·57; 95% CI 0·74, 3·31). When we ran a model assessing interaction, the hypertension χ social isolation term was statistically significant (p = 0·01).

Discussion

OUR findings are compatible with the notion that social networks reduce total mortality by lowering deaths from cardiovascular disease and accidents/suicides. In previous studies, the relative risks of total mortality among the most socially isolated individuals ranged from 1·8 (in the Evans County study) to 4·0 (in the Gothenburg study), whereas the present study found a multivariate relative risk of about 1·4. The smaller magnitude of risk found in the present study may be partly due to the high socioeconomic status and relative homogeneity of health professionals who continued our cohort. High socioeconomic status—associated with such resources as a high level of knowledge about health and disease, or access to health care and other material goods—may reduce some of the disadvantages of social isolation.[22 23] We were also able to adjust for a broader range of health behaviours and risk factors in this study compared with previous investigations.[34] In terms of the magnitude of the association, an adjusted relative risk of total mortality of 1·4 is comparable to the effect of cigarette smoking on total mortality reported in some studies.[24 25]

Four potential pathways have been proposed through which social relationships might affect health.[14] Firstly they may have an affect through the provision of instrumental support, such as financial assistance or services in kind. Such tangible assistance could contribute to the recovery and survival of patients after major illness (such

as stroke), independent of professional medical services. A second pathway is through the provision of information and advice that might assist individuals to seek medical care services, or to adopt more health promoting behaviours, such as smoking cessation. The existence of such a pathway is supported by two of our findings: that socially isolated men were less likely to undergo medical screening (table 1) and, secondly, that the effects of poor social networks were strongest among those who smoked or had hypertension. If risky health behaviours (such as smoking) are in the pathway through which poor social networks act, then control for such behaviours in multivariate analyses may constitute statistical over adjustment and attenuate the reported associations towards the null.

A third postulated pathway linking social networks to health is the provision of emotional support. A recent report[26] indicated that after an acute myocardial infarction, patients who lacked emotional support were nearly three times as likely to die during the first 6 months (odds ratio, 2·9; 95% CI 1·2, 6·9) compared with patients who received emotional support. A limitation of our study is that we did not collect data of such *functional* aspects of social ties. Thus, we are unable to distinguish the relative importance of different types of social support (eg, emotional, instrumental, informational) for the maintenance of health.

It has been suggested that social networks may directly influence host resistance and susceptibility to disease through alterations in neuroendocrine and immunological control systems.[11 27 28] For example, stress induces a sustained increase in cortisol and insulin levels, which in turn may lead to hyperlipidaemia and accelerate atherogensis.[29] However, few studies have actually demonstrated altered neuroendocrine control under conditions of stress.[30] Importantly, our data failed to corroborate the hypothesis of generalised disease susceptibility. Increased risks were found only for suicide (confirming Durkheim's original observation), and cardiovascular disease mortality.

Our analyses of coronary heart disease incidence suggest that social relationships affect *survival* following the onset of coronary heart disease, but not the incidence of new disease. A prospective study of social networks among Japanese-Americans residing in Hawaii[31] also found no association with incidence of non-fatal myocardial infarction. In our data, poor social ties were associated with an increased risk of fatal coronary heart disease, but only if sudden cardiac deaths were excluded as an end point. The finding that social networks have little or no influence on the risk of sudden cardiac death suggests that the protective mechanisms associated with social ties operate after the onset of illness. This interpretation is also consistent with several prospective studies among patients with *established* coronary heart disease,[26 32-35] in which social relationships were found to predict survival after acute myocardial infarction.

The association of strong social ties with reduced stroke mortality was previously described in the Alameda County study.[3] To our knowledge, no other study has reported a protective effect of social networks on stroke *incidence*. Several previous studies have reported a protective effect of social ties on cancer survival,[13 35 36] although the evidence has been inconsistent[37 38] depending on the stage of the cancer and the tumour site. We found no association of total cancer mortality with social ties, although our four year follow up period cannot exclude an effect on long term survival. We caution that some of our disease specific findings are based on limited duration of follow up with small numbers of cases. Nonetheless, our data suggest that social networks may improve the outcome of established disease, especially cardiovascular disease.

This study was supported by research grants HL 35464 and CA 55705 from the National Institutes of Health. We thank the participants of the health professionals follow up study for their continued cooperation and participation; and Mr Mark Shneyder, Ms Betsy Frost-Hawes, Ms Mitzi Wolff, Ms Kerry Pillsworth, Ms Karen Corsano, Mr Steve Stuart, and Ms Mira Koyfman for help with compiling the data and preparing the paper.

NOTES

1. Durkheim E. *Suicide*, New York: Free Press, 1951.

2. House JS, Landis KR, Umberson D. Social relationships and health. *Science* 1988;214:540–45.

3. Berkman LF, Syme SL. Social networks, host resistance and mortality: a nine-year follow-up study of Alameda County residents. *Am J Epidemiol* 1979;109:186–204.

4. House JS, Robbins C, Metzner HL. The association of social relationships and activities with mortality: prospective evidence from the Tecumseh Community health study. *Am J Epidemiol* 1982:116:123–40.

5. Schoenbach VJ, Kaplan BH, Fredman L, *et al*. Social ties and mortality in Evans County, Georgia. *Am J Epidemiol* 1986;123:577–91.

6. Kaplan GA, Salonen JT, Cohen RD, Brand RJ, Syme SL, Puska P. Social connections and mortality from all causes and from cardiovascular disease: prospective evidence from Eastern Finland. *Am J Epidemiol* 1988;128:370–80.

7. Orth-Gomer K, Johnson J. Social network interactoin and mortality. A six-year follow-up study of a random sample of the Swedish population. *J Chronic Dis* 1987;40:949–58.

8. Welin L, Tibblin G, Svardsudd K, *et al*. Prospective study of social influences on mortality. *Lancet* 1985;i:915–18.

9. Blazer DG, Social support and mortality in an elderly community population. *Am J Epidemiol* 1982;115:684–94.

10. Seeman TE, Berkman LF, Kohout F, LaCroix A, Glynn R, Blazer D. Inter-community variations in the association between social ties and mortality in the elderly: A comparative analysis of three communities. *Annals of Epidemiology* 1993;3:325–35.

11. Cassel J. The contribution of the social environment to host resistance. *Am J Epidemiol* 1976;104:107–23.

12. Berkman L, Breslow L. *Health and ways of living: findings from the Aladema County study*. New York: Oxford University Press, 1983.

13. Reynolds P, Kaplan GA. Social connections and risk for cancer: Prospective evidence from the Alameda County study. *Behav Med* 1990;16:101–10.

14. Berkman LF. The relationship of social networks and social support to morbidity and mortality. In: Cohen S, Syme SL eds. *Social Support and health.* New York: Academic Press, 1985;241–62.

15. Berkman LF. *Social networks, host resistance, and mortality: A follow-up of Alameda County residents.* University of California, Berkeley, 1977. PhD thesis.

16. Ascherio A, Rimm EB, Giovannucci EL, *et al.* A prospective study of nutritional factors and hypertension among US men. *Circulation* 1992;86:1474–84.

17. Stampfer MJ, Willett WC, Speizer FE, *et al.* Test of the National Death Index. *Am J Epidemiol* 1984;119:837–9.

18. Rose GA, Blackburn H. *Cardiovascular survey methods.* 2nd ed. Geneva, Switzerland. World Health Organization, 1982.

19. Walker AE, Robins M, Weinfeld FD. The National survey of stroke: clinical findings. *Stroke* 1981;12(suppl I):113–44.

20. Rothman KJ, Boice JD Jr. *Epidemiologic analysis with a programmable calculator.* NIH publication no 79–1649. Washington, DC: Public Health Service, 1979.

21. House JS, Kahn RL. Measures and concepts of social support. In: Cohen S, Syme SL eds. *Social support and health.* New York: Academic Press, 1985;83–108.

22. Kaplan, GA, Keil JE. Socioeconomic factors and cardiovascular disease: a review of the literature. *Circulation* 1993;88;1973–98.

23. Syme SL, Berkman LF. Social class, susceptibility and sickness. *Am J Epidemiol* 1976;104:1–8.

24. Doll R, Hill AB. Lung cancer and other causes of death in relation to smoking. A second report on the mortality of British doctors. *BMJ* 1956;ii:1071–81.

25. Hammond EC. Smoking in relation to the death rates of one million men and women. In: Haenszel W ed. *Epidemiological approaches to the study of cancer and other chronic diseases, National Cancer Institute Monograph 19.* Bethesda, MD: US Department of Health, Education and Welfare, Public Health Service, National Cancer Institute; 1966;127–204.

26. Berkman LF, Leo-Summers L, Horwitz RI. Emotional support and survival after myocardial infarction. A prospective, population-based study of the elderly. *Ann Intern Med* 1992;117:1003–9.

27. Antonovsky A. Breakdown: a needed fourth step in the conceptual armamentarium of modern medicine. *Soc Sci Med* 1972;6:537–44.

28. Cobb S. Social support as a moderator of life stress. *J Psychosom Med* 1976;38:300-14.

29. Brindley D, Rolland Y. Possible connections between stress, diabetes, obesity, hypertension and altered lipoprotein metabolism that may result in artherosclerosis. *Clin Sci* 1989;77:435–61.

30. McEwan BS, Stellar E. Stress and the individual. Mechanisms leading to disease. *Arch Intern Med* 1993;153:2093–101.

31. Reed D, McGee D, Yano K, Feinleib M. Social networks and coronary heart disease among Japanese men in Hawaii. *Am J Epidemiol* 1983;117:384–96.

32. Ruberman W, Weinblatt E, Goldberg JD, Chauhary BS. Psychosocial influences on mortality after myocardial infarction. *N Engl J Med* 1984;13:641–54.

33. Case RB, Moss AJ, Case N, McDermott M, Eberly S. Living alone after myocardial infarction. Impact on prognosis. *JAMA* 1992;267:515–19.

34. Williams RB, Barefoot JC, Califf RM, *et al.* Prognostic importance of social and economic resources among medically treated patients with angiographyically documented coronary artery disease. *JAMA* 1992;267:520–4.

35. Vogt TM, Mullooly JP, Ernst D, Pope CR, Hollis JF. Social networks as predictors of ischemic heart disease, cancer, stroke and hypertension: incidence, survival and mortality. *J Clin Epidemiol* 1992;45:659–66.

36. Goodwin JS, Hunt WC, Key CR, Samet JM. The effect of marital status on stage, treatment, and survival of cancer patients. *JAMA* 1987;258:3125–130.

37. Cassileth BR, Lusk EJ, Strouse TB, Miller DS, Brown LL, Cross PA, Tenaglin AN. Psychosocial status in chronic illness. *N Engl J Med* 1984;311:506–11.

38. Ell K, Nishimoto R, Mediansky L, Mantell J, Hamovitch M. Social relationships, social support and survival among patients with cancer. *J Psychosom Res* 1992;36:531–41.

Twenty

HEALTH AND SOCIAL COHESION: WHY CARE ABOUT INCOME INEQUALITY?

Ichiro Kawachi and Bruce P. Kennedy

SUMMARY

THROUGHOUT the world, wealth and income are becoming more concentrated. Growing evidence suggests that the distribution of income—in addition to the absolute standard of living enjoyed by the poor—is a key determinant of population health. A large gap between rich people and poor people leads to higher mortality through the breakdown of social cohesion. The recent surge in income inequality in many countries has been accompanied by a marked increase in the residential concentration of poverty and affluence. Residential segregation diminishes the opportunities for social cohesion. Income inequality has spillover effects on society at large, including increased rates of crime and violence, impeded productivity and economic growth, and the impaired functioning of representative democracy. The extent of inequality in society is often a consequence of explicit policies and public choice. Reducing income inequality offers the prospect of greater social cohesiveness and better population health.

INCOME INEQUALITY AND MORTALITY

THE world's wealth is becoming more concentrated. According to the 1996 United Nations *Human Development Report*, the world's 358 richest individuals control economic assets equivalent to the combined annual incomes of the poor countries that are home to 45% of the world's population.[1] In the past 20 years, many countries including the United States and Britain have experienced soaring rates of income inequality. Do these trends matter for the health of populations?

No one would dispute that poverty is bad for health. In general, the lower the material standard of living (as measured by indicators like income) the worse is the level of health, whether measured by mortality, morbidity, or quality of life. In the United States, which is supposedly the richest country in the world, poverty still accounts for nearly 6% of all adult mortality.[2]

Aside from the evidence on absolute deprivation, there is growing evidence that the relative distribution of income in a society matters in its own right for population health. This thesis,

---

Originally published in *British Medical Journal*, 1997.

which has become most closely identified with the work of Richard Wilkinson,[3 4] has been replicated in nearly a dozen studies internationally.[4] Although some questions have been raised about the international evidence linking income inequality to mortality,[5] three recent studies reported in this journal—two from the United States[6 7] and one from Britain[8]—have suggested that income inequality predicts excess mortality within individual countries. In the American study by Kennedy *et al*, income inequality at the state level was strongly correlated with total mortality rates ($r = 0.54$, $P<0.05$), even after median income, poverty rates, smoking prevalence, and race were taken into account.[6] Income inequality was measured in that study by the Robin Hood index, which is the proportion of aggregate income that needs to be redistributed from the rich to the poor so as to achieve equality of incomes. A 1% rise in the Robin Hood Index was associated with an excess mortality of 21.7 deaths per 100 000 (95% confidence interval 6.6 to 36.7), suggesting that even a modest reduction in inequality could have an important impact on population health. The maldistribution of income was related not only to total mortality but also to infant mortality, homicides, and deaths from cardiovascular disease and neoplasms.

SOCIAL COHESION
AND INCOME INEQUALITY

THE repeated corroboration of the hypothesis that income inequality is harmful to health has spurred the search for the mechanisms underlying this relation. Some hypothesised pathways include psychologically harmful effects of relative deprivation and the lack of investment in human capital that is frequently evident in societies that tolerate large income differentials.[9] It is also possible that some other exogenous factor, such as racial discrimination in the United States, accounts for both income inequality and excess mortality. Much work remains to be carried out in sorting through these possibilities.

One notion that has existed for some time is that a widening of the gap between the rich and poor might result in damage to the social fabric. In a seminal essay on the dysfunctions of social stratification published in 1953, Melvin Tumin speculated that "to the extent that inequalities in social rewards cannot be made fully acceptable to the less privileged in a society, social stratification systems function to encourage hostility, suspicion and distrust among the various segments of society and thus to limit the possibilities of extensive social integration."[10] In his latest book, Wilkinson provides case studies of societies that at certain points in history underwent either a rapid compression of the income distribution (Britain during the two world wars) or a rapid widening of income differentials (the Italian-American community of Roseto in Pennsylvania during the 1960s).[4] In wartime Britain, narrowing of income differentials was accompanied by a greater sense of solidarity and social cohesion as well as dramatic improvements in life expectancy. In contrast, in the originally closeknit town of Roseto, rapid economic change in the 1960s opened the gap between rich people and poor people. The resulting breakdown of community cohesion was followed by a sharp increase in deaths from coronary disease.[11]

Enhanced Wellbeing

That social cohesion enhances wellbeing is by now a well established fact. Ever since Durkheim's study of the causes of suicide,[12] numerous epidemiological studies have shown that people who are socially integrated live longer.[13-15] Socially isolated people die at two to three times the rate of well connected people, presumably reflecting the former's limited access to sources of emotional support, instrumental support (for example, financial aid), and other forms of support. But what has been missing from recent epidemiological studies of social relationships and health is the social context in which people lead their lives. In other words, by

Figure 1
Socially isolated people die at two or three times the rate of people with a network of social relationships and sources of emotional and instrumental support

focusing on the outcomes of socially isolated (or well connected) individuals, epidemiology has neglected the possibility that entire communities or societies might be lacking in social connections.

"Social Capital"

Fortunately, there has been a renaissance in the notion of community cohesiveness, with the publication in 1993 of a work by an American political scientist, Robert Putnam. In *Making Democracy Work* he sought to measure the strength of social cohesion—what he termed "social capital"—within regions of Italy.[16] The purpose of his 20 year study was to attempt to explain the performance of local governments, which were introduced to Italy in 1970. Local government performance in each region of Italy was assessed by its responsiveness to constituents and its efficiency in conducting the public's business. According to Putnam, the stock of social capital in a region—for example, as measured by the density of citizens' participation in community organisa-

tions (choral societies, soccer leagues, Rotary clubs, and the like) turned out to be the best predictor of local government performance. Citizens living in regions characterised by high levels of social capital were more likely to trust their fellow citizens and to value solidarity, equality, and mutual tolerance. They were also blessed with highly functioning governments.

What can public health learn from this quasi-experiment in Italy? Although much work is needed in refining the notion of social capital, Kawachi *et al* recently carried out an analysis of income inequality in the United States and its relation to social capital, as defined by two of the indicators described by Putnam: levels of civic trust and density of associational membership. Data on social capital were obtained in 39 states from a survey conducted by the National Opinions Research Center between 1986 and 1990.[17] The survey asked respondents in each state whether "Most people can be trusted—or would most people try to take advantage of you if they got the chance?" The percentage of citizens who thought that people try to take advantage (sug-

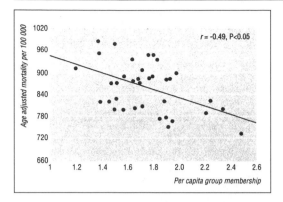

Figure 2
Relation of per capita group membership in United
States to age adjusted total mortality

gesting low levels of civic trust) was highly correlated with the degree of income inequality in
each state (r = 0.7, P<0.0001). Similarly, density
of associational life, as gauged by the per capita
membership of groups (church groups, sports
groups, fraternal organizations, labour unions,
and so on), was correlated with income inequality (r = -0.4, P<0.01). In turn, both the degree of
civic distrust and paucity of associated life were
strongly correlated with overall mortality (fig. 2).
The effect of income inequality on mortality thus
seemed to be mediated through the withering of
social capital.

THE INTERVENING EFFECTS OF
RESIDENTIAL SEGREGATION

CONCEPTS like income inequality and
social capital are inherently "ecological"—
that is, they are characteristics of places, not individuals. To understand the linkages between
such variables, further research needs to focus on
where people live rather than on the behaviours
of individuals.[18] Several researchers have attempted to separate out individual and area effects on mortality: is the health of people with
any given level of individual socioeconomic char-

acteristic better or worse according to whether
they live in a rich or poor area?[19-22] The assumption underlying such studies is that poor neighbourhoods are worse physical environments and
lack amenities such as public transportation, access to primary care, banking facilities, and retail
choice in healthy foods. Few of these studies
have dealt with the impact of inequality itself.
Indeed, not all studies have shown that poor
people have worse health if they live in a poor
area rather than in a rich one.[20] This lack of una-
nimity may be the result of the sense of relative
deprivation running counter to the effects of the
wider environment: a poor person living in an
affluent area may have a better environment but
may also feel relatively poorer.

Medical demographers have an established
tradition in studying the quantifiable characteristics of neighbourhoods. One such line of
research—on the health effects of residential
segregation—offers a promising approach by
which to link the effects of income inequality on
social disintegration.[23] Accompanying the surge

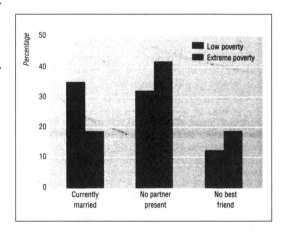

Figure 3
Social capital among black residents of Chicago
neighbourhoods with low poverty (20–30%) and ex-
treme (over 40%) poverty.[26] Reprinted by permis-
sion of Sage Publications

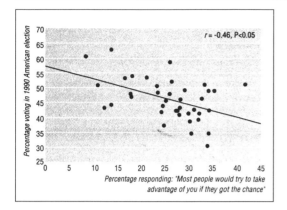

Figure 4
Relation of social distrust in United States to voter turnout in November 1990 elections

in income inequality in the United States since the mid-1970s, the spatial concentration of poverty has increased sharply. Between 1970 and 1990, the percentage of urban poor Americans living in non-poor neighbourhoods (defined as having poverty rates below 20%) declined from 45% to 31%, while the percentage living in poor neighbourhoods (poverty rates between 20% and 40%) increased from 38% to 41%. Meanwhile, the proportion living in very poor neighbourhoods (over 40% poverty) grew from 17% to 28%.[24] Such patterns of residential concentration impose a double burden on poor people: not only do they have to grapple with the multiple problems arising from their own lack of income. They also have to deal with the social effects of living in a neighbourhood where most of their neighbours are also poor.[25] Sociologist William Julius Wilson coined the term "concentration effects" to describe the cumulative disadvantages that are heaped on the residents of urban ghettos.[25] Wilson and Wacquant found that residents in extremely poor neighbourhoods were also less likely to report the presence of regular sources of social support, including a marital partner and close friends (fig 3).[26]

The trends in the special concentration of poor people fail to address what has happened at the opposite end of the income spectrum. According to Massey and Denton, affluence in the United States is even more highly concentrated spatially than poverty.[24] In 1970, the typical affluent American family—defined as having an income level at least four times the poverty rate—lived in a neighbourhood that was 39% affluent; by 1990, this had increased to 52%. In other words, the typical affluent person lived in a neighbourhood where more than half the residents were also rich. In contrast to people living in poverty stricken neighbourhoods, residents of affluent neighbourhoods benefit from better equipped public schools, higher quality public amenities, and more generous municipal services—all financed through higher property tax revenues. At the same time, the children of the privileged are more likely to socialise with other children of well educated and successful parents, thereby ensuring the social reproduction of material and cultural advantage.[25] Without question, the privileged classes actively invest in their own social capital when they retreat to affluent residential enclaves. But the segregated nature of the resulting forms of social capital will tend to undermine social cohesion within society at large.

THE SOCIAL CONSEQUENCES OF INCOME INEQUALITY

WHY should society really care about the extent of income inequality? Firstly, because income inequality induces "spillover" effects on quality of life, even for people not normally affected by material wants. Wide income disparities result in frustration, stress, and family disruption, which then increase the rates of crime, violence, and homicide.[4] Those who can afford to will be increasingly forced to flee to walled compounds equipped with round the clock security systems, as has already happened in some American communities. Middle class flight from poor neighbourhoods results in the progressive deterioration of the public education system and the erosion of support for public schools. As Kaplan and others have shown, wide income disparities tend to coexist with underinvestment in human capital, measured in a variety of ways including high school drop out rates, reduced public spending on education, and lower literacy rates.[7] The rise of an "underclass" of poorly educated and underskilled citizens means that society will ultimately pay the cost through low productivity and slow economic growth. Finally, as Putnam has suggested, the breakdown of social cohesion brought about by income inequality threatens the functioning of democracy. Low levels of civic trust spill over into lack of trust and confidence in government.[16] To give an example from the United States, there is a strong correlation between lack of civic trust and low voter turnout at elections (fig 4). It is already known that the votes of the poor are underrepresented at election time. Political representation is further distorted by inequalities in political campaign donations across different income groups. In the United States it is estimated that the richest 3% of the voting population accounts for 35% of all private campaign donations during presidential elections.[27]

To a large extent it is a matter of public choice as to how much inequality a society should tolerate. The danger is that society that becomes depleted of its stocks of social capital could enter into a vicious cycle—one in which lack of trust and civic engagement reinforces a kind of democracy in which public policy is no longer the outcome of collective deliberation about the public interest, but rather the residue of campaign strategy.[28] The alternative is to put a halt to the growth in income inequality, which offers the hope of revitalising social capital at the same time as improving the health of the whole population.

NOTES

1. United Nations. *Human development report 1996.* New York: Oxford University Press, 1996.

2. Hahn RA, Eaker ED, Barker ND, Teutsch SM, Sosniak WA, Krieger N. Poverty and death in the United States. *Int J Health Serv* 1996;26:673–90.

3. Wilkinson RG. Income distribution and life expectancy. *BMJ* 1992;304:165–8.

4. Wilkinson RG. *Unhealthy societies. The afflictions of inequality.* London: Routledge, 1996.

5. Judge K. Income distribution and life expectancy: a critical appraisal. *BMJ* 1995;311:1282–5.

6. Kennedy BP, Kawachi I, Prothrow-Stith D. Income distribution and mortality: cross sectional ecological study of the Robin Hood Index in the United States. *BMJ* 1996;312:1004–7.

7. Kaplan G, Pamuk E, Lynch JW, Cohen RD, Balfour JL. Inequality in income and mortality in the United States: analysis of mortality and potential pathways. *BMJ* 1996;312:999–1003.

8. Ben Shlomo Y, White IR, Marmot M. Does the variation in the socioeconomic characteristics of an area affect mortality? *BMJ* 1996;312:1013–4.

9. Kawachi I, Levine S, Miller SM, Lasch K, Amick B III. *Income inequality and life expectancy—theory, research and policy.* Boston: Health Institute, New England Medical Center, 1994.

10. Tumin MM. Some principles of stratification: a critical analysis. *American Sociological Review* 1953;18:387–94.

11. Bruhn JG, Wolf S. *The Roseto story.* Norman, OK: University of Oklahoma Press, 1979.

12. Durkheim E. *Suicide.* New York: Free Press, 1951. (First published 1897; trans. JA Spaulding, G Simpson.)

13. Berkman LF, Syme SL. Social networks, host resistance and mortality: a nine-year follow-up study of Alameda County residents. *Am J Epidemiol* 1979;109:186–204.

14. House JS, Landis KR, Umberson D. Social relationships and health. *Science* 1988;214:540–5.

15. Kawachi I, Colditz GA, Ascherio A, Rimm EB, Giovannucci E, Stampfer MJ, *et al.* A prospective study of social networks in relation to total mortality and cardiovascular disease in men in the U.S. *J Epidemiol Comm Health* 1996;50:245–251.

16. Putnam RD, *Making democracy work. Civic traditions in modern Italy.* Princeton, NJ. Princeton University Press, 1993.

17. Kawachi I, Kennedy BP, Lochner K, Prothrow-Stith D. Social capital, income inequality, and mortality. *Am J Public Health* (in press).

18. MacIntyre S, McIver S, Soloman A. Area, class and health: should we be focusing on places or people? *Journal of Social Policy* 1993;22:213–34.

19. Haan M, Kaplan GA, Camacho T. Poverty and health: prospective evidence from the Alameda County Study. *Am J Epidemiol* 1987;125:989–98.

20. Sloggett A, Joshi H. Higher mortality in deprived areas: community or personal disadvantage? *BMJ* 1994;309:1470–4.

21. Kaplan G. People and places: contrasting perspectives on the association between social class and health. *Int J Health Serv* 1996;26:507–19.

22. Shouls S, Congdon P, Curtis S. Modeling inequality in reported longterm illness in the UK—combining individual and area characteristics. *J Epidemiol Comm Health* 1996;50:366–76.

23. Massey DS, Denton NA. *American apartheid: segregation and the making of the underclass.* Cambridge, MA: Harvard University Press, 1993.

24. Massey DS. The age of extremes: concentrated affluence and poverty in the twenty-first century. *Demography* 1996;33:395–412.

25. Wilson WJ. *The truly disadvantaged.* Chicago: University of Chicago Press, 1987.

26. Wacquant LJD, Wilson WJ. The cost of racial and class exclusion in the inner city. *Annals of the American Academy of Political and Social Science* 1989;501:8–25.

27. Verba S, Schlozman KL, Brady HE. *Voice and equality.* Cambridge, MA: Harvard University Press, 1995.

28. Putnam RD. Bowling alone: America's declining social capital. *Journal of Democracy* 1995;6:65–78.

Twenty-One

UNDERSTANDING HOW INEQUALITY IN THE DISTRIBUTION OF INCOME AFFECTS HEALTH

John W. Lynch and George A. Kaplan

ABSTRACT

R ESEARCH on the determinants of health has almost exclusively focused on the individual but it seems clear we cannot understand or improve patterns of population health without engaging structural determinants at the societal level. This article traces the development of research on income distribution and health to the most recent epidemiologic studies from the USA that show how income inequality is related to age-adjusted mortality within the 50 states (r = -0.62, p = 0.0001) even after accounting for absolute levels of income. We discuss potential material, psychological, social and behavioral pathways through which income distribution might be linked to health status. Distributional aspects of the economy are important determinants of health and may well provide one of the most pertinent indicators of overall social well-being.

INTRODUCTION

I N this article, we are concerned with exploring the question of how inequality in the distribution of income affects patterns of population health. It is well-established that individual income level affects health, but income distribution is a characteristic of a social system—it is not measurable in individuals. Research on the determinants of health has almost exclusively focused on the individual, and this is certainly true in the field of health psychology, but it seems clear that we cannot understand or improve patterns of population health without engaging structural determinants at the societal level (Morris, 1990; M. Susser, & E. Susser, 1996).

One of our goals is to advance thinking abut health inequalities by moving from consideration of individual characteristics like income, or education, to properties of the social and economic systems in which people play out their daily lives. These structural properties may have

Originally published in *Journal of Health Psychology*, 1997.

important influences on health over and above the characteristics of the individuals who comprise these populations (Haan, Kaplan, & Camacho, 1987; Kaplan, 1996; Macintyre, MacIver, & Sooman, 1993). This should not be taken to mean that individual characteristics are unimportant determinants of health, but clearly there are structural aspects of our societies that play a large role in determining how individuals are sorted into the groups who receive good educations, get good jobs and receive adequate financial compensation. We believe that income inequality may be an important measure of one of these structural characteristics.

THE BACKGROUND

THE form of law which I should propose as the natural sequel would be as follows:

> In a state which is desirous of being saved from all plagues . . . there should exist among the citizens neither extreme poverty, nor, again, excess of wealth, for both are productive of both these evils. Now the legislator should determine what is to be the limit of poverty or wealth. Let the limit of poverty be the value of the lot; this ought to be preserved, and no ruler, nor any one else who aspires after a reputation for virtue, will allow the lot to be impaired in any case. This the legislator gives as a measure, and he will permit a man to acquire double or triple, or as much as four times the amount of this. (Plato, *Laws*, cited in Fraser, 1995, p. 528)

Concerns about social inequality are not new. They have been voiced throughout human history, and are germane to ideas of democracy and justice. For a variety of reasons inequality has often been seen as an undesirable characteristic of a society, because of its potentially disruptive effects on civic functioning, or its implications for the rise of reactionary political movements, or because of its offense to moral sensibilities. However, arguments have also been advanced that social inequality is merely the institutional reflection of 'natural' individual differences in

abilities and intelligence (Herrnstein & Murray, 1994). Both positions remain firmly entrenched in popular and scientific debates about economic, racial/ethnic and gender inequalities (Fischer, et al. 1996; Lewontin, 1991; Lewontin, Rose, & Kamin, 1984; Muntaner, Nieto, & O'Campor, 1996; Will, 1995). Scientific interest in this field would perhaps be limited to politics, philosophy, economics and sociology were it not for the overwhelming body of evidence that shows how social and economic inequalities are one of the most profound determinants of population health (Lynch, 1996). Almost without regard to how health status and position in the social structure have been measured, those with lower social and economic status experience poorer health (Antonovsky, 1967; Carroll, Davey Smith, & Bennett, 1996; Haan, Kaplan, & Syme, 1989; Kaplan & Keil, 1993; Krieger, Rowley, Hermann, Avery, & Phillips, 1993; Lynch, et al., 1994; Lynch, Kaplan, R. Salonen, Cohen, & J. Salonen, 1995; Lynch, 1996; Lynch, Kaplan, & J. Salonen, 1997; Marmot et al., 1991; Syme, 1992).

The vast majority of studies that have documented socio-economic health inequalities have conceptualized and measured socio-economic status (SES) as a property of an individual, and compared the health status of groups of individuals who differed in regard to their income, education or occupation. In this way, 'inequalities' in health status are due to the fact that individuals differ according to their educational achievement, or their absolute levels of income. Indeed, this makes sense because the skills and economic resources held by individuals are likely to influence things such as the type of housing they can afford, the neighborhood they live in, the quality of food they buy, or their access to leisure physical activity. However, it also leaves open the interpretation that there are other individual characteristics that explain why they have lower educational achievement, are not very well paid, or have 'bad' jobs—they are unintelligent, sick, lazy or genetically inferior. This focus on measuring SES as an individual characteristic has also been conceptually and methodologically consistent with the rise of modern, risk factor epidemiology which has focused almost exclusively on finding the individual biological, behavioral and psychosocial correlates of disease.

THE LITERATURE ON INEQUALITY OF INCOME DISTRIBUTION AND HEALTH

THE link between low income and poor health is highly consistent when individuals are compared *within* a country, but there is little association between low income and health status when compared *across* countries. Countries with higher average incomes do not invariably have better overall health status. For instance, Sen (1993) showed that Saudi Arabia and the Kerala region of India had similar life expectancies at birth of around 70 years, yet the absolute level of average income in Saudi Arabia was more than 30 times greater than that in Kerala. Similarly, average life expectancy at age 5 in Bangladesh was greater than it was for African Americans living in parts of New York City, despite the fact that African Americans on average had higher absolute incomes (McCord & Freeman, 1990). In this section of the article, we will briefly trace the development of research on income distribution and health from the early work in health economics and demography that focused on average absolute income level, to the most recent epidemiologic studies that have examined the health impacts of income distribution per se.

Part I

The need to look beyond the absolute level of income to understand its association with health status, became crystallized when mortality and life expectancy differences between countries were examined in relation to average income level. Evidence suggesting a relationship between income distribution and health began to accumulate in 1969, when Auster, Leveson and Sarachek (1969), in a comparison of the 50 United States, showed that average income tended to be positively associated with mortality. This surprising finding was not consistent with other evidence collected at the individual level. Fuchs (1974) found that per-capita income was not related to adult mortality in comparisons between developed countries.

In a seminal study, Preston (1975) examined the association between per-capita national income and life expectancy at birth, for three different decades of the twentieth century. He demonstrated that life expectancy in the 1900s, 1930s and 1960s exhibited a non-linear relationship with per-capita national income. Above a certain threshold, gains in life expectancy were not related to higher levels of average income. In addition, the relationship between income and life expectancy had shifted upwards during the twentieth century.

Preston made several points in discussing these findings that are pertinent to the topic of this article. First, he proposed that upward shifts in the life expectancy–income association were mainly due to 'exogenous' factors that strengthened the public health infrastructure (immunization, technological advances and specific disease-control campaigns) rather than income growth per se. Second, he suggested that over time, life expectancy had become progressively more dissociated from absolute income level and that at least some of the variation in life expectancy at the upper-income levels was likely due to variations in income distribution between countries.

Preston could not examine this issue in detail because the available data were inadequate, but he did show mathematically how income distribution could affect the total mortality burden of a population. He explained that because the association between income and life expectancy was asymptotic (increases in income produced diminishing returns on increased life expectancy), those with incomes below the average lost more years of life, than were gained by those with higher than average incomes. The non-linear association between income and mortality has been reported in some more recent studies on large US data sets (Backlund, Sorlie, & Johnson, 1996; Pappas, Queen, Hadden, & Fisher, 1993). Preston concluded that 'The distribution of income is clearly a likely source of variance in the basic relation between national life expectancy and average national income' (1975, p. 242).

Rodgers (1979) elaborated graphically and mathematically how income distribution was associated with population health. Additionally, in a sample of about 50 countries, he empirically tested a model that predicted life expectancy at birth, at age 5 and infant mortality as a function of mean income level, and income distribution. He found that income distribution was significantly and consistently related to mortality, after controlling for mean income (which was also an important predictor), and commented that 'The results for life expectancy at birth suggest that the differences in average life expectancy between a relatively egalitarian and a relatively inegalitarian country is likely to be as much as five to ten years' (p. 350).

Part II

Somewhat surprisingly, since these intriguing early findings, the relationship between income distribution and health has not been widely studied. Le Grand (1987) explored how different measures of inequality were related to mortality, and found that the greater the extent of inequality, the higher was the mortality. One of the most widely used measures of income distribution is the Gini coefficient. The Gini coefficient is an overall measure of income inequality derived from the relationship between cumulative proportions of the population, plotted against cumulative proportions of income. The Gini is calculated by comparing the area under the diagonal with the area under the actual income distribution, called the Lorenz curve. The Gini ranges from 0—perfect equality, to 1—perfect inequality of income distribution (Cowell, 1995). Perfect income distribution would be achieved if 10 percent of the population received 10 percent of the total income; 20 percent of the population received 20 percent of the total income and so on. If each percentile of the population received the equivalent share of total income, then the Gini coefficient would be 0. However, if only one household in the population received all the income, the Gini would be 1.

Flegg (1982) examined the infant mortality in a sample of less developed countries in terms of per-capita income, and the Gini coefficient, and found that absolute income was negatively related, and the Gini coefficient positively related to infant mortality. Weatherby, Nam and Isaac (1983) in a study of female mortality over the age of 50 years in a sample of 38 countries, found that countries with higher levels of income inequality had higher female all-cause mortality for ages 50–64, although the pattern of cause-specific mortality was not uniform among age groups. They also pointed out that the mortality effects of income inequality may be even stronger at ages less than 50. Pampel and Pillai (1986) used the Gini coefficient to examine infant mortality rates in 18 developed nations and found some support for the effect of income inequality. In a sample of 41 developed and developing countries Waldmann (1992) showed that the greater the total income share held by the top 5 percent of the population, the higher was the infant mortality. This finding received some support from another analysis of between 34 and 61 developing countries conducted by Crenshaw and Ameen (1993).

Wennemo (1993) used data from the Luxembourg Income Study to compare infant mortality in 18 industrialized countries, and confirmed that income inequality and relative poverty were of greater importance in understanding variations in infant mortality between countries, than was the absolute level of economic development. In

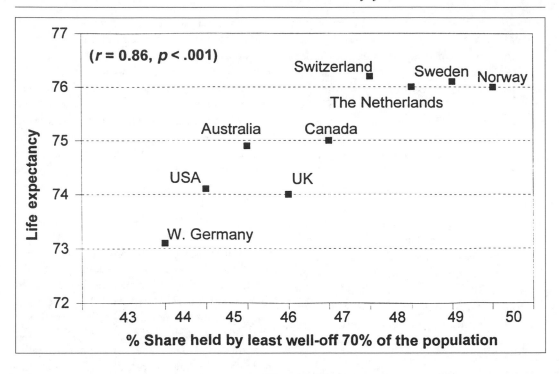

Figure 1
Association between life expectancy at birth and the share of post-tax and benefit income held by the least well-off 70 percent of the population (adapted from Wilkinson, 1992).

another study, that used a measure of the average income received by the bottom 10 percent of the population, although not strictly a measure of income distribution, Duleep (1995) argued that even for economically advanced countries, income inequality was an important determinant of mortality. In 1993, Merva and Fowles, used econometric modeling of cause-specific mortality and crime rates in 28 major metropolitan areas of the United States to examine the impact of unemployment, poverty and wage inequality. Among other things, they found that wage inequality was not associated with suicide, cardiovascular or stroke mortality, but was significantly related to homicides, accidents, aggravated assaults, larceny and motor vehicle thefts.

In a series of articles produced since the mid 1980s Richard Wilkinson has demonstrated im-

portant associations between income inequality and differences in mortality between industrialized countries (Wilkinson, 1986, 1989, 1993a & b, 1995). His most widely cited study, published in 1992, using income data from the Luxembourg Income Study, showed that the percentage share of total post-tax and benefit income held by the least well-off 70 percent of the population was cross-sectionally related to life expectancy at birth. This association was unaffected by adjustment for average absolute income level and was evident across a range of decile shares of the income distribution (Figure 1). Furthermore, using two other data sources, he showed how changes in income share were associated with changes in life expectancy. Wilkinson made extremely important observations not just because they could shed light on why income and health were related within, but not between countries, but because they had direct relevance to economic and public health policy.

Part III

A study by Ben-Shlomo, White and Marmot (1996) uses a measure of the variation in deprivation, as well as the absolute level of deprivation across local authority areas in Britain to show how both these factors contributed to mortality, although the absolute level appeared to be more strongly associated. In an intriguing analysis of post-transition countries in East Europe, Davey Smith and Egger (1996) report strong relationships between income inequality and life expectancy (1991–1993), as well as changes in inequality between 1987 and 1993 and changes in life expectancy over the same period. They comment that 'These countries have undergone a transformation from Stalinist pseudosocialism to the vagaries of the free market, and even the chief cheerleader for unfettered free market capitalism, the World Bank, was forced to ask: Is transition a killer?' (p. 1584).

Some of the most recent empirical work to examine specifically the effects of income inequality on health was conducted by two independent groups of investigators within the United States—George Kaplan's group at the University of Michigan, and by Kennedy, Kawachi and Prothrow-Stith at Harvard. The studies used different measures of income inequality to exam-

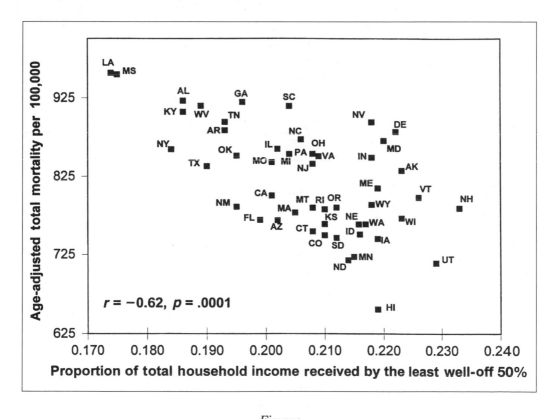

Figure 2
Association between age-adjusted mortality and the share of total income received by the least well-off 50 percent of the population in the 50 United States, 1990 (Kaplan et al., 1996b).

ine its association with mortality differences among the 50 United States. (Kaplan, Pamuk, Lynch, Cohen, & Balfour, 1996b; Kennedy, Kawachi, & Prothrow-Stith, 1996) These studies are important for a number of reasons. First, they examined the association between variations in state income inequality and mortality differences, at a different level of geopolitical aggregation than that between nations. Second, they overcame many of the data quality problems encountered in the previous between country analyses; and, third, the Kennedy and colleagues' (1996) study enabled an examination of how the association between income inequality and mortality differed by cause of death. (Please note: there were important corrections to these papers, published later in the *British Medical Journal 312*, 11 May 1996.) Finally, and perhaps most importantly, the study by Kaplan and colleagues (1996b) also examined a number of social and educational correlates of income inequality in an effort to understand how inequality might affect mortality.

Kaplan and colleagues (1996b) showed that the income share held by the least well-off 50 percent of the population in each state, was strongly cross-sectionally associated with overall mortality in 1990 ($r = -0.62$, $p = .0001$). This association was not affected by adjustment for median state income, was observed for almost all percentile shares of the income distribution; was consistent across age groups and in both sexes. Furthermore, the share of total state income held by the least well-off 50 percent of the population was strongly associated with a number of other health outcomes (Table 1), social indicators (Table 2) and educational indicators (Table 3). Moreover, the association between the share of the total income received by the least well-off 50 percent of the state population was consistently more strongly associated with mortality, other health outcomes, social and educational indicators than was the median absolute income in each state.

Table 1

Correlation between income inequality* and other health related outcomes (adjusted for median state income) (Kaplan et al., 1996b)

Health outcome	r	p value
% Live Births (<2500 gm)	− 0.65	.001
% Unable to work due to disability	− 0.33	.05
Violent crime/100K	− 0.7	.0001
Homicides/100K	− 0.74	.0001
Log per capita medical expenditures	− 0.67	.001
% Sedentary	− 0.34	.03
Smoker	− 0.35	.02
% Binge drinkers	0.32	.03

*Share of total income held by least well-off 50%.

Table 2

Correlation between income inequality and social indicators (adjusted for median state income) (Kaplan et al., 1996b)

Social indicator (%)	r	p value
Unemployed	− 0.48	.001
Prisoners	− 0.44	.01
Aid to families with dependent children (AFDC)	− 0.69	.001
Food stamps	− 0.72	.001
No health insurance	− 0.45	.002

In prospective analyses, income inequality levels in 1980 predicted changes in mortality between 1980 and 1990 ($r = -0.45$, $p < .001$). The higher the level of income inequality in 1980, the slower was the decline in mortality between 1980 and 1990. Simultaneous changes in income inequality and mortality between 1980 and 1990 were weakly related using the income share held by the least well-off 50 percent of the population, but changes in mortality were associated with simultaneous changes in the percentage share held

Table 3

Correlation between income inequality and educational indicators (adjusted fro median state income) (Kaplan et al., 1996b)

Educational indicators	r	p value
% No high-school degree	– 0.71	.001
% High-school dropout	– 0.5	.001
4th grade reading	0.58	.001
4th grade math	0.64	.001
Total education spending	0.32	.02
Library books per capita	0.42	.003

by the least well-off 10 percent of the population ($r = -0.53, p < .001$).

In similar analyses, Kennedy and colleagues (1996) used the Gini coefficient, and another Lorenz-based measure aptly called the 'Robin Hood Index', that approximated the share of total income from those above the mean that would have to be transferred to those below the mean to achieve equality of distribution, to examine the cross-sectional associations between income inequality and cause-specific mortality. Their findings were entirely consistent with those of Kaplan and colleagues (1996b), and showed how the Robin Hood Index was strongly related to infant mortality, coronary heart disease, malignant neoplasms and homicide (see corrections in *BMJ* cited earlier). They also calculated that each percentage increase in the Robin Hood Index was associated with an increase in total mortality of almost 22 deaths per 100,000. This meant that if Louisiana, the most unequal state, had the income distribution of the least unequal state (New Hampshire) there would be a reduction in the total mortality rate of 150 deaths per 100,000 in Louisiana. Taken together, the studies by Kaplan and colleagues (1996b), and Kennedy and colleagues (1996) have important and provocative implications for research and public policy on the economic determinants of health.

Part IV

Before proceeding to a discussion of the processes through which income inequality might affect health, we must address the recent criticisms of the research conducted in this field. In 1995, Ken Judge authored a critique of the work linking income inequality with mortality. In his critique, Judge focused exclusively on the work of Wilkinson (1992) and claimed that reanalysis of new data that had been added to the Luxembourg Income Study database (LIS) 'casts doubt on the hypothesis that inequalities in the distribution of income are closely associated with variations in average life expectancy at birth among the richest nations of the world' (p. 1282). More recently, these same criticisms have been repeated by Saunders (1996) who also showed that reanalysis of the updated LIS information failed to support a statistically significant association between income distribution and life expectancy or changes in life expectancy.

In new analyses, McIsaac and Wilkinson (1995) have shown how differences in response rates between countries recently added to the LIS database might shed some light on the inconsistent findings on life expectancy to which Judge (1995) and Saunders (1996) referred. These criticisms failed to consider the issue of data quality, nor did they provide an explanation for Wennemo's (1993) findings, also based on the newly added LIS data, that showed important associations between income inequality and infant mortality.

Nevertheless, Judge's and Saunders' criticisms of Wilkinson's research from 1992, deserve to be discussed. In our view, there were four basic issues. First, they claimed that there were problems with the validity of some of the data that Wilkinson used, that is, they were differentially unreliable, covered different years, and were not gathered for the purpose of examining income inequality and health. Second, the basic income data that were used to generate distributional measures of inequality were not adjusted for taxes, benefits and household size. The idea here is that use of 'raw' household income distributions would overstate the extent of inequality because neither did they reflect the number of people who were supported by the income in each household nor did they account for governmental policies that tax and transfer money and benefits from the rich to the poor. Third, Judge (1995) and Saunders (1996) claimed that there was no rationale for the selection of the income inequality measure, and the association between income inequality and mortality differed according to which measure was used. They claimed the choice of measure should be based on a theoretical rationale of how income distribution affects health. Finally, Judge argued that any examination of the income inequality, life expectancy association must use multivariate techniques that can adequately control for confounding.

These are potentially important considerations relevant to any study on income inequality and health, so it is indeed unfortunate that they were presented with such a personal focus on Wilkinson's work (1995). However, our purpose in this article is to evaluate the veracity of these criticisms in light of the more recent empirical findings within the United States. The basic points Judge (1995) and Saunders (1996) raised were largely addressed in the studies of income inequality and mortality in the 50 United States (Kaplan et al., 1996b; Kennedy et al., 1996). First, in our study, we used 1980 and 1990 US Census data that was based on pretax income from all sources, including governmental benefits, and examined mortality data from 1979–1981, and 1989–1991 provided by the National Center for Health Statistics in Washington, DC. Thus, the data are of high quality and collected in the same time frame as the mortality information. In addition, we showed that the association between income inequality and mortality was not highly sensitive to the measure employed, as has been argued by Saunders (1996). In fact, including information from the work by Kennedy, Kawachi and Prothrow-Stith (1996), the same substantive conclusions about the association between income inequality and health would be reached,

based on the use of the Gini coefficient, Robin Hood Index or any percentile share of total income between the 10th and the 80th.

Furthermore, in a new analysis conducted by Kawachi and Kennedy (in press) they examined the associations between eight different commonly used measures of income distribution and age-adjusted total mortality in the USA. All measures were highly correlated with each other, and showed significant associations with mortality, ranging from $r = 0.50$ to 0.66, even after adjustment for median income and poverty level. They state, 'Thus, the choice of income distribution measure does not appear to alter the conclusion that income inequality is linked to higher mortality.'

It is true, however, that the income distribution used in the original analyses by Kaplan and colleagues (1996b) and Kennedy and colleagues (1996) did not fully take into account the impact of taxes, transfers and household size, a point made by Judge (1996) in a more recent letter criticizing our study and the work of Kennedy and colleagues (1996). In response to his critique of our work, we addressed these concerns in two ways, by accounting for taxes, benefits and household size at both the aggregate and individual levels (Kaplan, Lynch, Pamuk, Cohen, & Balfour, 1996a).

In our original article, we reported an income-adjusted association between the share held by the least well-off 50 percent of the population and mortality of $r = -0.57$ (Kaplan et al., 1996b). This association was $r = -0.49$, after additional aggregate adjustment for average household size (a proxy for household composition); maximum welfare/food stamp payments; and the maximum difference between state income-tax brackets (a proxy for the redistributive effect of state income-tax). Subject to the limitations of ecologic adjustment of this association, taking account of these factors appears to make little difference.

To capture fully the effects of taxes, benefits

and household composition on the actual distribution of disposable income, we used data kindly provided by Professor Timothy Smeeding, the Director of the Luxembourg Income Study. The association between inequality and mortality in the United States was examined using disposable income distributions, adjusted at the household level for cash and near cash transfers, income and payroll taxes, including the Earned Income Tax Credit, and adjusted with a household size equivalence scale (Smeeding & Gottschalk, 1996). The LIS data were based on the US Current Population Survey (1990–1993), and included the share of household income received by the most and least well-off 20 percent of the population. We calculated directly comparable percentage shares in the 1990 US Census based data on gross income (Table 4).

The association between income inequality and mortality was virtually identical, although the absolute magnitude of income inequality in the States was reduced in LIS data. This suggests that there was no change in the ordering of the States with respect to income inequality. The relationship between income inequality and mortality was not affected by taking account of taxes, benefits and household size.

Judge has referred to the 'contentious' issue of the relationship between income distribution and mortality, but we are aware of only three criticisms of the data supporting this relationship: two are authored by Judge (1995, 1996) and

the third by Saunders (1996) merely repeats these same criticisms. Further progress on the relationship between income inequality and health will be made by examining different measures of income distribution, with a variety of health outcomes, across a number of geopolitical levels, and by careful consideration of how income distribution might influence the health of individuals and societies, and that is where we now turn our attention.

HOW MIGHT INEQUITABLE DISTRIBUTION OF INCOME IMPACT HEALTH?

WE have already alluded to the mathematical relationship between income distribution and population health, based on a positive asymptotic association between absolute income and health. For this reason, areas that have greater income inequality will have lower overall levels of population health because those at the bottom of the income distribution in a high inequality area will have lost more health than those at the top have gained. The proof of this association is set out in Preston (1975), Rodgers (1979) and by Kawachi, Levine, Miller, Lasch and Amick (1994). As Kawachi and colleagues argue, the non-linear relationship between income and mortality is a *'sufficient'* (1994, their emphasis) condition for income distribution to be a determinant of mortality, but it is

---

Table 4

Associations between inequality and mortality for the 50 United States, adjusted for median income (Kaplan et al., 1996a)

| | Share of total state income held by | |
	Least well-off 20%	Most well-off 20%
Disposable income (LIS)	− 0.60 ($p < .001$)	0.45 ($p < .001$)
'Raw income' (US Census)	− 0.61 ($p < .001$)	0.47 ($p < .001$)

probably not the most interesting or, indeed, most important part of understanding how income distribution impacts health.

We should point out there are very little data to inform this discussion. Furthermore, we are not trying to propose a particular causal pathway between income inequality and health, but rather suggest a range of factors that might be considered in developing a conceptual model of 'what fits where' in the association between income inequality and health. For this reason, the issues we discuss here are at least somewhat speculative, and highlight the need for more theoretical work to guide research. The importance of this task cannot be understated, because it is only through the development of comprehensive conceptual models, that we can sensibly address issues about adjustment for confounding that have been raised by Judge (1995). As we argue elsewhere, adjustment for confounding should be based on an underlying causal model relating a putative exposure and a health outcome, and is not primarily a technical or mechanical issue (Lynch et al., 1996, 1997).

Put in its simplest form, our basic hypothesis about the relation between income inequality and health has two intertwining strands. First, inequitable income distribution may be associated with a set of social processes and policies that systematically underinvest in human, physical, health and social infrastructure, and this underinvestment may have health consequences. Second, inequitable income distribution may have direct consequences on people's perceptions of their social environment that influence their health. In developing a conceptual framework for understanding how income distribution affects health, it may be worthwhile to reflect on what mechanisms and explanations have been proposed for how income affects health at the individual level. In an interesting and informative article, Macintyre (1997) has re-examined the Black Report (Townsend & Davidson, 1982) and developed both 'hard' and 'soft' interpreta-

tions of the explanations they proposed. The Black Report suggested four categories of explanation: artefactual; social selection; materialist; and cultural/behavioral/psychosocial. While these explanations were conceptualized at the individual level, a similar approach might be applied at the ecologic level. Perhaps by examining some ecologic counterparts we can begin to develop an understanding of how income inequality influences health. To some extent, we have already discussed the issues which would form the basis of an artefactual explanation for an association between income inequality and health status, in our comments about Judge's (1995, 1996) criticisms. For this reason, we will focus the discussion on material, cultural, behavioral and psychosocial factors at the ecologic level that may be linked with income inequality and influence health.

In thinking about how material, cultural, behavioral and psychosocial factors might be associated with income inequality and health status at the aggregate level, we feel that it is important to understand that some of these 'categories of explanation' are linked, as indeed they are at the individual level. At the outset, it may be helpful to pose the question like this: What sorts of characteristics and conditions are likely to exist in a country, state or region that also tolerates high levels of inequality in the distribution of income? In a general sense, we think the answer to this question is that areas that tolerate high-income inequality are also less likely to support the human, physical, cultural, civic and health resources in that area, independent of the absolute level of income.

For instance, what differences might exist between two areas that have the same average absolute level of income, but one allows a smaller share of the total income to be received by the least well-off 50 percent of the population? It may not be surprising to find that the higher inequality area also provides less equitable support for education, affordable housing, good roads or environmental protection. In fact there is some evidence for this in our study comparing the 50 States on inequality and mortality (Kaplan et al., 1996b). We showed in that study how states with more equitable income distribution had higher spending on education per capita ($r = 0.32$, $p = .02$); had more library books per capita ($r = 0.42$, $p = .002$); had lower proportions of their populations without any health insurance ($r = 0.45$, $p = .002$); had lower rates of violent crime ($r = -0.70$, $p = .0001$), and tolerated lower proportions of their population in jail ($r = 0.44$, $p = .01$), even after accounting for differences in the absolute level of median income in each state. In fact, the distributional measure of income we used in this study was more strongly associated with these characteristics than was the absolute income level.

There may be a plethora of other characteristics of high-income inequality areas that influence health status directly and indirectly. Do higher inequality areas have less immunization or tuberculosis control programs; fewer initiatives in public health education about smoking, diet or exercise; less strict environmental pollution standards; provide less support for cultural festivals, civic performances and art shows; have higher concentrations of cigarette and alcohol advertising; or are more likely to tolerate racial and gender discrimination? It is also important for us to point out that it is not just spending by governments on social programs that determines overall inequality of income distribution. In the popular press, it is commonplace to read reports about the ever widening gaps in wages within private-sector employment (Timmins, 1996). It is perhaps emblematic of the nature of income inequality that at the same time workers are pressured to restrict their claims for higher wages, the incomes and benefits received by some top executives in the private sector have risen to unprecedented levels.

It is also possible that high-income inequality creates an undesirable psychosocial climate which directly influences health by affecting the level of social cohesion. A recent paper by Kawachi, Kennedy, Lochner and Prothrow-Stith (in press) explored the relation between income inequality and social capital, defined as features of 'social organization, such as civic participation, norms of reciprocity, and trust in others, that facilitate cooperation and mutual benefit' (p. 5). The idea of 'social capital' was proposed by Coleman (1987, 1990) in the context of educational reform, and used by Putnam (1993) in relation to the performance of democratic institutions. Social capital refers to the stock of investments, resources and networks that produce social cohesion, trust and a willingness to engage in community activities. Kawachi and colleagues (in press) showed that income inequality (measured by the Robin Hood Index) was strongly associated with levels of social trust ($r = 0.73$, $p < .0001$) and group membership ($r = -0.46$, $p < .01$) for both blacks and whites. They concluded that social capital was an important mediating variable in the relation between income inequality and mortality.

> Unlike physical or human capital, which are private goods, social capital is a public good that is created as a by-product of social relationships. Like most types of public goods, social capital tends to be under-produced if left to the market. A major finding of this study (which needs to be confirmed in longitudinal studies) is that the size of the gap between the rich and the poor is powerfully, and negatively related to the level of investment in social capital. (p. 15)

However, more work needs to be done clarifying the pathways by which social capital, or the lack of it is related to health.

Wilkinson (1992) and Kawachi and colleagues (1994) argued that evidence for an association between income distribution and health, forces a shift in emphasis away from the absolute level of income to considerations of how relative income influences health. From a more materialist position, we have argued that income inequality (relative income) may be a marker for a set of other concrete societal characteristics and policies that influence health. However, it is also possible that income inequality directly influences health through individual appraisals of relative position in the social order. Wilkinson (1992, p. 168) states that 'The social consequences of people's differing circumstances in terms of stress, self esteem and social relations may now be one of the most important influences on health.'

Kawachi and colleagues (1994) elaborate this thinking by pointing out that most people living in poverty in industrialized nations, still have access to heat, water, electricity and television. By absolute standards, if they were living in less-developed countries, these same people would be considered rich, but in fact they are 'poor' in relation to those who live around them, not to some absolute standard. This is one of the reasons that the 'poverty level' must be periodically reset—it is not based on an absolute, rather it is defined by a society's changing living standards. To use a simple example: if there were two areas that had the same absolute income, but differed according to the distribution of that total income, people in the least well-off 50 percent of the population of the more unequal area would perceive themselves as being more relatively deprived than would the same group in a more equitable area. In other words, they would 'feel' the higher inequality around them.

It is this appraisal of relative well-being that many provide a psychosocially mediated link between income inequality and health status. Indeed, there are a number of theories for how such relational appraisals might be deleterious to health. In discussing how experiences of inequality might produce a gap between aspirations and rewards, Kawachi and colleagues (1994) suggested how these perceptions of inequality might translate into stress, frustration, depression, anxiety, hostility or, for that matter, any number of health damaging psychosocial characteristics and behaviors. Our point here is that there ap-

pears to be plausible theories within the field of health psychology to explain how living in a climate of income inequality might produce increased levels of psychosocial stress, or the initiation and maintenance of behaviors that could be detrimental to health. This psychosocial aspect of income inequality may also help to explain partly why those not quite at the top of the income distribution are thought to have somewhat poorer health than would those at the very top (Rose & Marmot, 1981). In rich countries, the negative impact of inequality on health would not be limited to the bottom of the social pyramid, because appraisal of relative position would extend to everyone in the hierarchy, so that even those with good incomes might feel 'relatively deprived' compared to the super rich.

However, it is vital to remind ourselves that any psychosocial understanding of income inequality is inextricably linked to the material features of the environment. It would be difficult to understand fully the psychologically 'immiserating' effects of relative position in the social order without appreciating the material factors that help to form the basis of this perception (Engels, 1848/1958; Marx, 1867/1967). Bourdieu (1984) has demonstrated in some detail how individuals embody and display their place in the social structure through their tastes for art, music, food and reading material. People use a variety of information about their environment to form perceptions of their relative position in the socioeconomic order, from material possessions and financial strain, to the levels of noise and pollution they experience, to how much violence and crime they encounter, to the friendliness of strangers on the streets where they live, to the choices available for housing, education and medical care. These individual perceptions are initiated and reinforced by the day-to-day conditions, events and experiences of living in a particular environment of income inequality, and it is not too difficult to imagine that the everyday experiences of living in a high inequality area presents different images from those encountered in a more equal environment. Although anecdotal evidence, it is commonplace to hear international visitors to certain parts of the United States, from more egalitarian countries, comment upon the stark contrast between homelessness and extreme wealth, that is less evident in their own countries.

WHERE TO FROM HERE?
CHALLENGES AND POSSIBILITIES

Research on the relationship between income distribution and health is in its infancy, so there are many issues to be explored. We conclude this article by briefly describing some of the challenges and important possibilities in better understanding the link between inequality of income distribution and health.

The Challenges

MEASURING INEQUALITY IN INCOME DISTRIBUTION

Although, there is some evidence presented in this article, to show that the cross-sectional association between income inequality and mortality within the 50 States was not sensitive to how income distribution was measured (Kaplan et al., 1996b; Kawachi & Kennedy, in press; Kennedy, Kawachi & Prothrow-Stith, 1996; and see corrections in *British Medical Journal 312*, 11 May 1996), it remains an open question, whether this is the case for prospective analyses, for other health outcomes, or for other levels of aggregation. Measures of income distribution may vary to the extent they differentiate between changes in the shape of particular parts of the income distribution. The choice of a measure of inequality would be aided by the development of a conceptual model of how income distribution affects a particular health outcome.

For example, it is possible to construct a variety of measures that express ratios of the total

income received by any particular proportion of the population. In studying how change in income distribution over time was related to health, we think it would be informative to know if changes in health status were related to the 'rich getting richer' or the 'poor getting poorer'. Consequently, inequality measures that assessed changes in the ratio of the income share held at the 90th compared to the 50th percentile (90:50), and the 50th compared to the 10th percentile (50:10) could begin to assess whether population health levels were more strongly related to how much those at the bottom of the income distribution were pushed away or toward the middle of the distribution (50:10), compared to income share gains or losses at the top of the income distribution (90:50) (Daly, Duncan, Kaplan, & Lynch, 1997).

In addition, it will be important to know more about how different definitions of income affect the association with health outcomes. Judge (1995, 1996) has correctly pointed out that failure to account for governmental policies that tax and transfer benefits will overstate the extent of inequality. One important issue here, may be whether there are particular types of tax and transfer benefits that blunt the health impacts of 'raw' market inequality. There are potentially important implications for public policy in this type of research, and, indeed, we are currently attempting to examine this issue with United States data.

One of the most important areas of future research on issues of income distribution and health involves measuring 'wealth' and not income. Wealth refers to the total value of assets net of outstanding debt, and typically includes financial wealth (bank accounts, stocks, bonds, life insurance, etc.), value of housing and businesses, consumer durables like cars and major appliances, plus the value of pensions and retirement programs. It is important to explore the association between the distribution of wealth and health, because wealth better captures the long-term capacity to ensure economic security from fluctuations in income level, and is powerfully related to the exercise of economic, political and social influence. For these reasons, income distribution may be a poor measure of how material, financial, political and social resources are actually distributed.

Krugman (1992) has shown that income distribution statistics may greatly underestimate the true concentration of wealth. In the United States while the top 1 percent of income earners receives about 12 percent of the total pretax income, they hold more than 37 percent of the wealth. From 1983 to 1989, the top 1 percent of wealth holders in the United States received 62 percent of the total gain in marketable net worth (Wolff, 1995). The next 19 percent of wealth holders received 37 percent of the gains, while the bottom 80 percent of the population received only 1 percent. 'This pattern represents a distinct turnaround from the 1962–83 period, when every group enjoyed some share of the overall wealth growth and the gains were roughly in proportion to the share of wealth held by each in 1962' (Wolff, 1995, p. 12).

GEOPOLITICAL AGGREGATION

To date, evidence of negative health effects of inequality in the distribution of income has been limited to studies comparing nations and among the 50 US States. Income distribution is a structural characteristic of a social system, however it is unclear how different levels of geopolitical aggregation might affect its association with health status. The basic question concerns deciding what level of geopolitical aggregation is an appropriate 'unit of analysis'. If inequitable income distribution is related to a variety of other structural characteristics, at what level should these factors influence health status—national, state or province, county or local authority, city or neighborhood? To some extent, we would expect the association between income distribution and health to weaken as the level of geopolitical aggregation became more local. For instance, if everyone in a neighborhood was unemployed, there would be little inequality in income distribution, but the health status of the neighborhood would be poor.

In terms of a more psychosocial interpretation of the link between income distribution and health, information about relative position in the social hierarchy may not only be derived from localized references to the immediate social and economic surroundings of a neighborhood, city or state. Technologies like television and movies allow comparisons across a wide economic, social, behavioral and cultural range. We are currently examining some of these issues by studying the association between income distribution and health outcomes in 283 metropolitan areas of the United States. We hope that analyses such as these may provide clues as to how income distribution impacts health status, as there will be both more variation in income distribution and mortality and greater potential for local features of the geopolitical environment (e.g. specifically focused local public initiatives on issues like affordable public housing, access to prenatal care or violence prevention) to exert their impact on the link between income distribution and health.

INTERPRETING THE ASSOCIATION BETWEEN INEQUITABLE INCOME DISTRIBUTION AND HEALTH

As we stated earlier, one important task in advancing understanding of the association between income distribution and health is the development of comprehensive conceptual models. Thinking about such frameworks will be aided by empirical investigations, and may need to consider issues like:

- the pathways through which income distribution impacts health, and distinguishing between 'confounders', and factors in the causal pathway
- how inequitable income distribution is related to health outcomes that have different latency periods (e.g. cardiovascular disease vs suicide or homicide)

- how to understand and model the separate and joint effects of absolute income and income distribution, and
- how to understand differences in the association of inequality in income distribution and health between the young and the old, the rich and the poor, men and women, or between racial and ethnic groups.

THE POSSIBILITIES

Studies on the relationship between inequality of income distribution and health could not be more timely. In recent years, there has been a surge of scientific interest, particularly in economics, to document the extent, nature and trends in income inequality both internationally and within individual countries (Danziger & Gottschalk, 1995; Reed, Haber, & Mameesh, 1996; Smeeding & Gottschalk, 1996). While interpretation of these data has been vigorously debated in political circles, there now seems little doubt about the validity of the evidence showing

increased income inequality since the 1980s (Krugman, 1992).

Table 5 presents data from the Luxembourg Income Study that shows changes in income inequality between 1967 and 1992 for a variety of selected countries. In addition, it shows changes in child poverty rates over the same time period. In countries like the United Kingdom and the United States, there have been large increases in income inequality and in child poverty rates. These data suggest that at the same time as overall income inequality has increased there has been a simultaneous assault on the youngest and most vulnerable members of the society, by pushing more families with children into the lower end of the income distribution. In addition to negative effects on the immediate health status of these children, there may well be longer term behavioral, psychosocial and health dividends to the reaped (Lynch et al., 1997). How-

Table 5

*Changes in income inequality and child poverty rate (1967–1992)**

Country	% Change in inequality	% Change in child poverty
UK	+ >30	+ >30
USA	+ 16−29	+ >30
Sweden	+ 16−29	− >5
Australia	+ 10−15	0
Denmark	+ 10−15	− >5
Norway	+ 5−10	+ 10−15
The Netherlands	+ 5−10	+ 5−10
Belgium	+ 5−10	+ 5−10
W. Germany	0	+ 5−10
Israel	0	+ 5−10
Spain	0	0
France	0	0
Finland	0	− >5
Canada	0	− >5
Italy	− >5	− >5

*Adapted from Smeeding & Gottschalk (1996).

ever, these data also show that there is no necessary relation between changes in income inequality and child poverty. While Sweden witnessed
similar increases in income inequality to
the USA, they were able enact policies that actually reduced child poverty levels.

As Davey Smith (1996, p. 988) has pointed
out, 'The only coherent argument against redistributive social policies is that they hinder overall
economic growth.' The standard political argument against income redistribution is almost always framed in terms of a 'trade-off' between
overall economic growth and equitable distribution of income. This is true whether the debate
concerns the economies of developed or developing countries, and has usually been cast so that
social spending, investment in public infrastructure and redistribution of social goods must
be curtailed or delayed to ensure overall growth
in the economy. The best way to improve the lot
of those at the bottom of the income distribution
is to enlarge the size of the 'economic pie'. The
unstated assumption in this 'trickle-down' approach is that equity is derivative of growth.
However, evidence is mounting that overall economic growth may be relatively ineffective in
helping the disadvantaged members of the population (Cutler & Katz, 1991). In short, the rising
tide does not lift all boats evenly (Danziger &
Gottschalk, 1993).

Bruno, Revallion and Squire (1995, p. 22) show
that

> there is no intrinsic trade-off between long-run ef-
> ficiency and equity. In particular, policies aimed at
> facilitating accumulation of productive assets by the
> poor—when adopted in a relatively non-distorted
> framework—are also important instruments for
> achieving higher growth. The problem should not
> be posed as that of choosing between growth and
> redistribution. (WHO/SIDA, 1996)

This is a vital issue for developing and developed
nations concerned not only with economic
growth but with equity in health and health care.

As Bruno and colleagues (1995) suggest, the
accumulation of productive assets enhances eco-

nomic growth. The material presented here suggests that one of these important productive
assets is health, and it is strongly related to the
extent of inequitable income distribution. We
hope that research on the link between inequality
in the distribution of income and health status
will force policy debates about income inequality
to be framed, in part, in terms of its health and
social consequences. Distributional aspects of
the economy are important determinants of
health, over and above the absolute level of income, and for those of us concerned with population health may well provide one of the most
pertinent indicators of overall social well-being.

REFERENCES

Antonovsky, A. (1967), Social class, life expectancy and overall mortality. *Millbank Memorial Fund Quarterly, 45,* 31–
735.

Auster, R., Leveson, I., & Sarachek, D. (1969). The production of health: An exploratory study. *Journal of Human
Resources, 4,* 411–436.

Backlund, E., Sorlie, P. D., & Johnson, N. J. (1996). The
shape of the relationship between income and mortality in
the United States: Evidence from the National Longitudinal Mortality Study. *Annals of Epidemiology, 6,* 1–9.

Ben-Shlomo, Y., White, I. R., & Marmot, M. (1996). Does
the variation in socioeconomic characteristics of an area
affect mortality? *British Medical Journal, 312,* 1013.

Bourdieu, P. (1984). *Distinction.* Cambridge, MA: Harvard
University Press.

Bruno, M., Ravallion, M., & Squire, L. (1995). *Equity and
growth in developing countries: Old and new perspectives on
the policy issues.* Paper prepared for the IMF Conference
on Income Distribution and Sustainable Growth, 1–2
June.

Carroll, D., Davey Smith, G., & Bennett, P. (1996). Some
observations on health and socio-economic status. *Journal
of Health Psychology, 1*(1), 13–39.

Coleman, J. S. (1987). Families and schools. *Educational Researcher* (August–September), 32–38.

Coleman, J. S. (1990). *The foundations of social theory.* Cambridge, MA: Harvard University Press.

Cowell, F. A. (1995). *Measuring inequality*. Hemel Hempstead: Prentice-Hall/Harvester Wheatsheaf.

Crenshaw, E., & Ameen, A. (1993). Dimensions of social inequality in the Third World. *Population Research and Policy Review, 12*, 297–313.

Cutler, D. M., & Katz, L. F. (1991). Macroeconomic performance and the disadvantaged. *Brookings Papers on Economic Activity, 2*, 1–74.

Daly, M., Duncan, G., Kaplan, G. A., & Lynch, J. W. (1997). *Macro-to-micro linkages in the inequality mortality relationship*. Manuscript submitted for publication.

Danziger, S. H., & Gottschalk, P. (Eds.). (1993). *Uneven tides: Rising inequality in America*. New York: Russell Sage.

Danziger, S. H., & Gottschalk, P. (1995). *America unequal*. New York: Russell Sage.

Davey Smith, G. (1996). Income inequality and mortality: Why are they related? *British Medical Journal, 312*, 987–988.

Davey Smith, G., & Egger, M. (1996). Commentary: Understanding it all—health, meta-theories, and mortality trends. *British Medical Journal, 313*, 1584–1585.

Duleep, H. O. (1995). Mortality and income inequality among economically developed countries. *Social Security Bulletin, 58*, 34–50.

Engels, F. (1958). *The condition of the working class in England*. (O. W. Henderson, & W. H. Chalones, Trans.). Stanford, CA: Stanford University Press. (Original work published 1848)

Fischer, C. S., Hout, M., Jankowski, M. S., Lucas, S. R., Swidler, A., & Voss, K. (1996). *Inequality by design: Cracking the Bell curve myth*. Princeton, NJ: Princeton University Press.

Flegg, A. T. (1982). Inequality of income, illiteracy and medical care as determinants of infant mortality in underdeveloped countries. *Population Studies, 36*, 441–458.

Fraser, G. R. (1995). Plato on social inequality [Letter to the editor]. *British Medical Journal, 310*, 528.

Fuchs, V. (1974). Some economic aspects of mortality in developed countries. In M. Perlman (Ed.), *The economics of health and medical care* (pp. 174–193). New York: Wiley.

Haan, M. N., Kaplan, G. A., & Camacho, T. (1987). Poverty and health: Prospective evidence from the Alameda County study. *Amnerican Journal of Epidemiology, 125*, 989–998.

Haan, M. N., Kaplan, G. A., & Syme, S. L. (1989). Socioeconomic status and health: Old observations and new thoughts. In J. P. Bunker, D. S. Gomby, & B. H. Kehrer (Eds.), *Pathways to health: The role of social factors*. (pp. 76–135). Menlo Park, CA: HJ Kaiser Family Foundation.

Herrnstein, R. J., & Murray, C. (1994). *The Bell curve: Intelligence and class structure in American life*. New York: Free Press.

Judge, K. (1995). Income distribution and life expectancy: A critical appraisal. *British Medical Journal, 311*, 1282–1285.

Judge, K. (1996). Income and mortality in the United States [Letter to the editor]. *British Medical Journal, 313*, 1206.

Kaplan, G. A. (1996). People and places: Contrasting perspectives on the association between social class and health. *International Journal of Health Services, 26*, 507–519.

Kaplan, G. A., & Keil, J. E. (1993). Socioeconomic factors and cardiovascular disease: A review of the literature. *Circulation, 88*, 1973–1998.

Kaplan, G. A., Lynch, J. W., Pamuk, E. R., Cohen, R. D., & Balfour, J. L. (1996a). Income and mortality in the United States [Letter to the editor]. *British Medical Journal, 313*, 1207.

Kaplan, G. A., Pamuk, E. R., Lynch, J. W., Cohen, R. D., & Balfour, J. L. (1996b). Inequality in income and mortality in the United States: Analysis of mortality and potential pathways. *British Medical Journal, 312*, 999–1003.

Kawachi, I., & Kennedy, B. P. (in press). The relationship of income inequality to mortality—Does the choice of indicator matter? *Social Science & Medicine*.

Kawachi, I., Kennedy, B.P., Lochner, K., & Prothrow-Stith, D. (in press). Social capital, income inequality, and mortality. *American Journal of Public Health*.

Kawachi, I., Levine, S., Miller, S. M., Lasch, K., & Amick, B. (1994). Income inequality and life expectancy—theory, research and policy. Boston, MA: Society and Health Working Group, Health Institute, New England School of Medicine.

Kennedy, B. P., Kawachi, I., & Prothrow-Stith, D. (1996). Income distribution and mortality: Cross-sectional ecologic study of the Robin Hood index in the United States. *British Medical Journal, 312*, 1004–1007.

Krieger, N., Rowley, D., Hermann, A. A., Avery, B., & Phillips, M. T. (1993). Racism, sexism, and social class: Implications for studies of health, disease, and well-being.

American Journal of Preventive Medicine, 9 (Suppl. 6), 82–122.

Krugman, P. (1992). The rich, the right and the facts. *The American Prospect, 2,* 19–31.

LeGrand, J. (1987). Inequalities in health. *European Economic Review, 31,* 182–191.

Lewontin, R. C. (1991). *Biology as ideology.* New York: Harper Perennial.

Lewontin, R. C., Rose, S., & Kamin, L. J. (1984). *Not in our genes: Biology, ideology and human nature.* New York: Pantheon.

Lynch, J. W. (1996). Social position and health. *Annals of Epidemiology, 6,* 21–23.

Lynch, J. W., Kaplan, G. A., Cohen, R. D., Kauhanen, J., Wilson, T. W., Smith N. L., & Salonen J. T. (1994). Childhood and adult socioeconomic status as predictors of mortality in Finland. *Lancet, 343,* 524–527.

Lynch, J. W., Kaplan, G. A., Cohen, R. D., Tuomilehto, J., & Salonen, J. T. (1996). Do cardiovascular risk factors explain the relation between socioeconomic status, risk of all-cause mortality, cardiovascular mortality and acute myocardial infarction? *American Journal of Epidemiology, 144,* 934–942.

Lynch, J. W., Kaplan, G. A., & Salonen, J. T. (1997). Why do poor people behave poorly? Variation in adult health behaviours and psychosocial characteristics by stages of the socioeconomic lifecourse. *Social Science & Medicine, 44,* 809–820.

Lynch, J. W., Kaplan, G. A., Salonen, R., Cohen, R. D., & Salonen J. T. (1995). Socioeconomic status and carotid atherosclerosis. *Circulation, 92,* 1786–1792.

Lynch, J. W., Krause, N., Kaplan, G. A., Cohen, R. D., Tuomilehto, J., & Salonen, J. T. (1997). Workplace conditions, socioeconomic status, and the risk of mortality and acute myocardial infarction: The Kuopio ischemic heart disease risk factor study. *American Journal of Public Health, 87*(4): 617–622.

Macintyre, S. (1997). The Black report and beyond: What are the issues? *Social Science & Medicine, 44,* 723–746.

Macintyre, S., Maciver, S., & Sooman, A. (1993). Area, class and health: Should we be focusing on places or people? *Journal of Social Policy, 22,* 213–234.

Marmot, M. G., Davey Smith, G., Stansfeld, D., Patel, C., North, F., Head, J., White, I., Brunner, E., & Fenney, A. (1991). Health inequalities among British civil servants: The Whitehall II study. *Lancet, 337,* 1387–1392.

Marx, K. (1967). *Capital: A Critique of Political Economy* (Vol. 1). New York: International Publishers. (Original work publsihed 1867)

McCord, C., & Freeman, H. P. (1990). Excess mortality in Harlem. *New England Journal of Medicine, 322,* 173–177.

McIsaac, S., & Wilkinson, R. G. (1995) *Cause of death, income distribution, and problems of response rates.* Luxembourg: Luxembourg Income Study Working Paper Series, No. 136.

Merva, M., & Fowles, R. (1993). *Effects of diminished economic opportunities and social stress: Heart attacks, stroke, crime.* Washington, DC: Economic Policy Institute.

Morris, J. N. (1990). Inequalities in health: Ten years and little further on. *Lancet, 336,* 491–493.

Muntaner, C., Nieto, F. J., & O'Campo, P. (1996). The Bell curve: On race, social class, and epidemiologic research. *American Journal of Epidemiology, 144,* 531–536.

Pampel, F. C., & Pillai, V. K. (1986). Patterns and determinants of infant mortality in developed nations, 1950–1975. *Demography, 23,* 525–524.

Pappas, G., Queen, S., Hadden, W., & Fisher, G. (1993). The increasing disparity in mortality between socioeconomic groups in the United States, 1960 and 1986. *New England Journal of Medicine, 329,* 103–109.

Preston, S. H. (1975). The changing relation between mortality and level of economic development. *Population Studies, 29,* 231–248.

Putnam, R. D. (1993). *Making democracy work.* Princeton, NJ: Princeton University Press.

Reed, D., Haber, M. G., & Mameesh, L. (1996). *The distribution of income in California.* San Francisco: Public Policy Institute of California.

Rodgers, G. B. (1979). Income and inequality as determinants of mortality: An international cross-section analysis. *Population Studies, 33,* 343–351.

Rose, G., & Marmot, M. G. (1981). Social class and coronary heart disease. *British Heart Journal, 45,* 13–19.

Saunders, P. (1996). *Poverty, income distribution and health: An Australian study,.* Sydney: Social Policy Research Centre, Reports and Proceedings No. 128.

Sen, A. (1993). The economics of life and death. *Scientific American* (May), 40–47.

Smeeding, T. M., & Gottschalk, P. (1996). The international evidence on income distribution in modern economies:

Where do we stand? In M. Kaser & Y. Mundlak (Eds.), *Contemporary economic development reviewed, Vol. 2, Labour, food and poverty*. London: Oxford University Press.

Susser, M., & Susser, E. (1996). Choosing a future for epidemiology: II. From black boxes to Chinese boxes and eco-epidemiology. *American Journal of Public Health, 86,* 674–677.

Syme, S. L. (1992). Social determinants of disease. In J. M. Last & R. B. Wallace (Eds.), *Maxcy-Rosenau public health and preventive medicine* (13th edn, pp. 687–700). Norwalk, CT: Appleton & Lange.

Timmins, N. (1996, 21 November). Gap between rich and poor 'too wide'. *Financial Times,* p. 9.

Townsend, P., & Davidson, N. (1982). *Inequalities in health: The Black report*. Harmondsworth: Penguin.

Waldmann, R. J. (1992). Income distribution and infant mortality. *Quarterly Journal of Economics, 107,* 1283–1302.

Weatherby, N. L., Nam, C. B., & Isaac, L. W. (1983). Development inequality, health care, and mortality at the older ages: A cross-national analysis. *Demography, 20,* 27–43.

Wennemo, I. (1993). Infant mortality, public policy and inequality—A comparison of 18 industrialized countries 1950–85. *Sociology of Health and Illness, 15,* 429–446.

Wilkinson, R. G. (1986), Income and mortality. In *Class and health: Research and longitudinal data* (pp. 88–114). London: Tavistock.

Wilkinson, R. G. (1989). Class mortality differentials, income distribution and trends in poverty 1921–1981. *Journal of Social Policy, 18,* 307–335.

Wilkinson, R. G. (1992). Income distribution and life expectancy. *British Medical Journal, 304,* 165–168.

Wilkinson, R. G. (1993a). Income and health. In *Health, wealth and poverty*. London: Medical World/SHA.

Wilkinson, R. G. (1993b). *Unfair shares*. Ilford: Barnardos.

Wilkinson, R. G. (1995). Commentary: A reply to Ken Judge: Mistaken criticisms ignore overwhelming evidence. *British Medical Journal, 311,* 1285–1287.

Will, G. (1995, 24 April). What's behind income disparity? *San Francisco Chronicle.*

Wolff, E. N. (1995). *Top heavy. A study of the increasing inequality of wealth in America*. New York: Twentieth Century Fund Press.

World Health Organization/Swedish International Development Cooperation Agency (1996). *Equity in health and health care: A WHO/SIDA initiative*. Geneva: WHO.

Twenty-Two

SOCIAL CAPITAL,
INCOME INEQUALITY, AND MORTALITY

Ichiro Kawachi, Bruce P. Kennedy,
Kimberly Lochner, and Deborah Prothrow-Stith

ABSTRACT

Objectives. Recent studies have demonstrated that income inequality is related to mortality rates. It was hypothesized, in this study, that income inequality is related to reduction in social cohesion and that disinvestment in social capital is in turn associated with increased mortality.

Methods. In this cross-sectional ecologic study based on data from 39 states, social capital was measured by weighted responses to two items from the General Social Survey: per capita density of membership in voluntary groups in each state and level of social trust, as gauged by the proportion of residents in each state who believed that people could be trusted. Age-standardized total and cause-specific mortality rates in 1990 were obtained for each state.

Results. Income inequality was strongly correlated with both per capita group membership ($r = -.46$) and lack of social trust ($r = .76$). In turn, both social trust and group membership were associated with total mortality, as well as rates of death from coronary heart disease, malignant neoplasms, and infant mortality.

Conclusions. These data support the notion that income inequality leads to increased mortality via disinvestment in social capital.

INTRODUCTION

A number of cross-national studies have indicated that the degree of income inequality in a given society is strongly related to the society's level of mortality.[1-5] In one investigation of nine nations included in the Luxembourg Income Study,[4] a correlation of .86 was reported between average life expectancy and proportion of income allotted to the 70% of the population at the lowest income levels. Two recent US studies independently demonstrated an association between income inequality and mortality.[6, 7] Kennedy et al.[6] examined the relationship between degree of household income inequality and state-level variation in all-cause and cause-specific mortality. The degree of income inequality in each state was estimated by the Robin Hood Index, which is equivalent to the propor-

Originally published in *American Journal of Public Health*, 1997.

tion of aggregate income that must be redistributed from households above the mean and transferred to those below the mean in order to achieve perfect equality in the distribution of household incomes.[8] The higher the Robin Hood Index, the more unequal the distribution of income. The overall correlation of the Robin Hood Index to all-cause mortality in 1990 was .54 (*P* < .0001). After adjustment for poverty, a 1% rise in the Robin Hood Index was associated with an increase in age-adjusted total mortality rate of 21.7 deaths per 100 000 (95% confidence interval [CI] = 6.6, 36.7).[6] The Robin Hood Index was also associated with deaths from specific causes, including coronary heart disease, cancer, and infant mortality.

In an independent study, Kaplan et al.[7] examined the association between income inequality—as measured by the share of aggregate income earned by the bottom 50% of households—and state-level variations in total mortality. A strong association was found between their measure of income inequality and age-adjusted total mortality rates in 1990 (*r* = -.62, *P* < .001). Moreover, the degree of income inequality in each state in 1980 was a powerful predictor of levels of total mortality 10 years later.

The pathways and mechanisms underlying the association between income inequality and mortality levels remain to be established.[9, 10] One hypothesis is that rising income inequality results in increased levels of frustration, which may have deleterious behavioral and health consequences.[9, 10] Societies that permit large disparities in income to develop also tend to be the ones that underinvest in human capital (e.g., education), health care, and other factors that promote health.[7, 9] Recently, it has been hypothesized that the growing gap between the rich and the poor has led to declining levels of social cohesion and trust, or disinvestment in "social capital."[6, 7, 9, 10] Social capital has been defined as the features of social organization, such as civic participation, norms of reciprocity and trust in others, that fa-

cilitate cooperation for mutual benefit.[11-13] Social capital is thus a community-level ("ecologic") variable whose counterpart at the individual level is measured by a person's social networks. A vast literature has linked social networks to health outcomes at the individual level.[14-16] By contrast, studies of social capital have so far been limited to attempts to explain the performance of civic institutions and the economic development of societies.[11-13]

In the present study, we tested three linked hypotheses: (1) that state variations in income inequality predict the extent of investment in social capital, (2) that the degree of investment in social capital predicts state variations in total and cause-specific mortality, and (3) that there is little residual direct association between state income inequality and mortality after investment in social capital has been controlled.

METHODS

Measurement of State Variations in Social Capital

The core concepts of social capital, according to its principal theorists,[11-13, 17] consist of civic engagement and levels of mutual trust among community members. Civic engagement refers to the extent to which citizens involve themselves in their communities, as most often measured by their membership in groups and associations. Following Putnam,[11, 12, 17] we used weighted data from the General Social Survey, conducted by the National Opinion Research Center,[18] to estimate state variations in group membership and levels of social trust. This nationally representative survey samples noninstitutionalized English-speaking persons 18 years of age or older living in the United States. The survey has been repeated 14 times over the last 2 decades and has included a set of questions on social trust and organizational membership. In the present study, we averaged 5 years of cumulated data (1986 through 1990) from the survey, representing 7654 individual observations from 39 states (mean number of respondents per state = 196, SD deviation = 146, range = 58 [Iowa] to 729 [California]). Although the survey is nationally representative, only 39 states were included, because, by chance, people residing in some of the less populous states (e.g., Alaska, Delaware) were not picked up by the sampling scheme.

Level of civic engagement was measured by the per capita number of groups and associations (e.g., church groups, labor unions, sports groups, professional or academic societies, school groups, political groups, and fraternal organizations) to which residents in each state belonged. The other component of social capital, trust in others, was assessed from responses to two General Social Survey items that asked "Do you think most people would try to take advantage of you if they got a chance, or would they try to be fair?" (perceived lack of fairness) and "Generally speaking, would you say that most people can be trusted or that you can't be too careful in dealing with people?" (social mistrust). For each state, we calculated the percentage of respondents who agreed with the first part of each statement. Belief in the goodwill and benign intent of others facilitates collective action and mutual cooperation and therefore adds to the stock of a community's social capital. Collective action, in turn, further reinforces community norms of reciprocity. In addition to the social trust items, we evaluated the response to another General Social Survey item as a marker of social capital: "Would you say that most of the time people try to be helpful, or are they mostly looking out for themselves?" (perceived helpfulness).

All responses to the General Social Survey were weighted to take account of the fact that the survey was developed to generate representative data at the national and regional levels but not at the state level (Dr T. Smith, verbal communication, June 1996). Poststratification weights were developed to adjust for the extent to which survey respondents may not have been representative of the states in which they resided. In order to construct the weights, we first examined demographic characteristics in the survey that were most predictive of responses to the social capital items. Younger age, Black race, and less than high school education were the characteristics most correlated with lower social capital scores (lower levels of social trust and group membership). We therefore developed postsratification weights based on the distribution of age, race, and educational attainment of survey respondents. These stratum-specific weights were calculated as follows:

$$w_{i,j,k,l} = P_{i,j,k,l}/p_{i,j,k,l},$$

where $w_{i,j,k,l}$ is the postsratification weight for the survey respondent residing in the ith state and being of jth age group, kth race, and lth level of education attainment; $P_{i,j,k,l}$ is the proportion of individuals with these characteristics residing in the ith state (obtained from the 1990 US census; and $p_{i,j,k,l}$ is the corresponding proportion of such respondents in the General Social Survey.

These weights were then used to adjust the individual responses to the social capital items in the General Social Survey (via the weight procedure in SAS). For example, in states where the survey oversampled younger, Black, and less educated respondents, levels of social trust were adjusted upward.

Measurement of State Variations in Income Inequality

Income, household size, and poverty data were obtained from 1990 US Census Population and Housing Summary Tape File 3A. This summary tape provides annual household income data for 25 income intervals. Counts of the number of households that fall into each income interval, along with total aggregate income and median household income, were obtained for each state. Income data represented income prior to taxes and benefits; equivalence scales adjusting for household size were not used. Our measure of income inequality, the Robin Hood Index, was estimated from shares of household income arranged by decile groups (an example of the derivation of the index can be obtained from the senior author). Income deciles were calculated via software developed by Ed Welniak (unpublished software, US Bureau of the Census, 1988). The index is calculated by taking those decile groups whose share of the total income exceeds 10%, and summing the excesses of these shares. This value approximates the proportion of aggregate household income in each state that has to be taken from households above the mean and transferred to those below the mean in order to achieve equality in distribution of incomes.[8] The higher the index value, the less egalitarian the distribution of income.

Measurement of State Variations in Poverty

There is some evidence to suggest that poverty is linked to depletion in social capital.[19] Since poverty is also a predictor of mortality,[20] we evaluated poverty as a potential confounder in the relationship between social capital and mortality. Census Summary Tape File 3A contains data on state-specific prevalence of poverty; households are classified as being above or below the poverty level based on the revised federal poverty index originally developed by the Social Security Administration in 1964. The current poverty index is purely wage-income based and does not reflect other sources of income such as noncash benefits from food stamps, Medicaid, and public housing. Poverty thresholds are updated annually to reflect changes in the Consumer Price Index. The poverty variable used in the analyses represents the percentage of households in a given state below the federal poverty level (in 1990, an income of less than $13 359 for households with four family members[21]).

Measurement of State Variations in Mortality

The age-adjusted mortality rates for each state in 1990 were obtained from the Compressed Mortality Files compiled by the National Center for Health Statistics of the Centers for Disease Control and Prevention (CDC). The data were obtained from the CDC's database via CDC WONDER/PC software.[22]

All mortality rates were directly age standardized to the US population and expressed as the number of deaths per 100 000 persons (except in the case of infant mortality, for which death rates were expressed per 1000 live births). In addition to all-cause mortality, we examined the following major causes of death: coronary heart disease (*International Classification of Diseases*, 9th revision [ICD-9] codes 410 through 414), malignant neoplasms (ICD-9 codes 140 through 239), cerebrovascular disease (ICD-9 codes 430 through 438), and unintentional injuries (ICD-9 codes 800 through 949, 970 through 999).

Data Analysis

Ordinary least squares regression was used to examine the relationships of social capital indicators to

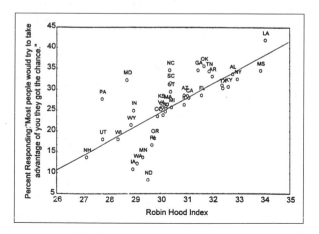

Figure 1
The relationship between income inequality, as measured by the Robin Hood Index, and lack of social trust.

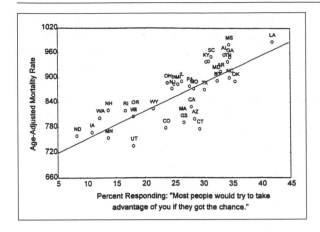

Figure 2
The relationship between age-adjusted mortality rates and lack of social trust.

out for themselves"—were highly correlated with each other (Table 1). Since these variables may not represent an exhaustive list of "social capital" indicators, we chose not to combine them into a single index. Instead, results of analyses are represented separately for each indicator.

A strong inverse relationship was found between degree of income inequality, as measured by the Robin Hood Index, and per capita group membership ($r = -.40$, $P < .01$). Income inequality was also strongly associated with lack of social trust, as measured by the perceived fairness variable ($r = .73$, $P < .0001$) (Figure 1.)

mortality rates. Two sets of models were examined for each outcome of interest. In the first set of models, we regressed the weighted social capital measures (e.g., weighted average group membership and weighted average social trust) against all-cause and cause-specific mortality rates. In the second set of models, we adjusted the regression models for state variations in prevalence of poverty. To examine the effects of inequality (as measured by the Robin Hood Index) and social capital (as measured by the social trust variable) on mortality, we carried out a path analysis[23] based on a causal model in which inequality affects mortality through its impact on social capital.

RESULTS

Relationships among Social Capital Measures and between Income Inequality and Social Capital

The four indicators of social capital—extent of participation in civic associations and the weighted proportions of respondents who agreed that "most people would try to take advantage of you if they got a chance," "you can't be too careful in dealing with people," or "people mostly look

Relationship between Social Capital and Mortality

SOCIAL TRUST

We examined the relationship between social trust (as measured by the perceived fairness variable) and all-cause and cause-specific mortality (see Table 2 and Figure 2). States that had high levels of social mistrust (i.e., high proportions of respondents who agreed that "most people would try to take advantage of you if they got the chance") had higher age-adjusted rates of total mortality ($r = .77$, $P < .0001$) (Figure 2). In our ecologic regression model, variations in level of social trust explained 58% of the variance in total mortality. Each percentage increment in people agreeing that others would take advantage of them was associated with an increase in overall mortality of 6.7 deaths per 100 000 (95% CI = 4.9, 8.5). Conversely, if the overall level of trust were to increase by one standard deviation or 10%, this would be associated with a decline in the overall age-adjusted mortality rate of about 67.1 per 100 000 (95% CI = 48.7, 85.5), representing about an 8% reduction in overall mortality. Lower levels of social trust were associated with higher rates of most major causes of death, including coronary

Table 1

Correlations among Indicators of Social Capital, Poverty, Income Inequality, and Mortality

	Poverty	Mortality	Robin Hood Index	Group Membership	Fairness	Trust
Mortality	.57*					
Robin Hood Index	.74*	.65*				
Group membership	−.20	−.49*	−.40*			
Perceived lack of fairness[a]	.49*	.77*	.73*	−.54*		
Social mistrust[b]	.52*	.79*	.71*	−.65*	.79*	
Perceived lack of helpfulness[c]	.63*	.71*	.71*	−.54*	.78*	.81*

[a]Measured by the percentage responding, "Most people would try to take advantage of you if they got a chance."
[b]Measured by the percentage responding, "You can't be too careful in dealing with people."
[c]Measured by the percentage responding, "People mostly look out for themselves."
*$P < .05$.

heart disease, malignant neoplasms, cerebrovascular disease, unintentional injury, and infant mortality (Table 2). Adjusting for state variations in poverty resulted in some attenuation of the regression coefficients; nevertheless, the coefficients for social trust remained highly statistically significant for total mortality, malignant neoplasms, infant mortality, and stroke; these coefficients were of borderline statistical significance for coronary heart disease mortality (Table 2). Only in the case of unintentional injury was there a substantial attenuation in the association between the social trust measure and mortality, suggesting a major role of poverty in explaining state variations in deaths from this cause.

OTHER SOCIAL CAPITAL MEASURES

We also examined the relationships of the perceived mistrust item (percentages of respondents agreeing that "you can't be too careful in dealing with people") and the perceived lack of helpfulness item (percentages of respondents agreeing that "people mostly look out for themselves") to total age-adjusted mortality. The effects of both of these variables on overall mortality were essentially identical to the effects of the trust variable

discussed earlier, with correlations of .79 ($P = <$ .0001) and .71 ($P < .0001$). Table 3 shows age- and poverty-adjusted regressions for the social mistrust variable, and Table 4 shows regressions for the perceived lack of helpfulness variable.

GROUP MEMBERSHIP

Per capita group membership was strongly inversely correlated with all-cause mortality ($r =$ .49, $P < .0001$). A one-unit increment in average per capita group membership was associated with a decline in total age-adjusted mortality of 83.2 deaths per 100 000 persons (95% CI = 34.2, 132.2). Level of group membership was also a predictor of coronary heart disease, malignant neoplasms, and infant mortality. These associations remained statistically significant after adjustment for poverty (with the exceptions of infant mortality and unintentional injury) (Table 5).

BLACK–WHITE DIFFERENCES

We separately examined the effects of social capital measures on White and Black Mortality rates. The social mistrust variable was strongly related to age-adjusted total mortality rates both

Table 2

The Effects of Perceived Lack of Fairness[a] on All-Cause and Cause-Specific Age-Adjusted Mortality Rates

Cause of Death (ICD-9 Codes)	*B*	SE	*t*	*P*	Adjusted R^2
Total mortality					
Unadjusted	6.71	0.91			.58
Adjusted for poverty	5.61	0.98	5.69	.0001	.63
Infant mortality					
Unadjusted	0.12	0.02			.42
Adjusted for poverty	0.10	0.03	4.01	.0005	.43
Heart Disease (410–414)					
Unadjusted	1.32	0.47			.15
Adjusted for poverty	1.08	0.54	2.00	.053	.15
Malignant neoplasms (140–239)					
Unadjusted	0.95	0.29			.20
Adjusted for poverty	1.03	0.34	3.03	.005	.18
Cerebrovascular disease (430–438)					
Unadjusted	0.48	0.16			.16
Adjusted for poverty	0.33	0.19	1.78	.083	.20
Unintentional injuries (800–949, 970–999)					
Unadjusted	0.51	0.15			.22
Adjusted for poverty	0.17	0.13	1.30	.202	.57

[a]Measured by the percentage responding, "Most people would try to take advantage of you if they got the chance."

in Whites (r = .70, P < .0001) and in Blacks (r = .34, P < .01). After adjustment for poverty, the relationship was somewhat attenuated for overall Black mortality (adjusted β = 2.92, P < .08) but remained strong for overall White mortality (adjusted β = 4.93, P < .0001). A 10% rise in level of perceived fairness (equivalent to about a one-standard-deviation increment) was associated with a decline in White mortality of 36.5 deaths per 100 000 (95% CI = 20.2, 52.9) and a decline in Black mortality of 23.9 deaths per 100 000 (95% CI = −3.4, 51.3) after adjustment for poverty. Levels of perceived fairness, adjusted for poverty, explained more of the variance in White mortality (adjusted R^2 = 52.3%) than in Black mortality

(adjusted R^2 = 11.4%). Per capita group membership was similarly predictive both of White and Black mortality rates.

Interrelationships between Income Inequality, Social Capital, and Mortality

The path analysis indicated that the primary effect of income inequality (as measured by the Robin Hood Index) on mortality is mediated by social capital (as measured by level of perceived fairness). According to our model, income inequality exerts a large indirect effect on overall mortality through the social capital variable (Figure 3). In Figure 3, as income inequality increases, so does the level of social mistrust, which

Table 3

The Effects of Social Mistrust[a] on All-Cause and Cause-Specific Age-Adjusted Mortality Rates

Cause of Death (ICD-9 Codes)	B	SE	t	P	Adjusted R^2
Total mortality					
Unadjusted	5.32	.68			.61
Adjusted for poverty	4.54	0.77	5.89	.0001	.64
Infant mortality					
Unadjusted	0.08	0.02			.30
Adjusted for poverty	0.06	0.02	2.81	.007	.32
Heart Disease (410–414)					
Unadjusted	0.98	0.37			.14
Adjusted for poverty	0.78	0.43	1.81	.07	.13
Malignant neoplasms (140–239)					
Unadjusted	0.84	0.23			.27
Adjusted for poverty	0.97	0.26	3.77	.0005	.26
Cerebrovascular disease (430–438)					
Unadjusted	0.42	0.12			.21
Adjusted for poverty	0.32	0.14	2.17	.03	.23
Unintentional injuries (800–949, 970–999)					
Unadjusted	0.42	0.11			.26
Adjusted for poverty	0.14	0.10	1.43	.16	.58

[a]Measured by the percentage responding, "You can't be too careful in dealing with people."

is in turn associated with increased mortality rates. The small path coefficient (.18) from income inequality to mortality suggests that the former is an instrumental variable. That is, income inequality was directly and strongly related to the postulated causal factor (disinvestment in social capital) but, when the causal factor was controlled, there was little residual direct association between the instrumental variable and the outcome (mortality).

DISCUSSION

IN his classic observations of America in the 1830s, Alexis de Tocqueville remarked on the density of associational life as the cornerstone of democracy in this country: "Americans of all ages, all stations in life, and all types of disposition are forever forming associations."[24(p114)] He went on to speculate that the equality brought about by democracy necessitated the formation of associations so that citizens could band together to achieve collective undertakings. According to evidence from a 35-nation survey conducted in 1991, America continues to rank high in associational membership and social trust.[17] Nevertheless, within the United States, we have demonstrated the existence of between-state variations in levels of social capital.

There is a wealth of literature linking social integration at the individual level to health

Table 4

The Effects of Perceived Lack of Helpfulness[a] on All-Cause
and Cause-Specific Age-Adjusted Mortality Rates

Cause of Death (ICD-9 Codes)	B	SE	t	P	Adjusted R^2
Total mortality					
Unadjusted	7.01	1.14			.49
Adjusted for poverty	5.69	1.45	3.91	.0003	.50
Infant mortality					
Unadjusted	0.14	0.02			.43
Adjusted for poverty	0.13	0.03	3.84	.0005	.42
Heart disease (410–414)					
Unadjusted	1.50	0.53			.15
Adjusted for poverty	1.29	0.69	1.85	.07	.14
Malignant neoplasms (140–239)					
Unadjusted	0.76	0.36			.08
Adjusted for poverty	0.86	0.46	1.86	.07	.06
Cerebrovascular disease (430–438)					
Unadjusted	0.54	0.19			.16
Adjusted for poverty	0.35	0.24	1.46	.15	.17
Unintentional injuries (800–949, 970–999)					
Unadjusted	0.69	0.16			.32
Adjusted for poverty	0.21	0.16	1.31	.19	.57

[a]Measured by the percentage responding, "People mostly look out for themselves."

outcomes[14-16]; to our knowledge, however, this is the first empirical demonstration of an association between social capital and mortality. Unlike physical or human capital, which are private goods, social capital is a public good created as a by-product of social relationships.[13] Like most types of public goods, social capital tends to be underproduced if left to the market. A major finding of this study (which needs to be confirmed in longitudinal studies) is that the size of the gap between the rich and the poor is powerfully and negatively related to level of investment in social capital. In other words, disinvestment in social capital appears to be one of the pathways through which growing income inequality exerts its effects on population-level mortality. It should be cautioned that an effect in the opposite direction is also possible (i.e., disinvestment in social capital resulting in income inequalities). Alternatively, there may exist unmeasured societal attitudes that underlie both social capital disinvestment and tolerance of income inequality. These considerations deserve further investigation.

Nonetheless, other studies have also noted an association between income inequality and reduced levels of social trust. In a pooled analysis of 20 years (1975 through 1994) of General Social

Table 5

*The Effects of Voluntary-Group Membership on All-Cause
and Cause-Specific Age-Adjusted Mortality Rates*

Cause of Death (ICD-9 Codes)	B	SE	t	P	Adjusted R^2
Total mortality					
Unadjusted	−83.17	24.24			.22
Adjusted for poverty	−66.75	20.77	−3.21	.003	.45
Infant mortality					
Unadjusted	−0.98	0.57			.05
Adjusted for poverty	−0.67	0.53	−1.27	.21	.21
Heart disease (410–414)					
Unadjusted	−25.99	9.14			.16
Adjusted for poverty	−23.03	9.11	−2.53	.016	.20
Malignant neoplasms (140–239)					
Unadjusted	−20.32	5.55			.25
Adjusted for poverty	−19.81	5.72	−3.46	.001	.23
Cerebrovascular disease (430–438)					
Unadjusted	−2.44	3.55			.01
Adjusted for poverty	−0.71	3.36	−.21	.83	.13
Unintentional injuries (800–949, 970–999)					
Unadjusted	−2.47	3.33			.01
Adjusted for poverty	0.58	2.26	0.25	0.80	.55

Surveys data involving more than 29 000 respondents,[25] rising income inequality (as measured by the Gini coefficient) was found to be a significant predictor of declining trust in others. In turn, a decline in social trust was predictive of diminished levels of civic engagement.[25] In our data, level of trust in others was strongly correlated with per capita group membership ($r = -.54$, $P < .0001$), low levels of social trust being associated with low per capita group membership. In his study of social capital in Italy, Putnam reported a correlation of .81 between income distribution and an index of civic engagement.[12(p224)]

The Nature of Social Capital

The aspect of social capital that makes it a classic public good is its property of nonexcludability; that is, its benefits are available to all living within a particular community, and access to it cannot be restricted. Hence, a socially isolated individual could potentially benefit from living in a neighborhood rich in social capital. As a hypothetical example, a widowed person living by herself could benefit from residing in a community in which neighbors organized and mingled at block parties, transported elderly residents to voting booths on election days, made sure that

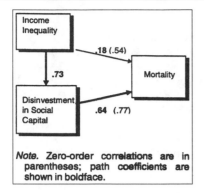

Note. Zero-order correlations are in parentheses; path coefficients are shown in boldface.

Figure 3
Path coefficients for the effects of income inequality and disinvestment in social capital (social mistrust, as measured by the percentage of respondents who agreed that "most people would try to take advantage of you if they got the chance") on age-adjusted mortality rates.

sidewalks were cleared when it snowed, and so on.

Conversely, we hypothesize that there are deleterious effects of living in a neighborhood that is depleted in social capital, irrespective of the stock of individual resources. William Julius Wilson coined the term "concentration effects" to describe the phenomenon of families that reside in deprived neighborhoods and face not only the constraints imposed by the larger society (e.g., unemployment) but also the behaviors and truncated aspirations of other jobless families in the neighborhood.[19, 26]

In each of the preceding instances, the actions of neighbors cannot be fully captured by measures of social networks and social support assessed at the individual level. In the foregoing example of the elderly, widowed resident, a conventional measure of social networks would classify her as a socially isolated individual. Yet she has access to the stock of social capital in her community, in the form of the passive surveillance and general regard for her welfare that her neighbors provide. In other words, measurement

of social capital at the ecologic level captures something distinct, over and above measurement of individual social connections.

The Ecologic Approach
The present study was an ecologic study of the "unmixed" type[27]; that is, our analyses used purely ecologic variables (social capital, income inequality, prevalence of poverty) to predict a purely ecologic outcome (population-level mortality). Hence, no cross-level bias occurred, since we avoided inferences about individuals from grouped data.[27, 28] Indeed, any study involving tests of hypotheses about income inequality or social capital must necessarily fall into the category of "obligate" ecological studies (to use Susser's[29] classification), since these variables are characteristics of groups rather than individuals.

Ecologic studies are susceptible to confounding, just as individual-level studies are.[28] In our theoretical model of the pathways leading to population-level mortality (Figure 3), we considered income inequality to be an antecedent to, rather than a confounder of, the relationship between social capital and mortality. The status of poverty is less well defined. If poverty is linked to depletion in social capital—as some work in deprived neighborhoods suggests[26]—then it may potentially confound the relationship between social capital and mortality. But in analyses that controlled for levels of poverty (Tables 3 and 5), the effects of social capital on mortality remained. Social trust and group membership are also strongly correlated with socioeconomic characteristics such as educational attainment. However, educational attainment is likely to lie in the pathway between income inequality and social capital. For example, Kaplan et al.[7] have demonstrated that there are strong relationships at the state level between degree of income inequality and underinvestment in education, as indexed by a high school education, the percentage of high school dropouts, and public spending on education. In examinations of the link between income inequality and social capital, adjusting for state differences in educational attainment may therefore result in statistical overadjustment.

Limitations

A major limitation of the present study is that the General Social Survey was designed to be representative at the national and regional levels but not at the state level. We attempted to overcome this limitation by using poststratification weights to adjust for oversampling (or undersampling) of certain demographic groups, which may have biased the responses to the survey. The results of the analyses using weighted survey responses were, in fact, quite similar to the results of the unweighted analyses. For example, the correlation between social distrust and total mortality changed from .81 (in the unweighted analysis) to .77 (in the weighted analysis), indicating that substantial bias is unlikely to have occurred. Nonetheless, appropriate caution must be exercised in interpreting the state-specific information in this study. For instance, there may be several other variables in addition to age, race, and educational attainment that are not measured in the General Social Survey, but are nonetheless potentially related to the representatives of estimates of social capital. Such parameters as urban/rural mix, percentage of minority residents, residential segregation, and religiosity may vary between states and be related to state variations in social capital and mortality rates.

An additional potential source of error in our estimates was the variability in state sample size in the General Social Survey. To address this issue, we conducted regression analyses of social capital and mortality weighted by the sample size from each state. The results of this analysis indicated that the coefficients and the standard errors were virtually unchanged, suggesting that bias due to variability in state sample sizes was un-

likely to be a problem. In a separate check of the validity of our findings, we carried out a regional analysis of social capital and mortality. The General Social Survey sample is valid for comparisons across the nine US regions. When we examined the relationship between income inequality across regions and social mistrust, we found a strong correlation (r = .91, P < .0001). In regression analyses, the associations of the social capital items to total mortality were not statistically significant, probably reflecting the lack of statistical power. Nonetheless, the beta coefficients continued to indicate a positive association between social mistrust and total mortality (β = 3.86, SE = 4.32, P = .39), as well as a negative association between group membership and total mortality (β = -122.8, SE = 157.8, P = .46). Moreover, the point estimates of these coefficients were consistent with the point estimates obtained in the weighted state-level analyses.

A second major limitation of the present study is that both the regression analyses and the path analysis were based on cross-sectional relationships between indicators of social capital and mortality. Cross-sectional analyses are limited in their ability to pin down direction of causality. Undoubtedly, there are bidirectional effects; for example, low levels of social capital seem to be associated with reduced confidence or trust in government performance,[25] which in turn seems to predict underinvestment in human capital (e.g., reduced public spending on education[7]) and, ultimately, widening income inequality. Ideally, longitudinal time series analyses should be carried out on long-term trends in income inequality, social capital, and mortality to test these linkages.

Finally, our model did not consider the full range of factors that may influence income inequality and social capital. Both income inequality and social capital may be derivative of some other unidentified factor that predicts state variations in mortality. For example, variables used to measure social capital may not, by themselves, cause mortality. Rather, the societies that disinvest in social capital may be those that fail to provide the social institutions directly responsible for the health of the population (e.g., health care for the elderly, income maintenance for poor women and children). In other words, a society with little trust in others may not necessarily suffer a high mortality rate unless such distrust also results in little popular support for policies that assist the needy.

Conclusions

The measures of social capital used in the present study reflect recent developments in political science and other fields.[11-13] Despite some important advances,[11-13, 30, 31] definition and measurement of this concept remain at nascent stages. Further work is needed to establish whether there are state-level, urban-rural, and other differences in the types of organizations to which people belong and whether these differences have an impact on health. Relatively little theoretical or empirical work has been done to distinguish between a growing array of potentially related notions, including community competency,[32, 33] collective efficacy, sense of community,[34, 35] and the "civil society."[36] A rigorous analysis of the core concepts common to these existing measures of community- or neighborhood-level characteristics would be timely.

There is no good theoretical account of how to build social capital. On the other hand, there are many accounts of how social capital can be destroyed by various social and economic forces.[17] Hence, there is an asymmetry in terms of our current state of knowledge about social capital. What our empirical data do appear to support is that the growing gap between the rich and the poor affects the social organization of communities and that the resulting damage to the social fabric may have profound implications for the public's health.

NOTES

1. Rodgers GB. Income inequality as determinant of mortality: an international cross-section analysis. *Popul Stud.* 1979;33:343–351.

2. Wilkinson RG. Income and mortality. In: Wilkinson RG, ed. *Class and Health: Research and Longitudinal Data.* London, England: Tavistock; 1986.

3. Wilkinson RG. Income distribution and mortality: a "natural" experiment. *Sociol Health Illness.* 1990;12:391–412.

4. Wilkinson RG. Income distribution and life expectancy. *BMJ.* 1992;304:165–168.

5. LeGrand J. Inequalities in health. Some international comparisons. *Eur Econ Rev.* 1987;31:182–191.

6. Kennedy BP, Kawachi I, Prothrow-Stith D. Income distribution and mortality: cross-sectional ecological study of the Rolbin Hood Index in the United States. *BMJ.* 1996;312:1004–1007.

7. Kaplan GA, Pamuk E, Lynch JW, Cohen RD, Balfour JL. Income inequality and mortality in the United States. *BMJ.* 1996;312:999–1003.

8. Atkinson AB, Micklewright J. *Economic Transformation in Eastern Europe and the Distribution of Income.* Cambridge, England: Cambridge University Press; 1992.

9. Kawachi I, Levine S, Miller SM, Lasch K, Amick B. *Income Inequaltiy and Life Expectancy: Theory, Research, and Policy.* Boston, Mass: Health Institute, New England Medical Center; 1994. Society and Health Working Paper 94–2.

10. Wilkinson RG. The epidemiological transition: from material society to social disadvantage? *Daedalus.* 1994;123: 61-77.

11. Putnam RD. The prosperous community. Social capital and economic growth. *Am Prospect.* Spring 1993:35–42.

12. Putnam RD. *Making Democracy Work.* Princeton, NJ: Princeton University Press; 1993.

13. Coleman JS. *The Foundations of Social Theory.* Cambridge, Mass: Harvard University Press; 1990:300–321.

14. House JS, Landis KR, Umberson D. Social relationships and health. *Science.* 1988;214:540–545.

15. Berkman LF, Syme SL. Social networks, host resistance and mortality: a nine-year follow-up study of Alameda County residents. *Am J Epidemiol.* 1979;109:186–204.

16. Kawachi I, Colditz GA, Ascherio A, et al. A prospective study of social networks in relation to total mortality and

cardiovascular disease in men in the US. *J Epidemiol Community Health.* 1996;50:245–251.

17. Putnam RD. Bowling alone. America's declining social capital. *J Democracy* 1995;6:65–78.

18. Davis JA, Smith TW. *General Social Survey Cumulative File.* Ann Arbor, Mich: University of Michigan, Interuniversity Consortium for Political and Social Research; 1972 through 1993.

19. Wilson WJ. Studying inner-city social dislocations: the challenge of public agenda research. *Am Sociol Rev.* 1991;56:1–14.

20. Hahn RA, Eaker E, Baker ND, Teutsch SM, Sosniak W, Krieger N. Poverty and death in the United States—1973 and 1991. *Epidemiology.* 1995;6:490–497.

21. *Income and Poverty* [CD-ROM]. Washington, DC: US Bureau of the Census; 1993.

22. Friede A, Reid JA, Ory HW. CDC WONDER: a comprehensive on-line public health information system of the Centers for Disease Control and Prevention. *Am J Public Health.* 1993;83:1289–1294.

23. Pedhazur EJ. *Multiple Regression in Behavioral Research.* New York, NY: Holt, Rinehart & Winston; 1973.

24. de Tocqueville A. *Democracy in America.* New York, NY: Vintage Books; 1945.

25. Brehm J, Rahn W. Individual-level evidence for the causes and consequences of social capital. *Am J Polit Sci.* 1997;41:999–1023.

26. Wilson WJ. *The Truly Disadvantaged: The Inner-City, the Underclass, and Public Policy.* Chicago, Ill: University of Chicago Press; 1987.

27. Susser M. The logic in ecological, I: the logic of analysis. *Am J Public Health.* 1994;84:825–829.

28. Schwartz S. The fallacy of the ecological fallacy: the potential misuse of a concept and the consequences. *Am J Public Health.* 1994;84:819–824.

29. Susser M. The logic in ecological, II; the logic of design. *Am J Public Health.* 1994;84:830–835.

30. Loury G. Why should we care about group inequality? *Soc Philosophy Policy.* 1987;5:249–271.

31. Bourdieu P. The forms of capital. In: Richardson JG, ed. *The Handbook of Theory: Research for the Sociology of Education.* New York, NY: Greenwood Press; 1986:241–258.

32. Eng E, Parker E. Measuring community competence in the Mississippi Delta: the interface between program evaluation and empowerment. *Health Educ Q.* 1994;21:199–220.

33. Cottrell LS Jr. The competent community. In: Kaplan BH, Wilson RN, Leighton AH, eds. *Further Explorations in Social Psychiatry.* New York, NY: Basic Books; 1976:195–209.

34. McMillan DW, Chavis DM. Sense of community: a definition and theory. *J Community Psychol.* 1986;14:6–23.

35. Chavis DM, Wandersman A. Sense of community in the urban environment: a catalyst for participation and community development. *Am J Community Psychol.* 1990;18:55–81.

36. Walzer M. The idea of civil society. *Dissent.* Spring 1991:293–304.

Twenty-Three

SOCIAL CAPITAL AND SELF-RATED HEALTH: A CONTEXTUAL ANALYSIS

Ichiro Kawachi, Bruce P. Kennedy, and Roberta Glass

ABSTRACT

Objective: Social capital has been defined as those features of social organization—such as the extent of interpersonal trust between citizens, norms of reciprocity, and voluntary group membership—which facilitate cooperation for mutual benefit. Social capital has been linked to lower mortality rates, as well as to fewer violent crimes. In the present study, we examined the cross-sectional relationship between social capital and individual self-rated health, adjusting for individual household income, health behaviors, and other covariates.

Methods: Self-rated health ("Would you say your overall health is excellent, very good, good, fair, or poor?") was assessed among 167,259 individuals residing in 39 U.S. states, sampled by the Center for Disease Control's Behavioral Risk Factor Surveillance System. Social capital indicators, aggregated to the state level, were obtained from the National Opinion Research Center's General Social Surveys. Indicators of social capital included levels of interpersonal trust (% citizens responding "Most people can be trusted"), norms of reciprocity (% citizens responding "Most people are helpful"), and per capita membership in voluntary associations. Logistic regression was carried out with the SUDAAN procedure to estimate the odds ratios of fair/poor health (vs. excellent/very good/good health), according to three levels of social capital.

Results: Strong associations were found between individual risk factors (e.g., low income, low education, smoking) and poor self-rated health. However, even after adjusting for these proximal variables, individuals living in states with low social capital were at increased risk of poor self-rated health. For example, the odds ratio for fair/poor health associated with living in areas with the lowest levels of social trust was 1.41 (95% confidence interval: 1.33 to 1.50) compared to living in high-trust states.

Conclusions: These results extend previous findings on the health advantages stemming from social capital. Social capital appears to exert an independent, contextual effect on self-rated health.

INTRODUCTION

SOCIAL scientists have long puzzled over the question: Why do some communities prosper, possess effective political institutions,

Originally published in *American Journal of Public Health*, 1998.

have law-abiding and healthy citizens, while other communities do not? To answer this question, researchers have begun to turn to the concept of social capital as a possible explanation. Social capital has been defined as those features of social organization—such as the extent of interpersonal trust between citizens, norms of reciprocity, and density of civic associations—which facilitate cooperation for mutual benefit.[1-3] Social capital has been claimed to be important for the enhancement of government performance and the functioning of democracy,[2] for the prevention of crime and delinquency,[4-6] and more recently, for the maintenance of population health.[7] Using U.S. data aggregated at the state level, Kawachi et al.[7] reported strong cross-sectional correlations between indicators of social capital and mortality rates. In that study, social capital (or the lack of it) was measured by responses to the General Social Surveys[8] about the degree of mistrust, levels of perceived reciprocity, and the per capita membership in voluntary associations of all kinds.[7] Each indicator of social capital was strikingly correlated with lower mortality rates (r = 0.79, 0.71, and -0.49, respectively), even after adjustment for state median income and poverty rates.[7]

Research dating back to Durkheim's study of the causes of suicide[9] has demonstrated that social integration can enhance population wellbeing. Epidemiologic investigations of social ties have found that individuals lacking in social connections are at two to three times the risk of dying from all causes compared to well connected individuals,[10, 11] But there is an important distinction to be drawn between social integration measured as an individual characteristic (which is how most epidemiological studies have measured social networks), and social integration measured as a collective characteristic (which is how social capital is conceptualized). The mechanisms linking social integration to health may differ depending on the level at which it is measured. For example, social capital measured

at the community level may determine patterns of political participation and policy-setting that are more egalitarian and health-promoting,[3] whereas social networks measured at the individual level may fail to capture these emergent group-level processes. In other words, collective features of society may not be reducible to the attributes of individuals living in it.[12]

Analyses of ecological concepts such as social capital are often susceptible to the ecological fallacy, i.e., correlations at the group level may not apply to individual risks.[13-15] We therefore undertook the present study to determine whether a contextual effect of social capital could be demonstrated for individual health. To address the problem in contextual analyses of misspecifying individual-level relations (and hence, arbitrarily interpreting residual differences as "contextual effects"[16, 17]), we controlled for a range of individual-level factors that predict health, including household income, race, health insurance coverage, and lifestyle behaviors.

METHODS

The Behavioral Risk Factor Surveillance System (BRFSS)

We used data from the Behavioral Risk Factor Surveillance System (BRFSS), which is a state-representative, random digit dial telephone survey of U.S. residents, conducted under the direction of the Behavioral Surveillance Branch of the National Center for Chronic Disease Prevention and Health Promotion, Centers for Disease Control and Prevention (CDC).[18] Each state uses probability samples in which all households with telephones have a non-zero chance of inclusion, designed to produce comparable state-level estimates for the civilian noninstitutionalized population aged 18 years or older. In 1993, the BRFSS began asking a question about perceived general health:[19] "Would you say that in general your health is: Excellent, Very Good, Good, Fair, or Poor?" From this item, we created a dichotomous outcome measure (1= fair or poor; 0=excellent, very good, or good). A recent review of twenty-seven community studies concluded that even such a simple global assessment appears to have high predictive validity for mortality, independent of other medical, behavioral, or psychosocial risk factors.[20] For most studies, odds ratios for subsequent mortality ranged from 1.5 to 3.0 among individuals reporting poor health compared to excellent health.[20] The risk of mortality for poor self-rated health often exceeded that of smoking when they were reported in the same study.[20] Furthermore, self-rated health has been demonstrated in longitudinal studies to predict the onset of disability.[21-25] In order to achieve stable estimates for individuals living in less populous states, we cumulated data from the 1993 and 1994 surveys.

Socio-demographic data available on the BRFSS include race (white, black, and other); gender; age (< 25, 25–39, 40–64, 65+ years); household income (< $10,000, $10,000–14,999, $15,000–19,999, $20,000–24,999, $25,000–34,999, and $35,000 or more per year; and unknown); and educational attainment (less than high school, high school graduate, some college or trade school, and college graduate). In addition, the BRFSS includes data on living arrangement (living alone vs. not alone), and health-related variables including current smoking status (yes/no), obesity (body mass index > 27.8 kg/m^{23} for males, and > 27.3 kg/m^2 for females), current health insurance coverage, and whether the individual had a health check-up within the past two years.

Social Capital Indicators

Indicators of social capital, aggregated to the state level, were obtained from the General Social Surveys (GSS), as previously described.[7] This nationally representative survey samples noninstituionalized English-speaking persons 18 years or older living in the United States. We av-

eraged 5 years of cumulated data (1986 through 1990) from the survey, representing 7654 individual observations from 39 states (mean number of respondents per state: 196, standard deviation: 146). Although the survey is nationally representative, only 39 states were included, because residents of less populous states (e.g., Delaware) were not sampled.

The extent of civic trust was assessed by responses to the GSS item: "Generally speaking, would you say most people can be trusted?" Collective perceptions of reciprocity was tapped by the item: "Would you say that most of the time people try to be helpful, or are they mostly looking out for themselves?" Finally, respondents in the GSS were asked about membership in a wide variety of voluntary associations, including church groups, sports groups, professional societies, political groups, and fraternal organizations. From this, we estimated the per capita membership of voluntary associations in each state.

Since the GSS was designed to be representative at the national and regional, but not the state level, we used a poststratification procedure to adjust the data for the extent to which survey respondents may not have been representative of the states in which they resided. All estimates were adjusted using weights based on the distribution of age, race, and educational attainment of survey respondents, as previously described.[7]

Data Analyses

The BRFSS employs a multistage cluster design,[26] based on selection of: clusters of phone numbers (based on the first 8 digits of 10 digit numbers); selection of households; and selection of respondents.[26] The primary sampling units (PSUs) are comprised of a list of random 8 digit numbers after excluding non-residential phone numbers. Within each PSU, the remaining 2 digits are assigned in random order, and interviewers call until three residences are recruited.

After a residence has been recruited, a respondent is randomly chosen from among household members aged 18 years or older. Weights are based on the probability of selection and adjusted for non-response and disproportionate sampling of subgroups relative to the state's population distribution.[18] The sampling procedure requires special statistical software to account for clustering. Data were analyzed using the SUDAAN logistic regression procedure,[27] which accounts for the sampling weights used in the BRFSS, as well as the probability that outcomes for individuals within states may be correlated.

States were grouped *a priori* into three levels of social capital (high/medium/low), based on cutpoints defined by 1.0 standard deviation on either side of the overall mean. For example, the mean level of mistrust (% responding "most people can't be trusted") was 43.2% (SD: 9.8%) across states. Low trust states were defined as those 1.0 SD above the mean (> 54.0% responding "others can't be trusted"), while high trust states were defined by those 1.0 SD below the mean (< 33.4%). The means (and SD) for reciprocity (% stating "others are helpful") was 32.8% (6.0); and for per capita group membership, it was 1.77 (0.32). Each individual in the BRFSS sample was assigned to a social capital category (high, medium, or low) based on their state of residence. Using this approach, approximately 20–30% of the sample ended up in the high or low social capital states.

Using SUDAAN, we then modelled the odds that an individual would report fair/poor health (as opposed to excellent/very good/good health) according to their state of residence. Models simultaneously controlled for individual sociodemographic and lifestyle characteristics.

RESULTS

OUR BRFSS sample consisted of 167,259 individuals (41.7% male and 58.3% female). The sample sizes from each state ranged from 1,259 (Wyoming) to 8,800 (Maryland). Perceived health was missing in just 386 (0.2%) individuals. Overall, 14.9 percent of individuals reported their health as being either fair (N = 17,651; 10.6%) or poor (N = 7,163; 4.3%); while 84.9 percent reported their health as excellent (N = 40,688; 24.3%), very good (N = 55,724; 33.3%), or good (N = 45,647; 27.3%). Table 1 displays the unweighted BRFSS sample characteristics, and the percent subjects reporting fair/poor health. Consistent with previous reports,[19, 20] poor perceived health was associated with black race, lack of health insurance coverage, overweight, current smoking, lower household income, and lower educational attainment. There was an eight-fold gradient in the proportion of individuals reporting fair/poor health across levels of household income. States with low social capital also had higher proportions of residents who reported that their health was only fair/poor.

The ecologic-level correlation between social mistrust and percentage of residents in fair/poor health was 0.71 (p < 0.0001) (Figure 1). The corresponding correlations between perceptions of reciprocity and fair/poor health was -0.66 (p < 0.0001); and -0.28 (p = 0.08) for per capita group membership. In turn, the social capital indicators were strongly correlated with each other: 0.78 (p < 0.0001) between mistrust and perceptions of reciprocity; -0.65 (p < 0.0001) between mistrust and per capita group membership; and -0.54 (p < 0.0003) between reciprocity and group membership.

We regressed individual health status on individual-level characteristics (Table 2). The strongest associations with fair/poor health were older age (e.g., odds ratio of 4.79 (95% CI: 4.51 to 5.09) among individuals over 65 years), and low income (odds ratio of 6.02 (95% CI: 5.65 to 6.41) comparing individuals with household income below $10,000 versus $35,000+). Living alone was associated with an odds ratio of 1.92 (95% CI: 1.33 to 2.78).

In Table 3 (Model 1), we examined the associations of three sets of social capital variables to fair/poor health, adjusting just for demographic

Table 1

Characteristics of Behavioral Risk Factor Surveillance System sample, 1993–94.

Characteristic	N (percent)	Percent reporting fair/poor health
Male	69,694 (41.7)	13.3
Famale	97,565 (58.3)	15.9
Race:[1]		
White	143,521 (85.8)	14.2
Black	16,225 (9.7)	20.6
Other	7,352 (4.4)	15.6
Health insurance[2]	146,546 (87.6)	14.5
No health insurance coverage	20,302 (12.1)	17.2
No health check-up in last 2 years	31,026 (18.6)	10.3
Check-up in last 2 years	136,233 (81.5)	15.9
Obese	43,747 (26.2)	21.0
Not obese	123,512 (73.8)	12.6
Current smoker	38,057 (22.8)	17.3
Non-smoker[3]	128,777 (77.0)	14.1
Household income:		
<$10,000	24,300 (14.5)	32.4
$10,000–14,999	14,989 (9.0)	24.3
$15,000–19,999	14,047 (8.4)	16.9
$20,000–24,999	15,105 (9.0)	13.2
$25,000–34,999	23,418 (14.0)	9.4
$35,000–49,999	25,024 (15.0)	6.3
$50,000 +	29,024 (17.5)	4.3
Missing	21,193 (12.7)	18.6
Educational status:		
No school	1,337 (0.8)	22.4
Elementary	9,397 (5.6)	46.1
Some high school	15,229 (9.1)	31.1
High school graduate	54,916 (32.8)	15.5
Some college/technical	44,034 (26.3)	10.1
College graduate	41,967 (25.1)	5.7
Mising	379 (0.2)	26.7
Living alone[4]	41,707 (25.0)	21.1
Not living alone	125,351 (75.0)	12.4

Table 1 (*continued*)

Characteristics of Behavioral Risk Factor Surveillance System sample, 1993–94.

Characteristic	N (percent)	Percent reporting fair/poor health
Residence in states characterized by:		
Low trust[5]	25,060 (15.0)	19.1
Medium trust	123,761 (74.0)	13.2
High trust	18,438 (11.0)	11.6
Low reciprocity[6]	25,270 (15.1)	18.8
Medium reciprocity	117,632 (70.30)	13.4
High reciprocity	24,357 (14.6)	10.7
Low group membership[7]	15,198 (9.1)	17.5
Medium membership	134,759 (80.6)	13.9
High membership	17,302 (10.3)	11.6

[1]Race missing in 160 individuals

[2]Health insuracne status missing in 411 individuals

[3]Smoking status missing in 425 individuals

[4]Living status missing in 201 individuals

[5]Percent responding on the General Social Surveys that "most people can't be trusted"

  Low trust states were: AL, AR, LA, MS, TN, WV (mean % mistrust = 59.4%; range: 56.0–61.6%).

  Medium trust states were: AK, CA, CO, CT, FL, GA. IL, IN, IA, KY, MD, MA, MI, MO, NH, NJ, NY, NC, OH, OK, OR, PA, RI, SC, TX, UT, VA, WA (mean % mistrust = 42.9%; range: 33.4–51.7%).

  High trust states were: KS, MN, ND, WI, WY (mean % mistrust = 26.7; range: 21.2–32.6%).

[6]Percent endorsing statement on the General Social Surveys that "most people look out for themselves"

  Low reciprocity states were: AR, GA, LA, MS, TN, WV (mean % endorsing statement = 44.2%; range: 41.4–51.5%).

  Medium reciprocity states were: AL, AK, CA, CO, CT, FL, IL, IN, KS, KY, MD, MA, MI, MO, NJ, NY, NC, OH, OK, OR, PA, RI, SC, TX, UT, VA, WA, WY (mean % endorsing statement = 33.0%; range: 26.6–38.8%).

  High reciprocity states were: IA, MN, NH, ND, WA (mean % endorsing statement = 22.0%; range: 19.8–24.2%).

[7]Per capita membership in voluntary associations, according to General Social Surveys

  Low membership states were: AL, AR, LA (mean number per capita groups = 1.3; range: 1.2–1.4).

  Medium membership states were: AK, CA, CO, CT, FL, GA, IL, IN, IA, KY, MD, MA, MI, MN, MS, MO, NH, NJ, NY, NC, OH, OK, OR, PA, RI, SC, TN, TX, VA, WV, WI (mean number per capita groups = 1.7; range: 1.4–2.0).

  High membership states were: KS, ND, UT, WA, WY (mean number per capita groups = 2.6; range: 2.2–3.5).

characteristics (gender, race, and age). Residing in a state with the lowest levels of social capital was associated with between a 45 to 73 percent increased odds of fair/poor health, compared to living in the highest social capital states. In Model 2 (Table 3), we examined the contextual effects of social capital, adjusting for the full range of individual-level variables. Although the associations of social capital of fair/poor health were attenuated by the inclusion of individual-

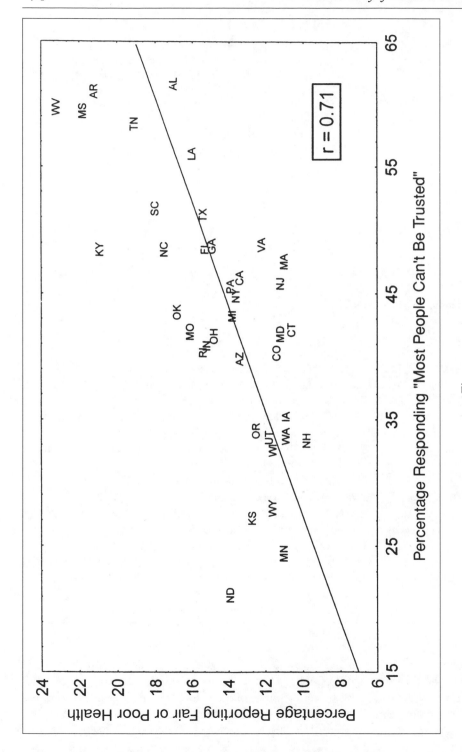

Figure 1

Scatterplot of levels of interpersonal trust and percent of residents in each state reporting fair/poor health, Behavioral Risk Factor Surveillance System, 1993–94.

Table 2

Associations between individual-level variables and fair/poor self-rated health, in the Behavioral Risk Factor Suveillance System, 1993–94.

Independent Variables	Odds ratio for fair/poor health (95% confidence interval)
Age:	
< 25 yrs	0.74 (0.67–0.81)
25–39	1.00
40–64	2.38 (2.26–2.51)
65+	4.79 (4.51–5.09)
Male	1.05 (1.01–1.09)
Race:	
Black	1.37 (1.30–1.44)
White	1.00
Other	1.42 (1.31–1.53)
Living alone	1.92 (1.33–2.78)
Income:	
< $10,000	6.02 (5.65–6.41)
$10,000–14,999	4.33 (4.40–4.64)
$15,000–19,999	3.30 (2.82–3.26)
$20,000–24,999	2.43 (2.26–2.61)
$25,000–34,999	1.88 (1.76–2.01)
$35,000+	1.00
Missing	3.00 (2.82–3.20)
Current smoker	1.51 (1.45–1.58)
Obese	1.70 (1.64–1.76)
Health insurance coverage	0.73 (0.69–0.77)
Recent checkup	1.39 (1.32–1.47)

level predictors, they nevertheless remained statistically significant. For example, living in areas with the lowest levels of trust was associated with an odds ratio (OR) for fair/poor health of 1.41 (95% CI: 1.33 to 1.50), compared to living in the high social capital states (Table 3, Model 2). Although the proximate, individual-level factors turned out to be the strongest predictors of fair/poor health, the magnitude of risk associated with living in a low social capital state nonetheless approached that of risk factors such as being a current smoker (OR = 1.51), or being obese (OR

Table 3

*Associations between social capital variables and fair/poor self-rated health
in the Behavioral Risk Factor Surveillance System, 1993–94.*

Social Capital Vairable	Odds ratio (95% confidence interval) for fair/poor health	
	Model 1[1]	Model 2[2]
Low trust	1.67 (1.56–1.75)	1.41 (1.33–1.50)
Medium trust	1.41 (1.35–1.45)	1.14 (1.08–1.21)
High trust	1.00	1.00
Low reciprocity	1.69 (1.61–1.79)	1.48 (1.41–1.57)
Medium reciprocity	1.33 (1.28–1.39)	1.24 (1.19–1.30)
High reciprocity	1.00	1.00
Low membership	1.43 (1.34–1.55)	1.22 (1.24–1.32)
Medium membership	1.18 (1.13–1.25)	1.11 (1.05–1.16)
High membership	1.00	1.00

[1]Adjusted for age group (<25, 25–39 (reference), 40–64, 65+ yrs), gender, and race.

[2]Adjusted for age-group (<25, 25–39 (reference), 40–64, 65+ yrs), gender, race, household income (<$10,000, $10,000–14,999, $15,000–19,999, $20,000–24,999, $25,000–34,999, ≥$35,000 (reference)), living alone, current smoking status, obesity, health insurance coverage, and health checkup in last 2 years.

= 1.70). The associations between social capital and perceived health remained unchanged when we substituted educational attainment for household income in the multivariate models (data not shown).

There appeared to be a "dose-response" gradient in the odds ratios for fair/poor health across levels of social capital indicators. When we repeated Model 2 (Table 3) using quartile cutpoints for social capital instead of cutpoints defined by 1.0 standard deviation, the gradient became a little stronger (e.g., odds ratio of 1.54 (95% CI: 1.47 to 1.61) comparing the lowest to highest quartile of trust).

The effects of social capital on perceived health was quite similar among men and women. Analyses were also stratified by different levels of household income (< $10,000, $10,000–14,999, $15,000–19,999, $20,000–24,999, $25,000–34,999, and $35,000 or more per year). The largest effects of social capital on health were observed in individuals with lowest income (< $10,000), where the odds ratio for fair/poor health was 1.51 (95% CI: 1.32 to 1.74) comparing low trust to high trust states. Nonetheless, an effect of social capital indicators of self-rated health was evident across most income groups, including among individuals from middle-class ranges of income (odds ratios of 1.40 and 1.18, respectively, among those earning $25,000–34,999, and > $35,000). Finally, we simultaneously examined the effects of household income inequality and social capital on self-rated health. Evidence both internationally[28, 29] and from within single countries[30-32] has suggested that income inequality is an independent, ecologic-level predictor of mortality and morbidity. Income distribution was measured by quartiles of the Gini coefficient derived from the 1990 Census.[30, 31] Simultaneously adjusting for income distribution attenuated the effects of social capital on self-rated health. Nevertheless, both the Gini and all three social capital indicators remained statistically significant predictors of self-rated health. For example, the odds ratio of fair/poor health for low trust compared to high trust states was 1.24 (95% CI: 1.15 to 1.33), whilst the odds ratio for the highest income inequality compared to the lowest inequality states was 1.24 (95% CI: 1.16 to 1.32). Tables of stratified analyses are available from the authors on request.

DISCUSSION

Mechanisms Linking Social Capital to Health

The mechanisms linking social capital to health outcomes have yet to be elucidated. Ample evidence suggests that socially-isolated *individuals* are at increased risk of poor health outcomes, due to their limited access to resources ranging from instrumental aid, information, and emotional support.[10, 11, 33] However, the mechanisms linking social capital to health might be different from those linking social networks to individual health. Here it is important to distinguish between the *contextual* effects of living in an area depleted of social capital, and any *compositional* effects of social capital. On the one hand, an ecologic-level correlation between social capital and poor health could be explained by the fact that more socially-isolated individuals reside in areas lacking in social capital (a compositional effect). Socially-isolated individuals are more likely to be concentrated in communities that are depleted in social capital, because such places provide fewer opportunities for individuals to form local ties.[34, 35] A limitation of our analysis is that we failed to account for individual-level indicators of social isolation (e.g., not having contacts with friends or relatives, not attending church or belonging to groups). Hence, we could not rule out a compositional effect of social capital on self-rated health.

The more challenging task remains to identify the mechanisms by which social capital may exert a contextual effect on individual health. Social capital may affect health through different pathways depending on the geographic scale at which it is measured, e.g., neighborhoods versus states. Although the present study did not measure social capital in neighborhoods, there are at least three plausible pathways by which social capital might influence individual health at this level. First, social capital may influence the health behaviors of neighborhood residents by: (a) promoting more rapid diffusion of health information[36]; (b) increasing the likelihood that healthy norms of behavior are adopted (e.g., physical activity); and (c) exerting social control over deviant health-related behavior. The theory of the diffusion of innovations[36] suggests that innovative behaviors (e.g., use of preventive services) diffuse much more rapidly in communities that are cohesive and where members know and trust each other. Alternatively, recent evidence from criminology[6] also suggests that the extent to which neighbors are willing to exert social control over deviant behavior (a characteristic that Sampson et al.[6] termed "collective efficacy") may be critical for the prevention of delinquency and crime. In turn, levels of collective efficacy are determined by the extent of trust in a neighborhood (or what we term "social capital"). We conjecture that collective efficacy may also help to prevent other forms of deviant behavior, such as adolescent smoking and drinking.

A second pathway by which neighborhood social capital may affect health is through increasing access to local services and amenities. Again, evidence from criminology suggests that socially cohesive neighborhoods are more successful at uniting to ensure that budget cuts do not affect local services.[6] The same kind of organizational processes could conceivably ensure access to services such as transportation, community health clinics, or recreational facilities, that are directly relevant to health.

Finally, neighborhood social capital could influence the health of individuals via psychosocial processes, by providing affective support and acting as the source of self-esteem and mutual respect.[29] Variations in the availability of psychosocial resources at the community level may help to explain the anomalous finding that socially-isolated individuals residing in cohesive communities (such as East Boston,[37] African-American in rural Georgia,[38] or Japanese-Americans in Hawaii[39]) do not appear to suffer the same ill health consequences as those living in less cohesive communities.

Each of the above mechanisms are empirically testable, and merit further investigation. Turning to mechanisms linking social capital at the *state* level to individual health (the subject of the present investigation), we hypothesize that more cohesive states produce better health via more egalitarian patterns of political participation that result in the passage of policies which ensure the security of all its members.[3, 40] Putnam[2] has demonstrated that social capital (measured by the same indicators used in the present study) is indispensable to the responsiveness and smooth functioning of civic institutions. Low levels of interpersonal trust correlate strikingly with low levels of trust and confidence in public institutions,[41] low levels of political participation (as measured by voting and other forms of engagement in politics),[2, 3, 42] and ultimately, reduced efficacy of government institutions.[2] Our own data demonstrate that states with low levels of interpersonal trust are less likely to invest in human security, and to be less generous with their provisions for social safety nets. For example, mistrust was highly inversely correlated (r = -0.76) with the maximum welfare assistance as a percentage of per capita income in each state. Needless to say, less generous states are likely to provide less hospitable environments for vulnerable segments of the population. Work is presently underway to document the links between social capital, political participation, and health outcomes.

Caveats and Limitations

Despite considerable progress in the conceptualization of social capital, some important caveats remain. First, there is a tendency to regard social capital as an unqualified social good.[43] Various commentators have warned against the tendency to overlook some of the more coercive and exclusive aspects of social capital.[43, 44] For instance, criminal organizations may provide social capital for its members, but contribute little to (or may be frankly destructive of) social cohesion.[45] Some forms of social capital may stifle individual choice, while other forms may not be available to all members of a community. Interestingly, we found that membership in civic organizations showed the weakest association with self-rated health. This may reflect the fact that a crude count of group membership is an imperfect measure of social capital. Civic associations vary along important dimensions that predict their contribution to overall social cohesion (Robert Putnam: personal communication). Thus, some groups may be more exclusive in their membership, compared to others that bridge social divisions along the lines of class, gender, and race/ethnicity; some associations have a mission that is more self-regarding (e.g., hobby groups) than other-regarding (e.g., charities); some associations are more likely to foster civic trust by encouraging face-to-face contact, while others merely involve the payment of membership dues, and so on. An important research task is to determine which of these characteristics matter for health.

Beyond these broad caveats, several specific limitations should be noted about our study. First, despite attempts to take account of a range of individual-level factors that determine self-rated health, it is still possible that the analyses omitted other variables that could account for the apparent contextual effect of social capital. Importantly, measures of social networks (beyond living arrangement) were unavailable in the BRFSS data-set, so that we could not rule out the possibility that the observed "contextual" effect was due to more socially-isolated individuals residing in low social capital states.

Additionally, caution must be exercised in interpreting the state-level social capital estimates generated from the General Social Surveys (GSS). As we have previously discussed,[7] we were able to account for a limited number of variables (age, education, race) in assessing the extent of representativeness of the state-level estimates derived from this national survey. Respondents in the GSS may have differed in other important ways that could have biased the state-level estimates.

Finally, our estimates of social capital were measured at a different time period (1986–90) than the outcome variable (1993–94). Although this preserves the temporal order of the hypothesized association (social capital → self-rated health), it may have introduced misclassification of the "exposure". Social capital in American society has been declining during the last 30 years.[45, 46] If the spread of social capital across states widened in recent years, then use of data from an earlier period may have under-estimated the degree of association between social capital and health. Finally, the direction of causality cannot be firmly established using the present design. Thus, it is possible that some states have a higher share of citizens with poor health (for whatever reason), and that illness leads to civic disengagement, not vice versa. A study is needed with repeated waves of data collection on social capital and health to unequivocally establish the causal direction.

NOTES

1. Coleman JS. *The Foundations of Social Theory*. Cambridge, MA: Harvard University Press, 1990: pp. 300–321.

2. Putnam RD. *Making Democracy Work*. Princeton, NJ: Princeton University Press, 1993.

3. Kawachi I, Kennedy BP. Health and social cohesion: why care about income inequality? Br Med J 1997; 314: 1037–40.

4. Sampson RJ, Groves WB. Community structure and crime: Testing social-disorganization theory. American Journal of Sociology 1989; 94, 774–802.

5. Kennedy BP, Kawachi I, Prothrow-Stith D, Lochner K, Gupta V. Social capital, income inequality, and firearm violent crime. Soc Sci Med 1998; 47: 7–17.

6. Sampson RJ, Raudenbush SW, Earls F. Neighborhoods and violent crime: a multilevel study of collective efficacy. Science 1997; 277: 918–924.

7. Kawachi I, Kennedy BP, Lochner K, Prothrow-Stith D. Social capital, income inequality, and mortality. Am J Public Health 1997; 87: 1491–8.

8. Davis JA, Smith TW. *General Social Survey Cumulative File*. Ann Arbor, Mich: University of Michigan, Interuniversity Consortium for Political and Social Research; 1972 through 1993.

9. Durkheim E. *Suicide* (1897). Ed. George Simpson, transl. J. A. Spaulding and G. Simpson. New York: The Free Press, 1951.

10. Berkman LF, Syme SL. Social networks, host resistance and mortality: a nine-year follow-up study of Alameda County residents. Am J Epidemiol 1979; 109: 186–204.

11. Kawachi I, Colditz GA, Ascherio A, Rimm EB, Giovannucci E, Stampfer MJ, Willett WC. A prospective study of social networks in relation to total mortality and cardiovascular disease in men in the US. J Epidemiol Comm Health 1996; 50: 245–51.

12. Marmot M. Improvement of social environment to improve health. Lancet 1998; 351: 57–60.

13. Susser M. The logic in ecological: I. The logic of analysis. Am J Public Health 1994; 84: 825–829.

14. Schwartz S. The fallacy of the ecologic fallacy: the potential misuse of a concept and the consequences. Am J Public Health 1994; 84: 819–824.

15. Diez-Roux, AV. Bringing context back into epidemiology: variables and fallacies in multilevel analysis. Am J Pub Health 1998; 88: 216–222.

16. Hauser R. Context and consex: A cautionary tale. Am J Sociol 1970; 75: 645–64.

17. Blalock H. Contextual-effects models; Theoretical and methodological issues. Am Rev School 1984; 10: 353–72.

18. Centers for Disease Control and Prevention. *Behavioral Risk Factor Surveillance System User's Guide*. Atlanta: US Department of Health and Human Services, 1997.

19. Hagan Hennessy C, Moriarty DG, Zack MM, Scherr PA, Brackbill R. Measuring health-related quality of life for public health surveillance. Public Health Reports 1994; 109: 665–72.

20. Idler EL, Benyamini Y. Self-rated health and mortality: A review of twenty-seven community studies. J Health and Social Behav 1997; 38: 21–37.

21. Ferraro KF, Farmer MM, Wybraniec JA. Health trajectories: long-term dynamics among black and white adults. J Health and Soc Behav 1997; 38: 38–54.

22. Idler EL, Kasl S. Self-ratings of health: do they also predict change in functional ability? J. Gerontol: Social Sciences 1995; 50B: S344–53.

23. Mor V, Murphy J, Materson-Allen S, Willey C, Razmpour A, Jackson ME, Greer D, Katz S. Risk of functional decline among well elders. J Clin Epidemiol 1989; 42: 895–904.

24. Wilcox VL, Kasl SV, Idler L. Self-rated health and physical disability in elderly survivors of a major medical event. J Gerontol: Social Sciences 1996; 51B: S96–104.

25. Farmer MM, Ferraro KF. Distress and perceived health: mechanisms of health decline. J Health Soc Behav 1997; 39: 298–311.

26. Waksberg JS. Methods for random digit dialing. J Am Stat Assoc 1978; 73: 40–46.

27. Shah BV. *Software for Survey Analysis (SUDAAN) Version 5.50.* Research Triangle Park, NC: Research Triangle Institute; 1991.

28. Wilkinson RG. Income distribution and life expectancy. Br Med J 1992; 304: 165–168.

29. Wilkinson RG. *Unhealthy Societies. The afflictions of inequality.* London: Routeldge, 1996.

30. Kennedy BP, Kawachi I, Prothrow-Stith D. Income distribution and mortality: cross-sectional ecological study of the Robin Hood Index in the United States Br Med J 1996; 312: 1004–1007. See also erratum: Br Med J 1996; 312: 1253.

31. Kawachi I, Kennedy BP. The relationship of income inequality to mortality—Does the choice of indicator matter? Soc Sci Med 1997; 45: 1121–1127.

32. Kaplan GA, Pamuk E, Lynch JW, Cohen RD, Balfour JL. Income inequality and mortality in the United States: analysis of mortality and potential pathways. Br Med J 1996; 312: 999–1003.

33. House JS, Landis KR, Umberson D. Social relationships and health. Science 1988; 214: 540–545.

34. Sampson RJ. Local friendship ties and community attachment in mass society: a multilevel model. Am Sociol Rev 1988; 53: 766–79.

35. Wacquant LJD, Wilson WJ. The cost of racial and class exclusion in the inner city. Annals of the American Academy of Political and Social Science 1989; 501: 8–25.

36. Rogers E. *Diffusion of Innovations.* New York: Free Press, 1983.

37. Seeman TE, Berkman LF, Kohout F, LaCroix A, Glynn R, Blazer D. Intercommunity variations in the association between social ties and mortality in the elderly. A comparative analysis of three communities. Annal Epidemiol 1993; 3: 325–35.

38. Reed D, McGee D, Yano K, Feinleib M. Social networks and coronary heart disease among Japanese men in Hawaii. Am J Epidemiol 1983; 117: 384–96.

39. Schoebach VJ, Kaplan BH, Fredman L, Kleinbaum DG. Social ties and mortality in Evans County, Georgia. Am J Epidemiol 1986; 123: 577–91.

40. Kawachi I, Kennedy BP, Lochner K. Long live community. Social capital as public health. The American Prospect 1997, November/December, 56–59.

41. Brehm J, Rahn W. Individual-level evidence for the causes and consequences of social capital. Am J Polit Sci 1997; 41: 999–1023.

42. Verba S, Lehman Schlozman K, Brady HE. *Voice and Equality. Civic voluntarism in American politics.* Cambridge, MA: Harvard University Press, 1991.

43. Woolcock M. Social capital and economic development: Toward a theoretical synthesis and policy framework. Theory and Society 1998; 27: 151–208.

44. Kaplan GA, Lynch JW. Whither studies on the socioeconomic foundations of population health? (editorial) Am J Public Health 1997; 87: 1409–11.

45. Putnam RD. Bowling alone. America's declining social capital. J Democracy 1995; 6: 65–78.

46. Putnam RD. The strange disappearnace of civic America. American Prospect 1996; 24: 34–48.

Twenty-Four

HEALTH AND CIVIC SOCIETY IN EASTERN EUROPE BEFORE 1989

Richard G. Wilkinson

AMONG less developed countries, and indeed in Central and Eastern Europe (CEE) until the mid 1970s, it appears that communism was good for health. Amartya Sen writing in 1981 looked at improvements in life expectancy among 100 developed and less developed countries between 1960 and 1977.[1] On the assumption that it is probably easier for countries with a lower, rather than a higher, starting point to add any given number of years to life expectancy, Sen measured progress in terms of the percentage decrease in the amount by which combined male and female life expectancy falls short of 80 years. Between 1960 and 1977 he finds that nine out of the ten communist countries in his list of 100 nations come within the top quartile in terms of the percentage reduction in the life expectancy short-fall they achieved. The nine were Albania, Bulgaria, Romania and Yugoslavia from Eastern Europe, as well as Vietnam, China, N. Korea, Mongolia and Cuba. Only Hungary (perhaps significantly with its uprising in 1956 and subsequent purges) failed to make such impressive progress. As he remarks "one thought that is bound to occur (to anyone looking at his table of results) is that communism is good for poverty removal".

Among the other high achieving countries were El Salvador, Malasia, Taiwan, Costa Rica, Hong Kong and Greece. The obvious link between some of these and the communist countries is their success in reducing the extremes of poverty. Some have achieved this mainly by narrowing income differences and others by effectively sharing the benefits of rapid economic growth throughout society. The distribution of income has been shown to have an important influence on national mortality rates throughout the course of economic development.[2-4]

Given that their living standards were substantially lower, what is perhaps most surprising about life expectancy in Eastern European countries is that it was ever comparable with life expectancy in Western Europe. Although figures on GNP per capita are rarely available for earlier years, what figure 1 (UN data) suggests is that even as late as 1990 the average life expectancy in most Eastern European countries appeared good in relation to their GNP per capita. This comparison of GNP per capita is not made at purchasing power parties and so is distorted by the

Originally published in *The East-West Life Expectancy Gap in Europe*, edited by C. Hertzman, S. Kelly, M. Bobak (Dordrecht: Kluwer, 1996).

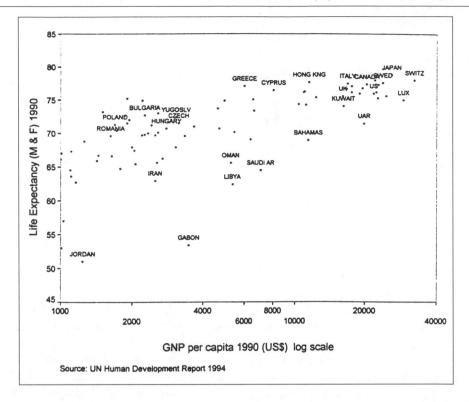

Figure 1
Life expectancy at birth and gross national product per capita, 1990, males and females

vagaries of exchange rates. It will also be affected by the first year of the decline in production which took place in Eastern Europe following the 1989 uprisings. However, if life expectancy increases very roughly with the log of GNP per capita, so that small differences in GNP will have no measurable impact on life expectancy, anything like the eight-fold differences found between Eastern and Western European countries means we would expect lower life expectancy in Eastern than Western Europe. Another implication of figure 1 is that two decades earlier, before the relative decline of Eastern European life expectancy, it must have been outstandingly good in relation to GNP per captia. This is not simply a result of preventive policies impacting on childhood infections and mortality: the same is true of life expectancy at age 15.

However, what has recently attracted attention about health in CEE countries is not that it had been extraordinary good, given their lower standard of living, but that their position compared to Western European countries has deteriorated since the early 1970s. The widening gap between average life expectancy in the 12 member states of the EC and the average in CEE (excluding the former Soviet Union) is shown in Figure 2. After a period in which several East European countries had higher life expectancy than some Western European ones (particularly East Germany, Bulgaria and Romania), from the early 1970s the East-West gap in life expectancy gradually widened.

Perhaps the right question to ask is why did communism, which had apparently been so good

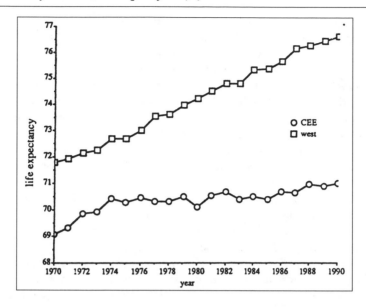

Figure 2
Life expectancy at birth in Eastern & Western Europe, 1970–1990

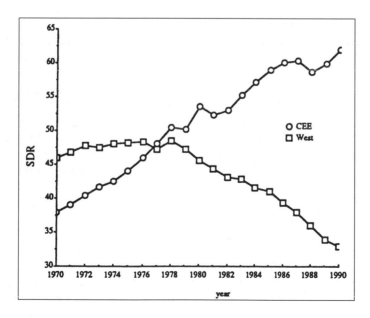

Figure 3
Age standardized death rates (SDR) for ischemic heart disease in Eastern & Western Europe, 1970–1991,
Males aged 0-64, (per 100,000)

for health, begin from the early 1970s to loose some of its advantages? To try to answer this question it would be easier to confine our attention to health trends in Eastern Europe, leaving out the comparison with the West. The comparison with the West adds substantially to the complexity of the explanatory problem because, as ??? as asking—for instance—why IHD rates continue to rise in Eastern Europe, we would also have to explain why rates in Western Europe reached a plateau in the later 1970s and then started to decline. If we do confine our attention to Eastern Europe, the obvious question is why did life expectancy, which had risen to impressively earlier fail to make any substantial advance after the early 1970s?

The change in trend in mortality in Eastern Europe is most pronounced among adult men. It is clearly visible in life expectancy at birth for both men and women, but the discontinuity is sharper in life expectancy at age 15 than at birth. The discontinuity is also sharper for life expect-

ancy at ages below age 65 than above. Peggy Watson has shown that the problem was concentrated particularly on single men and women.[3] She has also shown that the trends are common to the command economies and are quite distinct from those in Western Europe.

A number of important components of mortality show no marked change in trend over the period we are interested in. These include the rapid rise in heart disease. Figure 3 shows there was no marked acceleration in the rise of IHD rates in Eastern Europe over this period. Infant mortality also shows no dramatic change in trend: this time because it continues to fall almost as before (figure 4). While men's cancer rates continue to rise and women's to fall, neither shows a clear break in trend.

The causes where there is a marked change in trend during the mid 1970s include homicide and purposeful injury which rises sharply from the mid 1970s (figure 5), mental disorders, and diseases of the nervous system and sense organs which were falling and start to rise (figure 6), chronic liver disease and cirrhosis which starts to rise more rapidly than it did before (figure 7), endocrine, nutritional and metabolic diseases and immunity disorders which cease to fail and start to rise (figure 8) and infectious and parasitic diseases where the rate of progress declines substantially (figure 9).

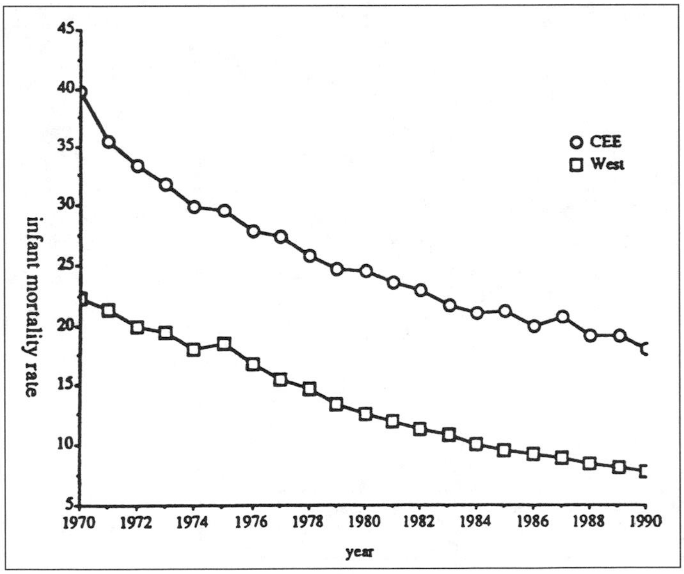

Simultaneous increases in deaths from homicide, mental disorders and cirrhosis, is strongly suggestive of a deteriorating social environment. If there had been a worsening of the social environment, then it would not be stretching a point to suggest that the unfavourable trends in deaths re-

Figure 4
Infant mortality rates in Eastern & Western Europe, 1970–1990, males and females (per 1000 live births)

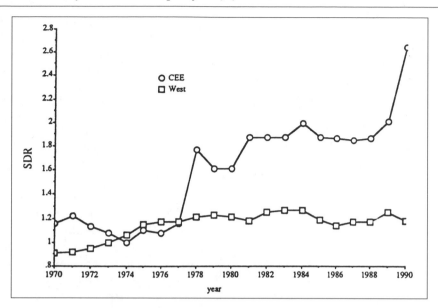

Figure 5
Age standardized death rates (SDR) for homicide and purposeful injury in Eastern & Western Europe 1970–1991, males and females aged 0–65, (per 100,000)

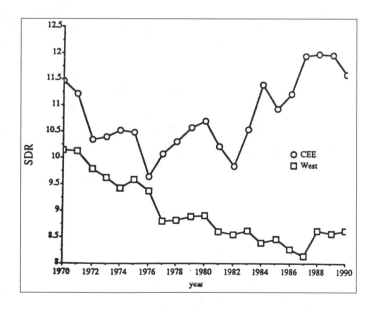

Figure 6
Age standardized death rates (SDR) for mental disorders and diseases of the nervous system and sense organs in Eastern & Western Europe, 1970–1990, Males aged 0–64, (per 100,000)

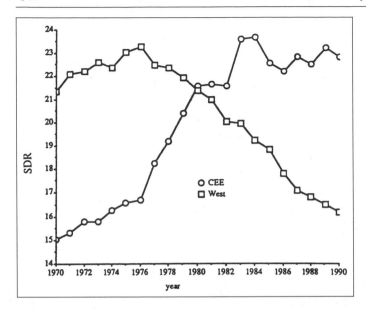

Figure 7
Age standardized death rates (SDR) for chronic liver disease and cirrhosis in Eastern & Western Europe, 1970–1990, males and females aged 0–64, (per 100,000)

lated to endocrine and immunity disorders and to infections could reflect its repercussions through psychosocial pathways.

If single people are affected more than the married, and adults more than children, this suggests that the main source of the problem is not to be found in family life. That the geographical boundaries of these trends are, as Peggy Watson showed, coterminous with the former political division of Europe, suggests an explanation in terms of processes emanating from the politico-economic structure. It is also worth pointing out that these trends were not shared by other communist countries. Centrally planned economies such as China, Cuba and Albania continued to see substantial improvements in health between 1970 and 1990. Although it is widely believed that economic growth continued throughout most of Eastern Europe in the 1970s and early '80s we should bear in mind that a large part of that

growth—if not all of it—may have been absorbed by increased military expenditure.

A useful starting point for an explanation of the health trends is Gorbachev's speech to the Central Committee of the Soviet Communist Party on 27th January 1987. In an extraordinary appeal for the party to renew its social and moral commitment, he spoke of the "loss of momentum", "stagnation", and of "unresolved problems piling up", which "seriously affected the economy and the social and spiritual spheres". He blamed the party saying "vigorous debates and creative ideas (had) disappeared . . . while authoritarian evaluations and opinions became unquestionable truths". "The social goals of the economy in the past few five-year plan periods were diluted and there emerged a deafness to the social issues." "Elements of social corrosion which emerged in the past few years had a negative effect on society's morale, and somehow, unnoticed, eroded the lofty moral values which have always been characteristic of our people . . ." ". . . interest in the affairs of society slackened, manifestations of callousness and scepticism appeared . . ."

"The stratum of people, some of them young people, whose ultimate goal in life was material well-being and gain by any means, grew wider. Their cynical stand was acquiring more and more aggressive forms, poisoning the mentality of those around them, and triggering a wave of consumerism. The spread of alcohol and drug abuse, and a rise in crime, became indicators of the decline of social mores.

Disregard for laws, distortion of reports, bribe taking and the encouragement of toadyism and adulation, had a deleterious influence on the moral atmosphere in society.

Real care for people, for the conditions of their life and work and for social well-being, were often replaced with political flirtation—the mass distribution of awards, titles and prizes. An atmosphere of permissiveness was taking shape, and attention to detail, discipline and responsibility were declining.

Serious shortcomings in ideological and political education were in many cases disguised with ostentatious activities, and campaigns and celebrations of numerous jubilees. The world of day to day realities, and that of make believe well-being, were increasingly diverging. The ideology and mentality of stagnation had their effect on the state of culture, literature and the arts."[6]

That is the situation as it appeared from above. The nearest Gorbachev came to dating it was to say that it "took shape in the late 1970s and early 1980s" That fits well with his criticism of "the last few five-year plans". In part his criticism was clearly a criticism of the Brezhnev administration from 1964–82, and his solution was openness and restructuring, glasnost and peristroika. After the crushing of the "Prague Spring" in Czechoslovakia in 1968, Brezhnev had announced what soon became known as the "Brezhnev doctrine" saying that Soviet Union would not remain inactive in the face of "anti-socialist degeneration" in the Soviet Block. This no doubt marked the beginning of a stronger Soviet influence in the political and economic life of Eastern European countries, and partly explains the similarity of their subsequent development.

Gorbachev's recognition of the problems of bureaucracy, cynicism, corruption, drugs and alcohol during the Brezhnev years seems to be echoed in deaths from homicide, mental disorders and cirrhosis. The atmosphere contrasted sharply with the remarkable confidence of the Khrushchev era (1953–64), when the economic growth rates of the centrally planned economies were widely believed to exceed what was achieved in all but the highest performing developed market economies. It was the widely held confidence (based on past differentials in growth rates and the Soviet launching of the first "sputnik" in 1957) that the Soviet block countries would overtake the West economically which Khrushchev expressed in his shoe-banging speech to the United Nations in 1960, when he predicted that the Soviet Union would bury capitalism.

The Brezhnev era must have brought a profound sense of disillusionment, specially for the older generations whose idealism and faith in the system had been partly rekindled when Khrushchev denounced the crimes and brutality of the Stalinist period. Although the signs of growing discontent had been clear from Hungary in 1956, Czechoslovakia in 1968, from the formation of Charter '77 and from the beginnings of Solidarity in 1981, for many people it must have been during Brezhnev's rule that they finally lost confidence in the whole system. In light of Antonovsky's research on the determinants of health, one could probably talk of the loss of a "sense of coherence" on a societal scale.[7]

The authorities' response to the growing discontent, made clear in the Brezhnev doctrine, was of course an increase in, or return to, the use of informers and secret police on a large scale throughout Eastern Europe. Vogel has described the effect of fear of informers on the quality of friendship in China.[8] If we are right in thinking that social affiliations make an important contribution to health, then it is likely that any increased reluctance among people to trust each other during this period may have had an impact on health. Indeed, one might expect it to have its greatest impact on just those single people without families who would be most isolated, whose death rates show the most marked change in trend. Vogel says:

". . . change in personal relationships arises principally from the uncertainty as to whether private conversation will remain private or whether it will one day be brought to the attention of the authorities. When one no longer confides in a friend for fear that he might pass on the information, whether intentionally or unintentionally, an element of trust is lost. When a person no longer invites a friend to his home for fear the friend might see something that he would later be called upon to describe, the nature of friendship is altered. When a person begins to watch carefully and think about what he might be revealing to his friend and wonders under what circumstances this information might be brought to the attention of the authorities, friendship as a relation of confidence and personal commitment is weakened."[8]

There is then a possibility that a change in the extent and perhaps the character of social networks may also have contributed to the lack of improvement in mortality rates in Eastern Europe. However there is another side to this issue. Writing primarily of the Soviet Union under Stalin, Gross describes the ability of everyone to act as informers as giving the arbitrary power of the state to every citizen to use against others.[9] He says "Everybody shared the power to bring down and destroy everyone else." So important was this power that Gross says "This ability to get anybody arrested was the great equaliser of Soviet citizens". As well as describing the growing sense that friends could no longer be trusted, in his paper on China Vogel also describes the growth of a "new ethic of comradeship" as a form of relationship between citizens. His paper is called "From Friendship to Comradeship: the Change in Personal Relations in Communist China." After describing the negative process of the breakdown of personal trust between people he goes on to describe the development of comradeship in more positive terms. Its essence was apparently not only loyalty to communism, but also in its universality, in the fact that every citizen is a fellow comrade. Vogel says that "part of the ethic underlying the concept of comrade is that there is an important way in which everyone in society is related to every other person." "The other side of the concept is that one should not have special relationships with certain people which would interfere with the obligations to everyone else.". An important element in comradeship in China was "helping other people" which, while this was apparently sometimes a euphe-

mism for getting other people to fall into line and pull their weight, also meant a genuine willingness to spend time to be of assistance to people in need. Vogel gives some examples:—

> "A student who is having trouble with his lessons should be helped by someone who can give the assistance. An old person on the street should be given assistance by someone located conveniently nearby. A new comer to a group should be helped by someone already on hand to become acquainted with the new place, to find all the facilities that he will need. There is a positive value placed on being of assistance to others, on spending time and energy to make things easier for them. Indeed, some refugees from mainland China find it difficult to adjust in Hong Kong to the fact that no longer are people really looking after them and caring for them.".

It is possible that the egalitarian quality of social relations and public values played a central role in why the so-called communist countries have traditionally had higher standards of health than would be expected given their per capita income. If so, then there is at least the possibility of explaining the diminishing health performance of Eastern European countries in the 1970s and '80s as due to a loss of an advantage they once shared with other communist countries. When Gorbachev complained of the erosion of "lofty moral values", a declining "interest in the affairs of society" and a growth in callousness and scepticism", he is surely referring to a decline in this quality of public life. Although it sounds very like a decline in what Putnam calls "civic community" in a pluralistic society like Italy,[10] in the countries of Eastern Europe these public values were fatally identified with support for the Party and the supposedly communist project. Being a good citizen appeared as an expression of support for the government and could only be maintained where there was still a degree of idealism. As that gave way to political cynicism, the nature of public life inevitably changed.

Before discussing how any such processes may have affected health in Eastern Europe, it is worth noting the similarities between the ethic of comradeship—as described by Vogel above—

and the character of social relations which people often say existed in Britain during the Second World War. The fact that it is referred to as a sense of "camaraderie", which existed between strangers in wartime Britain, is indicative. Camaraderie is used, like comradeship, to refer to a universal quality of social relations between citizens. That it is likely to have contributed to health is suggested by the fact that it was during the two World Wars that civilian life expectancy in Britain increased most rapidly this century, despite a deterioration in material circumstances, the overstretching of medical resources, and the diversion of productive capacity to the war effort. Both camaraderie in Britain and comradeship in communist countries were related to an egalitarian ethos. Income differentials narrowed substantially in Britain during the war.[11] The quality of social relations which these terms identify may be an important element in explaining why more egalitarian countries—with narrower income differences—tend so consistently to have better life expectancy.

The possibility that comradeship is an important health variable has the attraction of being able to explain a number of different things which it is usually assumed need different explanations. First it might explain why communist states have usually had a health advantage given their level of GNPpc. Secondly, the final disappearance of any egalitarian ethic of comradeship in Eastern Europe might also help to explain the loss of that advantage in the 1970s and '80s. Thirdly, it might also explain the uncomfortable fact that health progress was maintained in the countries where more "hard-line" governments survived the 1989 upheavals. It may not be stretching a point to suggest that health progress may have been maintained in hard-line countries like China and Albania for two reasons. First, because the commradely ethic of public life was so bound up with support for the system, it would have survived for longer in countries which managed to isolate themselves from awkward comparisons with the outside world and managed to clamp down on the growth of popular opposition. Second, the relationship described by Vogel and Gross between comradeship and the activities of informers and security services—(because "the ability to get anybody arrested was the great equaliser"), meant that one of the foundations of this "induced" comradeship was preserved in those countries. In addition, these ideas seem to find confirmatory echoes in the record wartime decline in civilian mortality in Britain and in the relationship between income distribution and national mortality rates.

We have no reliable assessments of what might have happened to friendships or to comradeship during the 1970s and '80s in Eastern Europe. But to suggest a contribution from this source need not rest on the misconception that Eastern Europe had, and then lost, a fully fledged post-revolutionary Chinese level of comradeship. As the British wartime experience indicates, this is likely to be a matter of degree. What may have happened is that the increased activities of the security services in Easter European countries during the 1970s may have increased the sense of insecurity about speaking openly to friends, but did so in the absence of the idealism needed to produce the compensating effect of a growth of comradeship. Indeed, the cynicism with which the purge (or "screening") was conducted in Czechoslovakia following the crushing of the Prague Spring meant that any remnants of idealism remaining in the party were rooted out. Describing the purges which lead to the removal of, a conservatively estimated, 100,000 from their jobs, Simecka says that "through the whole sorting operation the (Czech) Communist Party got rid of most of its active, idealistic and independently-thinking members"[12] (p.40) He says that the weeding out process valued above all else "obedience, loyalty, dependability, mediocrity, respectability, caution (and) moral weakness." (p.41) Although Czechoslovakia after 1968 was a special case, there was a general tightening of the security system throughout Europe and the Soviet Union to deal with growing dissension during the Brezhnev years. However, as Simecka also says, the operation "revealed how the State's total power over the economy could be used for purely political ends".

> "If any lesson of the Czechoslovak experience is of more general significance, then it is above all, the lesson of the crushing might of united personal departments from the ministry down to some local council work-site out in the sticks. It was not the tanks and infantry of the fraternal armies that crushed the orderly expression of the Czechoslovak people's aspirations . . . but the bureaucrats in charge of personal files at every level, who wielded the power to issue dismissal notices, reorganise or re-deploy the work-force, provide damning character references and use other ingenious methods, thereby avoiding bloodshed, fuss, trials and mass protests."[12] (p 65-6)

Whereas communist governments must initially have provided a sense of security, guaranteeing jobs and housing, they probably came to seem an ever-present threat to personal security among a population which had withdrawn its support. Insecurity—or more accurately job insecurity and the threat of unemployment—has several times been shown to affect health.[13]

When governments collapsed in 1989 the widespread signs of public resentment, not to say hatred, of members of the security services— whether the Stasi in East Germany, Securitate in Romania, the StB (State Security) in Czechoslovakia, or the UB (Security Police) in Poland— shows how much their presence was felt. The effect on employment and prospects for preferment throughout Eastern Europe must have affected most of the population.

The job insecurity, frustration and decline in work as an opportunity for the expression of a sense of purpose are likely to have had important effects on health in themselves. But there were also wider social effects—including those to which Gorbachev drew attention in 1987. To recap, when speaking of trends during the '70s and

'80s, he referred to the damage to the "social and spiritual spheres", to a "deafness to the social issues", to "elements of social corrosion", to "a negative effect on society's morale", and to increasing "callousness and scepticism". He also spoke of the growing stratum of people "whose ultimate goal in life was material well-being and gain by any means" and said "their cynical stand was . . . poisoning the mentality of those around them", and that . . . "The spread of alcohol and drug abuse and a rise in crime [were] indicators of the decline of social mores". Cynicism in the party "had a deleterious influence on the moral atmosphere in society." A "real care for people, for the conditions of their life and work and for social well-being" was declining he said.

No one suggests that even in the 1960s there was a thriving ethic of comradeship, but the indications are that whatever elements there where, were further weakened by a decline in public values as opposition to the regimes grew. The growing opposition also meant that the all pervading power of government would increasingly be experienced as threatening rather than as a source of the material security which is often lacking in market economies. Where at least some people had once gained a sense of meaning and purpose from their work as a contribution towards building a new society, that possibility would have disappeared as the role of the state was experienced increasingly as a resented imposition which stood in the way of the society's development. Together these processes would have forced a retreat into domestic life as public life and work ceased to be meaningful spheres of activity.

The process of demoralisation left its mark exclusively on the countries in the sphere of Soviet influence in Eastern Europe. Other countries with centrally controlled economies like China and Cuba continued to see rapid improvements in health during the 1970s and '80s. Most illuminating however is that fact that health in Albania, which was the only Eastern Europe state which was not in the Soviet sphere of influence, was also the only Eastern European state which continued to show impressive improvements in health.

Simecka describes the effect of the Soviet intervention in Czechoslovakia.[12] After recalling the early idealism among his circle of student friends in the Czech Party saying "every member was convinced that a new kind of fellowship was possible" (p.45), he says that they later began to feel there were "faults in the blueprint for the new society."[6] (p. 46) However, they devoted themselves to identifying the faults and "strove to have each of them recognised as such". ". . . it seemed that, slowly but surely, the worst faults were being eliminated and a way forward was being implemented. And that [he says] was true up to 21 August 1968" [the day that the Soviet tanks arrived]. (p.46) Although he soon came to look on their earliest views as naive youthful utopianism, it is clear that they remained hopeful and confident, right up to the invasion, that the system could respond.

Another indication of the importance of Soviet influence is surely Hungary. As well as being the first country to run into the Soviet buffers, its poor health performance dates back earlier than the other Eastern European countries. Despite being one of the most affluent of the Eastern European countries, by the 1980s it had the lowest life expectancy.

There can be little doubt that the loss of confidence in the state system in Eastern Europe, the decline in standards of public life which Gorbachev described, and the collapse of the remaining ethic of comradeship, are all intimately related. In the state planned economies morality, idealism, sense of purpose and public ethics were all uniquely bound up with the ideology of the political system. Rather than being a private moral value, comradeship was part of being a good communist citizen. Instead of having a large degree of autonomy, the ethics of public life were originally promoted as part of the political programme to transform society and always remained associated with support for the political

system. As governments became discredited under the Soviet yoke the crisis of legitimacy which ensued went much further into the economic, social and moral fabric of society than a similar crisis of legitimacy would have done in the West. In effect, public life as an arena in which people could express or gain any sense of meaning and purpose disappeared. Positive social values became politically tainted and cynicism became the natural expression of political opposition.

In a paper entitled "Social disintegration in Poland: civil society or amoral familism?", Tarkowska and Tarkowski describe the growing divide between public and private spheres of life in Poland.[14]

> "Throughout the 1970s, there was intense concern with family, friends and small social circles, in contrast to marked apathy towards public life. The politicisation of 1980–81 meant a revitalisation of the public sphere and the (brief) emergence of politics as an alternative. But with the introduction of martial law in December 1981, private life emerged supreme. . . . By 1989 a completely 'private society' had emerged.[14] [p. 103-4]

The psychosocial significance of these events was amply demonstrated by the dramatic, but temporary, fall in suicides in 1981 to which Peggy Watson drew attention[5]. After referring to the "boycott of public life", Tarkoska and Tarkowski say that economic shortages led to competition and antagonism between the small private social circles and tended to turn to create "aggression, social pathology and all the features of an 'unfriendly society' . . . divided between 'family members' and 'strangers'.[14] [p.104]

To Summarise

THE demoralisation of the period from the early 1970s to 1989 represented not only a reversal of the confidence in central planning of the early 1960s, but a growing crisis of legitimacy of the political system. The collapse of a political ideology which provided the moral linchpin of public conduct must have come to many as a source of disappointment and disillusionment amounting to a societal loss of a sense of coherence. The purges in Czechoslovakia and increased activity of the security services in other East European countries not only posed a threat to people's job security, but also reduced the chance that work would be experienced as a meaningful activity. At the same time, the activities of the security service would have reduced public confidence in friendships and weakened the contribution of social affiliations to health. The importance of unquestioned loyalty for advancement, both within the Party and outside, led to a lowering of the moral tone of the whole state machine and of public life. Any health advantage associated with an egalitarian ethic, public spiritedness and comradeship which remained in the 1960s would have disappeared in the 1970s.

These changes would have forced a retreat into private life leaving single people, particularly men, without any obvious source of self-fulfilment. This fits well with Watson's evidence of where the health trends were worst. The increased alcohol and drug consumption are other plausible social repercussions. The causes of death which show a marked change in trends from around the mid 1970s—alcohol related deaths, deaths from violence and from mental disorders, a slowing in the decline of deaths from infections and a rise in the group of endocrine, nutritional and metabolic diseases and immunity disorders—may be expressions of the psychosocial malaise.

NOTES

1. Sen, A. (1981) Public action and the quality of life in developing countries. *Oxford Bulletin of Economics and Statistics* 43, 287–319.

2. Wilkinson, R.G. (1994) Health, redistribution and growth, in A. Glyn and D. Miliband (eds.), *Paying for inequality: the economic cost of social injustice,* Rivers Oram Press, London, pp. 24–43.

3. Waldmann, R. J. (1992) Income distribution and infant mortality. *Quarterly Journal of Economics* 107, 1283–1302.

4. Rodgers, G.B. (1979) Income and inequality as determinants of mortality: an international cross-section analysis, *Population Studies* 33, 343–51.

5. Watson, P. (1994) *Explaining rising mortality among men in Eastern Europe,* Paper presented at an ESRC Research Seminar on Gender, Class and Ethnicity in Post-communist States held at Birkbeck College, University of London, 30 June 1994.

6. Gorbachev, M. (1987) "The way ahead . . . more democracy and openness", *The Guardian* (newspaper), February 2.

7. Lundberg, O. and Nystrom Peck, M. (1994) Sense of coherence, social structure and health, *European Journal of Public Health* 4, 252–7.

8. Vogel, E.F. (1965) From friendship to comradeship: the change in personal relations in communist China, *China Quarterly* 21, 46–70.

9. Gross, J.T. (1982) A note on the nature of Soviet totalitarianism. *Soviet Studies* 34, 367–76.

10. Putnam, R.D., Leonardi, R., and Nanetti, R.Y. (1993) *Making democracy work: civic traditions in modern Italy,* Princeton University Press, Princeton.

11. Wilkinson, R.G. (1989) Class mortality differentials, income distribution and trends in poverty 1921–1981, *Journal of Social Policy* 18, 307–35.

12. Simecka, M. (1984) *The restoration of order: the normalisation of Czechoslovakia,* Verso, London.

13. Bartley, M. (1994) Unemployment and ill-health: understanding the relationship, *Journal of Epidemiology and Community Health* 48, 333–7.

14. Tarkoska, E. and Tarkowski, J. (1991) Social disintegration in Poland: civil society or amoral familism?, *Telos* 89, 103–9.

Twenty-Five

THE ROLE OF SOCIAL CAPITAL
IN THE RUSSIAN MORTALITY CRISIS

Bruce P. Kennedy, Ichiro Kawachi,
and Elizabeth Brainerd

SUMMARY

E MERGING evidence suggests that the degree of social cohesion is an important determinant of population health status. Citizens living in societies with a high degree of social cohesion—characterized by strong social networks and high levels of interpersonal trust—seem to be healthier than those living in socially disorganized societies. Epidemiologists have become interested in notions of *civil society* and *social capital* to explain variations in health across societies. The purpose of the present paper was to examine the role of social capital in the Russian mortality crisis. Social capital has been defined as those features of social organization—such as the density of civic associations, levels of interpersonal trust, and norms of reciprocity—that act as resources for individuals, and facilitate collective action. A civil society is one that is rich in stocks of social capital. Various scholars have argued that one of the distinguishing characteristics of the Soviet regime was the paucity of civil society. Using household survey data from the All-Russian Center for Public Opinion research (VTsIOM), we carried out a cross-sectional, ecologic analysis of the association between indicators of social capital and mortality rates across 40 regions of Russia. We found associations between indicators of social capital (mistrust in government, crime, quality of work relations, civic engagement in politics) and life expectancy, as well as mortality rates. In the absence of civil society, it is believed that far more people in post-Soviet Russia rely on informal sources of support (friends, family) to deal with their day to day problems. Those lacking such sources of support may have been especially vulnerable to the economic hardships following the transformation to a market economy.

INTRODUCTION

S INCE the collapse of communism in 1989, many formerly socialist countries of Central and Eastern Europe have experienced major declines in life expectancy. The crisis has been par-

Originally published in *World Development*, 1998.

ticularly severe in Russia, where during 1989–94, life expectancy declined by 6.6 years in men, and by 3.6 years in women (Leon *et al.*, 1997). By 1994, male Russian life expectancy at birth (57.6 years) was lower than in countries such as Pakistan (60.9 years), Botswana (63.3 years), and Bolivia (58.0 years) (UNDP, 1996). Among Russian men, more than half of the excess deaths occurred in the age-group 25–59 years, and the major causes of excess death have been due to cardiovascular diseases and external causes (accidents, injuries, suicide) (Shkolnikov, Meslé and Vallin, 1995). In all, the upsurge in Russian mortality during this crisis has been estimated to amount to a staggering 1.3 to 2 million extra deaths (Chen, Witgenstein and McKeon, 1996).

Yet, the causes of the Russian mortality crisis remain to be established. The purpose of the present paper is to outline a broad sociocultural hypothesis of a potentially important contributor to the Russian mortality crisis, attributing the phenomenon to the lack of social capital in post-Soviet society.

Increasing evidence points to social cohesion as a crucial determinant of population health (Wilkinson, 1996; Kawachi and Kennedy, 1997; Kawachi, Kennedy and Lochner, 1997). There have been several examples across time and culture, where the presence or absence of social cohesion was strikingly correlated with population health status. Wilkinson (1996) offers several cases studies of societies that at certain points in history either enjoyed a high degree of social cohesion (e.g. Britain during the two world wars, as well as post-war Japan), or suffered a rapid deterioration in social cohesion (e.g. the Italian-American community of Roseto in Pennsylvania during the 1960s). In each instance, life expectancy in these societies closely mirrored the population health experience: the more cohesive the society, the lower the population mortality rates. In Britain, the wartime effort was accomplished by a greater sense of solidarity and social cohesion as well as dramatic improvements in life ex-

pectancy. For over 25 years, the rural town of Roseto has served as a population laboratory for researchers such as Stewart Wolf and colleagues (Bruhn and Wolf, 1979; Egolf *et al.*, 1992). The town originally came to the attention of medical researchers because the people who lived there had half the death rate from heart attack compared to neighboring towns, despite similar profiles of risk factors such as smoking, obesity, and fat intake. Wolf and colleagues eventually came to the conclusion that the protective factor was the close knit social relationships among inhabitants in the town. Beginning in the mid-1960s however, the town experienced rapid economic growth, which opened the gap between rich people and poor people. The resulting breakdown of community solidarity was followed by a sharp increase in deaths from coronary disease, such that Roseto "caught up" with neighboring towns.

The notion that social cohesion enhances well-being is by now a well-established fact (Kawachi and Kennedy, 1997). Ever since Durkheim's study of the causes of suicide (Durkheim, 1897), numerous epidemiological studies have shown that people who are socially integrated live longer (House, Landis and Umberson, 1988; Kawachi *et al.*, 1996). Socially isolated people die at two to three times the rate of well-connected people, presumably reflecting the former's limited access to sources of emotional support, instrumental support (for example, financial aid), and other forms of support. More recently, researchers have become interested in exploring the connections between a broader conception of social cohesion—or *social capital*—and health outcomes (Kawachi and Kennedy, 1997; Kawachi, Kennedy and Lochner, 1997).

Social capital has been defined as those features of social structures that facilitate the actions of members within them. According to Coleman (1990), three examples of the forms of social capital include: levels of trust within a social structure; appropriate social organizations (civic associations); norms and sanctions; and information channels. The first two of these forms—levels of trust and membership of civic associations—were used by Putnam (1993) in his empirical work on the factors predicting local government performance across the regions of Italy. According to Putnam, the stock of social capital in a region—for example, as measured by the density of citizens' participation in voluntary associations (choral societies, soccer leagues, Rotary clubs, and the like) turned out to be the best predictor of local government performance. Citizens living in regions characterized by high levels of social capital were more likely to trust their fellow citizens and to value solidarity, equality, and mutual tolerance. They were also blessed with high-functioning local governments.

The trustworthiness of the social environment is critical to the proper functioning of obligations and expectations, which are themselves forms of social capital. For example, if *A* does something for *B*, expecting *B* to reciprocate some time in the future, this establishes an expectation in *A* and an obligation on the part of *B*; but the success of the transaction depends crucially on the level of trust between *A* and *B* (Coleman, 1988). As an example of an appropriate social organization, Coleman describes a resident's organization in an urban housing project which formed for the initial purpose of pressuring builders to fix various problems (leaks, crumbling sidewalks, etc). After the problems were solved, the organization remained as available social capital the improved the quality of life for residents. The general point is that an organization, once brought into existence for one set of purposes can also be appropriated for other uses, thus constituting a form of social capital.

Most recently, Kawachi *et al.* (1997) tested the association between social cohesion and mortality rates across the 39 US states. Using indicators of "social capital" developed in political science and sociology (Coleman, 1990; Putnam, 1993; Putnam, 1995), they demonstrated that states characterized by low degrees of social cohesion tend to exhibit higher mortality rates from all causes, as well as cardiovascular disease, homicides, and infant mortality. The two indicators of social capital examined in this study were survey-based responses of citizens to questions about whether "other people could be trusted," and whether they belonged to a variety of civic and voluntary associations. Both indicators of social capital were strongly correlated with rates of age-adjusted mortality ($r = 0.79$ for social mistrust, and $r = -0.49$ for per capita membership of civic associations: $P < 0.05$ for both).

In contrast to the examples of democratic societies such as Italy and the United States, one of the hallmarks of a totalitarian regime (such as prevailed in Soviet Russia) is the absence of civil society, characterized by the lack of trust between citizens, lack of trust of state institutions, and the absence of active, private, nongovernmental organizations. A totalitarian regime, according to political scientist Carl Friedrich and Zbigniew Brzezinski, is marked by "a central control and direction of the entire economy through the bureaucratic coordination of formerly independent corporate entities, typically including most other associations and group activities" (quoted in Smith and Freedman, 1972, p. 33). Citizens living under such regimens are likely to minimize contact with the state and to rely upon dense horizontal networks of trusted friends to insulate themselves from the state. According to Rose, Mishler and Haerfer (1996), the reaction against totalitarian attempts to mobilize citizens resulted in the development of "an hourglass society" in Soviet Russia, characterized by a rich social life at the base, consisting of strong informal networks based on trust between friends, relatives and other face-to-face groups (Rose, 1995). At the top of the hour-glass, there developed a separate political and social life, as elites of the *nomenklatura* competed for power, wealth, and prestige. Thus:

> In the vast Russian State, cooperation within and between elites and institutions is the normal way for individual officials to secure their own goals. Such a society resembles a civil society insofar as a number of informal and formal institutions are tolerated and now even legally recognized by the state. Yet the result is not a civic community but an hourglass society, because the exchanges between the top and bottom are constricted and intended to be so (Rose, Mishler and Haerfer, 1996, p. 5).

Rose and colleagues go on to argue that the Soviet Union left a double legacy: individual Russians are likely to have a high degree of trust in their immediate social networks, and a high degree of distrust in the Russian state. In support of this thesis, several social surveys conducted in post-Communist Russia (such as the New Russia Barometer surveys) appear to confirm a high degree of distrust in political and civic institutions. In this climate, far more people in post-Communist Russia rely on informal social capital than on formal institutions of state and markets to deal with their problems. For example, when the 1996 New Russia Barometer asked people on whose help they rely, only 7% referred to formal organizations (including the state, trade unions, churches or charities). When problems arise, more than half rely on informal sources of social capital, i.e., their network of friends and relatives. Those without social capital rely principally on themselves (Rose, Mishler and Haerfer, 1996).

Thus the historic suppression of civil society in Russia is likely to have stranded a group of vulnerable citizens without means of support, when the state apparatus itself collapsed. The Barometer surveys consistently indicate that half or more of those who have been unemployed have not received any benefit payments from the state (Rose, Mishler and Haerfer, 1996). Informal social networks have then served as the major source of social security. Two-thirds of Russians

say that they have a friend who would loan them as much as a week's wages if their household was short of money, and more than two-thirds know someone who would help if they were ill (Rose, Mishler and Haerfer, 1996). But what happens if an individual is socially isolated, and has no friends or relatives to fall back on? Increasingly, evidence suggests that the excess of premature male mortality in post-Communist societies has been overwhelmingly concentrated in the non-married population (Watson, 1995). In other words, the devaluing of the public sphere and the overreliance on the private domain may have contributed to the rising health vulnerability of post-Communist societies.

In the present paper, we examined the relationships between total and cause-specific mortality, and measures of civil society and social cohesion in post-Soviet Russia.

METHODS

(a) *Measurement of Regional Variations in Social Capital*

The measures of social capital used in this study were estimated from a series of household surveys conducted in Russia by the All-Russian Center for Public Opinion Research (or VTsIOM, its Russian acronym) in April, May and June 1994. The surveys are based on a stratified random sample of the population and are nationally representative of the adult population of Russia age 16 and over. Each monthly survey comprises 3000 individuals in 121 areas of the country (92 urban areas and 29 rural areas).[1] These areas represent 40 of the 88 regions in Russia; these regions are roughly equivalent to US states. The total sample size for the three surveys used here is 8868 observations. Table A1 compares the demographic characteristics of the survey respondents with those of the general population. While the age structure and regional distribution of the population in these surveys are roughly similar to that of the population, women and university-educated people are slightly over-represented in the surveys relative to the population as a whole.

As indicators of the level of social capital across the regions, we took responses to questions regarding civic engagement, trust in government, and social cohesion. Civic engagement is reflected in the share of respondents who did not vote in the December 1993 Parliamentary elections, and in the percentage responding that "I am not at all interested in politics," when queried regarding their interest in politics. Respondents were also asked about their degree of trust in local and regional governments, as well as in the federal government. For each level of government and for each region in Russia, we calculated the percentage of people who responded that the respective government was "completely undeserving of trust." Items that directly inquired abut respondents' trust of other people (analogous to the General Social Surveys items in the United States) were not available on the VTsIOM surveys. It has been found in the past, however, that citizens' trust of state institutions correlate quite strongly with levels of social trust in general (Putnam, 1995; Brehm and Rahn, 1997); hence it was felt that citizens' trust of government was a reasonable proxy for social capital.

An additional measure of social cohesion that we used is given by the respondents' assessment of relations at their place of work, in particular the share responding that relations between people at work ". . . are strained, with conflicts." Finally, the occurrence of crime is increasingly regarded as an indicator of lack of social capital (Wilkinson, Kawachi and Kennedy, 1998). In numerous examples across time and place, crime appears to be a marker for social disorganization and strained social relations (Sampson, Raudenbush and Earls, 1997; Wilkinson, Kawachi and Kennedy, 1998); hence, we used registered crime rates across the regions as an additional proxy for social cohesion.

(b) *Measurement of Regional Variations in Income, Unemployment and Other Variables*

Regional data on average per capita income, unemployment rates and the reported crime rate were obtained from the 1996 *Russian Statistical Yearbook* (Goskomstat, 1996b). While average incomes are likely to be underreported due to tax avoidance in Russia, we used this measure because it is the best measure of regional income levels available, and because it is unlikely that the underreporting of income varies systematically across regions. Regional unemployment rates are relatively well-measured; the ILO definition of unemployment is used and rates are calculated from the regionally representative labor force survey of 580 000 people conducted in October 1994. The percentage of each region's population with incomes below the region's subsistence income level[2] is also included in the statistical work here as an indicator of relative hardship across regions; this measure is also from the 1996 *Statistical Yearbook*. In addition, we also used a variable capturing perceptions of economic hardship, or relative deprivation: the percentage of respondents in each region replying in the VTsIOM survey that "the economic situation in your city or region" is poor or very poor. Finally, divorce rates per 1000 population by region were obtained from the 1996 *Demographic Yearbook of Russia* (Goskomstat, 1996a).

We used a number of measures of mortality to test the relationships with the variables described above. These include male and female life expectancy at birth, and age-standardized death rates for men and women expressed as the number of deaths per 100 000 population (age standardization is based on the European age structure). We also examined the relationship between measures of social capital and the major causes of mortality, in particular circulatory diseases, neoplasms and external causes (accidents, homicides and poisonings) for both men and women. All of the mortality and life expectancy data were obtained from the 1996 *Demographic Yearbook of Russia* (Goskomstat, 1996a).

DATA ANALYSIS

ORDINARY least squares (OLS) regression was used to examine the relationships of the social capital indicators and other predictors to mortality rates. We regressed all-cause and cause-specific mortality rates for both males and females separately against the lead of the predictors, adjusting the regression models for region variations in the prevalence of poverty and per capita income.

RESULTS — RELATIONSHIP BETWEEN SOCIAL CAPITA AND MORTALITY

Trust in Government and Civic Engagement

We examined the relationship of trust in government (percentages of people who agreed that their local, regional and national governments respectively were "completely undeserving of trust.") to all-cause and major causes of mortality and life-expectancy (Tables 1–3; Figure 1). Regions with high levels of distrust in *local* government had higher male age-adjusted rates of total mortality (r = 0.33; *P* < 0.05) (Figure 1). In our regression model, variations in the level of trust in local government explained an additional 14% (R^2 = 0.31) of the variance in total male mortality after controlling for variations in per capita income and poverty (Table 2). A one unit change in the percentage of inhabitants agreeing that their local government was "completely undeserving of trust," was associated with an increase in overall male age-adjusted mortality rates of 6.33 deaths per 100 000. The effects of distrust of government were similar for women, accounting for an additional 7% of the variance in female age-adjusted overall mortality after controlling for per capita income and poverty, although the magnitude of the effect was not as large (*B* = 2.11, *t* = 1.93, *P* < 0.0611).

A higher level of distrust in local government was also associated with lowered life-expectancy for both men and women across regions independent of per capita income and poverty (Table 3). The relationship to major causes of mortality was strongest for circulatory disease rates in both males and females (Table 3). Distrust in local government was marginally associated with deaths due to neoplasms and external causes for males (*P* < 0.10) for meals but not for females (Table 3).

The effects of government distrust only held for the local government variable. Distrust in the *regional* government was only weakly associated with mortality and life-expectancy (Tablea 1–3) and the effects of distrust of the *national* government was actually inverse (r = – 0.30, Table 1) but in our multivariate regression models controlling for income and poverty this relationship approached zero (not shown). Thus, the relationship proximal institutions (local government), weaker for regional government, and nonexistent for distal (national) government.

The relationship between trust in governmental and civic engagement (interest in politics and voting participation) followed a similar pattern, where high levels of distrust in local government was associated with a higher percentage of persons not voting (r = 0.37, Table 1). This relationship was weaker at the levels of regional and national government (r = 0.10 and r = 0.13, respectively). In addition, disinterest in politics (percentage responding that "not at all interested in politics") was also strikingly associated with lack of voting participation (r = 0.45, Table 1). This civic engagement variable was in turn, strongly associated with male overall mortality, life-expectancy and deaths due to circulatory diseases when controlling for per capita income and poverty across regions (Tables 2 and 3). The relationship was similar for female mortality and life-expectancy, although only marginally significant for overall death rates after controlling for income and poverty (*B* = 2.86, *t* = 1.67, *P* < 0.10). As with the males, the relationships to

Table 1.

Correlations among region–level (n = 40) social capital indicators and male and female age–adjusted mortality rates.

	1	2	3	4	5	6	7	8	9	10	11	12	13	14
1 MDTH94 Male death rate	1.00													
2 FDTH94 Female death rate	0.93*	1.00												
3 LNINC94 Per capita income	0.45*	0.48*	1.00											
4 Pov94 Poverty	−0.29	−0.13	−0.37*	1.00										
5 UNEMP94 Unemployment rate	0.21	0.28	−0.19	0.30	1.00									
6 DIVCRD94 Divorce rate	0.44*	0.37*	0.33*	−0.01	0.03	1.00								
7 Crime94 Per capita crime rate	0.68*	0.73*	0.27	−0.06	0.29	0.34*	1.00							
8 ECSITB45 Economic situation poor	0.50*	0.50*	0.16	−0.07	0.17	0.33*	0.36*	1.00						
9 TRUSTLC3 Distrust of local government	0.33*	0.25	−0.05	0.18	0.23	0.37*	0.18	0.27	1.00					
10 TRUSTRG3 Distrust of regional government	0.16	0.15	−0.12	0.38*	0.27	0.33*	0.07	0.37*	0.73*	1.00				
11 TRUSTGV3 Distrust of national government	−0.30	−0.23	−0.24	0.18	−0.06	0.01	0.00	−0.10	0.27	0.46*	1.00			
12 EXPPOL7[a] Uninterested in politics	0.25	0.20	−0.06	−0.18	0.15	0.06	0.04	0.28	0.16	0.27	−0.07	1.00		
13 VOTED2[a] Percent not voting	0.13	0.07	−0.12	−0.15	0.08	0.09	0.23	−0.04	0.37*	0.10	0.13	0.45*	1.00	
14 RELWORK3[a] Work relations strained	0.30	0.19	−0.13	−0.26	0.03	−0.06	−0.01	0.40*	0.05	0.01	−0.37*	0.49*	0.34*	1.00

P<0.05.

[a]Due to missing data (regions 19, 52, 55, 70), correlations with these variables are based on 36 regions.

Table 2.

Effects of social capital variables on male age-adjusted mortality rates (40 regions)

Independent variables	Model													
	1		2		3		4		5		6		7	
	B (S.E.)	P <	B (S.E.)	P <	B (S.E.)	P <	B (S.E.)	P <	B (S.E.)	P <	B (S.E.)	P <	B (S.E.)	P <
LNINC94 Log Per capita income	348.74 (138.69)	0.016	340.53 (127.10)	0.0111	342.93 (133.22)	0.0143	288.34 (124.07)	0.0261	420.58 (135.87)	0.0041	372.11 (137.71)	0.0110	196.18 (108.36)	0.0736
POV94 Poverty	−5.72 (6.33)	0.3716	−8.65 (5.87)	0.1511	−10.58 (6.53)	0.1141	−5.51 (5.60)	0.3322	−0.39 (6.45)	0.9523	−3.018 (6.46)	0.6366	−6.74 (4.77)	0.1669
TRUSTLC3 Distrust of local government			6.33 (2.23)	0.0073										
TRUSTREG3 Distrust of regional government					5.28 (.259)	0.0497								
ECONSTB45 Economic situation poor							10.46 (3.12)	0.0019						
RELWORK3 Work relations strained									11.42 (4.83)	0.0241				
EXPOL7 Completely uninterested in politics											6.34 (3.70)	0.0964		
CRIME94*100 Per capita crime rate													34.17 (6.41)	0.0000
Adjusted R²	0.17		0.31		0.24		0.35		0.28[a]		0.22[a]		0.53	
$F_{3,36}$	5.01		6.74		5.06		8.08		5.50		4.35		15.67	
(P< . . . .)	(0.0110)		(0.0009)		(0.0049)		(0.0003)		(0.0036)		(0.0111)		(0.0000)	

Due to missing data (regions 19, 52, 55, 70) these models are based on 36 regions.

Table 3.

Effects of social capital variables on male and female cause specific mortality and life-expectancy adjusted for per capita income and poverty across 40 regions

Independent variables	Male mortality								Female mortality							
	MLIFEX94		MCIROC94		MINEO94		MEXT94		FLIFEX94		FCIRC95		MNEO94		FEXT94	
	B (S.E.)	P <	B (S.E.)	P <	B (S.E.)	P <	B (S.E.)	P <	B (S.E.)	P <	B (S.E.)	P <	B (S.E.)	B (S.E.)	B (S.E.)	P <
TRUSTLC3 Distrust of local government	-0.041 (0.016)	0.0167	3.97 (1.39)	0.0045	0.61 (0.32)	0.0709	1.77 (1.01)	0.0874	-0.029 (0.014)	0.0528	2.03 (0.82)	0.0187	0.17 (0.14)	0.2311	0.34 (0.35)	0.3351
TRUSTREG3 Distrust of regional government	-0.031 (0.019)	0.1516	4.35 (1.47)	0.0054	0.49 (0.36)	0.1811	1.24 (1.16)	0.2891	-0.021 (0.021)	0.2372	2.03 (0.93)	0.0362	0.057 (0.15)	0.7041	0.32 (0.39)	0.4284
ECONSTB45 Economic situation poor	-0.071 (0.023)	0.0069	5.43 (1.94)	0.0081	0.98 (0.45)	0.0371	3.67 (1.40)	0.0128	-0.057 (0.021)	0.0085	3.03 (1.19)	0.0154	0.25 0.19	0.2158	1.03 (0.48)	0.0411
RELWORK3[a] Work relations strained	-0.096 (0.033)	0.0069	1.78 (3.14)	0.5752	1.11 (0.72)	0.1277	2.87 (2.22)	0.2019	-0.063 (0.031)	0.0433	0.69 (1.91)	0.7194	0.042 (0.31)	0.8917	1.22 (0.72)	0.0996
EXPOL7[a] Completely uninterested in politics	-0.06 (0.025)	0.0167	4.55 (2.19)	0.0456	0.57 (0.54)	0.2914	0.31 (1.68)	0.8545	-0.045 (0.022)	0.0552	2.27 (1.35)	0.1037	0.03 (0.22)	0.9080	0.58 (0.55)	0.2912
CRIME94*100 Per capita crime rate	-0.22 (0.04)	0.0000	15.75 (4.36)	0.0009	3.39 (1.0)	0.0017	14.21 (2.78)	0.0000	-0.22 (0.04)	0.0000	11.27 (2.45)	0.0000	0.84 (0.45)	0.0736	4.15 (1.01)	0.0002

[a]Due to missing data (regions 19, 52, 55, and 70) these models are based on 36 regions.

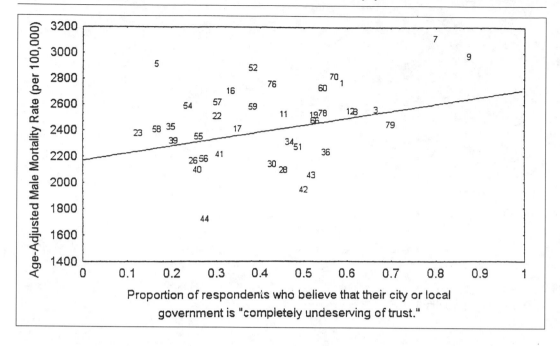

Figure 1
Age-adjusted male mortality rates by social capital (trust in government).

life-expectancy and deaths due to circulatory diseases were the strongest (Table 3).

Social Cohesion

Our two measures of social cohesion—crime and conflict at work (percentage responding that ". . . the relations between people at work are strained, with conflicts")—were both associated with overall male mortality (Table 2). Crime was a particularly strong predictor of both male and female life-expectancy, and associated with all major causes of death (Table 3). Work conflict also strongly predicted life-expectancy. Its association with major causes of death was less clear however (Table 3). Divorce rates were associated with male ($r = 0.44$) and female ($r = 0.48$) overall death rates in univariate analyses (Table 1). After controlling for income and poverty, however, these relationships were not statistically significant.

It is particularly interesting to note the *positive* relationships among divorce, crime and per capita income (Table 1), where higher per capita income is associated with higher crime and divorce rates. This may help to account for the surprising positive association between higher per capita income and higher mortality and lower life-expectancy (Tables 1 and 2). In fact, with crime in the regression model, the effects of per capita income and poverty on life-expectancy drop out (not shown). This was also seen for male overall mortality where the effects of per capita income, while still marginally significant, were reduced dramatically when crime was added to the model (Table 2). As a potential explanation for these paradoxical findings, we conjecture that rapid growth in some regions (measured by higher per capita income) has been associated with a socially destabilizing effect as evidenced by high divorce and crime rates.

Perceived Economic Hardship

Perceived economic hardship (percentage responding that "the economic situation in your city or region?" was poor or very poor) was associated with a number of the social capital variables as well as life-expectancy and mortality from a number of causes (Tables 1–3). Economic hardship was correlated with crime ($r = 0.36$) and divorce ($r = 0.33$) and although not statistically significant, it was positively associated with per capita income (Table 1). It was also associated with work conflicts ($r = 0.40$) and government distrust (Table 1).[3]

DISCUSSION

AMONG the many potential explanations for the recent Russian mortality crisis, we have attempted in the present paper to provide a test of a specific hypothesis—that the lack of social capital in Russian society is an important factor in the human security crisis. Although we were unable to examine secular trends in the stock of social capital in Russian society (i.e., before and after the collapse of the Soviet Union), our analysis nonetheless suggests that indicators of social capital could account for an important portion of the cross-sectional variation in mortality and life expectancy across the regions of the country. Social capital measured by a variety of indicators—trust in local government, political participation, crime and divorce rates, and conflicts in the work place—was strongly associated with all cause age-adjusted mortality, life-expectancy, and cause specific mortality (especially CHD) for both males and females. Moreover, the relationship of social capital to mortality persisted after controlling for per capita income and a measure of poverty.

Trust in government seemed to only matter at the local level and there was a clear gradient from local to national. This was true also for the economic situation variable where only the regional or city economic situation mattered and not beliefs about the national economy. This suggests a more localized effect of social capital where the proximally experienced social context is more significant to health than the general national economic and social context.

As with any cross-sectional data, there is difficulty in establishing casual relations in this study with any certainty, and thus, these results should be interpreted appropriate caution. Arguably, the mortality-social capital link could go either way—higher mortality rates in a region could serve to erode social cohesion rather the reverse. Indeed, crude death rates in 1980, (adjusted for the percentage of the population of retirement age) predict most of the variables used in our models.[4] This finding suggests that at least some of the observed relationship could be due to the influence of high mortality on social cohesion rather than the reverse. Although this finding complicates the picture somewhat, it is conceivable that regional differences in social capital were already present in 1980 and that these structural influences on mortality persist into the present. In fact, 1980 and 1994 crude death rates are quite strongly associated ($r = 0.79$) which suggests that some underlying structural variables may be accounting for the regional mortality differences. Whether one of these factors is social capital is difficult to tell due to the lack of historical data. As Rose (1995) has argued however, a key consequence of Soviet society was the distortion of social relations, and subsequently the erosion of civil society which may have made populations of certain regions more vulnerable to economic and social transformations.

Rose (1995) used the term "hour-glass society" to describe the bifurcation of social relations in Soviet society. At the top of the hour-glass, the ruling *apparatchik* maintained a mesh of social connections and mutual obligations. At the bottom of the hour-glass, Soviet citizens sought to minimize contact with the state, relying instead on dense horizontal networks of friends to insulate themselves from the state. Very little bridging occurred between these two poles of social relations, so that when the regime that created such behavior finally collapsed, the legacy was a country of citizens with an "uncivic" objective. According to the New Russia Barometer surveys conducted by Rose and colleagues, very few Russians work through civic associations to solve local problems:

> Only one in ten (Russian citizens) sometimes or often participated in local community associations. The very idea of locally initiated community associations appeared unfamiliar to many respondents socialized in a community in which the Communist Party was the guiding force. When Russians are asked to characterize what kind of people participate in local groups, as many as a third reply that they have no idea (Rose, 1995, p. 38).

Consistent with the VTsIOM surveys, the New Russia Barometer surveys also paint a picture of high levels of mistrust in Russian society. Although Russians trust people within their circle of intimate contacts. 75% respond that "other people can't be trusted". As a point of comparison, 63% of Americans responded the same way in the General Social Survey in 1993, up from 42% in 1960 (Putnam, 1995). Mistrust of political institutions in post-Soviet society is similarly very high. Political parties were actively distrusted by 83% of respondents in the 1994 New Russia Barometer. Distrust of Parliament was almost as high, 72%. The majority of trade union members distrust their union officials. Only 15% of Russian workers say they trust their national union officials (Rose, 1995).

To a considerable extent, mistrust of Russian government today may reflect the inability of the Russian Federation to guarantee its citizens an income. According to the 1995 New Russia Barometer:

> [O]ne in seven of the labor force has been unemployed in the past year, but only a third of those received any unemployment benefit while without work, and usually only for a fraction of the period of their unemployment. The ineffectiveness of the state to help the unemployed is compounded by the inability of employers to pay wages on time. More than half of Russian workers report that they have

been paid late or not at all for at least one month during the past year (Rose, 1995, p. 37).

Since people in an hour-glass society do not look to the state for protection, when they find themselves in trouble, they look to their friends. Again, as Rose (1995) said: "The ability of Russians to build strong social networks to keep the state out is historically understandable. In an inflationary era, 100 friends are worth far more than ten million rubles." The problem is when people have no friends they can turn to for support. The most vulnerable group in an uncivic society consists of those socially-isolated individuals who lack informal networks of support (spouses, friends, close relatives), and who are forced to rely on the official economy for their survival. Whereas such individuals were already vulnerable during the Soviet era (forced as they were to rely on the state for support), the collapse of the regime left them exposed to the turmoil of economic transformation. The more "uncivil" the region, the greater the vulnerability of those at the bottom of the hour-glass.

To be sure, social capital is abundantly evident today in the thriving enterprises of the new Russian entrepreneurs. After the collapse of the old regime, those individuals who had access to political and social connections (typically drawn from the ranks of the *apparatchik*) were able to capitalize on the new opportunities opened up by the economic reforms. But the social capital generated in such a context is likely to be segregated to the top of the hour-glass society. The result is an increasing polarization of social capital in Russian society. Those who have access to social capital get ahead: those who do not get sick and die.

Perhaps the most worrisome trend picked up by the New Russian Barometer is that a significant portion of Russians appear to be "anticitizens," actively wanting to keep the center of the hour-glass as narrow as possible in order to limit what the state can do to them (Rose, 1995). Unfortunately, as our study found, distrust in government is likely to translate into poorer voter turnout and disinterest in politics. In turn, a disengaged electorate is unlikely to give rise to good governance. Ultimately, the price that citizens will pay (and we argue, have already paid) will be in the form of the human toll of ill-health and diminished quality of life.

NOTES

1. The sample selection procedure is described in detail in Metodologia (1993) and Kozerenko (1994).

2. Each region's subsistence income level is calculated monthly, and reflects the income needed to purchase a minimal basket of goods in each region.

3. We also disaggregated the survey responses by gender (for example, trust in government) and used these to predict gender specific mortality rates. The results of these analyses suggested that there was little difference between using overall and gender specific responses. In addition, we also reran the analyses using White-corrected standard errors to adjusted for the possibility of heteroskedastic errors across regions. These analyses also indicated little change, suggesting that our initial models were robust.

4. For example, the partial correlation coefficient (after adjusting for age) for 1980 crude death rates and trust in local government was 0.33, $P<0.05$. The partial correlation with the 1994 crime rate was surprisingly strong ($r = 0.54$, $P<0.0003$).

REFERENCES

Brainerd, E. (1996) Death and the market. In *Distributional Consequences of Economic Reform in Russia and Eastern Europe*. Ph.D. dissertation, Department of Economics, Harvard University, Cambridge, MA.

Brehm, J. and Rahn, W. (1997) Individual-level evidence for the causes and consequences of social capital. *American Journal of Political Science* 41,(3),999–1023.

Bruhn, J. G. and Wolf, S. (1979) *The Roseto Story*. University of Oklahoma Press, Norman, OK.

Chen, L. C., Witgenstein, F. and McKeon, E. (1996) The upsurge of mortality in Russia: causes and policy implications. *Population and Development Review* 22, 517–530.

Coleman, J. S. (1988) Social capital in the creation of human capital. *American Journal of Sociology* 94,(Supplement),S95–S120

Coleman, J. S. (1990) *Foundations of Social Theory*. Harvard University Press, Cambridge, MA.

Durkheim, E. (1897) (reprinted 1951). *Suicide*. Transl. J. A. Spaulding. The Free Press, New York.

Egolf, B., Lasker, J., Wolf, S. and Potvin, L. (1992) The Roseto effect: a 50-year comparison of mortality rates. *American Journal of Public Health* 82, 1089–1093.

Goskomstat (1994) *Chislennost' naseleniya rosskiiskoi federatsii (Population of the Russian Federation)*. Goskomstat, Moscow.

Goskomstat (1995) *Trud i zanyatost' v rossii (Labor and employment in Russia)*. Goskomstat, Moscow.

Goskomstat (1996a) *Demograficheskii ezhegodnik rossii (The Demographic Yearbook of Russia)*. Goskomstat, Moscow.

Goskomstat (1996b) *Rossiiskii statisticheskii ezhegodnik (Russian Statistical Yearbook)*. Goskomstat, Moscow.

House, J. S., Landis, K. R. and Umberson D. (1988) Social relationships and health. *Science* 214. 540–545.

Kawachi, I. and Kennedy, B. P. (1997) Health and social cohesion: Why care about income inequality? *British Medical Journal* 314, 1037–1040.

Kawachi, I., Kennedy, B. P. and Lochner, K. (1997) Long live community. Social capital as public health. The American Prospect. November/December. 56–59.

Kawachi, I., Kennedy, B. P., Lochner, K. and Prothrow-Stith, D. (1997) Social capital, income inequality, and mortality. *American Journal of Public Health* 87, 1491–1498.

Kawachi, I., Colditz, G. A., Ascherio, A., Rimm, E. B., Giovannucci, E., Stampfer, M. J. *et al.* (1996) A prospective study of social networks in relation to total mortality and cardiovascular disease in men in the US. *Journal of Epidemiology and Community Health* 50, 245–251.

Kozerenko, E. V. (1994) Metoducheskiye problemy monitoringa. (Methodological problems of monitoring), in VTsIOM and InterCentre (Vse-rossiskii tsentr izucheniya obshchestvennogo mneniya and Mezhdistsiplinarnyi adakemicheskii tsentr sotsial'nykh nauk). *Ekonomicheskiye i sotsial'nye peremeny: monitoring obshchestvennogo mneniya (Economic and social changes: monitoring of public opinion)* 5, 50–52.

Leon, D. A., Chenet, L., Shkolnikov, V. M., Zakharov, S., Shapiro, J., Rakhmanova, G., Vassin, S. and McKee, M. (1997) Huge variation in Russian mortality rates 1984–94: Artefact, alcohol, or what? *Lancet* 350, 383–388.

Metodologia (Methodology) (1993) in VTsIOM and Inter-Centre (Vse-rossiiskii tsentr izucheniya obshchestven-nogo mneniya and Mezhdistsiplinarnyi adakemicheskii tsentr sotsial'nykh nauk). *Ekonomicheskiye i sotsial'nye peremeny: monitoring obshchestvennogo mneniya (Economic and social changes: monitoring of public opinion)* 1, 3–10.

Putnam, R. D. (1993) *Making Democracy Work. Civic Traditions in Modern Italy.* Princeton University Press, Princeton, NJ.

Putnam, R. D. (1995) Bowling alone: America's declining social capital. *Journal of Democracy* 6, 65–78.

Rose, R. (1995) Russia as an hour-glass society: A constitution without citizens. *East European Constitutional Review* 4(3), 34–42.

Rose, R., Mishler, W. and Haerfer, C. (1996) "Getting real": Social capital in post-Communist societies. Paper presented to the Society for Comparative Research Conference on "The Erosion of Confidence in Advanced Democracies," Brussels, November 7–9.

Shkolnikov, V., Mesle, F. and Vallin, J. (1995) Health crisis in Russia: I. Recent trends in life expectancy and causes of death from 1970 to 1993. *Population* 4–5, 907–944.

Sampson, R. J., Raudenbush, S. W. and Earls, F. (1997) Neighborhoods and violent crime: A multi-level study of collective efficacy. *Science* 277, 918–924.

Smith, C. and Freedman, A. (1972) *Voluntary Associations. Perspectives on the Literature.* Harvard University Press, Cambridge, MA.

United Nations Development Programme (UNDP) (1996) *Human Development Report, 1996.* Oxford University Press, New York.

Watson, P. (1995) Explaining rising mortality among men in Eastern Europe. *Social Science and Medicine* 41, 923–934.

Wilkinson, R. G. (1996) *Unhealthy Societies. The Afflictions of Inequality.* Routledge, London.

Wilkinson, R. G., Kawachi, I. and Kennedy, B. P. (1998) Mortality, the social environment, crime and violence. *Sociology of Health and Illness*, ed. M. Bartley, Special issue.

APPENDIX A: ABBREVIATIONS TO TABLES 1–3

	Variable descriptions
Dependent variables	
MLIFEX94	Male life expectancy at birth, 1994
FLIFEX94	Female life expectancy at birth, 1994
MDTH94	Standardized death rate per 100 000 population, men
MNEO94	Standardized death rate per 100 000 population due to neoplasms, men
MCIRC94	Standardized death rate per 100 000 population due to diseases of the circulatory system, men
MEXT94	Standardized death rate per 100 000 population due to accidents, poisoning and injuries, men
FDTH94	Standardized death rate per 100 000 population, women
FNEO94	Standardized death rate per 100 000 population due to neoplasms, women
FCIRC94	Standardized death rate per 100 000 population due to diseases of the circulatory system, women
FEXT94	Standardized death rate per 100 000 population due to accidents, poisoning and injuries, women
Independent variables	
LNINC94	Log of nominal income per capita, thousand rubles, 1994
POV94	Percent of population with incomes below the region subsistence minimum, 1994
UNEMP94	Unemployment rate, 1994
DIVCRD94	Divorce rate per 1 000 population, 1994
CRIME94	Number of registered crimes per 100 000 population, 1994
ECONSITB45	Percent responding that "the economic situation in your city or region?" was poor or very poor.
EXPPOL7	Percent responding that "I'm not at all interested in politics."
RELWORK3	Percent responding that ". . . the relations between people at . . . work are strained, with conflicts"
TRUSTGV3	Percent responding that "The Government of Russia . . . is not at all deserving of trust . . ."
TRUSTRG3	Percent responding that "The regional (state) organs of power . . . are not at all deserving of trust . . ."
TRUSTLC3	Percent responding that "The city or local organs of power . . . are not at all deserving of trust . . ."
VOTED2	Percent that didn't vote in last election

Table A1: SURVEY DATA BY REGION

Region number	Region	Number of survey respondents
1	Arkhangelskaya	232
3	Vologodskaya	63
5	Karelia	122
7	Leningradskaya obl.	170
8	St Petersburg	291
9	Pskovskaya	50
11	Vladmirskaya	311
12	Ivanovskaya	291
16	Moskovskaya	508
17	City of Moscow	560
19	Smolenskaya[a]	140
22	Nizhegorodskaya	276
23	Kirovskaya	51
26	Chuvash	183
28	Belgorodskaya	213
30	Voronezhskaya	259
34	Lipetskaya	247
35	Samarskaya	111
36	Penzenskaya	402
39	Saratovskaya	239
40	Tatarstan	222
41	Krasnodarsky krai	148
42	Rep. of Adygeya	251
43	Stavropol'skii krai	174
44	Karachaevo-Cherk.	207
51	Rostovskaya	410
52	Permskaya[a]	31
54	Sverdlovskaya	142
55	Chelyabinskaya[a]	125
56	Rep. of Bashkortosta	220
57	Udmurtskaya	212
58	Altaiskii krai	74
59	Gorny Altai Rep.	174
60	Kemerovskaya	435
66	Novosibirskaya	356
67	Krasnoyarskii krai	111
70	Khakassiya rep.[a]	43
76	Primorsky krai	39
77	Khabarovskii krai	242
79	Amurskaya obl.	74

[a]Data for the variables: EXPPOL7, VOTED2 and RELWORK3 were missing for these regions.

TABLE A2: REPRESENTATIVES OF SURVEY DATA

	VTsIOM survey survey data, Apr–Jun 1994	Official data, 1994
Sex (%) (population age 20–69)		
Men	40.1	46.4
Women	59.9	53.6
Age (%) (population age 15–72)		
15–19	3.3	3.5
20–24	9.4	9.9
25–29	11.7	9.8
30–49	60.0	58.2
50–54	7.4	7.7
55–59	5.8	7.4
60–72	2.4	3.5
Education (economically active population, age 16–72)		
Higher	24.4	17.5
Incomplete higher	2.8	1.7
Specialized secondary	30.8	32.0
Secondary	30.6	32.7
Incomplete secondary	9.8	13.8
Primary or less	1.6	2.3
Major region, all population (%)		
North	4.7	4.1
Northwest	5.8	5.5
Central (excluding Moscow)	14.1	14.4
Volga-Vyatsky	5.8	5.7
Central Chernozem	5.3	5.3
Povolzhsky	11.4	11.3
North Caucuses	11.3	11.8
Urals	14.6	13.8
Western Siberia	9.8	10.2
Eastern Siberia	5.8	6.2
Far East	5.0	5.2
Moscow City	6.3	5.9

Sources of official data: Goskomstat (1994) *Chislennost' naseleniya rosskiiskoi federatsii (Population of the Russian Federation)*, Moscow; Goskomstat (1995) *Trud i zanyatost' v rossii (Labor and employment in Russia)*, Moscow.

Twenty-Six

POVERTY, INCOME INEQUALITY, AND VIOLENT CRIME: A META-ANALYSIS OF RECENT AGGREGATE DATA STUDIES

Ching-Chi Hsieh and M. D. Pugh

In the late 1970s and early 1980s, several important reviews of the literature failed to establish a clear consensus on the relationship between economic conditions and violent crime. The research presented here applies the procedures of meta-analysis to 34 aggregate data studies reporting on violent crime, poverty, and income inequality. These studies reported a total of 76 zero-order correlation coefficients for all measures of violent crime with either poverty or income inequality. Of the 76 coefficients, all but 2, or 97 percent, were positive. Of the positive coefficients, nearly 80 percent were of at least moderate strength (>.25). It is concluded that poverty and income inequality are each associated with violent crime. The analysis, however, shows considerable variation in the estimated size of the relationships and suggests that homicide and assault may be more closely associated with poverty or income inequality than are rape and robbery.

SINCE 1980 a large body of research has been published on poverty, income inequality, and violent crime (assault, homicide, rape, and robbery). Some of these publications are largely or exclusively theoretical (Currie, 1985; Tittle, 1983), but the majority are empirical studies, and with a few important exceptions (Elliot & Huizinga, 1983) many of these recent works make use of cross-sectional, aggregate data at the national or subnational level of analysis. Today, there is a growing consensus that resource deprivation in general is an underlying cause of violent crime (Land, McCall, & Cohen, 1990; Messner & Golden, 1992) and that resource deprivation is especially associated with assault and homicide (McCall, Land, & Cohen, 1992). Assuming that poverty and income inequality are each an indicator of resource deprivation, a review of the previous research using the methods of meta-analysis should show evidence that poverty and income inequality are each correlated with violent crime and that these correlations are especially robust with respect to assault and homicide. Meta-analysis is intended as a way of establishing such basic facts, from which theories

Originally published in *Criminal Justice Review*, 1993.

can be built (Hunter & Schmidt, 1990; Wells & Rankin, 1991).

THEORETICAL ISSUES IN THE RECENT LITERATURE

IN the late 1970s and early 1980s, a number of important literature reviews cataloged a variety of studies on crime and economic conditions and all too frequently could not reach a clear conclusion on the existence of even the most simple bivariate associations (Box, 1987; Braithwaite & Braithwaite, 1980; Chiricos, 1987; Clelland & Carter, 1980; Elliott & Ageton, 1980; Tittle, Villemez, & Smith, 1978). We believe that what has been described as the "chaotic state" of this literature (Simpson, 1985) reflects major difficulties in making inferences from a body of empirical research that incorporates so many important conceptual and methodological variations, variations that may account for significant differences in findings. For example, Brownfield (1986) has concluded that the strength of the relationship between violent crime and economic indicators of social class depends primarily on the measure of class being used.

Previous reviews in this general area of research have necessarily distinguished between studies based on cross-sectional data and those based on longitudinal data. Lieberson (1985, pp. 179–183) has argued that such distinctions are important because the dynamic processes at work in longitudinal data may be obscured in cross-sectional studies. Similarly, the processes that account for relationships at the individual level of analysis may not be synonymous with those that operate at the level of aggregate data. In this regard, it is somewhat surprising that the conceptual linkages between either poverty or income inequality and violent crime rates in aggregate units (census tracts, neighborhoods, cities, metropolitan areas, states, or nations) are often assumed rather than explicitly described. Williams and Flewelling (1988), for example, have recently commented that investigators have

rarely explained in detail why variations in resource deprivation should be positively associated with variations in homicide rates across aggregate units (p. 423).

Ever since the work of Quetelet (1842), and despite recent challenges (Cantor & Land, 1985; Parker & Horwitz, 1986; Wilson & Herrnstein, 1985), it seems to be an accepted tenet of criminology that economic conditions (unemployment rates, income inequality, poverty rates) are associated with crime rates (Quinney & Wildeman, 1991). Furthermore, even in those studies where the conceptual linkages between either poverty or income inequality and violent crime in aggregate units are described rather than assumed, investigators have paid relatively little or no attention to important distinctions between the microanalytic and macroanalytic levels of explanation (Huber, 1991; Liska, 1990; Ritzer & Gindoff, 1992). With these distinctions in mind, why should poverty and income inequality be associated with violent crime rates in aggregate sampling units such as neighborhoods, cities, states, or nations?

Poverty and Violent Crime

Studies using subnational sampling units (census tracts, neighborhoods, cities, standard metropolitan statistical areas [SMSAs], and states) within the United States generally measure absolute poverty as the percentage of the population below poverty thresholds defined by the Social Security Administration and adopted by the U.S. Bureau of the Census.[1] In Lazarsfeld and Menzel's scheme for describing the properties of social collectivities or groups (1965), poverty is an "aggregate" variable, and the micro-macro linkage follows a simple rule of statistical aggregation (percentaging) similar to finding the mean income of a group. In this instance, explanations of "within group variation in micro actions" and "between group variation of macro aggregates" can be conceptually similar (Liska, 1990, p. 297). This is exactly the case for one of the most common explanations of the connection between poverty and violent crime: resource deprivation.

The typical argument (Arthur, 1991; Crutchfield, 1989; Messner, 1983b) is that resource deprivation or "material disadvantage" causes frustration, which in turn can result in diffuse hostility and violent aggression.[2] So, at the micro level, homicides are explained as an individual's reaction to resource deprivation, subsequent personal frustration, and diffuse hostility directed against targets of opportunity. At the macro level, between-group differences in homicide rates are explained, at least in part, by differences in group composition (that is, by differences in the percentage of poor across aggregate units).

Although resource deprivation, treated in this way, is a leading explanation of the connection between rates of poverty and violent crime in aggregate units, it is important to emphasize that it is just one of several possible explanations. Various subcultural explanations (Cohen, 1955; Miller, 1958; Wolfgang, 1967) do not explain variations in crime rates across aggregate units in terms of individual poverty as we have done. In Miller's theory, for example, delinquency is interpreted not in terms of individual poverty but in terms of a shared subculture of violence. Poverty and urban slums are conducive to subcultures valuing toughness, excitement, and fatalism, and these subcultural values supposedly bring young people into conflict with the police (Blau & Blau, 1982, p. 118). In Shaw and McKay's work (1942), an area's poor economic conditions are not interpreted in terms of individual poverty but rather are seen as contributing to social disorganization, low social cohesion, and the decreased effectiveness of social control.

We stress that these alternative explanations all provide rationales for finding a correlation between poverty and violent crime, but we believe that the typical argument relying on frustration and diffuse hostility directed against targets of opportunity may apply better to homicide and assault than to rape and robbery. Homicide and

assault are frequently associated spontaneous acts of rage and are often directed against known victims. Whether our speculation is valid or not, there is certainly substantial variation in the types of violent crime being measured in the current research literature.

Variation in Types of Violent Crimes

At the level of aggregate data, a substantial majority of all recent studies of violent crime rely on reported offense rates for assault, homicide, rape, or robbery as published in the Federal Bureau of Investigation's *Uniform Crime Reports* or, in the case of cross-national studies, in the yearly editions of INTERPOL's *International Crime Statistics*. This approach is certainly consistent with Braithwaite's assertion that "crime is not a unidimensional construct" and his warning that we "should not be overly optimistic about a general theory which sets out to explain all types of crime" (Braithwaite, 1989, p. 1). But we note that a number of studies published in recent years have employed variously defined global indices of violent crime (Arthur, 1991; Baron & Straus, 1988; Blau & Blau, 1982; Carroll & Jackson, 1983; Crutchfield, 1989; Hartnagel & Lee, 1990; Lieberman & Smith, 1986; Mladenka & Hill, 1976; Patterson, 1991). Nevertheless, global indices are problematic because they may obscure important differences in the strength of relationships between different types of violent crime and poverty or income inequality. On the other hand, global indices of violent crime may offer the advantage of yielding more consistent estimates of association to the extent that they minimize the effects of random variation in specific offense rates.

Income Inequality and Violent Crime

The explanation of the linkage between income inequality and violent crime differs from the preceding explanation because income inequality is not an "aggregate" variable in the same sense as poverty. Again using the traditional nomenclature of Lazarsfeld and Menzel (1965), income inequality is a structural variable. Structural variables refer to relationships between individuals in a group and therefore to such things as the distribution of power and income within an aggregate unit. In both national and subnational studies of violent crime the Gini index, however imperfect it may be, has become a nearly standard measure of income inequality.[3] The Gini index is a measure of income concentration developed independently by the American Max Lorenz and the Italian Corrado Gini (Bronfenbrenner, 1971). The Gini index ranges from "0" indicating perfect equality (where all persons have equal shares of aggregate income) to "1" indicating perfect inequality (where one person has all income and the rest have none).

The Gini index characterizes the distribution of income within a social unit or group of people and therefore has no analogue at the individual level of analysis. In such cases, making the linkage between individual action or agency and group structure requires the assumption of a relational, social process (Ritzer & Gindoff, 1992; Zelditch, 1991). What is needed is a construct linking variations in the subjective states and motives of actors to variations in their locations within a social structure. In this respect, Nettler (1984) has observed that "the principal interpretation given for the association between inequality and violent crime has focused on the process of relative deprivation as a stimulant to hostility" (p. 229). Although relative deprivation is experienced by individuals as a subjective state similar to absolute deprivation and may in fact be empirically indistinguishable from absolute deprivation in its effects on violent crime, it results from a process of social comparison. Furthermore, in making social comparisons, we have long recognized that a "critical contingency" is the actor's selection of a frame of reference (Messner & Tardiff, 1986, p. 300). Frames of reference indicate how people locate themselves within a structure or system. The recent literature on income inequality and violent crime

includes considerable discussion of what constitutes an appropriate frame of reference for the experience of relative deprivation.

Variation in the Size of Aggregate Sampling Units
Whereas many researchers have chosen to use states and nations as their sampling units, others have argued for increasingly smaller frames of reference and the use of correspondingly smaller aggregate sampling units. In the early 1980s, for example, Messner suggested that standard metropolitan statistical areas are a better sampling unit than states because SMSAs are more "meaningful aggregations than are states." Messner argued that states are "arbitrary statistical aggregations" and suggested that the boundaries of SMSAs are more likely to coincide with those of "genuine social communities" (Messner, 1982a, p. 106). Bailey (1984) has subsequently argued that SMSAs, in turn, are too large because they can mask important differences between central cities and their suburban or outlying areas (pp. 534–535). Bailey therefore recommended cities as an appropriate sampling unit. More recently, however, Messner and Tardiff (1986, pp. 298–299) have suggested that an even smaller unit of analysis such as residential and commercial neighborhoods should be used. They have argued that people experience relative deprivation as a result of gaining knowledge of income differences through direct experience with other members of a local community. This argument makes local communities theoretically more appropriate than states or nations as sampling units.

Nonetheless, it can also be argued that the mass media have made people aware of the full range of income differences across an entire nation and that people will react to perceived differences in comparison to "national norms" rather than to the frequently smaller income differences that they actually experience within their own local neighborhoods. In fact, Patterson's recent study (1991) concluded that the "theoretical utility" of income inequality would seem to be "more appropriate for larger units of aggregation, such as regions of country or nations themselves" (p. 771). Whether this argument over the appropriate type of population aggregate to employ in macro-level research on crime has any actual bearing on the distribution of effect parameters estimated in the existing literature can be evaluated using the methods of meta-analysis.

META-ANALYSIS
OF AGGREGATE DATA STUDIES

META-ANALYSIS is a method of statistically combining the results of independent studies using inferential statistics. It is a quantitative evaluation of an empirical body of research, as opposed to the traditional literature review that uses qualitative techniques to integrate the results of previous studies. Our first objective was to assess the size of the relationships between poverty and violent crime and between income inequality and violent crime. The principal null hypothesis was that neither poverty nor income inequality is associated with violent crime. Although meta-analysis provides procedures for estimating combined effect sizes (Hunter & Schmidt, 1990; Mullen, 1989; Mullen & Rosenthal, 1985; Rosenthal & Rubin, 1982), it is not intended as a way of evaluating complex causal chains or models. And it generally cannot be applied to multivariate statistics such as partial regression coefficients.[4]

Retrieval of Studies

To retrieve an initial set of studies focusing on poverty (percentage of the population below poverty level) or income inequality (the Gini index) and violent crime (assault, homicide, rape, and robbery) we used a combination of techniques. We started by searching various computer data bases *(Criminal Justice Periodical Index, National Criminal Justice Reference Service, Social Sciences Citation Index, Sociological Ab-*

stracts) and SOCIOFILE, a computerized reference index of about 1,600 journals from more than 50 countries. We then supplemented our computer searches with an "ancestry approach" (Mullen, 1989), which uses the bibliographies of previous reviews (Land et al., 1990; Patterson, 1991) to locate additional studies published at an earlier time.[5]

Although we make no claim that the results of our search are exhaustive, 53 aggregate data studies reporting on poverty, income inequality, and violent crime were located using the procedures just described. Not all of these studies were amenable to the methods of meta-analysis. Meta-analysis assumes that the findings of many studies can be expressed in terms of common statistics and metrics. Meta-analysis also treats the findings of previous studies as independent data points. A lack of common statistics, any lack of statistical independence, or a lack of common metrics is therefore an important preliminary consideration.

Criteria for Including Studies

We selected the correlation coefficient r as our common measure of effect size. This statistic is frequently used in meta-analysis because it is widely recognized and has a known statistical distribution, and because there are formulas for converting t, F, chi-square, p, and Z into values of r (Mullen & Rosenthal, 1985, p. 134). We therefore expected this decision to optimize the number of studies we could retain for our analysis. Nonetheless, three of the studies we located were not included in our analysis because estimates of r were not reported and were not otherwise available (Crutchfield, Geerken, & Gove, 1982; Devine, Sheley, & Smith, 1988; Williams, 1984).

We were also unable to include all of the studies—Blau & Blau, 1982; Blau & Golden, 1986; DeFronzo, 1983; Messner, 1982a, 1983a; Rosenfeld, 1986; and Simpson, 1985—that appeared to have used overlapping samples of

SMSAs for a single census year, 1970. Although there may be sound theoretical justifications for studies using various subsets of SMSAs, the overlapping of samples created by pooling these studies would pose a problem in that the statistical procedures of meta-analysis assume the complete independence of the findings under review (Mullen & Rosenthal, 1985, p. 20). Because the study by Blau and Blau (1982) is seminal in this area of research, we have used only their estimates of association for further analysis.[6]

In summary, 3 studies for which our common statistic *r* was not available were excluded from our analysis. Another 5 studies were not included in our analysis because they used overlapping samples of data from the same year. In addition, 11 studies that did not use reported offense rates as their measures of violent crime were also excluded. The outcome variables in these 11 studies were defined as arrest rates (Liska & Chamlin, 1984; Sampson, 1985a, 1985b; Williams & Drake, 1980), victimization rates (Messner & South, 1986; Patterson, 1991; Sampson & Castellano, 1982), sentencing practices (Myers, 1987), delinquency referrals (Chilton, 1964), canonical vectors (Harries, 1976), and even police violence (Jacobs & Britt, 1979). Our review was limited to aggregate data studies of violent crime as indicated by reported offense rates for assault, homicide, rape, and robbery and to global indices of violent crime based on reported offense rates. These problems in standardizing the results of

previous research reduced our initial set of 53 studies to a final pool of 34 studies.

RESULTS

A CURSORY inspection of the 34 studies included in our meta-analysis reveals considerable variation in their design or study characteristics (see Table 1). Column 1 indicates that 30 of the 34 studies (88%) were published in 1980 or thereafter. However, column 2, which shows the year of data collection, indicates that only 10 of the reviewed studies (30%) made use of any data collected as recently as 1980. Columns 3 and 4 indicate the independent and dependent variables employed in each of the reviewed studies. Here it is apparent that the great majority of the studies we found distinguished between different types of violent crime. This practice may derive from the premise that crime is not a unidimensional construct (Braithwaite, 1989, p. 1). It is also noteworthy that the type of sampling unit employed by these studies (column 5) varied in size from neighborhoods and census tracks to states and nations. This feature of the pooled studies almost certainly reflects the availability of data at varying levels of aggregation as much as theoretical differences regarding the appropriate size of aggregate sampling units. Sample size (*N*) varied from 13 to 408 aggregate sampling units (column 6). The correlation coefficients reported by each of the reviewed studies are shown in column 7.

Table 1

Summary of Studies in Meta-Analysis of Income Inequality, Poverty, and Violent Crime

(1) Study reference	(2) Year (data)	(3) Independ. var.	(4) Depend. var.	(5) Sample unit	(6) Sample size	(7) Corr. coef. (*r*)
Arthur	(1991)	1975	Poverty	V. crime	Counties	13	.37
		1980	Poverty	V. crime			.31
		1985	Poverty	V. crime			.41

Table 1 (continued)

Summary of Studies in Meta-Analysis of Income Inequality, Poverty, and Violent Crime

(1) Study reference		(2) Year (data)	(3) Independ. var.	(4) Depend. var.	(5) Sample unit	(6) Sample size	(7) Corr. coef. (r)
Avison & Loring	(1986)	1975 1967– 1971	Gini	Homicide	Nations	32	.62
Baily	(1984)	1950	Gini	Homicide	Cities	153	.53
		1960	Gini	Homicide	Cities	153	.56
		1970	Gini	Homicide	Cities	153	.47
Balkwell	(1990)	1979– 1982	Poverty Gini	Homicide Homicide	SMSAs	150	.65 .73
Baron & Straus	(1988)	1979– 1980	Poverty Poverty Gini Gini	Homicide V. crime Homicide V. crime	States	50	.43 .35 .53 .28
Blau & Blau	(1982)	1970	Poverty Poverty Poverty Poverty Poverty Gini Gini Gini Gini Gini	V. crime Assault Homicide Rape Robbery Assault Homicide Rape Robbery V. Crime	SMSAs	125	.30 .45 .49 .29 .05 .55 .63 .34 .28 .47
Carroll & Jackson	(1983)	1970	Gini Gini	Robbery V. Crime	Cities	93	.29 .30
Critchfield	(1989)	1979– 1981	Poverty Poverty Poverty Poverty Poverty	Assault Rape Robbery V. crime Homicide	Seattle census tracks	121	.62 .55 .56 .60 .47
Groves et al.	(1985)	1974	Gini	Homicide	Nations	50	.13
Hansmann & Quigley	(1982)	NA	Gini	Homicide	Nations	40	.41
Hartnagael & Lee	(1990)	1971 1976– 1977	Gini	V. crime	Cities	88	.31
Huff-Corzine, Corzine, & Moore	(1986)	1969– 1971	Gini	Homicide	States	50	.65

Table 1 (continued)

Summary of Studies in Meta-Analysis of Income Inequality, Poverty, and Violent Crime

(1) Study reference		(2) Year (data)	(3) Independ. var.	(4) Depend. var.	(5) Sample unit	(6) Sample size	(7) Corr. coef. (*r*)
Jackson	(1984)	1970	Poverty	Assault	Cities	408	.32
			Poverty	Homicide			.51
			Poverty	Rape			.18
			Poverty	Robbery			.11
			Poverty	V. crime			.14
Jacobs	(1981)	1970	Poverty	Robbery	SMSAs	195	.14
			Gini	Robbery			.11
Kennedy et al.		1976	Gini	Homicide	CMAs*	24	.18
	(1991)	1981	Gini	Homicide			.09
Kick & LaFree	(1985)	1968– 1972 1976	Gini	Homicide	Nations	40	.61
Krahn et al.		1971	Gini	Homicide	Nations	47	.26
	(1986)	1975	Gini	Homicide	Nations	47	.48
Krohn	(1976)	1972	Gini	Homicide	Nations	27	.6
Lieberman &		1971	Poverty	V. crime	SMSAs	65	.53
Smith	(1986)	1972	Poverty	V. crime			.39
		1973	Poverty	V. crime			.37
		1974	Poverty	V. crime			.39
		1975	Poverty	V. crime			.32
		1976	Poverty	V. crime			.24
		1977	Poverty	V. crime			.36
		1978	Poverty	V. crime			.27
		1979	Poverty	V. crime			.02
Loftin & Hill	(1974)	1967 1959– 1961	Gini	Homicide	States	48	.74
Loftin & Parker	(1985)	1970	Gini	Homicide	Cities	49	.48
Messner	(1980)	1952– 1970	Gini	Homicide	Nations	39	.40
Messner	(1982b)	1960s	Gini	Homicide	Nations	50	.38
Messner	(1983)	1969– 1971	Gini	Homicide	Cities	91	.32
			Poverty	Homicide			.13
			Gini	Homicide		256	.30
			Poverty	Homicide			.70
			Gini	Homicide		347	.31
			Poverty	Homicide		347	.55

Table 1 (continued)

Summary of Studies in Meta-Analysis of Income Inequality, Poverty, and Violent Crime

(1) Study reference		(2) Year (data)	(3) Independ. var.	(4) Depend. var.	(5) Sample unit	(6) Sample size	(7) Corr. coef. (r)
Messner	(1989)	1975 1980	Gini	Homicide	Nations	52	.19
Messner & Tardiff	(1986)	1985 1980	Gini Poverty	Homicide Homicide	Neighborhoods in Manhattan	26	.23 .55
Mladenka & Hill	(1976)	1970-1973	Poverty	V. crime	Houston police districts	19	.93
Parker & Smith	(1979)	1970-1978	Poverty	Homicide	States	50	.75
Patterson	(1991)	1977	Gini	V. crime	Neighborhoods	57	.10
Peterson & Bailey	(1988)	1980	Poverty Gini	Rape Rape	SMSAs	246	.19 .41
Smith & Bennet	(1985)	1979-1983 1980	Poverty	Rape	SMSAs	88	.34
Smith & Parker	(1980)	1973	Gini	Homicide	States	50	.51
Watts & Watts	(1981)	1970	Poverty	V. crime	Cities	152	.30
Williams & Flewelling	(1988)	1980-1984	Poverty	Homicide	Cities	168	.77

*Canadian Metroplitan Areas

Note: Several studies used log transformations of homicide rates (Bailey, 1984; Huff-Corzine et al., 1986; Krahn et al., 1986; Messner & Tardiff, 1986). One study (Blau & Blau, 1982) used a log (base 10) transformation of robbery, and another (Jacobs, 1981) took the square root of robbery. The study by Smith and Bennet (1985) used a log (base 10) transformation of rape. Messner's original result (1982b) was negative because he used (1-Gini) as his measure of equality. Williams and Flewelling (1988) used a log (base 10) transformation of homicide and poverty; the r coefficient was obtained from the author by mail. Patterson (1991) used "% < 5000" as a poverty index. Messner and Tardiff (1986) used 75% under the poverty line as a poverty index; the four coefficients were requested over the telephone. We combined regional cities (347 cities in total) from Messner's article (1983b) and used a weighted average coefficient in the current study.

Estimating Overall Effect Sizes

Table 2 shows the distribution of the correlation coefficients (*r*) for poverty and income inequality with all measures of violent crime. Our final pool of 34 studies yielded a total of 76 correlation coefficients (*r*). The great majority of these coefficients (58 out of 76) were reported either for homicide or for global indices of violent crime. Of the 76 estimates, all but two (97%) are positive. Both of the outlying negative coefficients are quite small (-.09 and -.14). The last column of Table 2 indicates that the positive coefficients are generally moderate in size. Of the 74 positive coefficients, nearly half (49%) are between .25 and .49, and another 30 percent are greater than .50.[7]

For any set of findings, the best estimate of overall association between two variables in meta-analysis is an *N*-weighted average coeffi-

cient (Hunter & Schmidt, 1990, pp. 100–101). The *N*-weighted average coefficient allows studies with larger *N*s, and correspondingly smaller errors of estimation, to make a relatively larger contribution to the overall estimate of association. The *N*-weighted average estimate of association for poverty with all types of violent crime (assault, homicide, rape, and robbery) in the 34 studies we analyzed was .44. Coincidentally, the *N*-weighted average coefficient for income inequality with all types of violent crime was also .44. Each of these combined estimates of effect size is statistically significant from zero ($t = 9.00$, $p < .005$, and $t = 11.55$, $p < .005$, respectively).[8]

Analyzing Variance in Effect Sizes

In meta-analysis the search for covariates of effect size often begins with a regression of the ob-

---

Table 2

Preliminary Distribution of Correlation Coefficients (r) *for Poverty and Income Inequality with Violent Crime*

Poverty

Coefficient size	Assault	Homicide	Rape	Robbery	V.C. index	Totals
-.500 — -.250						
-.249 — .000				1		1
.001 — .249		1	2	2	3	8
.250 — .499	3	4	2		12	21
.500 — 1.00		6	1	1	3	11
Total	3	11	5	4	18	41

Income inequality

Coefficient size	Assault	Homicide	Rape	Robbery	V.C. index	Totals
-.500 — -.250						
-.249 — .000		1				1
.001 — .249		4		1	1	6
.250 — .499		8	2	2	4	16
.500 — 1.00	1	11				12
Total	1	24	2	3	5	35

Note: The studies by Blau and Golden (1986), DeFronzo (1983), Messner (1982a), and Simpson (1985) were not included in this table because of overlapping 1970 samples. Lieberman and Smith's coefficient for 1970 (1986) was also excluded for the same reason.

served correlation coefficients on the study characteristics of the research from which they were taken. Based on our previous discussion, the study characteristics we chose to examine as covariates of effect size included differences in types of crime (assault, homicide, rape, and robbery) and differences in the areal size of sampling units (neighborhoods, cities, metropolitan areas, states, and nations). We began our preliminary analysis with two regressions. The first was a regression of the distribution of correlation coefficients for poverty with violent crime on the type of measure (assault, homicide, rape, and robbery) and the type of sampling unit (neighborhoods, cities, SMSAs, states, and nations) as well as each study's time period (the year of data collection) and sample size (N).[9] The second was a regression of the correlation coefficients for income inequality with violent crime with the same set of study characteristics as predictor variables.

The regression of the coefficients for poverty and violent crime was significant (F = 5.61, p < .001) and produced a multiple correlation of .76 (R-square = .58). With respect to type of measure, the beta coefficients were .168 for violent crime as indicated by assault rates (t = 1.77, p < .10), .241 for violent crimes as indicated by homicide rates (t = 3.82, p < .001), .006 for rape (t = 0.07, p > .94),. and -.129 for violent crime as measured by robbery (t = -1.52, p < .14). The beta coefficient for the type of sampling unit was -.107 (t = -2.21, p < .04). For time period the beta coefficient was .009 (t = 1.49, p < .15), and for sample size it was -.001 (t = -1.98, p < .06). The regression of the correlation coefficients for income inequality and violent crime was nonsignificant. Nonetheless, we have some preliminary evidence that the observed correlation coefficients based on homicide, and perhaps assault, are larger than those based on rape or robbery and that the coefficients from studies using larger aggregate sampling units tend to be smaller in size.[10]

In meta-analysis, tests of homogeneity can be performed to see whether the findings reported in previous research vary significantly around

their N-weighted average coefficient. When the resulting chi-square value is significant, the original analysis may have combined studies that were too dissimilar in their research designs. Moderator analyses can then be performed to determine whether estimates of effect size covary with any of the design characteristics of the studies. We began this phase of our analysis by considering the variability of the observed correlation coefficients regardless of the type of violent crime being measured or the type of sampling unit being employed.

When all types of violent crime (assault, homicide, rape, and robbery) are considered as a single category, and the type of sampling unit being employed is ignored, the data for both poverty (chi-square = 293.65, df = 21, p < .001) and income inequality (chi-square = 132.01, df = 28, p < .001) clearly indicate that the variance of the reported coefficients is so great that it is unlikely to have been the result of sampling variability alone. This result is entirely consistent with the preliminary findings of our regression analyses, which suggested that the size of the observed correlations may covary with both the type of measure and the type of sampling unit being employed.

We proceeded to group the available data into subsets according to the type of violent crime being measured. The N-weighted average estimates of association could then be recalculated for the grouped data (see Table 3). Unfortunately, the small number of studies examining poverty with assault, rape, and robbery makes our conclusions extremely tentative. Only the data for poverty and homicide appear to be reasonably reliable, and the N-weighted average coefficient for that relationship is r = .58.[11] As expected from our first regression, this combined estimate of association of poverty and homicide is significantly larger than the overall coefficients based on either rape or robbery (.577 vs. .318, t = 3.66, p < .01, and .577 vs. .163, t = 3.89, p < .01).[12] We also note that the difference between the values for income inequality with homicide (r = .46) and income

Table 3

Effects of Poverty and Income Inequality by Type of Violent Crime

Poverty	Comparison of estimates			Average estimates	
	Chip-sq.	*df*	*p*-value	Size	*N*
All types	293.65	21	< .001	.44	22
Assault	14.55	2	< .001	.47	3
Homicide	39.17	9	< .001	.58	10
Rape	19.62	4	< .001	.32	5
Robbery	44.23	3	< .001	.16	4
Violent crime index	70.49	17	< .001	.40	18

Income inequality	Comparison of estimates			Average estimates	
	Chi-sq.	*df*	*p*-value	Size	*N*
All types	132.01	28	< .001	.44	29
Assault	–	–	–	–	1
Homicide	90.12	22	< .001	.46	23
Rape	.54	1	> .30	.38	2
Robbery	3.34	2	> .10	.23	3
Violent crime index	6.87	4	> .10	.30	5

Note: The studies by Blau and Golden (1986), Defronzo (1983), Messner (1982a), and Simpson (1985) were not included in this table because of overlapping 1970 samples. Lieberman and Smith's coefficient for 1970 (1986) was also excluded for the same reason. A weighted average coefficient was used for the study by Messner (1983b).

inequality with robbery (r = .23) does approach statistical significance (t = 1.84, p < .10).

Table 4 fails to reveal any clear trend after the data have been grouped by the size of aggregate sampling units. With respect to poverty and violent crime, the coefficient for neighborhoods and cities (r = .52) is significantly larger than the coefficient for counties and SMSAs (r = .32) (t = 2.968, p < .05). With respect to income inequality, however, the coefficients based on neighborhoods and cities appear to be smaller than those based on larger sampling units. The comparison for the coefficient based on neighborhoods and cities (r = .35) with the coefficient for states (r = .57) is statistically significant (t = 2.212, p < .05).

The tests of homogeneity shown in tables 3 and 4 indicate that the variability of the previ-

ously reported correlation coefficients is not accounted for even after the coefficients are grouped by either the type of crime or the type of sampling unit. Table 5 shows the available data broken into subsets according to both the type of measure and the type of sampling unit employed by the reporting studies. Although simultaneous control of both of these study characteristics does produce some sets of homogeneous estimates, the relatively small number of studies being analyzed makes any conclusions extremely tentative. With respect to poverty, only the estimates of association with global indices of violent crime from studies using SMSAs as their sampling units represent a reasonably large number of study results. But this set of estimates was indeed homogeneous (chi-square = 12.00, df = 9, p > .01),

Table 4

Effects of Income Inequality on All Types of Violent Crime by Levels of Aggregation

Poverty	Comparison of estimates			Average estimates	
	Chi-sq.	*df*	*p*-value	Effect size	N
Neighborhoods & cities	236.178	15	< .001	.521	16
Counties and SMSAs	105.177	20	< .001	.324	21
States	10.046	2	< .001	.536	3
Income inequality	Comparison of estimates			Average estimates	
	Chi-sq.	*df*	*p*-value	Effect size	N
Neighborhoods & cities	25.160	8	< .01	.353	9
Counties and SMSAs	81.887	9	< .001	.387	10
States	11.138	3	> .01	.572	4
Nations	16.473	10	> .05	.430	11
States and nations	33.660	14	< .01	.471	15

and for this set of homogeneous coefficients the N-weighted average estimate of overall association was recalculated as $r = .32$.[13]

The two sets of coefficients for income inequality and homicide based on states and nations were homogeneous, but only the set of coefficients for nations was based on a relatively large number of studies (chi-square = 15.59, $df = 9$, $p > .01$). The corresponding N-weighted average estimate of association for income inequality with homicide was .43.[14] With respect to income inequality and homicide we note that the homogeneous sets of estimates were reported by studies using states and nations as their sampling units, not by studies using smaller sampling units such as cities and SMSAs.

DISCUSSION AND CONCLUSION

UNTIL now, the procedures of meta-analysis have never been applied to aggregate data studies of violent crime, poverty, and income inequality. It is possible to do so now because many of the studies published since 1980 have used nearly standard measures of poverty and income inequality and, to a lesser extent, comparable measures of violent crime. Assuming that resource deprivation is an underlying cause of violent crime and that poverty and income inequality are both indicators of resource deprivation, we expected to find an association between poverty and violent crime as well as between income inequality and violent crime. In addition, we assumed that these zero-order relationships would be more robust with respect to assault and homicide than with respect to rape and robbery.

Although the procedures of meta-analysis are intended to address these issues, they are somewhat limiting. Only 34 of the 53 studies we originally identified met our requirements for the standardization of study results. Of the 19 studies we excluded, 11 did not use reported offense rates as their measure of violent crime, and for 3 studies we were unable to obtain estimates of the correlation coefficient, r. Five additional studies were subsequently dropped from our analysis because of their overlapping samples and consequent lack of independent findings.

Table 5

*Correlation Coefficients for Poverty and Income Inequality Grouped
by Type of Violent Crime and Levels of Aggregation*

	Comparison of estimates			Average estimates	
	Chi-sq.	*df*	*p*-value	Size	*N*
Poverty and homicide					
Neighborhoods*	.23	1	> .50	.51	2
Cities	37.94	3	< .01	.56	2
Counties	–	–	–	–	–
SMSAs	3.65	1	> .01	.57	2
States	5.97	1	> .01	.61	2
Nations	–	–	–	–	

Income inequality and homicide	Comparison of estimates			Average estimates	
	Chi-sq.	*df*	*p*-value	Size	*N*
Neighborhoods	–	–	–	–	1
Cities	14.06	3	< .01	.47	4
Counties	–	–	–	–	–
SMSAs	26.25	3	< .01	.41	4
States	4.49	3	> .01	.62	4
Nations	15.59	9	> .01	.43	10
Poverty and V.C. index					
Neighborhoods	13.13	1	< .01	.83	2
Cities	3.10	1	> .01	.22	2
Counties	.67	2	> .01	.36	3
SMSAs	12.00	9	> .01	.32	10
States	–	–	–	–	1
Nations	–	–	–	–	–

*This category includes studies using neighborhoods, census tracks, and police districts.

Our final pool of 34 aggregate data studies reported a total of 76 zero-order correlation coefficients for all measures of violent crime with poverty or income inequality. Of the 76 coefficients, all but 2, or 97 percent, were positive, and nearly 80 percent of the positive coefficients were of at least moderate strength (> .25). These results provide strong support for the general assumption that poverty and income inequality are each positively associated with violent crime. The *N*-weighted average estimate of association for poverty with all types of violent crime in the studies we analyzed was *r* = .44. The *N*-weighted average coefficient for income inequality with all types of violent crime was also $r = .44$. Each of these estimates was statistically significant.

There was, however, substantial variability in the degree of association reported for poverty, income inequality, and violent crime. Our analysis of moderator effects generally suggests that the type of crime being measured is an important consideration. The N-weighted average coefficients for poverty with assault and poverty with homicide were .47 and .58, whereas the N-weighted average coefficients for poverty with rape and poverty with robbery were .32 and .16. The N-weighted coefficient for poverty with homicide was significantly larger than either of the coefficients based on rape or robbery. A similar pattern of results was also found when using income inequality as a measure of resource deprivation. Here we noted that the difference between the N-weighted value for income inequality with homicide ($r = .46$) and income inequality with robbery ($r = .23$) did approach statistical significance.

Even after the observed correlations were broken into subsets based on the type of crime being measured and the size of aggregate sampling units, there remained substantial variability in the size of the reported correlations. Controlling for both the type of crime and the type of sampling unit being employed, however, did produce two relatively large sets of homogeneous estimates. Specifically, using homogeneous sets of estimates, we were able to recalculate an overall estimate of association for poverty with global indices of violent crime ($r = .32$) as well as for income inequality with homicide ($r = .43$). Each of these estimates was based on a set of 10 reported correlation coefficients.

On balance, the results of our review are clearly consistent with the assumptions that resource deprivation is an underlying cause of violent crime and that poverty and income inequality are both indicators of resource deprivation. Resource deprivation, as indicated by either poverty of income inequality, appears to be more closely associated with homicide and as-

sault than with robbery or rape. With respect to arguments over the appropriate size of aggregate sampling units, our preliminary regression analyses did indicate that smaller population aggregates may produce more robust correlations, but the results of our meta-analysis also suggest that it may be too soon to favor lower levels of aggregation when studying the effects of resource deprivation. We found that homogeneous estimates of association between income inequality and homicide were reported by studies using states and nations as their sampling units, but not by studies using smaller sampling units such as cities and standard metropolitan statistical areas.

REFERENCES

Arthur, J. A. (1991). Socioeconomic predictors of crime in rural Georgia. *Criminal Justice Review, 16*, 29–41.

Avison, W. R., & Loring, P. L. (1986). Population diversity and cross-national homicide: The effects of inequality and heterogeneity. *Criminology, 24*, 733–749.

Bailey, W. C. (1984). Poverty, inequality and city homicide rates. *Criminology, 22*, 531–550.

Balkwell, J. W. (1990). Ethnic inequality and the rate of homicide. *Social Forces, 69*(1), 53–70.

Baron, L., & Straus, M. A. (1988). Cultural and economic sources of homicide in the United States. *The Sociological Quarterly, 29*(3), 371–390.

Bennett, R. R. (1991). Development and crime: A cross-national, time-series analysis of competing models. *The Sociological Quarterly, 32*(3), 343–363.

Blau, J. R., & Blau, P. M. (1982). The cost of inequality: Metropolitan structure and violent crime. *American Sociological Review, 47*, 114–129.

Blau, P. M., & Golden, R. M. (1986). Metropolitan structure and violence. *The Sociological Quarterly, 27*, 15–26.

Box, S. (1987). *Recession, crime and punishment.* Totowa, NJ: Barnes & Noble.

Braithwaite, J. (1989). *Crime, shame, and reintegration.* Cambridge, MA: Cambridge University Press.

Braithwaite, J., & Braithwaite, V. (1980). The effect of income inequality and social democracy on homicide. *British Journal of Criminology, 20*, 45–53.

Brofenbrenner, M. (1971). *Distribution theory.* New York, NY: Aldine-Atherton.

Brownfield, D. (1986). Social and violent behavior. *Criminology, 24,* 421–438.

Cantor, D., & Land, K. (1985). Unemployment and crime rates in the post-World War II U.S.A.: A theoretical and empirical analysis. *American Sociological Review, 50,* 317–332.

Carroll, L., & Jackson, P. I. (1983). Inequality, opportunity, and crime rates in central cities. *Criminology, 21,* 178–194.

Chilton, R. J. (1964). Continuities in delinquency area research: A comparison of studies for Baltimore, Detroit, and Indianapolis. *American Sociological Review, 29,* 71–83.

Chiricos, T. G. (1987). Rates of crime and unemployment: An analysis of aggregate research evidence. *Social Problems, 34,* 187–212.

Clelland, D., & Carter, T. J. (1980). The new myth of class and crime. *Criminology, 18,* 319–336.

Cohen, A. K. (1955). *Delinquent boys.* Glencoe, IL: Free Press.

Crutchfield, R. D. (1989). Labor stratification and violent crime. *Social Forces, 68*(2), 489–512.

Crutchfield, R. D., Geerken, M. R., & Gove, W. R. (1982). Crime rate and social integration. *Criminology, 20,* 467–478.

Currie, E. (1985). *Confronting crime.* New York, NY: Pantheon Books.

DeFronzo, J. (1983). Economic assistance to impoverished Americans. *Criminology, 21,* 119–136.

Devine, J. A., Sheley, J. F., & Smith, M. D. (1988). Macroeconomic and social-control policy influences on crime rate changes, 1948–1985. *American Sociological Review, 53,* 407–420.

Elliott, D. S., & Ageton, S. (1980). Reconciling race and class differences in self-reported and official estimates of delinquency. *American Sociological Review, 45,* 95.

Elliott, D. S., & Huizinga, D. (1978). Economic factors in crime and delinquency: A critical review of the empirical evidence. In House of Representatives, *Unemployment and crime: Hearings before the Subcommittee on Crime of the Committee on the Judiciary* (pp. 601–626). Washington, DC: U.S. Government Printing Office.

Elliott, D. S., & Huizinga, D. (1983). Social class and delinquent behavior in a national youth panel, 1976–1980. *Criminology, 21,* 149–177.

Engels, F. (1968). *The conditions of the working class in England,* Stanford, CA: Stanford University Press.

Engels, F. (1968). *The conditions of the working class in England.* Stanford, CA: Stanford University Press.

Groves, W. B., McCleary, R., & Newman, G. R. (1985). Religion, modernization, and world crime. *Comparative Social Research, 8,* 59–78.

Hansmann, H. B., & Quigley, J. M. (1982). Population heterogeneity and the sociogenesis of homicide. *Social Forces, 61,* 206–224.

Harries, K. D. (1976). Cities and crime: A geographic model. *Criminology, 14,* 369–386.

Hartnagel, T. F., & Lee, G. W. (1990, October). Urban crime in Canada. *Canadian Journal of Criminology, 32,* 591–606.

Huber, J. (1991). *Macro-micro linkages in sociology.* Newbury Park, CA: Sage Publications, Inc.

Huff-Corzine, L., Corzine, J., & Moore, D. C. (1986). Southern exposure: Deciphering the South's influence on homicide rates. *Social Forces, 64,* 906–924.

Hunter, J. E., & Schmidt, F. L. (1990). *Methods of meta-analysis.* Newbury Park, CA: Sage Publications.

Hyde, J. S., & Linn, M. C. (1986). *The psychology of gender: Advances through meta-analysis.* Baltimore, MD: Johns Hopkins University Press.

Jackson, P. I. (1984). Opportunity and crime: A function of city size. *Sociology and Social Research, 68,* 172–193.

Jacobs, D. (1981). Inequality and economic crime. *Sociology and Social Research, 66,* 12–28.

Jacobs, D., & Britt, D. (1979). Inequality and police use of deadly force: An empirical assessment of a conflict hypothesis. *Social Problems, 26*(4), 403–412.

Kennedy, L. W., Silverman, R. A. & Forde, D. R. (1991). Homicide in urban Canada: Testing the impact of economic inequality and social disorganization. *Canadian Journal of Sociology, 16*(4), 397–410.

Kick, E. L., & LaFree, G. D. (1985). Development and the social context of murder and theft. *Comparative Social Research, 8,* 37–58.

Krahn, H., Hartnagel, T. F., & Gartrell, J. W. (1986). Income inequality and homicide rates: Cross-national data and criminological theories. *Criminology, 24,* 269–295.

Krohn, M. D. (1976). Inequality, unemployment and crime: A cross-national analysis. *The Sociological Quarterly, 17,* 303–313.

Land, K. C., McCall, P. L., & Cohen, L. E. (1990). Structural covariates of homicide rates: Are there any invariances across time and social space? *American Journal of Sociology, 95,* 922–963.

Lazarsfeld, P., & Menzel, H. (1965). On the relations between individual and collective properties. In A. Etzioni (Ed.), *Complex organizations: A sociological reader* (pp. 422–440). New York, NY: Holt, Rinehart and Winston.

Lieberman, L., & Smith, A. B. (1986). Crime rates and poverty—A reexamination. *Crime and Social Justice, 25,* 166–177.

Lieberson, S. (1985). *Making it count: The improvement of social research and theory.* Berkeley, CA: University of California Press.

Liska, A. (1990). The significance of aggregate dependent variables and contextual independent variables for linking macro and micro theories. *Social Psychology Quarterly, 53,* 292–301.

Liska, A. E., & Chamlin, M. B. (1984). Social structure and crime control among macrosocial units. *American Journal of Sociology, 90,* 383–395.

Loftin, C., & Hill, R. H. (1974). Regional subculture and homicide: An examination of the Gastil-Hackney thesis. *American Sociological Review, 39,* 714–724.

Loftin, C., & Parker, R. N. (1985). An errors-in-variable model of the effect of poverty on urban homicide rates. *Criminology, 23,* 269–287.

McCall, P. L., Land, K. C., & Cohen, L. E. (1992). Violent criminal behavior: Is there a general and continuing influence of the South? *Social Science Research, 21,* 286–310.

Messner, S. F. (1980). Income inequality and murder rates: Some cross-national findings. *Comparative Social Research, 3,* 185–198.

Messner, S. F. (1982a). Poverty, inequality, and the urban homicide rate. *Criminology, 20,* 103–114.

Messner, S. F. (1982b). Societal development, social equality, and homicide: A cross-national test of a Durkheimian model. *Social Forces, 61,* 225–240.

Messner, S. F. (1983a). Regional and racial effects on the urban homicide rate: The subculture of violence revisited. *American Journal of Sociology, 88,* 997–1007.

Messner, S. F. (1983b). Regional differences in the economic correlates of the urban homicide rate: Some evidence on the importance of cultural context. *Criminology, 21,* 477–488.

Messner, S. F. (1989). Economic discrimination and societal homicide rates: Further evidence on the cost of inequality. *American Sociological Review, 54,* 597–611.

Messner, S. F., & Golden, R. M. (1992). Racial inequality and racially disaggregated homicide rates: An assessment of alternative theoretical explanations. *Criminology, 30,* 421–447.

Messner, S. F., & South, S. J. (1986). Economic deprivation, opportunity structure, and robbery victimization: Intra- and interracial patterns. *Social Forces, 64,* 975–991.

Messner, S. F., & Tardiff, K. (1986). Economic inequality and levels of homicide: An analysis of urban neighborhoods. *Criminology, 24,* 297–317.

Miller, W. B. (1958). Lower class culture as a generating milieu of gang delinquency. *Journal of Social Issues, 14,* 5–19.

Mladenka, K. R., & Hill, K. Q. (1976). A reexamination of the etiology of urban crime. *Criminology, 13,* 491–506.

Mullen, B. (1989). *Advanced BASIC meta-analysis.* Hillsdale, NJ: Lawrence Erlbaum.

Mullen, B., & Rosenthal, R. (1985). *Basic meta-analysis: Procedures and programs.* Hillsdale, NJ: Lawrence Erlbaum.

Myers, M. A. (1987). Economic inequality and discrimination in sentencing. *Social Forces, 65,* 746–766.

Nettler, G. (1984). *Explaining crime* (3rd ed.). New York, NY: McGraw Hill.

Parker, R., & Horwitz, A. (1986). Unemployment, crime, and imprisonment: A panel approach. *Criminology, 24,* 751–770.

Parker, R. N., & Smith, M. D. (1979). Deterrence, poverty, and type of homicide. *American Journal of Sociology, 85,* 614–624.

Patterson, E. B. (1991). Poverty, income inequality, and community crime rates. *Criminology, 29,* 755–776.

Peterson, R. D., & Bailey, W. C. (1988). Forcible rape, poverty, and economic inequality in U.S. metropolitan communities. *Journal of Quantitative Criminology, 4,* 99–119.

Quetelet, A. (1842). *A treatise on man.* Edinburgh, Scotland: Chambers.

Quinney, R., & Wildeman, J. (1991). *The problem of crime* (3rd ed.). Mountainview, CA: Mayfield Publishing Co.

Ritzer, G., & Gindoff, P. (1992). Methodological relationism: Lessons for and from social psychology. *Social Psychology Quarterly, 55,* 128–140.

Rosenfeld, R. (1986). Urban crime rates: Effects of inequality, welfare, dependency, region, and race. In J. M. Byrne & R. J. Sampson (Eds.), *The social ecology of crime* (pp. 116–129). New York, NY: Springer-Verlag.

Rosenthal, R. (1979). The "file drawer problem" and tolerance for null results. *Psychological Bulletin, 86,* 638–641.

Rosenthal, R., & Rubin, D. B. (1982). Comparing effect sizes of independent studies. *Psychological Bulletin, 92,* 500–504.

Sampson, R. (1985a). Race and criminal violence: A demographically disaggregated analysis of urban homicide. *Crime & Delinquency, 31,* 47–82.

Sampson, R. (1985b). Structural sources of variation in race-age-specific rates of offending across major U.S. cities. *Criminology, 23,* 647–673.

Sampson, R. J., & Castellano, T. C. (1982). Economic inequality and personal victimization. *The British Journal of Criminology, 22,* 363–385.

Shaw, C. R., & McKay, H. D. (1942). *Juvenile delinquency in urban areas.* Chicago, IL: University of Chicago Press.

Simpson, M. E. (1985). Violent crime, income inequality, and regional culture: Another look. *Sociological Focus, 18,* 199–208.

Smith, M. D., & Bennett, N. (1985). Poverty, inequality, and theories of forcible rape. *Crime and Delinquency, 31,* 295–305.

Smith, M. D., & Parker, R. N. (1980). Type of homicide and variation in regional rates. *Social Forces, 59,* 136–147.

Tittle, C. R. (1983). Social class and criminal behavior: A critique of the theoretical foundation. *Social Forces, 62,* 334–358.

Tittle, C. R., & Meier, R. F. (1990). Specifying the SES/delinquency relationship. *Criminology, 28,* 271–299.

Tittle, C. R., Villemez, W. J., & Smith, D. A. (1978). The myth of social class and criminality: An empirical assessment of the empirical evidence. *American Sociological Review 43,* 643–656.

Watts, A. D., & Watts, T. W. (1981). Minorities and urban crime. *Urban Affairs Quarterly, 16,* 423–436.

Wells, L. E., & Rankin, J. H. (1991). Families and delinquency: A meta-analysis of the impact of broken homes. *Social Problems, 38,* 71–93.

Williams, K. R. (1984). Economic sources of homicide: Re-estimating the effects of poverty and inequality. *American Sociological Review, 49,* 283–289.

Williams, K. R., & Drake, S. (1980). Social structure, crime and criminalization: An empirical examination of the conflict perspective. *The Sociological Quarterly, 21,* 563–575.

Williams, K. R., & Flewelling, R. L. (1988). The social production of criminal homicide: A comparative study of disaggregated rates in American cities. *American Sociological Review, 53,* 421–431.

Wilson, J. Q., & Herrnstein, R. J. (1985). *Crime and human nature.* New York, NY: Simon & Schuster.

Wolfgang, M. E. (1967). *The subculture of violence.* London, England: Tavistock Publications.

Zelditch, M. (1991). Levels in the logic of macro-historical explanation. In J. Huber (Ed.), *Macro-micro linkages in sociology* (pp. 101–106). Newbury Park, CA: Sage Publications.

NOTES

1. As an alternative approach, Loftin and Hill (1974) have defined a structural poverty index (SPI) based on six aggregate indicators including, for example, the percentage of children living with one parent and the percentage of the population failing the Armed Forces Mental Test. Several studies (Huff-Corzine, Corzine, & Moore, 1986; Smith & Parker, 1980) have reported using the SPI. Messner and South (1986) chose $4,000 of annual household income as a cutoff point for absolute poverty, which was close to the official poverty level for a family of four during the time of their data collection ($3,968).

2. In Engels' classic statement (1968), absolute deprivation dehumanizes rather then frustrates individuals and thereby frees them to commit violent crimes.

3. As an alternative to the Gini index, another possibility, used by Bennett (1991), is Ray and Singer's index of income concentration. In still another approach, a study by Watts and Watts (1981) used a dummy variable where 1 represented cities with above-average proportions of both poor and wealthy families.

4. For discussion see Hunter and Schmidt (1990), p. 502. Although it may be tempting to offer tallies of positive, negative, and null regression coefficients (Patterson, 1991), this approach is highly suspect for two reasons: The regression models reported in the existing literature often differ in their specifications of independent variables, and the current literature generally fails to account for significant inferential problems associated with multicollinearity. Aggregate sampling units such as cities, SMSAs, and states with high (or low) absolute deprivation (poverty levels) also tend to have high (or low) levels of relative deprivation (that is, income

inequality). Collinearity among regressors is associated with (a) large changes in estimated regression coefficients that occur as variables are added or deleted from regression models, (b) wide confidence intervals, sign reversals, and nonsignificant test statistics, and (c) an overall instability of regression coefficient estimates from sample to sample. Recent analyses have treated poverty and income inequality as indicators of an underlying factor called resource deprivation as a solution to the problem of collinearity. (See Land, McCall, & Cohen, 1990, and Messner & Golden, 1992, for further discussion.)

5. Although the omission of unpublished results could bias our analysis toward studies reporting significant positive correlations, the so-called "file drawer" problem would seem to be unlikely in the context of the current debate, which emphasizes the substantive importance of negative or null findings. In any case, where appropriate we will be calculating the number of "file drawer" studies yielding null results that would be needed to threaten the validity of our conclusions. (For a discussion of the calculation, see Rosenthal, 1979.)

6. Because the correlations reported by studies using the same or overlapping samples are not independent estimates, we felt it would be inappropriate to use an "average" of the reported coefficients. Although Messner's estimates (1982a) are based on a more inclusive set of SMSAs (*N* = 204) than those given by Blau and Blau (*N* = 125), Messner's data are only for homicide, whereas Blau and Blau also report estimates for assault, rape, and robbery. We also note that substituting Messner's estimated correlations for homicide with poverty and homicide with income inequality would not alter our general conclusions. The same lack of independence may occur when studies use overlapping samples of nations, but here the problem is not as severe. For example, Krahn, Hartnagel, and Gartrell (1986) and Messner (1989) appear to use similar samples of nations in the same year (1975), but the correlation coefficients that they report for homicide with the Gini index are not identical: .48 v. .19.

7. The 11 studies that were previously excluded from our analysis because they did not use reported offense rates as their measures of violent crime reported 11 positive correlation coefficients and 1 negative coefficient.

8. With respect to the so-called "file drawer" problem, at least 740 unretrieved studies reporting null findings would be required to threaten the validity of our result with respect to poverty, and 1,716 studies reporting null findings would be required with respect to income inequality (see Rosenthal, 1979, pp. 638–641.

9. Type of measure was coded as a set of four dummy variables where, for example, 1 = assault and 0 = not assault. Type of sampling unit was coded as follows: 1 = neighborhoods and cities, 2 = counties and SMSAs, 3 = states, and 4 = nations. This is a more parsimonious coding scheme for type of sampling unit than using four separate dummy variables and allows us to evaluate the contention in the literature that smaller areal units are more appropriate than larger areal units for analyzing the effects of relative deprivation.

10. The effect for sample size is marginally significant, indicating that studies using larger sample sizes (*N*) produce smaller observed correlations, but this effect is substantively small.

11. A minimum of 114 studies reporting null results would be required to invalidate this result.

12. When assault coefficients were compared with those involving either rape or robbery, the comparable test values were as follows: .47 vs. .32, *t* = 1.41, *p* < .20, and .47 vs. .16, *t* = 1.64, *p* < .20).

13. With respect to the file drawer problem, at least 28 new or unretrieved studies reporting null results would be required to reduce this coefficient to an insignificant size.

14. A minimum of 58 new or unretrieved studies would be required to jeopardize the validity of this result.

Twenty-Seven

LIFE EXPECTANCY, ECONOMIC INEQUALITY, HOMICIDE, AND REPRODUCTIVE TIMING IN CHICAGO NEIGHBORHOODS

Margo Wilson and Martin Daly

SUMMARY

IN comparison among Chicago neighbourhoods, homicide rates in 1988–93 varied more than 100-fold, while male life expectancy at birth ranged from 54 to 77 years, even with effects of homicide mortality removed. This "cause deleted" life expectancy was highly correlated with homicide rates; a measure of economic inequality added significant additional prediction, whereas median household income did not. Deaths from internal causes (diseases) show similar age patterns, despite different absolute levels, in the best and worst neighbourhoods, whereas deaths from external causes (homicide, accident, suicide) do not. As life expectancy declines across neighbourhoods, women reproduce earlier; by age 30, however, neighbourhood no longer affects age specific fertility. These results support the hypothesis that life expectancy itself may be a psychologically salient determinant of risk taking and the timing of life transitions.

INTRODUCTION

PSYCHOLOGISTS, economists, and criminologists have found that young adults, poor people, and criminal offenders all tend to discount the future relatively steeply.[1-6] Such tendencies have been called "impulsivity" and "short time horizons" or, more pejoratively, impatience, myopia, lack of self control, and incapacity to delay gratification. Behind the use of such terms lies a presumption that steep discounting is dysfunctional and that the appropriate weighting of present rewards against future investments is independent of life stage and socioeconomic circumstance.

There is an alternative view: adjustment of discount rates in relation to age and other variables is just what we should expect of an evolved psyche functioning normally.[5-11] Steep discounting may be a "rational" response to information that indicates an uncertain or low probability of surviving to reap delayed benefits, for example, and "reckless" risk taking can be op-

Originally published in *British Medical Journal*, 1997.

timal when the expected profits from safer courses of action are negligible.[7 8 12 13]

Hypothesis 1

Criminal violence can be considered an outcome of steep future discounting[6] and escalation of risk in social competition.[10] This is especially true of homicide in urban parts of the United States, where a large majority of cases involve competition for status or resources among unrelated men[7 9] and even marital homicides result from sexual proprietariness in the shadow of competition.[14 15] This line of reasoning suggests that criminal violence will vary in relation to local indicators of life expectancy, hence our first hypothesis: homicide rates will vary as a function of local life expectancy.

Hypothesis 2

Sensitivity to inequality is an expected feature of a psyche that adjusts risk acceptance as we envision, because those at the bottom may be especially motivated to escalate their tactics of social competition when it is clear that some "winners" are doing very well and when the expected payoffs from low risk tactics are poor.[12] This expectation accords with arguments that mortality is exacerbated by inequality itself, over and above the compromising effects of simply being poor on nutrition, access to medical care, safety, and other health promoting opportunities.[16 17] Recent papers in the *BMJ* have presented evidence that economic inequality predicts mortality in general, and moreover that it is most strongly related to "external" mortality of the sort affected by behavioural risk taking, especially homicide.[18 19] Accordingly, our second hypothesis is that economic inequality will account for additional variance in homicidal violence besides that accounted for by local life expectancy.

Previous demonstrations of the effects of inequality on homicide have focused primarily on comparisons between nations, American states, or cities.[18-21] The arguments presented above suggest that the relevant processes of social comparison might operate more locally, with the lives and deaths of people known personally being especially salient to one's mental model of life prospects. We have therefore compared neighbourhoods within a large city. This may also be a good level at which to detect the relations of interest because variables such as latitude, weather, urbanness, laws, history, and prevailing political practices complicate comparisons among larger jurisdictions.

Table 1

Effects of life expectancy ("cause deleted" with respect to death from homicide), income, and income inequality on homicide rates of neighbourhoods in Chicago 1988–93: bivariate correlations

	Homicide rate	Life expectancy for males	Life expectancy for females	Median household income*	Robin Hood index
Homicide rate	—				
Life expectancy for males	− 0.88	—			
Life expectancy for females	− 0.83	0.92	—		
Median household income	− 0.67	0.73	0.59	—	
Robin Hood index	0.75	− 0.75	− 0.66	− 0.86	—

*Effects of household size partialled out.

Table 2

Effects of life expectancy ("cause deleted" with respect to death from homicide), income, and income inequality on homicide rates of neighbourhoods in Chicago 1988–93: results of stepwise multiple regression predicting homicide rate of neighbourhoods from the other four variables in table 1

	β	t	p value
Variables in final equation			
Life expectancy of males	− 0.74	− 9.25	<0.0001
Robin Hood index	0.19	2.34	0.02
Variables not in final equation			
Life expectancy of females	− 0.19	− 1.43	0.16
Median household income	0.12	1.11	0.27

Hypothesis 3

Finally, if low life expectancy is indeed psychologically salient in the ways we envision, it will inspire short time horizons in other domains of behavioural decision making as well. Life expectancy cues might thus affect inclinations to invest in the future through education, preventive health measures, and savings, as well as decisions about the timing of major transitions and life events. Geronimus's studies of young mothers support these ideas: although early reproduction among urban poor people is commonly viewed as an instance of social pathology and failure to exercise choice, she has shown that teenage pregnancy is often an active decision, motivated in large part by expectations about a life course more compressed in time than that of more affluent people.[22][23] Her interviewees in urban ghettos in the United States expressly wished to become mothers and grandmothers while still young and competent because they anticipated problems of early "weathering" and poor health. Thus, our third hypothesis is that reproduction will occur earlier in the lifespan as one moves from neighbourhoods with high life expectancy to those with low expectancy.

Data Sources

There are 77 "community areas" with relatively stable boundaries in the American city of Chi-

cago. We used demographic data for 1988–93 for these 77 neighbourhoods (vital statistics obtained from the Illinois Department of Public Health) and population data from the 1990 census. Following Schoen's method,[24] we used these data to compute male and female life expectancies at birth for each neighbourhood, "cause deleted" in that effects of homicide mortality were removed. We also computed sex and age specific mortality for different causes of death and age specific birth rates. We used counts of the number of households in each of 25 income intervals, derived from 1990 United States Census population and housing summary tape file 3A, to compute the Robin Hood index of income inequality (the maximum deviation of the Lorenz curve of cumulative share of total income from the straight line that would represent zero income variance[19]) for each neighbourhood.

LIFE EXPECTANCY AND HOMICIDE

NEIGHBOURHOOD specific, cause deleted male life expectancy at birth (range 54.3 to 77.4 years) and homicide rates (range 1.3 to 156 per 100 000 per year) are highly correlated, confirming our first hypothesis (fig 1; $r = -0.88$, $P<0.0001$).

Table 1 shows the bivariate correlations among

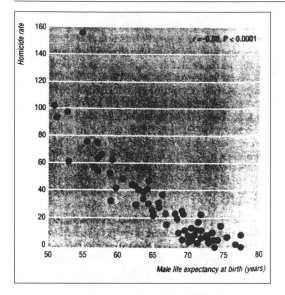

Figure 1
Neighbourhood specific homicide rates (per 100 000 population per year) in relation to male life expectancy at birth (with effects of homicide mortality removed) for 77 community areas of Chicago, 1988–93

homicide rates, cause deleted life expectancies, median household income (adjusted to remove effects of mean household size, which was correlated with median household income across the 77 neighbourhoods at $r = -0.32$), and a measure of income inequality. All pairs of measures were highly correlated (all P values <0.0001), but male life expectancy was more strongly related to both economic measures and to the homicide rate than was female life expectancy, and male life expectancy predicted the homicide rate better than either economic measure. Stepwise multiple regression indicated that economic inequality adds significantly to the prediction of homicide rate that is afforded by life expectancy, supporting our second hypothesis. The adjusted median household income is apparently of less relevance than inequality, a result that is consistent with previous findings from comparisons among larger politico-geographic units,[18-21] but since

the two economic measures are so highly correlated, this conclusion must be tentative.

Mortality Patterns
in Best and Worst Neighbourhoods

Figure 2 shows age specific and sex specific death rates, distinguishing death by homicide and other "external" causes (accidents and suicides) from death by "internal" causes (all other causes—that is, by disease, broadly construed). The figure includes data only for the 10 neighbourhoods with the shortest life expectancies (panels on right) and the 10 with the longest (panels on left). Neighbourhoods with low life expectancy have higher levels of all sorts of mortality in virtually all age-sex categories; however, although the pattern of risk of death from internal causes across the lifespan is similar in the best and worst neighbourhoods, age related patterns of external mortality are quite different. These patterns support the idea that differential rates of external mortality are largely a result of differentials in risk acceptance and future discounting, especially in young adults. (Although perpetrating a homicide, rather than becoming a victim, might be thought to reflect risk acceptance and future discounting, the age-sex patterns for perpetrators and victims are similar,[9] largely because homicides in Chicago arise primarily from competitive interactions between male victims and killers who are drawn from the same demographic groups.)

LIFE EXPECTANCY AND
AGE SPECIFIC BIRTH RATES

TABLE 2 shows age specific birth rates for the 10 neighbourhoods with the highest life expectancies, the 10 with the lowest, and the 10 nearest the median. Teenage birth rates are dramatically different, but the differentials decline rapidly and have vanished by age 30. The median age of women giving birth (the "generation time") was 22.6 years in the neighbourhoods with low life expectancy, compared with 25.4

Table 3

Age specific birth rates (per 1000 women per year) in 10 neighbourhoods with longest life expectancy, 10 with shortest life expectancy, and 10 nearest median life expectancy in Chicago, 1988–93

Age of mother (years)	Birth rate in neighbourhoods		
	Shortest life expectancy	Median life expectancy	Longest life expectancy
10–14	9	2	1
15–19	190	86	45
20–24	224	128	90
25–29	129	103	103
30–34	83	84	89
35–39	39	43	42
40–44	9	10	7

years in the intermediate neighbourhoods and 27.3 years in the neighbourhoods with long life expectancy. These differences are consistent with our third hypothesis and support Geronimus's suggestion[22] [23] that the relatively high birth rates in young women in the worst neighbourhoods often reflect a distinct family planning schedule rather than a mere absence of family planning.

EFFECT OF LIFE EXPECTANCY

LIFE expectancy reflects not only affluence but such additional considerations as local pathogen loads, health care, and risk of violent death, and it may thus provide a more encompassing quality of life index than economic measures alone. More than just providing a useful epidemiological index, however, an "expectation" of future lifespan may be psychologically salient in its own right, although it need not be a conscious expectation. The data presented here indicate that people behave as if they have adjusted their rates of future discounting and risk acceptance thresholds in relation to local life expectancy, and that they do so in the non-violent domain of reproductive decision making as well

as in the potentially violent domain of social competition.

How could such a statistical abstraction as life expectancy be a cause of anything? One possibility is that the human psyche produces what is in effect a semi-statistical apprehension of the distribution of local lifespans, based on the fates of other relevant people.[10] If a young man's grandfathers were both dead before he was born, for example, and some of his primary school classmates had already died, discounting the future could be a normal, adaptive reaction. Moreover, if much of this mortality seems to represent "bad luck" incurred more or less independently of the decedents' choices of action, then accepting more risks in the pursuit of immediate advantage would also make sense.

These inference processes are unlikely to be transparent to introspection, but they may be revealed in expressed attitudes and expectations. Ethnographic studies of urban poor people in American cities contain many articulate statements about the perceived risk of early death, the unpredictability of future resources, and the futility of long term planning.[25-28] One interesting question for psychological research is how the relevant mental models and subjective values de-

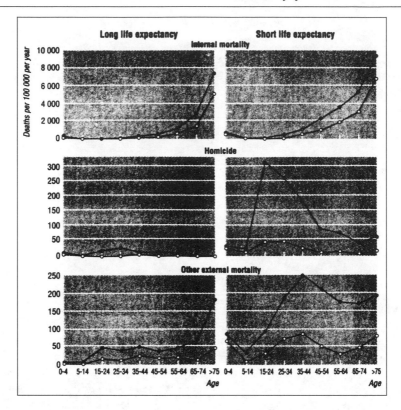

Figure 2
Age specific death rates per 100 000 population per year, according to sex (mail •; female ○) and cause of death for the 10 neighbourhoods with longest life expectancy (left panels) and the 10 with the shortest life expectancy (right panels), Chicago, 1988–93.

velop and are adjusted over the lifespan.[29] [30] Another is whether media representations, even fictitious ones, can affect such development in the same way as information about known relatives and neighbours. These questions may best be addressed from an evolutionary psychological perspective, which credits the mind with functional "design" for solving important problems of living in society and making decisions under uncertainty.[10] [29] [31] [32] Such an approach has already shed considerable light on detailed aspects of sex differences and age effects.[5] [9]

Feedback Effects

The regression analysis in table 1 and our emphasis on life expectancy as a predictive variable must not be taken to imply that economic inequality plays only a secondary role. Considerable evidence indicates that such inequality is itself a major determinant of life expectancy variations,[17] so the more basic (and remediable) causes of violence and other manifestations of steep future discounting are socioeconomic and structural. How our proposal differs from some other accounts is in suggesting that inequality has its effects not only by virtue of non-adaptive or maladaptive stress effects but also by inspiring a "rational" escalation of costly tactics of social competition.[7-10 33] This consideration complicates causal analysis, because it implies that the distribution of age specific mortality is more than an outcome variable, having feedback effects on its own causal factors and hence on itself. We excluded deaths due to homicide from the analyses in table 1 to eliminate spurious autocorrelational effects, but it is likely that local levels of homicidal violence affect expectations of future life, discount rates, and hence further violence.[8]

The number of likely feedback loops among the phenomena of interest is daunting. If many people react to a local socioecological milieu by discounting the future and lowering their thresholds for risk and violence, the behavioural consequences are likely to worsen the very problems that provoke them, as well as contributing to fear, distrust, and perhaps even economic inequality itself. Living where any resources that one accumulates are apt to be expropriated will also exacerbate these tendencies. Wilkinson has proposed that the behavioural and health effects of unequal resource distributions reflect breakdowns in social and community relations, a proposition that we do not dispute. But exactly how the correlated phenomena of poverty, inequality, injustice, and exogenous threats to life and wellbeing affect the perceptions, motives, and actions of individuals remains to be elucidated. The causal links are several and multidirectional, but we cannot let that deter us from trying to disentangle them.

We thank the Illinois Department of Public Health for the vital statistics data; Paula Robinson, Kevin Eva, and Vessna Jocic for data compilation and analyses; Richard Wilkinson for drawing our attention to relevant epidemiological literature and for comments on the manuscript; and Carolyn and Richard Block for getting us interested in Chicago homicides.

NOTES

1. Gottfredson MR, Hirschi T. *A general theory of crime.* Stanford, CA: Stanford University Press, 1980.

2. Green L, Fry AF, Myerson J. Discounting of delayed rewards: a life-span comparison. *Psychological Science* 1994;5:33–3.

3. Lawrance EC. Poverty and the rate of time preference: evidence from panel data. *Journal of Political Economy* 1991;99:54–77.

4. Loewenstein G, Elster J, eds. *Choice over time.* New York: Russell Sage, 1992.

5. Rogers AR. Evolution of time preference by natural selection. *American Economic Review* 1994;84:460–81.

6. Wilson JQ. Herrnstein RJ. *Crime and human nature.* New York: Simon and Schuster, 1985.

7. Wilson MI, Daly M. Competitiveness, risk-taking and violence: the young male syndrome. *Ethology and Sociobiology* 1985;6:59–73.

8. Daly M, Wilson MI. *Homicide.* Hawthorne, NY: Aldine de Gruyter, 1988.

9. Daly M, Wilson MI. Killing the competition. *Human Nature* 1990;1:83–109.

10. Daly M, Wilson MI. Crime and conflict: homicide in evolutionary psychological perspective. *Crime and Justice* 1997;22:251–300.

11. Charlton BG. What is the ultimate cause of socioeconomic inequalities in health? An explanation in terms of evolutionary psychology. *J R Soc Med* 1996;89:3–8.

12. Rubin PH, Paul CW. An evolutionary model of taste for risk. *Economic Inquiry* 1979;18:585–96.

13. Kacelnik A, Bateson M. Risky theories—the effects of variance on foraging decisions. *American Zoologist* 1996;36:402–34.

14. Wilson MI, Daly M. Who kills whom in spouse killings? On the exceptional sex ratio of spousal homicides in the United States. *Criminology* 1992;30:189–215.

15. Wilson MI, Daly M. The man who mistook his wife for a chattel. In: Barkow J, Cosmides L, Tooby J, eds. *The adapted mind.* New York: Oxford, 1992:289–322.

16. Wilkinson RG. Income distribution and life expectancy. *BMJ* 1992;304:165–8.

17. Wilkinson RG. *Unhealthy societies: the afflictions of inequality.* London: Routledge, 1996.

18. Kaplan GA, Kamuk ER, Lynch JW, Cohen RD, Balfour JL. Inequality in income and mortality in the United States: analysis of mortality and potential pathways. *BMJ* 1996;312:999–1003, 1253.

19. Kennedy BP, Kawachi I, Prothrow-Stith D. Income distribution and mortality: cross sectional ecological study of the Robin Hood index in the United States. *BMJ* 1996;312:1004–7, 1194.

20. Krahn H, Hartnagel TF, Gartrell JW. Income inequality and homicide rates: cross-national data and criminological theories. *Criminology* 1986;24:269–95.

21. Hsieh C-C, Pugh MD. Poverty, income inequality and violent crime: a meta-analysis of recent aggregate data studies. *Criminal Justice Review* 1993;18:182–202.

22. Geronimus AT. The weathering hypothesis and the health of African-American women and infants: evidence and speculation. *Ethnicity and Disease* 1992;2:207–21.

23. Geronimus AT. What teen mothers know. *Human Nature* 1996;7:323–52.

24. Schoen R. Calculating life tables by estimating Chiang's a from observed rates. *Demography* 1978;15:625–34.

25. Hagedorn JD. *People and folks.* Chicago: Lake View Press, 1988.

26. Jankowski MS. *Islands in the street.* Berkeley: University of California Press, 1992.

27. Waldman L. *My neighbourhood: the words and pictures of inner-city children.* Chicago: Hyde Park Foundation, 1993.

28. Wilson WJ. *The truly disadvantaged: the inner city, the underclass, and public policy.* Chicago: University of Chicago Press, 1987.

29. Hill EM, Ross LT, Low BS. The role of future unpredictability in human risk-taking. *Human Nature* (in press).

30. Nisbett RE, Cohen D. *Culture of honor: the psychology of violence in the South.* Boulder, CO: Westview Press, 1996.

31. Barkow J, Cosmides L, Tooby J, eds. *The adapted mind.* New York: Oxford, 1992.

32. Gigerenzer G, Goldstein DG. Reasoning the fast and frugal way: models of bounded rationality. *Psychol Rev* 1996;103:650–69.

33. Frank RH. *Choosing the right pond.* New York: Oxford, 1985.

Twenty-Eight

MORTALITY, THE SOCIAL ENVIRONMENT, CRIME AND VIOLENCE

Richard G. Wilkinson, Ichiro Kawachi, and Bruce P. Kennedy

ABSTRACT

Starting out from the relationship between income equality and indicators of social cohesion and social trust, this paper explores the social processes which might account for the relationship between greater income equality and lower population mortality rates. We note that: homicide shows an even closer relationship to income inequality than does mortality from all other causes combined; there are several reports that homicide rates are particularly closely related to all-cause mortality; and there is a growing body of research on crime in relation to social disorganisation.

We use US state level data to examine the relationships between various categories of income inequality, median state income, social trust and mortality. The data suggest that violent crime, but not property crime, is closely related to income inequality, social trust and mortality rates, excluding homicide.

The second half of the paper is devoted to literature on the antecedents of violence. Feeling shamed, humiliated and disrespected seem to be central to the picture and are plausibly related to the way in which wider income differences are likely to mean more people are denied access to traditional sources of status and respect. We suggest that these aspects of low social status may be central to the psychosocial process linking inequality, violence, social cohesion and mortality.

INTRODUCTION

THIS paper uses data on homicide and other categories of crime to explore the nature of the associations between income distribution, mortality and a measure of social cohesion in the United States.

Close associations between income distribution and population mortality rates have now been reported on independent data at least fifteen times (Wilkinson 1996). In different papers the relationship has been shown to withstand controlling for average incomes, expenditure on medical care, poverty, spoking and race (Kennedy *et al.* 1996, Kaplan *et al.* 1996). It has been reported among developed and developing countries and among administrative areas within developed countries (Ben Shlomo *et al.* 1996). Most analyses have used cross-sectional data but the relationship has also been demonstrated using data on changes over time (*e.g.* Wilkinson 1992; Kaplan *et al.* 1996).

When it was believed that the main determinants of health were likely to involve the direct physiological effects of exposure to features of the material environment and to health related behaviour, it was harder to imagine how social

Originally published in *Sociology of Health & Illness*, 1998.

relationships of inequality could be strongly associated with mortality. However, the growing body of epidemiological findings suggesting the importance of features of psychosocial life, such as sense of control, social affiliations and support, self-esteem, 'life events' and job security, is now coupled with a clearer understanding of the physiological pathways through which chronic psychosocial stress can have a wide range of health outcomes (Chrousos *et al.* 1995). There is also impressive evidence of the health-related physiological consequences of low social status from studies of non-human primates (Sapolsky 1993, Shively *et al.* 1994, Shively *et al.* 1997).

The difficulty is now more a matter of identifying which are the more important of a wide range of social processes that could plausibly contribute to a relationship between mortality and inequality. Particularly interesting is the question of whether people's health is only affected by income inequality through the impact of their individual relative income on their own health (*i.e.* through things like low self-esteem consequent on low social status, worry over debt, financial insecurity etc.), or whether there are more broadly based social processes which may lead to improvements in health more widely among people living in more egalitarian societies—at least partly independently of their own relative income. On this latter possibility, Kawachi *et al.* (1997) have shown statistical evidence suggesting that the relationship between income inequality and mortality among the states of the USA is mediated by 'social trust'—as measured by the proportion of people in each state agreeing with the statement 'most people would try to take advantage of you if they got the chance'. Similarly, Wilkinson (1996) discussed a number of examples of societies which were both unusually egalitarian and unusually healthy. They all showed a marked tendency to be more socially cohesive. However, not only is it unclear what aspects of social cohesion might be important to health, but it would be possible to

argue that rather than income inequality affecting health through social cohesion, the psychosocial effects of low relative income could rebound directly on both health and social cohesion without the latter being a pathway to the former.

In passing, we should mention that it has been suggested (Fiscella and Franks 1997) that the association between income inequality and mortality may reflect a greater incidence of absolute poverty and lower absolute levels of consumption among the less well off in areas of greater inequality. In other words, it has been argued that the relationship of income inequality to mortality simply reflects a compositional effect of more poor people (who are presumably at higher risk of death) residing in areas of high income disparity. We reject this explanation because it has been shown that, of the two variables income distribution and the percentage of households in each state living below the federal poverty threshold, income distribution but not poverty is independently related to mortality. In addition, when the weak relationship between mortality and median state income is controlled for income distribution, rather than the association being strengthened, it disappears altogether and mortality shows no independent relation to median income whatsoever (Kaplan *et al.* 1996, Kennedy *et al.* 1996).

Homicide

One of the intriguing aspects of the relationship between inequality and mortality is that it seems to be mirrored by a relationship between income distribution and homicide. Kaplan *et al.* (1996) reported close correlations between income inequality and both homicide ($r = 0.74$) and violent crime rates ($r = 0.70$) among the 50 states of the United States. Kennedy *et al.* (1996) examined the cross-sectional relationship between household income distribution and state-level variations in homicide rates. The greater the disparity in household incomes, the higher was the homicide rate at the state level. Relative deprivation was apparently an even stronger predictor of homicide rates than absolute deprivation. Homicide showed correlations with income inequality and household poverty rates of 0.74 and 0.53, respectively. Even after adjusting for poverty, income inequality accounted for 52 per cent of the between-state variance in homicide rates. An association between homicide and income inequality has also been found using international data (Messner 1983, Krahn *et al.* 1986). In addition, Wilson and Daly (1997) reported a correlation of 0.88 between homicide and all other causes of death (excluding homicide) among 77 'community areas' in the Chicago region. The link was confirmed in a meta-analysis of some 34 studies (Hsich 1993).

Social Disorganisation

There is a substantial body of research which suggests that crime rates reflect 'community social disorganisation'. Social disorganisation theory was originally developed by the Chicago School researchers Clifford Shaw and Henry McKay in their classic work, *Juvenile Delinquency and Urban Areas* (1942). Shaw and McKay demonstrates that the same socioeconomically disadvantaged areas in 21 US cities continued to exhibit high delinquency rates over a span of several decades, despite changes in their racial and ethnic composition, indicating the persistent contextual effects of these communities on crime rates, regardless of what populations experienced them. This observation led them to reject individualistic explanations of delinquency and to focus instead on community processes—like disruption of local community organisation and weak social controls—which led to the apparent trans-generational transmission of criminal behaviour. In general, social disorganisation is defined as the 'inability of a community structure to realise the common values of its residents and

maintain effective social controls' (Sampson and Groves 1989). The social organisational approach views local communities and neighbourhoods as complex systems of friendship, kinship, and acquaintanceship networks, as well as formal and informal associational ties rooted in family life and ongoing socialisation processes (Sampson 1995). From the perspective of crime control, a major dimension of social disorganisation is the ability of a community to supervise and control teenage peer groups, especially gangs. Thus Shaw and McKay (1942) argued that residents of cohesive communities were better able to control the youth behaviours that set the context for gang violence. Examples of such controls include: 'the supervision of leisure-time youth activities, intervention in street-corner congregation, and challenging youth "who seem to be up to no good". Socially disorganised communities with extensive street-corner peer groups are also expected to have higher rates of adult violence, especially among younger adults who still have ties to youth gangs' (Sampson 1995).

Recently, social disorganisation theory has been linked to the emerging concept of social capital (Sampson 1995). Social capital has been defined by its principal theorists (Coleman 1990, Putnam 1993) as those features of social organisation, such as networks, norms of reciprocity, and trust in others, that facilitate cooperation between citizens for mutual benefit. Lack of social capital is thus one of the primary features of socially disorganised communities (Sampson 1995). Although the conceptualisation and measurement of social capital are still evolving, two critical features of the concept appear to be the level of trust among citizens and the density and rate of participation in voluntary associations and local organisations (Putnam 1995).

Several empirical studies, reviewed by Sampson (1995), have corroborated the link between low stocks of social capital and high crime rates. Taylor and colleagues (1984) examined violent crimes (such as mugging, assault, murder, rape) across 63 street blocks in Baltimore. Based on interviews with 687 household respondents, Taylor *et al.* constructed block-level measures of the proportion of respondents who belonged to an organisation to which co-residents also belonged, and the proportion of respondents who felt responsible for what happened in the area surrounding their home. Both variables were significantly and negatively associated with rates of violence. Similarly, Sincha-Fagan and Schwartz (1986) collected survey information on 553 residents of 12 neighbourhoods in New York City, and found a significant negative relationship between the rate of self-reported delinquency and rates of organisational participation by local residents. A third set of studies conducted by Sampson and Groves (1989) in Great Britain reported that density of local friendship networks had a significant negative effect on robbery rates, while the level of organisational participation by residents had significant inverse effects on both robbery and stranger violence. Not only does participation in local organisations increase the level of community control, it may facilitate the capacity of communities to obtain extra-local resources—such as police and fire services, as well as block grants—that have indirect consequences for crime control (Burski and Grasmick 1993). In the most convincing demonstration to date of the link between social cohesion and crime. Sampson and colleagues (1997) surveyed 8,782 residents of 343 Chicago neighbourhoods to ask about their perceptions of social cohesion and trust in the neighbourhood. Respondents were asked how strongly they agreed (on a five point scale) that 'people around here are willing to help their neighbors', 'this is a close-knit neighborhood', 'people in this neighborhood can be trusted', 'people in this neighborhood generally don't get along with each other', and 'people in this neighborhood do not share the same values' (the last two items were reverse-coded). The resulting scale was then combined with responses to questions about the level of informal

social control (whether neighbours would intervene in situations where children were engaging in delinquent behaviour) to produce a summary index of 'collective efficacy'. Collective efficacy turned out to be significantly ($P < 0.01$) related to organizational participation ($r = 0.45$) and neighbourhood services ($r = 0.21$). In hierarchical statistical models adjusting for individual characteristics (age, socioeconomic status, gender, ethnicity, marital status, home ownership, and years in neighbourhood), the index of collective efficacy was significantly inversely associated with reports of neighbourhood violence, violent victimisation, as well as homicide rates. For example, a two standard deviation elevation in neighbourhood collective efficacy was associated with a 39.7% reduction in the expected homicide rate.

Given these reported links between crime and the nature of the local social environment we decided to use rates of different kinds of crime to re-examine the relationship between income inequality, social trust and mortality which had been identified in previous work (Kawachi *et al.* 1997). Using data for the states of the United States we decided to see whether there were informative differences in the way different kinds of crime fitted into these relationships. Our hope was that they would provide a guide to the social processes which mediate between income distribution and mortality.

DATA SOURCES

The Social Environment

A core feature of 'social capital', as presented by its principal theorists (Coleman 1990, Putnam 1993) consists of levels of interpersonal trust among community members. Following Putnam (1995), we used data from the General Social Surveys (GSS), conducted by the National Opinion Research Center to estimate state variations in levels of interpersonal trust. The GSS is a nationally representative survey of noninstitutionalised adults over 18 years living in the United States. The surveys have been repeated 14 times over the last two decades, and have included a set of questions on interpersonal trust. In the present study, we averaged five years of cumulated data (1986–1990), representing 7,679 individual observations. Of the 50 states, only 39 were sampled in the survey due to the small population of some states (*e.g.* Delaware, Rhode Island); hence, social capital data were not available in these states. Because the sampling design of the GSS was intended to be representative of regions rather than states, we adjusted individual responses using post-stratification weights to reflect the age, race/ethnic, and educational composition of each state. Detailed procedures for the post-stratification weighting are described elsewhere (Kawachi *et al.* 1997).

Our Social Trust variable was assessed from responses to the GSS item that asked: 'Generally speaking, would you say that most people can be trusted, or that you can't be too careful in dealing with people?' For each state, we calculated the percentage of residents who agreed that 'most people cannot be trusted.' Belief in the good will and benign intent of others facilitates collective action and mutual cooperation, and therefore adds to the stock of a community's social capital. In turn, collective action further reinforces community norms of reciprocity.

Based on the well-established association between male youth and violent crime rates, we also obtained Census-derived estimates of the proportion of the population in each state who were males aged 15 to 24 years.

Income Measures

Household income data for each state were obtained from the 1990 US Census Summary Tape File STF 3A. The data provide annual household income for 25 income intervals ($0–5,000 at the bottom, and $150,000 or more at the top). To calculate income inequality, counts of the number of households falling into each of the 25 income intervals were obtained for each state. These interval data were converted into income deciles using a programme developed by the US Census Bureau. Our measure of income inequality, the Robin Hood Index (RHI), was estimated for each state from the income decile distribution, which represents the share of total household income in each decile. The RHI is then calculated by summing the excess shares of income for those deciles whose shares of the aggregate income exceed 10 per cent (Atkinson and Micklewright 1992). For example in Massachusetts, the RHI is 30.26 per cent. This represents the share of total income from all households that would have to be transferred from those above the mean to those below the mean in order to achieve a perfectly equal income distribution. The higher the value of RHI, the greater is the degree of income inequality. We also obtained median gross household income for each state.

Mortality and Crime Rates

Age-adjusted mortality from all-causes and homicide rates were obtained for each state from the Compressed Mortality Files compiled by the National Center for Health Statistics, Center for Disease Control and Prevention (CDC). We subtracted homicide from all-cause mortality to provide two variables—homicide and all-causes mortality excluding homicide—which were entirely separate from each other. Mortality (excluding homicide) was taken for the year 1990, while data for years 1981–1991 were combined to provide more stable estimates of homicide rates.

Incidence rates of other crimes—rape, robbery, aggravated assault, burglary, larceny, and motor vehicle theft—were obtained from the Federal Bureau of Investigation's Uniform Crime Reports (UCR) for the years 1991–1994 (US Department of Justice 1991–1994). These rates are based on the incidents of crime reported to the police, and subsequently to the Federal

Bureau of Investigation (FBI) through the crime reporting programme. Incidence data, while subject to various biases related to variations in reporting, are nonetheless considered less susceptible to bias compared to arrest data (Reiss and Roth 1993). Table 1 shows a list of the variables and their definitions. Homicide, rape, robbery and aggravated assault are classified under the broad category of violent crimes, while burglary, larceny, and motor vehicle theft are classified under property crimes.

Results and Discussion

TABLE 2 shows the correlation matrix between all the variables. Data are presented for the 39 states covered by the General Social Surveys. Strong correlations with mortality in the expected direction are shown with income inequality (r = .63), social trust (r = 0.76), and homicide (r = 0.70) (see also Kawachi *et al.* 1997). Much weaker, though still statistically significant, correlations were found with the proportion of males 15–24, median income, and aggravated assault. Correlations between mortality and the other crime variables failed to reach statistical significance: while robbery, burglary and rape showed a weak direct association with mortality, motor vehicle theft showed no association and larceny was inversely correlated with mortality. It could be argued that the differences in the associations between mortality and different categories of crime were simply a reflection of differences in reporting, and that homicide shows a close association because the data are much more accurate. Nevertheless, the statistically significant direct correlations between higher median state income and higher rates of robbery and motor vehicle theft might indicate that some forms of property crime are influenced by the greater opportunities for theft which more prosperous states would provide.

As well as being closely associated with mortality, income inequality is significantly associated with homicide (r = 0.74), social trust (r = 0.73), assault (r = 0.50), burglary (r = 0.44), and robbery (r = 0.36). Inequality's correlations with rape and motor vehicle theft are weakly positive but there is no relationship with larceny.

The fact that violent crime, particularly homicide and aggravated assault, are more closely related both to mortality and to income inequality than are property crimes, may tell us something of the nature of the relationship between mortality and income inequality. If we assume that violent crime is indicative of some aspect of the social fabric, how does this factor fit into the relationship between mortality and both income inequality and social trust?

Regressing mortality simultaneously on income inequality and homicide shows that income inequality is not related to mortality independently of homicide (p = 0.76), though homicide is strongly related to mortality independently of income inequality (p = 0.0002). Regressing mortality against homicide and social trust shows that social trust is related significantly to mortality independently of homicide (p = 0.005), but the relationship between mortality and homicide independent of social trust fails to reach significance (p = 0.19).

What these results suggest is that the social conditions which produce homicide are near the heart of the relationships we want to understand between income distribution and mortality. The social conditions which produce homicide are also very closely related to social trust (the simple correlation between homicide and social trust is 0.82) but homicide does not wholly account for the relationship between social trust and mortality. Other forms of crime have either no relationship or a weaker relationship to this pattern. It would appear that homicide and larceny (or motor vehicle theft)—the most and least violent crimes—are at opposite extremes in how they are related to income distribution and mortality, with assault, burglary and robbery taking up intermediate positions. The associations with assault are most like those with homicide, so

Table 1

Definitions of variables used. (Abbreviations used in Table 2 listed in parentheses)

1. *Males 15–25 yrs* (% 15–24M):
   Percentage of state population who are males 15–24 years old.
2. *Social trust* (SOCTRUST):
   Level of interpersonal trust, measured by percentage of residents in state responding that 'Most people cannot be trusted'.
3. *Income inequality* (ROBINHD):
   The Robin Hood Index of income inequality measures the proportion of income which would need to be redistributed to gain total income equality (see text).
4. *Median income* (MEDINC):
   Median household income in state.
5. *Mortality* (MORTALITY):
   Age-standardised total mortality rate per 100,000 population in each state.
6. *Homicide* (HOMICIDE):
   Age-standardised homicide rate per 100,000 inhabitants in each state.
7. *Aggravated assault* (ASSAULT):
   Reported aggravated assault incidence in state (per 100,000 population). Defined as an unlawful attack by one person upon another for the purpose of inflicting severe or aggravated bodily injury.
8. *Rape* (RAPE):
   Reported rape incidence in state (per 100,000 population).
9. *Robbery* (ROBBERY):
   Reported robbery incidence in state (per 100,000 population). Defined as the taking or attempting to take anything of value from the care, custody, or control of a person or persons by force or threat of force or violence and/or putting the victim in fear.
10. *Burglary* (BURGLARY):
    Reported burglary rate in state (per 100,000 population). Defined as the unlawful entry of a structure to commit a felony or theft.
11. *Larceny* (LARCENY):
    Reported larceny–theft rate in state (per 100,000 population). Defined as the unlawful taking, carrying, leading, or riding away of property from the possession or constructive possession of another. It includes crimes such as shoplifting, pickpocketing, purse-snatching, thefts from motor vehicles, thefts of motor vehicle parts, bicycle thefts, etc., in which no use of force, violence or fraud occurs. This crime category does not include embezzlement, 'con' games, forgery and worthless cheques.
12. *Motor vehicle theft* (MVTHEFT):
    Reported rate of motor vehicle theft in state (per 100,000 population).

Table 2

Correlation matrix for all variables (data for 39 states) (Coefficients marked * are significant at P < 0.05)

Variable	% 15–24M	HOMICIDE	MORTALITY	ROBINHD	MEDINC
% 15–24M	1.00	.32*	.37*	.31	−.18
HOMICIDE	.32*	1.00	.70*	.74*	−.24
MORTALITY	.37*	.70*	1.00	.63*	−.38*
ROBINHD	.31	.74*	.63*	1.00	−.47*
MEDINC	−.18	−.24*	−.38*	−.47*	1.00
SOCTRUST	.32*	.82*	.76*	.73*	−.24
RAPE	.14	.38*	.13	.13	−.07
ROBBERY	−.04	.63*	.23	.36*	.38*
ASSAULT	.19	.73*	.35*	.50*	−.01
BURGLARY	.13	.67*	.17	.44*	−.04
LARCENY	−.07	.26	−.31	−.04	.12
MVTHEFT	−.05	.39*	−.01	.24	.54*

adding to the impression that we are dealing with a distinction between social conditions which lead to increased violence and those which lead to increased property crime. Rape, as a violent crime which lacks strong associations with income distribution or social trust, appears to be an exception to this pattern, but as rape statistics are notoriously affected by differences in reporting, it may be unwise to read much into this.

We are inclined to take the differences in the associational patterns of violence and property crime seriously partly because they echo earlier findings. In an analysis of data for 27 countries, Krohn (1976) found statistically significant relationship between higher homicide and greater income inequality which remained after controlling for GNPpc. However, he found the relationship with property crime was, if anything, the other way round. A number of other pieces of research also reveal a sharp distinction between violence and property crime. Field (1990) analyses fluctuations in crime in Britain in relation to the business cycle and shows sharply differing patterns: property crime is negatively related to changes in consumer's expenditure per capita

while violence is positively related. He suggests that property crime is a result of relative deprivation, whereas violence occurs more frequently when there are more people on the street and alcohol consumption is higher. Hennigan *et al.* (1982) examined the effects of the introduction of television in different parts of the United States in the 1950s and '60s on the rates of violent crime, burglary, auto theft and larceny. They found no effect on violence, burglary or auto theft, but a consistent association between the spread of television and rises in larceny.

What then are the differences between the social conditions conducive to homicide and those conducive to property crime, and what can the difference tell us about the way the social environment associated with greater income inequality affects health? We conjecture that one of the salient characteristics of social environments marked by wide income disparities is that they generate invidious social comparisons, which in turn engender a sense of exclusion and alienation among vulnerable individuals. Under such conditions, violent behaviour may be seen as an expression of the quest for respect from others. To shore up these arguments, we turn to evidence of a different nature, viz. narrative histories of violent individuals describing their quest for respect. In the section to follow, we move purposely from community-level analysis (the interrelationships among income inequality, social cohesion, and mortality) toward an individual-level description of the relationship between the psychological sense of exclusion and the expression of violent behaviour. The reason for making this macro-to-micro transition is to attempt to link the social environment (income inequality) to individual health outcomes, via intervening psychological variables, including the lack of self-esteem and the sense of not being respected.

Antecedents of Violence

Few authorities can match James Gilligan's detailed personal knowledge of men imprisoned for violence. He worked for 25 years as a psychiatrist in American prisons talking daily to violent offenders (Gilligan 1996). As a former director of the Centre for the Study of Violence at Harvard Medical School, he regards his book, *Violence*, as a contribution to public health and we shall quote from it extensively. Gilligan says:—

. . . the prison inmates I work with have told me repeatedly, when I asked them why they had as-

saulted someone, that it was because 'he disrespected me', or 'he disrespected my visit' (meaning/visitor'). The word 'disrespect' is central in the vocabulary, moral value system, and psychodynamics of these chronically violent men that they have abbreviated it into the slang term, 'he dis'ed me'. (1996: 106)

The challenge 'Are you dis'in' m?' has now also become the standard way young people on the streets of Britain threaten belligerence.

Gilligan continues:—

I have yet to see a serious act of violence that was not provoked by the experience of feeling shamed and humiliated, disrespected and ridiculed, and that did not represent the attempt to prevent or undo this 'loss of face'—no matter how severe the punishment, even if it includes death (1996: 110).

Describing one prisoner, he says

a very angry and violent inmate in his thirties, in prison for armed robbery, was referred to me because he had been yelling at, insulting, threatening, and assaulting another inmate. He had been doing this kind of thing for the past several weeks, and, off and on, for years . . . (and I had little) success in persuading him to stop his endlessly self-defeating power struggles with everyone around him, which inevitably resulted in his being punished more severely.

In an attempt to break through that vicious cycle with this man, I finally asked him, 'What do you

SOCTRUST	RAPE	ROBBERY	ASSAULT	BURGLARY	LARCENY	MVTHEFT
.32*	.14	−.04	.19	.13	−.07	−.05
.82*	.38*	.63*	.73*	.67*	.26	.39*
.76*	.13	.23	.35*	.17	−.31	−.01
.73*	.13	.36*	.50*	.44*	−.04	−.24
−.24	−.07	.38*	−.01	−.04	.12	.54*
1.00	.17	.45*	.61*	.54*	.01	.31
.17	1.00	.19	.43*	.53*	.57*	.20
.45*	.19	1.00	.64*	.49*	.29	.77*
.61*	.43*	.64*	1.00	.74*	.45*	.56*
.54*	.53*	.49*	.74	1.00	.63*	.55*
.01	.57*	.29	.45*	.63*	1.00	.32*
.31	.20	.77*	.56*	.55*	.32*	1.00

want so badly that you would sacrifice everything else in order to get it?' And he . . . replied with calm assurance, with perfect coherence and even a kind of eloquence: 'Pride. Dignity. Self-esteem.' And then he went on to say, again more clearly than before: 'And I'll kill every mother-fucker in that cell block if I have to in order to get it! My life ain't worth nothin' if I take somebody disrespectin' me and callin' me punk asshole faggot and goin' Ha, Ha! at me. Life ain't worth livin' if there ain't nothin' worth dyin' for. If you ain't got pride, you got nothin'. That's all you got! I've already got my pride'. He explained that the other prisoner was 'tryin'' to take that away from me. I'm not a total idiot. I'm not a coward. There ain't nothin I can do except snuff him. I'll throw gasoline on him and light him'. (1996: 106)

About the use of violence in robbery, Gilligan says:—

Some people think that armed robbers commit their crime in order to get money. And of course, sometimes that is the way they rationalize their behavior. But when you sit down and talk with people who repeatedly commit such crimes, what you hear is, 'I never got so much respect before in my life as I did when I first pointed a gun at somebody', or 'You wouldn't believe how much respect you get when you have a gun pointed at some dude's face'. For men who have lived for a lifetime on a diet of contempt and disdain, the temptation to gain instant respect in this way can be worth far more than the cost of going to prison, or even dying. (1996: 109)

Discussing the kind of events which can trigger violence, Gilligan says:—

. . . it is well known to anyone who reads the newspapers that people often seem to become seriously violent, even homicidal, over what are patently trivial events. (1996: 12)

It is the very triviality of the incidents that precipitate violence, the kinds of things that provoke homicide and sometimes suicide, whether in family quarrels or those that occur among friends and lovers on the street or in barrooms, that has often been commented on, with surprise and perplexity— being given a 'dirty look', having one's new shoes stepped on, being called a demeaning name, having a spouse or lover flirt with someone else, being

shoved by someone at a bar, having someone take food off one's plate, or refuse to move a car that is blocking one's driveway . . . (1996: 133)

Everyone has experienced 'trivial' insults that rankle. A child is teased for a difficult word mispronounced, a professional woman is asked to get the coffee. If these small incidents rankle people with power, prestige, and status, imagine their effect on people who don't have these advantages . . . (1996: 134)

. . . events that are utterly trivial from any moral or legal point of view may be of the very greatest importance and significance from a . . . psychological perspective. (1996: 135)

This view from a prison psychiatrist accords well with Jimmy Boyle's descriptions of himself. Once known as 'the most violent man in Scotland', Boyle wrote his autobiography in the 10th year of a sentence for manslaughter (Boyle 1977). Violence as a means of gaining status and respect is equally clear in his account.

There is no doubt that when I was sober, alone and faced with reality I hated myself . . . there was just this completely lost feeling . . . Yet . . . when I was with my pals, there was this feeling that it was okay and that having attacked a gang single handed the previous night, I had in some way proved myself and gained enough confidence to fight alongside them. I had this hunger to be recognised, to establish a reputation for myself and it acted as an incentive being with the top guys in the district at sixteen. There was this inner compulsion for me to win recognition amongst them. (1977: 79)

Talking of one spell in Barlinnie Prison: '. . . each of us had reputations, there had never been this sort of gathering of guys in the criminal element in Glasgow ever before. Although we were inside this was still the great motivating force—our reputation' (1977: 131).

Of a period of fundamental self-examination, Boyle said 'For the first time in my life, I was having to think very deeply about violence and other methods of gaining status' (1977: 240).

The contribution of low socioeconomic status to the need to earn respect through violence is shown not only in the association between homicide and income distribution, but also in the frequency with which Boyle mentions that fellow prisoners were also from the Gorbals (then the poorest slum area of Glasgow) and had sometimes even been to the same school as him.

Given that violence is a defense of status among those who have few sources of status and self-esteem, Gilligan suggests that there are three factors which make the difference between people who are violent and others. First, he says,

Many of the violent criminals who fill our maximum security prisons . . . desperately want to feel that they are big, tough, independent, self-assertive, self-reliant men, so as not to feel needy, helpless, frightened, inadequate, unskilled, incompetent, and often illiterate. . . . For we will never understand violence and violent crimes until we see through what is, in truth, a defensive disguise . . . (1996: 127)

He continues:

The second precondition for violence is met when these men perceive themselves as having no non-violent means of warding off or diminishing their feelings of shame or low self-esteem — such as socially rewarding economic or cultural achievement, or high social status, position or prestige. Violence is a 'last resort', a strategy they will use only when no other alternatives appear possible. (1996: 112)

On the third precondition for violence, Gilligan says

What is startling about the most violent people is how incapable they are, at least at the time they commit their violence, of feeling love, guilt, or fear. The person who is overwhelmed by feelings of shame is by definition experiencing a psychically life-threatening lack of love . . . (1996:113)

This accords well with Jimmy Boyle's statement (above) that in the cold light of day he hated himself. It is tempting to see this in the context of his description of the lack of physical affection in his family life. He says:

for some strange reason or other, actual physical contact in families that I knew was very limited. I would never think of coming into the house after all this long absence (on release from several years in prison) and cuddling my Ma or giving her a kiss or for that matter shaking my brothers by the hand or embracing them; these things just weren't done. That was sissy stuff, therefore not for us. (1977: 113)

We are left with a strong impression that homicide and violence are so closely related to income inequality because they come out of an extreme sensitivity to issues of personal social status to which people are particularly vulnerable when excluded from many of the usual sources of status. Although we have quoted material relating to violent offenders, it is clear that the same relationships hold in society more widely. The pervasive discrimination and exclusion of African-Americans from mainstream American society has been postulated to be the phenomenological explanation for younger blacks' preoccupation with respect (readers are referred, for example, to the eloquent qualitative work by American scholars like Elijah Anderson (1990) and Bourgois (1995)). The *Washington Post* reported, Nathan McCall, who grew up in a poverty-stricken neighbourhood in Virginia and served time in prison for violent crime, says in his autobiography: —

For as long as I can remember, black folks have had a serious thing about respect. I guess it's because white people disrespected them so blatantly for so long that blacks viciously protected what little morsels of self-respect they thought they had left. Some of the most brutal battles I saw in the streets stemmed from seemingly petty stuff . . . But the underlying issue was always respect. You could ask a guy, 'Damn, man, why did you bust that dude in the head with a pipe?'

And he might say, 'The motherfucka disrespected me!'

That was explanation enough. It wasn't even necessary to explain how the guy had disrespected him. It was universally understood that if a dude got disrespected, he had to do what he had to do. It's still that way today. Young dudes nowadays call it 'dissin''. They'll kill a nigger for dissin' them. Won't touch a white person, but they'll kill a brother in a heartbeat over a perceived slight. This irony was that white folks constantly disrespected us in ways seen and unseen, and we tolerated it. Most blacks understood that the repercussions were more severe for retaliating against whites than for doing each other in. It was as if black folks were saying, 'I can't do much to keep whites from dissin' me, but I damn sure can keep black folks from doing it'. (McCall 1994: 52)

Property Crime

What then of property crime—larceny and motor vehicle theft? The indications of the social milieu in which it is most common are less clear. While there have been several papers (cited above) which testify to a sharp distinction between patterns of violence and theft, there is little work which explores the differences in the social environment from which these crimes come. The finding that property crime increases in economic recessions (Field 1990), and that it also rose in response to the spread of television in the United States (Hennigan *et al.* 1982) both suggest that it is a response to relative deprivation. However, the broad pattern of correlations in Table 2 (above) shows that it is not even weakly related to income distribution. More surprising still is that larceny's weak association with mortality is an inverse association (Table 2), and that motor vehicle theft shows a significant positive relation with median income (r = 0.54) and no relation with mortality.

Using the World Values Survey (WVS) and the International Crime Victim Surveys, Halpern (1996) found that 'although moral values have little or no relationship with the covariants of crime and cannot therefore "explain" it, a specific sub-set of items tapping "self-interest" do covary (with crime) and therefore offer some explanations' (1996: 5). The WVS covered 50 countries, and common groupings of values were picked out using factor analysis before the factors were related to crime victimisation rates. In a subsequent more detailed analysis Halpern (personal communication) reported a correlation of 0.5 between international crime victimisation

rates and the 'self-interest' factor. Although these results come from data which make no distinction between kinds of crime, as theft is the most common form of crime in most countries, the patterns which emerge are likely to reflect its distribution.

Given that in our data larceny and motor vehicle theft are unrelated to income distribution and tend, if anything, to be more prevalent where median income is higher and mortality lower, one might then speculate—as Halpern (1996) indeed does—that theft arises from values rooted in something closer to self-interest and individualism, fuelled perhaps as much by the habit of consumption as by deprivation. Our data did not include fraud which is clearly a form of property crime not involving violence. Traditionally regarded as a 'white collar crime', fraud is likely to have even less association with deprivation than larceny and its inclusion would have led to an even sharper distinction between the pattern of violence and property crime.

Indeed, a limitation of our study is the lack of data addressing a broader conceptualisation of violence and property crime. Thus the routine reporting of violent *crime* ignores the many other forms of institutionalised violence in society: (a) those which are perpetrated by the State and its personnel (armed forces, warfare, police, and prisons); (b) those to which the State turns a blind eye (domestic violence, firearm ownership, motor vehicle violence—'road rage', speeding, and drunk driving); as well as (c) those which are professionalised, rarely apprehended, and a necessary part of illegal business activity (illegal drugs, loan sharking, prostitution, protection). Similarly, broader definition of property crime (*e.g.* extraction of surplus value, tax evasion, fraud and white collar crime) would have sharpened the distinctions we are trying to draw. Additionally, the usual caveats apply in attempting to interpret findings based on crime *statistics*, which are mediated via processes of report, arrest, charge, and trial; and are consequently biased against the poor, the inarticulate, and those with low social status.

CONCLUSIONS

OUR argument is not that the number of homicide victims account for the relationship between health and income distribution. It is that the violence associated with income inequality serves as an indicator of the psychosocial impact of wider income differences. What we can take away from this discussion is that the most pressing aspect of relative deprivation and low relative income is less the shortage of the material goods which others have, as the low social status and the desperate lack of sources of self-esteem which usually goes with it. If social cohesion matters to health, then perhaps the component of it which matters most is that people have positions and roles in society which accord them dignity and respect. We infer this from the fact that it is violence rather than property crime which varies so closely with income distribution, social trust and mortality. Unlike theft, which is in a sense a relationship with property, violence is a much more intensely social crime and seems above all to express a lack of adequate internal and external sources of self-esteem, dignity and social status.

As Miller and Ferroggiaro (1996) have pointed out 'Respect and self-respect are central components of an enlarged concept of citizenship . . . Respect affects how we are treated, what help from others is likely, what economic arrangements others are willing to engage in with us, when reciprocity is to be expected'. Respect acts as a resource for individuals, and should be considered a component of the norms of reciprocity, trust, and social obligation that are essential for minimising the risks of poor physical, psychological, or social health (Aday 1994). Indeed, mutual respect and the avoidance of inflicting humiliation on people is the central concept of Margalit's 'decent society' (Margalit 1996). As he

says, a decent society 'does not injure the civic honour of those belonging to it' (1996: 151). That honour and shame are so crucial to human social relations and may often become issues of life and death has long been recognised by social anthropologists (Peristiany 1965).

The impressive body of work on the physiological effects of the chronic stress experienced by low status baboons and macaques (Sapolsky 1993, Shively *et al.* 1994, Shively *et al.* 1997) suggests that there may be a number of health effects which spring directly from low social status among humans, and some of the same physiological effects of low social status have been found among humans as among these nonhuman primates (Brunner 1997). However, if issues round shame, respect, self-esteem, are how we conceptualise the most powerful psychosocial impact of low social status, then it is still difficult to distinguish between the individual and social effects of inequality on health status. As Pitt-Rivers (1965) says, 'Honour is the value of a person in his own eyes, but also in the eyes of society. It is his estimation of his own worth, his claim to pride, but it is also the acknowledgement of that claim . . . by society' (1965: 21).

Considerable research has already documented the contribution to the social gradient in health attributable to factors such as unemployment, job insecurity, sense of control and other sources of difficulty associated with disadvantages. Perhaps more attention should now be given to the psychosocial effects most directly inherent in low social status itself.

The authors wish to thank two anonymous reviewers for their helpful comments made on an earlier version of this manuscript.

REFERENCES

Aday, L.A. (1994) Health status of vulnerable populations, *Annual Review of Public Health*, 15, 487–509.

Anderson, E. (1990) *Streetwise: Race, Class, and Change in an Urban Community.* Chicago: Chicago University Press.

Atkinson, A.B. and Micklewright, J. (1992) *Economic Transformation in Eastern Europe and the Distribution of Income.* Cambridge: Cambridge University Press.

Ben-Shlomo, Y., White, I.R. and Marmot, M. (1996) Does the variation in the socioeconomic characteristics of an area affect mortality? *British Medical Journal* 312, 1013–14.

Bourgois, P.L. (1995) *In Search of Respect: Selling Crack in El Barrio.* Cambridge, New York: Cambridge University Press.

Boyle, J. (1977). *A Sense of Freedom.* London: Pan Books.

Burski, R.J. Jr. and Grasmick, H. (1993) *Neighborhoods and Crime: the Dimensions of Effective Community Control.* New York: Lexington.

Brunner, E. (1997) Stress and the biology of inequality. *British Medical Journal,* 314, 1472–6.

Chrousos, G.P., McCarty, R., Pacak, K., Cizza, G., Sternbery, E., Gold, P.W. and Kvetnansky, R. (eds) (1995) *Stress: Basic Mechanisms and Clinical Implications. Annals of the New York Academy of Sciences,* Vol. 771. New York: The New York Academy of Sciences.

Coleman, J.S. (1990) *The Foundations of Social Theory.* Cambridge, MA: Harvard University Press.

Field, S. (1990) *Trends in Crime and their Interpretation.* Home Office Research and Planning Unit Report. London: HMSO.

Fiscella, K. and Franks, P. (1997) Poverty or income inequality as predictors of mortality: longitudinal cohort study, *British Medical Journal,* 314, 1724–8.

Gilligan, J. (1996) *Violence: our Daily Epidemic and its Causes.* New York: G.P. Putnam.

Halpern, D. (1996) Changes in moral concepts and values: can values explain crime? Royal Society of Edinburgh, Causes of Crime Symposium, 5 June 1996.

Hennigan, K.M., Heath, L., Wharton, J.D., Del Rosario, M.L., Cook, T.D. and Calder, B.J. (1982) Impact of the introduction of television on crime in the United States: empirical findings and theoretical implications, *Journal of Personality and Social Psychology,* 42, 461–77.

Hsieh, C-C., Pugh M.D. (1993) Poverty, income inequality and violent crime: a meta-analysis. *Criminal Justice Review,* 18, 182–202.

Kaplan, G.A., Pamuk, E., Lynch, J.W., Cohen, R.D. and Balfour, J.L. (1996) Inequality in income and mortality in the United States: analysis of mortality and potential pathways, *British Medical Journal,* 312, 999–1003.

Kawachi, I., Kennedy, B.P., Lochner, K. and Prothrow-Stith, D. (1997) Social capital, income inequality and mortality, *American Journal of Public Health,* 87, 1491–8.

Kennedy, B.P., Kawachi, I. and Prothrow-Stith, D. (1996) Income distribution and mortality: cross sectional ecological study of the Robin Hood index in the United States, *British Medical Journal,* 312, 1004–7.

Krahn, H., Hartnagel, T.F. and Gartrell, J.W. (1986) Income inequality and homicide rates: cross-national data and criminological theories, *Criminology,* 24, 269–95.

Krohn, M.D. (1976) Inequality, unemployment and crime, *Sociological Quarterly,* 17, 303–13.

Margalit, A. (1966) *The Decent Society.* Harvard: Harvard University Press.

McCall, N. (1994) *Makes Me Wanna Holler. A Young Black Man in America.* New York: Random House.

Messner, S.E. (1982) Societal development, social equality and homicide, *Social Forces,* 61, 225–40.

Miller, S.M. and Ferroggiaro, K.M. (1996) Respect. *Poverty and Race,* 5, 1, 1–14.

Peristiany, J.G. (1965) *Honour and Shame: the Values of Mediterranean Society.* London: Weidenfeld and Nicolson.

Pitt-Rivers, J. (1965) Honour and social status. In Peristiany, J.G. (ed) *Honour and Shame: the Values of Mediterranean Society.* London: Weidenfeld and Nicolson.

Putnam, R.D. (1993). *Making Democracy Work. Civic Traditions in Modern Italy.* Princeton, NJ: Princeton University Press.

Putnam, R.D. (1995) Bowling alone: America's declining social capital, *Journal of Democracy,* 6, 65–78.

Reiss, A.J. and Roth, J.A. (eds) (1993) *Understanding and Preventing Violence.* Washington DC: National Academy Press.

Sampson, R.J. (1987) Urban black violence: the effect of male joblessness and family disruption. *American Journal of Sociology,* 93, 348–82.

Sampson, R.J. (1995) The community. In James, Q., Wilson, and Petersilia, J. (eds) *Crime.* San Francisco: Institute for Contemporary Studies.

Sampson, R.J., Raudenbush, S.W. and Earls, F. (1997) Neighborhoods and violent crime: a multilevel study of collective efficacy, *Science,* 277, 918–24.

Sampson, R.J. and Groves, W.R. (1989) Community structure and crime: testing social-disorganization theory, *American Journal of Sociology*, 94, 774–802.

Sapolsky, R.M. (1993) Endocrinology alfresco: psychoendocrine studies of wild baboons, *Recent Progress in Hormone Research*, 48, 437–68.

Shaw, C. and Mckay, H. (1942) *Juvenile Delinquency and Urban Areas*. Chicago: University of Chicago Press.

Shively, C.A. and Clarkson, T.B. (1994) Social status and coronary artery atherosclerosis in female monkeys, *Arteriosclerosis and Thrombosis*, 14, 721–6.

Shively, C.A., Laird, K.L. and Anton, R.F. (1997) The behavior and physiology of social stress and depression in female cynomolgus monkeys, *Biological Psychiatry*, 41, 871–82.

Simcha-Fagan, O. and Schwartz, J. (1986) Neighborhood and delinquency: an assessment of contextual effects, *Criminology*, 24, 667–704.

Skogan, W. (1991) *Disorder and Decline*. New York: Free Press.

Taylor, R., Gottfredson, S. and Brower, S. (1984) Block crime and fear: defensible space, local social ties, and territorial functioning, *Journal of Research in Crime and Delinquency*, 21, 303–31.

US Department of Justice, Federal Bureau of Investigation (1991–1994) Crime in the United States, 1991–1994, Uniform Crime Reports. Washington DC: Federal Bureau of Investigation, US Department of Justice.

Wacquant, L.J.D. and Wilson, W.J. (1989) The cost of racial and class exclusion in the inner city, *Annals of the American Academy of Political and Social Science*, 501, 8–25.

Wilkinson, R.G. (1992) Income distribution and life expectancy, *British Medical Journal*, 304, 165–8.

Wilkinson, R.G. (1996) *Unhealthy Societies. The Afflictions of Inequality*. London: Routledge.

Wilson, M. and Daly, M. (1997) Life expectancy, economic inequality, homicide, and reproductive timing in Chicago neighbourhoods, *British Medical Journal* 314: 1271–4.

Twenty-Nine

SOCIAL CAPITAL, INCOME INEQUALITY, AND FIREARM VIOLENT CRIME

*Bruce P. Kennedy, Ichiro Kawachi, Deborah Prothrow-Stith,
Kimberly Lochner, and Vanita Gupta*

Abstract

Studies have shown that poverty and income are powerful predictors of homicide and violent crime. We hypothesized that the effect of the growing gap between the rich and poor is mediated through an undermining of social cohesion, or social capital, and that decreased social capital is in turn associated with increased firearm homicide and violent crime. Social capital was measured by the weighted responses to two items from the U.S. General Social Survey: the per capita density of membership in voluntary groups in each state; and the level of social trust, as gauged by the proportion of residents in each state who believed that "most people would take advantage of you if they got the chance". Age-standardized firearm homicide rates for the years 1987–1991 and firearm robbery and assault incidence rates for years 1991–1994 were obtained for each of the 50 U.S. states. Income inequality was strongly correlated with firearm violent crime (firearm homicide, $r = 0.76$) as well as the measures of social capital: per capita group membership ($r = -0.40$) and lack of social trust ($r = 0.73$). In turn, both social trust (firearm homicide, $r = 0.83$) and group membership (firearm homicide, $r = -0.49$) were associated with firearm violent crime. These relationships held when controlling for poverty and a proxy variable for access to firearms. The profound effects of income inequality and social capital, when controlling for other factors such as poverty and firearm
availability, on firearm violent crime indicate that policies that address these broader, macro-social forces warrant serious consideration.

Introduction

"Take the people of Briançon. They allow the needy, the widows and orphans, to cut their hay three days earlier than the rest. When their homes are in ruins they repair them for nothing . . . In the past hundred years they have not had a single murder".

—Victor Hugo, *Les Misérables* (1862)

Intentional injuries resulting from violence make a significant contribution to the mortality and morbidity of the U.S. population. Injuries caused by violent behavior are estimated to cost American society approximately $26 billion dollars a year (Rice *et al.*, 1989). Currently, homicide is the leading cause of death for young African-American males and females (15–34) and the second leading cause of death for all 10–19 year-olds with an increasing number attributable to firearms (Hammett *et al.*, 1992; Fingerhut *et al.*, 1992).

Much of the recent policy debate concerning ways to reduce intentional injuries due to vio-

Originally published in *Social Science & Medicine*, 1998.

lence has focused on restricting access to lethal means such as firearms. Recent studies suggest a strong association between gun availability and homicide rates (Cook, 1991; McDowell *et al.*, 1992; Kellermann *et al.*, 1993). Furthermore, there has been an increase in adolescent self-reports of carrying firearms that may have contributed to the homicide problem, although whether the increase in weapon-carrying is due to increased access to weapons or some other factor remains unclear (Reiss and Roth, 1993).

Unfortunately, the debate about restricting access to firearms has focused attention on individual behaviors often to the exclusion of other important determinants of violent crime. The role that broader social factors, such as income inequality and poverty, play in determining the incidence of violent crime have been increasingly neglected in the current policy debate. Studies have shown that poverty and income inequality, whether at the city, state, or national level, are powerful predictors of homicide and violent crimes (Blau and Blau, 1986; Krahn *et al.*, 1986; Land *et al.*, 1990; Hsieh and Pugh, 1993). Income inequality, or other indices of relative deprivation, are considered to be stronger predictors of homicide and violent crime than indices of absolute deprivation, such as poverty (Baily, 1984; Messner, 1989). Recently, Kennedy *et al.* (1996) found that the Robin Hood Index, a measure of income inequality, predicted state-level variations in homicide rates. Even after adjusting for poverty, income inequality accounted for 52% of the between-state variance in homicide rates.

A number of theories have attempted to explain the observed relationship between income inequality and violent crime (Shaw and McKay, 1942; Blau and Blau, 1986; Wilson, 1987). Much of this work is built on an initial hypothesis by Shaw and McKay (1942) that inequality, and the concentration of poor economic conditions, lead to social disorganization through a breakdown of social cohesion and normlessness. It is hypothesized that communities lacking in social cohe-

sion (social capital) are less effective in exerting informal means of social control through establishing and maintaining norms to reduce violence compared to communities with higher levels of social capital (Sampson and Wilson, 1995).

The present study was undertaken to examine two related hypotheses: (1) state-level variations in income inequality predict firearm homicide, assault, and robbery rates independent of poverty and firearm availability; (2) state-level variations in social capital predict firearm homicide, assault, and robbery rates independent of poverty and firearm availability; and (3) the effect of income inequality on violent crime is mediated by its effect on social capital.

DATA AND METHODS

Measurement of Poverty and Income Inequality

Poverty and household income data for each state were obtained from the 1990 U.S. Census Summary Tape File STF 3A. The poverty variable represents the percentage of households in a state that were considered to be below the federal poverty index. The federal poverty index is a wage-income based measure that does not include income from other sources, such as public assistance programs. The index is updated annually to reflect cost of living changes in the Consumer Price Index. In 1990, this represented a household income of less than $13,359 for a household of four (U.S. Census, 1993). We also obtained median household income, per capita income, and the percentage of the population living in urban areas data for each state.

Data from the Census provides annual household income for 25 income intervals (0–$5,000 at the bottom and $150,000 or more at the top). To calculate income inequality, counts of the number of households falling into each of the 25 income intervals along with the total aggregate income were obtained for the state. The interval data was converted into income deciles using a program developed by Welniak (1988) at the U.S. Census Bureau for this purpose.

Our measure of income inequality, the Robin Hood Index (RHI), was established for each state from the income decile distribution (Atkinson and Micklewright, 1992), which represents the share of total household income in each decile (see Table 6 for an example derivation). The RHI is calculated by summing the excess shares of income for those deciles with shares that exceed 10%. In the case of Massachusetts, the RHI is 30.26% (Table 6). This represents the share of income that would have to be transferred from those above the mean to those below the mean to achieve an income distribution of perfect equality (Atkinson and Micklewright, 1992). Hence, the higher the value of the Index, the greater the degree of inequality in the distribution of incomes.

Measurement of Social Capital

Two core constructs of social capital, as presented by its principal theorists (Coleman, 1990; Putnam, 1993a,b, 1995), consist of levels of mutual trust among community members, and civic engagement. Civic engagement refers to the level of commitment of citizens to their communities and is reflected by their involvement in community affairs. Typically, this is measured by membership in civic-related and other associations and groups that bring members of a community together around shared interests. Following Putnam (1993a,b, 1995), we used weighted data from the general social survey (GSS), conducted by the National Opinion Research Center (Davis and Smith), to estimate state variations in group membership and levels of social trust. The GSS is a national survey that samples noninstitutionalized English-speaking persons 18 years or older living in the United States. The survey has been repeated 14 times over the last two decades, and has included a set of questions on social trust and organizational membership. In the present study, we averaged 5 years of cumulated data (1986–1990) from the GSS, representing 7,679 individual observations from 39 states.

Level of civic engagement was measured by the per capita number of groups and associations (e.g., church groups, labor unions, sport groups, professional or academic societies, school groups, political groups, and fraternal organizations) that residents belonged to in each state. The other component of social capital, trust in others, was assessed from responses to two GSS items that asked: "Do you think most people would try to take advantage of you if they got a chance, or would they try to be fair?" and "Generally speaking, would you say that most people can be trusted or that you can't be too careful in dealing with people?" For each state, we calculated the percentage of respondents who agreed with the first part of the above statements. Belief in the goodwill and benign intent of others facilitates collective action and mutual cooperation, and therefore adds to the stock of a community's social capital. Collective action, in turn, further reinforces community norms of reciprocity. In addition to the social trust items, we evaluated the response to another item on the GSS as a marker of social capital: "Would you say that most of the time people try to be helpful, or are they mostly looking out for themselves?"

The GSS was designed to provide a national and census region representative population sample, and as such, responses to the GSS are not necessarily representative of a state's population. To correct for this potential bias when disaggregating to the state level, we used post-stratification weights (as per Dr. Smith: personal communication) to adjust for the extent to which GSS respondents in a given state were over/under represented. To accomplish this, we developed post-stratification weights based on the distribution of age, race, and educational attainment of GSS respondents. The stratum-specific weights were calculated as follows:

$$w_{i,j,k,l} = P_{i,j,k,l}/p_{i,j,k,l}$$

where $w_{i,j,k,l}$ is the post-stratification weight for the GSS respondent residing in the i-th state, and being of j-th age-group, k-th race, and l-th level of education attainment; $P_{i,j,k,l}$ is the proportion of individuals with these characteristics residing in the i-th state, obtained from the 1990 U.S. Census; and $p_{i,j,k,l}$ is the corresponding proportion of such respondents in the GSS.

These weights were then used to adjust the individual responses to the social capital items in the GSS, using the *weight* procedure in SAS. For example, in states where the GSS over-sampled younger, black, and less educated respondents, the levels of social trust were adjusted upwards. In all of the subsequent analyses, we used the weighted responses.

Firearm Homicide and Violent Crime

Age-adjusted overall and race-specific homicide rates attributable to firearms (ICD 9th revision codes E965.0–E965.4) were obtained for each state from the Compressed Mortality Files compiled by the National Center for Health Statistics, Centers for Disease Control and Prevention (CDC). Data for years 1987–1991 were combined to provide more stable estimates of the firearm homicide rates. The firearm homicide rates were directly age-standardized to the U.S. population, and are expressed as the number of deaths per 100 000 population.

In addition to age-adjusted firearm homicide rates, firearm assault and firearm robbery incidence rates were calculated by combining data from the Federal Bureau of Investigation's Univorm Crime Reports (UCR) for the years 1991–1994 (these years were used instead of 1987–91 as the FBI only began collecting these data in 1991) (Federal Bureau of Investigation, 1991–1994). These rates are based on the number of *incidents* involving assaults or robberies with a firearm reported to police, and subsequently to the FBI through the crime reporting program.

Incidence data, while subject to various biases due to factors that influence reporting, is considered less susceptible to bias compared to arrest data (Reiss and Roth, 1993). The rates were calculated by summing the number of incidents for each state across the four years and dividing by the sum of the estimated total population for each state across the same four years. We used the state population data that is provided along with the incidence data in the UCR. Unlike the firearm homicide rates, these incidence rates could not be adjusted for age as this information was not available in the UCR. Nor could the data be disaggregated by race, so that rates represent crude overall firearm assault and robbery incidence rates.

Firearm Availability

As state-specific measures of gun ownership are not available, we used the fraction of *successful* suicides completed with a firearm as a surrogate for gun availability. This measure is the best currently available and has been used in numerous studies as a proxy for firearm availability (Cook, 1978; Lester, 1989, 1991). Suicide data were also obtained from the Compressed Mortality Files by combining years 1987–1991 (ICD-9 codes E955.0–E955.4; E950–E959).

Data Analysis

All analyses were conducted using Pearson's correlation and ordinary least squares (OLS) regression with variables in their nontransformed state. Due to problems of collinearity, the Robin Hood Index and social capital measures were not included in the same model. Instead, separate models were used to test for their effects on firearm violent crime. For each of these models we ran two separate regressions. In the first, we simply regressed each univariate predictor (group membership, social trust, RHI) on each of the measures of firearm violent crime (age-adjusted firearm homicide, firearm assault, firearm robbery). In the second set of regressions we examined the effects of each of the predictors adjusting for the effects of poverty and firearm availability (percentage of suicides completed with a firearm). To model the joint effects of income inequality (RHI) and social capital (as measured by social trust), we conducted a path analysis to decompose their relationship to the age-adjusted firearm homicide rate into direct and indirect effects (Pedhazur, 1973; Alwin and Hauser, 1975).

RESULTS

Relationship Between Income Inequality and Firearm Violent Crime

There was substantial variation in the degree of income inequality among the states. The overall RHI for the U.S. was 30.22%. New Hampshire (RHI = 27.13%) had the least income inequality and Louisiana (RHI = 34.05%) the greatest (Fig. 1). In the univariate analyses, RHI was significantly related to both the age-adjusted overall homicide (adjusted R^2 = 0.54) and age-adjusted firearm homicide (adjusted R^2 = 0.56) rates (Table 1). RHI was so significantly related to firearm assault (adjusted R^2 = 0.36) and robbery (adjusted R^2 = 0.23) rates, although these relationships were not as strong (Table 1). The association of RHI to all of the firearm violent crime variables remained highly statistically significant after adjusting for poverty and firearm availability in the multi-variate regression analyses: a one unit change in the RHI, which is the equivalent to transferring a one percent share of total income from the wealth to the less wealthy, was associated with a change in the age-adjusted firearm homicide rate of 1.55 per 100 000 (95% confidence interval [CI]: 1.12 to 1.99) (Table 2). This association was stronger for whites (adjusted R^2 = 0.55, p < 0.0001) than for blacks (adjusted R^2 = 0.20, p < 0.0006) in the univariate regression. RHI continued to be a statistically significant predictor of age-adjusted firearm homicide rates

after adjusting for poverty and firearm availability among both whites (B = 0.69; 95% CI: 0.45 to 0.92; p < 0.0001) and black (B = 4.82; 95% CI: 2.57 to 7.07; p < 0.0001).

To further determine the robustness of this relationship, we also examined the effects of RHI after adjusting for state variations in median household income, per capita income, and percentage of the population living in urban areas. None of these variables changed the association of the Robin Hood Index with firearm violent crime (data not shown).

Relationships Among Social Capital Variables and Firearm Violent Crime

All of the social capital measures were highly correlated with each other and with the violent crime measures (Table 3). Higher levels of social mistrust were associated with higher levels of firearm violent crime, while higher per capita group membership was associated with lower levels of firearm violent crime. Social trust (percentage of people who agreed that "most people would try to take advantage of you if they got a chance") was more strongly associated with firearm homicide rates (adjusted R^2 = 0.68) than per capita group membership (adjusted R^2 = 0.23) (Table 4). These relationships remained statistically significant after adjusting for poverty and firearm availability (Table 5). A one unit change in social trust (percentage of people who agreed that "most people would try to take advantage of you if they got a chance") was associated with a change in the age-adjusted firearm homicide rate of 0.27 (95% CI: 0.24 to 0.36) per 100 000 which is equivalent to about a 5% change in the age-adjusted firearm homicide rate. For per capita group membership, a one unit change in group membership was associated with a change in age-adjusted firearm homicide rates of 3.00 (95% CI: 1.22 to 4.78) per 100 000. As with the RHI, the social trust variable explained more of the between-state variance in age-adjusted firearm homicide rates among whites (adjusted R^2 = 0.53,

Figure 1(a).

Figure 1(b).

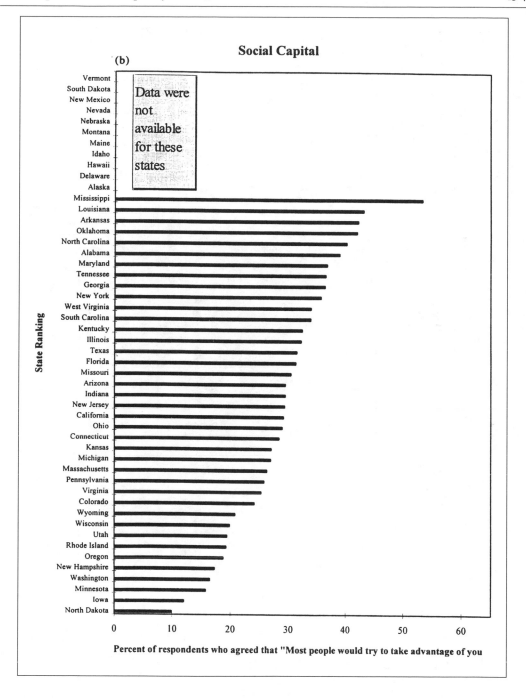

Figure 1(c).
State rankings on income inequality, social capital, and firearm homicide

Table 1.

Effects of income inequality on overall homicide and firearm homicide, assault, and robbery rates (50 states)

Violent Crime Rates	Years	B	S.e.	Adjusted R^2	$F_{1,48}$	$p <$
Overall homicide	1987–91	1.77	0.23	0.54	57.94	0.0001
Age-adjusted firearm homicide	1987–91	1.31	0.16	0.56	64.63	0.0001
Firearm assault	1991–94	28.56	5.30	0.36	28.08	0.0001
Firearm robbery	1991–94	23.75	6.04	0.23	15.47	0.0002

Table 2.

Effects of income inequality on overall homicide and firearm homicide, assault, and robbery rates, adjusted for poverty and firearm availability (50 states)

Violent Crime Rates	B	S.e.	$t, p <$	Adjusted R^2	$F_{3,46}$	$p <$
Age-adjusted homicide	2.04	0.33	6.11, 0.0001	0.56	21.80	0.0001
Age-adjusted firearm homicide	1.55	0.22	6.92, 0.0001	0.62	27.67	0.0001
Firearm assault	30.82	7.95	3.88, 0.0001	0.35	9.94	0.0001
Firearm robbery	40.22	8.45	4.76, 0.0001	0.30	8.08	0.0002

Table 3.

Correlations among indicators of social capital, income inequality, and firearm violent crime (39 states)

	1	2	3	4	5	6	7	8	9
1 age-adjusted homicide									
2 age-adjusted firearm homicide	0.99*								
3 firearm assault	0.61*								
4 firearm robbery	0.57*	0.56*	0.53*						
5 firearm suicide	0.41*	0.48*	0.50*	0.45*					
6 income inequality	0.73*	0.76*	0.48*	0.31*	0.43*				
7 group membership	−0.51*	−0.49*	−0.34*	−0.33*	−0.05	−0.40*			
8 trust 1[a]	0.82*	0.83*	0.55*	0.52*	0.49*	0.73*	−0.54*		
9 trust 2[b]	0.72*	0.73*	0.34*	0.46*	0.44*	0.71*	−0.65*	0.79*	
10 helpfulness[c]	0.72*	0.75*	0.60*	0.54*	0.51*	0.71*	−0.54*	0.81*	0.78*

*$p < 0.05$.

[a] Percent responding: "most people would try to take advantage of you if they got the chance".

[b] Percent responding: "you can't be too careful in dealing with people".

Table 4.

Effects of social capital on overall homicide and firearm homicide, assault, and robbery rates (39 states)

Violent Crime Rates	Years	B	S.e.	Adjusted R^2	$F_{1,37}$	$p <$
Social trust: Percentage of respondents who agreed that "most people would try to take advantage of you if they got a chance".						
Overall homicide	1987–91	0.41	0.05	0.66	75.42	0.0001
Age-adjusted firearm homicide	1987–91	0.30	0.03	0.68	80.39	0.0001
Firearm assault	1991–94	6.17	1.28	0.37	23.27	0.0001
Firearm robbery	1991–94	5.72	1.35	0.31	17.99	0.0001
Per capita group membership						
Overall homicide	1987–91	−5.06	1.37	0.25	13.67	0.0007
Age-adjusted firearm homicide	1987–91	−3.49	1.03	0.23	11.59	0.002
Firearm assault	1991–94	−65.39	29.89	0.09	4.79	0.035
Firearm robbery	1991–94	−72.10	29.75	0.11	5.87	0.02

Table 5.

Effects of social capital on overall homicide and firearm homicide, assault, and robbery rates, adjusted for poverty and firearm availability (39 states)

Violent Crime Rates	B	S.e.	$t, p <$	Adjusted R^2	$F_{3,35}$	$p <$
Social trust: Percentage of respondents who agreed that "most people would try to take advantage of you if they got a chance".						
Age-adjusted homicide	0.38	0.05	6.79, 0.0001	0.67	26.65	0.0001
Age-adjusted firearm homicide	0.27	0.04	6.85, 0.0001	0.69	28.69	0.0001
Firearm assault	5.52	1.53	3.59, 0.0009	0.35	7.83	0.0004
Firearm robbery	7.37	1.51	4.85, 0.0001	0.37	8.59	0.0002
Per capita group membership						
Age-adjusted homicide	−4.39	1.21	−3.63, 0.0009	0.44	11.09	0.0001
Age-adjusted firearm homicide	−3.00	0.88	−3.39, 0.002	0.45	11.22	0.0001
Firearm assault	−54.68	28.87	−1.87, 0.066	0.19	4.03	0.014
Firearm robbery	−67.34	31.14	−2.16, 0.037	0.08	2.05	0.124

$p < 0.0001$) than among blacks (adjusted R^2 = 0.21, $p < 0.002$). These effects persisted after adjusting for poverty and firearm availability: B = 0.10 (95% CI: 0.05 to 0.15; $p < 0.0001$) and B = 0.63 (95% CI: 0.23 to 1.04; $p < 0.003$) respectively. The results were similar for per capita group membership (data not shown).

We also examined the relationships of the other social trust item (percentage of respondents who agreed that "most people can be trusted") and the perceived helpfulness item (percentage of respondents who agreed that "most of the time people try to be helpful") to the firearm violent crime variables. The effects of both these variables on age-adjusted firearm homicide rates were essentially identical to the social trust variable discussed above: adjusted R^2 = 0.54 ($F_{1,37}$ = 423.95, $p < 0.0001$) and adjusted R^2 = 0.56 ($F_{1,37}$ $p < 0.0001$) respectively.

Relationships Among Inequality, Social Capital, and Age-adjusted Firearm Homicide: Path Analysis

State-level variations in income inequality (RHI) were strongly associated with lack of social trust: states with high inequality also had more respondents who agreed that "most people would try to take advantage of you if they got a chance" ($r = 0.73$, $p < 0.0001$). The other social capital measure, per capita group membership, was inversely related to the Robin Hood Index: states with low inequality had high per capita group membership ($r = -0.40$, $p < 0.003$).

The path analysis indicated that the effect of income inequality (as measured by the Robin Hood Index) on age-adjusted firearm homicide is mediated in part by social capital (as measured by level of social trust). According to our model, income inequality exerts a large indirect effect on age-adjusted firearm homicide through the social capital variable (Fig. 2). In Fig. 2, as income inequality increases so does the level of social mistrust which is in turn associated with increased age-adjusted firearm homicide rates.

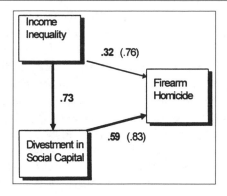

Figure 2

Path coefficients for the effects of income inequality and social capital on age-adjusted firearm homicide rates (39 states). Note: zero-order correlations are in parentheses, path coefficients are bold. Inequality is measured by the Robin Hood Index and social capital is measured by the percentage of respondents who agree that "most people would try to take advantage of you if they got a chance."

DISCUSSION

THE dominant current in the violence literature has sought to identify the individual factors that distinguish violent offenders from nonoffenders, whereas the purpose of the present study was to ask what societal characteristics—including income inequality, poverty, and social capital—predict differential rates of homicide and violent crime. More than half a century ago, Shaw and McKay (1942) argued in their classic work, *Juvenile Delinquency and Urban Areas,* that crime could be linked to broad social forces such as socioeconomic deprivation. Shaw and McKay demonstrated that in socioeconomically depressed areas in 21 U.S. cities, high rates of crime persisted over several decades despite changes in the racial and ethnic composition of the communities. The authors thereby rejected individualistic explanations of crime and focused instead on the processes by which criminal patterns of behavior were apparently transmitted across generations in areas of social disorganization and weak social controls.

Following the path breaking work of Shaw and McKay (1942), a number of studies throughout the 1970s and 1980s have investigated the relationships of poverty and income inequality to violent crimes, using cross-sectional, aggregate data at the national or subnational level (e.g., states, census tracts, cities, and standard metropolitan statistical areas [SMSAs]). Hsieh and Pugh (1993) have provided a meta-analysis of the 34 aggregate data studies that had been published on poverty, income inequality, and violent crime. Despite differences in methodology, the vast majority of studies agree that violent crime is related to poverty (pooled $r = 0.44$), as well as to income inequality (pooled $r = 0.44$). Interestingly, the effects of poverty were more homogeneous across the studies using lower levels of aggregation (e.g., cities). The converse was true for income inequality, which yielded more homogeneous effect sizes across studies using state and national levels of aggregation. This may be accounted for by the differences in how the two variables effect violent crime rates: income inequality, as a measure of *relative* deprivation, captures the effect of the individual's relationship to the larger society, whereas poverty, as a measure of *absolute* deprivation, captures the effect of resource deprivation on individuals. This is consistent with Richard Wilkinson's view that at lower levels of aggregation individual, or absolute income will matter more to health than income inequality—it is only within larger geographic areas that the social heterogeneity which is necessary for the effect of income inequality to occur that one finds a relationship between income inequality and health. As Wilkinson (1996) points out, it is not the inequality within Harlem that matters to its residents health, but rather the fact that so many are poor relative to the rest of the U.S.

Thus, there is growing consensus that

societal-level variables such as material deprivation may be a cause of crime. However, much less empirical work has been carried out to elucidate the pathways and mechanisms involved. According to one view, homicides and other violent crimes are explained as an individual's reaction to resource deprivation, subsequent personal frustrations, and diffuse hostility directed against targets of opportunity (Messner, 1983; Crutchfield, 1989; Arthur, 1991). Another view is that residential segregation and the concentration of deprived groups in urban slums have given rise to subcultures that value toughness, excitement, and fatalism, and these subcultural values supposedly bring young people in conflict with the law (Blau and Blau, 1982). Our aim in the present study was to test yet a third hypothesis: that a pronounced and highly visible gap in the *distribution* of income (as distinct from the absolute standard of living) may give rise to social disorganization and low social cohesion, as indexed by the level of mutual distrust among members of society, as well as their propensity to associate with each other. In turn, we hypothesized that lack of social cohesion (or "social capital") would predict aggregate rates of homicide and violent crime.

Our findings suggest that income inequality is powerfully related to the incidence of homicide and violent crimes via the depletion of social capital. These findings hold even when controlling for poverty and access to firearms. A variety of sociological and criminological evidence supports these claims. In a pooled analysis of 20 years (1975–1994) of data from the General Social Surveys, involving over 29 000 respondents, Brehm and Rahn (1997) found that rising income inequality was a significant predictor of declining trust in others. In turn, a decline in social trust was predictive of diminished levels of group membership. According to the work of Wilson (1987, 1991), Anderson (1990) and others, a critical factor responsible for the high incidence of delinquency and crime in urban settings has been the loss of social buffers that normally exist in middle class neighborhoods. Such buffers consist of formal and informal networks of organizations (church groups, business groups, neighborhood associations), as well as the presence of social norms concerning work and education. These buffers have become depleted in inner-city areas as a result of the increasing residential segregation of the poor. Conversely, a youth living in a neighborhood that includes a mixture of working and professional families "may observe increasing joblessness and idleness but he will also witness many individuals going to and from work . . . he may be cognizant of an increase in crime, but he can recognize that many residents in his neighborhood are not involved in criminal activity", (Wilson, 1987, p. 56).

While the work of Wilson (1987, 1991) and others refers to the situation of inner-city African-Americans, our data suggest that the relationships of income inequality and social capital to firearm violent crime holds equally for whites as well. Furthermore, these effects remain stable when controlling for poverty and the percentage of the population living in urban areas suggesting that income inequality, through its erosion of social capital, may have a broader social impact that extends beyond specific groups in high-risk urban settings. While our data are based upon analysis of aggregate data, the "ecological fallacy"—inferring individual relations based on grouped data—is not an issue here, since we have not made any cross-level inferences (Susser, 1994a,b). Our analyses have used purely ecologic variables (social capital, income inequality, prevalence of poverty) to predict purely ecological outcomes (population rates of firearm homicide and violent crime) and as such, do not provide the means for making predictions about individual behavior, yet can provide powerful indicators of macrosocial determinants of violent behavior (Schwartz, 1994; Susser, 1994a,b).

Table 6.

Data on derivation of Robin Hood Index
(example: Massachusetts)

Decile of households	Percent of total income
1	1.08
2	2.48
3	4.13
4	5.74
5	7.33
6	8.97
7	10.83
8	13.09
9	16.41
10	29.93

CONCLUSION

IN his review of poverty and inequality and their relationship to crime, Braithwaite (1979) concluded that programs that simply targeted groups living in poverty would not have a significant impact on the overall crime rates in society. In contrast, he argued "that gross economic measures to reduce the gap between the rich and the poor and the rest of the population" (pp. 231) are necessary if a significant reduction in crime is to be expected.

This view runs against the conventional violence prevention wisdom which usually *only* targets high risk individuals and groups rather than attempting to shift the underlying societal forces that give rise to a high incidence of violence in the population. This is not to say that the effects of poverty on violent crime are negligible (firearm homicide, $r = 0.49$), and we would certainly not argue against policies to reduce the burden on families living in impoverished settings. Nor would we argue that policies that restrict access to firearms be neglected as one of the means to reduce violent deaths. The proxy for access to firearms was highly correlated with firearm homicide ($r = 0.44$) indicating that it is also a powerful determinant of firearm homicide as has been shown in other studies rates (Cook, 1991; McDowell *et al.*, 1992; Kellermann *et al.*, 1993).

However, the profound effects of income inequality and social capital on firearm violent crime when controlling for both of these factors, indicate that policies and interventions that address these broader, macro-social forces warrant serious consideration.

REFERENCES

Alwin, D. F. and Hauser, R. M. (1975) The decomposition of effects in path analysis. *American Sociological Review* **40**, 37–47.

Anderson, E. (1990) *Street Wise*. University of Chicago Press, Chicago, IL.

Arthur, J. A. (1991) Socioeconomic predictors of crime in rural Georgia. *Criminal Justice Review* **16**, 29–41.

Atkinson, A. B., Micklewright, J. (1992) *Economic transformation in Eastern Europe and the distribution of income.* Cambridge University Press.

Baily, W. C. (1984) Poverty, inequality, and city homicide rates: Some not so unexpected findings. *Criminology* **22**, 531–550.

Blau, J. R. and Blau, P. M. (1982) The cost of inequality. Metropolitan structure and violent crime. *American Sociological Review* **47**, 114–129.

Blau, J. R. and Blau, P. M. (1986) The cost of inequality: Metropolitan structure and criminal violence. *Sociological Quarterly* **27**, 15–26.

Brehm, J. and Rahn, W. (1997) Individual-level evidence for the causes and consequences of social capital. *American Journal of Political Science* **41**, 999–1023.

Braithwaite, J. (1979) *Inequality, Crime and Public Policy.* Routledge and K. Paul, Boston.

Coleman, J. S. (1990) *The Foundations of Social Theory*. Harvard University Press, Cambridge, MA, pp. 300–321.

Cook, P. J. (1978) The effect of gun availability on robbery and robbery murder: A cross-section study of fifty cities. *Policy Studies Review Annual* **2**, 743–781.

Cook, P. J. (1991) The technology of personal violence: A review of the evidence concerning the importance of gun availability and use in violent crime, self defense, and suicide. *Crime and Justice: A Review of Research,* ed. M. Tonry, 14, pp. 1–71. University of Chicago Press, Chicago, IL.

Crutchfield, R. D. (1989) Labor stratification and violent crime. *Social Forces* **68**, 489–512.

Davis, J. A., Smith, T. W. *General Social Survey Cumulative File.* University of Michigan, Interuniversity Consortium and Social Research, Ann Arbor, MI.

Federal Bureau of Investigation (1991–1994) *Uniform Crime Reports.*

Fingerhut, L. A., Ingram, D. D. and Feldman, J. J. (1992) Firearm and nonfirearm homicide among persons 15 through 19 years of age. *JAMA* **267**, 3048–3053.

Hammett, M., Powell, K. E., O'Carroll, P. W. and Clanton, S. T. (1992) Homicide surveillance—United States, 1979–1988. *Morbidity and Mortality Weekly Report* **41**, 1–33.

Hsieh, C. C. and Pugh, M. D. (1993) Poverty, income inequality, and violent crime: A meta-analysis of recent aggregate data studies. *Criminal Justice Review* **18**, 182–202.

Kellermann, A. L., Rivera, F. P. and Rushforth, N. B. *et al.* (1993) Gun ownership as a risk factor for homicide in the home. *New England Journal of Medicine* **329**, 1084–1091.

Kennedy, B. P., Kawachi, I. and Prothrow-Stith, D. (1996) Income distribution and mortality: Test of the Robin Hood Index in the United States. *British Medical Journal* **312**, 1004–1007.

Krahn, H., Hartnagel, T. F. and Gartrell, J. W. (1986) Income inequality and homicide rates: Cross-national data and criminology theories. *Criminology* **24**, 269–295.

Land, K., McCall, P. and Cohen, L. (1990) Structural covariates of homicide rates: Are there any invariances across time and space? *American Journal of Sociology* **95**, 922–963.

Lester, D. (1989) Gun ownership and suicide in the United States. *Psychological Medicine* **19**, 519–521.

Lester, D. (1991) Crime as opportunity: A test of the hypothesis with European homicide rates. *British Journal of Criminology* **31**(2), 186–188.

McDowell, D., Loftin, C. and Wiersema, B. (1992) A comparative study of the preventive effects of mandatory sentencing laws for handgun crimes. *Journal of Criminal Law and Criminology* **83**, 378–394.

Messner, S. F. (1983) Regional differences in the economic correlates of the urban homicide rate. Some evidence on the importance of cultural context. *Criminology* **21**, 477–488.

Messner, S. F. (1989) Economic discrimination and societal homicide rates: Further evidence on the cost of inequality. *American Sociological Review* **54,** 597–611.

Pedhazur, E. J. (1973) *Multiple Regression in Behavioral Research.* Holt, Rinehart and Winston, New York.

Putnam, R. D. (1993a) The prosperous community. Social capital and economic growth. *The American Prospect* Spring, 35–42.

Putnam, R. D. (1993b) *Making Democracy Work.* Princeton University Press, Princeton, NJ.

Putnam, R. D. (1995) Bowling alone. America's declining social capital. *Journal of Democracy* **6,** 65–78.

Reiss, A. J., Roth, J. A., eds (1993) National Research Council. *Understanding and Preventing Violence.* National Academy Press, Washington, DC.

Rice, D. P., MacKenzie, E. J. and Associates (1989) *Cost of Injury in the United States: A Report to Congress.* Intitute for Health and Aging, USC and Injury Prevention Center, The Johns Hopkins University, San Francisco, CA.

Sampson, R. J., Wilson W. J. (1995) Toward a theory of race, crime, and urban inequality. In *Crime and Inequality,* eds. J. Hagan and R. D. Peterson. Stanford University Press, Stanford, CA.

Schwartz, S. (1994) The fallacy of the ecologic fallacy: The potential misuse of a concept and the consequences. *Am. J. Public Health* **84,** 819–824.

Shaw, C., McKay, H. (1942) *Juvenile Delinquency and Urban Areas.* University of Chicago Press, Chicago.

Susser, M. (1994a) The logic in ecological: II. The logic of design. *Am. J. Public Health* **84,** 830–835.

Susser, M. (1994b) The logic in ecological: I. The logic of analysis. *Am. J. Public Health* **84,** 825–829.

U.S. Bureau of Census (1993) Income and Poverty (CD-ROM).

Welniak, E. (1988) Unpublished software. U.S. Census Bureau.

Wilkinson, R. G. (1996) Income inequality and social cohesion. *American Journal of Public Health* **87,** 104–106.

Wilson, W. J. (1987) *The Truly Disadvantaged: The Inner City, the Underclass, and Public Policy.* University of Chicago Press, Chicago, IL.

Wilson, W. J. (1991) Studying inner-city social dislocations: The challenge of public agenda research. *American Sociological Review* **56,** 1–14.

Appendix

TABLE 6 shows the shares of income earned by each decile of household in Massachusetts in 1990. For example, the bottom 10% of households accounted for 1.08% of the total income in that state. If income were distributed perfectly equally, then each decile of household would account for exactly 10% of the share of total income. In the example of Massachusetts, households at or above the 70th percentile earned more than their "fair share" of total income.

The Robin Hood Index (RHI) is calculated by summing the excesses above the fair share of total income (i.e., > 10%) earned by each decile of households. In the case of Massachusetts,

$$RHI = (10.83 - 10.0) + (13.09 - 10.0)$$
$$+ (16.41 - 10.0) + (29.93 - 10.0)$$
$$= 0.83 + 3.09 + 6.41 + 19.93 = 30.26\%$$

The Index is equivalent to the approximate proportion of aggregate income that must be redistributed from households above the mean, and transferred to those below the mean in order to achieve perfect equality in the distribution of household incomes.

Thirty

NEIGHBORHOODS AND VIOLENT CRIME: A MULTILEVEL STUDY OF COLLECTIVE EFFICACY

Robert J. Sampson, Stephen W. Raudenbush, and Felton Earls

It is hypothesized that collective efficacy, defined as social cohesion among neighbors combined with their willingness to intervene on behalf of the common good, is linked to reduced violence. This hypothesis was tested on a 1995 survey of 8782 residents of 343 neighborhoods in Chicago, Illinois. Multilevel analyses showed that a measure of collective efficacy yields a high between-neighborhood reliability and is negatively associated with variations in violence, when individual-level characteristics, measurement error, and prior violence are controlled. Associations of concentrated disadvantage and residential instability with violence are largely mediated by collective efficacy.

FOR most of this century, social scientists have observed marked variations in rates of criminal violence across neighborhoods of U.S. cities. Violence has been associated with the low socioeconomic status (SES) and residential instability of neighborhoods. Although the geographical concentration of violence and its connection with neighborhood composition are well established, the question remains: why?

What is it, for example, about the concentration of poverty that accounts for its association with rates of violence? What are the social processes that might explain or mediate this relation?[1-3] In this article, we report results from a study designed to address these questions about crime and communities.

Our basic premise is that social and organizational characteristics of neighborhoods explain variations in crime rates that are not solely attributable to the aggregated demographic characteristics of individuals. We propose that the differential ability of neighborhoods to realize the common values of residents and maintain effective social controls is a major source of neighborhood variation in violence.[4, 5] Although social control is often a response to deviant behavior, it should not be equated with formal regulation or forced conformity by institutions such as the police and courts. Rather, social control refers generally to the capacity of a group to regulate its members according to desired principles—to realize collective, as opposed to forced, goals.[6] One central goal is the desire of community residents to live in safe and orderly environ-

Originally published in *Science*, 1997.

ments that are free of predatory crime, especially interpersonal violence.

In contrast to formally or externally induced actions (for example, a police crackdown), we focus on the effectiveness of informal mechanisms by which residents themselves achieve public order. Examples of informal social control include the monitoring of spontaneous play groups among children, a willingness to intervene to prevent acts such as truancy and street-corner "hanging" by teenage peer groups, and the confrontation of persons who are exploiting or disturbing public space.[5, 7] Even among adults, violence regularly arises in public disputes, in the context of illegal markets (for example, prostitution and drugs), and in the company of peers.[8] The capacity of residents to control group-level processes and visible signs of social disorder is thus a key mechanism influencing opportunities for interpersonal crime in a neighborhood.

Informal social control also generalizes to broader issues of import to the well-being of neighborhoods. In particular, the differential ability of communities to extract resources and respond to cuts in public services (such as police patrols, fire stations, garbage collection, and housing code enforcement) looms large when we consider the known link between public signs of disorder (such as vacant housing, burned-out buildings, vandalism, and litter) and more serious crime.[9]

Thus conceived, neighborhoods differentially activate informal social control. It is for this reason that we see an analogy between individual efficacy and neighborhood efficacy: both are activated processes that seek to achieve an intended effect. At the neighborhood level, however, the willingness of local residents to intervene for the common good depends in large part on conditions of mutual trust and solidarity among neighbors.[10] Indeed, one is unlikely to intervene in a neighborhood context in which the rules are unclear and people mistrust or fear one another. It follows that socially cohesive neighborhoods will prove the most fertile contexts for the realization of informal social control. In sum, it is the linkage of mutual trust and the willingness to intervene for the common good that defines the neighborhood context of collective efficacy. Just as individuals vary in their capacity for efficacious action, so too do neighborhoods vary in their capacity to achieve common goals. And just as individual self-efficacy is situated rather than global (one has self-efficacy relative to a particular task or type of task),[11] in this paper we view neighborhood efficacy as existing relative to the tasks of supervising children and maintaining public order. It follows that the collective efficacy of residents is a critical means by which urban neighborhoods inhibit the occurrence of personal violence, without regard to the demographic composition of the population.

WHAT INFLUENCES COLLECTIVE EFFICACY?

AS with individual efficacy, collective efficacy does not exist in a vacuum. It is embedded in structural contexts and a wider political economy that stratifies places of residence by key social characteristics.[12] Consider the destabilizing potential of rapid population change on neighborhood social organization. A high rate of residential mobility, especially in areas of decreasing population, fosters institutional disruption and weakened social controls over collective life. A major reason is that the formation of social ties takes time. Financial investment also provides homeowners with a vested interest in supporting the commonweal of neighborhood life. We thus hypothesize that residential tenure and homeownership promote collective efforts to maintain social control.[13]

Consider next patterns of resource distribution and racial segregation in the United States. Recent decades have witnessed an increasing geographical concentration of lower income residents, especially minority groups and female-headed families. This neighborhood concentration stems in part from macroeconomic changes related to the deindustrialization of central cities, along with the out-migration of middle-class residents.[14] In addition, the greater the race and class segregation in a metropolitan area, the smaller the number of neighborhoods absorbing economic shocks and the more severe the resulting concentration of poverty will be.[15] Economic stratification by race and place thus fuels the neighborhood concentration of cumulative forms of disadvantage, intensifying the social isolation of lower income, minority, and single-parent residents from key resources supporting collective social control.[1, 16]

Perhaps more salient is the influence of racial and economic exclusion on perceived powerlessness. Social science research has demonstrated, at the individual level, the direct role of SES in promoting a sense of control, efficacy, and even biological health itself.[17] An analogous process may work at the community level. The alienation, exploitation, and dependency wrought by resource deprivation act as a centrifugal force that stymies collective efficacy. Even if personal ties are strong in areas of concentrated disadvantage, they may be weakly tethered to collective actions.

We therefore test the hypothesis that concentrated disadvantage decreases and residential stability increases collective efficacy. In turn, we assess whether collective efficacy explains the association of neighborhood disadvantage and residential instability with rates of interpersonal violence. It is our hypothesis that collective efficacy mediates a substantial portion of the effects of neighborhood stratification.

RESEARCH DESIGN

THIS article examines data from the Project on Human Development in Chicago Neighborhoods (PHDCN). Applying a spatial definition of neighborhood—a collection of people and institutions occupying a subsection of a larger community—we combined 847 census tracts in the city of Chicago to crate 343 "neighborhood clusters" (NCs). The overriding consideration in formation of NCs was that they should be as ecologically meaningful as possible, composed of geographically contiguous census tracts, and internally homogeneous on key census indicators. We settled on an ecological unit of about 8000 people, which is smaller than the 77 established community areas in Chicago (the average size is almost 40,000 people) but large enough to approximate local neighborhoods. Geographic boundaries (for example, railroad tracks, parks, and freeways) and knowledge of Chicago's neighborhoods guided this process.[18]

The extensive racial, ethnic, and social-class diversity of Chicago's population was a major criterion in its selection as a research site. At present, whites, blacks, and Latinos each represent about a third of the city's population. Table 1 classifies the 343 NCs according to race or ethnicity and a trichotomized measure of SES from the 1990 census.[19] Although there are no low-SES Latino neighborhoods, there are black neighborhoods in all three cells of SES, and many heterogeneous neighborhoods vary in SES. Table 1 at once thus confirms the racial and ethnic segregation and yet rejects the common stereotype that minority neighborhoods in the United States are homogeneous.

To gain a complete picture of the city's neighborhoods, 8782 Chicago residents representing all 343 NCs were interviewed in their homes as part of the community survey (CS). The CS was designed to yield a representative sample of households within each NC, with sample sizes large enough to create reliable NC measures.[20] Henceforth, we refer to NCs as "neighborhoods," keeping in mind that other operational definitions might have been used.

Table 1.

Racial and ethnic composition by SES strata: Distribution of 343 Chicago NCs in the PHDCN design.

Race or ethnicity	SES		
	Low	Medium	High
≥ 75% black	77	37	11
≥ 75% white	0	5	69
≥ 75% Latino	12	9	0
≥ 20% Latino and ≥ 20% white	6	40	12
≥ 20% Latino and ≥ 20% black	9	4	0
≥ 20% black and ≥ 20% white	2	4	11
NCs not classified above	8	15	12
Total	114	114	115

MEASURES

"INFORMAL social control" was represented by a five-item Likert-type scale. Residents were asked about the likelihood ("Would you say it is very likely, likely, neither likely nor unlikely, unlikely, or very unlikely?") that their neighbors could be counted on to intervene in various ways if (i) children were skipping school and hanging out on a street corner, (ii) children were spray-painting graffiti on a local building, (iii) children were showing disrespect to an adult, (iv) a fight broke out in front of their house, and (v) the fire station closest to their home was threatened with budget cuts. "Social cohesion and trust" were also represented by five conceptually related items. Respondents were asked how strongly they agreed (on a five-point scale) that "people around here are willing to help their neighbors," "this is a close-knit neighborhood," "people in this neighborhood can be trusted," "people in this neighborhood generally don't get along with each other," and "people in

this neighborhood do not share the same values" (the last two statements were reverse coded).

Responses to the five-point Likert scales were aggregated to the neighborhood level as initial measures. Social cohesion and informal social control were closely associated across neighborhoods ($r = 0.80$, $P < 0.001$), which suggests that the two measures were tapping aspects of the same latent construct. Because we also expected that the willingness and intention to intervene on behalf of the neighborhood would be enhanced under conditions of mutual trust and cohesion, we combined the two scales into a summary measure labeled collective efficacy.[21]

The measurement of violence was achieved in three ways. First, respondents were asked how often each of the following had occurred in the neighborhood during the past 6 months: (i) a fight in which a weapon was used, (ii) a violent argument between neighbors, (iii) a gang fight, (iv) a sexual assault or rape, and (v) a robbery or mugging. The scale construction for perceived neighborhood violence, mirrored that for social control and cohesion. Second, to assess personal victimization, each respondent was asked "While you have lived in this neighborhood, has anyone ever used violence, such as in a mugging, fight, or sexual assault, against you or any member of your household anywhere in your neighborhood?".[22] Third, we tested both survey measures against independently recorded incidents of homicide aggregated to the NC level.[23] Homicide is one of the most reliably measured crimes by the police and does not suffer the reporting limitations associated with other violent crimes, such as assault and rape.

Ten variables were constructed from the 1990 decennial census of the population to reflect neighborhood differences in poverty, race and ethnicity, immigration, the labor market, age composition, family structure, homeownership, and residential stability (see Table 2). The census was independent of the PHDCN CS; moreover, the census data were collected 5 years earlier, which permitted temporal sequencing. To assess

Table 2

Oblique rotated factor pattern (Loadings ≥ 0.60) in 343 Chicago neighborhoods. (Data are from the 1990 census.)

Variable	Factor loading
Concentrated disadvantage	
Below poverty line	0.93
On public assistance	0.94
Female-headed families	0.93
Unemployed	0.86
Less than age 18	0.94
Black	0.60
Immigrant concentration	
Latino	0.88
Foreign-born	0.70
Residential stability	
Same house as in 1985	0.77
Owner-occupied house	0.86

whether a smaller number of linear combinations of census characteristics describe the structure of the 343 Chicago neighborhoods, we conducted a factor analysis.[24]

Consistent with theories and research on U.S. cities, the poverty-related variable given in Table 2 are highly associated and load on the same factor. With an eigenvalue greater than 5, the first factor is dominated by high loadings (>0.85) for poverty, receipt of public assistance, unemployment, female headed-families, and density of children, followed by, to a lesser extent, percentage of black residents. Hence, the predominant interpretation revolves around concentrated disadvantage—African Americans, children, and single-parent families are differentially found in neighborhoods with high concentrations of poverty.[25] To represent this dimension parsimoniously, we calculated a factor regression score that weighted each variable by its factor loading.

The second dimension captures areas of the city undergoing immigration, especially from Mexico. The two variables that define this dimension are the percentage of Latinos (approximately 70% of Latinos in Chicago are of Mexican descent) and the percentage of foreign-born persons. Similar to the procedures for concentrated disadvantages, a weighted factor score was created to reflect immigrant concentration. Because it describes neighborhoods of ethnic and linguistic heterogeneity, there is reason to believe that immigrant concentration may impede the capacity of residents to realize common values and to achieve informal social controls, which in turn explains an increased risk of violence.[1-5, 7]

The third factor score is dominated by two variables with high (>0.75) loadings: the percentage of persons living in the same house as 5 years earlier and the percentage of owner-occupied homes. The clear emergence of a residential stability factor is consistent with much past research.[13]

ANALYTIC MODELS

THE internal consistency of a person measure will depend on the intercorrelation among items and the number of items in a scale. The internal consistency of a neighborhood measure will depend in part on these factors, but it will hinge more on the degree of intersubjective agreement among informants in their ratings of the neighborhood in which they share membership and on the sample size of informants per neighborhood.[26] To study reliability, we therefore formulated a hierarchical statistical model representing item variation within persons, person variation within neighborhoods, and variation between neighborhoods. Complicating the analysis is the problem of missing data: inevitably, some persons will fail to respond to some questions in an interview. We present our hierarchical model as a series of nested models, one for each level in the hierarchy.[27]

Level 1 Model

Within each person, Y_{ijk}, the *i*th response of person *j* in neighborhood *k*, depends on the person's latent perception of collective efficacy plus error:

$$Y_{ijk} = \pi_{jk} + \sum_{p=1}^{9} \alpha_p D_{pijk} + e_{ijk} \qquad (1)$$

Here D_{pijk} is an indicator variable taking on a value of unity if response i is to item p in the 10-item scale intended to measure collective efficacy and zero if response i is to some other item. Thus, α_p represents the "difficulty" of item p, and π_{jk} is the "true score" for person jk and is adjusted for the difficulty level of the items to which that person responded.[28] The errors of measurement, e_{ijk}, are assumed to be independent and homoscedastic (that is, to have equal standard deviations).

Level 2 Model

Across informants within neighborhoods, the latent true scores vary randomly around the neighborhood mean:

$$\pi_{jk} = \eta_k + r_{jk}, \quad r_{jk} \sim N(0, \tau_\pi) \qquad (2)$$

Here η_k is the neighborhood mean collective efficacy, and random effects r_{jk} associated with each person are independently, normally distributed with variance τ_π, that is, the "within-neighborhood variance."

Level 3 Model

Across neighborhoods, each neighborhood's mean collective efficacy η_k varies randomly about a grand mean:

$$\eta_k = \gamma + u_k, \quad u_k \sim N(0, \tau_\eta) \qquad (3)$$

where γ is the grand mean collective efficacy, u_k is a normally distributed random effect associated with neighborhood k, and τ_n is the between-neighborhood variance. According to this setup, the object of measurement is η_k. The degree of intersubjective agreement among raters is the intraneighborhood correlation, $\rho = \tau_\eta/(\tau_\eta + \tau_\pi)$. The reliability of measurement of η_k depends

primarily on ρ and on the sample size per neighborhood. The entire three-level model is estimated simultaneously via maximum likelihood.[26]

The results showed that 21% of the variation in perceptions of collective efficacy lies between the 343 neighborhoods.[29] The reliability with which neighborhoods can be distinguished on collective efficacy ranges between 0.80 for neighborhoods with a sample size of 20 raters to 0.91 for neighborhoods with a sample size of 50 raters.

Controlling Response Biases

Suppose, however, that informant responses to the collective efficacy questions vary systematically within neighborhoods as a function of demographic background (such as age, gender, SES, and ethnicity), as well as homeownership, marital status, and so on. Then variation across neighborhoods in the composition of the sample of respondents along these lines could masquerade as variation in collective efficacy. To control for such possible biases, we expanded the level 2 model (Eq. 2) by incorporating 11 characteristics of respondents as covariates. Equation 2 becomes

$$\pi_{jk} = \eta_k + \sum_{q=1}^{11} \delta_q X_{qik} + r_{jk}, \quad r_{jk} \sim N(0, \tau_\pi)$$

$$(4)$$

where X_{qjk} is the value of covariate q associated with respondent j in neighborhood k and δ_q is the partial effect of that covariate on the expected response of that informant on the collective efficacy items. Thus, η_k is now the level of efficacy for neighborhood k after adjustment for the composition of the informant sample with respect to 11 characteristics: gender (1 = female, 0 = male), marital status (composed of separate indicators for married, separated or divorced, and single), homeownership, ethnicity and race (composed of indicators for Latinos and blacks), mobility (number of moves in past 5 years), years in neighborhood, age, and a composite measure of SES (the first principal component of education, income, and occupational prestige).

ASSOCIATION BETWEEN NEIGHBORHOOD SOCIAL COMPOSITION AND COLLECTIVE EFFICACY

THE theory described above led us to expect that neighborhood concentrated disadvantage (con. dis.) and immigrant concentration (imm. con.) would be negatively linked to neighborhood collective efficacy and residential stability would be positively related to collective efficacy, net of the contributions of the II covariates defined in the previous paragraph. To test this hypothesis, we expanded the level 3 model (Eq. 3) to

$$\eta_k = \gamma_0 + \gamma_1(\text{con. dis.})_k + \gamma_2(\text{stability}_k$$
$$+ \gamma_3(\text{imm. con.})_k$$
$$+ u_k, \quad u_k \sim N(0, \tau_\eta) \quad (5)$$

where γ_o is the model intercept and γ_1, γ_2, and γ_3 are partial regression coefficients.

We found some effects of personal background (Table 3): High SES, homeownership, and age were associated with elevated levels of collective efficacy, whereas high mobility was negatively associated with collective efficacy. Gender, ethnicity, and years in neighborhood were not associated with collective efficacy.

At the neighborhood level, when these personal background effects were controlled, concentrated disadvantage and immigrant concentration were significantly negatively associated with collective efficacy, whereas residential stability was significantly positively associated with collective efficacy (for metric co-efficients and *t* ratios, see Table 3). The standardized regression coefficients were -0.58 for concentrated disadvantage, -0.13 for immigrant concentration, and 0.25 for residential stability, explaining over 70% of the variability across the 343 NCs.

COLLECTIVE EFFICACY AS A MEDIATOR OF SOCIAL COMPOSITION

PAST research has consistently reported links between neighborhood social composition and crime. We assessed the relation of social composition to neighborhood levels of violence, violent victimization, and homicide rates, and asked whether collective efficacy partially mediated these relations.

Perceived Violence

Using a model that paralleled that for collective efficacy (Eqs. 1, 4, and 5), we found that reports of neighborhood violence depended to some degree on personal background. Higher levels of violence were reported by those who were separated or divorced (as compared with those who were single or married), by whites and blacks (as opposed to Latinos), by younger respondents, and by those with longer tenure in their current neighborhood. Gender, homeownership, mobility, and SES were not significantly associated with responses within neighborhoods. When these personal background characteristics were controlled, the concentrations of disadvantage (*t* = 13.30) and immigrants (*t* = 2.44) were positively associated with the level of violence (see Table 4, model 1). The corresponding standardized regression coefficients are 0.75 and 0.11. Also, as hypothesized, residential stability was negatively associated with the level of violence (*t* = − 6.95), corresponding to a standardized regression coefficient of -0.28. The model accounted for 70.5% of the variation in violence between neighborhoods.

Next, collective efficacy was added as a predictor in the level 3 model (Table 4, model 2). The analysis built in a correction for errors of measurement in this predictor.[30] We found collective efficacy to be negatively related to violence (*t* = − 5.95), net of all other effects, and to correspond to a standardized coefficient of -0.45. Hence, after social composition was controlled, collective efficacy was strongly negatively associated with

Table 3.

Correlates of collective efficacy.

Variable	Coefficient	SE	*t* ratio
Intercept	3.523	0.013	263.20
Person-level predictors			
Female	−0.012	0.015	−0.76
Married	−0.005	0.021	−0.25
Separated or divorced	−0.045	0.026	−1.72
Single	−0.026	0.024	−1.05
Homeowner	0.122	0.020	6.04
Latino	0.042	0.028	1.52
Black	−0.029	0.030	−0.98
Mobility	−0.025	0.007	−3.71
Age	2.09×10^{-3}	0.60×10^{-3}	3.47
Years in neighborhood	0.64×10^{-3}	0.82×10^{-3}	0.78
SES	3.53×10^{-2}	0.76×10^{-2}	4.64
Neighborhood-level predictors			
Concentrated disadvantage	−0.172	0.016	−10.74
Immigrant concentration	−0.037	0.014	−2.66
Residential stability	0.074	0.130	5.61
Variance components			
Within neighborhoods	0.320		
Between neighborhoods	0.026		
Percent of variance explained			
Within neighborhoods	3.2		
Between neighborhoods	70.3		

violence. Moreover, the coefficients for social composition were substantially smaller than they had been without a control for collective efficacy. The coefficient for concentrated disadvantage, although still statistically significant, was 0.171 (as compared with 0.277). The difference between these coefficients (0.277 - 0.171 = 0.106) was significant (*t* = 5.30). Similarly, the coefficients for immigrant concentration and for residential stability were also significantly reduced: The coefficient for immigrant concentration, originally 0.041, was now 0.018, a difference of 0.023 (*t* = 2.42); the coefficient for residential stability, which had been -0.102, was now -0.056, a

difference of -0.046 (*t* = − 4.18). The immigrant concentration coefficient was no longer statistically different from zero. As hypothesized, then, collective efficacy appeared to partially mediate widely cited relations between neighborhood social composition and violence. The model accounted for more than 75% of the variation between neighborhoods in levels of violence.

Violent Victimization

Violent victimization was assessed by a single binary item (Y_{jk} = 1 if victimized by violence in the neighborhood and Y_{jk} = 0 if not). The latent outcome was the logarithmic odds of victimization

π_{jk}. The structural model for predicting π_{jk} had the same form as before (Eqs. 4 and 5).[31] Social composition, as hypothesized, predicted criminal victimization, with positive coefficients for concentrated disadvantage and immigrant concentration and a negative coefficient for residential stability (Table 4, model 1). The relative odds of victimization associated with a 2-SD elevation in the predictor were 1.67, 1.33, and 0.750, respectively. These estimates controlled for background characteristics associated with the risk of victimization. When added to the model, collective efficacy was negatively associated with victimization (Table 4, model 2). A 2-SD elevation in collective efficacy was associated with a relative odds ratio of about 0.70, which indicated a reduction of 30% in the odds of victimization. Moreover, after collective efficacy was controlled, the coefficients associated with concentrated disadvantage and residential stability diminished to nonsignificance, and the coefficient for immigrant concentration was also reduced.

Homicide

To assess the sensitivity of the findings when the measure of crime was completely independent of the survey, we examined 1995 homicide counts (Y_k is the number of homicides in neighborhood k in 1995). A natural model for the expected number of homicides in neighborhood k is $E(Y_k) = N_k\lambda_k$, where λ_k is the homicide rate per 100,000 people in neighborhood k and N_k is the population size of neighborhood k as given by the 1990 census (in hundreds of thousands). Defining $\eta_k = \log(\lambda_k)$, we then formulated a regression model for η_k of the type in Eq. 5. This is effectively a Poisson regression model with a logarithmic link with extra-Poisson variation represented by between-neighborhood random effects.[32]

Although concentrated disadvantage was strongly positively related to homicide, immigrant concentration was unrelated to homicide,

and residential stability was weakly positively related to homicide (Table 4, model 1). However when social composition was controlled, collective efficacy was negatively related to homicide (Table 4, model 2). A 2-SD elevation in collective efficacy was associated with a 39.7% reduction in the expected homicide rate. Moreover, when collective efficacy was controlled, the coefficient for concentrated disadvantage was substantially diminished, which indicates that collective efficacy can be reviewed as partially mediating the association between concentrated disadvantage and homicide.[33]

Control for Prior Homicide

Results so far were mainly cross-sectional, which raised the question of the possible confounding effect of prior crime. For example, residents in neighborhoods with high levels of violence might be afraid to engage in acts of social control.[9] We therefore reestimated all models controlling for prior homicide: the 3-year average homicide rate in 1988, 1989, and 1990. Prior homicide was negatively related ($P < 0.01$) to collective efficacy in 1995 ($r = -0.55$) and positively related ($P < 0.01$) to all three measures of violence in 1995, including a direct association ($t = 5.64$) with homicide (Table 5). However, even after prior homicide was controlled, the coefficient for collective efficacy remained statistically significant and substantially negative in all three models.

FURTHER TESTS

ALTHOUGH the results have been consistent, there are still potential threats to the validity of our analysis. One question pertains to discriminant validity: how do we know that it is collective efficacy at work rather than some other correlated social process?[34] To assess competing and analytically distinct factors suggested by prior theory,[4, 5] we examined the measure of collective efficacy alongside three other scales derived from the CS of the PHDCN:

Table 4.

*Neighborhood correlates of perceived neighborhood violence,
violent victimization, and 1995 homicide events.*

Variable	Model 1: social composition			Model 2: social composition and collective efficacy		
	Coefficient	SE	t	Coefficient	SE	t
*Perceived neighborhood violence**						
Concentrated disadvantage	0.277	0.021	13.30	0.171	0.024	7.24
Immigrant concentration	0.041	0.017	2.44	0.018	0.016	1.12
Residential stability	− 0.102	0.015	− 6.95	− 0.056	0.016	− 3.49
Collective efficacy				− 0.618	0.104	− 5.95
Violent victimization†						
Concenterated disadvantage	0.258	0.045	5.71	0.085	0.054	1.58
Immigrant concentration	0.141	0.046	3.06	0.098	0.044	2.20
Residential stability	− 0.143	0.050	− 2.84	− 0.031	0.051	− 0.60
Collective efficacy				− 1.190	0.240	− 4.96
1995 homicide events‡						
Concentrated disadvantage	0.727	0.049	14.91	0.491	0.064	7.65
Immigrant concentration	− 0.022	0.051	− 0.43	− 0.073	0.050	− 1.45
Residential stability	0.093	0.042	2.18	0.208	0.046	4.52
Collective efficacy				− 1.471	0.261	− 5.64

*Estimates of neighborhood-level coefficients control for gender, marital status, homeownership, ethnicity, mobility, age, years in neighborhood, and SES of those interviewed. Model 1 accounts for 70.5% of the variation between neighborhoods in perceived violence, whereas Model 2 accounts of 77.8% of the variation. †Neighborhood-level coefficients are adjusted for the same person-level covariates listed in the first footnote. Model 1 accounts for 12.3% of the variation between neighborhoods in violent victimization, whereas Model 2 accounts for 44.4%. ‡Model 1 accounts for 56.1% of the variation between neighborhoods in homicide rates, whereas Model 2 accounts for 61.7% of the variation.

neighborhood services, friendship and kinship ties, and organizational participation.[35] On the basis of the results in Tables 3 to 5 and also to achieve parsimony, we constructed a violent crime scale at the neighborhood level that summed standardized indicators of the three major outcomes: perceived violence, violent victimization, and homicide rate.

Consistent with expectations, collective efficacy was significantly ($p < 0.01$) and positively related to friendship and kinship ties ($r = 0.49$), organizational participation ($r = 0.45$), and neighborhood services ($r = 0.21$). Nonetheless, when we controlled for these correlated factors in a multivariate regression, along with prior homicide, concentrated disadvantage, immigrant concentration, and residential stability, by far the largest predictor of the violent crime rate was collective efficacy (standardized coefficient = -0.53, $t = -8.59$). Collective efficacy thus retained discriminant validity when compared with theoretically relevant, competing social processes. Moreover, these results suggested that dense personal ties, organizations, and local services by themselves are not sufficient; reductions in violence appear to be more directly attributable to informal social control and cohesion among residents.[36]

A second threat stems from the association of racial composition with concentrated disadvantage as shown in Table 2. Our interpretation was that African Americans, largely because of housing discrimination, are differentially exposed to neighborhood conditions of extreme poverty.[15] Nonetheless, a counterhypothesis is that the percentage of black residents and not disadvantage accounts for lower levels of collective efficacy, and consequently, higher violence. Our second set of tests therefore replicated the key models within the 125 NCs where the population was more than 75% black (see the first row of Table 1), effectively removing race as a potential confound. Concentrated poverty and residential stability each had significant associations with collective efficacy in these predominantly black areas (t = 5.60 and t = 2.50, respectively). Collective efficacy continued to explain variations in violence across black NCs, mediating the prior effect of concentrated disadvantage. Even when prior homicide, neighborhood services, friendship and kinship ties, and organizational participation were controlled, the only significant predictor of the violent crime scale in black NCs was collective efficacy (r = − 4.80). These tests suggested that concentrated disadvantage more than race per se is the driving structural force at play.

DISCUSSION AND IMPLICATIONS

THE results imply that collective efficacy is an important construct that can be measured reliably at the neighborhood level by means of survey research strategies. In the past, sample surveys have primarily considered individual-level relations. However, surveys that merge a cluster sample design with questions tapping collective properties lend themselves to the additional consideration of neighborhood phenomena.

Together, three dimensions of neighborhood stratification—concentrated disadvantage, immigration concentration, and residential stability—explained 70% of the neighborhood variation in collective efficacy. Collective efficacy in turn mediated a substantial portion of the association of residential stability and disadvantage with multiple measures of violence, which is consistent with a major theme in neighborhood theories of social organization.[1−5] After adjustment for measurement error, individual differences in neighborhood composition, prior violence, and other potentially confounding social processes, the combined measure of informal social control and cohesion and trust remained a robust predictor of lower rates of violence.

There are, however, several limitations of the present study. Despite the use of decennial census data and prior crime as lagged predictors, the basic analysis was cross-sectional in design; causal effects were not proven. Indicators of informal control and social cohesion were not observed directly but rather inferred from informant reports. Beyond the scope of the present study, other dimensions of neighborhood efficacy (such as political ties) may be important, too. Our analysis was limited also to one city and did not go beyond its official boundaries into a wider region.

Finally, the image of local residents working collectively to solve their own problems is not the whole picture. As shown, what happens within neighborhoods is in part shaped by socioeconomic and housing factors linked to the wider political economy. In addition to encouraging communities to mobilize against violence through "self-help" strategies of informal social control, perhaps reinforced by partnerships with agencies of formal social control (community policing), strategies to address the social and ecological changes that best many inner-city communities need to be considered. Recognizing that collective efficacy matters does not imply that inequalities at the neighborhood level can be neglected.

Table 5.

Predictors of neighborhood level violence, victimization, and homicide in 1995, with prior homicide controlled. For violence and victimization as outcomes, the coefficients reported in this table were adjusted for 11 person-level covariates (see Table 3), but the latter coefficients are omitted for simplicity of presentation.

Variable	Violence as outcome			Victimization as outcome			Homicide in 1995 as outcome		
	Coefficient	SE	t	Coefficient	SE	t	Coefficient	SE	t
Intercept	3.772	0.379	9.95	−2.015	0.042	−49.24	3.071	0.050	62.01
Concentrated disadvantage	0.157	0.025	6.38	0.073	0.060	1.22	0.175	0.072	2.42
Immigrant concentration	0.020	0.016	1.25	0.098	0.045	2.20	−0.034	0.044	−0.77
Residential stability	−0.054	0.016	−3.39	−0.029	0.052	−0.56	0.229	0.043	5.38
Collective efficacy	−0.594	0.108	−5.53	−1.176	0.251	−4.69	−1.107	0.272	−4.07
Prior homicide	0.018	0.014	1.27	0.017	0.049	0.34	0.397	0.070	5.64
Variance									
Between-neighborhood variance	0.030			0.091			0.207		
Percent of variance explained between neighborhoods	78.0			43.8			73.0		

REFERENCES AND NOTES

1. For a recent review of research on violence covering much of the 20th century, including a discussion of the many barriers to direct examination of the mechanisms explaining neighborhood-level variations, see R. J. Sampson and J. Lauritsen, in *Understanding and Preventing Violence: Social Influences,* vol. 3, A. J. Reiss Jr. and J. Roth, Eds. (National Academy Press, Washington, DC, 1994), pp. 1–114.

2. J. F. Short Jr., *Poverty, Ethnicity, and Violent Crime* (Westview, Boulder, CO, 1997).

3. For a general assessment of the difficulties facing neighborhood-level research on social outcomes, see S.E. Mayer and C. Jencks, *Science* **243**, 1441 (1989).

4. R. Kornhauser, *Social Sources of Delinquency* (Univ. of Chicago Press, Chicago, IL, 1978); R. J. Bursik Jr., *Criminology* **26**, 519 (1998); D. Elliott *et al.*, *J. Res. Crime Delinquency* **33**, 389 (1996).

5. R. J. Sampson and W. B. Groves, *Am. J. Sociol.* **94**, 774 (1989).

6. M. Janowitz, *ibid.* **81**, 82 (1975).

7. E. Maccoby, J. Johnson, R. Church, *J. Social Issues* **14**, 38(1958); R. Taylor, S. Gottfredson, S. Bower, *J. Res. Crime Delinquency* **21**, 303 (1983); J. Hacker, K. Ho, C. Ross, *Social Problems* **21**, 328 (1974). A key finding from past research is that many delinquent gangs emerge from unsupervised spontaneous peer groups [F. Thrasher, *The Gang: A Study of 1,313 Gangs in Chicago* (Univ. of Chicago Press, Chicago, IL, 1963); C. Shaw and H. McKay, *Juvenile Delinquency and Urban Areas* (Univ. of Chicago Press, Chicago, IL, 1969), pp. 176–185; J. F. Short Jr. and F. Strodbeck, *Group Process and Gang Delinquency* (Univ. of Chicago Press, Chicago, IL, 1965)].

8. For example, about half of all homicides occur among nonfamily members with a preexisting relationship: friends, neighbors, casual acquaintances, associates in illegal activities, or members of a rival gang. Illegal markets are especially high-risk settings for robbery, assault, and homicide victimization, whether by an associate or a stranger [A. J. Reiss Jr. and J. Roth, Eds. *Understanding and Preventing Violence* (National Academy Press, Washington, DC, 1993), pp. 18, 79; A. J. Reiss Jr., in *Criminal Careers and "Career Criminals,"* A. Blumstein, J. Cohen, J. Roth, C. Visher, Eds. (National Academy Press, Washington, DC, 1986), pp. 121–160].

9. W. Skogan, *Disorder and Decline: Crime and the Spiral of Decay in American Neighborhoods* (Univ. of California Press, Berkeley, CA, 1990).

10. J. Coleman, *Foundations of Social Theory* (Harvard Univ. Press, Cambridge, MA, 1990); R. Putnam, *Making Democracy Work* (Princeton Univ. Press, Princeton, NJ, 1993).

11. A. Bandura, *Social Foundations of Thought and Action: A Social Cognitive Theory* (Prentice-Hall, Englewood Cliffs, NJ, 1986).

12. See, generally, J. Logan and H. Molotch, *Urban Fortunes: The Political Economy of Place* (Univ. of California Press, Berkeley, CA, 1987).

13. See also J. Kasardo and M. Janowitz, *Am. Sociol. Rev.* **39**, 328 (1974); Sampson, *ibid.* **53**, 766 (1988).

14. W. J. Wilson, *The Truly Disadvantaged* (Univ. of Chicago Press, Chicago, IL, 1987).

15. D. Massey and N. Denton, *American Apartheid: Segregation and the Making of the Underclass* (Havard Univ. Press, Cambridge, MA, 1993); D. Massey, *Am. J. Sociol.* **96**, 329 (1990).

16. J. Brooks-Gunn, D. Duncan, P. Kato, N. Sealand, *Am. J. Sociol.* **99**, 353 (1993); F. F. Furstenberg Jr., T. D. Cook, J. Eccles, G. H. Elder, A., Sameroff, *Urban Families and Adolescent Success* (Univ. of Chicago Press, Chicago, IL, in press), chap. 7. Research has shown a strong link between the concentration of female-headed families and rates of violence [see (1)].

17. D. Williams and C. Collins, *Annu. Rev. Sociol.* **21**, 349 (1995).

18. Cluster analyses of census data also helped to guide the construction of internally homogeneous NCs with respect to racial and ethnic mix, SES, housing density, and family organization. Random-effect analyses of variance produced intracluster correlation coefficients to assess the degree to which this goal had been achieved; analyses (37) revealed that the clustering was successful in producing relative homogeneity within NCs.

19. For purposes of selecting a longitudinal cohort sample, SES was defined with the use of a scale from the 1990 census that included NC-level indicators of poverty, public assistance, income, and education (37). Race and ethnicity were also measured with the use of the 1990 census, which defined race in five broad categories: "white," "black," "American Indian, Eskimo, or Aleut," "Asian or Pacific Islander," and "other." We use the census labels of white and black to refer to persons of European American and African American background, respectively. We use the term "Latino" to denote anyone of Latin American descent as determined from the separate census category of "Hispanic origin." "Hispanic" is more properly used to describe persons of Spanish descent (i.e., from Spain), although the terms are commonly used interchangeably.

20. The sampling design of the CS was complex. For purposes of a longitudinal study (37), residents in 80 of the

343 NCs were oversampled. Within these 80 NCs, a simple random sample of census blocks was selected and a systematic random sample of dwelling units within those blocks was selected. Within each dwelling unit, all persons over 18 were lsited, and a respondent was sampled at random with the aim of obtaining a sample of 50 households within each NC. In each of the remaining NCs ($n = 263$), nine census blocks were selected with probability proportional to population size, three dwelling units were selected at random within each block, and an adult respondent was randomly selected from a list of all adults in the dwelling unit. The aim was to obtain a sample of 20 in these 263 NCs. Despite these differences in sampling design, the selected dwelling units constituted a representative and approximately self-weighting sample of dwelling units within every NC ($n = 343$). ABT Associates (Cambridge, MA) carried out the data collection with the cooperation of research staff at PHDCN, achieving a final response rate of 75%.

21. "Don't know" responses were recoded to the middle category of "neither likely nor unlikely" (informal social control) or "neither agree nor disagree" (social cohesion). Most respondentes answered all 10 items included in the combined measure; for those respondents, the scale score was the average of the responses. However, anyone responding to at least one item provided data for the analysis; a person-specific standard error of measuremente was calculated on the basis of a simple linear item-response model that took into account the number and difficulty of the items to which each resident responded. The analyses reported here were based on the 7729 cases having sufficient data for all models estimated.

22. Respondents were also asked whether the incident occurred during the 6 months before the interview; about 40% replied affirmatively. Because violence is a rare outcome, we use the total violent victimization measure in the main analysis. However, in additional analyses, we examined a summary of the prevalence of personal and household victimizations (ranging from 0 to four) restricted to this 6-month window. This test yielded results very similar to those based on the binary measure of total violence.

23. The original data measured the address location of all homicide incidents known to the Chicago police (regardless of arrests) during the months of the community survey.

24. The alpha-scoring method was chosen because we are analyzing the universe of NCS in Chicago and are interested in maximizing the reliability of measures [H. F. Kaiser and J. Caffry, *Psychometrika* **30**, 1 (1965)]. We also estimated an oblique factor rotation, allowing the extracted dimensions to covary. A principal components analysis with varimax rotation nonetheless yielded substantively identical results.

25. For a methodological procedure and empirical result that are similar but that used all U.S. cities as units of analysis, see K. Land, P. McCall, L. Cohen, *Am. J. Sociol.* **95**, 922 (1990).

26. S. W. Raudenbush, B. Rowan, S. J. Kang, *J. Educ. Stat.* **16**, 295 (1991).

27. D. V. Lindley and A. F. M. Smith, *R. Stat. Soc. J. Ser. B Methodol.* **34**, (1972).

28. Although the vast majority of respondents answered all items in the collective efficacy scale, the measurement model makes full use of the data provided by those whose responses were incomplete. There is one less indicator D_{pijk}, than the number of items to identify the intercept π_{jk}.

29. This degree of intersubjective agreement is similar to that found in a recent national survey of teachers that assessed organizational climate in U.S. high schools [B. Rowan, S. Raudenbush, S. Kang, *Am. J. Educ.* **99**, 238 (1991)].

30. The analysis of collective efficacy and violence as outcomes uses a three-level model in which the level 1 model describes the sources of measurement error for each of these outcomes. The level 2 and level 3 models together describe the joint distribution of the "true scores" within and between neighborhoods. Given the joint distribution of these outcomes, it is then possible to describe the conditional distribution of violence given "true" collective efficacy and all other predictors, thus automatically adjusting for any errors of measurement of collective efficacy. See S. Raudenbush and R. J. Sampson (paper presented at the conference "Alternative Models for Educational Data," National Institute of Statistical Sciences, Research Triangle Park, NC, 16 October 1996) for the necessary derivations. This work is an extension of that of C. Clogg, E. Petkova, and A. Haritou [*Am. J. Sociol.* **100**, 1261 (1995)] and P. Allison (*ibid.*, p. 1294). Note that census blocks were not included as a "level" in the analysis. Thus, person-level and block-level variance are confounded. However, this confounding has no effect on standard errors reported in this manuscript. If explanatory variables had been measured at the level of the census block, it would have been important to represent blocks as an additional level in the model.

31. The resulting model is a logistic regression model with random effects of neighborhoods. This mode was estimated first with penalized quasi-likelihood as described by N. E. Breslow and D. G. Clayton [*J. Am. Stat. Assoc.* **88**, 9 (1993)]. The doubly iterative algorithm used is described by S. W. Raudenbush ["Posterior, modal estimation for hierarchical generalized linear models with applications to dichotomous and count data" (Longitudinal and Multilevel Methods Project. Michigan State Univ., East Lansing, MI, 1993)]. Then, using those results to model the marginal covariation

of the errors, we esetimated a population-average model with robust standard errors [S. Zeger, K. Liang, P. Albert, *Biometrics* **44**, 1049 (1988)]. Results were similar. The results based on the population-average model with robust standard errors are reported here.

32. The analysis paralleled that of criminal victimization, except that a Poisson sampling model and logarithmic link were used in this case. Again, the reported results on a population-average model with robust standard errors.

33. Although the zero-order correlation of residential stability with homicide was insignificant, the partial coefficient in Table 4 is significantly positive. Recall from Table 3 that stability is positively linked to collective efficacy. But higher stability without the expected greater collective efficacy is not a positive neighborhood equality according to the homicide data. See (*14*).

34. T. Cook, S. Shagle, S. Degimencioglu, in *Neighborhood Poverty: Context and Consequences for Children*, vol. 2, J. Brooks-Gunn, G. Duncan, J. L. Aber, Eds. (Russell Sage Foundation, New York, in press).

35. "Neighborhood services" is a nine-item scale of local activities and programs (for example, the presence of a block group, a tenant association, a crime prevention program, and a family health service) combined with a six-item inventory of services for youth (a neighborhood youth center, recreational programs, after-school programs, mentoring and counseling services, mental health services, and a crisis intervention program). "Friendship and kinship ties" is a scale that measures the number of friends and relatives that respondents report are living in the neighborhood. "Organizational participation" measures actual involvement by residents in (i) local religious organizations; (ii) neighborhood watch programs; (iii) block group, tenant association, or community council; (iv) business or civic groups; (v) ethnic or nationality clubs; and (vi) local political organizations.

36. Similar results were obtained when we controlled for a measure of social interaction (the extent to which neighbors had parties together, watched each other's homes, visited in each other's homes, exchanged favors, and asked advice about personal matters) that was positively associated wtih collective efficacy. Again the direct effect of collective efficacy remained, suggesting that social interaction, like friendship and kinship ties, is linked to reduced violence through its association with increased levels of collective efficacy.

37. R. J. Sampson, S. W. Raudenbush, F. Earls, data not shown.

38. Major funding for this project came from the John D. and Catherine T. MacArthur Foundation and the National Institute of Justice. We thank L. Eisenberg and anonymous reviewers for helpful comments; S. Buka and A. J. Reiss Jr. for important contributions to the research design; and R. Block, C. Coldren, and J. Morenoff for their assistance in obtaining, cleaning, geo-coding, and aggregating homicide incident data to the NC level. M. Yosef and D. Jeglum-Bartusch assisted in the analysis.

Thirty-One

WHAT IS AN UNHEALTHY ENVIRONMENT AND HOW DOES IT GET UNDER THE SKIN?

Shelley E. Taylor, Rena L. Repetti, and Teresa Seeman

ABSTRACT

This review explores the role of environments in creating chronic and acute health disorders. A general framework for studying the nesting of social environments and the multiple pathways by which environmental factors may adversely affect health is offered. Treating socioeconomic status (SES) and race as contextual factors, we examine characteristics of the environments of community, work, family, and peer interaction for predictors of positive and adverse health outcomes across the lifespan. We consider chronic stress/allostatic load, mental distress, coping skills and resources, and health habits and behaviors as classes of mechanisms that address how unhealthy environments get "under the skin," to create health disorders. Across multiple environments, unhealthy environments are those that threaten safety, that undermine the creation of social ties, and that are conflictual, abusive, or violent. A healthy environment, in contrast, provides safety, opportunities for social integration, and the ability to predict and/or control aspects of that environment.

HEALTH PSYCHOLOGY: WHAT IS AN UNHEALTHY ENVIRONMENT AND HOW DOES IT GET UNDER THE SKIN?

THE role of the environment in health and illness has been known since the time of Hippocrates. With the discovery that infectious agents produce disease, physicians and public health researchers directed their attention to the environmental conditions that give rise to these agents and permit them to breed. Following breakthroughs in water treatment, sewage control, food storage, and waste disposal, the incidence of many infectious diseases declined substantially, soon to be replaced by the slower-developing chronic illnesses to heart disease, cancer, and diabetes, among others. These diseases have come to be known as diseases of lifestyle, because behavioral risk factors are clearly involved in their etiology and progression. An unintended consequence of the focus on lifestyle has been to divert attention away from the role of

Originally published in *Annual Review of Psychology*, 1997.

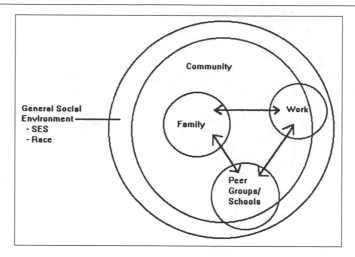

Figure 1
*Diagrammatic representation of social environments that have health-relevant implications. This represen-
tation assumes that the proximal environments of family, work, and peer groups are nested or partially nested
within neighborhood and fully nested within a larger social environment in which such factors as socioeconomic status (SES) and race have health implications.*

the environment in producing disease in favor of
an emphasis on behavior. As health psychologists
have increasingly identified what risk factors
people incur and how they incur them, the focus
of health prevention has moved from environmental interventions to individual behavior.
Some scientists have argued that this focus has
led to a culture of blame, whereby individuals are
held responsible for good health and blamed or
discredited for their illnesses (Becker 1993).

The role of the environment in producing
chronic as well as acute disease merits renewed
attention in the context of the current concerns
addressed by health psychology. Specifically, as
research has identified the individual difference
predictors of chronic illness, including health behaviors, use of health services, social factors such
as social support, and psychological factors such
as hostility and depression, it has become clear
that these predictors are nested within geographic, developmental, occupational, and social
environments. In this review, we focus attention

on these environments and the ways environmental characteristics may influence health and
also influence individual characteristics or behaviors that pose risks for health.

In so doing, our analysis gives primary status
neither to environmental characteristics nor to
their concomitant effects on individuals. Not all
individuals in the same environment are affected
by that environment in the same way, nor will all
individuals in a given environment sustain health
risks. Thus, we explicitly reject the notion that
the health effects of environments can be reduced to or explained by individual-level factors.
Rather, we maintain that individual characteristics are nested within social environments (see
Figure 1), with each level of analysis revealing information about the causes of health and illness
that consideration of one level alone cannot provide.

As we note below, social class and race provide
a context for understanding the effects of environment. These characteristics are well-

established predictors of all-cause mortality and a variety of specific diseases, and they are also reliably associated with individual differences in exposure to stress, the practice of health behaviors, coping strategies, and other factors of interest to psychologists (Adler & Matthews 1994, Williams & Collins 1995). With SES and race as background, we then examine community, family, work, and peer groups as specific environments that have a contributing role in health and illness (see Figure 1). Within each environment, we ask the question, "How do the health-relevant characteristics of this environment get under the skin?" For example, some children live in conflict-ridden families and others do not, and health risks sustained differ between the two groups. We ask how that environmental characteristic may translate into risks that have the identified health consequences. In so doing, we consider several general pathways in each of the environments. These general pathways, as well as more complex combinations of them, are illustrated in Figure 2.

Environments exert direct effects on health (Figure 2, Segment a) that may be largely unmediated or unmoderated by psychological and social processes, except insofar as they lay the initial groundwork for their occurrence. For example, the poor and African-Americans are disproportionately likely to contract certain kinds of cancers because of differential exposure to toxins at work or in their neighborhoods. At present, research has not progressed to the point of identifying whether there are social or psychological factors that contribute to these adverse effects.

Because this is a psychological review, the routes on which we focus most of our attention are psychosocial pathways for the development of health risks. A first route whereby environments may get under the skin is by differentially exposing people to chronic stress (Segments fk). That chronic stress may have a cumulative effect on the body was first observed by Hans Selye (1956) in his articulation of the General Adaptation Syndrome. Selye maintained that individu-

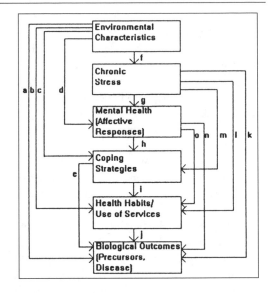

Figure 2

A range of models by which environmental characteristics may come to exert adverse biological outcomes on individuals. Segments b–o represent partial pathways that may concatenate to form more complex pathways.

als respond to stressful events with nonspecific reactions that, over time, produce wear and tear on the system. Repeated cycling through the three-phase syndrome of alarm, resistance, and exhaustion, Selye argued, leads to cumulative damage to the organism. Building on these ideas, McEwen & Stellar (1993) proposed that, beginning early in life, there are cascading relationships between environmental factors and genetic predispositions that lead to large individual differences in susceptibility to stress and, in some cases, to disease. Physiological systems within the body fluctuate to meet demands from external forces, a state termed allostasis. Over time, the allostatic load builds up, which is defined as the physiological costs of chronic exposure to fluctuating or heightened neural or neuroendocrine responses that result from repeated or chronic environmental challenges that an individual reacts to as stressful. For example, the hypothesized links between recurrent changes in autonomic reactivity produced by stress and the subsequent development of chronic hypertension (Anderson et al 1991) may be thought of as an allostatic load model. The allostatic load formulation, then, explicitly argues that stress produces cumulative identifiable damage that results in increased pathology (Seeman et al 1996).

A second route by which environments may have adverse health effects is via an impact on mental health or mental distress (Melamed 1995) (Segments dn). Negative emotions, such as depression, anxiety, and hostility, appear to play a significant role in health risks, including all-cause mortality (Martin et al 1995) and especially coronary heart disease risk (Booth-Kewley & Friedman 1987). These relations are apparently not due to behavior changes associated with affective disorders, such as increased smoking or alcohol consumption. Major depression, depressive symptoms, history of depression, and anxiety have all been related to the likelihood of cardiac events (Frasure-Smith et al 1995), and depression is a risk factor for mortality following myocardial infarction, independent of cardiac disease severity (Frasure-Smith et al 1995). State depression and clinical depression have both been related to sustained suppressed immunity (Herbert & Cohen 1993). Anger appears to be significant in the development of coronary artery disease and hypertension, at least among some individuals (Frasure-Smith et al 1995). These health effects of negative emotions may result from the activation of both the sympathetic-adrenal-medullary (SAM) system and the hypothalamic-pituitary-adrenocortical (HPA) axis. The former is manifested in increased blood pressure, heart rate, circulating levels of epinephrine and norepinephrine, and constriction of peripheral blood vessels. SAM activation is believed to contribute to the development of coronary artery disease (Manuck et al 1995), essential hypertension (Krantz & Manuck 1984), and susceptibility to infectious disease (Cohen & Herbert 1996). The

activation of HPA leads to high circulating levels of corticotrophin-releasing hormone, adrenocorticotropic hormone, and cortisol. HPA activation has been linked to atherosclerosis (Troxler et al 1977) and chronic inflammatory responses, as are found in rheumatoid arthritis and reactivity of the airways in people with asthma (McNeil 1987). Although biologically based predispositions appear to play some role in the relation of affective diseases to physical state changes, environmental factors are also reliably related to sustained depression, anxiety, and anger. As such, mental health/distress constitutes a second important route by which environments may get under the skin.

Coping strategies constitute a third explanatory route that may clarify how unhealthy environments adversely affect health (Segments ce). Individuals who find constructive ways of coping with stress, such as taking direct action or finding meaning in their experience, may be better able to withstand the potential adverse effects of stressful circumstances. In addition, there may be stressor-specific coping styles, such as expressing hostility or suppressing anger, that have health implications both generally and for specific disorders, such as cardiovascular disease and hypertension. In addition, environments influence the development of coping strategies, especially those involved in managing conflict and stress, and the ability to develop social ties.

Health habits are heavily implicated in the development of illness, especially chronic illness, as numerous reviews have documented (e.g. Adler & Matthews 1994) (Segments bj). They include smoking, alcohol and drug abuse, diet, exercise, the use of preventive and secondary health services, and adherence to treatment recommendations. Environments constitute the contexts in which health habits are learned, encouraged, and practiced. The family is an important context for the acquisition of health habits, and it lays the groundwork for a broad array of healthy and unhealthy behaviors (Taylor 1995). The peer group, first in adolescence and then in adulthood, is an important context within which many health-compromising behaviors are acquired and enacted, including smoking, alcohol, and drug abuse.

These, then, are the routes we consider in each of the environments analyzed. These routes are not independent or even discrete pathways by which unhealthy environments affect health; all represent routes in potential causal chains involving two or more of these processes. Thus, for example, a chronically stressful family environment may prevent the development of effective coping strategies (Segments fm), compromise the learning of health habits (Segments fl), and produce chronic anxiety and/or depression (Segments fg), all of which feed into enhanced health risks (Segments e, j, and n). In most areas, research has not progressed to the point where these complex pathways can be identified or tested in the context of particular health problems or disorders. Thus, Figure 2 is offered largely as a representation of potential routes, rather than established routes, by which pernicious environments exact adverse health effects.

SOCIOECONOMIC STATUS AND RACE

WE begin our consideration of the question "What is an unhealthy environment?" by examining SES and race differences in health. Because SES and race heavily determine the more proximal environments in which people live, such as neighborhood and work, they provide important contexts for understanding the features of these more proximal environments that may compromise health (Williams & Collins 1995).

SES is traditionally measured by education, income, and occupation. Using these criteria, an extensive, highly consistent literature documents the negative health outcomes that result as one moves lower on the SES gradient (for reviews, see Adler et al 1993, Williams & Collins 1995). Analyses of potential measurement artifacts or natural or social selection suggest that these in-

equalities are real and affected little by selection factors (see Macintyre 1997). SES is related to higher prevalence and incidence of most chronic and infectious disorders and to higher rates of nearly all major causes of morbidity and mortality across populations and across time (Adler et al 1993, Macintyre 1997, Williams & Collins 1995). Moreover, SES differentials in morbidity and morality appear to be widening rather than narrowing (e.g. Marmot 1994, Wagener & Schatzkin 1994).

The association of SES with morbidity and mortality is, for the most part, linear, with increasingly better health outcomes as one ascends the SES continuum. As such, the relation of SES to health and mortality involves more than the obvious role of inadequate financial resources or poor and dangerous living conditions associated with poverty. While SES differentials may be found among children (Durkin et al 1994) and among the elderly (e.g. Seeman et al 1994), the largest social inequalities in health and mortality are seen most frequently for those aged 40 to 65.

Substantial race differences also exist in health. On virtually every major index of health status, African-Americans look worse than whites, and these differences in health occur across the lifespan (Williams & Collins 1995). With the exception of race-specific disorders such as sickle-cell anemia, these black-white differences are apparently not due primarily to genetic or biological factors that differentiate blacks from whites (for discussion, see Anderson et al 1991, Williams & Collins 1995). Socioeconomic differences account substantially for these health status differences, inasmuch as approximately one third of the African-American population lives in poverty, compared with 11% of the white population. Nonetheless, poverty does not fully account for black-white differences in health (e.g. Rushing et al 1992). Within every level of SES, African-Americans typically have worse health than whites (Williams & Collins 1995).

Although SES and race are not themselves environments, they provide an important and often overlooked context for understanding the more immediate environments within which people live, namely communities, work, family, and social life. As such, they provide the environmental backdrop against which more specific environmental encounters occur.

COMMUNITY

CERTAIN characteristics of the communities in which people live have been shown to have adverse effects on health. Many of these arise because of the social class and racial composition of those communities. Consequently, they act as the proximal manifestation of these characteristics. For example, low-SES neighborhoods have higher rates of cancer, hypertension, heart disease, and upper-respiratory disorders, including asthma, bronchitis, and emphysema (Adler et al 1993). Other health-enhancing or health-compromising characteristics of environment are less dependent upon community social class or racial composition.

Chronic Stress

The degree of chronic stress experienced by individuals is heavily influenced by the characteristics of their communities. Residents of middle- and upper-income communities typically have access to high-quality housing, an abundance of shops, banks, health-care services and transportation. In poor neighborhoods, these resources are less likely to be available (Troutt 1993). Consequently, the lower one is on the SES continuum, the greater the amount of hassle and time needed to address basic tasks of living. Further contributing to the chronic stress of lower SES communities are characteristics such as police-documented higher crime rates (Macintyre et al 1993), greater perceived threat of crime and more local problems (Sooman & Macintyre 1995), more refused services (e.g. taxi, credit, ambulance; Sooman & Macintyre 1995), and poorer transportation and recreational facilities (Macin-

tyre et al 1993). Lower SES neighborhoods also have been linked to greater exposure to physical hazards such as air and water pollutants, hazardous wastes, pesticides, and industrial chemicals (Calnan & Johnson 1985) and to greater crowding and exposure to noise (Evans 1997).

Lack of available housing typically leads to overcrowding, both in the form of high density within the neighborhood and crowding within the home (defined as 1.5 persons or more per room). High density associated with higher all-cause mortality (Levy & Herzog 1974) and with higher rates of mortality due to cancer and stroke, but not heart disease (Levy & Herzog 1978). High-density living is also associated with death due to homicide, but negatively associated with death due to suicide, which appears to be tied to isolation and loss of family ties (Levy & Herzog 1978). A potential mediating pathway for these effects is suggested by the fact that high-density living is associated with both higher reports of chronic stress and with biochemical indices of stress, such as urinary excretion of norepinephrine and epinephrine (Fleming et al 1987). Crowding in the home has been related to increased likelihood of infections and to higher death rates from heart disease, to respiratory disorders, and to all-cause mortality (Levy & Herzog 1978). In addition to its association with crowding, substandard housing may affect health in other ways. Older buildings with poorly lit hallways and debris pose risks to safety and to health by attracting rodents and insects that may spread infection, for example.

Community studies of the effects of noise on physical health have identified few clear-cut relations to disease morbidity in the adult population. Acute noise produces short-lived elevations in cardiovascular and neuroendocrine functioning, but many adults appear to habituate to chronic noise. However, some studies suggest a relation of chronic noise to the development of hypertension, links that necessitate further investigation (Evans 1997). Recent evidence suggesting a relation of noise exposure to abnormal fetal development also merits continued consideration (Evans 1997). As noted below, noise may adversely affect health habits as well.

High rates of crime and delinquency are associated with a variety of adverse health characteristics, including a high rate of infant mortality, low birth rate, tuberculosis, and child abuse (Sampson 1992). Women living in high-violence neighborhoods are significantly more likely to experience pregnancy complications than women living in neighborhoods with little violence (Zapata et al 1992).

Because a number of the adverse characteristics of neighborhoods are intercorrelated, investigators have attempted to operationalize the concept of high-stress neighborhood. Harburg et al (1973) defined areas characterized by low socioeconomic status, high population density, high geographic mobility, high rates of marital breakup, and high crime as high stress; low-stress areas had more favorable ratings on all these variables. Harburg found higher rates of hypertension in the high-stress than low-stress locales, especially among dark-skinned black men. Others (e.g. Troutt 1993) have argued that in such neighborhoods there are low levels of economic opportunity, poor marriage pools, and poor transportation, which erodes the ability of residents, especially single mothers, to seek employment in the neighborhood, to marry, or to move to a better neighborhood. As noted below, such characteristics may have adverse effects on parenting, which affects the health of children.

Mental Health/Distress

Little research has addressed the impact of community characteristics on mental health, and still less has tied such effects to physical health outcomes. To date, the only community characteristic to receive systematic study is exposure to violence, especially for children. Osofsky (1995) argued that exposure to chronic community violence directly and adversely affects children's mental health. Children's reports of psychological distress are significantly related to their reports of witnessing acts of violence (Richters & Martinez 1993). Children who live in violent neighborhoods show signs of posttraumatic stress disorder, including disrupted patterns of eating and sleeping, difficulties in controlling attention and relating to others, anxiety responses and fear, and reexperiences of the violent episodes they have witnessed (for a review, see Osofsky 1995). Among adults, sleep disturbances, nightmares, and manifestations of anxiety are common (Pynoos 1993). Exposure to violence may also adversely affect the mental health of children and adults because of the need to deal with losses and to cope with grieving for family members, neighbors, and friends who have been killed. Such grieving may compromise immune functioning (Kiecolt-Glaser et al 1994).

Coping Skills and Resources

Community characteristics may affect coping skills and resources in several ways that have health implications. Repeated arousal of intense negative emotions due to exposure to chronic violence, for example, may lead to difficulty in the effective regulation of emotions among children (Osofsky 1993). The adverse effects of chronic exposure to violence may be partially offset if an individual has at least one supportive person in the neighborhood, a protective place to go, or certain personal resources such as an adaptable temperament or a high level of intelligence (Osofsky 1993). Low-SES neighborhoods may also compromise the development of coping skills relating to the recruitment and effective use of social contacts. Parents who are concerned about exposing their children to drugs and crime may keep their children inside and otherwise restrict social behavior. Thus, the ability to develop or utilize a supportive network may be somewhat compromised (Sampson 1992). Whether these disruptions in the formation of social ties have negative effects on health in childhood or cumulative effects on adult health is unknown.

The inherently social nature of communities affects coping and health at both the community level and the individual level. In particular, characteristics of communities influence the degree to which social capital may be created (Coleman 1990). Social capital exists when the relations among people make possible individual or joint achievements that otherwise would not be possible (Coleman 1990). Social capital involves parents and children in friendship networks and community organizations, both formal and informal, which are characterized by a set of obligations, expectations, and social ties that connect the adults, and that help to bring about the control and supervision of children. Through such a process, it is argued, information is exchanged, norms are established, and informal systems of social control are laid down. As such, a child is raised in a neighborhood environment with norms and sanctions that are not or cannot be brought about by one adult in isolation. The creation of social capital is virtually impossible to develop in unstable communities, and mere density of a community is insufficient to establish it. Social capital, then, constitutes a community-level coping variable.

"Social impoverishment," the absence of social capital, has been tied to several health-related outcomes. Such indicators predict high rates of child abuse (Garbarino & Sherman 1980), which is important as a cause of morbidity and mortality and also as a predictor of violence in adulthood (Widom 1989). Indicators of social capital are inversely related to levels of adolescent aggression and delinquency which, in turn, are predictors of homicide and suicide. Low levels of social organization are associated with high levels of adult crime as well. Social disorganization also predicts whether young girls will become pregnant (Osofsky 1990); whether they will be supported by a network in limiting high-risk maternal behavior such as smoking, drinking, and drug abuse (Wallace 1990); and whether they will abuse their children after birth (Sampson 1992). Overall, the more formal and informal ties exist

in a community, the more dense and multiplex the networks and the greater the constraints on deviant, often health-compromising behavior, both for adolescents and adults (Sampson 1992).

On the individual level, the lack of social capital may erode the quality of social support available to an individual. Rapid mobility in and out of an area reduces the marriage pool initially, and the likelihood of remarriage following divorce. Fear of crime fosters a distrust of others that can contribute to social isolation (Krause 1992). Social isolation has, in turn, been related to an array of adverse health outcomes (House et al 1988a), and it is known to compromise immunologic functioning (Kiecolt-Glaser et al 1994). In contrast, social opportunities provided via information networks, intergenerational networks, churches, and other community organizations may foster the creation of individual social ties that have a health-protective effect (Sampson 1992).

Health Habits and Behaviors

Community characteristics influence the degree to which certain health habits may be practiced. Because poorer neighborhoods have fewer facilities and resources, the adoption of public health recommendations such as obtaining a healthy diet and obtaining regular exercise sometimes cannot be met. High-stress neighborhoods, characterized by high density, high crime, and high mobility, may also lead to the development of health-compromising behaviors that act as efforts to cope with stress, such as smoking, alcohol consumption, and drug abuse. Noise appears to increase rates of smoking and the use of some drugs (Evans 1997).

Health habits are also affected by the social capital generated within communities. For example, pregnant women, especially young, single pregnant women, show higher levels of prenatal care in neighborhoods with strong social networks, perhaps because these networks put pressure on them to avoid compromising the health of their fetus and also provide them with more information about what constitutes effective prenatal care (Sampson 1992). Other health habits may be similarly affected.

The availability of health care varies substantially by neighborhood. Consistently poor health services are found in low-income, minority, and transient areas (Macintyre et al 1993, Williams 1990, Wyke et al 1992). Especially for children, the combination of rapid population loss coupled with inadequate health services is devastating. Communities experiencing poverty, overcrowding, and rapid population change show rises in infant mortality and low birth weight (Wallace & Wallace 1990). In contrast, the information networks that develop in stable communities transmit knowledge of and linkages to clinic services (Sampson 1992), including prenatal services, child health services, and general child care.

Conclusion

Documenting the effects of community characteristics on health is difficult. Studies that control for demographic characteristics, such as SES and race, on the one hand, and more proximal family characteristics, such as family income, on the other hand, may statistically underestimate the contribution of community to health by virtue of drawing off variance into these more distal and proximal predictors (G Duncan, J Connell & P Klebanov, unpublished observations). Moreover, estimating the dependent contribution of highly correlated community characteristics, such as population density, population mobility, and community SES level creates problems of data analysis and interpretation. In addition, community characteristics do not have uniformly positive or negative effects that consistently translate into health outcomes. For example, the presence of middle-SES neighbors appears to have a protective effect in reducing aggression and delinquency among low-SES youngsters, especially black males from low-income, single-parent homes, but it may simultaneously adversely af-

fect the ability to develop social relationships with their peers (Kupersmidt et al 1995).

Despite the difficulties with drawing inferences from community studies, the evidence suggests several community characteristics that have adverse effects on health, including crowding, air pollution, exposure to violence, and the absence of social networks and social ties. In addition, the protective effects of informal and formal social ties and networks appear to be robust. Exactly how community and neighborhood characteristics affect health is still largely unknown (Jencks & Mayer 1990); the evidence is strongest for chronic stress, the erosion of social ties, and development of poor health behaviors, although the links to physiology have yet to be established. The role of mental distress and coping skills other than those relating to social capital are less well studied.

THE FAMILY SOCIAL ENVIRONMENT

THE family environment clearly influences children's health. The link can be direct, as when a parent's behavior exposes a fetus to drugs in the womb (Neuspiel et al 1989). We focus on indirect links and highlight four characteristics of the family social environment that appear to influence child and adolescent health; (*a*) the quality of parenting, especially emotional aspects of the parent-child relationship; (*b*) the family's social climate, especially the amount of conflict and violence in the home; (*c*) the parents' mental health and other behavioral characteristics of the parents; and (*d*) variables associated with social-economic conditions of the household, such as whether the child lives with one or both parents and the educational level of parents.

Chronic Stress

Characteristics of a family environment that appear to be associated with health problems in children include a lack of warmth and emotional support from parents and a high level of conflict and violence. A cold and unresponsive parenting style has been associated with retarded infant growth and increased rates of illness in childhood (Bradley 1993, Gottman & Katz 1989). A stressful family environment can even influence prenatal development (Collins et al 1993). Quarreling and fighting at home have been linked to psychosomatic symptoms such as headaches and stomachaches in adolescents (Mechanic & Hansell 1989). When family dysfunction and conflict escalate to the point of abuse, the direct and indirect effects on child health can be lethal. Children with histories of physical abuse and neglect have an elevated mortality risk for all causes of death, including homicide, transportation injury, other unintentional injury, and disease (Sorenson & Peterson 1994). A history of sexual abuse can have health consequences years later, leading to increased rates of psychological distress, headache, asthma, diabetes, arthritis, HIV infection, gynecological problems, and various somatic symptoms (Braaten 1996). Some of the effects of sexual abuse on health may be mediated by poor health habits. Women with a history of childhood sexual abuse are more likely to smoke, abuse drugs, and engage in risky sexual behavior, and they are less likely to use medical care (Springs & Friedrich 1992). Other indirect effects of abuse may be mediated by conditions in the family. For example, the instability and social isolation that is often found in abusive families appear to mediate the effects of maltreatment on children's poor academic performance (Eckenrode et al 1995) and may influence health as well (House et al 1988b).

Repeated interference with homeostatic processes may be one physiologic pathway through which a chronically stressful family environment causes health problems in children. Experimental manipulations resembling two of the family characteristics considered, namely the presence of anger and conflict and the absence of emotional warmth and responsiveness, can disrupt patterns of cardiovascular and neuroendocrine regulation in children. For example, preschoolers respond to videotapes of angry adult interactions with increases in heart rate and blood pressure (El-Sheikh et al 1989), and separations from mothers lead to increased heart rates as well as elevations in norepinephrine and cortisol, particularly among socially shy children (Kagan et al 1987, 1988). However, a secure infant-mother attachment predicts lower stress response (as indexed by salivary cortisol) to new or strange situations (Hertsgaard et al 1995). Cortisol responses to separation are also attenuated in the presence of a responsive caregiver (Gunnar et al 1992). A buildup in allostatic load experienced by a child who is responding physiologically to repeated social challenges at home may help to explain the poor development and high rates of illness observed in children from stressful family environments.

Mental Health/Distress

Depression is clearly associated with deleterious health outcomes among children and adolescents, such as increased acute illness and physical symptoms and unhealthy behaviors such as smoking and substance abuse (Gore et al 1992, Lewinsohn et al 1994). Household economic conditions influence both the risk of childhood depression and its link to health. Risk factors for childhood depression include living in a single parent household, parental unemployment, and parents' poor education background (Gore et al 1992, Kaslow et al 1994, Lewinsohn et al 1994). Depression is more strongly linked to poor health among adolescents with a lower standard of living (Gore et al 1992).

More depressed children are also found among families whose members provide one another with little or no support, families that do not experience a sense of cohesiveness, and families characterized by high levels conflict, especially marital conflict (Kaslow et al 1994, Lewinsohn et al 1994). Characteristics of the parent-child relationship that are associated with depression include low levels of behavioral and emotional involvement, high levels of conflict and hostility, and a parenting style that is more autocratic, dominant, and controlling (Kaslow et al 1994, Lewinsohn et al 1994). Children of depressed mothers appear to be at increased risk for both depression and suicidal behavior, as well as a variety of other psychiatric diagnoses (Kaslow et al 1994). The behavior of depressed parents may contribute to this risk. Most studies find depressed mothers to be less responsive, more critical, negative, and irritable, and more controlling and intrusive with their children (Downey & Coyne 1990, Nolen-Hoeksema et al 1995).

Abuse within the family is also associated with depression and suicide (Malinosky-Rummell & Hansen 1993). Evidence suggests that the connection between a childhood history of family violence and recurrent depressions in adulthood is mediated by chronic interpersonal problems in the adult's life (Kessler & Magee 1994).

In summary, the links between family and parenting characteristics and depression in children and adolescents are clear. There is also evidence for negative short-term health effects in the form of increased rates of acute illness and suicide. Chronic or intermittent depression in childhood and adolescence may be associated with patterns of coping and/or physiologic responses to stress that contribute to long-term adverse health outcomes as well.

Coping Skills and Resources

Davies & Cummings (1994) suggested that emotionally secure children are better able to regulate their emotions in the face of stress and therefore cope more effectively with daily problems. According to their model, emotional security is threatened by destructive forms of family conflict, such as conflicts between parents that involve physical aggression, and by parent-child relationships marked by instability and a lack of personal warmth and responsiveness. Family social environments with features such as these, including abuse, discord, and parental psychopathology, are associated with maladaptive coping

in children, in particular difficulty with anger regulation (Crittenden 1992, Cummings & El-Sheikh 1991, Zahn-Waxler et al 1984). Because anger and its regulation have been tied to the development of heart disease and hypertension, there may be health risks associated wtih growing up in homes that have these characteristics.

Family experiences also influence how children learn to negotiate interpersonal situations involving frustration and anger. Violent boys are more likely to live in mother-headed households, or to have fathers who use spanking for discipline and rarely express affection for their sons (Sheline et al 1994). Prospective research indicates that the development of hostile attitudes and behaviors in male adolescents is associated with family interactions that are nonsupportive and have a negative affective tone (Matthews et al 1996). Parent-child conflict and ineffective parenting practices foster problems in social information processing and social skill deficits in children that, in turn, lead to poor coping in school, in particular during interactions with peers (Patterson et al 1989). Children from families in which there is greater organization and consistency in the home use fewer aggressive coping strategies in response to everyday stress (Hardy et al 1993).

Dysfunctional coping strategies in children and adolescents may persist into adulthood. Thus, maladaptive coping styles that are first acquired in response to a stressful family environment in childhood may be associated with greater autonomic reactivity and poorer health outcomes throughout the lifespan. For example, hostility measured in adolescence is linked to coronary risk factors (such as high lipid ratios, larger body mass, smoking, and caffeine consumption) assessed more than 20 years later (Siegler et al 1992).

Health Habits and Behaviors

The abuse of substances, such as alcohol, cigarettes, and illicit drugs, and risky sexual behavior are two health-threatening classes of behavior that are usually first observed during adolescence. In addition to their direct effects on health, these behaviors are linked with patterns of sleep, diet, and physical activity that indicate an unhealthy adolescent lifestyle (Donovan et al 1991).

The use of drugs by family members, both parents and siblings, is a reliable risk factor for adolescent drug usage (Denton & Kampfe 1994). Although genetics may play a role in cigarette smoking (Rowe & Linver 1995), the family's influence on adolescents' use of other drugs may be mediated by social environment factors. In addition to the imitation of behaviors observed at home, teens whose parents abuse substances appear to be more vulnerable to stress (Barrera et al 1995) and to acquire attitudes and coping styles that lead to increased affiliation with substance-using peers (Wills et al 1994). The experience of maltreatment in the home is also a risk factor for adolescent drug use (Malinosky-Rummell & Hansen 1993). In contrast, supportive and cohesive families help protect adolescents with problem-drinking fathers (Farrell et al 1995).

Drug-abusing teens are more likely to live in single-parent homes and homes from which they feel alienated (Denton & Kampfe 1994). A lack of support and sense of rejection and detachment from parents has been associated with adolescent substance use (Barrera et al 1993, Turner et al 1993). Deficits in parental support partially mediate the association between low parental education and increased substance use among teens (Wills et al 1995b). Prospective longitudinal data suggest that fathers' difficulty controlling anger predicts sons' future alcohol and drug abuse (D'Angelo et al 1995). Maternal behavior rated as cold, unresponsive, and underprotective when children were five years old has been associated with frequent drug usage during adolescence (Shedler & Block 1990). Findings like these do not rule out the possibility that the same stable personality traits in a child that undermine the development of supportive family relationships

may also increase the child's propensity of abuse substances (Wills et al 1995a).

There are conflicting findings regarding the role that parental control, supervision, and monitoring play in adolescent drug use. On the one hand, studies suggest that the homes of some abusing adolescents are overly controlling and that the children experience a lack of autonomy (Denton & Kampfe 1994, Webb et al 1991). On the other hand, longitudinal evidence relates abuse of drugs and smoking by teens to homes with less consistent enforcement of rules, less parental monitoring of the child's behavior, fewer parental demands of the child, and less imposition of structure and organization (Biglan et al 1995, Stice & Barrera 1995). In addition, some parents respond to their teen's use of drugs with fewer attempts at control and less support, which may signal the parents' acquiescence or sense of helplessness (Stice & Barrera 1995).

Many of the characteristics of families that are linked to substance abuse are also linked to adolescent sexual behavior. Teens growing up in single-parent households and those with histories of physical or sexual abuse show an increased probability of engaging in risky sexual behavior (Cunningham et al 1994, Jemmott & Jemmott 1992). Teens engage in more frequent sexual activity and more risky sexual behaviors when there is less parental monitoring and more permissiveness at home (Jemmott & Jemmott 1992, Metzler et al 1994). However, there is also evidence of increased sexual activity among adolescents whose parents overprotect them and fail to help them to learn to function independently (Turner et al 1993).

Conclusion

Research findings consistently point to three characteristics of family environments that can undermine the health of children and adolescents: (*a*) a social climate that is conflictual and angry or, worse, one that is violent and abusive; (*b*) relationships, particularly parent-child relationships, that are unresponsive and lacking in cohesiveness, warmth, and emotional support; and (*c*) parenting that is either overly controlling and dominating on the one hand or uninvolved with little monitoring of the child and little imposition of rules and structure on the other hand. These dimensions of a family environment are stressful for children, and they are associated with depression, maladaptive ways of coping with negative affect, and health-threatening behaviors in adolescence. The family characteristics identified as contributors to poor health outcomes in childhood are often embedded within households characterized by economic strain and few resources. Evidence suggests that parenting behavior may mediate some of the effects of economic strain (Huston et al 1994); however, economic strain may mediate the effects of other family characteristics, such as the number of parents in the home (Gore et al 1992).

The Peer Social Environment

Chronic Stress and Mental Health/Distress

Characteristics similar to the factors identified in stressful communities and families predict chronic stress in the peer and school environments: less adult attention and stability at school, and more conflict with and less acceptance by peers. For example, children who show greater cardiovascular reactivity are more prone to develop respiratory illnesses when they are enrolled in preschools that are unstable and unable to provide individual adult attention (e.g. those with high teacher-child ratios, high staff turnover, more part-time teachers, etc) (Boyce et al 1995). As highly reactive children in less stable and less attentive preschools repeatedly respond to social stressors in the environment, they may build up high allostatic load, which may result in more illnesses.

Adolescents spontaneously mention interpersonal stressors involving peers—such as conflicts with friends, feeling lonely or left out of peer groups, and boyfriend/girlfriend problems—as among the most common and most distressing problems that they face in daily life (Repetti et al 1996). Being neglected or rejected by peers has been associated in longitudinal studies with both increased aggression and depression (Kupersmidt & Patterson 1991). The complex interactions between the family and peer social environments are illustrated by research indicating that poor parenting practices often result in child behavior problems that can, in turn, lead to peer rejection (Patterson et al 1989).

Coping Skills and Resources

As youngsters move from childhood into their teenage years they spend less time with their families and (especially for girls) more time with peers (Larson & Richards 1991). Not surprisingly, then, adolescents often turn to their friends for support, especially when there is turmoil at home (Aseltine et al 1994). The presence of supportive peer relationships is usually associated with better mental health among children and adolescents, although that association partly reflects the impact of psychological functioning on the development of supportive friendships (Hirsch & DuBois 1992). The peer group may facilitate children's coping by enhancing self-esteem, perceptions of control, and the perceived security of social relations (Sandler et al 1989b). Empirical evidence for the stress-buffering role of peer social support has been mixed. Some studies suggest that support from friends can provide protection from the negative impact of stress on children's psychological adjustment (Dubow & Tisak 1989), but others do not find evidence of a moderating role of peer support (Cumsille & Epstein 1994). The effectiveness of peer support is likely to vary as a function of the stressor with which the adolescent is coping (Gore & Aseltine 1995).

Health Habits and Behaviors

Adolescents' beliefs about the prevalence and acceptance of alcohol and drug use by peers are risk factors for alcohol and drug use, with peer influence increasing as children age (Bailey & Hubbard 1990, Donaldson 1995). In addition to passive social pressures exerted by the perceived behavior and attitudes of peers, social contact with certain individuals may increase the availability of these substances (Dolcini & Adler 1994). For example, residence in a fraternity or sorority and the adoption of a party-centered lifestyle are reliable predictors of binge drinking among college students (Wechsler et al 1995).

Peer social influence affects other behaviors that pose significant threats to adolescent health. For example, high school students are more likely to engage in risky sexual behavior if their friends are sexually active or if they believe that a majority of their peers have had intercourse (Walter et al 1992). Consistent with data on other risky behaviors, one of the best-known predictors of adolescent smoking is association with peers who smoke (Biglan et al 1995). The appeal of smoking may derive, in part, from its function as a social signal suggesting adult role status and independence from parents (Rowe & Linver 1995).

The influence exerted by peers may be at least partially shaped by the family social environment. On the one hand, children are more likely to affiliate with substance-abusing peers if their parents abuse substances or inadequately supervise their activities (Biglan et al 1995, Wills et al 1994). On the other hand, the effect of peer drug use is much weaker when parenting is authoritative (i.e. parents are involved, make demands, and supervise while demonstrating acceptance and warmth) (Mounts & Steinberg 1995).

Conclusion

The social environments provided at school and by peers affect child and adolescent health at each point in Figure 2. There is particularly strong evidence for the stressfulness of conflicts and rejection by peers and for the social influence of peers over several categories of health-threatening behavior. An important finding is that the effects of the peer social environment must be understood within the context of the family environment.

ADULT SOCIAL ENVIRONMENT

A BROAD range of social ties has been examined concerning adult health. These ties include not only immediate family and other close relatives and friends but also ties to larger formal and informal groups. An extensive literature documents the range of negative health outcomes that accrue to those whose social environment is either structurally impoverished (i.e. characterized by fewer social ties) or functionally impoverished (i.e. characterized by a dearth of socially supportive interactions with others) (Berkman 1995, Broadhead et al 1983).

Although social ties have generally been seen as serving a health-promoting role, the social environment can also be a source of increased and potentially chronic stress, which contributes to increased rather than decreased health risks; that is, social relationships are characterized by costs as well as benefits. Such costs can take the form of requests/demands for assistance, criticism, or other forms of interpersonal conflict (Averill 1982). When such characteristics predominate in the social environment, they can result in increased risks for poor mental and physical health (for discussion and review, see Burg & Seeman 1994, Seeman et al 1996).

Chronic Stress

The health-promoting effects of the social environment are generally hypothesized to result from the stress-reducing effects of social integration within a nurturant, supportive milieu (Cohen 1992). Evidence linking social environment characteristics to physiologic stress responses supports this view, pointing to the potential importance of the social environment in the accumulation of allostatic load.

Although being married has been generally

associated with better immune responses as measured by various parameters of immune reaction (Kiecolt-Glaser et al 1994), spousal interaction characterized by greater hostility and conflict has been associated with greater cardiovascular and neuroendocrine reactivity and lower immune function (Kiecolt-Glaser et al 1994). The stress-inducing combination of emotional and physical demands of caring for a sick spouse had also been related to lowered immune function (e.g. among those with a spouse with cancer or those who are caring for a spouse with Alzheimer's disease) as well as elevated lipids and increased endocrine reactivity (for a review, see Kiecolt-Glaser et al 1994). Ambulatory monitoring of blood pressure at work and at home indicates that men show a reduction in blood pressure in the home environment whereas women do not (Unden et al 1991), which may be due to the greater demands of home and child care frequently assumed by women. Beyond the marital relationship, individuals reporting lower levels of support from close friends and family also exhibit higher heart rate and systolic blood pressure (Dressler et al 1986, Unden et al 1991), higher serum cholesterol and lower immune function (Thomas et al 1985), and higher levels of neuroendocrine activity (Seeman et al 1994).

Experimental studies also demonstrate the physiologic impacts of social interactions. Interpersonal challenge or hostility have been shown to elicit increased neuroendocrine and cardiovascular activity (Brown & Smith 1992, Krantz et al 1986). The presence of a friend or supportive confederate, however, generally attenuates cardiovascular reactivity in subjects confronted with challenging laboratory tasks (for a review, see Seeman & McEwen 1996). By contrast, the presence of a stranger observing the testing session produces increased reactivity (Syndersmith & Cacioppo 1992) as does the presence of others (friends or strangers) who disagree with the subject about some aspect of the session (Back & Bogdonoff 1964, Gerin et al 1992). Reactivity appears to be reduced by the presence of even one other person who agrees with the subject (Black & Bogdonoff 1964, Gerin et al 1992).

Mental Health/Distress

The positive and negative effects of the social environment on mental health have been extensively documented (for a review, see George 1989). Greater social integration, particularly as reflected in the presence of primary ties with spouse, children, and other kinds of supportive significant others are associated with lower risk of depression (George 1989), while marital disruption—either through bereavement, marriage dissolution, or the cognitive impairment of one's spouse—is associated with increased risks for psychological distress (Aseltine & Kessler 1993, Bloom et al 1978, Moritz et al 1989). The quality of existing relationships, however, appears equally important in predicting mental health outcomes. Relationships that are characterized by criticism, unwelcome advice or conflict, or demands for caregiving have been associated with increased psychological distress (Kessler et al 1985). Depression and/or negative affect in significant others is also associated with increased depression and psychological distress (Joiner 1994). Even in the absence of overtly negative social interactions, failure of the family or friends to provide anticipated or expected support can result in increased psychological distress (Brown & Harris 1989).

Women may be especially vulnerable to the psychological consequences of nonsupportive interactions with family or friends. Although men and women both report more supportive than negative social interactions, women report relatively more negative interactions with nondiscretionary family or kin ties (Lefler et al 1986, Schuster et al 1990) and appear to be more emotionally distressed by such negative interactions (Lefler et al 1986, Wethington et al 1987). Men benefit more consistently from greater social integration (House et al 1988a).

Coping Skills and Resources

Throughout life, one's family and friends serve as the social context within which events are appraised and coping strategies are evaluated and initiated (Cohen 1992). Family and/or friends can affect coping efforts through provision of actual instrumental and/or informational support and can serve as sources of emotional support (Cohen 1992). Such social resources may be particularly important in coping with lower-SES environmental demands: The relationship between lower occupational status and greater psychological vulnerability to life events disappears for lower-status women reporting high social support (Turner & Noh 1983).

The influence of the family or friends on coping, however, may not always be health promoting. The assistance provided by family and friends in coping with illness and/or disability can result in increased dependency and disability (for reviews, see Seeman et al 1996, Thompson & Sobolew-Shubin 1993) or poorer disease control. Diabetic men with larger support networks exhibit poorer control of their diabetes (e.g. significant increases in glycosylated hemoglobin, cholesterol and triglycerides, glucose and weight; Kaplan & Hartwell 1987) as do teenagers reporting greater satisfaction with their social-support systems (Kaplan et al 1985), possibly because members of the support network undermine diabetes-related diet behaviors. Studies also document limits to the effectiveness of social support in promoting better coping. In the face of severe stressors such as life-threatening disease, even the presence of close and apparently supportive relationships is not always associated with reductions in psychological distress or greater physical recovery (Bolger et al 1997, Coyne & Fiske 1992).

Health Habits and Behaviors

The social environment also serves as a source of learning and reinforcement for attitudes and behaviors that affect health. People who are more socially integrated exhibit greater preventive health behavior, including less smoking and drinking (Broman 1992) and more cancer screening (for a review, see Berkman 1995) and more successful risk reduction efforts such as reducing dietary fat, exercising, and stopping smoking (Bovbjerg et al 1995, Sallis et al 1989). Supportive family environments have also been related to better adherence in hemodialysis treatment (Christensen et al 1992). However, the social environments provided by family and friends also carry the potential for encouraging more detrimental health behaviors such as problem drinking (Seeman et al 1988), less successful efforts to quit smoking (Cohen 1992), and as indicated above, poorer control of diabetes. Family environments can also present more direct health threats in the form, for example, of second-hand smoke exposure from living with a smoker (Sandler et al 1989a) and physical abuse (Mercy & Saltzman 1989).

Evidence linking social environment characteristics to health-care utilization is neither extensive nor consistent. Consultations with family and friends can result in increased or decreased utilization, depending on the degree to which their attitudes and behaviors favor such utilization as well as their ability to provide assistance to facilitate utilization (Geertsen et al 1975, Penning 1995, Sampson 1992).

Conclusion

The characteristics of the social environment that relate most strongly to adult health outcomes—lack of social integration and poor quality of social relationships—also exhibit links with postulated pathways for these health effects. Specifically, social relationships characterized by conflict and hostility are associated not only with increased mental distress but also with increased physiologic arousal and lowered immune function, profiles of physiologic activity with known links to disease pathology (McEwen & Stellar 1993). In contrast with these health-damaging effects of impoverished social environments, environments characterized by supportive relationships appear to serve a stress-reducing, health-promoting function, enhancing psychological functioning and reducing physiologic arousal. In addition, the social environment can impact directly and importantly on health behaviors and health-care utilization.

WORK

THE work environment represents an important life arena for adults that contributes to life satisfaction. Controlling for SES and health, those who work report a higher quality of life than those who do not (Ruchlin & Morris 1991). Moreover, full-time employment predicts slower declines in perceived health and in physical functioning for both men and women (Ross & Mirowsky 1995). Nonetheless, adverse characteristics of the work environment have long been suspected to contribute to ill health. Work stressors are among the most common and upsetting stressors that people report, and because the majority of adults work full-time, they may be exposed to the health-compromising effects of these conditions over the long term.

The work environment may directly affect illness precursors or illness, including injuries, cancers, and respiratory and cardiovascular disease, by exposing workers to physical, chemical, and biological hazards (House & Smith 1985). Because this voluminous literature has not yet implicated psychosocial mechanisms in disease pathology, apart from the fact that such adverse exposure is strongly linked to SES and race, we do not review it here.

Chronic Stress

Chronic stress is the mechanism most commonly offered to explain the adverse effects of the work environment on health. Work overload is one of the chief factors studied. Workers who feel required to work too long and too hard at too many tasks report more stress (e.g. Caplan & Jones 1975), practice poorer health habits (Sorensen et al 1985), and report more health complaints than do workers not suffering from overload (Repetti 1993). Work overload appears to trigger neuroendocrine and cardiovascular reactions that, over time, can increase the likelihood of cardiovascular disease. Working 40 or more hours a week is a risk factor for producing babies of low birth weight among employed women (Peoples-Sheps et al 1991). Work pressure also predicts ill health. Men reporting high job pressure or demands sought medical attention more and showed more documented signs of pathology; a follow-up investigation revealed these men were more likely to die in the following decade (House et al 1986). Consistently, however, research demonstrates a stronger relationship between reported work overload and physical health complaints than between numbers of hours worked and poor health (e.g. Herzog et al 1991), which raises the possibility that psychological distress or negative affectivity is implicated in this relation.

Role conflict and role ambiguity have also been tied to illness precursors and illness (Caplan & Jones 1975). Role conflict occurs when an individual receives conflicting information about work tasks or standards. Chronically high blood pressure and elevated pulse have been tied to role conflict and role ambiguity (French & Caplan 1973).

Responsibility for others may contribute to ill health. For example, a study comparing illness rates of air-traffic controllers and second-class airmen found that hypertension was four times more common and diabetes and peptic ulcers twice as common among the air-traffic controllers than among the airmen, who did not have responsibility for the fates of others. Moreover, all three diseases were diagnosed at a younger age among the air-traffic controllers. Hypertension and ulcers were more common among controllers at busier airports (Cobb 1976).

The perception that one's career or job development has been inadequate may also contribute to ill health. People who feel they have been promoted too quickly or too slowly, who feel insecure about their jobs, and who feel that their ambitions are thwarted are more likely to report stress, to seek help for psychological distress, and to show higher rates of illness, especially cardiovascular disease (Catalano et al 1986).

Research has especially focused on the effects of a high-strain work environment defined as one with a high level of demands and a low level of decision latitude (Karasek & Theorell 1990). Considerable research has supported the hypothesized relation of high work strain to poor health (e.g. Landsbergis et al 1992). Work strain is significantly negatively associated with health-related quality of life, including physical functioning, role functioning related to physical health, vitality, social functioning, and mental health (Lerner et al 1994). Job strain has been linked to higher fibrinogen levels among working middle-aged women (Davis et al 1995) and to low birth weight (Woo 1994). Frankenhaeuser (1991) found that the catecholamine/cortisol balance is different in high- versus low-control situations, with cortisol levels lower in high-control situations. Not all studies find adverse effects of high levels of job demands and strain, however (Albright et al 1992), and studies relating job demands and decision latitude to coronary heart disease risk factors (cholesterol, smoking, and systolic and diastolic blood pressure) are inconsistent (Alterman et al 1994, Pieper et al 1989). Nonetheless, research suggests that the risk that role overload will lead to heart disease may be reduced when people are given a high degree of control in the work environment (Karasek & Theorell 1990).

Job uncertainty and unemployment have been associated with a variety of adverse mental and physical health outcomes, including depression, physical symptoms, physical illness (Hamilton et al 1990), alcohol abuse (Catalano et al 1993), and a heightened mortality rate (Sorlie & Rogot 1990). The negative effects of unemployment appear to be generated by the financial strain produced by unemployment and by the fact that unemployment creates vulnerability to other life events. Being unstably employed is also related to poor health (Pavalko et al 1993, Rushing et al 1992).

Research has focused increasingly not only on work stress but on its interactive effects with the stress induced by other roles, especially into the family. Much of this work has focused on married women with young children who are employed and who are chiefly responsible for household and child-care tasks. Overall, combining marital, parental, and occupational roles does not appear to significantly affect mortality (Kotler & Wingard 1989). However, attempting to juggle heavy responsibilities at both work and home reduces the enjoyment of all tasks (Williams et al 1991). On the other hand, employment can also be beneficial for women's well-being (Repetti et al 1989). Whether the effects of multiple roles are positive or negative appears to depend heavily on resources available. Having control and flexibility over one's work, having a good income, and having someone to help with the housework or child care all reduce the likelihood that combining multiple roles will produce psychological costs. (Lennon & Rosenfield 1992, Rosenfield 1992). Although less research has been conducted on men, what evidence there is suggests that for men, multiple roles are protective (Adelmann 1994).

Mental Health/Psychological Distress

Mental health or psychological distress has typically not been examined as a pathway to poor health in the work environment but has been treated as an outcome in its own right. This is because psychological distress often translates into outcomes of importance to employers, specifically job dissatisfaction, absenteeism, disability claims, and high rates of turnover. Overall research suggests that the factors that compromise physical health also compromise mental health (for a review, see Taylor 1995). Whether anxiety and depression generated by job stress constitute a route by which the chronic stress of the work environment translates into poor health outcomes is unknown.

Coping Skills and Resources

The role of coping strategies in moderating the relation between chronic work stress and adverse health outcomes is an understudied area. This may be true partly because objective work demands are often so powerful that individual coping strategies have little room in which to operate. In addition, understanding how people cope with job stress may necessitate the examination of coping strategies specific to a particular job (Dewe & Guest 1990). Nonetheless, active coping strategies have been associated with more effective coping in a variety of situations (for a review, see Haidt & Rodin 1995), and the Karasek model of work strain is consistent with such an argument in positing that the degree to which individuals have decision latitude reduces work strain. Nonetheless, under conditions of high psychological demands, decision latitude may have negative effects.

Social support has been extensively studied in the work environment, and its effects are generally beneficial. Social support can have both direct (e.g. Ganster et al 1986, Loscocco & Spitze 1990) and moderating effects (e.g. Repetti et al 1989) on reported stress and health problems in the workplace. Those who report being unable to develop satisfying relationships report more negative affect at work (Buunk et al 1993) and poorer physical and mental health (Repetti 1993). Poor social relations at work have been tied directly to heightened catecholamine levels (Cooper & Marshall 1976), to risk for coronary heart disease (Repetti 1993), and to heightened fibrinogen levels in working women (Davis et al 1995). A study of government workers found that high workload was related to high blood pressure, but this relationship was attenuated among employees who had supportive relationships with their supervisors (House 1981). Adverse ef-fects of unemployment also appear to be moderated by the seeking of social support (Turner et al 1991). Social support may be especially important for buffering work stress for minority group members (Gutierres et al 1996).

Health Habits and Behaviors

As noted, health habits are adversely affected by job stress and as such, may also play a moderating role in the relation between work stress and adverse health outcomes. People who feel they have more control over work are less likely to engage in risky health behaviors (Wickrama et al 1995). Substance abuse in the work environment has been extensively studied. Muntaner et al (1995) found that after adjusting for SES, alcoholism, and certain work conditions, drug abuse was higher in individuals with high-strain jobs. Job strain may not lead people to start smoking, but it does appear to lead to heavier smoking (Green & Johnson 1990). High job dissatisfaction is associated with heavy drinking, and negative consequences of drinking are associated with the job characteristics of low autonomy, little use of capacities, and lack of participation in decision making (Greenberg & Grunberg 1995). However, some research suggests that such abuse may be more related to general feelings of powerlessness, alienation, and lack of commitment than to specific job characteristics (Seeman et al 1988). Problem drinking in response to job characteristics may also depend on the degree to which alcohol consumption is perceived to be a useful means of coping (Greenberg & Grunberg 1995). Most studies relating job characteristics to health habits are cross-sectional, so it is difficult to determine whether job strain and health habits may be due to some third factor, such as emotional distress.

Conclusion

Research links work stress to a broad array of acute diseases, and evidence that it contributes to chronic disease such as cardiovascular disease, is mounting (Repetti 1993). The main psychosocial pathway from the work environment to poor health that has been studied involves chronic stress. Other potential routes, such as mental health or emotional distress, coping strategies, and health habits, have been studied not as pathways but as outcomes in their own right. The research on occupational stress could clearly profit from a consideration of more complex and multiple causal routes in relating chronic stress to adverse health outcomes.

CONCLUSIONS

INDIVIDUAL experiences and behaviors predictive of health outcomes are nested within geographic, social, developmental, and economic environments. The initial context for this observation is the recognition that social class and race are related to all-cause mortality and morbidity associated with a wide range of disorders. Those in the lower ends of the social class distribution and African-Americans disproportionately live in high-stress communities, occupy jobs characterized by high demands and low control, and live in family and social environments where they are disproportionately exposed to violence, conflict, and abuse. The type of community in which one lives and the demands of the work environment feed into the family environment and the kinds of social ties external to the family that may be developed. Thus, social environments influence health in a complex and interactive fashion.

The health effects of individual characteristics such as hostility, or the health effects of a family environment characteristic such as a high level of conflict, must be understood within the larger environments in which these behaviors are learned and expressed. At the very least, such an analysis should alert the psychologist to the potential risks of "psychologizing" or "biologizing" health-predictive variables without considering the contexts in which they occur. For example, recent empirical studies identifying a genetic

component to the perception of social support (Kendler et al 1991) and suggesting that social support is partly a function of individual dispositions in personality (Cohen et al 1986) must be balanced by the recognition that environments play an important role in fostering or undermining the ability to create social ties. Psychosocial predictors of health outcomes do not occur and should not be studied in an economic, racial, developmental, and social vacuum. With respect to interventions, the implications of such a viewpoint are complex. On the one hand, considering multiple levels of analysis simultaneously suggests multiple intervention points ranging from the individual through the family to the community. On the other hand, any intervention focus must acknowledge the interrelatedness of these environments and the fact that change induced at one level may have modest long-term effects, if corresponding changes do not occur at other levels.

Substantial evidence relates characteristics of environments to health-relevant outcomes, including all-cause mortality and a wide range of chronic diseases. Manifold pathways, reviewed above, have been implicated, including the exposure of individuals to chronic stress and the increased allostatic load that may result, the creation of chronic or intermittent emotional distress, the development or use of ineffective coping strategies and the inability to form and make use of social ties, and the acquisition and practice of health habits that are dependent upon environmental factors that limit personal and social resources. Empirically, the links from environmental characteristics to chronic stress to identifiable biological endpoints have most commonly been made. Pathways involving the other routes are less well studied, and more complex concatenations of these pathways, as suggested by Figure 2, have barely been studied at all. Each of the environments studied provides suggestive evidence about likely pathways that may guide research in the future.

At the outset, we asked "What is an unhealthy

environment and how does it get under the skin?" Answering such a question definitively is currently beyond the scope of any review, because much of the research one would like to see has not yet been conducted. Nonetheless, despite the gaps in the literature, the beginning of an answer is emerging. Consistently across the environments examined—community, family, work, and peers—those that threaten personal safety; that limit the ability to develop social ties; or that are characterized by conflictual, violent, or abusive interpersonal relationships are related to a broad array of adverse health outcomes. These effects appear to occur across the lifespan, beginning prenatally and carrying through into old age. Likewise, a picture of the healthy environment is coming into view. Environments are healthy to the degree that they provide safety and opportunities for social integration. In addition, the ability to experience a sense of personal control may be important, within certain parameters.

People have evolved as social animals and as such appear to be sensitively "tuned in" to others in the social world. Therefore, it should not be surprising that the social environment has such potential to affect physiology, both positively and negatively. Evidence continues to accumulate that throughout the lifespan, the structure and quality of social interactions have profound effects on psychological, behavioral, and physiologic functioning, and ultimately on our health and well-being.

ACKNOWLEDGMENTS

FUNDS for this review were provided in part by the MacArthur Foundation's SES Planning Initiative on Health. Preparation of this manuscript was also supported by MH 42152 from the National Institute of Mental Health to the first author and by FIRST Award R29-48593 from the National Institute of Mental Health to the second author. The third author was supported, in part, by a grant from the MacArthur Research Network on Successful Aging and by NIA-SERCA grant AG-00586. The authors gratefully acknowledge the helpful comments of Sheldon Cohen on a prior draft.

LITERATURE CITED

Adelmann PK. 1994. Multiple roles and psychological well-being in a national sample of older adults. *J. Gerontol.: Soc. Sci.* 49: S277–85

Adler NE, Boyce WT, Chesney MA, Folkman S, Syme SL. 1993. Socioeconomic inequalities in health: no easy solution. *J. Am. Med. Assoc.* 269:3140–45

Adler NE, Matthews KA. 1994. Health and psychology: Why do some people get sick and some stay well? *Annu. Rev. Psychol.* 45:229–59

Albright CL, Winkleby MA, Ragland DR, Fisher J, Syme SL. 1992. Job strain and prevalence of hypertension in a biracial population of urban bus drivers. *Am. J. Public Health* 82:984–89

Alterman T, Shekelle RB, Vernon SW, Burau KD. 1994. Decision latitude, psychologic demand, job strain, and coronary heart disease in the Western Electric study. *Am. J. Epidemiol.* 139:620–27

Anderson NB, McNeilly M, Myers H. 1991. Autonomic reactivity and hypertension in blacks: a review and proposed model. *Ethn. Dis.* 1:163–70

Aseltine RG, Kessler RC. 1993. Marital disruption and depression in a community sample. *J. Health Soc. Behav.* 34:237–51

Aseltine RH Jr, Gore S, Colten ME. 1994. Depression and the social developmental context of adolescence. *J. Pers. Soc. Psychol.* 67:252–63

Averill JR. 1982. *Anger and Aggression: An Essay on Emotion.* New York: Springer-Verlag

Back KW, Bogdonoff MD. 1964. Plasma lipid responses to leadership, conformity, and deviation. In *Psychobiological Approaches to Social Behavior*, ed. HP Leiderman, D Shapiro, pp. 24–42. Stanford, CA: Stanford Univ. Press

Bailey SL, Hubbard RL. 1990. Developmental variation in the context of marijuana initiation among adolescents. *J. Health Soc. Behav.* 31:58–70

Barrera M, Chassin L, Rogosch F. 1993. Effects of social support and conflict on adolescent children of alcoholic and nonalcoholic fathers. *J. Pers. Soc. Psychol.* 64:602–12

Barrera M, Li SA, Chassin L. 1995. Effects of parental alcoholism and life stress on Hispanic and non-Hispanic Caucasian adolescents: a prospective study. *Am. J. Community Psychol.* 23:479–507

Becker MH. 1993. A medical sociologist looks at health promotion. *J. Health Soc. Behav.* 34:1–6

Berkman LF. 1995. The role of social relations in health promotion. *Psychosom. Med.* 57:245–54

Biglan A, Duncan TE, Ary DV, Smolkowski K. 1995. Peer and parental influences on adolescent tobacco use. *J. Behav. Med.* 18:315

Bloom BL, Asher SJ, White SW, 1978. Marital disruption as a stressor: a review and analysis. *Psychol. Bull.* 85:867–94

Bolger N, Foster M, Vinokur AD, Ng R. 1997. Close relationships and adjustment to a life crisis: the case of breast cancer. *J. Pers. Soc. Psychol.* In press

Booth-Kewley S, Friedman HS. 1987. Psychological predictors of heart disease: a quantitative review, *Psychol. Bull.* 101:343–62

Bovbjerg VE, McCann BS, Brief DJ, Follette WC, Retzlaff BM, et al. 1995. Spouse support and long-term adherence to lipid-lowering diets. *Am. J. Epidemiol.* 141:451–60

Boyce, WT, Chesney M, Alkon A, Tschann JM, Adams S, et al. 1995. Psychobiologic reactivity to stress and childhood respiratory illness: results of two prospective studies. *Psychosom. Med.* 57:411–22

Braaten LS, 1996. Sexual dysfunction in sexually traumatized women. *Health Psychol.* 18:6

Bradley RH. 1993. Children's home environments, health, behavior, and intervention efforts: a review using the home inventory as a marker measure. *Genet. Soc. Gen. Psychol. Monogr.* 119:437–90

Broadhead EW, Kaplan BH, James SA, Wagner EH, Schoenbach VJ, et al. 1983. The epidemiologic evidence for a relationship between social support and health. *Am. J. Epidemiol.* 117:521–37

Broman C. 1992. Social relationships and health-related behavior. *J. Behav. Med.* 16:335–50

Brown GW, Harris TO, eds. 1989. *Life Events and Illness.* New York: Guilford

Brown PC, Smith TW, 1992. Social influence, marriage, and the heart: cardiovascular consequences of interpersonal control in husbands and wives. *Health Psychol.* 11:88–96

Burg MM, Seeman TE. 1994. Families and Health: the negative side of social ties. *Ann. Behav. Med.* 16:109–15

Buunk BP, Doosje BJ, Jans LGJM, Hopstaken LEM. 1993. Perceived reciprocity, social support, and stress at work: the role of exchange and communal orientation. *J. Pers. Soc. Psychol.* 65:801–11

Calnan M, Johnson B. 1985. Health, health risks, and inequalities: an exploratory study of women's perceptions. *Sociol. Health Ill.* 7:55–75

Caplan RD, Jones KW. 1975. Effects of work load, role ambiguity, and Type A personality on anxiety, depression, and heart rate. *J. Appl. Psychol.* 60:713–19

Catalano R, Dooley D, Wilson G, Hough R. 1993. Job loss and alcohol abuse: a test using data from the epidemiological catchment area. *J. Health Soc. Behav.* 34:215–25

Catalano RA, Rook K, Dooley D. 1986. Labor markets and help-seeking: a test of the employment security hypothesis. *J. Health Soc. Behav.* 27:277–87

Christensen AJ, Smith TW, Turner CW, Holman JM Jr, Gregory MC, Rich MA. 1992. Family support, physical impairment, and adherence in hemodialysis: an investigation of main and buffering effects. *J. Behav. Med.* 15:313–25

Cobb S. 1976. Social Support as a moderator of life stress. *Psychosom. Med.* 38:300–14

Cohen S. 1992. Stress, social support, and disorder. In *The Meaning and Measurement of Social Support*, ed. HOF Veiel, U Baumann, pp. 109–24. New York: Hemisphere

Cohen S, Herbert TB. 1996. Health psychology: psychological factors and physical disease from the perspective of human psychoneuroimmunology. *Annu. Rev. Psychol.* 47:113–42

Cohen S, Sherrod DR, Clark MS. 1986. Social skills and the stress-protective role of social support. *J. Pers. Soc. Psychol.* 50:963–73

Coleman JS. 1990. *Foundations of Social Theory.* Cambridge, MA: Harvard Univ. Press

Collins NL, Dunkel-Schetter C, Lobel M, Scrimshaw SCM. 1993. Social support in pregnancy: psychosocial correlates of birth outcomes and postpartum depression. *J. Pers. Soc. Psychol.* 65:1243–58

Cooper CJ, Marshall J. 1976. Occupational sources of stress: a review of the literature relating to coronary heart disease and mental ill health. *J. Occup. Psychol.* 49:11–28

Coyne JC, Fiske V. 1992. Couples coping with chronic and catastrophic illness. In *Family Health Psychology*, ed. TJ

Akamatsu, SC Crowther, SE Hobfoll, MAP Stevens, pp. 129–49. Washington, DC: Hemisphere

Crittenden PM. 1992. Children's strategies for coping with adverse home environments: an interpretation using attachment theory. *Child Abuse Negl.* 16:329–43

Cummings EM, El-Sheikh M. 1991. Children's coping with angry environments: a process-oriented approach. In *Life-Span Developmental Psychology: Perspectives on Stress and Coping*, ed. EM Cummings, AL Greene, KH Karraker, pp. 131–50. Hillsadale, NJ: Erlbaum

Cumsile PE, Epstein N. 1994. Family cohesion, family adaptability, social support, and adolescent depressive symptoms in outpatient clinic families. *J. Fam. Psychol.* 8:202–14

Cunningham RM, Stiffman AR, Dore P, Earls F. 1994. The association of physical and sexual abuse with HIV risk behaviors in adolescence and young adulthood: implications for public health. *Child Abuse Negl.* 18:233–45

D'Angelo LL, Weinberger DA, Feldmann SS. 1995. Like father, like son? Predicting male adolescents' adjustment from parents' distress and self-restraint. *Dev. Psychol.* 31:883–96

Davies PT, Cummings EM. 1994. Marital conflict and child adjustment: an emotional security hypothesis. *Psychol. Bull.* 116:387–411

Davis MC, Matthews KA, Meilahn EN, Kiss JE. 1995. Are job characteristics related to fibrinogen levels in middle-aged women? *Health Psychol.* 14:310–18

Denton RE, Kampfe CM. 1994. The relationship between family variables and adolescent substance abuse: a literature review. *Adolescence* 29:475–95

Dewe PJ, Guest DE. 1990. Methods of coping with stress at work: a conceptual analysis and empirical study of measurement issues. *J. Organ. Behav.* 11:135–50

Dolcini MM, Adler NE. 1994. Perceived competencies, peer group affiliation, and risk behavior among early adolescents. *Health Psychol.* 13:496–506

Donaldson SI, 1995. Peer influence on adolescent drug use: a perspective from the trenches of experimental evaluation research. *Am. Psychol.* 50:801–2

Donovan JE, Jessor R, Costa FM. 1991. Adolescent health behavior and conventionality-unconventionality: an extension of problem-behavior theory. *Health Psychol.* 10:52–61

Downey G, Coyne JC. 1990. Children of depressed parents: an integrative review. *Psychol. Bull.* 108:50–76

Dressler WW, Dos Santos EJ, Viteri FE. 1986. Blood pressure, ethnicity, and psychosocial resources. *Psychosom. Med.* 48:509–19

Dubow EF, Tisak J. 1989. The relation between stressful life events and adjustment in elementary school children: the role of social support and social problem-solving skills. *Child Dev.* 60:1412–23

Durkin MS, Davidson LL, Kuhn L, O'Connor P, Barlow B. 1994. Low-income neighborhoods and the risk of severe pediatric injury: a small-area analysis in northern Manhattan. *Am. J. Public Health* 84:587–92

Eckenrode J, Rowe E, Laird M, Brathwaite J. 1995. Mobility as a mediator of the effects of child maltreatment of academic performance. *Child Dev.* 66:1130–42

El-Sheikh M, Cummings EM, Goetsch V. 1989. Coping with adults' angry behavior: behavioral, physiological, and self-report responding in preschoolers. *Dev. Psychol.* 25:490–98

Evans GW. 1997. Environmental stress and health. In *Handbook of Health Psychology*, ed. A Baum, T Revenson, JE Singer. Hillsdale, NJ: Erlbaum

Farrell MP, Barnes GM, Banerjee S. 1995. Family cohesion as a buffer against the effects of problem-drinking fathers on psychological distress, deviant behavior, nad heavy drinking in adolescents. *J. Health Soc. Behav.* 36:377–85

Fleming I, Baum A, Davidson LM, Rectanus E, McArdle S. 1987. Chronic stress as a factor in physiologic reactivity to challenge. *Health Psychol.* 6:221–37

Frankenhaeuser M. 1991. The psychophysiology of workload, stress, and health: comparison between the sexes. *Ann. Behav. Med.* 13:197–204

Frasure-Smith N, Lesperance F, Talajic M. 1995. The impact of negative emotions on prognosis following myocardial infarction: is it more than depression? *Health Psychol.* 14:388–98

French JRP Jr, Caplan RD. 1973. Organizational stress and the individual strain. In *The Failure of Success*, ed. AJ Marrow. New York: AMACON

Ganster DC, Fusilier MR, Mayes BT. 1986. Role of social support in the experience of stress at work. *J. Appl. Psychol.* 71:102–10

Garbarino J, Sherman D. 1980. High-risk neighborhoods and high-risk families: the human ecology of child maltreatment. *Child Dev.* 51:188–98

Geertsen R, Klauber MR, Rindflesh M, Kane R, Gray R. 1975. A re-examination of Suchman's view on social factors in health care utilization. *J. Health Soc. Behav.* 16:226–37

George LK. 1989. Stress, social support, and depression over the life-course. In *Aging, Stress, Social Support, and Health*, ed. K Markides, C Cooper, pp. 241–67. London: Wiley

Gerin W, Pieper C, Levy R, Pickering TG. 1992. Social support in social interaction: a moderator of cardiovascular reactivity. *Psychosom. Med.* 54:324–36

Gore S, Aseltine RH Jr. 1995. Protective processes in adolescence: matching stressors with social resources. *Am. J. Community Psychol.* 23:301–27

Gore S, Aseltine RH Jr, Colten ME. 1992. Social structure, life stress and depressive symptoms in a high school-aged population. *J. Health Soc. Behav.* 33:97–113

Gottman JM, Katz LF. 1989. Effects of marital discord on young children's peer interaction and health. *Dev. Psychol.* 25:373–81

Green KL, Johnson JV. 1990. The effects of psychosocial work organization on patterns of cigarette smoking among male chemical plant employees. *Am. J. Public Health* 80:1368–71

Greenberg ES, Grunberg L. 1995. Work alienation and problem alcohol behavior. *J. Health Soc. Behav.* 36:83–102

Gunner MR, Larson MC, Hertsgaard L, Harris ML, Brodersen L. 1992. The stressfulness of separation among nine-month-old infants: effects of social context variables and infant temperament. *Child Dev.* 63:290–303

Gutierres SE, Saenz DS, Green BL. 1996. Job stress and health outcomes among Anglo and Hispanic employees: a test of the person-environment fit model. In *Stress in the 90's*, ed. G Keita, S Sauter. Washington, DC: Am. Psychol. Assoc. In press

Haidt J, Rodin J, 1995. *Control and Efficacy: An Integrative Review.* Rep. John D and Catherine T MacArthur Found. Prog. Ment. Health Hum. Dev. Univ. Michigan, Ann Arbor

Hamilton VL, Broman CL, Hoffman WS, Renner DS. 1990. Hard times and vulnerable people: initial effects of plant closing on autoworkers' mental health. *J Health Soc. Behav.* 31:123–40

Harburg E, Erfurt JC, Havenstein LS, Chape S, Schull WJ, Schork MA. 1993. Socioecological stress, suppressed hostility, skin color, and black-white male blood pressure: Detroit. *Psychosom. Med.* 35:176–96

Hardy DF, Power TG, Jaedicke S. 1973. Examining the relation of parenting to children's coping with everyday stress. *Child Dev.* 64:1829–41

Herbert TB, Cohen S. 1993. Depression and immunity: a meta-analytic review. *Psychol. Bull.* 113:472–86

Hertsgaard L, Gunnar M, Erickson FM, Nachmias M. 1995. Adrenocortical responses to the strange situation in infants with disorganized/disoriented attachment relationships. *Child Dev.* 66:1100–6

Herzog AR, House JS, Morgan JN. 1991. Relation of work and retirement to health and well-being in older age. *Psychol. Aging* 6:202–11

Hirsch BJ, DuBois DL. 1992. The relation of peer social support and psychologiocal symptomatology during the transition to junior high school: a two-year longitudinal analysis. *Am. J. Community Psychol.* 20:333–47

House JS. 1981. *Work Stress and Socail Support.* Reading, MA: Addison-Wesley

House JS, Landis KR, Umberson D. 1988a. Social relationships and health. *Science* 241:540–45

House JS, Smith DA. 1985. Evaluating the health effects of demanding work on and off the job. In *Assessing Physical Fitness and Physical Activity in Population-Base Surveys*, ed. TF Drury, pp. 481–508. Hyattsville, MD: Natl. Cent. Health Stat.

House JS, Strecher V, Meltzner HL, Robbins CA. 1986. Occupational stress and health among men and women in the Tecumseh Community health study. *J. Health Soc. Behav.* 27:62–77

House JS, Umberson D, Landis KR. 1988b. Structures and processes of social support. *Annu. Rev. Sociol* 14:293–318

Huston AC, McLoyd VC, Coll CG. 1994. Children and poverty: issues in contemporary research. *Child Dev.* 65:275–82

Jemmott LS, Jemmott JB III. 1992. Family struture, parental strictness, and sexual behavior among inner-city black male adolescents. *J. Adolesc. Res* 7:192–207

Jencks C, Mayer S. 1990. The social consequencs of growing up in a poor neighborhood. In *Inner-City Poverty in the United States,* ed. L Lynn, M McGeary, pp. 111–86. Washington, DC: Natl. Acad.

Joiner TE Jr. 1994. Contagious depression: existence, specificity to depressed symptoms, and the role of reassurance seeking. *J. Pers. Soc. Psychol.* 67:287–96

Kagan J, Reznick JS, Snidman N. 1987. The physiology and psychology of behavioral inhibition in young children. *Child Dev.* 58:1359–473

Kagan J, Reznick JS, Snidman N. 1988. Biological bases of childhood shyness. *Science* 240:167–71

Kaplan M, Chadwick MW, Schimmel LE. 1985. Social learning intervention to promote metabolic control in Type I diabetes mellitus: pilot experiment results. *Diabetes Care* 8:152–55

Kaplan RM, Hartwell SL. 1987. Differential effects of social support and social network on physiological and social outcomes in men and women with Type II diabetes mellitus. *Health Psychol.* 6:387–98

Karasek R, Theorell T. 1990. *Healthy Work: Stress, Productivity, and the Reconstruction of Working Life.* New York: Basic Books

Kaslow NJ, Deering CG, Racusin GR. 1994. Depressed children and their families. *Clin. Psychol. Rev.* 14:39–59

Kendler KS, Kessler RC, Heath AC, Neale MC, Eaves LJ. 1991. Coping: a genetic epidemiological investigation. *Psychol. Med.* 21:337–46

Kessler RC, MacLeod JD, Wethington E. 1985. The costs of caring: a perspective on the relationship between sex and psychological distress. In *Social Support: Theory, Research and Applications,* ed. IG Sarason, BR Sarason, pp. 491–506. Dordrecht: Martinus Nijhoff

Kessler RC, Magee WJ. 1994. Childhood family violence and adult recurrent depression. *J. Health Soc. Behav.* 35:13–27

Kiecolt-Glaser JK, Malarkey WB, Cacioppo JT, Glaser R. 1994. Stressful personal relationships: immune and endocrine function. In *Handbook of Human Stress and Immunity,* ed. R Glaser, J Kiecolt-Glaser, pp. 312–39. San Diego: Academic

Kotler P, Wingard DL. 1989. The effect of occupational, marital, and parental roles on mortality: the Alameda County study. *Am. J. Public Health* 79:607–12

Krantz DS, Manuck SB. 1984. Acute psychophysiologic reactivity and risk of cardiovascular disease: a review and methodologic critique. *Psychol. Bull.* 96:435–64

Krantz DS, Manuck SB, Wing RR. 1986. Psychological stressors and task variables on elicitors of reactivity. In *Handbook of Stress, Reactivity, and Cardiovascular Disease,* ed. KA Matthews, SM Weiss, T Demtre, TM Dembroski, B Falkner, et al, pp. 85–107. New York: Wiley

Krause, N. 1992. Stress and isolation form close ties in later life. *J. Gerontol.* 46:S183–94

Kupersmidt JB, Griesler PC, DeRosier ME, Patterson CJ, Davis PW. 1995. Childhood aggression and peer relations in the context of family and neighborhood factors. *Child Dev.* 66:360–75

Kupersmidt JB, Patterson CJ. 1991. Childhood peer rejection, aggression, withdrawal, and perceived competence as predictors of self-reported behavior patterns in preadolescence. *J. Abnorm. Child Psychol.* 19:427–49

Landsbergis PA, Schnall PL, Deitz D, Friedman R, Pickering T. 1992. The patterning of psychological attributes and distress by "job strain" and social support in a sample of working men. *J. Behav. Med.* 15:379–414

Larson R, Richards MH. 1991. Daily companionship in late childhood and early adolescence: changing developmental contexts. *Child Dev.* 62:284–300

Lefler A, Krannich RS, Gillespie DL. 1986. Contact, support and friction: three faces of networks in community life. *Sociol. Perspect.* 29:337–55

Lennon MC, Rosenfeld S. 1992. Women and mental health: the interaction of job and family conditions. *J. Health Soc. Behav.* 33:316–27

Lerner DJ, Levine S, Malspeis S, D'Agostino RB. 1994. Job strain and health-related quality of life in a national sample. *Am. J. Public Health* 84:1580–85

Levy L, Herzog A. 1974. Effects of population density and crowding on health and social adaptation in The Netherlands. *J. Health Soc. Behav.* 15:228–40

Levy L, Herzog A. 1978. Effects of crowding on health and social adaptation in the city of Chicago, *Hum. Ecol.* 3:327–54

Lewinsohn PM, Roberts RE, Seeley JR, Rohde P, Gotlib IH, Hops H. 1994. Adolescent psychopathy. II. Psychosocial risk factors for depression. *J. Abnorm. Psychol.* 103:302–15

Loscocco KA, Spitze G. 1990. Working conditions, social support, and the well-being of female and male factory workers. *J. Health Soc. Behav.* 31:313–27

Macintyre S. 1997. The black report and beyond: What are the issues? *Soc. Sci. Med.* In press

Macintyre S, Maciver S, Solomon A. 1993. Area, class and health: Should we be focusing on places or people? *Int. Soc. Policy* 22:213–34

Malinosky-Rummell R, Hansen DJ. 1993. Long-term consequences of childhood physical abuse. *Psychol. Bull.* 114:68–79

Manuck SB, Marsland AL, Kaplan JR, Willimas JK. 1995. The pathogenicity of behavior and its neuroendocrine mediation: an example from coronary artery disease. *Psychosom. Med.* 57:275–83

Marmot MG. 1994. Social differentials in health within and between populations. *Heatlh Wealth: J. Am. Acad. Arts Sci.* 123:197–216

Martin LR, Friedman HS, Tucker JS, Schwartz JE, Criqui MH, et al. 1995. An archival prospective study of mental health and longevity. *Health Psychol.* 14:381–87

Matthews KA, Woodall KL, Jacob T, Kenyon K. 1996. Negative family environment as a predictor of boys' future status on measures of hostile attitudes, interview behavior, and anger expression. *Health Psychol.* 15:30–37

McEwen BS, Stellar E. 1993. Stress and the individual: mechanisms leading to disease. *Arch. Intern. Med.* 153:2093–101

McNeil GN, 1987. Depression. In *Handbook of Psychiatric Differential Diagnosis*, ed. SM Soreff, GN McNeil, pp. 56–126. Littleton, MA: PSG

Mechanic D, Hansell S. 1989. Divorce, family conflict, and adolescents' well-being. *J. Health Soc. Behav.* 30:105–16

Melamed BG, ed. 1995. Special section: the interface of mental and physical health. *Health Psychol.* 14:371–426

Mercy JA, Saltzman LE. 1989. Fatal violence among spouses in the United States 1976–85. *Am. J. Public Health* 79:595–99

Metzler CW, Noell J, Biglan A, Ary D, Smolkowski K. 1994. The social context for risky sexual behavior among adolescents. *J. Behav. Med.* 17:419–38

Moritz DJ, Kasl SV, Berkman LF. 1989. The health impact of living with a cognitively impaired elderly spouse: depressive symptoms and social funtioning. *J. Gerontol: Soc. Sci.* 44:S17–27

Mounts NS, Steinberg L. 1995. An ecological analysis of peer influence on adolescent grade point average and drug use. *Dev. Psychol.* 31:915–22

Muntaner C, Anthony JC, Crum RM, Eaton WW. 1995. Psychosocial dimensions of work and the risk of drug dependence among adults. *Am. J. Epidemiol.* 142:183–90

Neuspiel DR, Rush D, Butler NR, Golding J, Buur PE, Kurzon M. 1989. Parental smoking and post-infancy wheezing in children: a prospective cohort study. *Am. J. Public Health* 79:168–71

Nolen-Hoeksema S, Wolfson A, Mumme D, Guskin K. 1995. Helplessness in children of depressed and nondepressed mothers. *Dev. Psychol.* 31:377–87

Osofsky JD. 1990. *Gender issues in the development of deviant behavior: the case for teenage pregnancy.* Presented at the Prog. Hum. Dev. Crim. Behav., Radcliffe Coll.

Osofsky JD. 1993. Applied psychoanalysis: how research with infants and adolescents at high psychosocial risk informs psychoanalysis. *J. Am. Acad. Psychoanal.* 41:193–207

Osofsky JD. 1995. The effects of exposure to violence on young children. *Am. Psychol.* 50:782–88

Patterson GR, DeBaryshe BD, Ramsey E. 1989. A developmental perspective on anti-social behavior. *Am. Psychol.* 44:329–35

Pavalko EK, Elder GH Jr, Clipp EC. 1993. Worklives and longevity: insights from a life course perspective. *J. Health Soc. Behav.* 34:363–80

Penning MJ. 1995. Health, social support, and the utilization of health services among older adults. *J. Gerontol.* 50B:S330–39

Peoples-Sheps MD, Siegel E, Suchindran CM, Origasa H, Ware A, Barakat A. 1991. Characteristics of maternal employment during pregnancy: effects on low birthweight. *Am. J. Public Health* 86:1007–12

Pieper C, LaCroix AZ, Karasek RA. 1989. The relation of psychosocial dimensions of work with coronary heart disease risk factors: a meta-analysis of five United States data bases. *Am. J. Epidemiol.* 129:483–94

Pynoos RS. 1993. Traumatic stress and developmental psychopathology in children and adolescents. In *American Psychiatric Press Review of Psychiatry*, ed. JM Oldham, MB Riba, A Tasman, Vol. 12. Washington, DC: Am. Psychiatric Assoc.

Repetti RL. 1993. The effects of workload and the social environment at work on health. In *Handbook of Stress*, ed. L Goldberger, S Bresnitz, pp. 368–85. New York: Free Press

Repetti RL, Matthews KA, Waldrun I. 1989. Employment and women's health. *Am. Psychol.* 44:1394–401

Repetti RL, McGrath EP, Ishikawa SS. 1996. Daily stress and coping in childhood and adolescence. In *Handbook of Pediatric and Adolescent Health Psychology*, ed. AJ Goreczny, M Hersen. Allyn & Bacon. In press

Richters JE, Martinez P. 1993. The NIMH community violence project: Vol. 1: children as victims of and witnesses to violence. *Psychiatry* 56:7–21

Rosenfield S. 1992. The cosrts of sharing: wives' employment and husbands' mental health. *J. Health Soc. Behav.* 33:213−25

Ross CE, Mirowsky J. 1995. Does employment affect health? *J. Health Soc. Behav.* 36:230−43

Rowe DC, Linver MR. 1995. Smoking and addictive behaviors: epidemiological, individual, and family factors. In *Behavior Genetic Approaches in Behavioral Medicine*, ed. JR Turner, LR Cardon, JK Hewitt, pp. 67−84. New York: Plenum

Rushing B, Ritter C, Burton RPD. 1992. Race differences in the effects of multiple roles on health: longitudinal evidence from a national sample of older men. *J. Health Soc. Behav.* 33:126−39

Ruchlin HS, Morris JN. 1991. Impact of work on the quality of life in community-residing young elderly. *Am. J. Public Health*, 81: 498−500

Sallis JF, Hovell MF, Hofstetter CR, Faucher P, Elder JP, et al. 1989. A multivariate study of determinants of vigorous exercise in a community sample. *Prev. Med.* 18:20−34

Sampson RJ. 1992. Family management and child development: insights from social disorganization theory. In *Facts, Frameworks, and Forecasts: Advances in Criminological Theory*, ed. J McCord, 3:63−93. New Brunswick, NJ: Transaction

Sandler DP, Helsing KJ, Comstock GW, Shore DL, 1989a. Factors associated with past household exposure to tobacco smoke. *Am. J. Epidemiol.* 129:380−87

Sandler IN, Miller P, Short J, Wolchik SA. 1989b. Social support as a protective factor for children in stress. In *Children's Social Networks and Social Support*, ed. D Belle, pp. 277−304. New York: Wiley

Schuster TL, Kessler RC, Aseltine RH Jr. 1990. Supportive interactions, negative interactions, and depressed mood. *Am. J. Community Psychol.* 18:423−38

Seeman M, Seeman AZ, Budros A. 1988. Powerlessness, work, and community: a longitudinal study of alienation and alcohol use. *J. Health Soc. Behav.* 29:185−98

Seeman TE, Berkman LF, Blazer D, Rowe J. 1994. Social ties and support and neuroendocrine function: MacArthur Studies of Successful Aging. *Ann. Behav. Med.* 16:95−106

Seeman TE, Bruce ML, McAvay G. 1996. Social network characteristics and onset of ADL disability. *J. Gerontol.: Soc. Sci.* In press

Seeman TE, McEwen BS. 1996. Social environment characteristics and neuroendocrine function: the impact of social

ties and support on neuroendocrine regulation. *Psychosom. Med.* In press

Selye H. 1956. *The Stress of Life*. New York: McGraw-Hall

Shedler J, Block J. 1990. Adolescent drug use and psychological health: a longitudinal inquiry. *Am. Psychol.* 45:612−30

Sheline JL, Skipper BJ, Broadhead WE. 1994. Risk factors for violent behavior in elementary school boys: Have you hugged your child today? *Am. J. Public Health* 84:661−63

Siegler IC, Peterson BL, Barefoot JC, Williams RB. 1992. Hostility during late adolescence predicts coronary risk factors at mid-life. *Am. J. Epidemiol.* 136:146−54

Snydersmith MA, Cacioppo JT. 1992. Parsing complex social factors to determine component effects. I. Autonomic activity and reactivity as a function of human association. *J. Soc. Clin. Psychol.* 11:263−78

Sooman A, Macintyre S. 1995. Health and perceptions of the local environment in socially contrasting neighborhoods in Glasgow. *J. Health Place.* 1:15−26

Sorensen G, Pirie P, Folsom A, Luepker R, Jacobs D, Gillum R. 1985. Sex differences in the relationship between work and health: the Minnesota heart survey. *J. Health Soc. Behav.* 26:379−94

Sorenson SB, Peterson JG. 1994. Traumatic child death and documented maltreatment history, Los Angeles. *Am. J. Public Health* 84:623−27

Sorlie PD, Rogot E. 1990. Mortality by employment status in the national longitudinal mortality study. *Am. J. Epidemiol.* 132:983−92

Springs FE, Friedrich WN. 1992. Health risk behaviors and medical sequelae of childhood sexual abuse. *Mayo Clin.* 67:527−32

Stice E, Barrera M Jr. 1995. A longitudinal examination of the reciprocal relations between perceived parenting and adolescents' substance use and externalizing behaviors. *Dev. Psychol.* 31:322−34

Taylor SE. 1995. *Health Psychology*. New York: McGraw-Hill. 3rd ed.

Thomas PD, Goodwin JM, Goodwin JS. 1985. Effect of social support on stress-related changes in cholesterol level, uric acid level, and immune function in an elderly sample. *Am. J. Psychiatry* 142:735−37

Thompson SC, Sobolew-Shubin A. 1993. Perceptions of overprotection in ill adults. *J. Appl. Soc. Psychol.* 23:85−97

Trout DD. 1993. *The Thin Red Line: How the Poor Still Pay More*. San Francisco: Consum. Union US West Coast Reg. Off.

Troxler RG, Sprague EA, Albanese RA, Fuchs R, Thompson, AJ. 1977. The association of elevated plasma cortisol and early atherosclerosis as demonstrated by coronary angiography. *Atheroscleroses* 26:151–62

Turner JB, Kessler RC, House JS. 1991. Factors facilitating adjustment to unemployment: implications for intervention. *Am. J. Community Psychol.* 19:521–42

Turner RA, Irwin CE Jr, Tschann JM, Millstein SG. 1993. Autonomy, relatedness, and the initiation of health risk behaviors in early adolescence. *Health Psychol.* 12:200–8

Turner RJ, Noh S. 1983. Class and psychological vulnerability among women: the significance of social support and personal control. *J. Health Soc. Behav.* 24:2–15

Unden AL, Orth-Gomér K, Elofsson S. 1991. Cardiovascular effects of social support in the work place: twenty-four-hour ECG monitoring of men and women. *Psychosom. Med.* 53:50–60

Wagener DK, Schatzkin A. 1994. Temporal trends in the socioeconomic gradient for breast cancer mortality among US women. *Am. J. Public Health* 84:1003–6

Wallace R. 1990. Urban desertification, public health and public order: "planned shrinkage," violente deaeth, substance abuse and AIDS in the Bronx. *Soc. Sci. Med.* 31:801–13

Wallace R, Wallace D. 1990. Origins of public health collapse in New York City: the dynamics of planned shrinkage, contagious urban decay and social disintegration. *Bull. NY Acad. Med.* 66:391–434

Walter HJ, Vaughan RD, Gladis MM, Ragin DF, Kasen S, Cohall ST. 1992. Factors associated with AIDS risk behaviors among high school students in an AIDS epicenter. *Am. J. Public Health* 82:528–32

Webb JA, Baer PE, McLaughlin RJ, McKelvey RS, Caid CD. 1991. Risk factors and their relations to initiation of alcohol use among early adolescents. *J. Am. Acad. Child Adolesc. Psychiatry* 30:563–68

Wechsler H, Dowdall GW, Davenport A, Castillo S. 1995. Correlates of college student binge drinking. *Am. J. Public Health* 85:921–26

Wethington E, McLeod JD, Kessler RC. 1987. The importance of life events in explaining sex differences in psychological distress. In *Gender and Stress*, ed. RC Barnett, LB Biener, GK Baruch, pp. 144–56. New York: Basic Books

Wickrama K, Conger RD, Lorenz FO. 1995. Work, marriage, lifestyle, and changes in men's physical health. *J. Behav. Med.* 18:97–112

Widom C. 1989. The cycle of violence. *Science* 244:160–66

Williams DR. 1990. Socioeconomic differentials in health: a review and redirection. *Soc. Psychol. Q.* 53:81–99

Williams DR, Collins C. 1995. US socioeconomic and racial differences in health: patterns and explanations. *Annu. Rev. Sociol.* 21:349–86

Williams KJ, Suls J, Alliger GM, Learner SM, Wan CK. 1991. Multiple role juggling and daily mood states in working mothers: an experience sampling study. *J. Appl. Psychol.* 76:664–74

Wills TA, DuHamel K, Vaccaro D. 1995a. Activity and mood temperament as predictors of adolescent substance use: test of a self-regulation mediational model. *J. Pers. Soc. Psychol.* 68:901–16

Wills TA, McNamara G, Vaccaro D. 1995b. Parental education related to adolescent stress-coping and substance use: development of a mediational model. *Health Psychol.* 14:464–78

Wills TA, Schreibman D, Benson G, Vaccaro D. 1994. Impact of parental substance use on adolescents: a test of a mediation model. *J. Pediatr. Psychol.* 19:537–56

Woo G. 1994. *Strain in daily activities during pregnancy: associatoins of physical exertion, psychological demand, and personal control with birth outcomes*. PhD thesis. Univ. Calif., Los Angeles

Wyke S, Campbell G, MacIver S. 1992. Comparison of the provison of, and patient satisfaction with, primary care services in a relatively affluent and a relatively deprived area of Glasgow. *Br. J. Gen. Pract.* 42:271–75

Zahn-Waxler C, Cummings EM, McKnew DH, Radke-Yarrow M. 1984. Altruism, aggression, and social interactions in young children with a manic-depressive parent. *Child Dev.* 55:112-22

Zapata BC, Rebolledo C, Atalah E, Newman B, King M-C. 1992. The influence of social and political violence on the risk of pregnancy complications. *Am. J. Public Health* 82:685–90

Thirty-Two

PROTECTIVE AND DAMAGING EFFECTS OF STRESS MEDIATORS

Bruce S. McEwen

OVER 60 years ago, Selye[1] recognized the paradox that the physiologic systems activated by stress can not only protect and restore but also damage the body. What links these seemingly contradictory roles? How does stress influence the pathogenesis of disease, and what accounts for the variation in vulnerability to stress-related diseases among people with similar life experiences? How can stress-induced damage be quantified? These and many other questions still challenge investigators.

This article reviews the long-term effect of the physiologic response to stress, which I refer to as allostatic load.[2] Allostasis—the ability to achieve stability through change[3]—is critical to survival. Through allostasis, the autonomic nervous system, the hypothalamic-pituitary-adrenal (HPA) axis, and the cardiovascular, metabolic, and immune systems protect the body by responding to internal and external stress. The price of this accommodation to stress can be allostatic load,[2] which is the wear and tear that results from chronic overactivity or underactivity of allostatic systems.

THE PHYSIOLOGIC RESPONSE TO STRESS

STRESSFUL experiences include major life events, trauma, and abuse and are sometimes related to the environment in the home, workplace, or neighborhood. Acute stress (in the sense of "fight or flight" or major life events) and chronic stress (the cumulative load of minor, day-to-day stresses) can both have long-term consequences. The effects of chronic stress may be exacerbated by a rich diet and the use of tobacco and alcohol and reduced by moderate exercise.

Genetic factors do not account for all the individual variability in sensitivity to stress, as evinced by the lack of concordance between identical twins in many disorders.[4,5] Moreover, genetic factors do not explain the gradients of health across socioeconomic levels in Western societies.[6] Two factors largely determine individual responses to potentially stressful situations: the way a person perceives a situation[7] and a person's general state of physical health, which is determined not only by genetic factors but also by behavioral and lifestyle choices (Fig. 1).

Originally published in *New England Journal of Medicine*, 1998.

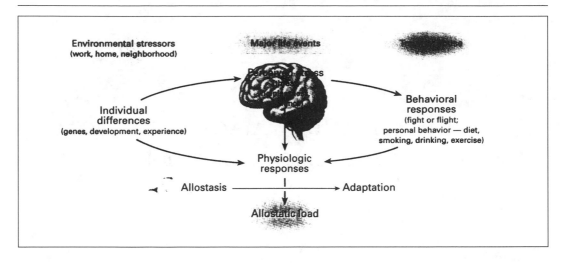

Figure 1.   The Stress Response and Development of Allostatic Load
The perception of stress is influenced by one's experiences, genetics, and behavior. When the brain perceives an experience as stressful, physiologic and behavioral responses are initiated, leading to allostasis and adaptation. Over time, allostatic load can accumulate, and the overexposure to mediators of neural, endocrine, and immune stress can have adverse effects on various organ systems, leading to disease.

Whether one perceives a situation as a threat, either psychological or physical, is crucial in determining the behavioral response—whether it is fleeing, fighting, or cowering in fear—and the physiologic response—calmness or heart palpitations and elevated cortisol levels.

The ability to adjust or habituate to repeated stress is also determined by the way one perceives a situation. For example, most people react initially to the challenge of public speaking with activation of the HPA axis. After repeated public speaking, however, most people become habituated and their cortisol secretion no longer increases with the challenge. But approximately 10 percent of subjects continue to find public speaking stressful, and their cortisol secretion increases each time they speak in public.[8] Others are prone to a cardiovascular stress response, as shown by a recent study of cardiovascular responses to a stressful arithmetic test. Blood-pressure responses to this experimental stress predicted elevated ambulatory blood pressure during periods

of perceived stress in everyday life.[9] Genetics may also have a role in susceptibility to cardiovascular stress; many people whose blood pressure remains elevated for several hours after the stress of an arithmetic test have a parent with hypertension.[10]

One's physical condition has obvious implications for one's ability to mount an appropriate physiologic response to stressful stimuli, and there may be a genetic component to the response as well. In inbred BioBreeding (BB) rats, an animal model of insulin-dependent diabetes, exposure to repeated stress increased the incidence of diabetes.[11] In children, family instability increases the incidence and severity of insulin-dependent diabetes.[12] Chronic stress, defined as feelings of fatigue, lack of energy, irritability, demoralization, and hostility, has been linked to the development of insulin resistance,[13] a risk factor for non-insulin-dependent diabetes. Deposition of abdominal fat, a risk factor for coronary heart disease and diabetes,[14] is increased by the psychosocial stress of colony reorganization in nonhuman primates[15] and may also be increased by stress in humans.[16]

ALLOSTASIS AND ALLOSTATIC LOAD

I N contrast to homeostatic systems such as blood oxygen, blood pH, and body temperature, which must be maintained within narrow ranges, allostatic (adaptive) systems have much broader boundaries. Allostatic systems enable us to respond to our physical states (e.g., awake, asleep, supine, standing, exercising) and to cope with noise, crowding, isolation, hunger, extremes of temperature, danger, and microbial or parasitic infection.

The core of the body's response to a challenge—whether it is a dangerous situation, an infection, living in a crowded and unpleasant neighborhood, or a public-speaking test—is twofold, turning on an allostatic response that initiates a complex adaptive pathway, and then shutting off this response when the threat is past. The most common allostatic responses involve the sympathetic nervous systems and the HPA axis. For these systems, activation releases catecholamines from nerves and the adrenal medulla and leads to the secretion of corticotropin from the pituitary. The corticotropin, in turn, mediates the release of cortisol from the adrenal cortex. Figure 2 shows how catecholamines and glucocorticoids affect cellular events. Inactivation returns the systems to base-line levels of cortisol and catecholamine secretion, which normally happens when the danger is past, the infection is contained, the living environment is improved, or the speech has been given. However, if the inactivation is inefficient (see below), there is overexposure to stress hormones. Over weeks, months, or years, exposure to increased secretion of stress hormones can result in allostatic load[2] and its pathophysiologic consequences.

Four situations are associated with allostatic load (Fig. 3). The first and most obvious is fre-

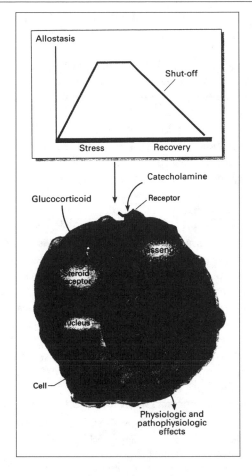

Figure 2. Allostasis in the Autonomic Nervous System and the HPA Axis

Allostatic systems respond to stress (upper panel) by initiating the adaptive response, sustaining it until the stress ceases, and then shutting if off (recovery). Allostatic responses are initiated (lower panel) by an increase in circulating catecholamines from the autonomic nervous system and glucocorticoids from the adrenal cortex. This sets into motion adaptive processes that alter the structure and function of a variety of cells and tissues. These processes are initiated through intracellular receptors for steroid hormones, plasma-membrane receptors, and second-messenger systems for catecholamines. Cross-talk between catecholamines and glucocorticoid-receptor signaling systems can occur.

quent stress. For example, surges in blood pressure can trigger myocardial infarction in susceptible persons,[17] and in primates repeated elevations of blood pressure over periods of weeks and months accelerate atherosclerosis,[18] thereby increasing the risk of myocardial infarction.

In the second type of allostatic load (Fig. 3), adaptation to repeated stressors of the same type is lacking, resulting in prolonged exposure to stress hormones, as was the case for some of the people subjected to the repeated-public-speaking challenge.[8]

In the third type of allostatic load (Fig. 3) there is an inability to shut off allostatic responses after a stress is terminated. As we have noted, the blood pressure in some people fails to recover after the acute stress of an arithmetic test,[10] and hypertension accelerates atherosclerosis.[18] Women with a history of depressive illness have decreased bone mineral density, because the allostatic load of chronic, moderately elevated serum cortisol concentrations inhibits bone formation.[19] Intense athletic training also induces allostatic load in the form of elevated sympathetic and HPA-axis activity, which results in weight loss, amenorrhea, and the often-related condition of anorexia nervosa.[20,21]

The failure to turn off the HPA axis and sympathetic activity efficiently after stress is a feature of age-related functional decline in laboratory animals,[22-24] but the evidence of this in humans is limited.[25,26] Stress-induced secretion of cortisol and catecholamines returns to base line more slowly in some aging animals with other signs of accelerated aging,[22-24] and the negative-feedback effects of cortisol are reduced in elderly humans.[26] One other sign of age-related impairment in rats is that the hippocampus fails to turn off the release of excitatory amino acids after stress,[27] and this may accelerate progressive structural damage and functional impairment (see below).

One speculation is that allostatic load over a lifetime may cause the allostatic systems to wear out or become exhausted.[25] A vulnerable link in the regulation of the HPA axis and cognition is the hippocampal region. According to the "glucocorticoid-cascade hypothesis," wear and tear on this region of the brain leads to dysregulation of the HPA axis and cognitive impairment.[23,28] Indeed, some but not all aging rats have impairment of episodic, declarative, and spatial memory and hyperactivity of the HPA axis, all of which can be traced to hippocampal damage.[29] Recent data suggest that similar events may occur in humans.[30,31]

In the fourth type of allostatic load (Fig. 3), inadequate responses by some allostatic systems trigger compensatory increases in others. When one system does not respond adequately to a stressful stimulus, the activity of other systems increases, because the underactive system is not providing the usual counterregulation. For example, if cortisol secretion does not increase in response to stress, secretion of inflammatory cytokines (which are counterregulated by cortisol) increases.[32] The negative consequences of an enhanced inflammatory response are seen, for example, in Lewis rats; these animals are very susceptible to autoimmune and inflammatory disturbances, because of a genetically determined hyporesponsiveness of the HPA axis.[33]

In another model, rats that become subordinate in a psychosocial living situation called the "visible-burrow system" have a stress-induced state of HPA hyporesponsiveness.[34,35] In these rats, the response to stressors applied by the experimenter is very limited, and concentrations of corticotropin-releasing hormone messenger RNA in the hypothalamus are abnormally low.[36] Human counterparts with HPA hyporesponsiveness include adults with fibromyalgia[37,38] and chronic fatigue syndrome[39,40] and children with atopic dermatitis.[41] In post-traumatic stress disorder, basal HPA activity is also low,[42,43] although reactivity to stress may not be blunted.

Feelings of anticipation and worry can also contribute to allostatic load.[44] Anticipation participates in the reflex that prevents us from black-

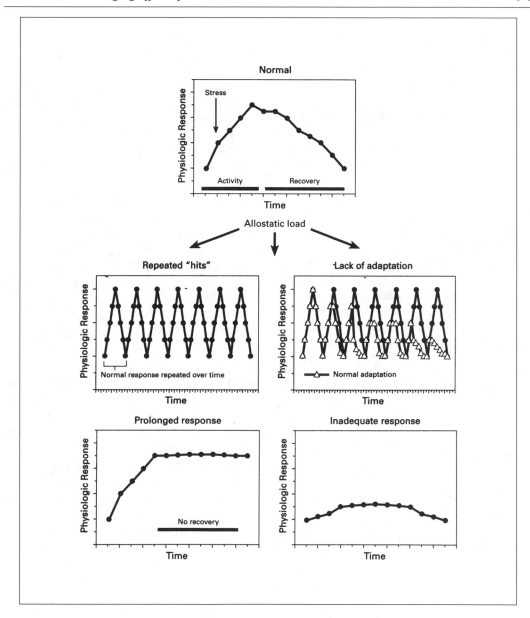

Figure 3.   Three Types of Allostatic Load

The top panel illustrates the normal allostatic response, in which a response is initiated by a stressor, sustained for an appropriate interval, and then turned off. The remaining panels illustrate four conditions that lead to allostatic load: repeated "hits" from multiple stressors; lack of adaptation; prolonged response due to delayed shutdown; and inadequate response that leads to compensatory hyperactivity of other mediators (e.g., inadequate secretion of glucocorticoids, resulting in increased concentrations of cytokines that are normally counterregulated by glucocorticoids).

ing out when we get out of bed in the morning[3] and is also part of worry, anxiety, and cognitive preparation for a threat. Anticipatory anxiety can drive the secretion of mediators like corticotropin, cortisol, and epinephrine, and for this reason, prolonged anxiety and anticipation are likely to result in allostatic load.[44] For example, salivary cortisol concentrations increase within 30 minutes after waking in people who are under considerable psychological stress due to work or family matters.[45] In a related fashion, intrusive memories of a traumatic event (as in post-traumatic stress disorder) can produce a form of chronic stress and can drive physiologic responses.[46]

Allostasis and allostatic load are also affected by the consumption of tobacco and alcohol, dietary choices, and the amount of exercise (Fig. 1). These forms of behavior are integral to the overall notion of allostasis—the way people cope with a challenge—and also contribute to allostatic load by known pathways (e.g., a high-fat diet accelerates atherosclerosis and progression to non-insulin-dependent diabetes by increasing cortisol secretion, leading to fat deposition and insulin resistance[47]; smoking elevates blood pressure and accelerates atherogenesis[48]; and exercise protects against cardiovascular disease[49]).

Examples of Allostatic Load

Cardiovascular and Metabolic Systems

The best-studied system of allostasis and allostatic load is the cardiovascular system and its links to obesity and hypertension. In nonhuman primates, the incidence of atherosclerosis is increased among the dominant males of unstable social hierarchies and in socially subordinate females.[50,51] In humans, lack of control on the job increases the risk of coronary heart disease,[52] and job strain (high psychological demands and lack of control) results in elevated ambulatory blood pressure at home and an increased left-ventricular-mass index,[53] as well as increased progression of atherosclerosis.[54] Chronic stress

(feelings of fatigue, lack of energy, irritability, and demoralization) and hostility are linked to increased reactivity of the fibrinogen system and of platelets, both of which increase the risk of myocardial infarction.[55,56]

Quantifying allostatic load, a major challenge, has been attempted with the use of measures of metabolic and cardiovascular pathophysiology. In a recent analysis,[57] data from the MacArthur Studies of Successful Aging were used to assess eight measures of increased activity of allostatic systems between 1988 and 1991. Allostatic load was approximated by determining the number of measures for which a person had values in the highest quartile from among the following: systolic blood pressure, overnight urinary cortisol and catecholamine excretion, the ratio of the waist to the hip measurement, the glycosylated hemoglobin value, and the ratio of serum high-density lipoprotein in the total serum cholesterol concentration; and the number of the following for which the person had values in the lowest quartile: serum concentration of dehydroepiandrosterone sulfate and serum concentration of high-density lipoprotein cholesterol. In cross-sectional analyses of base-line data, subjects with higher levels of physical and mental functioning had lower allostatic-load scores and a lower incidence of cardiovascular disease, hypertension, and diabetes. During the three years of follow-up (1988 to 1991), people in this higher-functioning group with higher allostatic-load scores at base line were more likely to have incident cardiovascular disease and were significantly more likely to have declines in cognitive and physical functioning. Among women in this group, increased cortisol secretion predicted a decline in memory.[31]

The Brain

Repeated stress affects brain function, especially in the hippocampus, which has high concentrations of cortisol receptors.[58] The hippocampus participates in verbal memory and is particularly important for the memory of "context," the time and place of events that have a strong emotional bias.[59,60] Moreover, glucocorticoids are involved in remembering the context in which an emotionally laden event took place.[61] Impairment of the hippocampus decreases the reliability and accuracy of contextual memories. This may exacerbate stress by preventing access to the information needed to decide that a situation is not a threat.[62] The hippocampus also regulates the stress response and acts to inhibit the response of the HPA-axis to stress.[63,64]

The mechanism for stress-induced hippocampal dysfunction and memory impairment is twofold. First, acute stress increases cortisol secretion, which suppresses the mechanisms in the hippocampus and temporal lobe that subserve short-term memory.[65,66] Stress can impair memory in the short term, but fortunately these effects are reversible and relatively short-lived.[67] Second, repeated stress causes the atrophy of dendrites of pyramidal neurons in the CA3 region of the hippocampus through a mechanism involving both glucocorticoids and excitatory amino acid neurotransmitters released during and after stress.[68] This atrophy is reversible if the stress is short-lived, but stress lasting many months or years can kill hippocampal neurons.[23,69] Magnetic resonance imaging has shown that stress-related disorders such as recurrent depressive illness, post-traumatic stress disorder, and Cushing's disease are associated with atrophy of the hippocampus.[70,71] Whether this atrophy is reversible or permanent is not clear.

Long-term stress also accelerates the appearance of several biologic markers of aging in rats, including the loss of hippocampal pyramidal neurons and the excitability of pyramidal neurons in the CA1 region by a calcium-dependent mechanism.[72] Glucocorticoids may mediate these effects by enhancing calcium currents in the hippocampus,[73] since calcium ions have a key role in destructive as well as plastic processes in hippocampal neurons.[74-76] The persistent release of the excitatory amino acid glutamate in the hippocampus after stress in aged rats may

also contribute to age-related neuronal damage[27] and may potentiate atrophy and possibly even neuronal loss.

Early stress and neonatal handling influence the course of aging and age-related cognitive impairment in animals. Early experiences are believed to set the level of responsiveness of the HPA axis and autonomic nervous system. These systems overreact in animals subjected to early unpredictable stress and underreact in animals exposed to neonatal handling.[77] In the former condition, aging of the brain is accelerated, whereas in the latter, aging of the brain is reduced.[29,77]

The Immune System

The immune system responds to pathogens or other antigens with its own form of allostasis that may include an acute-phase response as well as the formation of an immunologic "memory." At the same time, other allostatic systems, such as the HPA axis and the autonomic nervous system, tend to contain acute-phase responses and dampen cellular immunity.[78] However, not all the effects are suppressive. Acute stress causes lymphocytes and macrophages to be redistributed throughout the body and to "marginate" on blood-vessel walls and within certain compartments, such as the skin, lymph nodes, and bone marrow. This "trafficking" is mediated in part by glucocorticoids.[78-82] If an immune challenge is not encountered and the hormonal-stress signal ceases, immune cells return to the bloodstream. When a challenge occurs, however, as is the case is delayed-type hypersensitivity, acute stress enhances the traffic of lymphocytes and macrophages to the site of acute challenge.[83,84]

The immune-enhancing effects of acute stress depend on adrenal secretion and last for three to five days. Acute stress has the effect of calling immune cells to their battle stations, and this form of allostasis enhances responses for which there is an established immunologic "memory."[83-85] If the immunologic memory is of a pathogen or a tumor cell, the result of stress is presumably beneficial. If, on the contrary, the immunologic memory leads to an autoimmune or allergic response, then stress is likely to exacerbate a pathologic state. When allostatic load is increased by repeated stress, the outcome is completely different; the delayed hypersensitivity response is substantially inhibited[86] rather than enhanced. The consequences of suppressed cellular immunity resulting from chronic stress include increased severity of the common cold, accompanied by increased titers of cold-virus antibody.[87] In laboratory animals, repeated stress also leads to recurrent endotoxemia, which decreases the reactivity of the HPA axis to a variety of stimuli and decreases production of the cytokine tumor necrosis factor *a*.[88]

Implications of Allostatic Load in Human Society

The gradients of health across the range of socioeconomic levels[6] relate to a complex array of risk factors that are differentially distributed in human society.[89,90] Perhaps the best example is offered by the Whitehall studies of the British civil service, in which mortality and morbidity were found to increase stepwise from the lowest to the highest of the six grades of the British civil service.[91] Hypertension was a sensitive index of job stress,[92] particularly among factory workers, other workers with repetitive jobs and time pressures,[93] and workers whose jobs were unstable because of departmental privatization (Marmot MG: personal communication). Plasma fibrinogen concentrations, which predict an increased risk of death from coronary heart disease, are elevated among men in the lower British civil-service grades.[56] In less stable societies, conflict and social instability have been found to accelerate pathophysiologic processes and increase morbidity and mortality. For example, cardiovascular disease is a major contributor to the increase of almost 40 percent in the death rate among Russian men during the social collapse that followed the fall of Communism.[94] Blood-

pressure surges and sustained elevation are linked to accelerated atherosclerosis[18] as well as to an increased risk of myocardial infarction.[17]

Another stress-linked change is abdominal obesity (see above), measured as an increased waist-to-hip ratio. The waist-to-hip ratio is increased at the lower end of the socioeconomic-status gradient in Swedish men[95] and in the lower civil-service grades in the Whitehall studies.[96] Immune-system function is also a likely target of psychosocial stress,[97] increasing vulnerability to such infections as the common cold.[87,98]

Therapeutic Implications

A consideration of allostatic load is increasingly important in the diagnosis and treatment of many illnesses. Allostatic load is also important in illuminating the relation between disease and social instability, job loss, dangerous living environments, and other conditions that are chronically stressful. Medical illness itself is a source of stress, producing anxiety about prognosis, treatment, disability, and interference with social roles and relationships.

Physicians and other health care providers can help patients reduce allostatic load by helping them learn coping skills, recognize their own limitations, and relax. Patients should also be reminded of the interactions of a high-fat diet and stress in atherosclerosis, the role of smoking in cardiovascular disease and cancer, and the beneficial effects of exercise. But the patients themselves must change their behavior patterns appropriately.[99,100]

Beyond these obvious steps, other types of interventions must be considered. Two important causes of allostatic load appear to be isolation[101] and lack of control in the work environment.[52] Interventions that increase social support and enhance coping prolong the life spans of patients with breast cancer,[102] lymphomas,[103] and malignant melanoma.[104] Interventions designed to increase a worker's control over his or her job, such as the reorganization of auto production at Volvo, have also improved health and attitudes toward work.[93]

DISCUSSION

DR. JEFFREY FLIER: Is there any known correlation between lifelong stress (and therefore allostatic load) and Alzheimer's disease?

DR. McEWEN: There are a few anecdotes from admissions personnel at Veterans Affairs hospitals but nothing concrete. It is interesting, however, that education appears to have a "protective" role against the development of Alzheimer's disease.[105] It is not clear, though, whether education protects against the disease or provides more redundancy in the brain, which delays the symptoms.[106]

DR. BARBARA B. KAHN: What are the important differences between men and women in the biology of stress?

DR. McEWEN: Estrogens appear to protect the cardiovascular system, and at menopause, women's risk of cardiovascular disease increases to that of age-matched men. The decline in estrogen secretion at menopause also increases the activity of the HPA axis,[107] a development that has been linked to greater cognitive decline among elderly women than among elderly men.[31] A decline in androgen secretion in older men affect HPA function, although to a lesser extent. In rats, castration increases HPA activity.[108] Finally, there are structural and functional differences between the sexes in hippocampal formation in rodents,[109-111] and behavioral evidence suggests functional and possibly structural sex differences in humans, as well.[112] We do not yet know whether these differences influence the vulnerability of the hippocampus to severe stress, although a number of studies now suggest that female rodents and primates may be less vulnerable than males.[69,113]

DR. FLIER: Is there any evidence that humans are more susceptible to the effects of stress than animals because of the greater human capacity for cognition and insight, as well as the human ability to feel guilt?

DR. McEWEN: I believe that humans are more at risk for allostatic load than animals, because of the enormous individual differences in stress responsiveness and aging among humans, which relate to life experiences, personality, and physiologic phenotype. However, stress responsiveness and aging also differ among rats, so I don't thin we can be definitive about the importance of cognition in our own species.

A PHYSICIAN: What mechanisms underlie the differences between immune responses to acute stress and those to chronic stress?

DR. McEWEN: These mechanisms are just beginning to be understood. One key process is the redistribution, or trafficking, of immune cells. Acute stress enhances this response to delayed-type hypersensitivity. Chronic stress impairs delayed-type hypersensitivity, with the result that the blood is depleted of fewer lymphocytes. The greater the impairment of delayed-type hypersensitivity, the less the blood is depleted of lymphocytes (Dhabhar FS: unpublished data). Glucocorticoids are responsible for the trafficking of lymphocytes and for the stress enhancement of delayed-type hypersensitivity, but they do not act alone. Various cytokines function as more-local signals, emanating from a site of infection or challenge, and Dr. Firdaus Dhabhar at Rockefeller University is investigating their involvement. Beyond that, it is well known that stress hormones modulate immune function and influence the class of the immune response by their ability to increase the expression of some cytokines and decrease the expression of others.[78]

I am indebted to the Health Program of the John D. and Catherine T. MacArthur Foundation and its Network on Socioeconomic Status and Health for contributions to the concepts discussed in this article, and to Dr. Firdaus Dhabhar for assistance with Figure 3.

REFERENCES

1. Selye H. Syndrome produced by diverse nocuous agents. Nature 1936;138:32

2. McEwen BS, Stellar E. Stress and the individual: mechanisms leading to disease. Arch Intern Med 1993;153:2093–101.

3. Sterling P, Eyer J. Allostasis: a new paradigm to explain arousal pathology. In: Fisher S, Reason J, eds. Handbook of life stress, cognition and health. New York: John Wiley, 1988:629–49.

4. Berg K. Genetics of coronary heart disease. Prog Med Genet 1983;5:35–90.

5. Plomin R. The role of inheritance in behavior. Science 1990;248:183–8.

6. Adler NE, Boyce T, Chesney MA, et al. Socioeconomic status and health: the challenge of the gradient. Am Psychol 1994;49:15–24.

7. Lazarus RS, Folkman S. Stress, appraisal and coping. New York: Springer-Verlag, 1984.

8. Kirschbaum C, Prussner JC, Stone AA, et al. Persistent high cortisol responses to repeated psychological stress in a subpopulation of healthy men. Psychosom Med 1995;57:468–74.

9. Matthews KA, Owens JF, Allen MT, Stoney CM. Do cardiovascular responses to laboratory stress relate to ambulatory blood pressure levels? Yes, in some of the people, some of the time. Psychosom Med 1992;54;686–97.

10. Gerin W, Pickering TG. Association between delayed recovery of blood pressure after acute mental stress and parental history of hypertension. J Hypertens 1995;13:603–10.

11. Lehman C, Rodin J, McEwen BS, Brinton R. Impact of environmental stress on the expression of insulin-dependent diabetes mellitus. Behav Neurosci 1991;105:241–5.

12. Hagglof B, Blom L, Dahlquist G, Lonnberg G, Sahlin B. The Swedish childhood diabetes study: indications of several psychological stress as a risk factor for type 1 (insulin-dependent) diabetes mellitus in childhood. Diabetologia 1991;34:579–83.

13. Raikkonen K, Keltikangas-Jarvinen L, Adlercreutz H, Hautenen A. Psychosocial stress and the insulin resistance syndrome. Metabolism 1996;45:1533–8.

14. Bjorntorp P. "Portal" adipose tissue as a generator of risk factors for cardiovascular disease and diabetes. Arteriosclerosis 1990;10:493–6.

15. Jayo JM, Shively CA, Kaplan JR, Manuck SB. Effects of exercise and stress on body fat distribution in male cynomolgus monkeys. Int J Obes Relat Metab Disord 1993;17:597–604.

16. Moyer AE, Rodin J, Grilo CM, Cummings N, Larson LM, Rebuffe-Scrive M. Stress-induced cortisol response and fat distribution in women. Obes Res 1994;2:255–61.

17. Muller JE, Tofler GH, Stone PH. Circadian variation and triggers of onset of acute cardiovascular disease. Circulation 1989;79:733–43.

18. Kaplan JR, Pettersson K, Manuck SB, Olsson G. Role of sympathoadrenal medullary activation in the initiation and progresson of atherosclerosis. Circulation 1991;84:Suppl VI;:VI–23–VI–32.

19. Michelson D, Stratakis C, Hill L, et al. Bone mineral density in women with depression. N Engl J Med 1996;335:1176–81.

20. Boyar RM, Hellman LD, Roffwarg H, et al. Cortisol secretion and metabolism iln anorexia nervosa. N Engl J Med 1977;296:190–3.

21. Loucks AB, Mortola JF, Girton L, Yen SSC. Alterations inthe hypothalamic-pituitary-ovarian and the hypothalamic-pituitary-adrenal axes in athletic women. J Clin Endocrinol Metab 1989;68:402–11.

22. McCarty R. Sympathetic-adrenal medullary and cardiovascular responses to acute cold stress in adult and aged rats. J Auton Nerv Syst 1985;12:15–22.

23. Sapolsky RM. Stress, the aging brain and the mechanisms of neuron death. Cambridge, Mass.: MIT Press, 1992.

24. McEwen BS. Re-examination of the glucocorticoid hypothesis of stress and aging. In: Swaab DF, Hofman MA, Mirmiran M, Ravid R, van Leeuwen FW, eds. Progress in brain research. Vol. 93. The human hypothalamus in health and disease. Amsterdam: Elsevier Science, 1992:365–83.

25. Seeman TE, Robbins RJ. Aging and hypothalamic-pituitary-adrenal response to challenge in humans. Endocr Rev 1994;15:233–60.

26. Wilkinson CW, Peskind ER, Raskind MA. Decreased hypothalamic-pituitary-adrenal axis sensitivity to cortisol feedback inhibition in human aging. Neuroendocrinology 1997;65:79–90.

27. Lowy MT, Wittenberg L, Yamamoto BK. Effect of acute stress on hippocampal glutamate levels and spectrin proteolysis in young and aged rats. J Neurochem 1995;65:268–74.

28. Sapolsky RM, Krey LC, McEwen BS. The neuroendocrinology of stress and aging: the glucocorticoid cascade hypothesis. Endocr Rev 1986;7:284–301.

29. Meaney MJ, Aitken DH, van Berkel C, Bhatnagar S, Sapolsky RM. Effect of neonatal handling of age-related impairments associated with the hippocampus. Science 1988;239:766–8.

30. Lupien S, Lecours AR, Lussier I, Schwartz G, Nair NPV, Meaney MJ. Basal cortisol levels and cognitive deficits in human aging. J Neurosci 1994;14:2893–903.

31. Seeman TE, McEwen BS, Singer BH, Albert MS, Rowe JW. Increase in urinary cortisol excretion and memory declines. MacArthur studies of successful aging. J Clin Endocrinol Metab 1997;82:2458–65.

32. Munck A, Guyre PM, Holbrook NJ. Physiological functions of glucocorticoids in stress and their relation to pharmacological actions. Endocr Rev 1984;5:25–44.

33. Sternberg EM, Young WS III, Bernardini R, et al. A central nervous system defect in biosynthesis of corticotropin-releasing hormone is associated with susceptibility to streptococcal cell wall-induced arthritis in Lewis rats. Proc Natl Acad Sci U S A 1989;86:4771–5.

34. Blanchard DC, Sakai RR, McEwen BS, Weiss SM, Blanchard RJ. Subordination stress: behavioral, brain, and neuroendocrine correlates. Behav Brain Res 1993;58:113–21.

35. McKittrick CR, Blanchard DC, Blanchard RJ, McEwen BS, Sakai RR. Serotonin receptor binding in a colony model of chronic social stress. Biol Psychiatry 1995;37:383–93.

36. Albeck DS, McKittrick CR, Blanchard DC, et al. Chronic social stress alters expression of corticotropin-releasing factor and arginine vasopressin mRNA in rat brain. J Neurosci 1997;17:4895–903.

37. Crofford LJ, Pillemer SR, Kalogeras KT, et al. Hypothalamic-pituitary-adrenal axis perturbations in patients with fibromyalgia. Arthritis Rheum 1994;37:1583–92.

38. Heim C, Ehlert U, Hanker J, Hellhammer DH. Abuse-related post-traumatic stress disorder and alterations of the hypothalamo-pituitary-adrenal axis in women with chronic pelvic pain. Psychosom Med (in press).

39. Poteliakhoff A. Adrenocortical activity and some clinical findings in acute and chronic fatigue. J Psychosom Res 1981;25:91–5.

40. Ur E, White PD, Grossman A. Hypothesis: cytokines may be activated to cause depressive illness and chronic fatigue syndrome. Eur Arch Psychiatry Clin Neurosci 1992;241:317–22.

41. Buske-Kirschbaum A, Jobst S, Psych D, et al. Attenuated free cortisol response to psychosocial stress in children with atopic dermatitis. Psychosom Med 1997;59:419–26.

42. Yehuda R, Giller EL, Southwick SM, Lowy MT, Mason JW. Hypothalamic-pituitary-adrenal dysfunction in posttraumatic stress disorder. Biol Psychiatry 1991;30:1031–48.

43. Yehuda R, Teicher MH, Trestman RL, Levengood RA, Siever LJ. Cortisol regulation in posttraumatic stress disorder and major depression: a chronobiological analysis. Bio. Psychiatry 1996;40:79–88.

44. Schulkin J, McEwen BS, Gold PW. Allostasis, amygdala, and anticipatory angst. Neurosci Biobehav Rev 1994;18:385–96.

45. Schulz P, Kirschbaum C, Pruessner J, Hellhammer DH. Increased free cortisol secretion after wakening in chronically-stressed ilndividuals due to work overload. Stress Med (in press).

46. Baum A, Cohen L, Hall M. Control and inrusive memories as possible determinants of chronic stress. Psychosom Med 1993;55:274–86.

47. Brindley DN, Rolland Y. Possible connections between stress, diabetes, obesity, hypertension and altered lipoprotein metabolism that may result in atherosclerosis. Clin Sci 1989;77:453–61.

48. Verdecchia P, Schillaci G, Borgioni C, et al. Cigarette smoking, ambulatory blood pressure and cardiac hypertrophy in essential hypertension. J Hypertens 1995;13:1209–15.

49. Bernadet P. Benefits of physical activity in the prevention of cardiovascular diseases. J Cardiovasc Pharmacol 1995;25:Suppl 1:S3–S8.

50. Manuck SB, Kaplan JR, Adams MR, Clarkson TB. Studies of psychosocial influences on coronary artery atherogenesis in cynomolgus monkeys. Health Psychol 1988;7:113–24.

51. Shively CA, Clarkson TB. Social status and coronary aartery atherosclerosis in female monkeys. Arterioscler Thromb 1994;14:721–6.

52. Bosma H, Marmot MG, Hemingway H, Nicholson AC, Brunner E, Stansfeld SA. Low job control and risk of coronary heart disease in Whitehall II (prospective cohort) study. BMJ 1997;314:558–65.

53. Schnall PL, Schwartz JE, Landsbergis PA, Warren K, Pickering TG. Relation between job strain, alcohol, and ambulatory blood pressure. Hypertensin 1992;19:488–94.

54. Everson SA, Lynch JW, Chesney MA, et al. Interaction of workplace demands and cardiovascular reactivity in progression of carotid atherosclerosis: population based study. BMJ 1997;314:553–8.

55. Raikkonen K, Lassila R, Keltikangas-Jarvinen L, Hautanen A. Association of chronic stress wtih plasminogen activator inhibitor-1 in healthy middle-aged men. Arterioscler Thromb Vasc Biol 1996;16:363–7.

56. Markowe HLJ, Marmot MG, Shipley MJ, et al. Fibrinogen: a possible link between social class and coronory heart disease. BMJ 1985;291:1312–4.

57. Seeman TE, Singer BH, Rowe JW, Horwitz RI, McEwen BS, Price of adaptation—allostatic load and its health consequences: MacArthur studies of successful aging. Arch Intern Med 1997;157:2259–68.

58. McEwen BS, De Kloet ER, Rostene W. Adrenal steroid receptors and actions in the nervous system. Physiol Rev 1986;66:1121–88.

59. Eichenbaum H, Otto T, Cohen NJ. The hippocampus—what does it do? Behav Neural Biol 1992;57:2–36.

60. LeDoux JE. In search of an emotional system in the brain: leaping from fear to emotion and consciousness. In: Gazzaniga M, ed. The cognitive neurosciences. Cambridge, Mass.: MIT Press, 1995:1049–61.

61. Pugh CR, Tremblay D, Fleshner M, Rudy JW. A selective role for cortiosterone in contextual-fear conditioning. Behav Neurosci 1997;111:503–11.

62. Sapolsky RM. Stress in the wild. Sci Am 1990;262:116–23.

63. Jacobson L, Sapolsky R. The role of the hippocampus in feedback regulation of the hypothalamic-pituitary-adrenocortical axis. Endocr Rev 1991;12:118–34.

64. Herman JP, Cullinan WE. Neurocircuitry of stress: central control of the hypothalamo-pituitary-adrenocortical axis. Trends Neurosci 1997;20:78–84.

65. Kirschbaum C, Wolf OT, May M, Wippich W, Hellhammer DH. Stress- and treatment-induced elevations of cortisol levels associated with impaired declarative memory in healthy adults. Life Sci 1996;58:1475–83.

66. McEwen BS, Sapolsky RM. Stress and cognitive function. Curr Opin Neurobiol 1995;5:205–16.

67. Lupien SJ, McEwen BS. The acute effects of corticosteroids on cognition: integration of animal and human model studies. Brain Res Brain Res Rev 1997;24:1–27.

68. McEwen BS, Albeck D, Cameron H, et al. Stress and the brain: a paradoxical role for adrenal steroids. Vitam Horm 1995;51:371–402.

69. Uno H, Tarara R, Else JG, Suleman MA, Sapolsky RM. Hippocampal damage associated with prolonged and fatal stress in primates. J Neurosci 1989;9:1705–11.

70. Sapolsky RM. Why stress is bad for your brain. Science 1996;273:749–50.

71. McEwen BS, Magarinos AM. Stress effects on morphology and function of the hippocampus. Ann N Y Acad Sci 1997;821:271–84.

72. Kerr DS, Campbell LW, Applegate MD, Brodish A, Landfield PW. Chronic stress-induced acceleration of electrophysiologic and morphometric biomarkers of hippocampal aging. J Neurosci 1991;11:1316–24.

73. Kerr DS, Campbell LW, Thibault O, Landfield PW. Hippocampal glucocorticoid receptor activation enhances voltage-dependent Ca2 + conductances: relevance to brain aging. Proc Natl Acad Sci U S A 1992;89:8527–31.

74. Choi DW. Calcium-mediated neurotoxicity: relationship to specific channel types and role in ischemic damage. Trends Neurosci 1988;11:465–9.

75. Mills LR, Kater SB. Neuron-specific and state-specific differences in calcium homeostasis regulate the generation and degeneration of neuronal architecture. Neuron 1990;4:149–63.

76. Mattson MP. Calcium as sculptor and destroyer of neural circuitry. Exp Gerontol 1992;27:29–49.

77. Meaney MJ, Tannenbaum B, Francis D, et al. Early environmental programming; hypothalamic-pituitary-adrenal responses to stress. Semin Neurosci 1994;6:247–59.

78. McEwen BS, Biron CA, Brunson KW, et al. The role of adrenocorticoids as modulators of immune function in health and disease: neural, endocrine and immune interactions. Brain Res Brain Res Rev 1997;23:79–113.

79. Dhabhar FS, Miller AH, Stein M, McEwen BS, Spencer RL. Diurnal and acute stress-induced changes in distribution of peripheral blood leukocyte subpopulations. Brain Behav Immun 1994;8:66–79.

80. Dhabhar FS, Miller AH, McEwen BS, Spencer RL. Effects of stress on immune cell distribution: dynamics and hormonal mechanisms. J Immunol 1995;154:5511–27.

81. Miller AH, Spencer RL, Hassett J, et al. Effects of selective type I and II adrenal steroid agonists on immune cell distribution. Endocrinology 1994;135:1934–44.

82. Herbert TB, Cohen S. Stress and immunity in humans: a meta-analytic review. Psychosom Med 1993;55:364–79.

83. Dhabhar FS. Stress-induced enhancement of antigen-specific cell-mediated immunity: the role of hormones and leukocyte trafficking. New York: Rockefeller University, 1996.

84. Dhabhar FS, McEwen BS. Stress-induced enhancement of antigen-specific cell-mediated immunity. J Immunol 1996;156:2608–15.

85. Dhabhar FS, Miller AH, McEwen BS, Spencer RL. Stress-induced changes in blood leukocyte distribution: role of adrenal steroid hormones. J Immunol 1996;157:1638–44.

86. Dhabhar FS, McEwen BS. Moderate stress enhances, and chronic stress suppresses, cell-mediated immunity in vivo. Soc Neurosci 1996;22:1350. abstract.

87. Cohen S, Tyrrell DAJ, Smith AP. Psychological stress and susceptibility to the common cold. N Engl J Med 1991;325:606–12.

88. Hadid R, Spinedi E, Giovambattista A, Chautard T, Gaillard RC. Decreased hypothalamo-pituitary-adrenal axis response to neuroendocrine challenge under repeated endotoxemia. Neuroimmunomodulation 1996;3:62–8.

89. Taylor SE, Repetti RL, Seeman T. Health psychology: what is an unhealthy environment and how does it get under the skin? Annu Rev Psychol 1997;48:411–47.

90. Lynch JW, Kaplan GA, Cohen RD, Tuomilehto J, Salonen JT. Do cardiovascular risk factors explain the relation between socioeconomic status, risk of all-cause mortality, cardiovascular mortality, and acute myocardial infarction? Am J Epidemiol 1996;144:934–42.

91. Marmot MG, Smith GD, Stansfeld S, et al. Health inequalities among British civil servants: the Whitehall II study. Lancet 1991;337:1387–93.

92. Pickering TG, Devereux RB, James GD, et al. Environmental influences on blood pressure and the role of job strain. J Hypertens Suppl 1996;14:S179–S185.

93. Melin B, Lundberg U, Soderlund J, Granqvist M. Psychological and physiological stress reactions of male and female assembly workers: a comparison between two different forms of work organization. J Organizat Psychol (in press).

94. Bobak M, Marmot M. East-West mortality divide and its potential explanations: proposed research agenda. BMJ 1996;312:421–5.

95. Larsson B, Seidell J, Svardsudd K, et al. Obesity, adipose tissue distribution and health in men—the study of men born in 1913. Appetite 1989;13:37–44.

96. Brunner EJ. The social and biological basis of cardiovascular disease in office workers. In: Blane D, Brunner EJ, Wilkinson RG, eds. Health and social organization. London: Routledge, 1996:272–313.

97. Cohen S, Kaplan JR, Cunnick JE, Manuck SB, Rabin BS. Chronic social stress, affiliation and cellular immune response in nonhuman primates. Psychol Sci 1992;3:301–4.

98. Cohen S, Doyle WJ, Skoner DP, Rabin BS, Gwaltney JM Jr. Social ties and susceptibility to the common cold. JAMA 1997;277:1940–4.

99. Redelmeier DA, Rozin P, Kahneman D. Understanding patients' decisions: cognitive and emotional perspectives. JAMA 1993;270:72–6.

100. Horwitz RI, Horwitz SM. Adherence to treatment and health outcomes. Arch Intern Med 1993;153:1863–8.

101. Seeman TE, McEwen BS. The impact of social environment characteristics on neuroendocrine regulation. Psychosom Med 1996;58:459–71.

102. Spiegel D, Bloom JR, Kraemer HC, Gottheil E. Effect of psychosocial treatment on survival of patients with metastatic breast cancer. Lancet 1989;2:888–91.

103. Richardson JL, Shelton DR, Krailo M, Levine AM. The effect of compliance with treatment on survival among patients with hematologic malignancies. J Clin Oncol 1990;8:356–64.

104. Fawzy FI, Fawzy NW, Hyun CS, et al. Malignant melanoma: effects of an early structured psychiatric intervention, coping, and affective state on recurrence and survival 6 years later. Arch Gen Psychiatry 1993;50:681–9.

105. Stern Y, Alexander GE, Prohovnik I, et al. Relationship between lifetime occupation and parietal flow: implications for a reserve against Alzheimer's disease pathology. Neurology 1995;45:55–60.

106. Stern Y, Alexander GE, Prohovnik I, Mayeux R. Inverse relationship between education and parietotemporal perfusion deficit in Alzheimer's disease. Ann Neurol 1992;32:371–5.

107. Van Cauter E, Leproult R, Kupfer DJ. Effects of gender and age on the levels and circadian rhythmicity of plasma cortisol. J Clin Endocrinol Metab 1996;81:2468–73.

108. Handa RJ, Nunley KM, Lorens SA, Louie JP, McGivern RF, Bollnow MR. Androgen regulation of adrenocorticotropin and corticosterone secretion in the male rat

following novelty and foot shock stressors. Physiol Behav 1994;55:117–24.

109. Juraska JM, Fitch JM, Henderson C, Rivers N. Sex differences in the dendritic branching of dentate granule cells following differential experience. Brain Res 1985;333:73–80.

110. Gould E, Westlind-Danielsson A, Frankfort M, McEwen BS. Sex differences and thyroid hormone sensitivity of hippocampal pyramidal cells. J Neurosci 1990;10:996–1003.

111. Roof RL. The dentate gyrus is sexually dimorphic in prepubescent rats: testosterone plays a significant role. Brain Res 1993;610:148–51.

112. Kimura D. Sex differences in the brain. Sci Am 1992; 267:118–25.

113. Mizoguchi K, Kunishita T, Chui DH, Tabira T. Stress induces neuronal death in the hippocampus of castrated rats. Neurosci Lett 1992;138:157–60.

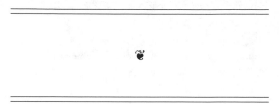

Thirty-Three

SOCIAL STATUS AND CORONARY ARTERY ATHEROSCLEROSIS IN FEMALE MONKEYS

Carol A. Shively and Thomas B. Clarkson

Abstract

While coronary heart disease is the leading cause of death in women in the United States, research in the area is lacking, especially concerning psychosocial risk factors. The purpose of this experiment was to study the effect of a known psychosocial risk factor in female monkeys, social status, and the effect of alteration of social status on coronary artery atherosclerosis. In previous experiments it has been demonstrated that social status is an enduring characteristic of the individual and that socially subordinate female monkeys have poor ovarian function and exacerbated coronary artery atherosclerosis. In the present experiment, adult female monkeys were fed an atherogenic diet and housed in small social groups, and social status was altered in half of the animals (subordinates became dominant and dominants became subordinate). The manipulation of social status had minimal effects on risk factors but significantly affected coronary artery atherosclerosis, supporting the hypothesis that social status affects atherogenesis in these females. However, all animals that changed social positions had worsened coronary artery atherosclerosis whether they became dominant or became subordinate, and this effect was independent of ovarian function. Subordinates that became dominant had 44% more and dominants that became subordinate had 500% more atherosclerosis than their counterparts that did not change social status. Thus, modification of this psychosocial risk factor was not effective in reducing coronary artery atherosclerosis. The manipulation of social status may have deleteriously altered a complex interaction between individuals and their psychosocial environment.

P SYCHOSOCIAL factors may increase the risk of coronary heart disease in women. Female cynomolgus monkeys (*Macaca fascicularis*) have been used for several years to identify psychosocial factors associated with coronary heart disease and to understand the mechanisms through which these factors increase coronary heart disease risk. This species is a useful animal model because, like humans, females are pro-

Originally published in *Arteriosclerosis and Thrombosis*, 1994.

tected against coronary artery atherosclerosis (CAA) relative to their male counterparts,[1] they have menstrual cycles similar in length and hormonal fluctuations to those of women,[2] and they rely on complex social relationships.[3]

Previously, it was reported that adult female cynomolgus monkeys that are socially subordinate have more extensive CAA than socially dominant females. Additionally, subordinate females have impaired ovarian function, characterized by fewer menstrual cycles and lower sex steroid concentrations than dominant females. Thus, it was hypothesized that social subordination may impair ovarian function and increase atherogenesis.[4] It was not clear from previous studies whether there was an effect of social status on CAA independent of ovarian function.

Social status is important to the individual because it has physiological as well as behavioral ramifications. Socially subordinate females are thought to be stressed because their adrenal glands hypersecrete cortisol, they are frequent subjects of aggression, and they spend considerable time alone, ie, socially isolated.[5-8] Intriguingly, social status appears to be a reliable characteristic of the individual. It has been observed that among females that live for a short period in each of a series of social groups, those that were dominant in the first social group were typically dominant in subsequent social groups. Likewise, those that were subordinate in the first social group typically were subordinate in subsequent social groups.[9]

In the experiment reported here, it was hypothesized that if social subordination causes exacerbation of atherosclerosis, then altering social status should result in a change in extent of atherosclerosis. If dominants became subordinate increased atherosclerosis would be expected, whereas if subordinates became dominant decreased atherosclerosis would be expected. Thus, we chose to manipulate social status, a known psychosocial risk factor, and measure the effect on CAA in adult females housed in social

groups. Manipulation of social status may be expected to alter behavioral responses as well as involve a change in the social environment. In addition to examining the effects of psychosocial risk factor modification, this experiment provides further evidence addressing the nature of the relationship between social status and CAA in females.

METHODS

Subjects

Forty-eight adult female monkeys were obtained from Charles River Research Primates. The animals were estimated to be 6 to 12 years of age based on dentition. These females were chosen from a pool of 72 adult female monkeys that were fed the experimental diet (described below) for 1 month before the onset of the experiment. Total plasma cholesterol (TPC) and high-density lipoprotein (HDL) cholesterol concentrations were determined using the methods described below, and monkeys falling in the upper two thirds of the distribution of the ratio of TPC to HDL (TPC-HDL) cholesterol were chosen for study. These females were selected to represent the subset of the adult female population that is at increased risk of developing atherosclerosis. Six animals died from causes unrelated to the experiment (primarily diarrheal diseases), resulting in 42 study animals.

Diet

The monkeys were fed a moderately atherogenic diet that contained 0.25 mg cholesterol per calorie and 40% of calories as fat (Table 1) ad libitum for 32 months. Based on previous studies this diet was expected to induce moderate hypercholesterolemia and significant amounts of atherosclerosis in the coronary arteries.[10]

Experimental Design

The experimental design is depicted in Fig. 1. The monkeys began consuming the atherogenic

Table 1

Diet Composition

Ingredient	Amount, g/100 g
Casein, USP	8.0
Lactalbumin	8.0
Wheat flour	35.4
Dextrin	6.0
Sucrose	5.0
Applesauce	4.5
Lard	9.5
Butter	3.0
Beef tallow	7.0
Dry egg yolk	3.5
Safflower oil	0.5
Complete vitamin mixture	2.6
Ausman-Hayes mineral mixture	5.0
Sodium chloride	2.0

Adapted from Reference 10.

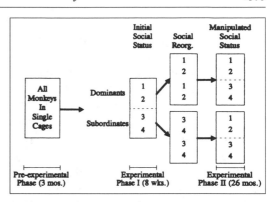

Figure 1

Schematic representation showing design of experiment. After a 3-month preexperimental phase, monkeys were assigned randomly to four-member social groups for 8 weeks (experimental phase 1) during which social status stabilized and was determined (initial social status). First- and second-ranking females were considered dominant, and third- and fourth-ranking females were considered subordinate. Animals were then assigned to new social groupings of four animals each, based on their social status, for 26 months (experimental phase 2). Animals that were previously dominant (two first- and two second-ranking monkeys) were housed together, and animals that were previously subordinate (two third- and two fourth-ranking monkeys) were housed together. Linear social status hierarchies reformed: half of the subordinate animals became dominant, and half of the dominant animals became subordinate (manipulated social status). This manipulation resulted in a change in social status in half of the animals: those that were initially subordinate and became dominant and those that were initially dominant and became subordinate.

diet 1 month before the onset of the experiment to aid subject selection (see above) and continued to consume this diet throughout the experiment. They were housed for 3 months in single cages when preexperimental measures of plasma cholesterol concentrations, adiposity, carbohydrate metabolism, and blood pressure were collected (preexperimental phase). The details of the sampling procedures are described below. The monkeys were then assigned randomly to four-member social groups for an 8-week period during which their social status stabilized and was determined (experimental phase 1). The animals were designated first, second, third, or fourth ranking. First- and second-ranking females were considered dominant, and third- and fourth-ranking females were considered subordinate. The animals were then assigned to new social groupings of four animals each, based on their social status, for the remaining 26-month experimental period. Animals that were previously dominant were housed together, and animals that were previously subordinate were housed together. Linear social status hierarchies reformed, and half of the subordinate animals became dominant, and half of the dominant animals became subordinate (experimental phase 2). In most cases, new social status positions were decided within hours of social reorganization, and aggression dropped to prereorganization levels in less than 2 weeks. This manipulation produced four experimental groups: (1) females that were initially dominant and remained dominant after social grouping (n=11), (2) females that were initially dominant and became subordinate after regrouping (n=11), (3) females that were initially subordinate and became dominant after social regrouping (n=8), and (4) females that were initially subordinate and remained subordinate after regrouping (n=12). This resulted in 2x2 study design: initial social status$_{dom,sub}$x manipulated social status$_{dom.sub.}$ It is important to note that the monkeys were in their final social groups over 90% of the time they were consuming an atherogenic diet.

Sampling Procedures

Several known or suspected atherosclerosis risk variables were measured periodically throughout the preexperimental phase and experimental phase 2. All procedures involving animals were performed in accordance with federal and state regulations and with the approval of the institutional animal care and use committee.

PLASMA CHOLESTEROL CONCENTRATIONS
TPC and HDL cholesterol concentrations were determined once during the preexperimental phase and every 4 months during experimental phase 2.[11,12] Multiple measures made during experimental phase 2 were averaged for analysis.

ADIPOSITY
Anthropometric measures of adiposity were taken once during the preexperimental phase and every 4 months during experimental phase 2.

Body weight (BW) and body mass index (BMI, measured as BW/[ventral trunk length in square centimeters]) were measured. Subscapular, suprailiac, triceps, and thigh skinfolds were measured during spring-loaded calipers, and waist, hip, and thigh circumferences were measured using a steel tape measure.[13] Multiple measures made during experimental phase 2 were averaged for analysis.

CARBOHYDRATE METABOLISM
Blood glucose and insulin concentrations were determined, following an 18-hour fast, during the preexperimental phase and during experimental phase 2.[14,15]

BLOOD PRESSURE
Systolic (SBP) and diastolic (DBP) blood pressures were measured once during the preexperimental phase and every 4 months during experimental phase 2.[16] Multiple measures made during experimental phase 2 were averaged for analysis.

MENSTRUAL CYCLE DETERMINATIONS
The monkeys were trained to present themselves for vaginal swabbing to detect menses and for femoral venipuncture for blood sample collection three times a week throughout experimental phase 2. Blood samples were used for progesterone determination by radioimmunoassay (Diagnostic Products Corp). Luteal-phase progesterone concentration was used as an indicator of the quality of a menstrual cycle. High progesterone concentrations (>4 ng/mL) indicate that ovulation has occurred, whereas low progesterone concentrations (<2 ng/mL) indicate an anovulatory cycle.[17,18] The highest progesterone value found during the luteal phase was used to represent that menstrual cycle, and mean peak progesterone concentrations were calculated for analysis. Average cycle length and the number of cycles each female had during experimental phase 2 were also calculated for analysis.

SOCIAL STATUS

The social status of an individual refers to that individual's ability to defeat other members of its social group in agonistic or competitive interactions. Social status was determined monthly throughout experimental phases 1 and 2 by recording the outcomes of aggressive interactions between cage mates. The animal in each social group that defeated all other group members was designated the first-ranking monkey. The animal that defeated all but the first-ranking monkey was designated the second-ranking monkey, and so forth. The resulting social status hierarchies for each social group were stable over time.[9] Animals that were first or second ranking on average were considered dominant, while those that were third or fourth ranking on average were considered subordinate.

Monkeys that changed social status when their social environment was altered also changed their behavior. Those that were subordinate and became dominant defeated the majority of individuals in their final social group, whereas those that were dominant and became subordinate wee defeated by the majority of others in their final social group.

Necropsy and Measurement of Artherosclerosis

At the time of necropsy, the animals were anesthetized deeply with pentobarbital (60 mg/kg). Each cardiovascular system was flushed with saline and perfused with 10% neutral buffered formalin under a pressure of 100 mm Hg. After pressure fixation, five serial blocks were taken from each of the left circumflex, left anterior descending, and right coronary arteries. One section from each block was stained with Verhoeff-van Gieson's stain and projected, and the area occupied by the intima and intimal lesion was measured in square millimeters with a digitizer by a technician blinded to the experimental group assignments of the animals.[19] The mean of the 15 sections from the three arteries was calculated for analysis.

Statistical Analysis

Logarithmic transformation of all variables was used to reduce skewness and equalize group variances. Unless otherwise indicated, all data presented are untransformed values in the original units derived from the mean of the transformed distribution. Pearson's r correlation, 2x2 (initial status x manipulated status) ANOVA and ANCOVA, and multiple regression were used for statistical analyses. All probability values are the result of two-sided tests. A value of $P<.05$ was considered significant.

RESULTS

Preexperimental Phase Characteristics of the Animals

Preexperimental measures of risk factors suggested that there was little difference between experimental groups before the onset of the experiment (Table 2). Plasma lipid and glucose concentrations did not differ between experimental groups during the preexperimental phase. SBP appeared to be slightly higher in females that were initially subordinate (effect of initial social status, $P<.07$), and insulin concentrations tended to be higher during the preexperimental phase in those females that became dominant in the experimental phase (effect of manipulated social status, $P<.08$); however, neither of these reached significance. Most measures of adiposity also were not different. However, among initially subordinate animals, those that became dominant had smaller thigh circumferences, whereas among initially dominant animals, those that became subordinate had larger thigh circumferences (initial social status x manipulated social status interaction, $P<.02$). Preexperimental values of plasma cholesterol concentrations were significantly associated with CAA extent (TPC, $r=.34$; HDL cholesterol ratio, $r=-.30$; TPC-HDL cholesterol: $r=.38$; all $P<.05$). No other risk variables measured during the preexperimental phase were associated with CAA.

Table 2

Preexperimental Mean Values of Coronary Artery Atherosclerosis Risk Factors

	Initial Social Status			
	Subordinate		Dominant	
	Manipulated Social Status			
	Sub (n=12)	Dom (n=8)	Sub (n=11)	Dom (n=11)
Body weight, kg	3.0	3.0	2.8	3.1
Body mass index, kg/m^2	40.4	40.1	40.7	39.1
Thigh circumference*†, cm	12.8	12.3	12.0	12.9
Total plasma cholesterol, mg/dL	344	312	325	309
HDL cholesterol, mg/dL	42.5	36.4	41.0	41.8
TPC-HDL cholesterol ratio*	8.1	8.6	7.9	7.4
Glucose, mg/dL	65.4	69.1	61.2	67.5
Insulin, μU/mL	28.8	48.3	27.3	39.3
Systolic blood pressure, mm Hg	91	106	88	88
Diastolic blood pressure, mm Hg	56	69	55	56

Sub indicates subordinate; Dom, dominant; HDL, high-density lipoprotein, and TPC, total plasma cholesterol.
*Significant preexperimental predictors of coronary artery atherosclerosis extent ($P<.05$).
†Initial social status x manipulated social status interaction ($P<.05$).

Changing Social Status and CAA Extent

The extent of CAA found in each female in each group is depicted in Fig 2. After transformation to reduce the skewness and heterogeneity of variance, ANOVA revealed a significant interaction effect (initial social status x manipulated social status interaction, $P<.03$). Among initially subordinate females, those that became dominant had somewhat more extensive CAA, whereas among initially dominant females, those that became subordinate had more extensive CAA.

Although the experimental groups had quite similar risk factor values before the onset of the experiment, small differences between the groups were present, particularly in the thigh cir-cumference. To control for small differences present before the onset of the experiment and to reduce variability, the means of all potential risk factors that were measured during the preexperimental phase were entered as eligible predictors in a multiple regression analysis (after grouping variables were in the equation) to determine significant preexperimental predictors (all variables with values of $P<.10$) of CAA extent (Table 2). The preexperimental ratio of TPC-HDL cholesterol ($P=.01$) and thigh circumference ($P=.05$) were significant preexperimental predictors of CAA extent and together accounted for 35% of the variance in CAA.

To control for this variation in preexperimen-

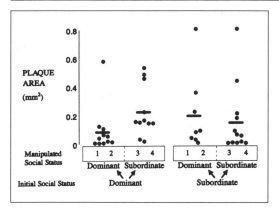

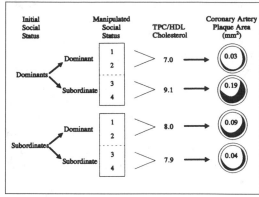

Figure 2

Graph showing coronary artery atherosclerosis extent expressed as the raw mean cross-sectional plaque area in square millimeters for each animal in each treatment group. Initial social status indicates the characteristic of females during 8 weeks in their first social group (experimental phase 1); manipulated social status, social status during 26 months in their second social group (experimental phase 2).

Figure 3

Schematic representation of effects of changing social status on total plasma cholesterol/high-density lipoprotein cholesterol (TPC-HDL) ratio and coronary artery atherosclerosis. Adjusted mean values of coronary artery atherosclerosis extent are expressed as cross-sectional plaque area (in square millimeters). Adjusted for preexperimental predictors of atherosclerosis extent: thigh circumference and TPC-HDL cholesterol ratio. Initial social status indicates the characteristic of females during 8 weeks in their first social group (experimental phase 1); manipulated social status, social status during 26 months in their second social group (experimental phase 2). Lipids were measured in experimental phase 2, during which the monkeys occupied their manipulated social status.

tal risk factors and to reduce variability caused by individual differences within experimental groups, we used ANCOVA to examine the effects of initial and manipulated social status, adjusted for significant preexperimental risk factors (thigh circumference and ratio of TPC-HDL cholesterol). These adjusted mean values of CAA extent represent the best estimate of the overall effect of social status and changing social status on CAA (Fig 3). Among initially subordinate females, those that became dominant had 44% greater CAA extent than subordinates that did not change social status. However, among initially dominant females, those that became subordinate had 500% greater CAA extent than those that did not change social status (initial social status x manipulated social status interaction, $P<.006$). Thus, females that changed social status had worsened atherosclerosis irrespective of whether they were dominant or subordinate for

the 26 months they lived in their final social groups. Those that were initially dominant and became subordinate were most deleteriously affected.

Risk Factors and CAA in Experimental Phase 2

There were relatively few differences between the experimental groups in risk factors measured during experimental phase 2 (Table 3). Glucose concentrations were slightly lower in females that were initially subordinate (effect of initial social status glucose, $P<.04$). Among initially subordinate animals, those that changed social status and became dominant had higher blood pressures. Among initially dominant animals, those that changed social status and became subordinate had higher blood pressures (initial social status x manipulated social status interaction: for SBP, $P<.03$; for DBP, $P<.05$). There were no differences in adiposity or in any measures of plasma cholesterol (TPC, HDL, or TPC-HDL cholesterol ratio) or insulin concentrations (2x2

ANOVA, all $P>.10$). However, mean peak luteal-phase progesterone concentrations were higher in females that were dominant in their manipulated social groupings, indicating an overall higher quality of ovarian function relative to their subordinate counterparts (manipulated social status, $P=.02$).

Plasma cholesterol and insulin concentrations in experimental phase 2 were significantly associated with CAA extent (TPC, $r=.59$; HDL cholesterol, $r=-.43$; TPC-HDL cholesterol ratio,

Table 3

Experimental Phase 2 Values of Coronary Artery Atherosclerosis Risk Factors

	Initial Social Status			
	Subordinate		Dominant	
	Manipulated Social Status			
	Sub (n=12)	Dom (n=8)	Sub (n=11)	Dom (n=11)
Body weight, kg	3.1	3.2	3.0	3.4
Body mass index, kg/m^2	41.1	43.4	42.0	42.0
Thigh circumference, cm	13.5	13.1	13.3	13.8
Total plasma cholesterol, mg/dL	345	303	363	323
HDL cholesterol, mg/dL	49.4	46.3	46.5	54.4
TPC-HDL cholesterol ratio*	7.9	8.0	9.1	7.0
Glucose‡, mg/dL	55.2	56.3	59.2	64.4
Insulin*, μU/mL	16.5	20.9	30.1	20.8
Systolic blood pressure†, mm Hg	104	114	105	98
Diastolic blood pressure†, mm Hg	63	71	62	56
Progesterone§, ng/mL	5.8	9.7	7.6	9.0

Sub indicates subordinate; Dom, dominant; HDL, high-density lipoprotein; and TPC, total plasma cholesterol.
*Significant experimental phase 2 correlates of coronary artery atherosclerosis extent ($P<.01$)
†Initial social status x manipulated social status interaction ($P<.05$).
‡Initial social status ($P<.05$).
§Manipulated social status ($P=.02$).

r=.65; insulin, r=.39; all P≤.01). No other risk variables measured during experimental phase 2 were associated with CAA extent (all P>.10).

To determine whether any of the risk factors measured during the experimental phase could have accounted for the effects of social status on CAA, all experimental phase 2 risk factors that, in addition to preexperimental phase predictors, significantly (P≤.10) predicted CAA extent were added to the model. TPC-HDL cholesterol and insulin concentrations were significant predictors. Whereas both variables accounted for a significant proportion of the variance in CAA, both were independent of the effect of social status (initial social status x manipulated social status interaction, P=.008). Thus, none of the risk factors considered appears to mediate the effect of social status on CAA.

DISCUSSION

THE results of this study are congruent with the results of prior investigations. Previously it has been observed among females that were randomly assigned to social groups that those that were subordinate also had more extensive CAA than those that were dominant.[1,4,8] In the present experiment, if all females that were subordinate for the majority of the experiment (ie, experimental phase 2) are compared with all females that were dominant for the majority of the experiment, CAA was more extensive on average in subordinate animals.

However, the results of the current experiment extend those of previous contributions because (1) social status was manipulated rather than observed, supporting the hypothesis of a causal relationship between social status and atherosclerosis; (2) after the manipulation, it became clear that changing social status exacerbates CAA; and (3) social status had an effect independent of ovarian function. All animals with altered social positions (dominants that became subordinate and subordinates that became dominant)

had worsened CAA. Atherosclerosis was exacerbated, although relatively modestly, even among those that became socially dominant. However, it appears that those monkeys that were characteristically dominant and occupied subordinate social positions for the majority of the experiment were most deleteriously affected on average.

The effects of changing social status on CAA appeared to be independent of any other differences between the groups before the onset of the study. For example, whereas the preexperimental plasma cholesterol response to the atherogenic diet was a significant predictor of CAA extent, the predictive power of preexperimental plasma cholesterol was independent of the effects of social status. Preexperimental thigh circumference was also predictive of atherosclerosis extent independent of social status; however, it was lowest in those females that eventually changed rank in response to the social manipulation. Patterns of fat distribution and muscle development both affect thigh circumference, and both may be affected by factors that influence metabolism, such as sex steroid concentrations.

Initial and manipulated social status, as well as changing social status, influenced few risk factors. Most obvious was the lack of an effect of experimental grouping on plasma cholesterol concentration, even though the latter was a strong predictor of CAA extent. Glucose concentrations were significantly higher in females that were initially dominant versus subordinate, perhaps indicating that it is a stable characteristic of the individual that co-occurs with the initial social status of that individual. Altered social status increased blood pressure, irrespective of whether the females were dominant or subordinate in their final social groupings. Whereas the pattern of this effect was similar to the pattern of the effect of social status on CAA extent, SBP and DBP measured during experimental phase 2 were not significantly correlated with CAA extent.

Manipulated social status influenced ovarian function. Females that were socially subordinate during the 26 months in their manipulated social groups had lower mean peak luteal-phase plasma progesterone concentrations. In general, luteal-phase progesterone concentrations are indicative of the quality of the menstrual cycle, with higher concentrations indicating normal ovulatory cycles and lower concentrations indicating impaired menstrual cycles that may be anovulatory or characterized by abnormally low sex hormone concentrations.[17,18] In prior experiments in which females were placed in social groups randomly without respect to their social status, subordinates had impaired ovarian function and exacerbated CAA. From these experiments, it was not possible to determine whether social status made an independent contribution to CAA risk. In the present experiment, ovarian function was especially sensitive to the current social status of the individual. Current subordinates had lower hormone concentrations than current dominants, irrespective of whether they had changed rank or not. Because CAA was worsened by a change in social status, whether to a subordinate or a dominant position, changing social status disassociated atherosclerosis extent from ovarian function. Thus, in the present experiment, social status had an effect on CAA independent of ovarian function.

Values of risk factors during the experiment, specifically plasma cholesterol and insulin concentrations in experimental phase 2, were significantly correlated with CAA extent; however, none of these appeared to be affected by initial or manipulated social status or changing social status.

Social subordination is thought to be a stressor and therefore deleterious to the health of monkeys. The assumption that subordinates are stressed is based on the observations that subordinates receive more aggression, spend more time alone, hypersecrete cortisol, and have suppressed reproductive function relative to domi-

nants. The results of the present study suggest that it is also deleterious to health to change social status. Previous observations suggest that social status is a reliable characteristic of the animal that is expressed similarly in different social environments.[9] Compelling an animal to behave in an uncharacteristic fashion, whether by making dominants subordinate or subordinates dominant, may be stressful. The mechanism of the effect of changing social status on CAA is unknown. The results of this experiment suggest that it was not due to social status effects on lipid or carbohydrate metabolism, blood pressure, reproductive function, or body size or composition. Other possible mechanisms yet to be considered include vasomotor, heart rate, and blood pressure reactivity as well as other systems known to be stress responsive, such as the hypothalamic-pituitary-adrenal axis.

The modification of physiological risk factors, such as plasma cholesterol concentrations, results in lowered risk in humans.[20,21] The efficacy of psychosocial risk factor modification (such as the modification of coronary-prone behavior pattern) is less certain.[22-27] In the present study, an established psychosocial risk factor for female monkeys was modified, and this change was not effective in reducing CAA. An important aspect of the relationship between psychosocial stress and CAA may be the congruity between an individual's behavior and the psychosocial environment.[28] Psychosocial risk factor modification may be a difficult undertaking because it is an attempt to alter a complex interaction between individuals and their psychosocial environment.

THIS research was supported in part by grants HL-39789 and HL-14164 from the National Heart, Lung, and Blood Institute, National Institutes of Health, Bethesda, Md. The authors would like to thank John Colwell, MD, PhD, his laboratory staff, and Kathy Laber-Laird, DVM, for collection of blood samples for carbohydrate metabolism assessments and insulin assays.

NOTES

1. Hamm TE Jr, Kaplan JR, Clarkson TB, Bullock BC. Effects of gender and social behavior on the development of coronary artery atherosclerosis is cynomolgus macaques. *Atherosclerosis.* 1983;48:221–233.

2. Mahoney CJ. A study of the menstrual cycle in *Macaca irus* with special reference to the detection of ovulation. *J Reprod Fertil.* 1970;21:153–163.

3. Shively CA, Kaplan JR, Adams MR. Effects of ovariectomy, social instability and social status on female *Macaca fascicularis* social behavior. *Physiol Behav.* 1986;36:1147–1153.

4. Adams MR, Kaplan JR, Clarkson TB, Koritnik DR. Ovariectomy, social status, and atherosclerosis in cynomolgus monkeys. *Arteriosclerosis.* 1985;5:192–200.

5. Kaplan JR, Adams MR, Koritnik DR, Rose JC, Manuck SB. Adrenal responsiveness and social status in intact and ovariectomized *Macaca fascicularis. Am J Primatol.* 1986;11:181–193.

6. Shively CA, Clarkson TB, Kaplan JR. Social. deprivation and coronary artery atherosclerosis in female cynomolgus monkeys. *Atherosclerosis.* 1989;77:69–76.

7. Shively CA, Manuck SB,. Kaplan JR, Koritnik DR. Oral contraceptive administration, interfemale relationships, and sexual behavior in *Macaca fascicularis. Arch Sex Behav.* 1990;19:101–117.

8. Clarkson TB, Shively CA, Morgan TM, Koritnik DR, Adams MR, Kaplan JR. Oral contraceptives and coronary artery atherosclerosis of cynomolgus monkeys. *Obstet Gynecol.* 1990;75:217–222.

9. Shively CA, Kaplan JR. Stability of social status rankings of female cynomolgus monkeys, of varying reproductive condition, in different social groups. *Am J Primatol.* 1991;23:239–245.

10. Adams MR, Kaplan JR, Manuck SB, Koritnik DR, Parks JS, Wolfe MS, Clarkson TB. Inhibition of coronary artery atherosclerosis by 17-beta estradiol in ovariectomized monkeys. *Arteriosclerosis.* 1990;10:1051–1057.

11. Rush RL, Leon L, Turrell J. Automated simultaneous cholesterol and triglyceride determination on the auto analyzer II instrument. In: Baraton EC, DuCros EJ, Erdrich MM, eds. *Advances in Automated Analysis. Technician International Congress 1970.* Mt Kisco, NY: Futura Publishing; 1971:503–507.

12. Lipid Research Clinics Program. Manual of Laboratory Operations: *Lipid and Lipoprotein Analysis.* Bethesda,

MD: National Institutes of Health; 1974. US Dept of Health, Education, and Welfare publication 75–628.

13. Jayo JM, Shively CA, Kaplan JR, Manuck SB. Effects of exercise and stress on body fat distribution in male cynomolgus monkeys. *Int J Obes.* 1993;19:597–604.

14. Alpert NL. Glucose analyzer and BUN analyzer. *Lab World.* 1973;24:40.

15. Meis PJ, Kaplan JR, Koritnik DR, Rose JD. Effects of gestation on glucose tolerance and plasma insulin in cynomolgus monkeys (*Macaca fascicularis*). *Am J Obstet Gynecol.* 1982;144:543–545.

16. Corbett WT, Schey HM, Lehner NDM, Greene AW. Standardized methods for recording blood pressure in anesthetized *Macaca fascicularis. Lab Anim.* 1981;15:37–40.

17. Wilks JW, Hodgen GD, Ross GT. Luteal phase defects in the rhesus monkey: the significance of serum FSH:LH ratios. *J Clin Endocrinol Metab.* 1976;43:1261–1267.

18. Wilks JW, Hodgen GD, Ross GT. Endocrine characteristics of ovulatory and anovulatory menstrual cycles in the rhesus monkey. In: Hafez ESE, ed. *Human Ovulation.* Amsterdam, the Netherlands: Elsevier/North-Holland Biomedical Press; 1979:205–218.

19. Clarkson TB, Bond MG, Marzetta CA, Bullock BC. Approaches to the study of atherosclerosis regression in rhesus monkeys: interpretation of morphometric measurements of coronary arteries. In: Gotto AM Jr, Smith LC, Allen B, eds. *Atherosclerosis V: The Fifth International Symposium on Atherosclerosis.* New York, NY: Springer-Verlag; 1980:739–748.

20. Lipid Research Clinics Program. The Lipid Research Clinics Coronary Primary Prevention Trial results, I. reduction in incidence of coronary heart disease. *JAMA.* 1984;251:351–364.

21. Lipid Research Clinics Program. The Lipid Research Clinics Coronary Primary Prevention Trial results, II. the relationship of reduction in incidence of coronary heart dieseases to cholesterol lowering. *JAMA.* 1984;251:365–374.

22. Friedman M, Thoresen CE, Gill JJ, Ulmer D, Powell LH, Price VA, Brown B, Thompson L, Rabin DD, Breall WS, Boug E, Levy R, Dixon T. Alteration of type A behavior and its effect on cardiac recurrences in postmyocardial infarction patients: summary results of the Recurrent Coronary Prevention Project. *Am Heart J.* 1986;112:653–665.

23. Rahe RM, Ward HW, Hayes V. Brief group therapy in myocardial infarction rehabilitation: three to four year follow-up of a controlled trial. *Psychosom Med.* 1979;41:229–242.

24. Nunes EV, Frank RA, Kornfield DS. Psychologic treatment for the type A behavior pattern and for coronary heart disease: a meta-analysis of the literature. *Psychosom Med.* 1987;48:159–173.

25. Jenkins CD. Psychosocial risk factors for coronary heart disease. *Acta Med Scand Suppl.* 1982;660:123–136.

26. Davidson MJ, Cooper CL. Type A coronary-prone behavior in the work environment. *J Occup Med.* 1980;22:375–383.

27. Friedman M. Effect of modifying type A behavior after myocardial infarction on recurrence rate. *Mt Sinai J Med.* 1987;51:47–55.

28. Levi L. *Society, Stress and Disease.* New York, NY: Oxford University Press; 1981.

29. Levi L. Work, stress and health. *Scand J Work Environ Health.* 1984;10:495–500.

Thirty-Four

BEHAVIOR AND PHYSIOLOGY OF SOCIAL STRESS AND DEPRESSION IN FEMALE CYNOMOLGUS MONKEYS

Carol A. Shively, Kathy Laber-Laird, and Raymond F. Anton

Abstract

The hypothesis that social subordination is stressful, and results in a depressive response in some individuals, was examined in socially housed female cynomolgus monkeys. Social status was manipulated such that half of the previously subordinate females became dominant and half of the previously dominant females became subordinate. Current subordinates hypersecreted cortisol, were insensitive to negative feedback, and had suppressed reproductive function. Current subordinates received more aggression, engaged in less affiliation, and spent more time alone than dominants. Furthermore, they spent more time fearfully scanning the social environment and displayed more behavioral depression than dominants. Current subordinates with a history of social subordination were preferentially susceptible to a behavioral depression response. The results of this experiment suggest that the stress of social subordination causes hypothalamic-pituitary-adrenal and ovarian dysfunction, and support the hypothesis that chronic, low-intensity social stress may result in depression in susceptible individuals.

Introduction

A SIGNIFICANT proportion of the population experiences a clinically significant depression that interferes with the conduct of their lives, and the rate of occurrence of depression may be increasing (Fombonne 1994). Depression is also linked with the incidence of other disorders such as coronary heart disease (Kaplan 1985; Ahern et al 1990; LaCroix 1994). Depression occurs approximately twice as frequently in women as in men. The lifetime prevalence of depression in women has been estimated to be as high as 21%, and several lines of evidence suggest an association between depression and reproductive function in women (Mackenzie 1986; Schwartz 1991; Yonkers and Chantillis 1995; Pearlstein 1995).

The heterogeneous nature of depression is well recognized. Depression appears to be a family of related disorders which thus far defy con-

Originally published in *Biological Psychiatry*, 1997.

structive classification. Depression may be mild or profound, acute or chronic, and may co-occur with anxiety (Phillipp et al 1992; Hirschfeld 1994; Boulanger and Lavallée 1993; Wittchen and Essau 1993; Stahl 1993). Social stress is believed to be associated with depression; however, that relationship has been difficult to demonstrate in some studies (Breslau and Davis 1986; Richardson 1991; Vilhjalmsson 1993; Brown et al 1994). A recent series of reports suggests that adverse experiences in childhood and adolescence increase risk of anxiety and depression in adulthood (Brown and Harris 1993). In adulthood, loss may precipitate a depressive episode, a severely threatening event that is dangerous (e.g., marital violence) may provoke anxiety, and danger and loss together appear to precipitate the onset of mixed depressive and anxiety disorders (Brown et al 1993, 1995; Brown 1993; Brown and Moran 1994).

Data are accumulating describing plausible neurobiological mechanisms through which social stress might cause depression (Anisman and Zacharko 1990; Iny et al 1994; Peeters and Broekkamp 1994; Berendsen 1995; Brown and Gershon 1993; Pearson Murphy 1991). It is difficult to study the biological mechanisms underlying the relationship between social stress and depression in human beings because the social stressors cannot be controlled and are hard to qualify, subjects cannot be randomized to treatment groups, and some experimental assessments that might be illuminating are inappropriate in studies involving human subjects. An appropriate animal model would be helpful to address the relationship between stress and depression, and the relationship between the depressive response to stress and susceptibility to other disease processes. Since rates of depression are so high in women, and depression appears to be associated with reproductive function, an animal model of depression in females would be especially helpful.

Nonhuman primates are an appropriate animal model to study responses to stress because of their dependence on social relationships, their ability to engage in complex cognitive processes, and the similarities to human beings in central nervous system (CNS) function. Reproductive system function of female cynomolgus monkeys (*Macaca fascicularis*) is similar to that of women, and their behavior varies with reproductive status, indicating relationships between reproductive system function and behavior (Dukelow 1977; Shively et al 1986, 1990; Yen 1991).

Social status hierarchies and kinship ties are the two most prominent central organizing features of macaque societies. Members of matrilines have similar rank; matrilines are ranked with respect to each other. Thus, females have the rank of their mother from birth. Given a few exceptions, the only escape for a female from her social status destiny in wild groups is generally group fission which is not a frequent event. The natural history and social dynamics of dominance are different in males. Males have a rank similar to their mother's while juveniles; however, they leave the natal group and live alone or in all-male bands for awhile. Eventually, they may join a new group in which they acquire their rank, which is correlated with tenure in the new group (Sugiyama 1976; Sade 1967). Among female cynomolgus monkeys, social subordinates receive more aggression and have exacerbated diet-induced coronary artery atherosclerosis, poor ovarian function, and adrenal hypersecretion of cortisol (Kaplan et al 1986; Shively et al 1986; Shively et al in press). These observations suggest that social subordination in female macaques is stressful and affects health. Furthermore, it appears that social status in female cynomolgus monkeys is an enduring trait of the individual that is expressed similarly in different social environments. The social status rankings of 41 adult female cynomolgus monkeys were documented while they lived in eight different small social groups over a two-year period. It was found that 71% of the females were stable dominants or stable subordinates irrespective of the social group (Shively and Kaplan 1991). Thus, adult female cynomolgus monkeys may be a useful animal model to investigate the relationship between stress, depression, and other disease processes relevant to women.

In the following experiment the hypothesis that social subordination is stressful, and in some individuals results in a depressive response, was tested in adult female cynomolgus monkeys. Social status was manipulated, and the effects of this manipulation on social behavior, ovarian, and hypothalamic-pituitary-adrenal function were measured.

METHODS

Subjects

Forty-eight adult female cynomolgus monkeys were obtained from Charles River Research Primates (Port Washington, NY). The animals were estimated to be 6–12 yrs of age based on dentition. During the course of the experiment six animals died from causes unrelated to the experiment (primarily diarrheal diseases), resulting in 42 study animals. (Those that died were about equally distributed between treatment groups.) All procedures involving monkeys were conducted in accordance with state and federal laws, standards of the Department of Health and Human Services, and guidelines established by the institutional Animal Care and Use Committee.

Diet

The monkeys were part of an experiment to evaluate social and reproductive effects on atherosclerosis and were thus fed a moderately atherogenic diet ad libitum, for 32 months, which contained 0.25 mg cholesterol/Cal and 40% of calories as fat (Shively and Clarkson 1994).

Experimental Design

The experimental design is depicted in Figure 1. The monkeys were housed in quarantine for 3 months in single cages (preexperimental phase), and then assigned randomly to four-member social groups for an 8-week period during which their social status stabilized and was determined (experimental phase I). The animals were designated first, second, third, or fourth ranking. First and second ranking females were considered dominant, and third and fourth ranking females were considered subordinate. The animals were then assigned to new social groupings of four animals each, based on their social status, for the remaining 26-month experimental period. Animals that were previously dominant were housed together and animals that were previously subordinate were housed together. Linear social status hierarchies reformed, such that half of the subordinate animals became dominant, and half of the dominant animals became subordinate (experimental phase II). The majority of their new social status positions were decided within hours of social reorganization, and rates of aggression dropped to prereorganization levels in less than 2 weeks. This manipulation produced four experimental groups: 1) females that were initially dominant, and remained dominant after social regrouping ($n = 11$); 2) females that were initially dominant and became subordinate after regrouping ($n = 11$); 3) females that were initially subordinate and became dominant after social regrouping ($n = 8$); and 4) females that were initially subordinate and remained subordinate after regrouping ($n = 12$). This resulted in a 2×2 study design: Initial social status$_{dom,sub}$ × manipulated social status$_{dom,sub}$. It is important to note that the monkeys were in their final social groups for over 90% of the experimental period. Since young female cynomolgus monkeys acquire their social status early in life and it tends to be stable, in the experiment reported here, initial social status may be considered a longstanding behavioral characteristic of the individual, whereas current social status represents an experimentally manipulated state of social environmental stress.

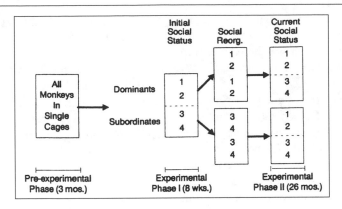

Figure 1

Following a 3-month quarantine, monkeys were assigned to four-member social groups for 8 weeks during which social status was determined (initial social status). First and second ranking females were considered dominant, and third and fourth ranking females were considered subordinate. Animals were then assigned to new social groupings of four animals each, based on their social status, for 26 months. Animals that were previously dominant (two first- and two second-ranking monkeys) were housed together, and animals that were previously subordinate (two third- and two fourth-ranking monkeys) were housed together. Linear social status hierarchies reformed: half of the subordinate animals became dominant, and half of the dominant animals became subordinate (current social status). This manipulation resulted in a change in social status in half of the animals: those that were initially subordinate and became dominant, and those that were initially dominant and became subordinate.

Sampling Procedures

All physiological and behavioral evaluations were done during experimental phase II.

HYPOTHALAMIC-PITUITARY-ADRENAL (HPA) FUNCTION

Cortisol response to an adrenocorticotropin (ACTH) challenge was the first test administered. The purpose of this test is to assess adrenocortical secretion of cortisol to exogenous ACTH independent of hypothalamic-pituitary activity. Following an overnight fast the animals were administered dexamethasone (0.5 mg/kg) to suppress hypothalamic-pituitary activity. Four hrs later they were sedated (ketamine hydrochloride 15 mg/kg), and a blood sample was taken quickly for baseline measures of cortisol. The animals were administered the ACTH challenge (Cortrosyn®, 10 ng/kg, IV), and blood samples were taken at 15 and 30 min following ACTH infusion and assayed for cortisol concentrations (Kaplan et al 1986). This test was done after the monkeys had lived for 21 mos in their final social groups.

The second test administered was the dexamethasone suppression test. The purpose of this test is to assess the sensitivity of the hypothalamus and pituitary to negative feedback from circulating levels of cortisol (Davidson et al 1984; Mossman and Somoza 1989). Since dexamethasone binds with great affinity to the cortisol receptor, it is used in relatively small amounts to test the sensitivity to negative feedback. A morning (8:00 hrs) blood sample was taken for a baseline measure of cortisol. That evening (22:00 hrs) a low dose (130 µg/kg BW, IM) of dexamethasone was administered. The next morning (8:00 hrs) another blood sample was taken for cortisol assay. Blood samples were taken rapidly following capture and sedation with ketamine hydrochloride (10 mg/kg). The difference between the first and second morning cortisol concentrations is used as an indicator of sensitivity to negative feedback (Kalin and Carnes 1984). This test was done after the monkeys had lived for 25 months in their final social groups.

MENSTRUAL CYCLE DETERMINATIONS

The monkeys were trained to present themselves for vaginal swabbing to detect menses, and for femoral venipuncture for blood sample collection, three times/week throughout experimental phase II. Blood samples were assayed for serum progesterone concentrations (ng/mL) by radioimmunoassay (Diagnostic Products Corp., Los Angeles, CA).

A menstrual cycle was defined in relation to the time preceding menses. Thus the number of menstrual cycles each monkey had during the experimental phase II was equivalent to the number of menses detected during that time period. Luteal phase progesterone concentrations were used as an indicator of the quality of a menstrual cycle. The highest progesterone value that occurred during the luteal phase was used to represent that menstrual cycle. High progesterone concentrations (greater than 4 ng/mL) indicated that ovulation had occurred, whereas low progesterone concentrations (less than 2 ng/mL) indicated an anovulatory cycle. Peak luteal phase progesterone concentrations that fell between these two categories (greater than or equal to 2.0 ng/mL, and less than 4.0 ng/mL) were considered indicative of a menstrual cycle that was impaired (Wilks et al 1979). Mean peak luteal phase progesterone concentrations, the proportion that were ovulatory, anovulatory, and impaired, and the number of cycles each female had during experimental phase II were calculated for analysis.

BEHAVIORAL CHARACTERIZATION

The social status of an individual refers to that individual's ability to defeat other members of its social group in agonistic or competitive interactions. Social status was determined monthly throughout experimental phases I and II by recording the outcomes of aggressive interactions between cagemates. The animal in each social group that defeated all other group members was designated the first ranking monkey. The animal that defeated all but the first ranking monkey was designated the second ranking monkey, and so forth. The resulting social status hierarchies for each social group were stable over time (Shively and Kaplan 1991). Animals that were first or second ranking, on average, were considered dominant, while those that were third or fourth ranking, on average, were considered subordinate.

A limited number of social behaviors were recorded twice a week throughout experimental phase II, using a 30-min group ad libitum observation method, punctuated with scan samples every 10 minutes (Altmann 1974). During the ad libitum sampling a continuous log of a limited number of behaviors of all members of a social group was recorded to indicate the frequency of agonistic behavior. The scan samples were used to estimate the duration of time that females spent in affiliative interaction (grooming, sitting in passive body contact, or sitting close—within arm's reach) or alone (see Shively et al 1986 for operational definitions). Body contact, close and alone was further characterized as either vigilant (visually scanning the social environment), resting (eyes closed), or depressed (slumped or collapsed body posture, relatively unresponsive to environmental stimuli to which other monkeys are attending [Suomi et al 1975]). Also during close and alone, time spent in stereotypic behavior (a repetitive motor behavior that occurs at least three times in quick succession) directed at herself or the environment was recorded.

Analysis

Statistical analyses included Pearson *r* and Spearman's rho correlations between dependent variables, $2_{\text{initial status}} \times 2_{\text{manipulated status}}$ analysis of variance, and $2_{\text{initial status}} \times 2_{\text{manipulated status}} \times 3$ repeated measures analysis of variance for the ACTH challenge test. When necessary, transformation was used prior to parametric analyses to reduce skewness and increase homogeneity of variance. The percent of time spent in a collapsed posture tended to be distributed bimodally. Females either did or did not engage in this behavior. Thus, a Chi^2 test was used to determine the significance of the difference between groups in the number of individuals observed in the collapsed, depressed posture, and a Spearman rho correlation was used to measure the association between time spent in the depressed posture and physiological variables. All p values are the result of two-sided tests. Means and standard errors from the distribution of raw data are depicted in figures and tables.

RESULTS

Hypothalamic-Pituitary-Adrenal (HPA) Function

Adrenal function was assessed by an ACTH challenge test (Figure 2). Following a relatively large dose of dexamethasone (0.5 mg/kg), cortisol concentrations were low (less than 10 μg/mL) and similar between the experimental groups. ACTH administered intravenously caused a significant increase in plasma cortisol over the next half hour (changes over time, $p < 0.001$). Females that were currently dominant tended to secrete less cortisol in response to ACTH than those that were currently subordinate ($p = 0.09$). Initial social status did not affect the cortisol response to ACTH ($p = .023$). Neither current social status nor initial social status significantly interacted with each other or with changes over time to affect cortisol concentrations (all p's > 0.17).

The sensitivity of the hypothalamic-pituitary portion of the HPA axis to negative feedback was assessed with a dexamethasone suppression test (Figure 3). Morning baseline cortisol concentrations were lower in females that were currently

dominant compared to those that were currently subordinate ($p < 0.02$). Initial social status had no main effect on baseline cortisol concentrations ($p = 0.30$). The interaction between initial and current social status did not reach significance, although currently subordinate females that initially had been subordinate had higher cortisol concentrations, on average, than animals in the other three treatment groups ($p = 0.10$).

After a relatively modest dose of dexamethasone (130 μg/mL), females that were currently dominant secreted less cortisol than those that were currently subordinate ($p = 0.003$). There was no main effect of initial social status ($p = 0.28$) or interaction between initial and current social status ($p = 0.63$). Examination of the percentage change between baseline and suppressed values revealed that currently dominant females had a greater percent suppression of cortisol in response to dexamethasone than currently subordinate females ($p = 0.02$; Figure 4). There was no main effect of initial social status ($p = 0.69$) or interaction between initial and current social status ($p = 0.34$).

Reproductive Function

Mean peak luteal phase progesterone concentrations for each group during experimental phase II are depicted in Figure 5. Females that were currently dominant had significantly higher luteal phase mean peak serum progesterone concentrations than those that were currently subordinate ($p < 0.03$). There was no effect of initial social status ($p = 0.76$) or interaction between current initial social status ($p = 0.32$). Most females exhibited some variability in the quality of their menstrual cycles over the 26-month experimental phase II as indicated by peak luteal phase serum progesterone concentrations. Current subordinates had fewer ovulatory menstrual cycles than current dominants ($p < 0.03$; Table 1). Current subordinates had more impaired menstrual cycles, on average, than current dominants

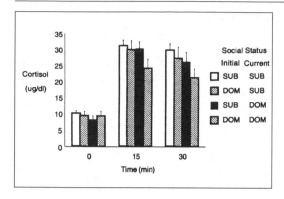

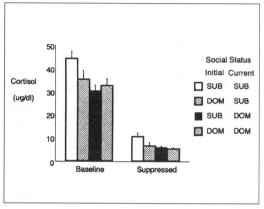

Figure 2
Plasma cortisol response to ACTH challenge follow-ing dexamethasone suppression. Current subordi-nates (SUB) tended to have adrenal hypersecretion of cortisol compared to current dominants (DOM, p = 0.09).

Figure 4
Percent suppression (baseline response to dexamethasone/baseline × 100) of cortisol in a dex-amethasone suppression test. Current dominants (DOM) suppressed cortisol secretion more than cur-rent subordinates (SUB) in response to dexametha-sone (p = 0.02).

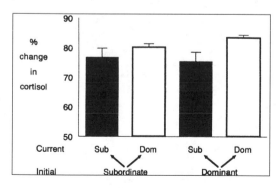

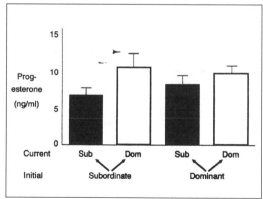

Figure 3
Plasma cortisol response to dexamethasone suppres-sion. Current subordinates (SUB) had higher base-line cortisol concentrations (p < 0.02) and secreted more cortisol after dexamethasone suppression (p = 0.003) than current dominants (DOM).

Figure 5
Mean peak luteal phase progesterone concentrations determined during experimental phase II. Current dominants (DOM) had higher progesterone concen-trations than current subordinates (SUB, p < 0.03).

although this difference did not reach significance ($p < 0.08$; Table 1). The interaction between current and initial social status also did not reach significance ($p = 0.10$), although as is apparent in Table 1, among initial subordinates, those that became dominant had fewer impaired cycles, on average, than those that remained subordinate. In contrast, among initial dominants there was very little difference in the proportion of cycles that were impaired between those that remained dominant, and those that became subordinate. There was no effect of initial social status, or interaction between current and initial social status (other than the trend just described), on the other measures presented in Table 1 (all p's > 0.21). There was also no effect of current social status, initial social status, or interaction between current and initial social status on the number of menstrual cycles detected during experimental phase II (Table 1, all p's ≥ 0.60). Thus, social status did not influence the incidence of amenorrhea.

Behavioral Characteristics

In addition to physiological indicators of stress, behavioral observations revealed a more stressful social experience for current subordinates compared to current dominants (Table 2). Current subordinates were involved in more agonistic encounters in which they were aggressed and submitted to cagemates than current dominants ($p < 0.001$), and current dominates received submissions from cagemates more frequently than current subordinates ($p < 0.001$). Current subordinates spent more time vigilantly scanning their social group than current dominants ($p = 0.05$). Vigilant scanning occurred principally while the animal was alone, and to a lesser degree while in body contact. Current subordinates appeared to be tracking the movements of dominants to avoid agonistic interactions. Affiliative behavior also differed by experimental group. Current subordinates were groomed less ($p < 0.001$), and they spent more time alone than current dominants ($p < 0.001$).

Furthermore, nearly all observations of the collapsed posture, which is indicative of behavioral depression in primates (and the operational definition of behavioral depression used in this experiment) occurred in current subordinates. The collapsed posture was primarily observed when the animal was alone, less frequently while the animal was in body contact, and infrequently while the animal was within arm's reach of a cagemate. The percentage of time spent in the

Table 1

Quality of Menstrual Cycles[a]

Initial status	Subordinate		Dominant		Effect of current status
Current status	Subordinate	Dominant	Subordinate	Dominant	$p \leq$
# of Cycles	15.2 (0.94)	15.4 (1.03)	14.4 (1.52)	15.1 (1.1)	0.60
% Ovulatory	68.1 (9.19)	91.4 (3.36)	81.6 (6.34)	88.4 (4.42)	0.03
% Impaired	19.4 (5.21)	4.2 (1.65)	8.4 (2.8)	8.1 (2.60)	0.08
% Anovulatory	12.5 (6.00)	4.5 (2.21)	9.9 (5.44)	3.5 (2.76)	0.17

[a]Means and standard errors.

collapsed posture was significantly higher in current subordinates than current dominants ($p <$ 0.05) and tended to be higher among initial subordinates compared to initial dominants ($p =$ 0.10, data not shown); however, the distribution of this variable made the results of parametric statistical analyses suspect because of the high proportion of zero scores. Females either did or did not engage in this behavior, thus nonparametric analyses were used to determine whether the proportions of individuals in each experimental group that engaged in this behavior were different. A significantly higher proportion of individuals that were observed in the collapsed posture were current subordinates, particularly those that had been subordinate also in their initial social groups ($p < 0.002$, Table 2).

There were no other significant effects of current or initial social status on behavior (all p's > 0.20).

Correlations among Dependent Variables

Correlations between behavioral and physiological variables are given in Table 3. The cortisol concentrations measured at 0, 15, and 30 minutes following ACTH challenge were not significantly correlated with any behavioral variables and thus are not included in the table.

Agonistic behavior was associated with ovarian and HPA axis function (Table 3). The frequency of submission was negatively correlated with indices of the quality of ovarian function (percent of cycles that were ovulatory, mean peak progesterone concentrations, both p's < 0.05) and with the sensitivity to negative feedback in the HPA axis (percent change in cortisol $p < 0.05$). Frequency of submission was positively correlated with cortisol concentrations at baseline and in response to dexamethasone (both p's < 0.001). The frequency of submissions received was positively correlated with the percent of cycles that were ovulatory ($p < 0.05$), and negatively correlated with the cortisol response to dexamethasone ($p < 0.05$). The percent of time spent vigilantly scanning the social environment was positively associated with baseline cortisol concentrations ($p < 0.02$).

Affiliative behavior (or lack thereof) was asso-

Table 2

Behavioral Characteristics[a]

Initial status	Subordinate		Dominant		
Current status	Subordinate	Dominant	Subordinate	Dominant	$p \leq$
Submission senet[c]	7.4 (0.80)	1.5 (0.73)	8.5 (1.33)	1.0 (0.38)	0.001[b]
Submission received[c]	2.0 (0.58)	6.7 (0.80)	2.8 (0.87)	8.1 (1.2)	0.001[b]
Vigilant scanning[c]	57.2 (1.67)	51.0 (3.60)	54.9 (2.64)	51.4 (1.86)	0.05[b]
Be groomed[d]	7.5 (0.81)	15.9 (3.24)	7.4 (1.55)	13.3 (1.21)	0.001[b]
Alone[d]	52.0 (3.21)	33.0 (4.71)	56.6 (3.76)	46.5 (2.36)	0.001[b]
Depressed posture[e]	10 (83%)	2 (25%)	4 (36%)	0 (0.0%)	0.002

[a] Means and standard errors from the distribution of raw data.
[b] p values for the effect of current social status.
[c] Frequency/hour.
[d] Percent time.
[e] Number and percent of monkeys that were observed in the depressed posture.

Table 3

Correlations between Dependent Variables[a]

	Submission	Submission received	Vigilant scanning	Be groomed	Alone	Depressed
% Ovulatory cycles	−0.32	0.34	−0.23	0.24	−0.29	−0.28
% Impaired cycles	0.24	−0.19	0.23	−0.27	0.28	0.31
% Anovulatory cycles	0.26	−0.34	0.14	−0.11	0.17	0.17
Mean peak progesterone	−0.34	0.28	−0.28	0.30	−0.32	−0.25
Baseline cortisol	0.51	−0.22	0.38	−0.47	0.35	0.21
Cortisol response to dexamethasone	0.56	−0.34	0.29	−0.39	0.15	0.37
% Change cortisol	−0.32	0.29	−0.05	0.11	0.09	−0.42

[a] $r_{cv} = 0.30$ for $p < 0.05$.

ciated with ovarian and HPA axis function (Table 3). The percent of time being groomed was positively associated with mean peak progesterone concentrations ($p < 0.05$), and negatively associated with the magnitude of cortisol at baseline and in response to dexamethasone ($p < 0.01$). Time spent alone was also negatively associated with mean peak progesterone concentrations and positively associated with baseline cortisol concentrations (both p's < 0.05).

There were also significant associations between indices of ovarian function and HPA function. The sensitivity of the negative feedback loop to dexamethasone (percent change in cortisol in response to dexamethasone) was associated with the percent of cycles that were ovulatory ($r = 0.31$, $p < 0.05$) and anovulatory ($r = -0.37$, $p < 0.02$) and the cortisol response to dexamethasone was associated with the percent of cycles that were anovulatory ($r = 0.37$, $p < 0.02$).

Spearman's rho correlations between physiological variables and time spent in the collapsed posture are reported because of the nature of the distribution of this behavioral variable. (Parametric correlations were similar to the nonparametric correlations reported in Table 3.) Time spent in the depressed posture was negatively associated with the sensitivity of the HPA axis to

negative feedback (percent change in cortisol, $p < 0.01$), and positively associated with the cortisol response to dexamethasone ($p < 0.05$).

Behavioral Depression Response to Stress

The bimodal nature of the expression of behavioral depression (collapsed posture) suggested that it may be useful to consider this behavior as a categorical variable (Table 4). Thus, females were divided into two groups (collapsed across initial and current social status categories): those that were ever observed in the depressed posture ($n = 16$), and those that never exhibited behavioral depression ($n = 26$). Females that were ever observed in the depressed posture spent more time vigilantly scanning their social environment than those that never exhibited behavioral depression ($p = 0.01$). Females that were never observed in the depressed posture were not different from nondepressed females in baseline cortisol concentrations; however, females with behavioral depression had higher cortisol concentrations in response to dexamethasone suppression ($p < 0.001$), and did not suppress cortisol as well in response to dexamethasone (percent suppression, $p = 0.006$) compared to their nondepressed counterparts. On the other hand there

Table 4

Characteristics of Females Exhibiting Behavioral Depression

	Females with behavioral depression ($n = 16$)	Females without behavioral depression ($n = 26$)	$p \leq$
Baseline cortisol	39.3 (2.57)	33.8 (2.31)	0.14
Cortisol response to dexamethasone	10.5 (1.44)	5.9 (0.34)	0.001
% Suppression of cortisol	74.3 (2.51)	81.5 (1.19)	0.006
% Time spent vigilant	57.7 (1.6)	51.6 (1.5)	0.01

[a] Physiological data were transformed prior to analysis, thus mean values shown here are derived from the transformed distribution. Mean and standard errors from the raw data distribution are given for behavioral variables.

was no difference in females with and without behavioral depression in the quality of ovarian function measured by mean peak luteal phase progesterone concentrations, or percentage of cycles that were ovulatory, impaired or anovulatory (all p's > 0.10, data not shown).

Of the 16 females displaying behavioral depression, 14 were currently socially subordinate (88%), whereas among the 26 females never displaying behavioral depression, nine were currently subordinate (35%). Thus, while the expression of behavioral depression was closely tied to the stress of social subordination, many subordinates did not respond to the current social situation with behavioral depression. The comparisons between those with and without behavioral depression made above were limited to current subordinates only ($n = 23$). The only significant physiological difference between these two subgroups was the cortisol response to dexamethasone (the second morning sample following the small dose of dexamethasone given the previous evening), which was higher in current subordinates with behavioral depression than current subordinates without behavioral depression ($p = 0.02$).

DISCUSSION

IN this experiment, adult female monkeys were subjected to the stress of social subordination, a characteristic of this species when living in groups in the wild. Many laboratory investigations of behavioral and physiological effects of stress use physical or biochemical stressors that are not typically a part of human life. Unlike those stressors, the stress of social subordination has face validity in that it is a type, intensity, and duration of stressor that is frequently experienced in human society. In the experiment reported here the physiological and behavioral responses to chronic, long-term social stress, of relatively low intensity, were studied.

Previous studies of the behavioral and physiological characteristics of social status in nonhuman primates have concentrated on male macaques and baboons. Sapolsky observed that hypercortisolemia was characteristic of subordinate males in stable social status hierarchies, but not when unstable status relationships were examined (Sapolsky 1989, 1992). The hypercortisolemia observed in stable subordinates appeared to originate from a CNS defect, as these males were dexamethasone resistant and there were no rank-related differences in sensitivity to ACTH

(Sapolsky 1989). In contrast, Kaplan reported a hypercortisolemic response to an ACTH challenge test following dexamethasone suppression in adult female cynomolgus monkeys (Kaplan et al 1986). The findings reported here are consistent with this observation, and extend the findings of the earlier study. This is the first report of which we are aware that describes a comprehensive assessment of the relationships between social status, behavior, hypothalamic-pituitary-adrenal, and reproductive system dysfunction in female monkeys.

Previously, we have demonstrated that social status is an enduring characteristic of the individual that is expressed similarly in different social groups among female cynomolgus monkeys (Shively and Kaplan 1991). Since young female cynomolgus monkeys acquire their social status early in life and it tends to be stable, in the experiment reported here, initial social status may represent a longstanding behavioral characteristic of the individual, whereas current social status represents an experimentally manipulated state of social environmental stress. Among all the behavioral and physiological responses to social subordination stress described here, only three had a tendency to be influenced by initial social status. Initial social status may have interacted with current social status to influence baseline cortisol concentrations, and the proportion of menstrual cycles that were impaired; however, neither of these effects reached significance at the $p < 0.05$ level. Behavioral depression occurred most frequently among subordinate females that were initially of subordinate social status.

The non-random distribution of behavioral depression is of particular interest. The behavioral depression observed in this experiment was among monkeys that were still able to function in their group and so may be considered relatively mild. Females displaying behavioral depression had impaired suppression of cortisol concentrations in a dexamethasone suppression test. Likewise, patients with endogenous depression are frequently hyercortisolemic, and there is some evidence that treating the hypercortisolemia results in improvements in the depression (Pearson Murphy 1991; Peeters and Broekkamp 1994). These monkeys also spent more time in fearful vigilant scanning of their social environment than females without behavioral depression. This scanning was frequently accompanied by continuous lipsmacking and grimacing, two facial expressions implying fear and appeasement in this species. It may be that fearful vigilant scanning is a behavioral indicator of anxiety in response to a threatening social situation. This behavior may indicate that a degree of anxiety accompanied the mild depression in these monkeys.

Behavioral depression was expressed by only a subset of current subordinates (14 of 23) suggesting that certain individuals were susceptible to a depressive response to the social stress of subordination. Over 70% of the current subordinates that displayed behavioral depression were also initially subordinate. These data suggest that females with a history of social subordination are preferentially susceptible to a behavioral depression response to a currently socially stressful environment. Whether this preferential susceptibility to behavioral depression is influenced by genetic make up, early experience, or is an epigenetic phenomena remains to be determined; however, four current areas of research are instructive to consider in regard to this question. First, we have recently observed that subordinate female cynomolgus monkeys differ from dominants in their prolactin response to a fenfluramine challenge test. This observation suggests that central serotonergic systems are functioning differently in dominant and subordinate female monkeys (Shively et al 1995). Furthermore, recent studies suggest that mild maternal stress during gestation causes long-term alterations in postnatal behavioral development and HPA function of rhesus monkeys (Schneider 1992, Clarke et al 1994). Subordinate mothers are subject to more aggression than dominant mothers, and they are likely to produce female offspring that are also socially subordinate. In addition, the propensity for a depressive response to stress accompanied by alterations in HPA function is reminiscent of the long-term responses to stress that are observed in posttraumatic stress disorder (Charney et al 1993). Finally, it has been observed in women that the onset of depression and anxiety is often provoked by a severely threatening recent event, and that early adverse experiences also increase the risk of both depression and anxiety later in life (Brown et al 1993). These studies suggest that subsequent, long-term physiological and behavioral responses to stress may be canalized by previous experience.

The remainder of the behavioral and physiological responses to social stress were affected only by current social status, suggesting that for these endpoints, the extent of stress in the current social environment, irrespective of prior history, had the greatest impact.

Current subordinates had high baseline cortisol concentrations, were insensitive to negative feedback, and may have had adrenal hypersensitivity to ACTH. Hypersensitivity to ACTH has been previously observed in female cynomolgus monkeys (Kaplan et al 1986), and we have subsequently replicated this finding in another group of female monkeys (Shively in press). Taken together, these findings indicate that subordinates were hypercortisolemic, that their adrenal glands were hypersensitive to ACTH, and that they were dexamethasone resistant. Thus, it is likely that the tissues of these subordinates were chronically exposed to excess cortisol. The most profound malfunction was the insensitivity of the cortisol negative feedback loop, which indicates that the principal disturbance in the HPA axis was centrally mediated. It appears that these characteristics of HPA axis function are responsive to the current level of social stress, as they

were found in current subordinates, whether they had been dominant or subordinate in the past.

Current subordinates had suppressed reproductive function. Poor ovarian function has been observed in socially subordinate macaques previously; however, this is the first report of the effects of experimental manipulation of social status on ovarian function in macaques. Apparently when social status changes, ovarian function also changes. Thus, ovarian function is also acutely sensitive to the immediate social environment. The effect of social subordination on reproductive function has implications for other aspects of health. Female cynomolgus monkeys with poor ovarian function have exacerbated coronary artery atherosclerosis (Shively and Clarkson 1994), impaired coronary vasomotor responses to neuroendocrine challenge (Williams et al 1994), lower bone density (Shively et al 1991), and perturbations in serum biomarkers of bone metabolism (Register et al 1993). Poor ovarian function has obvious implications for infertility. The importance of the relationships between social stress-induced poor ovarian function and these disease processes is underscored by the relationships between estrogen deprivation and increased risk of coronary heart disease and osteoporosis in postmenopausal women. Less widely appreciated, however, are reports that among premenopausal women, stress may cause ovarian dysfunction (Matteo 1987), and that poor ovarian function is associated with increased risk of breast cancer (Whelan et al 1994), coronary heart disease (La Vecchia et al 1987), and loss of bone mass (Prior et al 1990). It is important to note that stress did not cause amenorrhea, but had deleterious effects on sex hormone concentrations. Women, too, may have ovarian dysfunction severe enough to cause infertility and still have regular menstrual cycles (Wu 1990). Thus, women who appear to have normal reproductive function based on the frequency of menses may still be at enhanced risk for the diseases noted above due to stress effects on sex hormones.

In the experiment reported here, current subordinates received more aggression, engaged in less affiliative behavior, and spent more time alone than dominants. While differences in rates of aggression and submission between dominants and subordinates have been widely reported and are well recognized, the increases in social isolation of subordinates implied by less time spent in affiliative behavior, and more time spent alone has not received attention. Social isolation is associated with depression as well as increased mortality in human beings, and with exacerbated coronary artery atherosclerosis in female cynomolgus monkeys (Shively et al 1989). It is intriguing that time spent alone correlates significantly with basal cortisol and mean peak luteal phase progesterone concentrations. Social isolation may be an important aspect of subordination stress. Furthermore, current subordinates spent more time in fearful vigilant scanning of the social environment than current dominants, apparently to avoid conflict with dominants. Fearful vigilant scanning may be a behavioral indicator of increased anxiety.

Taken together the results of this study suggest that the social stress of subordination causes hypothalamic-pituitary-adrenal and hypothalamic-pituitary-ovarian dysfunction in adult female cynomolgus monkeys. Furthermore, females with a history of social subordination are preferentially susceptible to a behavioral depression response to current subordination-induced stress. These behavioral and physiological responses of female cynomolgus monkeys to social stress suggest that they may be a useful model for further research into the relationship between social stress, depression, and their relationships with other disease processes.

This research was supported in part by grants HL-39789 and HL-14164 from the National Heart, Lung, and Blood Institute.

We are especially grateful for the critical review of this manuscript by Dr. Kathy Grant.

REFERENCES

Ahern DK, Gorkin L, Anderson JL, Tierney C, Hallstrom A, Ewart C, Capore RJ, Schron E, Kornfield D, Herd JA (1990): Biobehavioral variables and mortality or cardiac arrest in the Cardiac Arrhythmia Pilot Study (CAPS). *Am J Cardiol* 66:59−62.

Altmann J (1974): Observational study of behavior: Sampling methods. *Behaviour* 48:1−41.

Anisman H, Zackarko RM (1990): Multiple neurochemical and behavioral consequences of stesses: Implications for depression. *Pharmacol Ther* 46:119−136.

Berendsen HHG (1995): Interactions between 5-hydroxytryptamine receptor subtypes: Is a disturbed receptor balance contributing to the symptomatology of depression in humans? *Pharmacol Ther* 66:17−37.

Boulenger J-P, Lavallée Y-J (1993): Mixed anxiety and depression: Diagnostic issues. *J Clin Psychiatry* 54(1, suppl):3−8.

Breslau N, Davis GC (1986): Chronic stress and major depression. *Arch Gen Psychiatry* 43:309−314.

Brown AW, Gershon S (1993): Dopamine and depression. *J Neural Transm Gen Sect* 91:75−109.

Brown GW (1993): Life events and affective disorder: Replications and limitations. *Psychosom Med* 55:248−259.

Brown GW, Harris TO (1993): Aetiology of anxiety and depressive disorders in an inner-city population. 1. Early adversity. *Psychol Med* 23:143−154.

Brown GW, Harris TO, Eales MJ (1993): Aetiology of anxiety and depressive disorders in an inner-city population. 2. Comorbidity and adversity. *Psychol Med* 23:155−165.

Brown GW, Harris TO, Hepworth C (1994): Life events and endogenous depression. A puzzle reexamined. *Arch Gen Psychiatry* 51:523−534.

Brown GW, Harris TO, Hepworth C (1995): Loss, humiliation and entrapment among women developing depression: A patient and non-patient comparison. *Psychol med* 25:7−21.

Brown GW, Moran P (1994): Clinical and psychosocial origins of chronic depressive episodes. 1: A community survey. *Br J Psychiatry* 165:447−456.

Charney DS, Deutch AY, Krystal JH, Southwick SM, Davis M (1993): Psychobiologic mechanisms of posttraumatic stress disorder. *Arch Gen Psychiatry* 50:294−305.

Clarke AS, Wittwer AS, Abbott DH, Schneider ML (1994): Long-term effects of prenatal stress on HPA axis activity in juvenile rhesus monkeys. *Dev Psychobiol* 27:257–269.

Davidson J, Lipper S, Zung WWK, Strickland R, Krishman R, Mahorney S (1984): Validation of four definitions of melancholia by the dexamethasone suppression test. *Am J Psychiatry* 141:1220–1223.

Dukelow WR (1977): Ovulatory cycle characteristics in *Macaca fascicularis. J Med Primatol* 6:33–42.

Fombonne E (1994): Increased rates of depression: Update of epidemiological findings and analytical problems. *Acta Psyciatr Scand* 90:145–156.

Hirschfeld RMA (1994): Major depression, dysthymia and depressive personality disorder. *Br J Psychiatry* 165(suppl. 26):23–30.

Iny LJ, Pecknold J, Suranyi-Cadotte BE, Bernier B, Luthe L, Nair NPV, Meany MJ (1994): Studies of a neurochemical link between depression, anxiety, and stress from [3H]imipramine and [3H]paroxetine binding on human platelets. *Biol Psychiatry* 36:281–291.

Kalin NH, Carnes M (1984): Biological correlates of attachment bond disruption in humans and nonhuman primates. *Prog Neuropsychopharmacol Biol Psychiatry* 8:459–469.

Kaplan G (1985): Psychosocial aspects of chronic illness: Direct and indirect associations with ischemic heart disease mortality. In Kaplan R, Criqui M (eds), *Behavioral Epidemiology and Disease Prevention.* New York: Plenum, pp 237–269.

Kaplan JR, Adams MR, Koritnik DR, Rose JC, Manuck SB (1986): Adrenal responsiveness and social status in intact and ovariectomized *Macaca fascicularis. Am J Primatol* 11:181–193.

LaCroix AZ (1994): Psychosocial factors and risk of coronary heart disease in women: An epidemiologic perspective. *Fertil Steril* 62:133S–139S.

La Vecchia C, Descarli A, Franceschi S, Gentile A, Negri E, Parazzini F (1987): Menstrual and reproductive factors and the risk of myocardial infarction in women under fifty-five years of age. *Am J Obstet Gynecol* 157:1108–1112.

Mackenzie TB (1986): Lifetime prevalence of psychiatric disorders in women with perimenstrual difficulties. *J Affect Disord* 10:15–19.

Matteo S (1987): The effect of job stress and job interdependency on menstrual cycle length, regularity, and synchrony. *Psychoneuroendocrinology* 12:467–476.

Mossman D, Somoza E (1989). Maximizing diagnostic information from the dexamethasone suppression test. *Arch Gen Psychiatry* 46:653–660.

Pearson Murphy BE (1991): General Review. Steroids and depression. *J Steroid Biochem Mol Biol* 38:537–559.

Pearlstein TB (1995): Hormones and depression: What are the facts about premenstrual syndrome, menopause, and hormone replacement therapy? *Am J Obstet Gynecol* 173:646–653.

Peeters BW, Broekkamp CL (1994): Involvement of corticosteroids in the processing of stressful life-events. A possible implication for the development of depression. *J Steroid Biochem Mol Biol* 49:417–427.

Philipp M, Delmo CD, Buler R, Schwarze H, Winter P, Maier W, Benkert O (1992): Differentiation between major and minor depression. *Psychopharmacology* 106:S75–S78.

Prior JC, Vigna YM, Schecter MT, Burgess AE (1990): Spinal bone loss and ovulatory disturbances. *N Engl J Med* 323:1221–1227.

Register TC, Jerome CP, Jayo MJ, Shively CA (1993): Ovarian function and bone metabolism in cynomolgus macaques. *Am J Primatol* 30:344.

Richardson JS (1991): Animal models of depression reflect changing views on the essence and etiology of depressive disorders in humans. *Prog Neuropsychopharmacol Biol Psychiatry* 15:199–204.

Sade DS (1967): Determinants of dominance in a group of free-ranging rhesus monkeys. In S. Altmann (ed), *Social Communication Among Primates.* Chicago: University of Chicago Press, pp 99–114.

Sapolsky RM (1989): Hypercortisolism among socially subordinate wild baboons originates at the CNS level. *Arch Gen Psychiatry* 46:1047–1051.

Sapolsky RM (1992): Cortisol concentrations and the social significance of rank instability among wild baboons. *Psychoneuroendocrinology* 17:701–709.

Schneider ML (1992): Prenatal stress exposure alters postnatal behavioral expression under conditions of novelty challenge in rhesus monkey infants. *Dev Psychobiol* 25:529–540.

Schwartz S (1991): Women and depression: A Durkheimian perspective. *Soc Sci Med* 32:127–140.

Shively CA, Clarkson TB (1994): Social status and coronary artery atherosclerosis in female monkeys. *Arterioscler Thromb* 14:721–726.

Shively CA, Clarkson TB, Kaplan JR (1989): Social deprivation and coronary artery atherosclerosis in female cynomolgus monkeys. *Atherosclerosis* 77:69–76.

Shively CA, Kaplan JR (1991): Stability of social status rankings of female cynomolgus monkeys, of varying reproductive condition, in different social groups. *Am J Primatol* 23:239–245.

Shively CA, Fontenot MB, Kaplan JR (1995): Social status, behavior, and central serotonergic responsivity in female cynomolgus monkeys. *Am J Primatol* 37:333–339.

Shively C, Jayo MJ, Weaver DS, Kaplan JR (1991): Reduced vertebral bone mineral density in socially subordinate female cynomolgus macaques. *Am J Primatol* 24:135.

Shively CA, Kaplan JR, Adams MR (1986): Effects of ovariectomy, social instability and social status on female *Macaca fascicularis* social behavior. *Physiol Behav* 36:1147–1153.

Shively CA, Manuck SB, Kaplan JR, Koritnik DR (1990): Oral contraceptive administration, interfemale relationships, and sexual behavior in *Macaca fascicularis*. *Arch Sex Behav* 19:101–117.

Shively CA, Watson SL, Williams JK, Adams MR (in press): Social stress, reproductive hormones, and coronary heart disease risk in primates. In K. Orth-Gomer, M. Chesney, R. Wenger (eds), *Women, Stress and Heart Disease*, Hillsdale, NJ: Lawrence Erlbaum Associates.

Stahl SM (1993): Mixed anxiety and depresssion: Clinical implications. *J Clin Psychiatry* 54(1, suppl):33–38.

Sugiyama Y (1976): Life history of male Japanese monkeys. *Adv Stud Behav* 7:255–284.

Suomi SJ, Eisle CD, Grady SA, Harlow HF (1975): Depressive behavior in adult monkeys following separation from family enviornment. *J Abnorm Psychol* 84:576–578.

Vilhjalmsson R (1993): Life stress, social support and clinical depression: A reanalysis of the literature. *Soc Sci Med* 37:331–342.

Whelan EA, Sandler DP, Root JL, Smith KR, Weinberg CR (1994): Menstrual cycle patterns and risk of breast cancer. *Am J Epidemiol* 140:1081–1090.

Wilks JW, Hodgen GD, Ross GT (1979): Endocrine characteristics of ovulatory and anovulatory menstrual cycles in the rheus monkey. In Hafez ESE (ed): *Human Ovulation.* Amsterdam: Elsevier/North-Holland Biomedical Press, pp 205–218.

Williams JK, Shively CA, Clarkson TB (1994): Determinants of coronary artery reactivity in premenopausal female cynomolgus monkeys with diet-induced atherosclerosis. *Circulation* 90:983–987.

Wittchen H-U, Essau CA (1993): Comorbidity and mixed anxiety-depressive disorders: Is there epidemiologic evidence? *J Clin Psychiatry* 54(1, suppl):9–15.

Wu CH (1990): Ovulatory disorders and infertility in women with regular menstrual cycles. *Curr Opin Obstet Gynecol* 2:398–404.

Yen SSC (1991): The human menstrual cycle. In Yen SSC, Jaffe RB (eds), *Reproductive Endocrinology: Physiology, Pathophysiology and Clinical Management.* Philadelphia: WB Saunders Co, 1991, pp 278–308.

Yonkers KA, Chantillis SJ (1995): Recognition of depression in obstetric/gynecology practices. *Am J Obstet Gynecol* 173:632–638.

Thirty-Five

HYPERCORTISOLISM ASSOCIATED WITH SOCIAL SUBORDINANCE OR SOCIAL ISOLATION AMONG WILD BABOONS

Robert M. Sapolsky, Susan C. Alberts, and Jeanne Altmann

ABSTRACT

Background: The phenomena of basal hypercortisolism and dexamethasone resistance have long intrigued biological psychiatrists, and much is still unknown as to the causes and consequences of such adrenocortical hyperactivity in various neuropsychiatric disorders. We have analyzed basal cortisol concentrations and adrenocortical responsiveness to dexamethasone in a population of wild baboons living in a national park in Kenya. We tested whether social subordinance in a primate is associated with dexamethasone resistance. Furthermore, we examined whether individual differences in adrenocortical measurements were predicted by the extent of social affiliation in these animals.

Methods: Seventy yellow baboons (*Papio cynocephalus*) were anesthetized and injected with 5 mg of dexamethasone; the cortisol response was monitored for 6 hours. The animals were of both sexes in a range of ages and had known ranks in the dominance hierarchies within their troops. Extensive behavioral data were available for a subset of 12 adult males who were anesthetized under circumstances that also allowed for the determination of basal cortisol concentrations.

Results: The socially subordinate baboons were less responsive to dexamethasone than were the dominant ones; as one manifestation of this, postdexamethasone cortisol values were more than 3 times higher in the dozen lowest-ranking animals compared with the dozen highest. In addition, socially isolated males had elevated basal cortisol concentrations and showed a trend toward relative dexamethasone resistance.

Conclusions: Our findings indicate that social status and degree of social affiliation can influence adrenocortical profiles; specifically, social subordinance or social isolation were associated in our study with hypercortisolism or feedback resistance.

Originally published in *Archives of General Psychiatry*, 1997.

GLUCOCORTICOIDS, the adrenal steroids secreted in response to stress, are critical for the successful adaptation to acute physical stressors. However, hypersecretion of glucocorticoids can have deleterious effects on immune defenses, metabolism, reproductive physiology, tissue repair, and neurologic status.[1] As such, it is not surprising that there exists a complex array of neuroendocrine regulatory mechanisms to maintain glucocorticoid concentrations within a desirable range,[2] and the failure of such regulation in some neuropsychiatric conditions is worth examining.

Hypercortisolism (taking the form of basal hypersecretion of cortisol and/or manifestations of glucocorticoid feedback resistance) occurs in approximately half of the individuals with primary effective disorders.[3] In addition, hypercortisolism occurs in individuals with anorexia nervosa[4] and Alzheimer disease,[5-7] aging humans in general and those aging "unsuccessfully" in particular,[8-10] individuals of varying maladaptive coping styles,[10-12] and chronically stressed individuals.[13-15] Despite this wealth of correlations, it remains unsettled precisely what psychological traits or disease subtypes are most likely to give rise to hypercortisolism, what pathophysiologic consequences it might have, and what prognostic value it might serve.

A cornerstone of much basic research in biological psychiatry is that there is considerable homology in the psychobiology of human and nonhuman primates, allowing more confident generalizations between them than between humans and other species. To that end, one of us (R.M.S.) has studied the psychoendocrinology of a population of wild olive baboons (*Papio anubis*) living freely in a national reserve in East Africa. These studies produced indirect evidence for dexamethasone resistance in socially subordinate baboons in that subordinance was associated with basal hypsercortisolism,[16] which was, in turn, associated with dexamethasone resistance.[17] Moreover, an absence of social affiliation among dominant males was associated with basal hypercortisolism as well.[18,19] In this article, we expand on these findings in many ways. First, we examine these issues in a different species of baboon. Second, we test directly, for the first time, whether social subordinance in a primate is associated with dexamethasone resistance. Finally, we examine the relationship between adrenocortical end points and social affiliation in more behavioral detail and over the entire rank range.

SUBJECTS AND METHODS

BACKGROUND on baboon life histories and social organization research was conducted on yellow baboons (*Papio cynocephalus*) in Amboseli National Park, a semiarid savanna in southern Kenya, during 1989 and 1990. Baboons are among the largest, most sexually dimorphic, and most ground-dwelling monkeys. They live in semiclosed matrilocal social troops consisting of males and females of all ages. Baboons are omnivores that forage long distances daily. Detection of and protection from predators is such an important benefit of troop living for these animals that individual baboons make extreme efforts to remain with their troop, even shortly after parturition or when encumbered by illness or aging.

Like most anthropoid primates, female baboons stay in their troop of birth throughout their lives and, from about 6 years of age, produce a single infant per gestation at 1- to 2-year intervals. After a subadult period, from 6 to 8 years of age, most males leave their natal troop and, if successful, reproduce in 1 or a succession of other troops; immigration is mostly into nearby troops.[20] Under stable demographic conditions, animals older than 6 years usually constitute half of the 60 or so animals in a troop, and a few of each sex are usually older than 16 years.[21-23]

Subjects

W E studied adult and juvenile baboons in 3 social groups in and around Amboseli National Park.[24,25] This population has been under continuous, near daily, observation since 1971,[26-29] resulting in extensive information on demography, life history, reproductive behavior, and agonistic and affiliative interactions. The animals were individually recognized and habituated to observers. Two of the study groups (the Hook group and the Alto group) subsist entirely on wild foods; the third group (the Lodge group) partially forages at a garbage dump adjacent to a tourist lodge. The difference in food source affects time spent in various activities,[30,31] body size and composition,[32] and energy expenditure (but not intake) for adult females.[30,31]

For baboons born into the study groups, birth dates were known to within a few days.[33] For males who first appeared in the study groups as subadults or adults, birth-date estimates were made on the basis of patterns of physical growth, testicular enlargement, and on other physical characteristics, the scoring for which was developed by assessing known-age males and by observing aging patterns in long-term members of the population.[29]

Methods

Determination of Dominance Rank

The baboons in the study groups were assigned dominance ranks within their age-sex classes. Agonistic behaviors were recorded ad libitum as part of routine monitoring and were defined according to Hausfater.[34] Based on these interactions, the animals were assigned rank numbers according to the number of animals within their age-sex class with whom they lost agonistic encounters. Thus, for example, an adult female of rank 4 consistently lost encounters with just 3 adult females and won encounters with all other adult females. Rank relationships were virtually always linear. Rank relationships among adult females are usually stable over many years;[35] those of adult males and juveniles are age-dependent and change more often.[29, 36, 37]

Determination of Social Connectedness and Social Isolation

In addition to routine data collection on life history, demography, reproductive behavior, and dominance rank, detailed data about adult male social behavior were collected by one of us (S.C.A.) during the 2 months prior to darting for anesthetization. These data were collected as part of a larger multiyear study about adult male baboon social behavior and presented an opportunity to examine detailed social correlates of hypercortisolism for the subset who were successfully darted (n=12). A total of 40 hours of observational data were collected about these animals during 40-minute focal animal samples[38] between 8 AM and 4 PM, excluding noon. All affiliative and agonistic interactions, as well as the identity of interactant, were recorded. Data about the number of "neighbors" (other baboons within 3 m) were collected as instantaneous scan samples[38] every 2 minutes during the focal sample. Data were also collected on sexual consortships obtained by each male. Consortships are periods of close, persistent following and guarding of an adult estrous female and are the typical mating pattern for this species.

A set of 8 social measurements deemed to be representative of the entire spectrum of male social interactions was extracted from these data. These measurements included rates of affiliative interactions per hour with adult females and adult males, rates of agonistic interactions per hour with adult males and adult females, proportion of time spent in social proximity (ie, other baboons within 3 m of the subject), average number of baboons within 3 m (neighbors) during periods when the subject was not alone, number of reciprocal grooming relationships (in which the subject was the groomer as often as was groomed), and the proportion of available sexual consortships with adult females obtained by the subject. This was calculated as that male's proportion of the total hours of consortships in the group during that 2-month period.

For each male, a cumulative measurement of "social connectedness" was calculated as the subject's deviation from the median for each of these 8 behaviors:

$$S = \frac{\displaystyle\sum_{i=1}^{8} \frac{X_1}{\text{Median}_i}}{8}.$$

The result was an index for each subject of whether male was on average above or below the median value for social connectedness. Scores above 1 indicated males with more social interactions and a richer social environment than average; scores below 1 indicated males with a relative lack of social interaction.

Acquisition of Blood Samples

Plasma was obtained by anesthetizing subjects with 75 mg of tiletamine hydrochloride and 75 mg of zolazepam hydrochloride (Telazol) per animal (male weight range, 16–38 kg; female weight range, 10–24 kg) injected from a propelled syringe fired from a blowgun at 10 m. No pregnant females beyond the first trimester was darted. Time constraints made it impossible to dart all of the baboons in the study groups. We attempted to maximize the representation of adults in the sample, but it was impossible to be selective while darting; instead, we darted opportunistically, anesthetizing the animals only when their backs were turned, to preclude anticipatory stress, and when the attention of other group members was elsewhere. Thus, the sample represents most of the adult males, many of the nonpregnant adult females, and a smaller representation of juveniles. The Lodge group is most

heavily represented because they were the largest, most accessible group. All subjects were darted between 7:30 AM and 10:30 AM during the summers of 1989 and 1990 to control for seasonal and circadian hormone fluctuations. Blood samples were obtained at the earliest opportunity after the baboons became unconscious, which was within 12 minutes. The subjects were kept anesthetized throughout the procedure. Reanesthetization was carried out when movement and muscle tension precluded obtaining a blood sample or the animal resting safely. This typically resulted in redosing with 25 mg of tiletamine hydrochloride approximately every 2 hours until the completion of the experiment, at 7 hours. Subjects recovered in a cage near their group and were released when fully conscious the next morning. The animals did not lose habituation to observers or experience difficulty in rejoining the groups. There was no relationship between basal cortisol concentrations and the time of day of darting (r=0.06, P=.75), precluding the possibility of a circadian confound (eg, that less socially affiliated baboons were easier to dart and, thus, were sampled closer to the circadian peak).

Dexamethasone Suppression Test

A second blood sample was obtained 1 hour after the initial darting. Immediately following that, 5 mg of dexamethasone (Decadron phosphate) was administered to the animals intramuscularly and subsequent samples were obtained 3 and 6 hours later (4 and 7 hours postdarting). Thus, this protocol differs from the classic dexamethasone suppression test.[39] First, of necessity, the animals had to be anesthetized throughout. Second, the 7-hour postdarting sample represented the latest time point at which samples could be obtained for the animals to still safely recover by the next morning; thus, the lengthy postdexamethasone follow-up done in the typical dexamethasone suppression test could not be carried out. Finally, an extremely large concentration of dexamethasone was used (approximately 15-fold higher on a body weight basis than in the standard 1-mg human protocol); this was to induce feedback suppression of the adrenocortical axis within the limited time available for monitoring the animals. This protocol was suppressive within this period in a previous study with wild baboons.[17] This modified dexamethasone suppression test was carried out on 70 animals.

Assay of Cortisol Concentrations

Samples were centrifuged on site and plasma was frozen in dry ice until they were returned to the United States. Cortisol concentrations were determined by radioimmunoassay[28] with an antibody with less than 0.1% cross-reactivity with dexamethasone (antibody F21−53, Endocrine Sciences, Tarzana, Calif). Intra-assay and inter-assay coefficients of variation were 0.07 and 0.11, respectively.

STATISTICAL ANALYSIS

IN our studies correlating basal cortisol concentrations with a number of behavioral measurements, baboons were excluded from analysis if the initial "basal" sample was collected more than 15 minutes after darting. This was because our prior studies with chair-restrained, catheterized baboons[16] indicated that cortisol concentrations had probably elevated markedly in those samples from true basal values.

Statistical procedures were performed using a statistical software package (JMP 3.0, SAS, Cary, NC).[40] For initial analyses, data were pooled across social groups. Among these baboons, garbage feeding was associated with markedly higher rates of aggression,[41] probably associated with intense competition for a highly localized food resource. Thus, we also analyzed data as a function of membership in the wild-feeding group vs the higher aggression, garbage-feeding group. Descriptive statistics were obtained for cortisol concentrations at darting

and at 1, 4, and 7 hours after darting. A single classification analysis of variance was used to determine whether cortisol concentrations changed significantly over time. Simple linear regressions were employed to examine the effects of social connectedness on basal cortisol concentrations and on dexamethasone responsiveness, which is defined as the circulating cortisol concentrations 6 hours after dexamethasone administration. Previous work on this population has shown that the incidence of hypercortisolism increases with age.[28] Therefore, multiple regressions were employed to examine the effects of social rank and age on basal cortisol concentrations and on dexamethasone responsiveness.

RESULTS

SIX hours of dexamethasone exposure caused a significant decline in cortisol concentrations ($F[3, 235] =4.8$, $P<.01$) (**Table 1**). Such dexamethasone responsiveness occurred in both sexes and both feeding conditions (Table 1). This seemed to represent a true suppression by dexamethasone, rather than the normal circadian decline in concentrations that occurs at that time of day or the inhibitory effects of the benzodiazepine zolazepam contained in the anesthetic. As evidence, under identical darting and anesthetization conditions without dexamethasone, cortisol concentrations increased to 860 ± 60 nmol/L (mean ± SEM) in wild baboons by the 6-hour mark.[42]

Basal cortisol concentrations were not predicted by dominance rank; however, social connectedness was a strong predictor of such concentrations. Specifically, for the 12 males from whom we had data on social connectedness as well as basal cortisol concentrations, socially isolated males had significantly higher basal concentrations than males that were well-connected socially (R^2=0.50, P=.01, n=12) (**Figure 1**). Age did not contribute to the variance in basal cortisol concentrations when it was included in a multiple regression with social connectedness (R^2

Table 1

Cortisol Concentrations After Darting With Anesthesia and After Administration of Dexamethasone*

Time, h†	All Subjects (N=33-70)	Wild Diet		High Aggression‡	
		Female (n=24-28)	Male (n=9-14)	Female (n=8)	Male (n=9-10)
1	500±40	440±80	80±110	470±80	410±110
4	360±30	360±60	390±80	330±60	410±60
7	300±30	300±80	330±110	330±60	250±80

* Data are expressed as nanomoles per liter (±SEM). Sample size varied because of the exigencies of field conditions (ie, it might be impossible to obtain a correctly timed sample on an animal if a second animal had been darted and was being tracked in the bush).

† Time indicates hours after darting and anesthesia. Dexamethasone was administered immediately after the 1-hour sample.

‡ High aggression indicates the garbage-feeding group.

[adjusted]=0.39, P=.04, n=12). This is a somewhat weaker regression than the linear regression of basal cortisol concentrations on social connectedness alone.

Dexamethasone responsiveness declines with age in this population of baboons.[28] A multiple regression revealed that social rank as well as age predicted dexamethasone responsiveness (R^2 [adjusted]=0.15, P=.002; partial F for social rank=6.00, P=.017; partial F for age=7.01, P=.01) (**Figure 2**). Specifically, the more socially subordinate an individual baboon, the higher its cortisol concentrations 6 hours after dexamethasone administration. As one manifestation of this, cortisol concentrations were more than 3 times higher in the dozen lowest-ranking animals compared with the dozen highest. This relative dexamethasone resistance occurred in subordinate animals on both feeding conditions, with the effect being stronger for animals from the high-aggression, garbage-feeding group and for those animals when divided by sex (**Figure 2**). The relative dexamethasone resistance among subordinate animals probably does not reflect the stress of nutritional deprivation; as evidence, so-

cially subordinate adult females do not weigh less than their high-ranking counterparts (r=-0.12, P=.68).

For the 12 males for whom we had data about social connectedness, dexamethasone responsiveness showed a nonsignificant tendency to decline with increasing social isolation. Males below the median for social connectedness had postdexamethasone cortisol concentrations 2-fold higher than males above the median for social connectedness (650±210 nmol/L vs 300±210 nmol/L: P<.20, unpaired t test). There was no correlation between rank and social connectedness (r=-0.24, P=.44).

COMMENT

IN our study, we observed that social subordinance and social isolation are associated with manifestations of hypercortisolism in wild baboons. Specifically, socially subordinate animals were less responsive to dexamethasone than were dominant animals; to our knowledge, this is the first explicit demonstration of this with a social primate. Moreover, socially isolated males

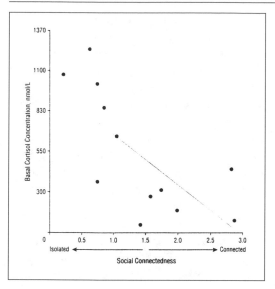

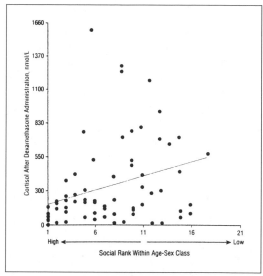

Figure 1

Basal cortisol concentrations were predicted by social connectedness for adult males (R^2=0.50. P=.01, n= 12). Each dot represents the value for 1 baboon. Social connectedness is an index of the extent to which males score high (connected) or low (isolated) on 8 social measurements; measurements of social connectedness were available for 12 males.

Figure 2

Dexamethasone resistance (circulating cortisol 6 hours after dexamethasone administration) was predicted by social rank. Each dot represents the value for 1 baboon. Because previous work on this population had shown that the incidence of dexamethasone resistance increases with age, we included age and social rank in a multiple regression analysis of dexamethasone resistance (R^2 [adjusted]=0.15, P =.002, n=70) (Table 2). The fitted line in the Figure corresponds to a simple linear regression of dexamethasone resistance on social rank (R^2=0.09, P=.011, n=70).

had elevated basal cortisol concentrations and a trend toward relative dexamethasone resistance.

The linking of dexamethasone resistance with social subordinance coincides with knowledge about the effects of chronic stress on glucocorticoid secretion. In the adrenocortical axis, elevated circulating glucocorticoid concentrations exert a negative feedback effect, inhibiting subsequent secretion.[2] Repeated stressors can cause glucocorticoid feedback resistance in rodents,[43-45] primates,[46,47] and humans.[13-15] Moreover, the onset of affective disorders involving dexamethasone resistance is often preceded by major stressors.[48] In stable dominance hierarchies among baboons (as were the ones studied),

subordinance is associated with far more stressors than is dominance (a situation that is quite different in unstable, shifting hierarchies). Dominant animals have the lowest rates of aggression, are rarely challenged by subordinates, and have highly predictable control over resources and sources of social support. In contrast, subordiante animals have the highest rate of losses in agonistic interactions, have reduced feeding efficiency (at least partly because of the interference by high-ranking males[49,50]), and re-

Table 2

Results of Multiple Regressions of Dexamethasone Responsiveness on Age and on Social Rank Within Age-Sex Class

Conditions	No. of Subjects	R^2 (Adjusted)	P
All conditions pooled	70	0.15	.002
High-aggression garbage feeders			
Sexes pooled	28	0.34	.002
Females only	10	0.72	.005
Males only	18	0.29	.03
Wild feeders			
Sexes pooled	42	0.11	.04
Females only	14	0.01	.38
Males only	28	0.11	.09

duced access to favored resources.[49,51-53] They are also subject to the highest rates of displaced aggression and disruption of social grooming; the stressfulness of such unpredictable events is well documented.[54] The social rank-dexamethasone responsiveness link was particularly strong in the group that had higher rates of aggression than in the other 2 groups.[33] This aggressiveness is most likely owing to that group's subsisting on garbage, which entails intense competition for localized food resources, an association long recognized in troop-living primates.[55,56]

Dominance systems among yellow baboons differ by sex. Male social rank changes frequently as males age and migrate between groups, which they do periodically.[29,37] In contrast, females remain in their natal group throughout their lifetime and inherit dominance rank from their mothers.[36] The linking of dexamethasone resistance to social subordinance in these 2 different dominance systems as well as to 2 distinct feeding conditions suggests it is a rather robust association.

Our study offers no data regarding the neuroendocrine mechanisms of hypercortisolism or dexamethasone resistance; however, some laboratory data are relevant. Sustained or repeated stress can down-regulate (decrease) glucocorticoid receptor numbers and levels of receptor messenger RNA in rodents[57-59] and primates.[60] This is particularly pronounced in the hippocampus. This structure, in turn, helps mediate glucocorticoid feedback regulation, inhibiting subsequent glucocorticoid secretion.[61] Down-regulatory loss of hippocampal glucocorticoid receptors weakens such feedback regulation, producing feedback resistance.[62] These data, derived primarily from rodents, may apply to primates in that dexamethasone resistance, depletion of glucocorticoid receptors in the hippocampus, and a history of social instability have been linked in macaque monkeys.[47] In that context, it was surprising that the feedback resistance of the subordinate animals did not also involve basal hypercortisolism, a feature seen among subordinate animals in many, but not all, social species and populations (including the closely related olive baboon[63]). However, basal hypercortisolism and dexamethasone resistance can dissociate in human depressives.[3]

We observed that social isolation was also associated with hypercortisolism, manifesting itself as elevated basal cortisol secretion and a trend toward dexamethasone resistance. In a previous study with a wild population of closely related olive baboons (*P anubis*), we observed that among dominant males, those with the lowest rates of grooming with females and social interactions with infants had markedly elevated basal cortisol concentrations[18,19]; the present data show the link between social isolation and hypercortisolism in greater behavioral detail. These studies cannot reveal whether there is any causality in this link (ie, if hypercortisolemia makes animals less socially affiliated or if social isolation stimulates adrenocortical secretion). However, studies with rodents and captive primates demonstrate the power of social proximity or affiliation to blunt the adrenocortical response to various stressors,[54] suggesting that these baboons are hypercortisolemic because they lack the stress-reducing advantages of social affiliation. This notion is supported by studies on the role played by dominance interactions and social affiliation in reducing social tension and maintaining cohesion in the social group.[64]

This association echoes the classic finding in behavioral medicine that social isolation represents a highly notable mortality risk factor across a wide range of maladies in humans[65] (although the effects of social isolation on adrenocortial profiles have not, to our knowledge, been studied systematically in humans). A key finding in those studies was that no particular form of social affiliation (a spouse, a close friend, or strong involvement in a community group) was more protective than the others, but that the association instead emerged from the aggregate of social connections of an individual baboon. Similarly, we did not observe any single 1 of the 8 measurements of social connectedness to predict adrenocortical status; instead, it was their aggregate that was highly predictive.

CONCLUSIONS

THE challenge remains in biological psychiatry to understand the causes and consequences of hypercortisolism. Classic studies of the parents of children with cancer demonstrated that the adrenocortical axis responds to external stressors (such as the illness) and internal coping styles.[11] Our study repeats this theme in showing the relevance of the external factor of rank and an individual's affiliative style. When coupled with other studies showing adrenocortical correlates of personality styles in nonhuman primates,[18,19,66] our findings emphasize the relevance of such studies to understanding the behavioral biology of humans as well as the subtle complexity of these animals in their own right.

This study was supported by the Harry Frank Guggenheim Foundation (Dr Sapolsky) and the Chicago Zoological Society, Chicago, Ill (Dr Altmann).

We thank the Office of the President, Republic of Kenya; the Kenya Wildlife Services, its Amboseli staff and wardens, and its director at the time of this study, Richard Leakey; the Institute of Primate Research, Karen, Nairobi, Kenya, its staff, its director, M. Isahakia, and former director, J. Else, for permits, sponsorship and assistance.

We also thank Stuart Altmann, PhD, David Chai, DVM, Robert Eley, PhD, Richard Kones, Phillip Muruthi, PhD, Raphael Mututua, Graham Reid, DVM, Serah Saiyallel, Kathy Snyder, BA, Lisa Share, PhD, Jonathan Somen, BA, and Mbaruk Suleman, DVM, for their assistance with the field work, and Deborah Hargrove, for assistance with data tabulation, and entry.

REFERENCES

1. Munck A, Guyre P, Holbrook N. Physiological functions of glucocorticoids during stress and their relation to pharamacological actions. *Endocr Rev.* 1984;5:25−51.

2. Dallman M, Akana S, Cascio C, Darlington D, Jacobson L, Levin N. Regulation of ACTH secretion: variations on a theme of B. *Recent Prog Horm Res.* 1987;43:113−141.

3. American Psychiatric Association Taskforce on Laboratory Tests in Psychiatry. The dexamethasone suppression test: an overview of its current status in psychiatry. *Am J Psychiatry.* 1987;144:1253−1278.

4. Newman M, Halmi K. The endocrinology of anorexia nervosa and bulimia nervosa. *Endocrinol Metab Clin North Am.* 1988; 17:195-212.

5. Greenwald B, Mathe A, Mohs R, Levy M, Johns C, Davis K. Cortisol in Alzheimer's disease. II: dexamethasone suppression, dementia severity and affective symptoms. *Am J Psychiatry.* 1986;143:442-450.

6. Hatzinger M, Z'Brun A, Hemmeter U, Seifritz E, Baumann F, Holsboer-Trachsler E, Heuser I. HPA system function in patients with Alzheimer's disease. *Neurobiol Aging.* 1995;16:205. Abstract.

7. Krishnan K, Heyman A, Ritchie J, Utley C, Dawdon D, Rogers H. Depression in early onset Alzheimer's disease: clinical and neuroendocrine correlates. *Biol Psychiatry.* 1988:24:937−942.

8. Sapolsky R. The adrenocortical axis. Schneider E, Rowe J. *Handbook of the Biology of Aging.* 3rd edition. New York, NY. Academic Press Inc. 1990:330–348.

9. Lupien S, Lecours A, Lussier I, Schwartz G, Nair N, Meaney M. Basal cortisol levels and cognitive deficits in human aging. *J Neurosci.* 1994; 14:2893–2903.

10. Seeman T, Berkman L, Blazer D, Rowe J. Social ties and support and neuroendocrine function: the MacArthur studies of successful aging. *Ann Behav Med.* 1994;16:95–106.

11. Wolff C, Friedman S, Hofer M, Mason J. Relationship between psychological defenses and mean urinary 17-hydroxycorticosteroid excretion rates. *Psychosom Med.* 1964;26:576–588.

12. Brown L, Tomarken A, Orth D, Loosen P. Individual differences in repressive-defensiveness predict basal salivary cortisol levels. *J Pers Social Psychol.* 1996;70:362–369.

13. Baumgartner A, Graf K, Kurten I. The dexamethasone suppression test in depression, schizophrenia and during experimental stress. *Biol Psychiatry.* 1985;20:675–682.

14. Ceulemans D, Westenberg H, van Praag H. The effect of stress on the dexamethasone suppression test. *Psychiatry Res.* 1985;14:189–197.

15. Reincke M, Allolio B, Wurth G, Winkelmann W. The HPA axis in critical illness: response to dexamethasone and CRH. *J Clin Endocrinal Metab.* 1993;77:151–158.

16. Sapolsky R. The endocrine stress-response and social status in the wild baboon. *Horm Behav.* 1982;15:279–284.

17. Sapolsky R. Individual differences in cortisol secretory patterns in the wild baboon: role of negative feedback sensitivity. *Endocrinology.* 1983;113:2263–2269.

18. Sapolsky R, Ray J. Styles of dominance and their endocrine correlates among wild olive baboons *(Papio anubis). Am J Primatol.* 1989;18:1–13.

19. Ray J, Sapolsky R. Styles of male social behavior and their endocrine correlates among high-ranking wild baboons. *Am J Primatol.* 1992;28:231–250.

20. Samuels A, Altmann J. Baboons of the Amboseli basin: demographic stability and change. *Int J Primatol.* 1991; 12:1–19.

21. Altmann S, Altmann J. Demographic constraints on behavior and social organization. In: Berstein I, Smith E. *Primate Ecology and Human Origins.* New York, NY: Garland Press; 1979:31–47.

22. Strum S, Western J. Variations in fecundity with age and environment in olive baboons *(Papio anubis). Am J Primatol.* 1982;3:61–76.

23. Altmann J, Hausfater G, Altmann S. Demography of Amboseli baboons: 1963–1983. *Am J Primatol.* 1985;8:113–125.

24. Altmann S, Altmann J. *Baboon Ecology.* Chicago, Ill: University of Chicago Press; 1970.

25. Western D, van Praet C. Cyclical changes in the habitat and climate of an East African ecosystem. *Nature.* 1973;241:104–106.

26. Altmann J, Altmann S, Hausfater G, McCuskey S. Life histories of yellow baboons: physical development, reproductive parameters, and infant mortality. *Primates.* 1977;18:315–330.

27. Altmann J, Altmann S, Hausfater G. Physical maturation and age estimates of yellow baboons. *Papio cynocephalus,* in Amboseli National Park, Kenya. *Am J Primatol.* 1981;1:389–399.

28. Sapolsky R, Altmann J. Incidence of hypercortisolism and dexamethasone resistance increases with age among wild baboons. *Biol Psychiatry.* 1991;30:1008–1016.

29. Alberts S, Altmann J. Balancing costs and opportunities: dispersal in male baboons. *Am Nature.* 1995;145:279–306.

30. Altmann J, Muruthi P. Differences in daily life between semi-provisioned and wild-feeding baboons. *Am J Primatol.* 1988;15:213–221.

31. Muruthi P, Altmann J, Atlmann S. Resource base, parity, and reproductive condition affect females' feeding time and nutrient intake within and between groups of a baboon population. *Oecologia.* 1991;87:467–472.

32. Altmann J, Schoeller D, Altmann S, Muruthi P, Sapolsky R. Body size and fatness of free-living baboons reflect food availability and activity levels. *Am J Primatol.* 1993;30:149–161.

33. Altmann J. *Baboon Mothers and Infants.* Cambridge, Mass: Harvard University Press; 1980.

34. Hausfater G. *Dominance and Reproduction in Baboons* (Papio cynocephalus). Basel, Switzerland: Karger; 1975.

35. Hausfater G, Altmann J, Altmann S. Long-term consistency of dominance relations among female baboons *(Papio cynocephalus). Science.* 1982;217:752–755.

36. Packer C. Male dominance and reproductive activity in *Papio anubis. Anim Behav.* 1979;27:37–45.

37. Pereira M. Agonistic interactions of juvenile savanna baboons. I: fundamental features. *Ethology.* 1988;79:195–217.

38. Altmann J. Observational study of behavior: sampling methods. *Behaviour.* 1974;48:1–27.

39. Carroll B. The dexamethasone suppression test for melancholia. *Br J Psychiatry.* 1982;140:292–304.

40. SAS Institute. In: *JMP: Statistics for the Apple Macintosh From SAS Institute Inc.* Cary, NC: SAS Institute Inc; 1994.

41. Muruthi P. *Food Intake and Energy Expenditure in Savannah Baboons.* University of Nairobi; 1989. Thesis.

42. Sapolsky R. Stress-induced suppression of testicular function in the wild baboon: role of glucocorticoids. *Endocrinology.* 1985;116:2273–2278.

43. Vernikos J, Daolman M, Bonner C, Katzen A, Shinsako J. Pituitary-adrenal function in rats chronically exposed to cold. *Endocrinology.* 1982;110:413–421.

44. Young E, Akana S, Dallman M. Decreased sensitivity to glucocorticoid fast feedback in chronically stressed rats. *Neuroendocrinology.* 1990;51:536–542.

45. Bhatnager S, Viau V, Meaney M. HPA responses to acute restraint stress following chronic exposure to cold in handled and nonhandled rats. *Soc Neurosci Abstr.* 1991;17:621–623.

46. Kalin N, Cohen R, Kraemer G, Risch S, Shelton S, Cohen, McKinney W, Murphy D. The dexamethasone suppression test as a measure of hypothalamic-pituitary feedback sensitivity and its relationship to behavioral arousal. *Neuroendocrinology.* 1981;32:92–95.

47. Brooke S, de Haas-Johnson A, Kaplan J, Manuck S, Sapolsky R. Dexamethasone resistance among nonhuman primates associated with a selective decrease of glucocorticoid receptors in the hippocampus and a history of social instability. *Neuroendocrinology.* 1994;60:134–140.

48. Post R. Transduction of psychosocial stress into the neurobiology of recurrent affective disorder. *Am J Psychiatry.* 1992;149:999–1010.

49. Dittus W. The social regulation of population density and age-sex distribution in the toque monkey. *Behaviour.* 1977;63:281–322.

50. Post D, Hausftaer G, McCuskey S. Feeding behavior of yellow baboons (*Papio cynocephalus*): relationship to age, gender and dominance rank. *Folia Primatol (Basel).* 1980;34:170–195.

51. Wrangham R. Drinking competition in vervet monkeys. *Anim Behav.* 1981;29:904–910.

52. Wrangham R, Waterman P. Feedilng behaviour of vervet monkeys on *A. tortilis* and *A. xanthophloea* with special reference to reproductive strategies and tannin production. *J Anim Ecol.* 1981;50:715–731.

53. Whitten P. Diet and dominance among female vervet monkeys (*Cercopithecus aethiops.*) *Am J Primatol.* 1983;5:139–159.

54. Levine S, Wiener S, Coe C. The psychoneuroendocrinology of stress: a psychobiological perspective. In: Levine S, Brush F. *Psychoendocrinology.* New York, NY: Academic Press Inc: 1989.

55. Southwick C. An experimental study of intragroup agonistic behavior in rhesus monkeys. *Behaviour.* 1967;28:182–209.

56. Belzung D, Anderson J. Social, rank and responses to feeding competition in rhesus monkeys. *Behav Processes.* 1986;12:307–316.

57. Sapolsky R, Krey L, McEwen B. Stress downregulates corticosterone receptors in a site-specific manner in the brain. *Endocrinology.* 1984;114:287–295.

58. Herman J, Adams D, Prewitt C. Regulatory changes in the neuroendocrine stress-integrative circuitry produced by a variable stress paradigm. *Neuroendocrinology.* 1995;61:180–190.

59. Makino S, Smith M, Gold P. Increased expression of CRH and vasopressin mRNA in the hypothalamic paraventricular nucleus during repeated stress: association with reduction in glucocorticoid receptor mRNA levels. *Endocrinology.* 1995;136:3299–3307.

60. Johren O, Flugge G, Fuchs E. Hippocampal glucocorticoid receptor expression in the tree shrew: regulation by psychosocial conflict. *Cell Mol Neurobiol.* 1994;14:281–288.

61. Jacobson L, Sapolsky R. The role of the hippocampus in feedback regulation of the hypothalamic-pituitary-adrenocortical axis. *Endocrine Rev.* 1992;12:118–140.

62. Sapolsky R, Krey L, McEwen B. Glucocorticoid-sensitive hippocampal neurons are involved in terminating

the adrenocortical stress response. *Proc Natl Acad Sci U S A.* 1984;81:6174–6179.

63. Sapolsky R. Endocrinology alfresco: psychoendocrine studies of wild baboons. *Recent Prog Horm Res.* 1993;48:437–465.

64. de Waal F. The integration of dominance and social bonding in primates. *Q Rev Biol.* 1986;61:459–479.

65. House J, Landis K, Umberson D. Social relationships and health. *Science.* 1988;241:540–546.

66. Virgin C, Sapolsky R. Styles of male social behavior and their endocrine correlates among low-ranking baboons. *Am J Primatol.* In press.

☙

Thirty-Six

ATTENUATED CORTISOL RESPONSE TO A STANDARDIZED STRESS TEST IN LITHUANIAN VS. SWEDISH MEN: THE LiVICORDIA STUDY

Margareta Kristenson, Kristina Orth-Gomér,
Zita Kucinskienë, Björn Bergdahl,
Henrikas Calkauskas, Irena Balinkyniene,
and Anders G. Olsson

Abstract

CARDIOVASCULAR mortality rates of middle aged men are four times higher in Lithuania than in Sweden. The difference is not explained by standard risk factors, but our previous findings of pronounced psychosocial stress in Lithuanian men offer a possible explanation.

We investigated cortisol and cardiovascular reactivity to a standardised laboratory stress test in population based random samples of 50-year-old men from Vilnius, Lithuania and Linköping, Sweden.

Repeated measures analysis of variance showed that cortisol responses differed between cities (p's<0.001). Mean change of serum cortisol from baseline to 30 minutes was 18.1 and 88.4 nmol/l for Vilnius and Linköping men, respectively (p<0.001). In a multivariate analysis, a low peak cortisol response was significantly related to high baseline cortisol, current smoking and to vital exhaustion.

The findings suggest a physiological mechanism of chronic psychosocial stress, which may contribute to increased risk for cardiovascular death.

Introduction

THE importance of stress in the development of disease has long been recognised.[1] A main area where psychosocial factors and stress can predict morbidity and mortality is coronary heart disease (CHD).[2,3] CHD mortality has increased dramatically in Eastern and Central Europe during recent decades, while it has decreased in Western Europe.[4-6] In 1994 the CHD mortality for 50–54-year-old men was more than four times higher in Lithuania than in

Originally published in *International Journal of Behavioral Medicine*, 1998.

Sweden (436 vs 100 per 100 000, national statistics). Earlier studies[7,8] have failed to show differences in traditional risk factors which could explain these trends. The LiVicordia study (Linköping-Vilnius-coronary-risk-assessment study) is a cross-sectional study, designed to find possible new explanations. Small differences in traditional risk factors were found; blood pressure was higher in Vilnius men, cholesterol levels higher in Linköping men and smoking similar.[9] Psychosocial strain due to the political and socio-economic situation in Eastern Europe has been suggested as a possible causal factor.[6,10] We found consistent differences in psychosocial risk factors for CHD between the two groups. Vilnius men were characterised by higher job strain, lower social support, and higher vital exhaustion.[11]

Several studies have shown that psychosocial strain affects cardiovascular, immunological and neuroendocrine parameters.[12-15] Laboratory stress tests have been developed to study cardiovascular and hormonal responsiveness by which psychosocial strain may lead to CHD.[16,17] Regarding hormones, the response along the hypothalamo-pituitary-adreno-cortical axis (HPA-axis) has evoked special interest. Cortisol secretion, originally characterised as a non-specific response to any stressor,[1] is now seen as specific to situations described as unpleasant, threatening or involving elements of helplessness or loss of control.[17] The importance of an interaction between chronic stress and responsiveness to acute stressors has also been pointed out.[18,19]

The aim of this part of the study was to investigate cardiovascular and cortisol responses to acute stressors in two study groups representing populations with a marked difference in CHD mortality.

METHODS

Subjects and Study Design

The cross-sectional LiVicordia study compared randomly selected 50-year-old men from Vilnius, Lithuania and Linköping, Sweden between October 1993 and May 1994.[9] The experimental set-up was thoroughly standardized between and within the two centres. Exclusion criteria were serious acute or chronic diseases.[9] For the stress test additional exclusion criteria were systolic blood pressure (SBP) >180 mm Hg and/or diastolic blood pressure (DBP) > 105 mm Hg, acute myocardial infarction or stroke less than 3 months ago, unstable angina pectoris and insulin treated diabetes. Response rate in the full study was 83 percent in both cities. In the stress test 89 men in Linköping and 94 in Vilnius were included. Reasons for exclusion are given in Table 1, and general characteristics of the groups in Table 2.

Procedures

The investigation rooms in Linköping and Vilnius were decorated with the same picture (spring landscape). Room temperature was kept at 20°C. Only the two researchers were in the room together with the volunteer. The researchers had a neutral attitude; apart from instructions, silence was maintained at all times. The participants came to the hospitals on a fasting stomach, after a night's sleep. Prescribed drugs were taken before the test. Half of the stress tests

---

Table 1

Reasons for excluding volunteers from stress test

	Vilnius	Linköping
Included total	109	101
SBP>180 and/or DBP>105	11	5
Angina pectoris	0	2
Insulin treated diabetes	0	1
Refused	2	2
Fainted during session*	2	2
Included in stress test	94	89

*One volunteer fainted during cold pressor session in Sweden, the others fainted during blood sampling.

Table 2

Characteristics of Vilnius and Linköping men included in the stress test (means ± SEM);
SEM = standard error of the mean; SBP = systolic blood pressure; DBP = diastolic blood pressure;
HDL = high density lipoprotein; LDL = low density lipoprotein

	Vilnius n=94	Linköping n=89	p
Body mass index, kg/m2	26.8 ± 0.3	25.3 ± 0.4	< 0.01
Sagittal diameter, cm	21.1 ± 0.3	21.1 ± 0.3	0.99
SBP, mm Hg	136 ± 2	130 ± 2	< 0.05
DBP, mm Hg	86 ± 1	85 ± 1	0.60
Heart rate, beats/minute	64 ± 1	62 ± 1	0.12
Current smokers % (n)	36 (34)	27 (24)	0.15*
Total cholesterol, mmol/l	5.07 ± 0.10	5.51 ± 0.11	< 0.01
Triglycerides, mmol/l	1.48 ± 0.15	1.56 ± 0.13	0.71
HDL cholesterol, mmol/l	1.15 ± 0.03	1.13 ± 0.03	0.58
LDL cholesterol, mmol/l	3.25 ± 0.09	3.68 ± 0.11	< 0.01
ß-blocker for hypertension % (n)	0 (0)	7 (6)	0.012#
Use of tranquilizers % (n)	2 (2)	2 (2)	not calculated
Vital exhaustion (scale score range 19–57)	33.8 ± 0.6	29.6 ± 0.8	< 0.001

* p-value calculated using Chi-square test, # p-value according to Fishers exact test, all other p-values are according to Student's t-test.

started at 7:30 AM, half at 9:30 AM, usually on a Monday or a Tuesday. During the initial 45 minutes, the participants rested. They lay down on a bed reclining comfortably. During the stress test, SBP, DBP and HR were measured by an OM-RON ®Auto-Inflation digital sphygmomanometer (model HEM-703-C, Tokyo, Japan), calibrated against a mercury manometer and given accurate measures. The participant was instructed to relax.[20] SBP, DBP and HR were recorded every second minute for 10 minutes. The average of the last two measurements was defined as the baseline value (Figure 1). The difference between these two measure of SBP was less than 5 mm Hg in 72 and 79 percent of the subjects in Vilnius and Linköping, respectively. Mean baseline SBP was 6 mmHg lower than the mean resting SBP in both cities. Samples for analyses of cortisol in serum and saliva were taken before and after the stress test (Figure 1). Saliva was collected with Salivetti ® cotton wool swabs (Sarstedt, Landskrona, Sweden). The first sample was taken immediately after baseline while the volunteer was still calmly resting, i.e. before initiating venepuncture to avoid a possible stress effect. Venepuncture was followed by inserting a soft cannule into the vein. A blood sample for analysis of cortisol was drawn directly after venepuncture i.e. 8 minutes before the start of the stress test as described.[21] Blood samples were centrifuged within 30 minutes at 2000 G for 10–15 minutes and serum frozen at -70°C. Saliva samples were stored at +4°C, for up to 24 hours and then frozen at -70°C. Ten saliva samples in each city could not be analysed because of too small amounts of recovered saliva.

Stress Test

The stressors were presented in a fixed sequence with 2-minute intervals in between, to allow time for instructions (Figure 1). The first stressor was the "anger recall."[22] The participant was instructed to recall an event that made him angry, frustrated or upset and had 6 minutes in which to relate what had happened and how he had felt. The second stressor was a mental arithmetic test.[16] The participant was instructed to count backwards, 700 minus 7 as quickly and correctly as possible and to try to reach zero within 4 minutes. The third stressor was the cold pressor test.[23] The participant put his left hand up to the radial styloid process in iced water (between 0 and +4°C) for 90 seconds. Then he was again instructed to relax. BP and HR were recorded until they had returned to baseline or until 32 minutes after the start of the first stressor (Figure 1). Instructions for anger recall and mental arithmetic tests were read word by word. The Swedish and Lithuanian teams were trained together. In a pi-

lot study the researchers performed the anger recall test in the same group of volunteers and reached similar BP and HR responses.

Cortisol Analyses

Cortisol was analysed with radioimmunoassay procedures; in serum by RIA Cortisol I 125, Orion Diagnostica (Espoo, Finland) and in saliva by Coat-A Count, Cortisol-saliva DPC (Los Angeles, USA). Samples from the two groups were analysed in random order. Interassay analysis showed coefficients of variation between 2.2–6.0% in saliva and 1.7–3.1% in serum, using low, median and high concentration batches.

Lifestyle and Psychosocial Characteristics

These were measured by questionnaires which have earlier been described.[9,11] An instrument derived from the Maastricht scale was used to describe vital exhaustion. One of the characteristic statements of this construct is "I feel so tired as if my batteries were emptied".[24]

Calculations and Statistical Analyses

Cardiovascular reactivity measures were calculated as the average of all readings during each of the free stressors (Figure 1), i.e. for anger recall recordings at 0, 2, 4 and 6 minutes after the start of the test, for mental arithmetic at 8, 10 and 12

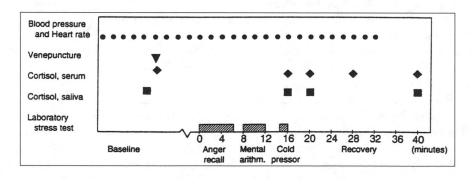

Figure 1
Standardised laboratory stress test; time schedule for procedures.

minutes, for cold pressor test at 15 and 16 minutes. Recovery was defined as the average of the recordings at 28, 30 and 32 minutes. Individual change scores were calculated as the arithmetic difference between reactivity or recovery measures and baseline for SBP, DBP, HR and cortisol. Differences between group means were analysed by two-tailed Student's t-test. For skewed distributions, Mann-Whitney's test was also used, but this did not substantially alter the results. Therefore, only results from the t-tests will be presented. For dichotomous data chi-square test was applied. Repeated measures analyses of variance[25] were performed for all change scores, with city as the between factor and time, i.e. the measurements periods, as the within factor. These analyses were performed with and without introduction of the three covariates baseline measure, current smoking and vital exhaustion;[26] the latter two expressing chronic stress. Greenhouse-Geisser corrections were performed when appropriate, but in the result section the degrees of freedom are presented in the uncorrected form. The level of significance was set at p<0.05.

RESULTS

Cardiovascular Reactivity

At baseline, Vilnius men had higher SBP and DBP than Linköping men (Table 3, Figure 2). Substantial increases in SBP, DBP and HR were observed in both groups during all stressors, but differences between the countries were small and insignificant (Table 3). Recovery change scores were small in both countries with no significant difference between the countries (Table 3). Repeated measures analyses of heart rate, systolic and diastolic blood pressure change scores, showed no significant interactions between time and city.

Cortisol Reactivity

Repeated measures analysis showed that interactions between time and city were significant for

Table 3

Cardiovascular reactivity during stress test. Baseline values and change scores at stress and recovery, (means ± SEM). SBP = systolic blood pressure; DBP = diastolic blood pressure; HR=heart rate; bpm=beats per minute.

	Vilnius n = 94	Linköping n = 89	p
SBP, mm HG			
Baseline	130±2	124±1	<0.01
Anger recall	+22±1	+20±1	=0.42
Mental arithmetic	+22+1	+21±1	=0.65
Cold pressor	+23±1	+26±1	=0.13
Recovery	+3±1	+3±1	=0.95
DBP, mm Hg			
Baseline	86±1	82±1	<0.01
Anger recall	+15±1	+16±1	=0.37
Mental arithmetic	+14±1	+14±1	=0.85
Cold pressor	+14±1	+17±1	<0.05
Recovery	+3±0	+3±1	=0.83
HR, bpm			
Baseline	64±1	61±1	=0.09
Anger Recall	+9±1	+8±1	=0.59
Mental arithmetic	+12±1	+10±1	=0.10
Cold pressor	+4±1	+4±1	=0.93
Recovery	+1±1	0±0	=0.26

both serum and saliva cortisol measurements; F (degrees of freedom; 3/525) = 23.5, p<0.001 and $F_{(2/276)}$ = 9.98, p<0.001, for serum and saliva respectively. Vilnius men had lower cortisol responses to the stress test than Linköping men, both in serum and saliva samples (Table 4, Figure 3a and 3b).

At 30 minutes after the start of the stress test, mean serum cortisol change score ± SEM (standard error of the mean) was 18.1±11 in Vilnius and 88.4±14 in Linköping (p<0.001). Vilnius men tended to have higher baseline cortisol levels compared to Linköping men, both in saliva and serum, significantly so (Vilnius 463,3±20, Linköping 413,9±15, p=0.05) when comparing serum levels in the groups starting at 7:30 A.M. In both

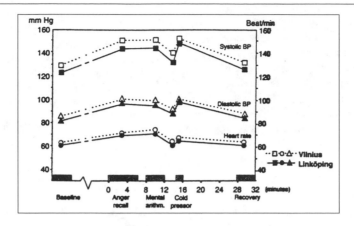

Figure 2
Mean levels of SBP, DBP and HR during stress test.

cities, the group starting at 7:30 A.M. had significantly higher mean baseline cortisol, but no difference in change scores compared to the group starting at 9:30 A.M. Partial correlations, controlled for city, between serum and saliva cortisol at baseline showed r=0.60 (p<0.001) and at 40 minutes after the start of the stress test r=0.75 (p<0.001).

Parameter estimates showed significnat effects of all three covariates on cortisol levels in serum at 30 minutes (baseline cortisol; B=0.33, p<0.001, smoking; B=48.4, p=0.007, and vital exhaustion; B=-3.02, p=0.013) the effect of city (Linköping vs Vilnius) was still significant (B= 47.7, p=0.006). In saliva no samples were taken at 30 minutes; at 40 minutes the effects of covariates were marginally significant (baseline cortisol; B=-2.36, p=0.007, smoking; -2.47, p=0.06, vital exhaustion; B=0.15, p=0.09) and likewise the effect for city (B= 2.23, p=0.07).

DISCUSSION

STRESS reactivity was compared between men from an Eastern European city (Vilnius) and men from a Western European city

(Linköping). In Vilnius men, compared to Linköping men, we found an attenuated cortisol response to acute stress and a tendency towards higher baseline cortisol levels but no difference in cardiovascular reactivity.

Our findings are in line with results from other studies in several settings. An attenuated cortisol response and absence of effect on cardiovascular responsiveness was seen in a study of chronic stress in high school teachers.[18] A pattern of combined high baseline cortisol and attenuated cortisol response was seen in extremely trained athletes with a daily stress of strenuous exercise,[27] in male addicts with symptomatic HIV infection,[28] and in women with metastatic breast cancer compared to healthy controls.[29] An attenuated cortisol response but no differences in baseline levels was found among sober alcoholics compared to non-alcoholic controls in a stress test using mental arithmetic and cold pressor test,[30] and also comparing habitual smokers to non-smokers using a psychological stressor.[19,31] Also in our study, smokers had a lower cortisol response. In animal studies, elevated basal corti-

Table 4

Cortisol in serum and saliva, nmol/l, during stress test. Baseline values and change scores (means±SEM)

Serum	Vilnius n = 94	Linköping n = 89	p
Baseline	415±15	397 ±12	=0.33
+ 16 min	+17±9	+21*±9	=0.76
+ 20 min	+19±10	+49***±10	<0.05
+ 30 min	+18±11	+88***±14	<0.001
+ 40 min	-8±11	+60***±14	<0.001

Saliva	Vilnius n = 84	Linköping n = 79	p
Baseline	10.3±0.6	9.0 ±0.5	=0.12
+ 16 min	+1.6* ±0.6	+1.7* ±0.6	=0.95
+ 20 min	+1.8* ±0.7	+3.1***±0.8	=0.21
+ 40 min	+2.0**±0.7	+5.8***±1.1	<0.01

*represent significant changes from baseline;*p<0.05,**p<0.01,***p<0.001

costerone levels were demonstrated in rats with a prior history of chronic stress,[32] and raised basal cortisol levels were found in subordinate monkeys, who are characterised by high psychosocial strain.[33] In these studies of severe chronic stress of different origin, cortisol response to acute stress were strikingly similar.

Cross-cultural comparisons involve several methodological problems. Different cortisol responses could be due to differences in methodology. Volunteers' understanding of stressors may differ between countries. However, the study methodology was carefully standardised. The very similar magnitude and pattern of cardiovascular response across all stressors, indicates a similar understanding of the three stressors in both countries. Also, within the cities, men in the low socioeconomic groups showed, as compared to men in the high socioeconomic groups, the same differences as Vilnius men compared to Linköping men, i.e. higher psychosocial strain, higher baseline (in Vilnius only) and lower cor-

tisol response, but no difference in cardiovascular response (to be published).

Retest reliability of stress tests improves if more than one type of stressor is used.[13] Therefore three stressors were included, and we analysed the summary effects of the fixed combination. Correlations between serum and saliva cortisol levels were high, in line with earlier studies.[34] Two of the stressors were psychological and one, i.e. the cold pressor test, was physical. However, all these three tests have both psychological and physical effect components. This has been shown especially for the cold pressor test where the setting is important for the outcome.[16] For this reason, we paid special attention to standardise both the physical and the psychological environment during the test.

Cardiovascular reactivity has been shown to be higher in hypertensives and in hyperlipidemics.[12,35] According to these findings, Vilnius men, with a higher resting blood pressure, would have been expected to exhibit stronger cardiovas-

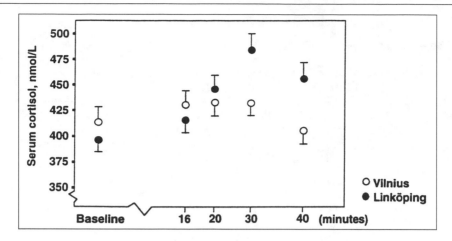

Figure 3a
Mean concentrations of serum cortisol during stress test, error bars representing SEM.

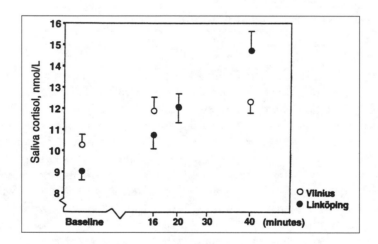

Figure 3b
Mean concentrations of saliva cortisol during stress test, error bars representing SEM.

cular responses. Similarly, the Linköping men, with a higher plasma cholesterol, would have been expected to exhibit stronger cardiovascular responses. Possibly, these two effects have counteracted and balanced each other, and the net effect in this case would be no significant difference.

The difference in response might to some extent be determined by genetic or developmental factors. However, our findings of the same differences in response pattern between different socio economic groups within, as well as between, countries argues against a strong genetic determinant. Early environmental conditions seem to effect individual vulnerability of the HPA-axis.[36] We have no individual data on the childhood of these men, but the situation in Lithuania during and after the second world war was indeed stressful. This still does not seem to be a main explanation, as official data show an increased IHD mortality for Lithuanian men also in cohorts born before the war.

Vilnius men had higher levels of several indicators of psychosocial strain, as expressed by higher job strain, lower social support and higher vital exhaustion.[11] Vital exhaustion has been described as a "chronic state of burnout," fitting into the third stage of Selye's general adaption syndrome.[26] This measure significantly contributed to explain low cortisol response.

Chronic stress can be described as repeated episodes of sustained, rather than appropriately self-limited activation of the corticotropin releasing hormone and the locus-ceruleus-norepinephrine system, and has been suggested as a possible precursor of depression.[37] In depression the feed-back system within the HPA axis is often impaired. Depression is conceptually related to vital exhaustion. We measured depression only in a second part of the LiVicordia study, and not in men who underwent the stress test. Depression and vital exhaustion were found to correlate closely in both groups; for Linköping men r=0.77 and for Vilnius men 0.45; p<0.001 for both.[11]

It is generally accepted that cortisol plays a critical role in maintaining the organism under conditions of stress.[38] Even more important than keeping homeostasis is the capacity to respond to meet new demands. This dynamic capacity, allostasis, is lost in states of chronic arousal.[39] As allostatic load, i.e. the cost of a chronic exposure to increased neuroendocrine response, may act as a predisposing factor for harmful effects of acute stressful life events.[40]

To conclude, we found, in Vilnius men as compared to Linköping men, an attenuated cortisol response to a standardised stress test. This response, which earlier has been found to relate to chronic stress, was significantly related to levels of vital exhaustion. We suggest that this, chronic stress related, inability to adequately respond to acute stress warrants more research to be assessed as an independent risk factor for CHD.

ACKNOWLEDGEMENTS

THIS study was supported by grants from the Swedish Research Council no 6962, The Royal Swedish Academy of Sciences, the Swedish Institute, Linköping University, Procordia Research Fund and Åke Wibergs' Fund. We thank nurses Susanne Wärjerstam-Elf and Regina Milasiené, assistant Snaige Jermaliené and biomedical analysts Siv-Britt Babtist, Britt Sigfridsson and Ylva Svensson for skilful technical assistance, PhD Carin Kullberg for help with statistical analyses, psychologist Alexander Perski and professor John Carstensen for advice on statistical interpretation.

REFERENCES

1. Selye H. The general adaptation syndrome and the diseases of adaptation. J Clin Endocrinol Metab 1946;6:117–230.

2. Theorell T. The psycho-social environment, stress, and coronary heart disease. In: Marmot M, Elliott P, eds. Coronary Heart Disease Epidemiology. New York: Oxford Univesity Press, 1992: 256–273.

3. Schneiderman N, Orth-Gomér K. Blending traditions: A concluding perspective on behavioral medicine approaches to coronary heart disease prevention. In: Orth-Gomér K, Schneiderman N, eds. Behavioral medicine approaches to cardiovascular disease prevention. Mahwah, New Jersey: Lawrence Erlbaum Associates, 1996: 279–301.

4. Feachem R. Health decline in Eastern Europe. Nature 1994;367:313–314.

5. WHO. Health for all database. Copenhagen: 1991.

6. UNICEF. Crises in mortality, health and nutrition. Florence 1994.

7. Bosma H, Appels A, Sturmans F, Grabauskas V, Gostautas A. Differences in mortality and coronary heart disease

between Lithuania and the Netherlands: Results from the WHO Kaunas-Rotterdam intervention study (KRIS). Int J Epidemiol 1994;23:12–18.

8. Pajak A, Kuulasmaa K, Tuomilehto J, Ruokokoski E. Geographical variation in the major risk factors of coronary heart disease in men and women aged 35–64 years. The WHO MONICA project. World Health Stat Q 1988;41:115–139.

9. Kristenson M, Ziedén B, Kucinskiene Z, Schäfer-Elinder L, Bergdahl B, Elwing B, Abaravicius A, Razinkoviene L, Calkauskas H, Olsson AG. Antioxidant state of mortality from coronary heart disease in Lithuanian and Swedish men: concomitant cross sectional study of men aged 50. BMJ 1997;314:629–633.

10. Bobak M, Marmot E. East-West mortality divide and its potential explanations: Proposed research agenda. BMJ 1996;312:421–425.

11. Kristenson M, Kucinskiene Z, Bergdahl B, Calkauskas H, Urmonas V, Orth-Gomér K. Increased psychosocial strain in Lithuanian vs Swedish men: The LiVicordia study. Psychosomatic Medicine, in press 1997.

12. Manuck S, Krantz D. Psychophysiologic reactivity in coronary heart disease and essential hypertension. In: Matthews K, Weiss S, Detre T, eds. Handbook of stress, reactivity and cardiovascular disease. New York: John Wiley & Sons, 1986: 11–34.

13. Manuck S. Cardiovascular reactivity in cardiovascular disease. "Once more unto the breach". Int J Behav Med 1994;1:4–31.

14. Zacharie R. Mind and immunity. Psychological modulation of immunological and inflammatory parameters [Thesis]. Aarhus university, Aarhus, 1996.

15. Herd J A. Neuroendocrine mechanisms in coronary heart disease. In: Matthews K, Weiss S, Detre T, eds. Handbook of Stress, Reactivity and Cardiovascular disease. New York: John Wiley & Sons, 1986: 49–70.

16. Schneiderman N, McCabe PM. Psychophysiologic strategies in laboratory research. In: Schneiderman N, Weiss SM, Kaufmann PG, eds. Handbook of research methods in cardiovascular behavioural medicine. New York: Plenum Publishing Corporation, 1989: 349–364.

17. Kuhn C. Adrenocortical and gonadal steroids in behavioural cardiovascular medicine. In: Schneiderman N, Weiss S, Kaufmann P, eds. Handbook on research methods in cardiovascular behavioural medicine. New York: Plenum Publishing Corporation, 1989: 185–204.

18. Benschop R, Brosschot J, Ballieux R. Chronic stress effects immunologic but not cardiovascular responsiveness to acute stess in humans. Am J Physiol 1994;266:R75–R80.

19. Roy MP, Steptoe A, Kirschbaum C. Association between smoking status and cortisol stress responsivity in healthy young men. Int J Behav Med 1994;3:264–283.

20. Weidner G, Messina C R. Cardiovascular reactivity to mental stress and cardiovascular disease. In: Orth-Gomér K, Chesney M, Wenger N, eds. Women, stress and heart disease. New Jersey: Laurence Erlbaum Associates Publishers, 1996.

21. Nyström F H. Ambulatory blood pressure and components of the metabolic syndrome in the population [Thesis]. Linköping University, 1997.

22. Ironson G, Taylor B, Boltwood M, Bartzokis T, Dennis C, Chesney M, Spitzer S, Segall GM. Effects of anger on left ventricular ejection fraction in coronary artery disease. Am J Cardiol 1992;70:281–285.

23. Keys A, Taylor HL, Blackburn H, Brozek J, Anderson JT, Simonson E. Mortality and coronary heart disease among men studied for 23 years. Arch Intern med 1971;128: 201–214.

24. Appels A, Höppener P, Mulder P. A questionnaire to assess premonitory symptoms of myocardial infarction. Int J Cardiol 1987;17:15–24.

25. Armitage P, Berry G. Multiple measurements. In: Statistical methods in medical research. 3rd. Oxford: Blackwell scientific publications, 1994: 312–386.

26. Appels A, Mulder P. Excess fatigue as a precursor of myocardial infarction. Eur Heart J 1988;9:758–764.

27. Luger A, Deuster P, Kyle S, Gallucci W, Montgomery L, Gold P, Loriaux L, Chrousos G. Acute hypothalamic-pituitary-adrenal responses to the stress of treadmill exercise. N Engl J Med 1987;316:1309–1315.

28. Biglino A, Limone P, Forno B, Pollono A, Carii G, Molinatti GM, Gioannini P. Altered adrenocorticotropin and cortisol response to corticotropin-releasing hormone in HIV-1 infection. Eur J Endocrinol 1995;133:173–179.

29. van der Pompe G, Antoni MH, Heijnen CJ. Elevated basal cortisol levels and attenuated ACTH and cortisol responses to a behavioral challenge in women with metastatic breast cancer. Psychoneuroendocrinology 1996;21:361–374.

30. Errico A, Parsons O, King A, Lovallo W. Attenuated cortisol response to biobehavioural stressors in sober alcoholics. J Stud Alcol 1993;54:393–398.

31. Kirschbaum C, Strasburger J, Langkrär J. Attenuated cortisol response to psychological stress but not to CRH or ergometry in young habitual smokers. Pharmacol Biochem Behav 1993;44:527−531.

32. Katz RJ. Acute and chronic stress effects on open field activity in the rat: Implications for a model of depression. Neurosci Biobehav Res 1981;5:247−251.

33. Sapolsky R. Endocrinology Alfresco: Psychoendocrine studies of wild baboons. Recent Progr Horm Res 1993;48:437−468.

34. Burke P M, Reichler R J, Smith E, Dugaw K, McCauley E, Mitchell J. Correlation between serum and salivary cortisol levels in depressed and non-depressed children and adolescents. Am J Psychiatry 1985;142:1065−1067.

35. Fredrikson M, Lundberg U, Toumisto M. Serum lipid levels and cardiovascular reactivity. J Psychophysiol 1991;5:89−95.

36. Meaney M J, Bhatnagar S, Larocque S, McCormick C, Shanks N, Sharma S, Smythe J, Viau V, Plotsky PM. Individual differences in the hypotalamic-pituitary-adrenal stress response and the hypothalamic CRF system. Annals of the New York Academy of Science 1996;794:70−85.

37. Gold PW, Goodwin FK, Chrousos GP. Clinical and biochemical manifestations of depression. N Engl J Med 1988;319:413−420.

38. Munck A, Guyre P, Holbrook N. Physiological functions of glucocorticoids in stress and their relation to pharmacological actions. Endocrine Rev 1984;5:25−44.

39. Sterling P, Eyer J, Allostasis: A new paradigm to explain arousal pathology. In: Fisher S, Reason J, eds. Handbook on life stress, cognition and health. Chichester. John Wiley & Sons, 1990: 629−649.

40. McEwen BS, Stellar E. Stress and the individual. Mechanisms leading to disease. Arch Intern med 1993;153: 2093−2101.

☙

Part Four

EFFECTS OF INCOME INEQUALITY
ACROSS RACE AND GENDER

Part Four

EFFECTS OF INCOME INEQUALITY ACROSS RACE AND GENDER

THE READINGS

37. Yllo K (1983). Sexual equality and violence against wives in American states. *Journal of Comparative Family Studies* XIV, No. 1 (Spring): 67–8

38. Kennedy BP, Kawachi I, Lochner K, Jones CP, Prothrow-Stith D (1997). (Dis)respect and black mortality. *Ethnicity & Disease* 7: 207–14.

39. Kawachi I, Kennedy BP, Gupta V, Prothrow-Stith (1999). Women's status and health of women and men: A view from the States. *Social Science & Medicine.*

40. Wilkinson RG (1998). The culture of inequality.

COMMENT

IN Part IV, we turn to the effects of vertical social stratification (income inequality) on stratification along the ascriptive (horizontal) dimensions of race/ethnicity and gender. Health disparities by race and gender have been extensively documented (see Krieger et al. 1993, for a comprehensive review). At the individual level, these disparities have been attributed to a host of factors, ranging from biology (e.g., genetic and hormonal differences between men and women, whites and blacks), psychology (e.g., differences in perceptions of, and responses to, illness symptoms), through to the direct and mediated effects of discrimination (e.g., differential treatment by health care institutions; discrimination in the labor market, education system, and judicial institutions).

In contrast to the wealth of research on the individual basis of race/gender disparities, relatively little work has been carried out at the eco-logical level. In fact, there are enormous variations in the health status of women and ethnic minorities across geographic areas, whether defined by countries, or smaller regions within nations. Moreover, the health status of women and minorities map closely on to the patterns of income inequality: areas with the highest disparities in income exhibit the worst health statistics for women (Kawachi et al. 1999) and African-Americans (Kennedy et al. 1997). Indeed, there seems to be a "culture of inequality" (Wilkinson, 1998), which is characterized by the exercise of patriarchal power by men over women, as well as high levels of collective prejudice against racial minorities. The health status of subordinated groups in society thus seems to be inextricably linked to the general quality of the social environment, and hence to economic inequality.

The questions and debates raised by the readings in this section include:

- How does vertical stratification (income inequality) play out along horizontal (ascriptive) dimensions of gender and race/ethnicity?
- Can we measure the quality of the social environment for subordinate groups in society? Can we devise measures of patriarchy, or collective prejudice? How do these relate to income inequality?
- Are there consequences of patriarchy for the health of men? Are there consequences of holding prejudiced views for the health of the racial majority?

SUGGESTIONS FOR FURTHER READINGS

Wacquant LJD, Wilson WJ (1989). The cost of racial and class exclusion in the inner city. *Annals of the*

American Academy of Political and Social Science, 501, 8–25.

Krieger N, Rowley DL, Herman AA, Avery B, Phillips MT (1993). Racism, sexism, and social class: implications for studies of health, disease, and well-being. *American Journal of Preventive Medicine* 9: 82–122.

Institute for Women's Policy Research (1996). *The Status of Women in the States*. Washington DC: Institute for Women's Policy Research (Library of Congress Card Catalogue Number 96–79874.

Blau FD, Kahn LM (1992). The gender earnings gap—learning from international comparisons. *American Economic Review* 82: 533–8.

🦅

Thirty-Seven

SEXUAL EQUALITY AND VIOLENCE AGAINST WIVES IN AMERICAN STATES

Kersti Yllo

THE relationship between sexual inequality and wife-beating has been the subject of some debate. This relationship has been considered by a number of authors (Dobash and Dobash, 1979; Martin, 1976), who point out that wife abuse is not a new social problem. These authors discuss the traditional position of women as property and offer horror stories of their abuse through the centuries and across cultures. The right to physically chastise one's wife is regarded as part of the historic foundation of patriarchy within the family and in society at large. The authors suggest that this right varies with status of women. In most contemporary societies, where the status of women is relatively high, for example, wife-beating is no longer legal (although it may still be condoned by the legal system). Nevertheless, there are no empirical data available regarding changes in the actual incidence of wife-beating over time. So, while the historical analyses suggest links between the status of women and levels of wife abuse, they offer only anecdotal evidence.

It has been readily assumed by many authors that a reduction in current sexual inequality would serve to reduce the level of violence against wives. Schuyler contends that

heading the list of cultural variables accounting for the phenomenon of wife abuse is the tradition of male subjection of females (1976:489)

She argues that the reduction of sexual inequality will lower the incidence of conjugal violence by making it less acceptable and more likely to come to the attention of the authorities. In addition, as the status of women in society improves, wives have more options and greater freedom to leave abusive husbands.

Pogrebin (1974) takes the same position as Schuyler. She maintains that many women have been "tied to a violent man by economic dependency . . ." She blames this dependency on the inability of women to obtain equal wages, advancements, and educational opportunities within a sexist society.

The question of equality and marital assault has also been taken up by Straus in an article entitled "Sexual Inequality, Cultural Norms, and Wife-Beating" (1976). In this piece he begins to show that wife-beating is not a personal abnormality but rather has its roots in the cultural norms and sexist organization of society and family. Straus suggests that one way to reduce the amount of force necessary to maintain a vi-

Originally published in *Journal of Comparative Family Studies*, 1983.

able pattern of family life is to reduce the degree of inequality between the sexes. He writes that

> the goals of the women's liberation movement are centered on elimination of . . . violence producing inequalities. . . . Since these are fundamental factors accounting for the high level of physical assaults on women by their husbands, it is clear that the achievement of the goals of the feminist movement is tremendously important for any reduction in the level of marital victimization (1976:555).

The women's movement's impact may not be limited to its effect on women and their values and options. A growing literature is focused on changing male roles (Pleck & Sawyer, 1974; Farrell, 1974; Tooley, 1980). As sex role socialization diminishes and males begin to develop their nurturant side, we may see a decline in the use of violence by husbands against their wives.

On the basis of the discussion to this point it would seem that sexual equality and marital violence are negatively related. As wider educational and economic opportunities, greater legal rights, and more egalitarian norms take hold, we would expect fewer women to feel "trapped" in violent marriages and less likely to stay in them. Further, husbands may adopt more egalitarian attitudes and may place less value on domination. Greater sexual equality could, in this way, be related to decreased levels of wife abuse.

However, there are also persuasive arguments which suggest that violence against wives may increase as women's status changes. It may be that where the status of women is lowest, women are more likely to tolerate their subordinate position. Acceptance of a male dominant ideology and recognition of limited options by wives may lessen the need for husbands to maintain control through force. Where women's subordination is questioned and more alternatives to marriage are available, conflicts and violence between spouses may be greater.

Toby's (1974) treatment of the "compulsive masculinity" theory of violence is relevant here. He suggests that one cause of violence in males is the desire to prove their masculinity. Toby argues that violence as an expression of masculinity will be highest where men cannot prove their masculinity symbolically (for example, by being the primary wage-earner and having authority over others both with the family and at work). Whether the movement to liberate men from their rigid sex roles is having an impact is not currently known. It may be, then, that as the status of women increases and the traditional symbols of masculinity diminish some males may turn to violence to assure themselves and others of their masculinity.

Whitehurst (1974) and Marsden (1978) consider the possibility of more violence as society becomes more egalitarian from a somewhat different angle. Rather than simply regarding violence as a symbol of masculinity, they focus on the issue of control. Changes such as greater legal rights, economic opportunities, and physical mobility are seen as creating strain and frustration for males attempting to retain their dominant position. Violence against wives may be a response to moves by women to question and reduce the degree of sexual domination. It may be a means by which males attempt to maintain control.

Steinmetz and Straus comment on Whitehurst's analysis. They write that if it is correct,

> it will not be until a generation of men and women reared under egalitarian conditions and subscribing to equalitarian rather than male-superiority norms takes over that we can expect to see a reduction in violent encounters between spouses. In the meantime, the conflict between the emerging equalitarian social structure and the continuing male superiority norms will tend to increase rather than decrease conflict and violence between husbands and wives (1974:76).

How increasing sexual equality affects rates of wife-beating is not at all clear. Both sides of the debate offer strong arguments as to what the effects on family violence are and will be. It may be, as Straus suggests, that the *long-run* consequences may be to lessen the frequency of wife abuse. But, the *short-run* impact may be the opposite. A sizable number of men will not easily give up their traditional dominate roles (1976:556).

This controversy is the central focus of this study. This research goes beyond the psychological and interpersonal variables which have dominated family violence research to empirically consider the impact of the societal status of women on wife-beating. In this study, the structured status of women in each American state is regarded as an important macro-sociological variable related to the micro-level interactions within the family, particularly wife abuse.

SEXUAL INEQUALITY: DEFINING AND MEASURING THE STATUS OF WOMEN

Definition

For the most part, discussions of sexual inequality and women's status have focused on the specific definition of these concepts. These terms are often used as a label almost any discussion of women in society.

A thoughtful analysis of "the status of women" is presented in a paper by Regina Hommes in *Demographic Aspects of the Changing Status of Women in Europe* (1978). Having reviewed the various approaches to the concept, she develops a definition of the status of women which seems useful for a range of purposes including this research. "The status of women is the position women have as a group, compared with the position of men as a group, in different fields of society" (1978:27−28).

Measurement: The Status of Women Index

This research focuses on American status as units of analysis for assessing women's status. While the state is often the unit of analysis in other social sciences (political science in particular), it is

rarely used as such in sociology. Although there is less precedent for this approach within our discipline, it appears most appropriate for the purposes of this research for a number of reasons.

First, the states are theoretically appropriate units for the comparative study of the status of women. Despite the sense that America is becoming increasingly "nationalized" due to the growth of centrally-controlled media, corporations, and the federal government, states are still more than different colored areas on the map. They are often the initiators of legislation and programs and are frequently the unit of implementation of federal policies.

In *The Maligned States* (1972), Ira Sharkansky takes up the issue of state and regional diversity. He maintains that "state differences go back to the beginning of this country, and account for basic features of our society and government. These differences do produce some problems in unequal citizen opportunities from one state to another . . ." (1972:20). The degree of such inequalities, as they concern women, is a major focus of the present study.

The second reason that this research takes the state as its unit of analysis is a practical one. Many of the variables of interest here are gathered by the census bureau on a state by state basis. In addition, a number of other agencies gather state-level data (for example the Eagleton Institute's data on women in politics and N.O.W.'s information on women and education). The uniformity of data from state to state make it most useful for comparative purposes. Variables from different sources can easily be related to one another.

There were two main considerations in the selection of indicators of women's status: first, that they be of theoretical relevance and second, that state-level data be available on them. Listed below are the items which met these general criteria. The items are worded so that the higher the percentage score for each item, the higher the status of women. While this makes for somewhat awkward phrasing for some items, it facilitates the mathematical construction of the index. A fuller specification of the items is given in Appendix B and the sources for the data are listed in Appendix C.

Economic Dimension

EC1, % of women in the labor force

EC2, % female in professional and technical occupations

EC3, % female in managerial, administrative occupations

EC4, Unemployment: Male rate as % of female rate

EC5, Median income: female as % of male, for full-time workers

ECX, Economic status of women index

Educational Dimension

ED1, High school graduation: Female rate as % of male rate

ED2, Post-secondary enrollment: % female

ED3, High school interscholastic athletes: % female

ED4, High School Administrators: % female

EDX, Educational status of women index

Political Dimension

POL1, Members in U.S. Congress: % female

POL2, Members of state senate: % female

POL3, Members of state house: % female

POL4, Judges on major appellate and trial courts: % female

POLX, Political status of women index

Legal Dimension

L1, No occupations barred to women

L2, Equal pay laws

L3, Fair employment practices act

L4, No man. hours restrictions for females

L5, Proof of resistance not req. for rape conviction

L6, Corrob. testimony not req. for rape conviction

L7, Husband and wife jointly resp. for family support

L8, Husband and wife have equal right to sue for pers. injury

L9, Hus. and wife have eq. right to sue for loss of consortium

L10, Wife's property rights unrestricted

L11, Wife's right to use maiden name unrestricted

L12, Wife's right to maintain sep. domicile unrestr.

L13, Ratified federal Equal Rights Amendment

L14, Passed a state Equal Rights Amendment

LEGX, Legal status of women index

The individual indicators were standardized and then added into the four dimension indexes. The total Status of Women Index (SWI) was obtained by summing the four dimension scores. The alpha coefficient of reliability for the SWI is a moderate .54. Given the range of indicators included in the index, an alpha of this magnitude is grounds for some confidence that the index is reliable relative to most measures used in the social sciences.

VIOLENCE AGAINST WIVES: DEFINITION AND MEASUREMENT

VIOLENCE is defined here as an act carried out with the knowledge that the likely consequences of it will be physical injury or pain to another person. The terms violence against wives, wife-beating, and wife abuse are used interchangeably in this paper to reduce redundancy. It is recognized that these terms are not identical in meaning.

The term violence against husbands denotes acts of physical aggression against husbands by wives. The use of the terms "husband abuse" and "husband-beating" are explicitly avoided here. The victimization and injuries implied by these terms do not warrant their use. Domestic violence is measured here through the use of the

Conflict Tactics Scale (discussed in detail in Straus, *et al.*, 1980). The rate of violence against wives is the proportion of couples who indicated that the husband had used any of the following tactics against the wife in the year prior to the interview: kicked, bit, or hit with a fist; hit or tired to hit with something; beat up; threatened with knife or gun; used a knife or gun. (See Appendix A.) A state Violence rate of 10%, for example, indicated that ten percent of the husbands perpetrated serious acts of violence against their wives within the past year. Note that more "minor" forms of violence, such as pushing, shoving, or slapping are not included in the calculation of the rate. This is not because such acts are condoned here, but that they are so common an element of family conflict that their inclusion would weaken the discrimination power of the index.

The violence rates are based on data from a national area-probability sample of 2143 adult Americans. To be included in the sample, individuals had to be living with a person of the opposite sex. (Over 98% were legally married.) Interviews, focusing on family background, conflicts, and violence, were conducted in the subjects home. Each interview lasted approximately one hour and was completely confidential and anonymous. Further, interviewers were of the racial group predominant in the interviewing area. Interviews were conducted in Spanish where necessary.

The present study is based on a secondary analysis of these data. This survey of violence in the American family provides the best estimate or rates of wife-beating currently available. (For a thorough discussion of the original study see Straus *et al.*, 1980.)

The individual state samples, which are the units of analysis on this study, could be assumed to be representative in that, initially, every person in every state had an equal probability of being included in the sample. This assumption is not wholly justified, however. Since only certain ar-

eas of states were included after the first stage of sampling, the concern arose that the areas might not be representative of the whole state, particularly in those states in which only one or two areas were selected.

The representativeness of state data was checked by comparing key variables (such as husband's income) from the survey data with parallel variables from census data, which we know to be representative. The survey rates paralleled census figures for the most part. Six states (with sample sizes of under 20) appeared unrepresentative and were dropped from the analysis, leaving an N of thirty states to work with. (Only 36 states were sampled in the national survey.) In the analysis reported here states were grouped by the status of women because the mean violence rate for a group of states is more reliable than individual state rates in that it is based on a larger number of cases. States were grouped into quintiles (6 states in each group), so that reliability could be improved, yet a range of status levels could be examined. (Centiles, for example, would decrease the number of states in each group to only three and reduce reliability.)

The Status of Women and Violence Against Wives

THE findings of this exploratory study represent the first empirical evidence about the relationship between the social status of women and spousal violence. The data suggest that the various theoretical arguments regarding this relationship each explain a different part of the total picture.

Figure 1 gives a picture of the overall relationship between women's status and wife-beating. In this graph, the economic, educational, political, and legal dimensions of women's status, as well as the overall Status of Women Index (SWI), are identified. Each indicator is divided into quintiles (20% of states in each group), and then the relationship between status and violence is graphed.

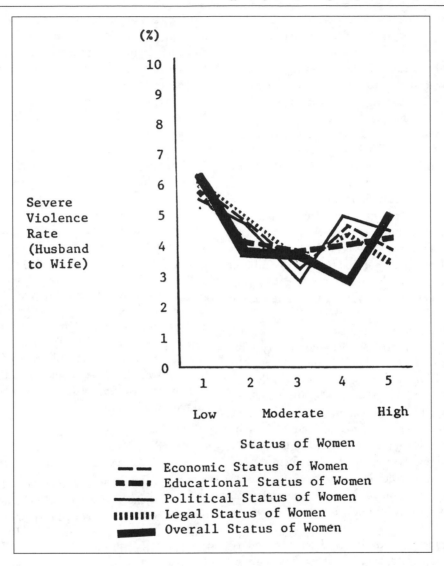

Figure 1
Violence Against Wives by the Status of Women

In Figure 1 a curvilinear pattern emerges. The level of violence is highest in those states where the overall status of women is lowest and then drops as status improves. This pattern then reverses as we consider the quintile of states in which the status of women is highest. In those states the level of violence is almost as high as in the lowest status states.

Moreover, we find that the pattern for the combined index of the status of women is clearer than for any of the dimension indicators. Of particular interest is the fact that combining dimension indicators results in more than an additive effect. States that fall in the lowest or highest quintiles on the total indicator have higher violence rates than any of the dimension indicators alone predict.

The graph of the violence rate for overall status is not simply the average of the dimension rates for a particular quintile group. For example, the quintile of states scoring highest on a particular dimension are not necessarily the same states which score highest on the overall SWX. A state that is high on economic status may be moderate on educational status and consequently end up in the moderately high quintile on overall status. The fact that the violence rate graphed for the SWX differs from that graphed for any particular dimension is a reflection of the interaction of the dimensions.

The Pearson correlation coefficient (r) for the bivariate relationship between overall status and violence is -.21 (p<.13). The correlations between the dimension indicators and violence are as follows: economic status, -.19 (p<.16); educational status, -.04 (p<.42); political status, -.07 (p<.35); and legal status, -.26 (p<.08). Due to the small number of cases (30 states), these correlations are not statistically significant at levels regarded as standard, such as .05 or .01, in the social sciences. However, these are standards generally applied to individual-level research based on a large number of cases. Aggregate level analyses such as this one are necessarily limited to smaller N's because each case represents some larger unit rather than an individual respondent. Significance levels are reported here for information sake. However, they should be considered with the nature of the data in mind.

The Pearson r statistic expresses how well a linear regression line explains the variation in the dependent variable. Since our graph of the data (Figure 1) indicates that the bivariate relationship is not linear, it is understandable that r fails to reach significance.

An alternative to r is the Eta statistic, which is basically the same type of measure as r except that

the mean within categories of the independent variable rather than the regression equation, is used to predict the dependent variable score (Loethner and McTavish, 1974). Eta and r are identical where subcategory means fall along the regression line; that is, when the relationship is linear. When Eta is greater than r in magnitude (not in direction, as Eta is always positive), we can infer that the nature of the relationship is curvilinear. For the status women-wife abuse relationship, Eta is .46, more than double the r statistic. Thus, the curvilinear pattern explains 21% (eta^2) of the variance between these variables as compared with 4% (r^2) explained by the linear pattern.

The graph and statistical analysis indicate that where the status of women is lowest, wives are most likely to be physically assaulted by their husbands and that violence decreases as status of women is highest, violence against wives is also high.

The fact that violence against wives is greatest in states which fall at the two extremes of women's status requires closer examination. It has been suggested that low status states might have the most wife-beating because greater force may be necessary to keep women "in their place" and because women in these states have fewer alternatives to violent marriages. On the other hand, the possibility was considered that violence could be greater in high status states because these were the states which had undergone the most rapid social change and in which husbands may feel most threatened. It seems plausible that domestic conflict may increase in these areas where women are achieving equality most quickly. While the traditional formula and norms for the relationship between husbands and wives disappears, new patterns or guidelines are not yet institutionalized. As Moore states in *Social Change*, the probability of conflict is related to rapid social change (even if it is favorable change) and to the decreased predictability of interpersonal relations (1974:68). It seems likely that changes of this sort would also result in increased conflict in marriages.

The empirical evidence suggests that both of these processes may be at work. Women in states where their economic, educational, political, and legal status is low are the victims of the greatest violence at the hands of their husbands. Yet, at the same time, wives in states where women have achieved the greatest equality also suffer high levels of physical aggression from their husbands.

Reciprocity of Violence

Considering the large discrepancy between these two groups of women with regard to the status of women in the areas in which they live, it seems likely that the violence they endure results from somewhat different factors and may be dealt with differently. In order to investigate this latter possibility, violence *by* wives against husbands was taken into consideration.

Figure 2 presents the rates of violence against husbands by the status of women as well as rates of violence against wives. The graph of violence against husbands shows a fairly clear positive relationship to women's status. The rate in highest status states is double that in the lowest quintile of states (5.9% vs. 2.9%). The Pearson r for this relation is +.42 and is significant at the .01 level.

By comparing the rate of violence against wives with that against husbands, a striking pattern becomes evident. In those states where the status of women is lowest, the rate of violence against wives is double the rate of violence by them (6.2% vs. 2.9%). In sharp contrast, the amount of violence by husbands and wives is comparable in those states in which the status of women is highest (5.1% vs. 5.9%).

The findings presented in Figure 2 suggest how the status of women influences spousal violence. In low status states, wife-beating is high and physical aggression is generally not reciprocated by wives. That is, the wives in these states appear to take the beatings without fighting back. Perhaps because alternatives for these

wives are so limited, they are forced to tolerate abuse from their husbands. On the other hand, wives who live in states where their economic, educational, political and legal status is relatively high, seem to react to violence by their husbands quite differently. They fight back.

It would constitute an ecological fallacy to directly conclude that the equivalence of husband and wife violence rates is due to reciprocal violence in all individual relationships in the high status states. It is, however, a plausible explanation for the findings. It is almost certain that there are some marriages in these states in which only the wife is violent. However, it is quite unlikely, based on previous research (Straus, 1980c), that a majority of these violent relationships are of this sort.

It appears then that the general status of women has some influence on wives' acceptance of unilateral physical aggression. It may be that in states where women have achieved some measure of equality in society at large, that violence by husbands is no longer regarded as legitimate behavior and that illegitimate acts are reciprocated in kind.

In addition, there may also be other factors at work which result in the dramatic increase in violence by wives in higher status states. Perhaps because wives perceive themselves as less dependent on their husbands, a larger portion than previously will directly attack their spouse when conflict or hostility occurs. In a sense, greater societal status may free some women, who would not otherwise strike out due to a greater sense of dependence, to respond with physical aggression. It may be that more wives turn to violence first. This violence may then be reciprocated by husbands who may not have turned to physical aggression otherwise. It is important to note, however, that individual acts of violence by wives are as common as acts of violence by husbands in these states. This is *not* taken as evidence of equal victimization, however. Given the differences in size and strength between most husbands and

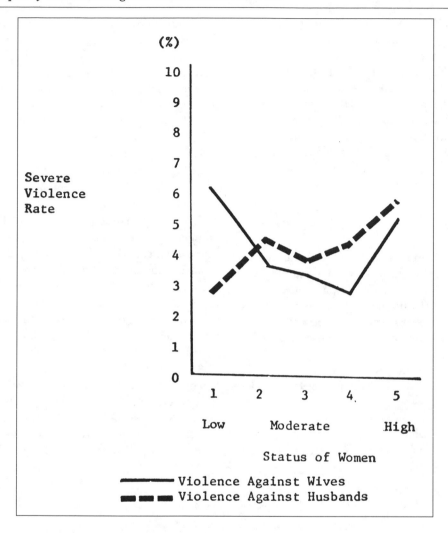

Figure 2
Violence Against Wives and Violence Against Husbands by the Status of Women

wives, wives are more likely to be injured in any violent marital interchange.

As women gain equality in more and more spheres of life, sex differences in various behaviors previously associated with one sex or the other are likely to diminish. A review of the research on human aggression by Robert Baron (1977) indicates that there has been a disappearance of clear-cut sex differences in aggression in both laboratory and field studies in the last fifteen years. He suggests that this disappearance may be related to changes in sexual roles and stereotypes. These changes may serve to render women less inhibited about responding physically to direct provocation. "In short," he concludes, "the two sexes may gradually become equal in their propensity for violence, as well as their tendencies toward more desireable forms of behavior" (1977:221). As Kalmuss (1981) points out, an egalitarian society is not necessarily a non-violent one.

It is likely that a number of factors combine to push up rates of violence *by* wives as the status of women increases. The data upon which this study is based do not allow us to distinguish between the possible factors and their interactions. Confirmation of such increased rates and exploration of the reasons for it must await future research.

THE IMPACT OF OTHER STATE FACTORS

I N order to more thoroughly examine the interrelationship between state status of women and spousal violence, a number of control variables were introduced. Specifically, urbanization, per capita income, educational level and overall level of violent crime were taken into consideration.

Before reporting on the analysis, the measurement of these variables needs to be clarified. Urbanization is indicated by the proportion of a state's population which resides in large urban areas. State educational level is the proportion of adult residents who have completed high school.

State per capita income is drawn from the 1976 Census Bureau survey, as are the urbanization and education variables. The violent crime rate, an indicator of "violent climate," is the number of reported violent crimes per 100,000 population in 1976. (See Appendix C for source references for these variables.)

In order to get a sense of how these control variables and our focal variables are interconnected, zero-order correlations between them were calculated. These correlations are presented in Table 1.

A brief explanation of Table 1 reveals that a number of these variables are, not surprisingly, intercorrelated. We find that the higher the per capita income and educational level of a state, the higher the status of women in that state. While this relationship is not unexpected, this research is the first (based on this review of the literature) which empirically documents this for the United States.

Also expected, and previously documented, are the high positive correlations between urbanization and violent crime, and between urbanization, per capita income, and education. However, the purpose of considering these control variables is not to determine how they are interre-

Table 1

Zero-Order Correlations Between Control Variables, the Status of Women, and the Level of Violence Against Wives

(1) Violence against Wives	(2) Status of Women	(3) Urbanization	(4) Education	(5) Violent Crime	(6) Per Capita Income
(1) 1.00					
(2) −.21	1.00				
(3) −.40*	.19	1.00			
(4) −.07	.50**	.18	1.00		
(5) −.37*	.01	.52**	−.03	1.00	
(6) −.34*	.55**	.54**	.52**	.36**	1.00
	(* p < .05	** p < .01)			

Table 2

Correlations of Status of Women with Violence Against Wives Controlling for Violent Crime,
Urbanization and State Per Capita Income

Control Variable	r
Violent Crime	−.22
Urbanization	−.15
Per Capita Income	−.03

lated with one another, but how they impact upon the status of women-wife abuse relationship. Since urbanization, violent crime, and income are all significantly negatively correlated with violence against wives, these variables were considered more closely.

Table 2 presents first-order partial correlation coefficients. The status of women-wife abuse relationship is controlled for each of these three variables.

Violent Climate

The state rate reported violent crime was taken into account because of the possibility that it is the "violent climate" or culture of violence of particular states that explains the women's status-wife abuse relationship. This is, the possibility that low status states may have more overall violence and therefore more violence against wives, needed to be considered. The data indicate that this is not the case. For one thing, reported violent crime and the rate of wife abuse are negatively related. Further, the partial correlation analysis indicates that controlling for this factor does not affect our focal relationship.

Urbanization

Urbanization was introduced as a control variable because of the possibility that it might be antecedent to both women's status and domestic violence. Again, the control variable proved unimportant with regard to the focal relationship of the research. Controlling for degree of urbaniza-

tion does diminish the women's status-wife abuse correlation slightly. However, since the level of urbanization of a state and the status of women are not significantly correlated, there is little reason to pursue the effect of this variable further.

State Per Capita Income

The most critical control variable, it turns out, is state per capita income. This control was introduced on the grounds that the status of women and violence against wives may both depend on state income level. As Table 2 shows, income has a strong impact on the correlation of status and violence.

Nevertheless, as Figure 3 shows, the relationship does retain a curvilinear shape within income groups. So, while per capita income is an important variable and is closely entwined in this complex of relationships, it does not negate the curvilinear relationship between women's status and wife-beating.

SUMMARY AND CONCLUSIONS

THE purpose of this research was to examine the relationship between the status of women in American states and the level of violence against wives. Visual displays of the data and statistical analysis indicate that there is a curvilinear relationship between these two variables. In states where the status of women is lowest, wives are most likely to be physically assaulted by their husbands. Violence does decrease as wom-

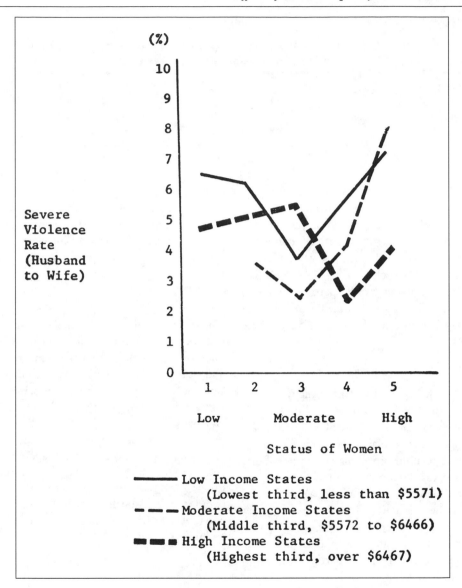

Figure 3
Violence Against Wives by the Status of Women, Controlling for State Per Capita Income

en's status increases—to a point. In those states where the status of women is highest, the level of violence against wives is also quite high.

It was suggested that the high level of violence in low-status states might be due to the need to use greater amounts of force to keep women "in their place." In addition, the more limited options to violent marriage in these states may serve to keep battered women in their marriages. The high level of violence against wives in high status states, in contrast, is likely to be a result of other factors. In states where the general status of women is relatively high, husbands may feel threatened by the rapid social change and the breakdown of traditional husband-wife roles. Increased domestic conflict may be a consequence of women's move toward equality.

Further, it was found that violence against wives is not directly paralleled by violence against husbands. In states where women's status is relatively low, wives are twice as likely as husbands to be the victims of severe violence at the hands of their spouse. In contrast, the rates of violence *by* wives is comparable to that *against* them in states where women's status is high. It is suggested that a context of relative equality may result in husbands' violence being seen as illegitimate, and being reciprocated in kind. Moreover, the decline of sexual inequality in all spheres may be related to a reduction in sex differences in various types of behaviors, including violence.

Finally, a number of control variables were introduced in an attempt to determine if the findings regarding the status of women-wife abuse relationship are confounded by other factors. State educational level, urbanization, and "violent climate" proved to have no significant impact on the original relationship. Per capita income turned out to be the only salient control variable.

However, graphing the status-violence relationship within high, medium and low categories of income provided evidence of the independent existence of a curvilinear relationship. The pattern is less pronounced within income categories (except for the low income states). Nevertheless, the status of women does show an impact on levels of wife-beating separate from income effects.

The central theme of this research is that the status of women is related to the level of violence against wives. However, that relationship is much more complex than the theoretical discussions of it to date have led us to believe.

On the one hand are the authors and social scientists who have argued that a reduction of sexual inequality will result in a reduction of wife-beating (Dobash and Dobash, 1979; Martin, 1976; Schuyler, 1976). On the other are those who contend that violence against wives may increase as the general status of women improves as men attempt to retain control (Toby, 1974; Whitehurst, 1974; Marsden, 1978).

The problem common to both of these formulations is oversimplification. For one thing, the impact of increased equality between the sexes on marital violence is not of the magnitude implied by those who have debated this issue. As the research on family violence mounts, it becomes increasingly clear that there is no single cause of such abuse. A complicated web of factors are at work. Some of these factors are embedded in the social structure and culture; others grow out of socialization experiences or day-to-day stresses (Straus, Gelles, and Steinmetz, 1980). While the status of women is an important consideration, changing the status alone will not eradicate wife-beating. The uni-causal assumptions which underlie the discussions of women's status and violence in the literature are unfounded.

Another oversimplification in discussions to date is the assumption of a linear relationship between sexual equality and wife-beating. Whether they argue that the relationship is positive or negative, commentators generally regard it as linear.

In a brief commentary, Steinmetz and Straus (1974) do consider the possibility that the short-run and long-run effects of increasing equality may not be identical. They suggest that the transition period in which patriarchal and egalitarian structures and norms clash may be characterized by increased marital conflict and violence. This particular discussion of theirs (they do revert to linear explanations in some other works) comes closest to the empirical evidence uncovered in this research.

The distinction between short-run and long-

Appendix A

CONFLICT TACTICS SCALE

No matter how well a couple gets along, there are times when they disagree on major decisions, get annoyed about something the other person does, or just have spats or fights because they're in a bad mood or tired or for some other reason. They also use many different ways of trying to settle their differences. I'm going to read a list of some things that you and your (wife/partner) might have done when you had a dispute, and would first like you to tell me for each one how often you did it in the past year.

RESPONDENT-IN PAST YEAR

		NEVER	ONCE	TWICE	3–5 TIMES	6–10 TIMES	11–12 TIMES	MORE THAN 20 TIMES	DON'T KNOW
a.	Discussed the issue calmly	0	1	2	3	4	5	6	X
b.	Got information to back up (your/her) side of things	0	1	2	3	4	5	6	X
c.	Brought in or tried to bring in someone to help settle things	0	1	2	3	4	5	6	X
d.	Insulted or swore at the other one	0	1	2	3	4	5	6	X
e.	Sulked and/or refused to talk about it	0	1	2	3	4	5	6	X
f.	Stomped out of the room or house (or yard)	0	1	2	3	4	5	6	X
g.	Cried	0	1	2	3	4	5	6	X
h.	Did or said something to spite the other one	0	1	2	3	4	5	6	X
i.	Threatened to hit or throw something at the other one	0	1	2	3	4	5	6	X
j.	Threw or smashed or hit or kicked something	0	1	2	3	4	5	6	X
k.	Threw something at the other one	0	1	2	3	4	5	6	X
l.	Pushed, grabbed, or shoved the other one	0	1	2	3	4	5	6	X
m.	Slapped the other one	0	1	2	3	4	5	6	X
n.	Kicked, bit, or hit with a fist	0	1	2	3	4	5	6	X
o.	Hit or tired to hit with something	0	1	2	3	4	5	6	X
p.	Beat up the other one	0	1	2	3	4	5	6	X
q.	Threatened with a knife or gun	0	1	2	3	4	5	6	X
r.	Used a knife or gun	0	1	2	3	4	5	6	X
s.	Other (PROBE): _____	0	1	2	3	4	5	6	X

And what about your partner? Tell me how often she (ITEM) in the past year.

run effects of increasing equality is an important one. The findings of this research *do not* indicate that sexual equality is related to increased domestic violence. The states in which the status of women is relatively high can by no means be considered egalitarian. They are just somewhat less inequitable than the others.

The results of this study do suggest that many wives are victims of violence where women's status is low. Further, they suggest that the change toward equality is not an easy one and that the "battle of the sexes" is literally being waged in many homes. It may be that when and if the era of transition ends and equality is institutionalized, violence against wives will be reduced. Unfortunately, the investigation of the long-run consequences of sexual equality must await future generations.

Appendix C

SOURCES OF DATA FOR THE STATUS OF WOMEN INDEX AND STATE CONTROL VARIABLES

Items from Source are listed in parentheses.

Alexander, Shana. 1975. Women's Legal Rights. Los Angeles: Wollstonecraft, Inc. (LI–LI4)

Council of State Governments. 1975. Book of the States. Lexington, KY.: The Council of State Governments. (POLI–POL4)

Johnson, Marilyn and Kathy Stanwick. 1978. Profile of Women Holding Office. New Brunswick, N.J.: Eagleton Institute of Politics. (POLI–POL4)

Project on Equal Education Rights. 1979. "Back to School Line-up: Where Girls and Women Stand in Education Today." Washington, D.C.: National Organisation for Women. (ED3–ED4)

U.S. Bureau of the Census. 1977. Statistical Abstract of the U.S. Washington, D.C. (EDI–ED2)

U.S. Department of Labor. 1978. Survey of Income and Education, Spring, 1976. Washington, D.C.: Bureau of Labor Statistics, Report 536. (ECI–EC5)

The author would like to thank Murray Straus and the members of the University of New Hampshire Family Violence Research Program for their valuable comments, criticisms, and support throughout this research project.

REFERENCES

Alexander, S. 1975. Women's Legal Rights. Los Angeles: Wollstonecraft.

Baron, Robert. 1977. Human Aggression. New York: Plenum Press.

Collins, R. 1975. Conflict Sociology, New York: Academic Press.

Cromwell, R. and D. Olson. 1975. Power in Families. New York: John Wiley and Sons.

Dobash, R.E. and R.P. Dobash. 1979. Violence Against Wives. New York: The Free Press.

Farrell, W. 1974. The Liberated Man. NY: Bantam Books.

Gelles, R. and MLA. Straus. 1979. "Determinants of violence in the family: toward a theoretical integration." In W. Burr et al. (Eds.) Contemporary Theories about the Family, Vol. 1. New York: The Free Press.

Hommes, R. 1978. "The Status of Women: in Nipheus-Nell, M. (Ed.) Demographic Aspects of the Changing Status of Women in Europe. Boston: Martin-Dyboff.

Kalmuss, K. 1981. "Resolving Family Violence: Non-Sexism or Non-Violence?" Paper presented to the National Conference for Family Violence Researchers, Durham, N.C. July, 1981.

Marsden, D. 1978. "Sociological perspectives on family violence." In J.P. Martin (Ed.) Violence and the Family. New York: John Wiley and Sons.

Martin, D. 1976. Battered Wives. San Francisco: Glide Pub.

Moore, Wilbert. 1974. Social Change. Englewood Cliffs, N.J.: Prentice-Hall (2nd edition).

Pleck, J. and J. Sawyer (Eds). 1974. Men and Masculinity. Englewood Cliffs, N.J.: Prentice-Hall Pub.

Pogrebin, L.C. 1974. "Do women make men violent?" Ms. Magazine III:5

Schuyler, M. 1976. "Battered wives: an emerging social problem." Social Work Nov: 488–491.

Steinmetz, S. and N.A. Straus. 1974. Violence in the Family. New York: Dodd, Mead, and Co.

Straus, M.A. 1976. "Sexual inequality, cultural norms, and wife-beating." Victimology 1:54–76

——1980a. "Victims and aggressors in marital violence." American Behavioral Scientist 23:681–704.

————1980b. Indexing and Scaling for Social Science Research with SPSS. (Book in Progress).

Straus, M.A., R. Gelles and Steinmetz. 1980. "Behind Closed Doors; NY: Doubleday.

Toby, J. 1974. "Violence and the masculine ideal: some qualitative data." In S. Steinmetz and M.A. Straus (Eds.). Violence in the Family. New York: Dodd, Mead, and Co.

Tooley, K. 1980. "Johnny, I Hardley Knew Ye" Toward a Revision of the Theory of Male Psychosexual Development." In A. Skolnick & J. Skolnick (Eds.) Family in Transition. Boston: Little, Brown, and Co.

U.S. Dept. of Labor. 1979. Employment in Perspective: Working Women. No. 1, Report 565.

Whitehurst, R. 1973. "Violence in Husband-wife interaction." In S. Steinmetz and M.A. Straus (Eds.). Violence in the Family. New York: Dodd, Mead, and Co.

Thirty-Eight

(DIS)RESPECT AND BLACK MORTALITY

Bruce P. Kennedy, Ichiro Kawachi,
Kimberly Lochner, Camara P. Jones, and
Deborah Prothrow-Stith

Abstract

Objectives: A growing number of studies have documented the deleterious health consequences of the experience of racial discrimination in African Americans. The present study examined the association of racial prejudice—measured at a collective level—to black and white mortality across the United States.

Methods: Cross-sectional ecologic study, based on data from 39 states. Collective disrespect was measured by weighted responses to a question on a national survey, which asked: "On the average blacks have worse jobs, income, and housing than white people. Do you think the differences are: (A) Mainly due to discrimination? (yes/no); (b) Because most blacks have less in-born ability to learn? (yes/no); (c) Because most blacks don't have the chance for education that it takes to rise out of poverty? (yes/no); and (d) Because most blacks just don't have the motivation or will power to pull themselves up out of poverty? (yes/no)." For each state, we calculated the percentage of respondents who answered in the affirmative to the above statements. Age-standardized total and cause-specific mortality rates in 1990 were obtained for each state.

Results: Both measures of collective disrespect were strongly correlated with black mortality (r = 0.53 to 0.56), as well as with white mortality (r = 0.48 to 0.54). A 1 percent increase in the prevalence of those who believed that blacks lacked innate ability was associated with an increase in age-adjusted black mortality rate of 359.8 per 100,000 (95% confidence interval: 187.5 to 532.1 deaths per 100,000).

Conclusions: These data suggest that racism, measured as an ecologic characteristic, is associated with higher mortality in both blacks and whites.

Introduction

COMPARED to white Americans, African Americans have higher mortality rates for nearly all causes of death, except suicide and chronic obstructive pulmonary disease.[1,2] In 1992, the life expectancy gap between whites and African Americans was 6.9 years, and the gap appears to be widening in men.[1] Various explana-

Originally published in *Ethnicity and Disease*, 1997.

tions have been put forth to account for the African American deficit in life expectancy—for example, differential access to medical care; socioeconomic disadvantage stemming from multiple forms of segregation (occupational, residential, political); and exposure to a variety of environmental and psychosocial stressors, such as toxic waste sites, violence and crime, and tobacco advertising.[3,4]

A hitherto neglected area of research has been documentation of the effects of racism on the health of African Americans. Racism involves "harmful and degrading beliefs and actions expressed and implemented by both institutions and individuals, as linked to their membership in racially defined groups."[3] A handful of epidemiologic studies has focused on the health effects of racism, mainly in research documenting the relationship of elevated blood pressure to the experience of racial discrimination.[5,6,7,8] These studies suggest that the experiences of racial discrimination and unfair treatment predict elevated blood pressure among African Americans. In the studies by Krieger,[7] and Krieger and Sidney,[8] it appeared to be the internalized response to racial discrimination that was associated with increased blood pressure.

The studies to date have thus examined the health consequences of racial discrimination at the individual level. However, it is also possible to conceptualize discrimination as an *ecological* characteristic. In other words, whole societies may vary in their levels of discriminatory attitudes and behaviors, whether expressed through the opinions of the members of that society, or in the practices of its institutions. Consequently, the chances that a member of a minority group might be exposed to discrimination and unfair treatment can vary systematically according to place of residence.

Collective discrimination can be conceptualized as a lack of respect one group displays toward another. In the words of Miller and Ferroggiaro,[9] "respect and self-respect are central components of an enlarged concept of citizenship . . . Respect affects how we are treated, what help from others is likely, what economic arrangements others are willing to engage in with us, when reciprocity can be expected." In other words, respect acts as a resource for individuals, and should be considered a component of the stock of *social capitals* in society—i.e., a component of the norms of reciprocity, trust and social obligation that are essential for minimizing the risks of poor physical, psychological, or social health.[10] A lack of respect (or disrespect) is usually accompanied by a breakdown of social trust between members or groups within society, and the consequent disinvestment in social capital. Poor health status arises in such societies because the community fails to invest in, and assume responsibility for, the collective well-being of its members.[10,11,12]

Disrespect between races can take many forms, including institutional (e.g., stereotyping of blacks in the media, absence of representation), interpersonal (prejudice, physical violence, etc), and intrapersonal (e.g., internalized diminution of self-respect as a result of being the constant target of disrespect). In the present study, we examined the relationship of one form of collective disrespect, racial prejudice as expressed through racial stereotypes, to black and white mortality rates within the United States.

METHODS

Measures of Disrespect

States were used as the unit of analysis. Collective disrespect was measured by weighted responses to a question on a national survey which asked: "On the average, blacks have worse jobs, income, and housing than white people. Do you think the differences are: (a) Mainly due to discrimination? (yes/no); (b) Because most black have less in-born ability to learn? (yes/no); (c) Because most blacks don't have the chance for education that it takes to rise out of poverty?

(yes/no); and (d) Because most blacks just don't have the motivation or will power to pull themselves up out of poverty? (yes/no)." For each state, we calculated the percentage of respondents who answered in the affirmative to each of the above statements.

Data were obtained from the General Social Survey (GSS), conducted by the National Opinion Research Center.[13] The GSS is a nationally representative survey that samples non-institutionalized English-speaking persons 18 years or older living in the United States. The survey has been repeated 14 times over the last two decades, and has included a set of questions on social trust organizational membership. In the present study, we averaged 5 years of cumulated data (1986–1990) from the GSS, representing 7,679 individual observations from 39 states. Although the GSS is nationally representative, only 39 states were included in the survey, because, by chance, people residing in some of the less populous states (e.g., Alaska, Delaware) were not picked up by the sampling scheme.

All responses to the GSS were weighted to take into account of the fact that the survey was developed to generate representative data at the national and regional levels, but not at the state level. Post-stratification weights were developed to adjust for the extent to which respondents in the GSS may not have been representative of the states in which they resided. In order to construct the weights, we first examined demographic characteristics in the GSS that were most predictive of responses to the collective disrespect items. Younger age, white race, and less than high school education were the most correlated with the disrespect items. We therefore developed post-stratification weights based on the distribution of age, race, and educational attainment of GSS respondents.

The stratum-specific weights were calculated as follows:

$$w_{i,j,k,l} = P_{i,j,k,l} / p_{i,j,k,l}$$

where $w_{i,j,k,l}$ is the post-stratification weight for the GSS respondent residing in the $i\text{-}th$ state, and being of $j\text{-}th$ age-group, $k\text{-}th$ race, and $l\text{-}th$ level of educational attainment; $P_{i,j,k,l}$ is the proportion of individuals with these characteristics residing in the $i\text{-}th$ state, obtained from the 1990 US Census; and $p_{i,j,k,l}$ is the corresponding proportion of such respondents in the GSS.

These weights were then used to adjust the individual responses to the collective disrespect items in the GSS, using the *weight* procedure in SAS.

Measurement of State Variations in Median Income and Poverty

Some evidence suggests that low income and poverty are linked to depletion in social capital.[14] Since income levels and poverty are also potential predictors of mortality,[15] we evaluated these variables as potential confounders in the relationship between collective disrespect and mortality. The Census Summary Tape File 3A contains data on the state-specific median incomes as well as prevalence of poverty, where households are classified as being above or below the poverty level based on the revised federal poverty index originally developed by the Social Security Administration in 1964. The current poverty index is purely wage-income based and does not reflect other sources of income such as non-cash benefits from food stamps, Medicaid, or public housing. Poverty thresholds are updated annually to reflect changes in the Consumer Price Index. The poverty variable used in the analyses represents the percentage of households in a given state that were below the federal poverty level. In 1990, this represented an income of less than $13,359 for households with 4 family members.[16]

Measurement of State Variations in Race-specific Mortality

The race-specific age-adjusted mortality rates for each state in 1990 were obtained from the

Compressed Mortality Files compiled by the National Center for Health Statistics, Centers for Disease Control and Prevention (CDC). The data were obtained from the CDC's database using the CDC WONDER/PC software.[17] Black and white mortality rates were analyzed separately. All mortality rates were directly age-standardized to the U.S. population of blacks and whites, and expressed as the number of deaths per 100,000 persons.

DATA ANALYSIS

OLS regression was used to examine the relationships of collective disrespect items to mortality rates. Two sets of models were examined for each outcome of interest. In the first set of models, we regressed all-cause black and white age-adjusted mortality rates against the weighted disrespect items. In the second set of models, we adjusted the regression models for state variations in median income and prevalence of poverty.

RESULTS

Relationships Among Measures of Collective Disrespect, and Between Median Income and Poverty Levels

The two indicators of collective disrespect, the proportion of respondents from each state who responded that blacks had less innate ability, or less willpower, were highly correlated with each other ($r = 0.81$) (Table 1). In turn, these indicators were strongly negatively correlated with the proportion of respondents who believed that blacks were in a worse socioeconomic position compared to whites because of discrimination, or lack of opportunities for education. Both disrespect indicators were strongly correlated with both black mortality rates ($r = 0.53$ to 0.56), as well as with white mortality rates ($r = 0.48$ or 0.54). They were also moderately correlated with poverty rates and median income. Black mortality rates were positively correlated with white mortality rates ($r = 0.48$), so that states with higher black death rates also tended to have higher white death rates.

Table 1

Correlation Matrix of Disrespect Variables With Poverty Rates, Median Income, and Black and White Age-Adjusted Mortality Rates

	Poverty Rates	Median Income	Black Mortality	White Mortality	Ability	Will Power	Discrimination
Median income	− 0.81*						
Black mortality	0.31	− 0.20					
White mortality	0.56*	− 0.40*	0.48*				
Ability[1]	0.38*	− 0.34*	0.56*	0.48*			
Will power[2]	0.46*	− 0.36*	0.53*	0.54*	0.81*		
Discrimination[3]	− 0.41*	0.31	− 0.51	− 0.47*	− 0.72*	− 0.78*	
Education[4]	− 0.56*	0.48*	− 0.52*	− 0.62*	− 0.64*	− 0.80*	0.72*

* $P < 0.05$.

[1] Proportion of survey respondents who agreed that blacks do less well than whites because "most blacks have less in-born ability to learn."

[2] Proportion of survey respondents who agreed that blacks do less well than whites because "most blacks just don't have the motivation or will power to pull themselves up out of poverty."

[3] Proportion of survey respondents who agreed that blacks do less well than whites "mainly due to discrimination."

[4] Proportion of survey respondents who agreed that blacks do less well than whites "because most blacks don't have the chance for education that it takes to rise out of poverty."

Relationship Between Disrespect and Black Mortality

The disrespect variables predicted age-adjusted black mortality rates in the regression models. A 1 percent increase in the prevalence of those who believed that blacks lacked innate ability was associated with an increase in age-adjusted black mortality rate of 359.8 per 100,000 (95% confidence interval: 187.5 to 532.1 deaths per 100,000) (Figure 1, Table 2). The effect of disrespect on black mortality remained almost unchanged after adjusting for median income and poverty levels (Table 3). Together with median income and poverty, the disrespect items could account for between 22 and 28 percent of the between-state variance in black mortality.

Relationship Between Disrespect and White Mortality

The disrespect variables were similarly strongly predictive of white mortality rates, although the magnitude of the effects was smaller (Table 4). Adjusting for poverty rates and median income, a one percent increase in the proportion who believed that blacks had less ability was associated with an increase in white mortality rate of 182.4 deaths per 100,000 (95% CI: 41.5 to 323.3 per 100,000) (Table 5). The proportion of respondents who agreed that blacks encountered discrimination or lack of educational opportunities was strongly inversely associated with both black and white mortality rates.

DISCUSSION

OUR findings demonstrate the existence of geographic differences in the levels of collective prejudice and disrespect toward African Americans. Therefore, some African Americans may be more likely to routinely encounter such attitudes in their daily lives, depending on where they reside. Furthermore, there appears to be an association between widely held racist views and increased black mortality.

The mechanisms are manifold by which collective disrespect may lead to increased mortality in the oppressed group. The variable we chose to examine—disrespect—is a form of prejudice that reflects lack of social trust between races. This lack of social trust has several consequences. For instance, in the area of employment, racial prejudices may carry over into hiring and firing

Table 2

Regression Coefficients for Disrespect Variables on Age-Adjusted Total Black Mortality

Disrespect Variable	B	SE	t (P Value)	Adjusted R^2
No ability[1]	359.8	87.9	4.09 (0.0002)	29.3
No will power[2]	270.6	71.5	3.78 (0.0005)	25.9
Discrimination[3]	− 318.7	88.5	− 3.60 (0.0009)	23.9
Lack of educational opportunity[4]	− 240.4	65.7	− 3.65 (0.0008)	24.5

[1] Proportion of survey respondents who agreed that blacks do less well than whites because "most blacks have less in-born ability to learn."

[2] Proportion of survey respondents who agreed that blacks do less well than whites because "most blacks just don't have the motivation or will power to pull themselves up out of poverty."

[3] Proportion of survey respondents who agreed that blacks do less well than whites "mainly due to discrimination."

[4] Proportion of survey respondents who agreed that blacks do less well than whites "because most blacks don't have the chance for education that it takes to rise out of poverty."

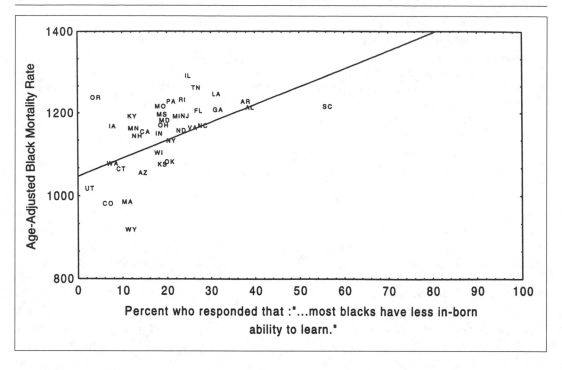

Figure 1
Age-Adjusted Black Mortality Rate by Disrespect

decisions, and hence directly affect the life chances of African Americans.

Kirschenman and Neckerman[18] carried out an interview survey of 185 Chicago-area employers to ascertain the extent of racial stereotypes in hiring decisions. The employers' characterizations of black workers mirrored pervasive racial stereotypes. Common among the traits listed were that black workers were "unskilled, uneducated, illiterate, dishonest, lacking initiative, unmotivated, involved with drugs and gangs, did not understand work, had no personal charm, were unstable, lacked a work ethic, and had no family life or role models."[18] As the authors pointed out, such discriminatory attitudes have the tendency to become self-fulfilling prophecies. For example, employers' expectations about group differences in productivity may bias evaluation of job performance. Such expectations may also in-

fluence job placement: workers perceived to have lower productivity may be given less on-the-job training. Finally, antagonism between workers and their employers, supervisors, or customers may indeed diminish productivity. Furthermore, lower expectations of African American workers may lead to less collaborative work and fewer joint initiatives.

Discrimination in hiring, in turn, reduces the chances that the disrespected groups can lead productive lives. The result, as Miller and Ferroggiaro[9] point out, "is a vicious cycle: members of disrespected groups and classes stand a substantial chance of needing public assistance because of the obstacles they encounter in trying to achieve a decent outcome." In turn, negative views of welfare recipients expressed by members of society at large have resulted in the steady erosion of benefits over time. Low incomes, and the

Table 3

Multivariate Regression Coefficients for Disrespect on Black Mortality,
Adjusted for Poverty Rates and Median Income

Disrespect Variable	B	SE	t (P value)	Adjusted R²
No ability[1]	336.5	93.4	3.60 (0.0009)	28.2
No will power[2]	256.1	83.6	3.06 (0.004)	22.3
Discrimination[3]	− 290.1	99.0	− 2.93 (0.006)	20.9
Lack of educational opportunity[4]	− 246.9	83.9	− 2.94 (0.006)	21.0

[1] Proportion of survey respondents who agreed that blacks do less well than whites because "most blacks have less in-born ability to learn."

[2] Proportion of survey respondents who agreed that blacks do less well than whites because "most blacks just don't have the motivation or will power to pull themselves up out of poverty."

[3] Proportion of survey respondents who agreed that blacks do less well than whites "mainly due to discrimination."

[4] Proportion of survey respondents who agreed that blacks do less well than whites "because most blacks don't have the chance for education that it takes to rise out of poverty."

associated inability to fully participate in the life of the community, further reinforces low collective respect, as well as low self-respect.

Most interestingly, we found an association between levels of collective prejudice and increased mortality in the *majority* group. Although this finding needs to be replicated, it seems to imply that there are deleterious health consequences of racism for those who hold such views, as well as for those who are the targets of prejudice. Thus groups with low levels of respect and trust for members of another group, may also tend, on average, to hold lower levels of respect for members of their own group. Alternatively, it is possible that both levels of prejudice and mortality rates (for both blacks and whites) are derivative of some other, unmeasured, factor.

A major limitation of the present study is that the General Social Survey was designed to be representative at the national and regional levels, but not at the state level. We have attempted to overcome this limitation by using post-stratification weights to adjust for over- (or under) sampling of certain demographic groups which may have biased the responses to the GSS. The results of the analyses using weighted re-sponses to the GSS were, in fact, quite similar to the unweighted analyses. For example, the correlation between the prejudice items and black mortality ranged from 0.50 to 0.57 (in the unweighted analysis), and from 0.53 to 0.56 (in the weighted analysis), so that substantial bias is unlikely to have occurred. Nonetheless, appropriate caution must be exercised in interpreting the individual state-specific information in this study, particularly since there are other variables not available in the GSS which may have nonetheless affected the representativeness of the state estimates.

A final limitation of the present study is its cross-sectional design. It is unknown whether levels of collective disrespect fluctuate across time, and whether these can be linked to changes in mortality rate. Furthermore, the reasons why racist attitudes vary cross-sectionally by region remain unexplained. In the South, high levels of prejudice may reflect the historical legacy of a slavery society. In other parts of the US, collective prejudice may reflect more recent patterns of economic downturns. For instance, according to Wilson,[19] minority groups, especially urban minorities, have been particularly vulnerable to

Table 4

Regression Coefficients for Disrespect Variables on Age-Adjusted Total White Mortality

Disrespect Variable	B	SE	t (P Value)	Adjusted R²
No ability[1]	253.5	77.0	3.29 (0.002)	20.6
No will power[2]	228.6	58.6	3.90 (0.0003)	27.2
Discrimination[3]	− 241.7	75.1	− 3.22 (0.003)	19.7
Lack of educational opportunity[4]	− 239.3	49.7	− 4.82 (0.0001)	36.9

[1] Proportion of survey respondents who agreed that blacks do less well than whites because "most blacks have less in-born ability to learn."

[2] Proportion of survey respondents who agreed that blacks do less well than whites because "most blacks just don't have the motivation or will power to pull themselves up out of poverty."

[3] Proportion of survey respondents who agreed that blacks do less well than whites "mainly due to discrimination."

[4] Proportion of survey respondents who agreed that blacks do less well than whites "because most blacks don't have the chance for education that it takes to rise out of poverty."

structural changes in the economy, such as the shift from goods-producing to service-producing industries; the increasing polarization of the labor market into low-wage and high-wage sectors; and the relocation of manufacturing industries out of central cities. These structural changes have produced large numbers of jobless minorities in certain areas, and collective disrespect may possibly reflect a process of "victim-blaming" that is taking place.

The novel contribution of this preliminary study is that we have conceptualized and measured the health effects of racism and a *societal* characteristic, as opposed to an individual-level

Table 5

Multivariate Regression Coefficients for Disrespect Variables on White Mortality, Adjusted for Poverty Rates and Median Income

Disrespect Variable	B	SE	t (P Value)	Adjusted R²
No ability[1]	182.4	71.9	2.53 (0.01)	37.5
No will power[2]	148.5	62.5	2.37 (0.02)	36.3
Discrimination[3]	− 147.1	75.0	− 1.96 (0.06)	33.4
Lack of educational opportunity[4]	− 173.8	60.3	− 2.88 (0.007)	40.2

[1] Proportion of survey respondents who agreed that blacks do less than whites because "most blacks have less in-born ability to learn."

[2] Proportion of survey respondents who agreed that blacks do less than whites because "most blacks just don't have the motivation or will power to pull themselves up out of poverty."

[3] Proportion of survey respondents who agreed that blacks do less than whites "mainly due to discrimination."

[4] Proportion of survey respondents who agreed that blacks do less than whites "because most blacks don't have the chance for education that it takes to rise out of poverty."

phenomenon. Our findings suggest that researchers should be attempting to develop measures of racism on a variety of different levels (institutional, interpersonal, internalized), as well as widening the scope of investigation to document the effects of prejudice on those who hold such views.

Acknowledgements

THIS research was supported by a Robert Wood Johnson Foundation Investigator Award in Health Policy Research to Drs. Kennedy and Kawachi.

References

1. National Center for Health Statistics. Advance Report of Final Mortality Statistics, 1992. *Monthly Vital Statistics Report*, 1995;43:1–76.

2. Kochanek KD, Maurer JD, Rosenberg HM. Why did black life expectancy decline from 1984 through 1989 in the United States? *Am J Public Health*. 1994;84:938–944.

3. Krieger N, Rowley DL, Herman AA, Avery B, Phillips MT. Racism, sexism, and social class: implications for studies of health, disease, and well-being. *Am J Prev Med*. 1993; 9(Suppl 2):82–122.

4. King G, Williams DR. Race and health: a multidimensional approach to African American health. In: Amick BC III, Levine S, Tarlov AR, Chapman Walsh D (eds). *Society and Health*. New York, NY: Oxford University Press; 1995:93–130.

5. James SA, LaCroix AZ, Kleinbaum DG, Strogatz DS. John Henryism and blood pressure differences among black men. II. The role of environmental stressors. *J Behav Med*. 1984;7:259–275.

6. Dressler WW. Lifestyle, stress, and blood pressure in a southern black community. *Psychosom Med*. 1990;52:182–198.

7. Krieger N. Racial and gender discrimination: risk factors for high blood pressure? *Soc Sci Med*. 1990;30:1273–1281.

8. Krieger N, Sidney S. Racial discrimination and blood pressure: the CARDIA Study of young black and white adults. *Am J Public Health* 1996;86:1370–1378.

9. Miller SM, Ferroggiaro KM. *Poverty and Race*. 1996;5(1): 1–14.

10. Aday LA. Health status of vulnerable populations. *Annu Rev Public Health*. 1994;15:487–509.

11. Tesh SN. *Hidden Arguments: Political Ideology and Disease Prevention Policy*. New Brunswick, NJ: Rutgers University Press; 1988.

12. Kawachi I, Kennedy BP. Health and social cohesion: why care about income inequality? *BMJ* 1997;314:1037–1040.

13. Davis JA, Smith TW. *General Social Survey Cumulative File*. Ann Arbor, MI: University of Michigan, Interuniversity Consortium for Political and Social Research.

14. Wilson WJ. Studying inner-city social dislocations: the challenge of public agenda research. *Am Social Rev*. 1991;56:1–14.

15. Hahn RA, Eaker E, Barker ND, Teutsch SM, Sosniak W, Krieger N. Poverty and death in the United States—1973 and 1991. *Epidemiology*. 1995;6:490–497.

16. U.S. Bureau of Census, *Income and Poverty* (CD-ROM), 1993.

17. Friede A, Reid JA, Ory HW. CDC WONDER: a comprehensive on-line public health information system of the Centers for Disease Control and Prevention. *Am J Public Health*. 1993;83: 1289–1294.

18. Kirschenman J, Neckerman KM. "We'd love to hire them, but . . ." *The Meaning of Race for Employers*. In: Jencks C, Peterson PE, eds. Washington DC: The Brookings Institution; 1991.

19. Wilson WJ. *The Truly Disadvantaged*. Chicago, Ill: Chicago University Press; 1987.

Thirty-Nine

WOMEN'S STATUS AND THE HEALTH OF WOMEN AND MEN: A VIEW FROM THE STATES

Ichiro Kawachi, Bruce P. Kennedy,
Vanita Gupta, and Deborah Prothrow-Stith

ABSTRACT

WE examined the status of women in the 50 American states in relation to women's and men's levels of health. The status of women in each state was assessed by four composite indices measuring women's political participation, economic autonomy, employment and earnings and reproductive rights. The study design was cross-sectional and ecologic. Our main outcome measures were total female and male mortality rates, female cause-specific death rates and mean days of activity limitations reported by women during the previous month. Measures of women's status were strikingly correlated with lower female mortality rates (r = -0.51), as well as lower activity limitations (-0.47). A smaller wage gap between women and men was associated with lower female mortality rates (-0.30) and lower activity limitations (-0.31) (all correlations, P < 0.05). Indices of women's status were also strongly correlated with male mortality rates, suggesting that women's status may reflect more general underlying structural processes associated with material deprivation and income inequality. However, the indices of women's status persisted in predicting female mortality and morbidity rates after adjusting for income inequality, poverty rates and median household income. Associations were observed for specific causes of death, including stroke, cervical cancer and homicide. We conclude that women experience higher mortality and morbidity in states where they have lower levels of political participation and economic autonomy. Living in such states has detrimental consequences for the health of men as well. Gender inequality and truncated opportunities for women may be one of the pathways by which the maldistribution of income adversely affects the health of women.

INTRODUCTION

RESEARCHERS had employed a variety of theoretical 'lenses' through which to view and analyze gender differences in health

---

Originally published in *Social Science & Medicine*, 1998.

(Walsh Chapman et al., 1995). At the most micro level, the biomedical 'lens' seeks to explain gender differences in health in terms of genetic, hormonal, anatomic or physiological differences between men and women. The biochemical model may be contrasted with the psychosocial 'lens' which focuses on variables at the intrapsychic and interpersonal levels, including sex differences in personality, coping behaviors, self-efficacy and the experience and reporting of signs and symptoms. Further up the levels of conceptual organization, the epidemiologic 'lens' seeks to identify population patterns of 'risk factors'—behaviors and exposures—that might help to explain gender differences in health. Finally, at the most macro level of analysis, Walsh Chapman et al. (1995) have proposed the so-called 'society-and-health lens', which attempts to analyze the large-scale cultural, social, economic and political processes in society that produce differential health risks in women and men. What is distinctive about this perspective is its emphasis on how health outcomes 'are ordained and constrained by crucial mechanisms of social control and distribution of resources and power. Current epidemiological research on gender and health takes for granted a social-stratification system that allocates resources and power on the basis of gender-determined social roles and leaves the underlying social processes unidentified, unquestioned and unexplored' (Walsh Chapman et al., 1995, p.149).

According to Connell (1987), two fundamental social processes that explain and constrain the relationships between women and men are the division of labour and structures of power. The division of labour includes, among other facts, the segregation of labour markets and the associated inequalities in wages, discrimination in hiring and promotion and the distinction between paid and unpaid work. Power structures refer to the machinery of authority, control and coercion. They include government and business

hierarchies, the regulation and surveillance of sexuality and reproduction and the dynamics of authority within domestic relationships.

With the exception of some innovative work on the predictors of domestic violence (Yllo, 1983), relatively few attempts have been made to incorporate the 'society and health' lens into investigations of women's health. In 1983, Yllo reported an ecological analysis (based at the U.S. state level) of the relationship between gender inequality and violence against wives. Starting with the observation that battered women are often tied to violent men by economic dependency, Yllo reasoned that in states where women were more dependent, marital violence would be more frequent. To test this hypothesis, the researcher constructed four composite indices of women's status, covering their level of economic autonomy (e.g., the size of the female/male earnings gap, the percentage of women in managerial occupations); women's educational attainment; women's political participation (e.g., percent female members in Congress and state legislatures); and an index of women's legal status (e.g., equal pay laws, property rights, rape laws). According to all four indices of women's status, rates of severe marital violence against women were highest in the states where gender inequality was the greatest (Yllo, 1983). Of interest, violence by women against their husbands tended to be higher in states which accorded greater equality to women.

Despite growing interest in the characteristics of *places* as determinants of population health status (Macintyre, 1997), researchers have not attempted to examine women's status, modelled as an ecological characteristic, in relation to female (and male) mortality and morbidity rates. In 1996, the Institute for Women's Policy Research in Washington DC released a set of social indicators that benchmarked the status of women in the fifty American states (Institute for Women's Policy Research, 1996). These indicators—which measure the economic and political autonomy of women as well as their reproductive rights—provided an opportunity to test the relationship between the status of women in society and women's health through the 'society-and-health lens'.

METHODS

Indices of Women's Status

The indices of women's status used in the present analysis were developed and published by the Institute for Women's Policy Research (Washington DC, 1996). Women's status was examined in four separate domains: political participation, employment and earnings, economic autonomy and reproductive rights. The *political participation composite index* combined 4 aspects of women's political status: voter registration, voter turnout, representation in elected office and women's institutional resources. Women's representation in elected office was calculated for several levels: state representatives, state senators, state-wide elected executive officials, as well as US representatives, senators and governors. The number of women office-holders in each state was weighted according to the degree of political influence of the position, e.g., state representatives were given a weight of 1.0, compared to 1.75 for US senators. Examples of women's institutional resources include the presence of state commissions on the status of women or legislative caucuses for women. To construct the composite index, each of the 4 component indicators was standardized by subtracting the mean value for all 50 states from the observed value and dividing by the standard deviation. The standardized scores were then weighted: 1.0 each for voter registration and turnout; 3.0 for women in elected office and 1.0 for women's institutional resources. The overall index score was then calculated by summing the weighted, standardized values for the 4 component indicators. The higher the index score, the higher the level of women's political participation.

The *employment and earnings composite index* combined 4 indicators of women's economic status: their earnings, the male/female wage gap, women's representation in managerial and professional jobs and women's participation in the labor force. Each of the 4 indicators was standardized by dividing the observed value (in 50 states) by the mean value for the entire USA. The resulting ratios were summed for each state to create the composite index, with each composite indicator given equal weight.

The *economic autonomy composite index* combined 4 aspects of women's economic well-being: access to health insurance, educational attainment, business ownership, and percent of women above the poverty level. Educational attainment was obtained from the 1990 Census as the percent of women aged 25 yr or older with 4 or more years of college education. Again, each component was standardized and given equal weight, before summing to give the overall Index.

Finally, the *reproductive rights composite index* incorporated each state's scores on eight legislative and political indicators reflecting women's reproductive well-being and autonomy. These included access to abortion services without mandatory parental consent laws for minors, access to abortion services without a waiting period, public funding for abortions under any circumstances if a woman is eligible, percent of counties that have at least one abortion provider, whether the governor or state legislature is pro-choice, public funding of infertility treatments, existence of a maternity stay law and whether gay/lesbian couples can adopt. To construct this composite index, each component was assigned a weight ranging from 0 to 1.0 (depending on the existence of legal provisions and services), prior to summing. Further information on the data sources for each indicator, as well as the method of weighting, are reported in detail by the Institute for Women's Policy Research (1996).

Total and Cause-specific Mortality

State-specific, age-standardized mortality rates for women were obtained from the 1990 compressed mortality files compiled by the National Center for Health Statistics, Centers for Disease Control and Prevention (CDC). Data were obtained using the CDC WONDER/PC software (Friede et al., 1993). Age-standardized male all-cause mortality rates were obtained at the same time.

Self-reported Days of Activity Limitations

State-specific estimates of self-reported morbidity were obtained from the behavioral risk factor surveillance system (BRFSS) conducted by the National Center for Chronic Disease Prevention and Health Promotion. The BRFSS is a state-based, random telephone survey of community-dwelling US adults aged 18 yr and over. Between 1993 and 1996, 350 000 respondents answered the quality-of-life module of the survey, which included an item on the number of days during the previous month in which poor physical or mental health kept the respondent from performing their usual activities, such as self-care, work or recreation (Centers for Disease Control and Prevention, 1994; Hennessy et al., 1994). From this survey, we calculated for each state (with the exception of Wyoming where data were unavailable), the mean number of days in the previous month during which women reported activity limitations.

Other Ecologic Covariates Related to Health Status

It has been previously reported that income distribution and poverty rates are ecologic predictors of mortality rates at the U.S. state level (Kennedy et al., 1996; Kawachi and Kennedy, 1997). Therefore, where appropriate, we adjusted for these state-specific economic characteristics when examining the relationships between indicators of women's status and health outcomes. State-specific data on income distribution were obtained from unpublished statistics courtesy of the Luxembourg Income Study (Timothy Smeeding, Project Director: personal communication). Gini coefficients in each state were calculated from disposable income, adjusted for Federal and state income and payroll taxes, as well as for cash or near-cash benefits including food stamps, the earned income tax credit (EITC) and school lunches. Adjustment for household size was accomplished using a household equivalence scale, with equivalence elasticity set at 0.5 (Atkinson et al., 1995; Kawachi and Kennedy, 1997). Data for adjusted Gini coefficients were calculated from the pooled 1991, 1992 and 1993 Current Population Surveys (Luxembourg Income Study: unpublished data).

Data on median household income and poverty rates were obtained from the 1990 US census population and housing summary tape file 3A (US Bureau of the Census, 1993). Households were classified as being above or below the poverty level based on the federal poverty index originally developed by the social security administration in 1964. The current poverty index is based purely on income from wages and does not reflect other sources of income such as non-cash benefits from food stamps, Medicaid and public housing. Poverty thresholds are updated annually to reflect changes in the consumer price index. The poverty variable we used represents the percentage of households in a given state that were below the federal poverty threshold. In 1990, this represented an income of less than $13,359 for households with 4 family members (US Bureau of the Census, 1993).

Data Analysis

Ordinary least squares regression was used to examine the relationships between indicators of women's status and health outcomes. When examining the health impact of women's political participation and reproductive rights, we simultaneously adjusted for income distribution (using the adjusted Gini coefficients), median income and poverty rates. In our analyses of women's employment and earnings, we adjusted for income distribution and poverty rates, but not median income, since women's earnings was already incorporated in the composite index. In the case of women's economic autonomy, we adjusted only for income distribution, since poverty rates were already incorporated in the composite index and median income was highly collinear with educational attainment.

RESULTS

Distribution of the Composite Indices of Women's Status

The political participation index ranged from a high of 8.78 (Kansas) to a low of -7.29 (Tennessee). The employment and earnings index ranged from a high of 4.63 (Alaska) to a low of 3.34 (West Virginia). The economic autonomy index ranged from a high of 4.50 (Maryland) to a low of 3.45 (Mississippi). The reproductive rights index ranged from a high of 5.25 (Hawaii) to a low of 0.03 (Nebraska). A consistent pattern was observed whereby states in the South-East (Kentucky, Virginia, West Virginia, Tennessee, Georgia, Mississippi and Louisiana) showed up

in the worst third of at least two out of the four composite indices. By contrast, Midwestern states (Minnesota, Wisconsin, Iowa, Kansas, Missouri) were more likely to be represented among the best third on two or more indices. The correlation among the 4 indices were high, ranging from 0.50 to 0.89, with the sole exception of the correlation between women's political participation and reproductive rights (r = 0.24) (Table 1).

Relationships of Women's Status to Women's and Men's Health

Total and Cause-specific Mortality

The political participation composite index was strikingly correlated with female mortality rates (r = -0.51): the higher the level of women's political participation, the lower their mortality rates (Table 1; Fig. 1). In regression analysis, a one unit improvement in the political participation index was associated with 7.3 fewer deaths per 100 000 women (95% confidence interval, CI: 3.8 to 10.9), equivalent to about a 11% lower age-adjusted female mortality rate with each unit increase in female political participation (Table 2). In models adjusting for median income, Gini index and

---

Table 1

Correlations Among Composite Indicators of Women's Status and Total Mortality, Major Causes of Death and Self-reported Mean Days of Activity Limitations

	POL	EMPL	ECON	REPRO	Mortality	Disease	Stroke	Neoplasm	DAYS
POL	1.00	0.50*	0.62*	0.24	− 0.51*	− 0.43*	− 0.38*	− 0.07	− 0.47
EMPL		1.00	0.89	0.62	− 0.25	− 0.24	− 0.39*	0.18	− 0.43*
ECON			1.00	0.61*	− 0.42*	− 0.33*	− 0.50*	0.03	− 0.52*
REPRO				1.00	− 0.14	− 0.08	− 0.33*	0.11	− 0.27
Total Mortality					1.00	0.53*	0.49*	0.65*	0.39*
Heart Disease						1.00	0.12	0.46*	0.31*
Stroke							1.00	− 0.06	0.28
Malignant Neoplasm								1.00	0.15
DAYS									1.00

* P < 0.05. POL: political participation composite index; EMPL: employment and earnings composite index; ECON: economic autonomy composite index; REPRO: reproductive rights composite index; DAYS: mean days of self-reported activity limitations (from the behavioral risk factor surveillance system, based on data from 49 states).

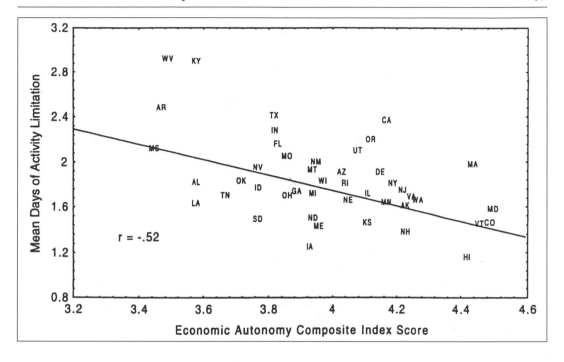

Figure 1
Women's political participation and female mortality rates.

poverty, the political participation index remained significantly associated with overall female mortality rates (ß = -5.1, s.e. = 2.1, p = 0.02). Interestingly, higher female political participation was also associated with higher overall mortality in men and the relationship was in fact slightly stronger than in women. A one unit increment in the political participation index was associated with 17.0 fewer age-adjusted deaths per 100 000 men (95% confidence interval, CI: 11.2 to 22.7), equivalent to about a 15% lower male mortality rate per unit increase in the index (Table 2, row 2).

Higher political participation was associated not only with lower overall female mortality, but also with certain specific causes of death (Table 2). In univariate models, higher female political participation was associated with lower rates of death from ischaemic heart disease, stroke, cer-

vical cancer, homicide and infant mortality (where male and female infant deaths were combined). However, only the associations with ischaemic heart disease and cervical cancer mortality remained statistically significant after adjustment for median income, income inequality and poverty rates. Malignant neoplasms, breast cancer and suicide showed no association with higher political participation either before or after adjustment for income distribution and poverty rates (Table 2).

In contrast to the political participation index, the employment and earnings composite index was statistically significantly associated with overall male mortality rates in both univariate and multivariate models, but not to female mortality rates (Table 3). Despite the lack of an association with overall female mortality, higher levels of women's employment and earnings

Table 2

Relationship of Political Participation Composite Index to Total and Cause Specific Mortality Rates and Mean Days of Activity Limitation

Cause of death	ICD code (9th revision)	Univariate model					Multivariate model adjusted for median income, income inequality and poverty						
		B	s.e.	adjusted R^2	$F_{1,48}$	$p <$	B	s.e.	$t, p <$	adjusted R^2	$F_{4,45}$	$p <$
Total female mortality		−7.33	1.80	0.24	16.68	0.0002	−5.09	2.15	2.36, 0.0227	0.29	6.08	0.0005
Total male mortality		−16.96	2.95	0.39	32.97	0.0000	−11.98	3.55	3.35, 0.0016	0.44	10.44	0.000
Female cause-specific mortality												
Ischaemic heart disease	410--414	−2.73	0.83	0.17	10.85	0.0019	−2.12	1.02	2.08, 0.0432	0.19	3.83	0.0092
Cerebrovascular disease	430--438	−0.75	0.27	0.12	7.87	0.0072	−0.37	0.32	1.16, 0.2535	0.18	3.69	0.0111
Malignant neoplasms	140–239	−0.27	0.53	0.00	0.26	0.6154	−0.41	0.62	0.66, 0.5119	0.1	2.38	0.0655
Breast Cancer	174	−0.01	0.08	0.00	0.00	0.9572	−0.10	0.09	1.13, 0.2661	0.14	2.99	0.0285
Cervical cancer	180	−0.07	0.01	0.34	26.12	0.0001	−0.06	0.02	3.58, 0.0008	0.34	7.20	0.0001
Suicide	950–959	0.03	0.05	0.00	0.36	0.5488	−0.10	0.06	1.68, 0.1006	0.04	1.47	0.2275
Homicide	960–969	−0.20	0.05	0.24	16.31	0.0002	−0.07	0.05	1.35, 0.1848	0.49	12.97	0.0000
Infant mortality (male and female)		−0.18	0.05	0.18	11.48	0.0014	−0.11	0.06	1.70, 0.0961	0.18	3.65	0.0117
Mean days limited activity (females)		−0.05	0.01	0.21	13.62	0.0006	−0.03	0.02	1.75, 0.871	0.25	5.05	0.002

Table 3

Relationship of Employment and Earnings Composite Index to Total and Cause Specific Mortality Rates and Days of Activity Limitation

Cause of death	ICD code (9th revision)	Univariate model					Multivariate model adjusted for income inequality and poverty					
		B	s.e.	adjusted R^2	$F_{1,48}$	$p <$	B	s.e.	$t, p <$	adjusted R^2	$F_{3,46}$	$p <$
Total female mortality		−46.98	26.12	0.04	3.23	0.0783	−36.87	31.69	1.16, 0.2507	0.24	6.16	0.0013
Total male mortality		−143.16	45.04	0.16	10.53	0.002	−119.99	53.17	2.26, 0.0288	0.37	10.61	0.0000
Female cause ± specific mortality												
Ischaemic heart disease	410–414	−19.55	11.57	0.04	2.85	0.0976	−27.13	14.53	1.87, 0.0682	0.18	4.60	0.0067
Cerebrovascular disease	430–438	−10.03	3.45	0.13	8.44	0.0055	−10.16	4.53	2.25, 0.0295	0.19	4.95	0.0046
Malignant neoplasms	140–239	8.79	6.75	0.01	1.70	0.1988	1.12	8.84	0.13, 0.8997	0.09	2.57	0.0654
Breast cancer	174	1.28	1.02	0.01	1.58	0.2144	−1.32	1.28	1.03, 0.3067	0.15	3.93	0.014
Cervical cancer	180	−0.50	0.21	0.09	5.59	0.0222	−0.56	0.26	2.14, 0.0379	0.24	6.14	0.0013
Suicide	950–959	−0.31	0.67	0.00	0.21	0.6450	0.66	0.90	0.73, 0.4693	0.00	0.91	0.4451
Homicide	960–969	−1.07	0.72	0.02	2.17	0.1473	0.51	0.73	0.70, 0.4905	0.47	15.2	0.0000
Infant mortality (male and female)		−1.75	0.70	0.10	6.26	0.0158	−1.36	0.90	1.50, 0.1397	0.18	4.66	0.0063
Mean days limited activity		−0.54	0.17	0.17	10.56	0.0021	−0.49	0.22	2.24, 0.0299	0.26	6.70	0.0008

Table 4

Relationship of Economic and Earnings Composite Index to Total and Cause Specific Mortality Rates and Mean Days of Activity Limitation

Cause of death	ICD code (9th revision)	Univariate model					Multivariate model adjusted for income inequality					
		B	s.e.	adjusted R^2	$F_{1,48}$	$p <$	B	s.e.	t, $p <$	adjusted R^2	$F_{2,47}$	$p <$
Total female mortality		-82.58	25.55	0.16	10.45	0.0022	-54.55	25.11	2.17, 0.0349	0.29	11.11	0.0001
Total male mortality		-217.39	41.40	0.35	27.57	0.0000	-170.87	40.49	4.22, 0.0001	0.46	21.72	0.0000
Female cause-specific mortality												
Ischaemic heart disease	410–414	-28.19	11.76	0.09	5.75	0.0204	-17.69	11.96	1.47, 0.1458	0.18	6.22	0.0040
Cerebrovascular disease	430–438	-13.56	3.38	0.24	16.06	0.0002	-11.63	3.57	3.25, 0.0021	0.26	9.41	0.0003
Malignant neoplasms	140–239	1.42	7.17	0.00	0.03	0.8432	-6.22	9.29	0.67, 0.5067	0.06	2.66	0.0801
Breast cancer	174	1.57	1.05	0.02	2.22	0.1427	1.93	1.13	1.71, 0.0938	0.02	1.51	0.2311
Cervical cancer	180	-0.71	0.21	0.18	11.52	0.0014	-0.51	0.21	2.43, 0.0187	0.26	9.80	0.0003
Suicide	950–959	-0.35	0.69	0.00	0.25	0.6187	-0.29	0.75	0.38, 0.7002	0.00	0.14	0.8647
Homicide	960–969	-2.44	0.69	0.19	12.56	0.0009	-1.37	0.60	2.28, 0.0272	0.46	21.98	0.0000
Infant mortality (male and female)		-2.63	0.68	0.22	15.03	0.0003	-2.17	0.17	3.06, 0.0037	0.26	9.59	0.0003
Mean days limited activity		-0.68	0.16	0.26	17.84	0.0001	-0.56	0.17	3.35, 0.0016	0.31	11.56	0.0000

Table 5

Relationship of Reproductive Rights Composite Index to Total and Cause Specific Mortality Rates, and Mean Days of Activity Limitation

Cause of death	ICD code (9th revision)	Univariate model					Multivariate model adjusted for income inequality, poverty, median income						
		B	s.e.	adjusted R^2	$F_{1,48}$	$p <$	B	s.e.	$t, p <$	adjusted R^2	$F_{4,45}$	$p <$	
Total female mortality		5.97	5.92	0.00	1.01	0.3188	−6.53	6.59	0.99, 0.3278	0.22	4.51	0.0038	
Total male mortality		−20.61	10.63	0.05	3.75	0.0585	−11.84	11.44	1.03, 0.3065	0.31	6.52	0.0003	
Female cause-specific mortality													
Ischaemic heart disease	410–414	−1.38	2.64	0.00	0.27	0.6033	0.21	3.11	0.07, 0.9452	0.11	2.51	0.0552	
Cerebrovascular disease	430–438	−1.89	0.78	0.09	5.79	0.0199	−1.00	0.94	1.06, 0.2926	0.18	3.62	0.0121	
Malignant neoplasms	140–239	1.16	1.52	0.00	0.59	0.4461	−0.89	1.81	0.49, 0.6235	0.10	2.32	0.0709	
Breast cancer	174	0.08	0.23	0.00	0.11	0.7374	−0.18	0.27	0.69, 0.4952	0.12	2.74	0.0398	
Cervical cancer	180	−0.07	0.05	0.03	2.39	0.1282	−0.07	0.06	1.23, 0.2235	0.18	3.60	0.0124	
Suicide	950–959	−0.16	0.15	0.00	1.23	0.2728	−0.04	0.19	0.19, 0.8502	0.00	0.73	0.5757	
Homicide	960–969	−0.18	0.16	0.00	1.23	0.2733	−0.17	0.15	1.17, 0.2462	0.49	12.75	0.0000	
Infant mortality (male and female)		−0.37	0.16	0.10	5.84	0.0195	−0.39	0.18	2.08, 0.0431	0.20	4.10	0.0064	
Means days limited activity		−0.07	0.04	0.05	3.55	0.0657	−0.03	0.05	0.71, 0.4817	0.12	3.19	0.0325	

were nonetheless significantly associated with lower mortality from specific causes after adjusting for median income, income inequality and poverty rates, including cerebrovascular disease (p = 0.03), cervical cancer (p = 0.04) and marginally to ischaemic heart disease (p = 0.07).

The economic autonomy composite index was strongly associated with both male and female total mortality rates, in univariate as well as multivariate models (Table 4). Once again, the association was stronger for males than for females. In multivariate models, women's economic autonomy was related to female death rates from cerebrovascular disease, cervical cancer, homicide and to infant mortality.

The reproductive rights composite index was the only index that was not associated with female total mortality, nor any specific cause of death except infant mortality (Table 5). Higher reproductive rights for women was marginally significantly (p = 0.06) associated with male mortality rates (Table 5, row 2), but this association did not hold up in analyses adjusting for income inequality, poverty and median income.

In sum, indices of women's political participation and economic autonomy were strikingly related to overall female and male mortality rates. For various reasons that we will discuss below, male mortality rates appeared to be even more strongly linked to indices of women's status than female mortality rates. Turning to cause-specific mortality among women, deaths from cerebrovascular disease and cervical cancer (and less consistently, heart disease, homicide and infant mortality) were associated with the status of women in both univariate and multivariate models, even in instances where the composite indices were not related to overall female mortality. Among the major causes of death, breast cancer was unrelated to any of the indices of women's status, even indicating a weak positive relationship to the index of women's economic autonomy (p = 0.09, Table 4).

Self-reported Mean Days of Activity Limitations Among Women

Three of the 4 indices of women's status were significantly and inversely correlated with the man number residing in the fifty states: political participation (r = -0.47); employment and earnings (r = -0.43) and economic autonomy (r = -0.52) (Table 1). In regression models, women's political participation was only marginally related to activity limitation (p = 0.09) after adjusting for median income, inequality and poverty (Table 2, bottom row). On the other hand, two of the composite indices—employment and earnings (Table 3) and economic autonomy (Table 4; Fig. 2)—remained strongly associated with fewer days of activity limitations among women, even in multivariate models. No relationship was observed between reproductive rights and activity limitations (Table 5).

Relationships of Individual Component Indicators of Women's Status to Women's Health

Given the strength of the associations found between composite indices of women's status and the health of both men and women, we proceeded to examine the relationships with the individual, component indicators that made up each index of women's status (Table 6). Of the 4 indicators that make up the political participation composite index, the percentage of women who voted in each state had the strongest inverse relationship to female mortality rates (r = -0.54), followed by women's representation in elected office (r = -0.38) and the present women registered to vote (r = -0.35). Among the 4 indicators that make up the employment and earnings composite index, the percent of women in the labor force (r = -0.55) and the female/male earnings ratio (r = -0.30) showed the strongest relationships to mortality. All 4 indicators that make up the economic autonomy composite index were about equally correlated with female mortality rates (Table 6). In all, 8 of the 12 component indicators of women's status were statis-

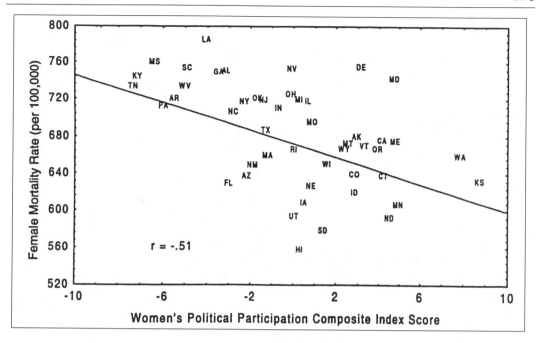

Figure 2
Women's economic autonomy and mean number of days of self-reported activity limitation

tically significantly correlated ($p < 0.05$) with women's reported mean days of activity limitation (Table 6).

Relationships of Women's Status Indicators to Men's Health

At the state level, female mortality rates were extremely tightly correlated with male mortality rates ($r = 0.93$). As a result, predictors of female mortality rates could be expected to correlate with male mortality rates. As described above, 3 of the 4 composite indicators of women's status also predicted male mortality rates. The correlations were -0.64 for political participation, -0.60 for women's economic autonomy, -0.42 for employment and earnings and -0.27 for reproductive rights. These correlations may partly reflect the fact that gender inequalities are manifestations of *general* inequalities. For example, the indices for female political participation and economic autonomy were both correlated ($r = -0.49$ and -0.36, respectively) with the Gini coefficient of income inequality (although neither the index of women's employment and earnings ($r = -.014$) nor reproductive rights ($r = -0.08$) were correlated with the Gini index).

In turn, income inequality has been previously demonstrated to be strongly correlated with both male and female mortality rates at the cross-country (Wilkinson, 1992; Wilkinson, 1996) and cross-regional level (Kaplan et al., 1996; Kennedy et al., 1996). Thus, measures of gender inequality may be confounded by more general processes (such as income inequality) or alternatively, truncated opportunities for women may be a potential pathway through which income inequality produces adverse health effects for both sexes. Both types of effects are plausible and given the tight correlation between male and female mor-

Table 6

Correlations Between Component Indicators of Women's Status and Mortality Rates and Activity Limitations

Component indicators	Female mortality rates	Male mortality rates	White female mortality	Black female mortality	Mean days of activity limitations (females)	Mean days of activity limitations (males)
Political participation composite index						
Women in elected office	− 0.38*	− 0.55*	− 0.26	− 0.33*	− 0.34*	− 0.35*
Percent women registered to vote in 1992/94	− 0.35*	− 0.26	− 0.42*	− 0.18	− 0.39*	− 0.29*
Percent women who voted in 1992/94	− 0.54*	− 0.56*	− 0.53*	− 0.20	− 0.49*	− 0.47*
Number of institutional resources available to women	0.16	0.10	0.18	0.13	0.13	− 0.01
Emloyment and earnings composite index						
Median annual earnings for full-time women	0.02	− 0.19	0.10	− 0.01	− 0.23	− 0.21
Earnings ratio between women and men	− 0.30*	− 0.29*	− 0.28*	− 0.25	− 0.31*	− 0.14
Percent women in labor force	− 0.55*	− 0.54*	− 0.55*	− 0.09	− 0.55*	− 0.44*
Percent women in managerial or professional occupations	− 0.12	− 0.31*	− 0.05	− 0.16	− 0.27	− 0.22
Economic autonomy composite index						
percent women with 4 or more years of college	− 0.33*	− 0.49*	− 0.29*	− 0.20	− 0.50*	− 0.38*
Percent women without health insurance	0.36*	0.39*	0.30*	0.13	0.37*	0.37*
Percent women in poverty	0.39*	0.55*	0.26	0.14	0.45*	0.48*
Percent of businesses owned by women	− 0.31*	− 0.50*	− 0.19	− 0.26	− 0.21	− 0.27

* $p < 0.05$.

tality rates at the state level, our analyses could not distinguish between the two.

In multivariate regression models adjusting for income inequality, indices of women's political participation, employment and earnings and economic autonomy continued to predict overall male mortality rates. The strength of these associations were undiminished when we examined the *difference* in male/female mortality rates across states: where women's status was low, women's mortality rates were higher, but male mortality rates tended to be even higher, so that the difference in male/female mortality rates were, if anything, even greater.

In contrast to mortality rates (where males have higher rates), morbidity rates are almost always higher in women. The zero-order correlations between indices of women's status and reported days of activity limitations among men were -0.49 for political participation, -0.34 for employment and earnings, -0.46 for economic autonomy and -0.20 for reproductive rights. However, in contrast to mortality, none of the indices of women's status predicted male activity limitations in multivariate regression models after adjusting for income inequality, poverty rates and median income, whereas they continued to predict women's activity limitations. Close examination of the individual component indicators of women's status (Table 6) similarly indicates that the associations are generally stronger for activity limitations among women than among men.

Women's Status and Mortality Among White Women Versus Black Women

As can be seen on Figs. 1 and 2, the Southern states in the USA tend to score poorly in terms of indices of women's status. These also tend to be the states where more African-Americans live and hence our findings could reflect confounding by other processes such as the effects of racial discrimination on health (Kennedy et al., 1997).

However, when we separately examined the relationships of women's status to mortality rates among white women and African-American women, we found that whereas the component indicators were consistently related to mortality rates among the former, none of them (with the exception of % women elected to political office) were related to mortality rates among black women (Table 6). Such a pattern suggests that confounding by racism is unlikely to explain our principal findings. The lack of association with black women's mortality may reflect the aggregated nature of our composite indices, i.e., the results may have been different if indicators had been developed specifically to reflect African-American women's status.

There were too few African-American women in the behavioral risk factor surveillance system to derive stable state-specific estimates of the mean days of activity limitations in this group.

DISCUSSION

P UBLIC health has increasingly recognized that women's unequal status in society jeopardizes their health and well-being (Cook, 1994; Fee and Krieger, 1994; Doyal, 1995). The 1994 Cairo conference on Population and Development expanded the conceptual framework of women's health to encompass previously unacknowledged components of health, including socioeconomic inequality, women's empowerment, unequal burdens of domestic labour, constraints on women to determine their own sexuality and reproduction, political participation, literacy and the epidemic of male violence against women (United Nations, 1994). In seeking to uncover the societal level determinants of women's health, the present study examined four composite indices of women's status: women's political participation, employment and earnings, economic autonomy and reproductive rights. Indicators of women's status in society turned out to be closely linked to female total and cause-specific mortality (with breast cancer, all malignant neoplasms and suicide being notable exceptions), as well as to morbidity.

Women's Status Predicts Men's Health

A noteworthy finding of our study was that indices of women's status also strongly predicted male mortality rates (though not male activity limitations). A possible interpretation of these results is that states with greater gender inequality are also more unequal in general, thereby raising both male and female mortality rates. For example, high poverty rates among woman may be correlated with (and hence act as a proxy for) high prevalence of poverty among men, so that female poverty rates end up predicting both male and female mortality rates. Alternatively, it is possible that indices of women's status are confounded by other ecologic variables that are detrimental to the health of both sexes—such as the degree of inequality in household incomes—which have been shown previously to explain variations in health status across states (Kaplan et al., 1996; Kennedy et al., 1996), as well as between countries (Wilkinson, 1992, 1996). We attempted to overcome this potential confounding by adjusting for known ecologic predictors of mortality, including the Gini index of household income, percent of households under the poverty threshold and median household income. Nevertheless, indices of women's status continued to predict both male and female mortality rates in multivariate regression models. The processes by which patriarchy and unequal status for women might spill over into worse health status for men therefore need to be further explored.

One mechanism for the association between women's status and male mortality is the fact that factors which adversely affect women's economic security also affect the material wellbeing of male members of the households to which women belong: including spouses, partners, sons and fa-

thers. Some of the indicators of women's status examined in the present analysis—for example, women's labor force participation and median earnings—could potentially affect the wellbeing of both men and women. Since dual earners characterized 70 percent of married-couple families in 1994 (Institute for Women's Policy Research, 1996), women's labor force participation and earnings could directly influence the economic well-being (and thereby the health status) of such families, including any male members.

In contrast to total mortality, our analyses of activity limitations yielded more unambiguous associations with between women's status and women's health. Greater economic autonomy, as well as employment and earnings among women were strongly associated with less activity limitations in women but not in men.

The Societal Costs of Gender Inequality

Discussion of patriarchy have tended to focus on the subordination of women by men, where the latter are assumed to benefit from such arrangements. Thus: "the material base of patriarchy is men's control over women's labor power. That control is maintained by excluding women from access to necessary economically productive resources and by restricting women's sexuality. Men exercise their control in receiving personal service work from women, in not having to do housework or rear children, in having access to women's bodies for sex and in feeling powerful and being powerful" (Hartmann, 1994, p. 572). While none could deny that men benefit from patriarchal arrangements in all the manners described, an overlooked feature of patriarchy is the costs of such a system for society as a whole. Hartmann (1994) has argued that it is crucial to examine hierarchy *among* men and their differential access to patriarchal benefits. Thus, certain types of gender inequality, such as reduced female earnings, are themselves patterned by class, race and other socioeconomic characteristics. In other words, the ill health burden of gender inequality is disproportionately borne by women—and men—with preexisting socioeconomic disadvantage. As well, women of different class, race, martial status or sexual orientation are subjected to different degrees of patriarchal power. Women may themselves exercise class, race or national power, or even patriarchal power (through their family connections) over men lower in the patriarchal hierarchy than their own male kin (Hartmann, 1994). Men's exploitation of women may be most evident when patriarchal systems are observed at the level of individual relationships, e.g., within domestic settings. But when society itself becomes the focus of analysis, the costs of patriarchy are no longer borne solely by women. Considered as a whole, a society that tolerates gender inequalities is also likely to be a more unhealthy place to live for both men and women, compared to a more egalitarian one. To paraphrase the Beijing Declaration and Platform for Action, the well-being of a society depends upon women's economic and political status within that society (United Nations, 1995).

Limitations

A number of important limitations should be noted about our analyses. The cross-sectional and ecologic nature of the data limits our ability to make causal inferences and to draw inferences about individuals. For instance, we were unable to exclude the possibility of reverse causation, i.e., that higher geographic concentrations of unhealthy women result in diminished economic autonomy and political participation in those areas. Ecologic analyses similarly do not permit us to say whether *individual* women with diminished economic autonomy suffer from increased mortality or disability risks. Statements of this type involve the risk of committing the ecologic fallacy. Our findings would have been strengthened if data were available on the health of individual women residing in different states. Such

data would help to identify which subgroups of women (and perhaps men)—defined by class, age or race/ethnicity—are most vulnerable to the risks of ill health imposed by gender inequality. Ecologic analyses of the type presented here only permit us to observe that more unequal states are unhealthier in general compared to more egalitarian places. A further caveat regarding the interpretation of our data is the possibility that some as yet unidentified, omitted variables could have confounded the observed relationship between indicators of women's status and women's health. Although we attempted to adjust for some of the major predictors of population health status, we lacked data on some variables (e.g., household division of labour and economic resources), while still other variables (e.g., patriarchal culture) remain poorly conceptualized.

Most of the economic indicators of women's status (e.g., median earnings, female:male earnings ratio, poverty level an educational attainment) were obtained from the 1990 Census of Population (Institute for Women's Policy Research, 1996). However, other indicators, such as those related to women's political participation, were based on data collected from 1993 onwards, so that strictly speaking, they post-dated our mortality data (which were 1990), though not our morbidity data (which were obtained between 1993 and 1996). Given the varying timing of the data assembled in our analyses, we have had to assume that there was sufficient stability in the rankings of states via á vis women's political circumstances reaching back in time. This assumption may not be warranted, since certain indicators such as legislation affecting women's reproductive rights, may change over a relatively short span of time. Additionally, we have not taken account of induction times between the start of exposure to a particular social environment and specific health outcomes. For instance, mortality from cardiovascular diseases (heart attack and stroke), homicide and infant mortality may respond more quickly to changes in the social milieu than other causes of death such as neoplasms. The finding in the present study of a relationship between women's status and mortality from cervical cancer was notable in that the disease possibly reflects the extent of women's control over sexual relationships (e.g., negotiating around use of barrier contraceptive methods). If the finding on cervical cancer is real, then this would suggest to us that the indices of women's status reflect stable, long-term processes.

Finally, analyses of the type presented here need to be repeated and tested for a much fuller set of health outcomes, including domestic violence, mental health, functional status, health behaviors and other measures that capture women's health experience across the life course.

CONCLUSIONS

DESPITE the limitations mentioned, the present study has demonstrated the potential utility of extending studies of gender inequality and women's health to the societal (ecologic) domain. Geographic and political units even within a single country vary in the level of status accorded to women, in ways that have measurable consequences for the health. Women's health and the formulation of effective strategies for improving women's status must thus be a central concern not only in feminist politics, but in broader campaigns for public health and social justice.

REFERENCES

Atkinson, A.B., Rainwater, L., Smeeding, T.M., 1995. Income Distributon in OECD Countries. Evidence from the Luxembourg Income Study. Organization for Economic Co-operation and Development, Paris.

Centers for Disease Control and Prevention, 1994. Quality of life as a new public health measure—Behavioral risk factor surveillance system. 1993. MMWR 43 (20), 375–380.

Connell, R. W., 1987. Gender and Power. Stanford University Press, Stanford, CA.

Cook, R.J., 1994. Women's Health and Human Rights. World Health Organizations. Geneva.

Doyal, L., 1995. What Makes Women Sick: Gender and the Political Economy of Health. Rutgers University Press, New Jersey.

Fee, E., Krieger, N. (Eds.). 1994. Women's Health, Politics, and Power. Baywood Publishing Co., New York.

Friede, A., Reid, J.A., Ory, H.W., 1993. CDC WONDER: a comprehensive on-line public health information system of the centers for disease control and prevention. Am. J. Public Health 83, 1289–1294.

Hartmann, H., 1994. The unhappy marriage of Marxism and feminism: towards a more progressive union. In: Grusky, D.B. (Ed.), Social Stratification in Sociological Perspective. Westview Press, Boulder, CO, pp. 570–576.

Hennessy, C.H., Moriarty, D.G., Zack, M.M., Scherr, P.A., Brackbill, R., 1994. Measuring health-related quality of life for public health surveillance. Public Health Rep. 109, 665–672.

Institute for Women's Policy Research, 1996. The Status of Women in the States. Institute for Women's Policy Research (Library of Congress Card Catalogue Number 96–79874), Washington, DC.

Kaplan, G., Pamuk, E., Lynch, J.W., Cohen, R.D., Balfour, J.L., 1996. Inequality in income and mortalty in the United States: analysis of mortality and potential pathways. BMJ 312, 999–1003.

Kawachi, I., Kennedy, B.P., 1997. The relationship of income inequality to mortality—Does the choice of indicator matter? Soc. Sci. Med. 45, 1121–1127.

Kennedy, B.P., Kawachi, I., Prothrow-Stith, D., 1996. Income distribution and mortality: cross sectional ecological study of the Robin Hood Index in the United States. BMJ 312, 1004–1007.

Kennedy, B.P., Kawachi, I., Lochner, K., Jones, C.P., Prothrow-Stith, D., 1997. (Dis)respect and black mortality. Ethnic Disease 7, 207–214.

Macintyre, S., 1997. The black report and beyond: what are the issues? Soc. Sci. Med. 44 (6), 723–745.

United Nations, 1994. Programme of Action of the International Conference on Population and Development. Cairo. United Nations. New York, NY.

United Nations, 1995. Report of the Fourth World Conference on Women. Beijing Declaration and Platform for Action. United Nations. New York, NY.

US Bureau of the Census (1993). CD-ROM, income and poverty. US Bureau of the Census. Washington, DC.

Walsh Chapman, D., Sorensen, G., Leonard, L., 1995. Gender, health, and cigarette smoking. In: Amick III, B.C., Levine, S., Tarlov, A.R., Chapman Walsh, D. (Eds.), Society and Health. Oxford University Press, Oxford.

Wilkinson, R.G., 1992. Income distribution and life expectancy. Br. Med. J. 304, 165–168.

Wilkinson, R.G., 1996. Unhealthy Societies. The Afflictions of Inequality. Routledge, London.

Yllo, K. (1983). Sexual equality and violence against wives in American states. J. Comp. Fam. Stud. XIV, No. 1 (Spring), 67–68.

☙

Forty

THE CULTURE OF INEQUALITY

Richard Wilkinson

A S the papers collected together in this book show, there are powerful connections between the scale of income inequality and population death rates. Indeed, it is not the richest of the developed countries, but the most egalitarian, which have the best health. More than 20 papers have reported this association using international data and data for large areas within countries—such as the 50 US states or 282 Standard Metropolitan Areas (see papers in Part One above). As well as cross sectional associations, *changes* in income distribution have also been found to be related to changes in death rates (Kaplan et al 1996 in Part Two; Wilkinson 1992 in Part One; Wilkinson 1994). These relationships have withstood controlling for variables such as GNP per capita or median income, absolute poverty, expenditure on medical care, and smoking. Against more than 20 papers confirming this relation there are only two which do not—and both of them used the same data set (see papers in Part Two above).

This relationship is as important for what it tells us about how social structure affects subjective welfare as it is for what it tells us about health. The quality of life is after all just as important as its length. The crucial determinants of population health and of health inequalities in most of the developed world turn out to be less a matter of medical care or the direct effects of ex-

posure to hazardous material circumstances, as of the effects of the social environment as structured by social hierarchy.

Increasingly it looks as if the most powerful influences on population health in the developed world are psychosocial. For example, research on unemployment and health shows that health worsens before people become unemployed, when redundancies are first announced and they start worrying about the future (Ferrie et al 1995). Similarly, the three-fold differences in death rates between senior and junior civil servants working in London offices (almost all of whom would call themselves middle class) are most strongly related to psychosocial variables such as the amount of job control they have (Marmot et al 1997; Davey Smith et al 1990). Likewise, research into the effects of social hierarchy among monkeys shows that low social status has many of the same physiological effects as are found among low status civil servants—even when the social status of the monkeys is experimentally manipulated and diet and environment are controlled (Shively et al 1994, 1997, and Sapolsky 1997—all in Part Three above; Brunner 1997). It is hard to explain the biological results as reflecting anything except the direct psychosocial effects of low social status itself. Health inequalities therefore are not simply the direct result of exposure to material factors like bad housing and diet. Instead, low social status leads to chronic anxiety, permanent increases in levels of stress hormones such as cortisol, more atherosclerosis, and poorer immunity. In many ways the end result is analogous to more rapid ageing (Sapolsky 1994).

The most important reason why more egalitarian societies are healthier seems to be that they enjoy a better quality of social relations. In chapter 6 of my book (Wilkinson 1996) I showed circumstantial evidence that societies which were unusually egalitarian and unusually healthy were also unusually *cohesive*. Similarly, Robert Putnam (1993), in his study of the strength of civic society in the Italian regions, noted that his index of civic community is closely correlated with income distribution and said that more egalitarian social attitudes are "an essential feature of the civic community" (p.105). Since then measures of social relations such as the extent to which people *trust* each other in different US States (Kawachi et al 1997), levels of hostility in different cities (Williams et al 1995) and rates of homicide and violent crime have all been shown to be strongly related to the extent of income inequality. The relationship with homicide has been found to be particularly robust: a meta-analysis of some 34 studies shows that homicide and violence are related to income inequality over a wide range of conditions (Hsieh et al 1993).

What we are seeing is not the health effects of any single measure of the social environment but the result of a general shift in the nature of social relations throughout a society: not only lower levels of trust and more hostility and violence, but also lower levels of social support, weaker social networks and almost certainly more domestic conflict as well. There seems to be what we should probably call a *"culture of inequality"* which is less supportive, more aggressive and macho—or "laddish". As well as being suggested by measures of social relations, this picture is also supported by the pattern of mortality related to inequality. Although inequality is associated with increased death rates from most of the ma-

jor causes of death, it seems to have a particularly dramatic effect on violence, accidents and alcohol related deaths (Kaplan et al 1996; McIsaac et al 1997 in section B; Wilkinson 1996b; Walberg et al 1998).

A close interaction between income distribution and the social environment could not fail to have a powerful impact on health. As many well controlled studies show, two of the most powerful influences on population health in developed countries are *social status* and the quality of *social networks*. (Shively et al 1994, 1997, and Sapolsky 1997—all in Part Three above; Brunner 1997; House et al 1988; Berkman 1995) But in an important sense, social status and social relations are probably opposite sides of the same coin. Friendship is about mutuality, reciprocity and a recognition of each other's needs. Social status, at least in the form of animal pecking orders, is about differential access to resources based on power and coercion—regardless of each other's needs. Interestingly, Putnam (1994) refers to the relationships between equals which contribute to a strong civic community as *horizontal* and contrasts them with the *vertical* patron/client relations up and down the hierarchy in less civic places. Similarly, among non-human primates there is also a clear contrast between the horizontal alliances or friendships and the vertical social ranking system. Animals form grooming alliances, incurring obligations of reciprocity, which serve to protect or improve their position in the social hierarchy.

The recognition that inequality is inimical to friendship is of course not new. Plato (*The Laws*) said "How correct the old saying is, that 'equality leads to friendship'! It's right enough and it rings true . . ." (p.229) Indeed the connection is so taken for granted that the Cambridge Scale for classifying occupations by social status (Prandy 1990) works by asking a sample of people their own occupation and the occupations of their friends. The occupations are then hierarchically ordered on the assumption that those with many friendship links between them have a similar social status whereas those with few such links between them will be those separated by large social status differences.

In addition to its sensitivity to social status and friendship, health provides a third pointer to the nature of the important underlying psychosocial processes. This is the powerful influence which early childhood emotional development has on health in adulthood. Emotional trauma, domestic conflict and poor attachment cast a long shadow forward over health in later life (Lundberg 1993; Fonagy 1999 in press; Montgomery et al 1997; Wadsworth 1984). Much the most plausible interpretation is that friendship, low social status and early childhood experience point to the same issues of insecurity, fears of personal inadequacy and inferiority. We use these same words not only to talk both about the results of poor early emotional attachment but also about the insecurities induced in relation to the social status hierarchy in adult life. Another similarity is that they both lead to higher basal levels of stress hormones such as cortisol, and it is also clear that early emotional insecurity increases our vulnerability to the status insecurities generated in relation to the social hierarchy.

Whether or not we have friends reflects the same underlying issue of confidence: friends feed back feelings of acceptance and belonging, they are validating and confirm our personal adequacy; their absence leads to feelings of inadequacy, self doubt and rejection. It would seem then that income inequality not only dramatically exacerbates status problems, cutting more people off from the normal sources of status and respect, but, through the strains which relative poverty imposes on domestic life, it also increases the number of people made vulnerable by growing up with domestic conflict (James 1995).

Central here is the emotional complex involving a sense of inferiority, lack of confidence and shame which Scheff (1988) called the *"deference-emotion system"*. Thomas Scheff notes "there has been a continuing suggestion in the literature that shame is *the* primary social emotion, gener-

ated by the virtually constant monitoring of the self in relation to others" (Scheff 1990 p.79). In part this echoes both Goffman (1967) who said that embarrassment plays a prominent role in every social encounter, and Darwin (1872) who, in his chapter on blushing (and its relation to shame), asserted that shame "depends in all cases on . . . a sensitive regard for the opinion, more particularly the depreciation of others". In the same vein, Paul Gilbert (1992) has suggested that "shame" is distantly related to an evolved 'submission' response of subordinate animals to superiors in the social hierarchy. In that the social hierarchy presents itself as an ordering of human competency, from the most competent at the top to the least competent at the bottom, the approach also fits well with the findings of Sennett and Cobb's (1973) study *The Hidden Injuries of Class.*

Scheff (1989) explains:

"shame involves painful feelings that are not identified as shame by the person experiencing them. Rather they are labelled with a wide variety of terms that serve to disguise the experience of shame: having low self-esteem, feeling foolish, stupid, ridiculous, inadequate, defective, incompetent, awkward), exposed, vulnerable, insecure, helpless." (These terms) occur . . . in contexts (which) involve a perception of self as negatively evaluated, by either self or others—the basic context for shame . . . In these instances, the negative evaluation of self appears to cause so much pain that it interferes with the fluent production of thought or speech, even though the pain is mislabeled." (p.182)

It is the unacknowledged or repressed nature of shame which "explains how shame might be ubiquitous, yet usually escape notice" (Scheff 1988 p.183). Scheff suggests that unacknowledged shame also leads to anger in a "shame-rage spiral." "As humiliation increases, rage and hostility increases proportionately to defend against loss of self-esteem." ". . . hostility can be viewed as an attempt to ward off feelings of humiliation (shame) generated by inept, ineffectual moves, a sense of incompetence, insults, and a lack of power to defend against insults". This ties up closely with the literature on violence which suggests how frequently it is triggered by people feeling they are being disrespected (Wilkinson et al 1998 in Part Three). James Gilligan (1996), a prison psychiatrist for 25 years, says in his book on violence "I have yet to see a serious act of violence that was not provoked by the experience of feeling shamed and humiliated, disrespected and ridiculed, and that did not represent the attempt to prevent or undo this "loss of face"—no matter how severe the punishment" (p. 110). Descriptions of street violence—even from participants—make much the same point (Wilkinson et al 1998 in Part Three, section B).

The centrality of disrespect would seem to explain the link between violence and greater inequality. At the same time it also explains the apparent paradox that the violence accompanying greater inequality is not primarily between rich and poor but tends instead to be concentrated in the poorest areas where people are denied access to the usual sources of status and respect. Interestingly, studies of the social behaviour of non-human primates have often recorded how, when an animal loses a battle for status, it then shows what is often described simply as "displaced aggression" towards others below it in the social hierarchy. The phenomenon is however more systematic than that and probably represents a reassertion of position over those below it, perhaps to prevent a catastrophic loss of status. It is known in German as the *"Radfahrer-reaktion"* (bicycling-reaction) because, having lost a battle for status, the animal—as Volker Sommer explained to me (personal communication)—"shows its back to those above it (in the domestic hierarchy) while kicking downwards at the animals below it". Among non-human primates, Sommer said it is very common that, after having received aggression from a higher ranking individual, it will then "redirect aggression towards lower ranking animals, sometimes in a chain reaction—so that alpha slaps beta, beta slaps gamma, gamma slaps delta etc.". Virgin and Sapolsky (1997) report that baboons showing this

kind of "displaced aggression" in response to domination from above often have lower basal cortisol levels suggesting that it may be an effective way of alleviating some of the stress of social subordination.

It looks as if this may also be relevant to the pattern which links economic hardship to increased discrimination against vulnerable minorities. We see this not only in the tendency for migrants and other ethnic and religious minorities to be scapegoated when unemployment is high, but presumably also in other areas including the tendency for sex offenders to be treated particularly brutally by other inmates in prisons, or for men who have been humiliated to be more likely to take it out on their wives. Institutional violence from above becomes overt violence against the most vulnerable lower down. Kennedy et al (1997 in this section) show that racial prejudice in the United States is greater where income inequality is greater, and the political and economic status of women (discussed in relation to health by Kawachi et al 1999 this section) is lower where the income distribution is wider. This is an important aspect of the more aggressive, more macho culture of inequality. Gloria Anzaldua, who grew up near the US-Mexican border, where the term "macho" developed its current connotations, explained the links thus:—

"For men like my father, being 'macho' meant being strong enough to protect and support my mother and us, yet being able to show love. Today's macho has doubts about his ability to feed and protect his family. His 'machismo' is an adaptation to oppression and poverty and low self-esteem. It is the result of hierarchical male dominance. The Anglo, feeling inadequate and inferior and powerless, displaces or transfers these feelings to the Chicano by shaming him. In the Gringo world, the Chicano suffers from excessive humility and self-effacement, shame of self and self-deprecation.

The loss of a sense of dignity and respect in the macho breeds a false machismo which leads him to put down women and even to brutalize them. Co-existing with his sexist behavior is a love of the mother which takes precedence over that of all others. Devoted son, macho pig. To wash down the shame of his acts, of his very being, and to handle the brute in the mirror, he takes to the bottle, the snort, the needle and the fist." (p.83)

It is not difficult to imagine how much the same processes may lie behind the association between greater inequality and more racial discrimination which has been demonstrated statistically in the United States (Kennedy et al 1997 in Part IV). Just as high status is built—by definition—at the expense of others who are rendered low status, so the relatively deprived can regain some shreds of the sense of self-worth taken from them by treating the most vulnerable as their inferiors—by discrimination and violence against them. The structural sources of these kinds of discrimination perhaps means that blame for them is not confined to those who overtly practice discrimination.

This paper has suggested that the relationship between wider income differences and lower standards of population health is likely to spring partly from the way a more unequal, more hierarchical, society increases people's sense of inferiority, shame and incompetence. The most plausible way of explaining the powerful influence which social status, social affiliations and poor emotional attachments in early childhood all have on health is that they are all linked to the chronic anxiety which arises from sources of insecurity involved in processes of social comparison. Such a perspective would bring together the psychological literature emphasising the importance of early childhood with the sociological literature on social stratification.

But rather than the importance of the social environment allowing us to ignore material inequalities, as some would wish, the implication is quite the reverse: the statistics show that somewhere between one-third and two-thirds of the differences in violence, social cohesion and life expectancy between societies is determined by differences in income inequality alone. Rather than the psychosocial taking us into individualism, it shows instead that the psychosocial welfare of populations is powerfully affected by structural factors. Indeed, because the social environment is built on economic foundations, it means we have—at last—a potent policy handle on the real social quality of life. Nor does everything depend on creating a totally egalitarian utopia: the evidence in this book comes entirely from analyses of the importance of existing differences in inequality between and within developed market democracies.

One additional point, which comes as a byproduct of this work, is that it tends to confirm the suggestion that the need to maintain or improve social status is a powerful force fuelling consumption. Income differences appear to be related to health only within countries where they map onto differences in social status. Large differences in average incomes between developed countries are, at most, only weakly related to health. Even where, among the 50 US states, there is less noise introduced by cultural differences, median income is only very weakly related to health and, after controlling for income inequality within each state, even that weak relation disappears altogether (Kaplan et al 1996; Wilkinson 1997). The contrasting close relation between income and health *within* societies and the weak or non-existent relation *between* developed societies is very striking. It provides additional evidence that income differences matter most where they map onto social status differences, that we are dealing with relative rather than absolute income. Following economists Robert Frank (1985) and Juliet Schor (1998) who have both argued that consumption is powered by concern over relative social status, it may not be too much of an exaggeration to suggest that if the individual desire for more income is largely a desire for improved social position, then it is not legitimate to assume that those individual desires can be summed into a desire for economic growth. That leads simply to a zero-sum game. If we are to achieve sustainable levels of economic activity it will surely be necessary to reduce the social stimulus to consumption.

REFERENCES

Anzaldua G. (1987) *Borderlands*. Aunt Lute Books, San Francisco.

Berkman LF. The role of social relations in health promotion. *Psychosomatic Research* 1995; 57: 245–54.

Brunner E. (1997) Stress and the biology of inequality. *British Medical Journal*; 314: 1472–6.

Darwin C. (1872). *The Expression of Emotion in Men and Animals*. John Murray, London.

Davey Smith G, Shipley MJ, Rose G. (1990) Magnitude and causes of socioeconomic differentials in mortality: further evidence from the Whitehall Study. *Journal of Epidemiology and Community Health*; 44: 265–70.

Frank RH. (1985) *Choosing the right pond: human behavior and the quest for status*. Oxford University Press.

Ferrie JE, Shipley MJ, Marmot MG, Stansfield S, Davey Smith G. (1995) Health effects of anticipation of job change and non-employment: longitudinal data from the Whitehall II study. *British Medical Journal*; 311: 1264–9.

Fonagy P. (1998) Early influences on development and social inequalities: an attachment theory perspective. Paper presented at the Kansas Conference on Health and its Social Determinants. Wichita.

Gilbert P. (1992) *Depression: the Evolution of Powerlessness*. Erlbaum, Hove.

Gilligan J. (1996) *Violence: Our Deadly Epidemic and its Causes*. G.P. Putnam.

Goffman E. (1967) *Interaction Ritual*. Anchor Doubleday, Garden City N.Y.

House JS, Landis KR, Umberson D. (1988) Social relationships and health. *Science*; 241: 540–5.

Hsieh CC, Pugh MD. (1993) Poverty, income inequality, and violent crime: a meta-analysis of recent aggregate data studies. *Criminal Justice Review*; 18: 182–202.

James O. (1995) *Juvenile violence in a winner-looser culture*. Free Associations Books.

Kaplan GA, Pamuk E, Lynch JW, Cohen RD, Balfour JL. (1996) Inequality in income and mortality in the United States: analysis of mortality and potential pathways. *British Medical Journal*; 312: 999–1003.

Kawachi I, Kennedy BP, Lochner K, Prothrow-Stith D. (1997) Social capital, income inequality and mortality. *American Journal of Public Health*; 87: 1491–8.

Kawachi I, Kennedy BP, Gupta V, Prothrow-Stith D. (1999) Women's status and the health of women: a view from the States. *Social Science and Medicine* 48: 21–32.

Kennedy BP, Kawachi I, Lochner K, Jones CP, Prothrow-Stith D. (1997) (Dis)respect and black mortality. *Ethnicity & Disease*; 7: 207–214.

Lundberg O. (1993) The impact of childhood living conditions on illness and mortality in adulthood. *Social Science and Medicine*; 36: 1047–52.

Marmot MG, Bosma H, Hemmingway H, Brunner E, Stansfeld S. (1997) Contribution of job control and other risk factors to socal variations in coronary heart disease incidence. *Lancet*; 350, 9073: 235–239.

McIsaac SJ, Wilkinson RG. (1997) Income distribution and cause-specific mortality. *European Journal of Public Health*; 7: 45–53.

Montgomery SM, Bartley MJ, Wilkinson RG. (1997) Family conflict and slow growth. *Archives of the Diseases of Childhood*; 77: 326–30.

Plato (translated by T.J. Saunders) (1979) *The Laws*. Penguin.

Prandy K. (1990) The revised Cambridge scale of occupations. *Sociology*; 24(4): 629–655.

Putnam RD, Leonardi R, Nanetti RY. (1993) *Making democracy work: civic traditions in modern Italy*. Princeton U.P.

Sapolsky RM. (1994) *Why zebras don't get ulcers. A guide to stress, stress-realted disease and coping*. WH Freeman, N.Y.

Sapolsky RM, Alberts SC, Altmann J. (1997) Hypercortisolism associated with social subordinance or social isolation among wild baboons. *Archives of General Psychiatry*; 54, 12: 1137–1143.

Scheff TJ, Retzinger SM, Ryan MT. (1989) Crime, violence, and self-esteem: review and proposals. In: *The social importance of self-esteem*. Edited by Mecca AM, Smelser NJ, Vasconcellos J. University of California Press, Berkeley.

Scheff TJ. (1988) Shame and conformity: the deference-emotion system. *American Sociological Review*; 53: 395–406.

Scheff TJ. (1990) *Microsociology: discourse, emotion and social structure*. University of Chicago Press.

Schor J. (1998) *The overspent American: when buying becomes you*. Basic Books.

Sennett R, Cobb J. (1973) *The Hidden Injuries of Class*. Knopf, N.Y.

Shively CA, Clarkson TB. (1994) Social status and coronary artery atherosclerosis in female monkeys. *Arteriosclerosis and Thrombosis*; 14: 721–6.

Shively CA, Laird KL, Anton RF. (1997) The behavior and physiology of social stress and depression in female cynomolgus monkeys. *Biological Psychiatry*; 41: 871–82.

Virgin CE, Sapolsky RM. (1997) Styles of male social behaviour and their endocrine correlates among low-ranking baboons. *American Journal of Primatology*; 42, 1: 25–39.

Wadsworth MEJ. (1984) Early stress and associations with adult health, behaviour and partenting. In: *Stress and disability in childhood*. Edited by Butler NR, Corner BD. Wright, Bristol.

Walberg P, McKee M, Shkolnikov V, Chenet L, Leon DA. (1998) Economic change, crime, and mortality crisis in Russia: regional analysis. *British Medical Journal*; 317: 312–8.

Wilkinson RG. (1992) Income distribution and life expectancy. *British Medical Journal*; 304: 165–8.

Wilkinson RG. (1994) Health, redistribution and growth. In: *Paying for inequality: the economic cost of social injustice.* Edited by A. Glyn and D. Miliband. Rivers Oram Press, London.

Wilkinson RG. (1996) *Unhealthy Societies: the afflictions of inequality*. Routledge, London.

Wilkinson RG. (1996b) Health and civic society in Eastern Europe before 1989. In: *The East-West life expectancy gap in Europe*. Edited by C. Hertzman, S. Kelly, M. Bobak. Kluwer, Dordrecht.

Wilkinson RG. (1997) Health inequalities: relative or absolute material standarsd? *British Medical Journal*; 314:591–5.

Wilkinson RG, Kawachi I, Kennedy B. (1998) Mortality, the social environment, crime and violence. *Sociology of Health and Illness*; 20(5): 578–97.

Williams RB, Feaganes J, Barefoot JC. (1995) Hostility and death rates in 10 US cities. *Psychosomatic Medicine*; 57 (1): 94.

APPENDIX

General Sources on Income Inequality Trends and Measurement

Atkinson AB, Rainwater L, Smeeding TM (1995). *Income distribution in OECD countries. Evidence from the Luxembourg Income Study.* Paris: Organization for Economic Co-operation and Development.

Cowell FA (1977). *Measuring Inequality.* Oxford: Philip Allan.

Danziger S and Gottschalk P (1995). *America Unequal.* Cambridge, MA: Harvard University Press.

Wolff E (1995; updated edition, 1996). *Top Heavy. The increasing inequality of wealth in America and what can be done about it.* New York: The New Press.

Massey DS (1996). The age of extremes: concentrated affluence and poverty in the twenty-first century. Demography 33: 395–412.

Hacker A (1997). *Money. Who has how much and why.* New York: Scribner.

Galbraith JK (1998). *Created Unequal. The Crisis in American Pay.* New York: The Free Press.

The relationship between equity and economic growth falls outside the scope of this book, but because of its potential importance, we offer the following list of references to interested readers.

Rodrik D (1998). Where did all the growth go? External shocks, social conflict, and growth collapses. *National Bureau of Economic Research Working Paper Series (No. 6350).*

Buchele R, Christiansen J (1992). Industrial relations and productivity growth: a comparative perspective. *International Contributions to Labour Studies* 2:77–97.

Gordon DM (1996). Conflict and cooperation: an empirical glimpse of the imperative of efficiency and redistribution. *Politics and Society* 24(4):433–456.

Organization for Economic Cooperation and Development (1996). Growth, equity, and redistribution. *OECD Economic Outlook,* December.

Bruno M, Ravallion M, Squire L (1995). Equity and growth in developing countries: old and new perspectives on the policy issues. IMF Conference on Income Distribution and Sustainable Growth. June 1–2.

Benabou R (1996). Inequality and growth. *Luxembourg Income Study Working Paper 142.* Luxembourg, June.

Slemrod J (1995). What do cross-country studies teach about government involvement, prosperity and economic growth? *Brookings Papers on Economic Activity* 2:373–431.

World Bank (1993). *The East Asian Miracle.* Oxford: Oxford University Press.

Birdsall N, Ross D, Sabot R (1995). Inequality and growth reconsidered—lessons from East Asia. *World Bank Economic Review* 9(3):477–508.

Persson T, Tabellini G (1994). Is inequality harmful for growth? Theory and evidence. *American Economic Review* 84(3):600–621.

Alesina A, Perotti R (1993). Income distribution, political instability, and investment. *National Bureau of Economic Research Working Paper 4486.* Cambridge, MA.

Leonardi R (1995). Social capital and the Mezzogiorno. *Oxford Review of Economic Policy.* 11:165–178.

Glyn A, Miliband D (1994). Introduction. In: A. Glyn and D. Miliband (eds). *Paying for Inequality: The Costs of Social Injustice.* London: Rivers Oram Press.

Osberg L (1995). The equity/efficiency trade-off in retrospect. *Canadian Business Economics.* Spring: 5–19.

❧

PERMISSIONS

12. Fiscella and Franks, "Poverty or Income Inequality as a Predictor of Mortality" originally appeared in *British Medical Journal*, 314: 1724–1728. © 1997 by the BMJ Publishing Group. Reprinted by permission.

13. Kawachi and Kennedy, "The Relationship of Income Inequality to Mortality" originally appeared in *Social Science & Medicine*, 45: 1121–1127. Reprinted by permission.

14. McIsaac and Wilkinson, "Income Distribution and Cause-Specific Mortality" originally appeared in *European Journal of Public Health*, 7: 45–53. Reprinted by permission.

15. Kennedy, Kawachi, Glass, and Prothrow-Smith, "Income Distribution, Socioeconomic Status, and Self-Rated Health" originally appeared in *British Medical Journal*, 317: 917–921. © 1998 by the BMJ Publishing Group. Reprinted by permission.

16. Wilkinson, "Health Inequalities" originally appeared in *British Medical Journal*, 314: 591–595. © 1997 by the BMJ Publishing Group. Reprinted by permission.

17. House, Landis, and Umberson, "Social Relationships and Health" originally appeared in *Science*, 214: 540–545. © 1998 by the American Association for the Advancement of Science. Reprinted by permission.

18. Berkman, "The Role of Social Relations in Health Promotion" originally appeared in *Psychosomatic Medicine*, 57: 245–254. © Lippincott Williams & Wilkins, reprinted by permission.

19. Kawachi, Colditz, Ascherio, Rimm, Giovannucci, Stampfer, and Willett, "A Prospective Study of Social Networks in Relation to Total Mortality and Cardiovascular Disease Incidence in Men" originally appeared in *Journal of Epidemiology & Community Health*, 50: 245–251, © 1996 by the BMJ Publishing Group. Reprinted by permission.

20. Kawachi and Kennedy, "Health and Social Cohesion" originally appeared in *British Medical Journal*, 314: 1037–1040. © 1997 by the BMJ Publishing Group. Reprinted by permission.

21. Lynch and Kaplan, "Understanding How Inequality in the Distribution of Income Affects Health" originally appeared in *Journal of Health Psychology*, 2 (3): 297–314, © 1997 by Sage Publications Ltd. Reprinted by permission.

22. Kawachi, Kennedy, Lochner, and Prothrow-Smith, "Social Capital, Income Inequality, and Mortality" originally appeared in *American Journal of Public Health*, 87: 1491–1498. © 1997 by the American Public Health Association. Reprinted by permission.

23. Kawachi, Kennedy, and Glass, "Social Capital and Self-Rated Health" originally appeared in *American Journal of Public Health*, 1999. © 1999 by the American Public Health Association. Reprinted by permission.

24. Wilkinson, "Health and Civil Society in Eastern Europe before 1989" originally appeared in *The East-West Life Expectancy Gap in Europe*, edited by Clyde Hertzman, pp.195–209. © 1996 by Kluwer Academic Publishers. Reprinted by kind permission of Kluwer Academic Publishers.

25. Kennedy, Kawachi and Brainerd, "The Role of Social Capital in the Russian Mortality Crisis" originally appeared in *World Development*, 26: 2029–2043. Reprinted by permission.

26. Hsieh and Pugh, "Poverty, Income Inequality, and Violent Crime" originally appeared in *Criminal Justice Review*, 18 (2): 182–202. © 1993 by the Criminal Justice Review. Reprinted by permission.

27. Wilson and Daly, "Life Expectancy, Economic Inequality, Homicide, and Reproductive Timing in Chicago Neighborhoods" originally appeared in *British Medical Journal*, 314: 1271–

1274. © 1997 by the BMJ Publishing Group. Reprinted by permission.

28. Wilkinson, Kawachi, and Kennedy, "Mortality, the Social Environment, Crime, and Violence" originally appeared in *Sociology of Health & Illness*, 20 (5): 578–597. © 1998 by Blackwells Publishers. Reprinted by permission.

29. Kennedy, Kawachi, Prothrow-Stith, Lochner, and Gupta, "Social Capital, Income Inequality, and Firearm Violent Crime" originally appeared in *Social Science & Medicine*, 47: 7–17. Reprinted by permission.

30. Sampson, Raudenbush, and Earls, "Neighborhoods and Violent Crime" reprinted with permission from *Science*, 277: 918–924. © 1998 by the American Association for the Advancement of Science.

31. Taylor, Repetti, Seeman, "What Is an Unhealthy Environment and How Does It Get Under the Skin?" reprinted with permission from the *Annual Review of Psychology*, 48: 411–447, © 1997 by Annual Reviews, *www.AnnualReviews.org*"

32. McEwen, "Protective and Damaging Effects of Stress Mediators" originally appeared in *New England Journal of Medicine*, 338 (3): 171–179. © 1998 by the Massachusetts Medical Society. All rights reserved. Reprinted by permission.

33. Shively and Clarkson, "Social Status and Coronary Artery Atherosclerosis in Female Monkeys" originally appeared in *Arteriosclerosis and Thrombosis*, 14: 721–726. Reprinted by permission.

34. Shively, Laird, and Anton, "The Behavior and Physiology of Social Stress and Depression in Female Cynomolgus Monkeys" originally appeared in *Biological Psychiatry*, 41: 871–882. Reprinted by permission.

35. Sapolsky, Alberts, and Altman, "Hypercortisolism Associated with Social Subordinance or Social Isolation Among Wild Baboons" originally appeared in *Archives of General Psychiatry*, 54 (12): 1137–1143. © 1997 by the American Medical Assocation. Reprinted by permission.

36. Kristenson et al., "Attenuated Cortisol Response to a Standardized Stress Test in Lithuanian versus Swedish Men" originally appeared in *International Journal of Behavioral Medicine*, 5 (1): 17–30. © 1998 by Lawrence Erlbaum Associates, Inc. Reprinted by permission.

37. Yllo, "Sexual Equality and Violence Against Wives in American States" originally appeared in *Journal of Comparative Family Studies*, 14 (1): 67–68. © 1983 by the *Journal of Comparative Family Studies*. Reprinted by permission.

38. Kennedy, Kawachi, Lochner, Jones, and Prothrow-Stith, "(Dis)respect and Black Mortality" originally appeared in *Ethnicity and Disease*, 7: 207–214. Reprinted by permission.

39. Kawachi, Kennedy, Gupta, and Prothrow-Stith, "Women's Status and the Health of Women and Men" originally appeared in *Social Science & Medicine*, 1999. Reprinted by permission.

40. Wilkinson, "The Culture of Inequality" is published here for the first time.

ABOUT THE CONTRIBUTORS

Susan C. Alberts, Department of Organismal and Evolutionary Biology, Harvard University.

Jeanne Altman, Department of Ecology and Evolution, University of Chicago.

Raymond F. Anton, Department of Psychiatry & Behavioral Sciences, Medical University of South Carolina.

Alberto Ascherio, Department of Nutrition, Harvard School of Public Health.

Jennifer L. Balfour, Human Population Laboratory, Department of Health Services, Berkeley, California.

Irena Balinkyniene, Department of Gastroentrology, Vilnius Unviersity, Lithuania.

Yoav Ben-Shlomo, Lecturer in Clinical Epidemiology, International Center for Health and Society, Department of Epidemiology and Public Health, University College London Medical School.

Bjorn Bergdahl, Department of Medicine and Care, Linkoping University, Sweden.

Lisa F. Berkman, Department of Epidemiology and Public Health, Yale University School of Medicine.

Elizabeth Brainerd, Williams College.

Henrikas Calkauskas, Department of Gastroentrology, Vilnius Unviersity, Lithuania.

Thomas B. Clarkson, Department of Comparative Medicine, Bowman Gray School of Medicine, Wake Forest University.

Richard D. Cohen, Human Population Laboratory, Berkeley, California.

Graham A. Colditz, Department of Medicine, Brigham and Women's Hospital and Harvard Medical School.

Martin Daly, Professor, Department of Psychology, McMaster University, Canada.

Felton Earls, Harvard School of Public Health.

Kevin Fiscella, Associate Professor, Department of Family Medicine, University of Rochester School of Medicine and Dentistry.

Peter Franks, Professor, Department of Family Medicine, University of Rochester School of Medicine and Dentistry.

Edward Giovannucci, Department of Medicine, Brigham and Women's Hospital and Harvard Medical School.

Roberta Glass, Division of Public Health Practice at the Harvard School of Public Health.

Hugh Gravelle, Professor, National Primary Care Research Centre, University of York.

Vanita Gupta, Harvard School of Public Health

James S. House, Professor and Chair of Sociology at the Survey Reseraach Center, University of Michigan.

Ching-Chi Hsieh, Department of Sociology, Bowling Green State University.

Camara Jones, Department of Health and Social Behavior, Harvard School of Public Health.

Ken Judge, Director, King's Fund Policy Institute in London.

George A. Kaplan, Professor and Chair of the Department of Epidemiology, University of Michigan School of Public Health.

Ichiro Kawachi, Associate Professor in the Department of Health and Social Behavior at the Harvard School of Public Health.

George A. Kaplan, Professor and Chair, Department of Epidemiology, School of Public Health, University of Michigan.

Bruce P. Kennedy, Deputy Director of the Division of Public Health Practice at the Harvard School of Public Health.

Margareta Kristenson, Department of Environment and Health, Linkoping University, Sweden.

Zita Kucinskiene, Department of Physiology and Biochemistry, Vilnius Unviersity, Lithuania.

Kathy Laber-Laird, Department of Comparative Medicine, Medical University of South Carolina.

Karl R. Landis, Department of Sociology, University of Michigan.

Kimberly Lochner, Department of Health and Social Behavior, Harvard School of Public Health.

John W. Lynch, Assistant Research Scientist, Department of Epidemiology, School of Public Health,University of Michigan.

Michael Marmot, Professor of Epidemiology and Public Health, International Cener for Health and Society, Department of Epidemiology and Public Health, University College London Medical School.

Bruce S. McEwen, Harold and Margaret Milliken Hatch Laboratory of Neuroendocrinology, Rockefeller University.

Sandra J. McIsaac, Department of Applied Social Studies, University of Keele.

Anders G. Olsson, Department of Medicine and Care, Linkoping University, Sweden.

Kristina Orth-Gomér, Department of Public Health Sciences, Karolinska Institute, Stockholm, Sweden.

Elsie R. Pamuk, National Center for Health Statistics.

Deborah Prothrow-Smith, Professor, Harvard School of Public Health.

M.D. Pugh, Department of Sociology, Bowling Green State University.

Stephen W. Raudenbush, College of Education, Michigan State University.

Rena L. Repetti, Department of Psychology, University of California at Los Angeles.

Eric B. Rimm, Department of Epidemiology, Harvard School of Public Health.

G.B. Rodgers, Head of the Research Wing, Population and Labour Policies Branch, International Labour Organisation.

Robert J. Sampson, Department of Sociology, University of Chicago.

Teresa Seeman, Andrus Gerontology Center, University of Southern California.

Carol A. Shively, Professor, Department of Comparative Medicine, Bowman Gray School of Medicine, Wake Forest University.

Meir J. Stampfer, Department of Epidemiology, Harvard School of Public Health.

Robert M. Sapolsky, Department of Biological Sciences, Stanford University.

Shelley E. Taylor, Department of Psychology, University of California at Los Angeles.

Debra Umberson, Assistant Professor, Department of Sociology, University of Texas at Austin.

Robert J. Waldmann, Department of Economics, European University Institute, Florence, Italy.

Ian R. White, Lecturer in Medical Statistics, London School of Hygiene and Tropical Medicine.

Richard G. Wilkinson, Professorial Research Fellow, Trafford Centre for Medical Research, University of Sussex.

Walter C. Willett, Department of Nutrition, Harvard School of Public Health.

Margo Wilson, Professor, Department of Psychology, McMaster University, Canada.

Irene H. Yen, School of Public Health, University of California, Berkeley.

Kersti Yllo, Department of Sociology, Wheaton College.

ABOUT THE EDITORS

Ichiro Kawachi is an Associate Professor in the Department of Health and Social Behavior at the Harvard School of Public Health where he is also the Director of the Center for Society and Health. He is the author of numerous articles and book chapters with a focus on social epidemiology, in particular, the social determinants of health. With Bruce Kennedy, he received a 1996 Robert Wood Johnson Foundation Investigator Award in Health Policy Research to study the effects of income inequality and social capital on population health. Kawachi is also a core member of the MacArthur Foundation Network on Socioeconomic Status and Health. He is co-editor (with Lisa Berkman) of a forthcoming textbook on Social Epidemiology to be published by Oxford University Press.

Richard G. Wilkinson is Professor of Social Epidemiology at the University of Sussex and Visiting Professor at University College London where he is also Associate Director of the International Center for Health and Society. He has worked for many years on the social and economic determinants of health inequalities, and

has focused primarily on the relation between the extent of income inequality and population health. His previously published books include: *Class and Health: Research and Longitudinal Data* (Tavistock 1986); *Unhealthy Societies: The Afflictions of Inequality* (Routledge 1996); and *Health and Social Organization* (with David Blane and Eric Brunner, Routledge 1996).

Bruce P. Kennedy is the Deputy Director of the Division of Public Health Practice at the Harvard School of Public Health where he teaches courses on adolescent health, as well as social inequalities in health. His current research focuses on developing models of the social determinants of health. With Ichiro Kawachi, he was the recipient of the 1996 Robert Wood Johnson Foundation Investigator Award in Health Policy Research to study the effects of income inequality and social capital on population health.